MAGICAL BOOK SERIES

Advanced DATA INTERPRETATION (High Level)

1000+ MCQs

YOUACE PUBLICATIONS

(A Unit of BSC Publishing Co. Pvt. Ltd.)

NOIDA (UP) - 201301

Phone: 9560483938

e-mail: bsckkundan@gmail.com

youacepublications@gmail.com

YOUACE PUBLICATIONS

First Edition – 2025
Second Edition – 2026

ISBN: 978-81-69162-83-8

DISCLAIMER

Every effort has been made to avoid errors or omissions in the publication. In spite of this, some errors might have crept in. The publisher shall not be responsible for the same. Any mistake, error or discrepancy noted may be brought to our notice which shall be taken care of in the next edition. It is notified that neither the publisher nor the authors or sellers will be responsible for any damage or loss of action of any one, of any kind, in any manner, therefrom.

PRICE: Rs 290.00

K Kundan
Email: bsckkundan@gmail.com
youacepublications@gmail.com

Printed at
REPRO INDIA LIMITED

Contents

OUR PUBLICATIONS

OUR BEST SELLING BOOKS

- QUICKER MATHS (Price: Rs 390)
- ANALYTICAL REASONING (Price: Rs 450)
- ENGLISH IS EASY (Price: Rs 420)
- PRACTICE BOOK ON QUICKER MATHS (Price: Rs 640)
- क्विकर मैथ्स (Price: Rs 400)

FOR BANKING AND INSURANCE EXAMS

- MAGICAL BOOK ON PUZZLE (Price: Rs 540)
- प्रैक्टिस बूक पजल एवं बैठक व्यवस्था (Price: Rs 430)
- PRACTICE BOOK ON PUZZLE AND SEATING ARRANGEMENT (Price: Rs 570)
- MAGICAL BOOK ON DATA INTERPRETATION (Price: Rs 570)
- ADVANCED DATA INTERPRETATION FOR BANKING EXAMS (Price: Rs 350)
- PRACTICE BOOK QUANT FOR BANKING EXAMS (Price: Rs 620)
- MASTERING CALCULATION FOR BANKING EXAMS (Price: Rs 260)
- VERBAL REASONING FOR BANKING EXAMS (Price: Rs 640)
- ADVANCED VERBAL REASONING FOR BANKING EXAMS (Price: Rs 670)
- PRACTICE BOOK ADVANCED ENGLISH FOR BANKING EXAMS (Price: Rs 410)
- TEST OF ENGLISH LANGUAGE FOR BANKING EXAMS (Price: Rs 630)
- 15 MOCK TESTS IBPS PO PT EXAMS (Price: Rs 190)
- 15 MOCK TESTS IBPS CLERK PT EXAMS (Price: Rs 170)
- 15 MOCK TESTS SBI PO PT EXAMS (Price: Rs 200)
- 15 MOCK TESTS SBI CLERK PT EXAMS (Price: Rs 180)
- 15 MOCK TESTS IBPS RRB PO PT EXAMS (Price: Rs 160)
- 15 MOCK TESTS IBPS RRB CLERK PT EXAMS (Price: Rs 140)

FOR ALL COMPETITIVE EXAMS

- ENGLISH VOCABULARY (Price: Rs 290)
- COMMON ERRORS IN ENGLISH (Price: Rs 390)
- ENGLISH GRAMMAR (Price: Rs 250)
- PRACTICE BOOK ERROR DETECTION & SENTENCE IMPROVEMENT (Price: Rs 220)
- MASTERING READING COMPREHENSION WITH WORD-MEANING (Price: Rs 190)
- MASTERING VOCAB PRACTICE BOOK (Price: Rs 220)
- MASTERING GK BASED ON NCERT (Approx. 6000 MCQs) (Price: Rs 390)
- हिन्दी व्याकरण (सभी प्रतियोगिता परीक्षाओं के लिए) (Price: Rs 160)

FOR SSC EXAMS

- ADVANCED MATHS (Price: Rs 370)
- एडवान्स्ड मैथ्स (Price: Rs 400)
- 15 MOCK TESTS SSC CGL TIER I EXAMS (ENGLISH MEDIUM) (Price: Rs 150)
- 15 MOCK TESTS SSC CGL TIER I EXAMS (HINDI MEDIUM) (Price: Rs 150)
- 15 MOCK TESTS SSC CHSL TIER I EXAMS (ENGLISH MEDIUM) (Price: Rs 150)
- 15 MOCK TESTS SSC CGL TIER I EXAMS (HINDI MEDIUM) (Price: Rs 150)

FOR MBA EXAMS

- QUANT FOR CAT (Price: Rs 840)

Practice Set 1

Directions (Q. 1-5): Study the following graph carefully to answer the given questions:

The bar graph shows the population of City P and City Q over the years

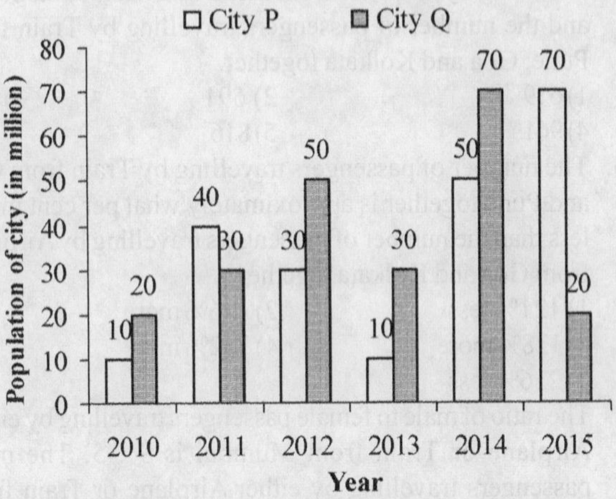

The table shows the percentage distribution of male and female population in City P and Q in different years.

Years	City P		City Q		% literate
	% male	% female	% male	% female	
2010	–	65	28	–	28
2011	35	–	32	–	72
2012	–	48		65	62
2013	42	–	–	27	65
2014	–	38	38		45
2015	62	–	45	–	55

Note: Literacy percentage remains the same for either of the cities; eg 28% population is literate in City P in 2010 and 28% population is literate in City Q in the same year.

1. What is the approximate average female population of City P for all the years together? (in million)
   1) 16.4 2) 32.4 3) 28.3 4) 23.4 5) 36.5
2. The illiterate population in City Q in the year 2014 is approximately what per cent of the total male population in City Q in the same year?
   1) 72% 2) 92% 3) 32% 4) 48% 5) 89%
3. What is the percentage increase in the female population in City Q from 2013 to 2014?
   1) 162.27% 2) 192.32% 3) 168.25%
   4) 133.33% 5) None of these
4. What is the difference between the total literate population in City P from 2010 to 2012 and the total illiterate population of City Q from 2013 to 2015?
   1) 4.8 million 2) 6.8 million 3) 7.2 million
   4) 8.5 million 5) 7.8 million
5. What is the ratio of the total female population of City Q in the year 2012 and 2013 together to the total literate population of City P in the year 2013 and 2014 together?
   1) 145 : 147 2) 203 : 145 3) 145 : 203
   4) 147 : 203 5) 203 : 148

Directions (Q. 6-11): Study the following table carefully to answer the questions that follow.

The table shows the number of candidates who appeared in online exam and the percentage of the candidates who appeared in offline exam from four towns and the total candidates who did not complete the exam (online or offline)

Note: 1. Total candidates appeared in the exam from a town = Total candidates appeared in the online exam + Total candidates appered in the offline exam.

2. Total candidates appeared in the exam from a town = Total candidates who completed the exam + Total candidates who did not complete the exam.

Town	Candidates appeared in online exam	Candidates appeared in offline exam	Candidates who did not complete the exam (online + offline)
P	320	36%	120
Q	500	60%	90
R	440	45%	105
S	460	54%	170

6. The total number of candidates who completed the exam from town R is how many more or less than the total number of candidates who completed the exam from town Q?
   1) 456 2) 465 3) 564
   4) 645 5) None of these
7. If the number of candidates who didn't complete the online exam and that who didn't complete the offline exam from town P are equal, then the number of candidates who completed the online exam from town P is approximately what per cent more than the number of candidates who completed the offline exam from the same town?

1) 97% 2) 107% 3) 117%
4) 102% 5) None of these

8. If the ratio of the numbers of candidates who didn't complete the online and offline exam from town S is 6 : 11 and 50% of the candidates who completed the online exam are males and 40% of the candidates who completed the offline exam are females, then find the difference between the number of female candidates who completed the online exam and the number of male candidates who completed the offline exam.
1) 70 2) 60 3) 56 4) 67 5) None of these

9. The number of candidates who completed the online and offline exam together from town R is what per cent of the total candidates who appeared in online and offline exam together from town S?
1) 65.5% 2) 62.5% 3) 59%
4) 69.5% 5) 73.5%

10. What is the sum total of the difference between the number of candidates who appeared in online and offline exams from all the four towns?
1) 520 2) 465 3) 550
4) 460 5) None of these

11. What is the approximate difference between the average of the number of candidates who appeared in online exam from all four towns and the average of the number of candidates who appeared in offline exam from all the four towns?
1) 21 2) 28 3) 32 4) 24 5) None of these

Directions (Q. 12-16): Study the following pie-charts and answer the questions that follow:

The pie-charts show the percentage distribution of passengers travelling by Airplane and Train from six different cities.

Note: If it is said that the number of passengers travelling by either airplane or train then it means the sum of the passengers travelling by airplane and train.

Total passengers travelling by Airplane = 2200

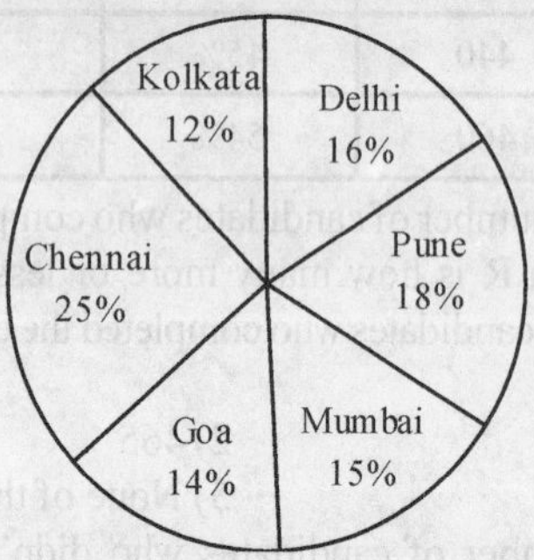

Total passengers travelling by train = 3400

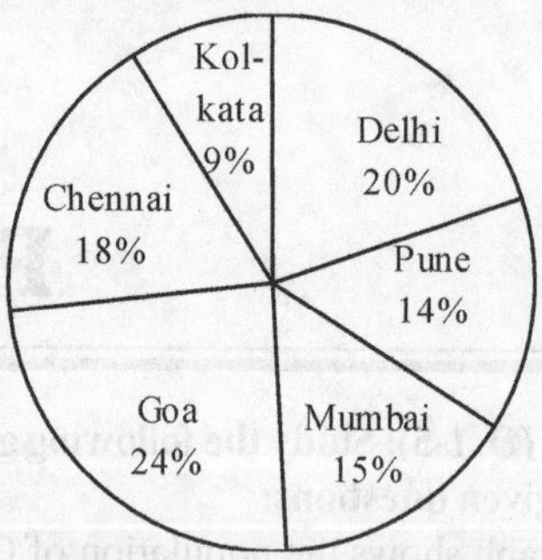

12. Find the difference between the number of passengers travelling by Airplane from Delhi and Mumbai together and the number of passengers travelling by Train from Pune, Goa and Kolkata together.
1) 619 2) 691 3) 916
4) 961 5) 816

13. The number of passengers travelling by Train from Goa and Pune together is approximately what per cent more/less than the number of passengers travelling by Airplane from Goa and Kolkata together?
1) 121% less 2) 126% more
3) 128% more 4) 162% more
5) 216% less

14. The ratio of male to female passengers travelling by either Airplane or Train from Mumbai is 9 : 5. The male passengers travelling by either Airplane or Train from Mumbai is approximately what per cent of the passengers travelling by Train from Kolkata?
1) 167% 2) 156% 3) 192%
4) 176% 5) None of these

15. If $\frac{7}{11}$ of the passengers from Chennai travelling by Airplane are males and $\frac{5}{17}$ of the passengers from Goa travelling by Train are females, then find the sum of the female passengers travelling by Airplane from Chennai and the male passengers travelling by Train from Goa.
1) 776 2) 767 3) 677
4) 766 5) None of these

16. What is the difference between the number of passengers travelling either by Airplane or by Train from Goa and the number of passengers travelling by Train from Mumbai and Kolkata together?
1) 380 2) 308 3) 803
4) 408 5) None of these

Directions (Q. 17-20): Study the following bar graph carefully and answer the questions that follow:

The bar graph shows the percentage of right products manufactured by five different companies in 2010 and 2015.

Note: Total manufactured products = right products + defective products

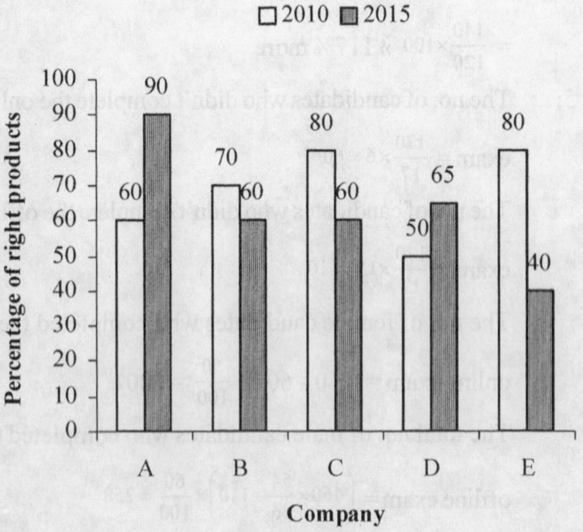

17. If the total number of products manufactured in 2010 was 20% more than the total number of products manufactured in 2015 by Company B, then find the ratio of the number of defective products manufactured in 2010 to the number of defective products manufactured in 2015 by the same company.

1) 5 : 1 2) 9 : 10 3) 7 : 5 4) 1 : 7 5) 3 : 5

18. What is the difference between the number of defective products manufactured by Company C in the given two years, if the number of right products manufactured by that company in 2015 was 3000, which is 25% more than the number of right products manufactured by the same company in 2010?

1) 1200 2) 1500 3) 1700
4) 1400 5) None of these

19. The number of total products manufactured by Company D in 2015 is what per cent more or less than that manufactured by Company B in 2010, if the ratio of the number of right products manufactured by Company B in 2010 to the number of defective products manufactured by Company D in 2015 is 12 : 5?

1) $15\frac{2}{3}$% less 2) $11\frac{3}{2}$% more

3) $16\frac{2}{3}$% less 4) $11\frac{5}{2}$% more

5) None of these

20. What is the number of total products manufactured by Company A and E in 2010, if the number of right products manufactured by Company A in 2010 is 6600, which is 10% more than the number of right products manufactured by Company E in 2010?

1) 16000 2) 18500 3) 17500
4) 14500 5) None of these

Directions (Q. 21-25): Study the following information carefully and answer the questions given below:

There are five companies A, B, C, D and E. The total number of employees in all the companies is 8000. The number of employees in Company A is 15% and that in Company B is 30% of the total employees in all the companies. Company D and E have equal number of employees. 25% of the employees of Company A know only Hindi. 35% employees of Company D know only English. There are 12 more employees in Company B who know only English than the number of employees of Company D who know only English. The number of employees of Company C is 40% that of Company A. Two-thirds of the employees of Company B know both the languages. 30% employees of Company A know both the languages. 20% employees of Company C know only English and the number of employees of Company C who know both the languages is equal to the number of employees who know only Hindi. The number of employees who know only Hindi from Company E is equal to the number of employees who know only English from Company D. The number of employees who know only English from Company E is 30 more than the number of employees who know only English from Company C. The number of employees of Company D who know only Hindi is 40 more than the number of employees who know both the languages from Company E. Each employee knows at least one of the two languages Hindi and English.

21. For which company is the difference between the number of employees who know only Hindi and only English the maximum?

1) C 2) B 3) E 4) D 5) None of these

22. What is the difference between the number of students who know Hindi and that of those who know only English?

1) 3708 2) 3780 3) 2708
4) 2920 5) None of these

23. What is the percentage of the number of employees who know both the languages?

1) 40.235% 2) 42.325% 3) 32.225%
4) 28.425% 5) None of these

24. What is the ratio of the total number of employees from Company A and C who know both the languages to the total number of employees from Company D?

1) 627 : 518 2) 267 : 958 3) 276 : 985
4) 138 : 490 5) 271 : 403

25. The number of employees of Company E who know only Hindi is how many times that of Company D who know only English?

1) 2 2) 2.5 3) 3
4) 1 5) 1.5

Answers and explanations

1. 1; Required average of female population

$$= \frac{10\times\frac{65}{100}+40\times\frac{65}{100}+30\times\frac{48}{100}+10\times\frac{58}{100}+50\times\frac{38}{100}+70\times\frac{38}{100}}{6}$$

$$= \frac{1}{6}\times(6.5+26+14.4+5.8+19+26.6)$$

$= \frac{1}{6}\times 98.3 = 16.38$ million » 16.4 million

2. 5; Reqd % $= \frac{55\% \text{ of } 70}{62\% \text{ of } 70}\times 100 = \frac{55}{62}\times 100$

$= 88.70\% \approx 89\%$

3. 5; Female population in City Q in 2013

$= 27\%$ of $30 = 8.1$ million

Female population in City Q in 2014

$= 38\%$ of $70 = 26.6$

Reqd % increase $= \frac{26.6-8.1}{8.1}\times 100$

$= \frac{18.5}{8.1}\times 100 = \frac{18500}{81} = 228.39\%$

4. 2; Reqd difference = (35% of 30 + 55% of 70 + 45% of 20) − (28% of 10 + 72% of 40 + 62% of 30) = (10.5 + 37.5 + 9) − (2.8 + 28.8 + 18.6) = 57 − 50.2 = 6.8 million

5. 2; Reqd ratio $= \frac{65\% \text{ of } 50 + 27\% \text{ of } 30}{65\% \text{ of } 10 + 45\% \text{ of } 50}$

$= \frac{32.5+8.1}{6.5+22.5} = \frac{40.6}{29} = \frac{406}{290} = \frac{203}{145} = 203:145$

6. 2; Total number of candidates who completed the exam from Town R

$= \left[\frac{440}{55}\times 100 - 105\right] = [800-105] = 695$

Total number of candidates who completed the exam from Town Q

$= \left[\frac{500}{40}\times 100 - 90\right] = [1250-90] = 1160$

∴ Reqd number = 1160 − 695 = 465 less

7. 3; Total number of candidates who appeared in offline exam from Town P $= \frac{320}{64}\times 36 = 180$

The number of candidates who didn't complete the exam from town P in online and offline exams $= \frac{120}{2}\times 1$

= 60 online, 60 offline

So, the total number of candidates who completed the offline exam from Town P = 180 − 60 = 120

The total number of candidates who completed the online exam from Town P = 320 − 60 = 260

∴ Reqd % more $= \frac{260-120}{120}\times 100$

$= \frac{140}{120}\times 100$ » 117% more

8. 5; The no. of candidates who didn't complete the online exam $= \frac{170}{17}\times 6 = 60$

The no. of candidates who didn't complete the offline exam $= \frac{170}{17}\times 11 = 110$

The no. of female candidates who completed the online exam $= (460-60)\times\frac{50}{100} = 200$

The total no. of male candidates who completed the offline exam $= \left(460\times\frac{54}{46} - 110\right)\times\frac{60}{100} = 258$

∴ Reqd difference = 258 − 200 = 58

9. 4; The number of candidates who completed the online and offline exam from Town R

$= \left[\frac{440}{55}\times 100 - 105\right] = [800-105] = 695$

Total number of appeared candidates in online and offline exams from Town S $= \frac{460}{46}\times 54 = 1000$

∴ Reqd % $= \frac{695\times 100}{1000} = 69.5\%$

10. 3; Reqd sum $= \left[\left(320 - \frac{320}{64}\times 36\right) + \left(\frac{500}{40}\times 60 - 500\right)\right.$

$\left. + \left(440 - \frac{440}{55}\times 45\right) + \left(\frac{460\times 54}{46} - 460\right)\right]$

= 140 + 250 + 80 + 80 = 550

11. 2; Average number of candidates who appeared in online exam from all four towns

$= \frac{320+500+440+460}{4} = \frac{1720}{4} = 430$

Average number of candidates who appeared in offline exam from all the four towns

$$= \frac{320\times\frac{36}{64} + \frac{500}{40}\times 60 + 440\times\frac{45}{55} + \frac{460}{46}\times 54}{4}$$

$= \frac{180+750+360+540}{4} = \frac{1830}{4} = 457.5$

∴ Reqd difference = 457.5 − 430 = 27.5 » 28

12. 3; Reqd difference

$$= \left[3400\times\frac{(14+24+9)}{100} - 2200\times\frac{(16+15)}{100}\right]$$

$$=(34\times47)-(22\times31)=1598-682=916$$

13. 2; Reqd % $= \dfrac{34(24+14)-22(14+12)}{22(14+12)}\times100$

$$= \frac{1292-572}{572}\times100 = \frac{720}{572}\times100$$

= 125.87 more » 126% more

14. 4; No. of passengers travelling by Airplane or Train from Mumbai = 22 × 15 + 34 × 15 = 15 × 56 = 840

Male passengers travelling by either Airplane or Train from Mumbai = $\dfrac{840}{14}\times9=540$

$\therefore$ Reqd % = $540\times\dfrac{100}{34\times9} = \dfrac{54000}{306} = 176.47$ » 176%

15. 1; The number of females from Chennai who travelled by Airplane = $1-\dfrac{7}{11}=\dfrac{4}{11}$

And the number of males from Goa who travelled by Train = $1-\dfrac{5}{17}=\dfrac{12}{17}$

Reqd sum = $22\times25\times\dfrac{4}{11}+34\times24\times\dfrac{12}{17}$

$=25\times8+24\times24=200+576=776$

16. 2; Reqd difference = (22 × 14 + 34 × 24) − 34(15 + 9) = 22 × 14 = 308

17. 2; Let the total no. of manufactured products in 2015 by Company B be x.

Then, total no. of manufactured products in 2010

$$=\frac{120x}{100}$$

$\therefore$ Reqd ratio = $\dfrac{\frac{120x}{100}\times\frac{30}{100}}{x\times\frac{40}{100}} = \dfrac{36}{40} = 9:10$

18. 4; No. of defective products manufactured by Company C in 2015 = $3000\times\dfrac{100}{60}\times\dfrac{40}{100}=2000$

No. of right products manufactured by Company C in 2010 = $3000\times\dfrac{100}{125} = 3000\times\dfrac{4}{5} = 2400$

$\therefore$ No. of defective products manufactured by Company C in 2010 = $2400\times\dfrac{100}{80}\times\dfrac{20}{100}=600$

$\therefore$ Reqd difference = 2000 − 600 = 1400

19. 3; Let the no. of total products manufactured by Company B in 2010 be x and the total no. of products manufactured by Company D in 2015 be y.

$$\therefore \frac{x\times\frac{70}{100}}{y\times\frac{35}{100}}=\frac{12}{5} \quad \therefore \frac{x}{y}=\frac{6}{5}$$

$\therefore$ Reqd % = $\dfrac{1}{6}\times100=16\dfrac{2}{3}$% less

20. 2; Total no. of manufactured products by A in 2010 = $6600\times\dfrac{100}{60}=11000$

Total no. of manufactured products by E in 2010 = $6600\times\dfrac{100}{110}\times\dfrac{100}{80}=7500$

$\therefore$ Total no. of products manufactured by A and E together in 2010 = 11000 + 7500 = 18500

(21-25):

Company	Total	Only Hindi	Only English	Both Hindi and English
A	15% of 8000 = 1200	25% of 1200 = 300	540	30% of 1200 = 360
B	30% of 8000 = 2400	102	686+12 = 698	2400×2/3 = 1600
C	40% of 1200 = 480	192	20% of 480 = 96	192
D	1960	1148+40 = 1188	35% of 1960 = 686	86
E	1960	686	96 + 30 = 126	1148

21. 2; For A, Reqd difference = 540 − 300 = 240
For B, Reqd difference = 698 − 102 = 596
For C, Reqd difference = 192 − 96 = 96
For D, Reqd difference = 1188 − 686 = 502
For E, Reqd difference = 686 − 126 = 560
Hence the maximum difference is for B.

22. 1; Reqd difference = [(300 + 102 + 192 + 1188 + 686) + (360 + 1600 + 192 + 86 + 1148)] − [(540 + 698 + 96 + 686 + 126)] = 5854 − 2146 = 3708

23. 2; Reqd % = $\dfrac{(360+1600+192+86+1148)}{8000}\times100$

$$=\frac{3386}{8000}\times100=42.325\%$$

24. 4; Reqd ratio = (360 + 192) : (1960)
= 552 : 1960 = 276 : 980 = 138 : 490

25. 4; Reqd answer = $\dfrac{686}{686}=1$

Practice Set 2

Directions (Q. 1-5): Study the following table carefully to answer the questions given below.

The table shows various statistics of five different products.

Product	Cost price	MP	Profit/Loss (Percentage)	Profit/Loss (in ₹)	SP
Laptop	₹30000	–	–	–	–
Mobile	₹15500	–	–	+1450	–
Scanner	–	₹25140	–	–	₹20350
Printer	–	₹20550	–	–	–
Monitor	–	–	–	–	₹15640

Note: MP = Marked price
SP = Selling Price

1. A shopkeeper marks 25% above the cost price on the laptop, but he offers 12% discount on the laptop to all his customers. He further offers a discount of 5% on the reduced price to those customers who pay in cash. What will be the purchase price for a customer who wishes to purchase in cash?
1) ₹35250 2) ₹39525 3) ₹31530
4) ₹31350 5) None of these

2. If the cost price of a printer is ₹15000, then find the percentage profit of a shopkeeper who offers a discount of 20% on the marked price of the same article.
1) 9.6% 2) 8.7% 3) 11.6%
4) 5% 5) 12.8%

3. A shopkeeper sold a monitor at a discount of 8% on the marked price. He would have earned a profit of 36%, had there been no discount. What was the actual percentage of profit earned?
1) 19.12% 2) 21.02% 3) 25.12%
4) 27.12% 5) 15.15%

4. A shopkeeper marked the price 25% and 20% above the cost price of mobiles and scanners respectively. What is the difference between the cost price of a scanner and the selling price of a mobile?
1) ₹6900 2) ₹7205 3) ₹6800
4) ₹5505 5) None of these

5. A shopkeeper sold a mobile at a discount of 8%. If on this the sales tax is 10%, then find the selling price of the mobile.
1) ₹11286 2) ₹15686 3) ₹12866
4) ₹97260 5) None of these

Directions (Q. 6-10): Study the following information to answer the given questions.

In a company there are five departments P, Q, R, S and T. The ratio of the number of officers in all the departments together to that of clerks is 3 : 4. The ratio of the number of male officers to the number of female officers is 7 : 5. The ratio of male clerks to female clerks is 9 : 7. The number of male officers in department P is 140. The number of male clerks in department R is 25% more than that of the number of male clerks in department Q. The number of male officers in department T is $\frac{1}{3}$ of the number of male clerks in department R. The number of male clerks in department Q is 20% more than that of male officers in department P. The number of male clerks in all the departments together is 900. The ratio of the number of male officers in department S to that of females is 3 : 2. The number of male officers in department S is 210. The number of male officers in department Q is 15 more than that of male clerks in the same department. The number of male clerks in department S is $\frac{2}{3}$ times that of R. The number of female clerks in department R and T each is $\frac{5}{7}$ times that of male clerks in department S. The number of male clerks in department P is 1.3 times that of female clerks in department R. The number of female clerks in department P is 160. The number of female officers in department R is two more than that of female clerks in department P. The number of female officers in department P is 10% less than that of female clerks in the same department. The number of female officers in department T is $\frac{2}{5}$ that of male officers. The number of female clerks in department Q is $\frac{3}{4}$ times that of male clerks in the same department.

6. What is the difference between the number of officers in department P and T together and the number of officers in department Q and R together?
1) 60 2) 72 3) 96
4) 86 5) None of these

7. The number of female officers in department Q is approximately what per cent of the number of male officers in that department?
1) 12% 2) 14% 3) 18% 4) 8% 5) 20%

8. The total number of male clerks is approximately what per cent more than that of male officers?
1) 39% 2) 21% 3) 29%
4) 19% 5) None of these

9. What is the ratio of the number of female clerks in department P, Q and S together to the number of male officers in department Q and T together?
1) 500 : 253 2) 400 : 131 3) 300 : 253
4) 253 : 500 5) 700 : 623

10. What is the approximate average number of employees in department P, Q, R and S?
1) 312 2) 220 3) 420
4) 512 5) None of these

Directions (Q. 11-15): Study the following pie-chart to answer the following questions.

The pie-chart shows the distance travelled by six persons.

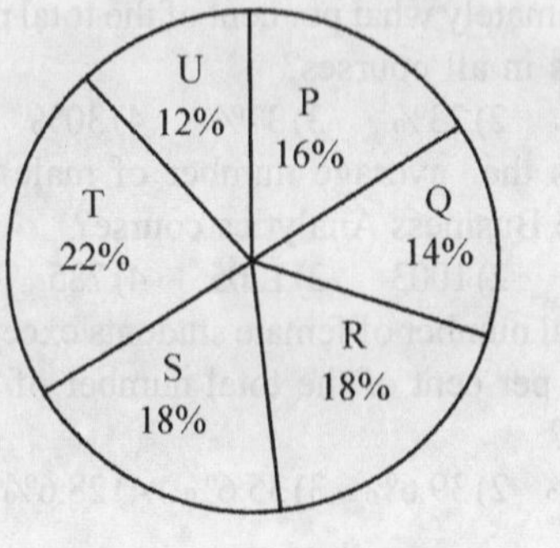

Total distance = 3200 km

11. T travels 70 km daily. After travelling for 2 days, T doubles his speed. Find the total time taken by him to reach his destination.
1) $5\frac{2}{7}$ days 2) $6\frac{1}{35}$ days 3) $7\frac{2}{29}$ days
4) $8\frac{3}{22}$ days 5) None of these

12. R started travelling at the rate of 48 km/hr so as to reach just in time. After 1 hour he realised that he had left his purse at the starting point, so he went back and after collecting his purse he began to travel at an increased speed, and reached his destination on time. What was the increase in speed?
1) 9.6 km/hr 2) 10.2 km/hr 3) 12 km/hr
4) 15 km/hr 5) 11 km/hr

13. Q travels at the rate of 40 km/hr for the first 200 km by scooty and then he travels by auto for the rest of the journey. However, had he travelled 200 km by auto and the remaining distance by scooty he would have taken $\frac{1}{4}$ hour longer to complete the journey. Find the speed of the auto (in km/hr).
1) 35.25 2) 52.25 3) 58
4) 45.71 5) 42

14. S's speed is 10 km/hr less than the speed of R and $\frac{5}{8}$ the speed of U. If U takes 8 hours to cover $\frac{5}{3}$ of his total distance, then what time will be taken by R to complete the whole journey? (in hours)
1) 7.5 2) 9.6 3) 8.2
4) 5 5) 11.2

15. P travels 212 km by air, 240 km by train and the remaining distance by car, taking altogether 8 hours. The speed of the aircraft is 2 times that of the train and the speed of the train 2 times that of the car. What is the speed of P in air?
1) 126 km/hr 2) 116.5 km/hr
3) 120 km/hr 4) 112 km/hr
5) None of these

Directions (Q. 16-20): The line graph given below shows the export of tea (in tonnes) from India and the import of tea (in tonnes) to Russia in six different years. Study the graph carefully and answer the questions that follow:

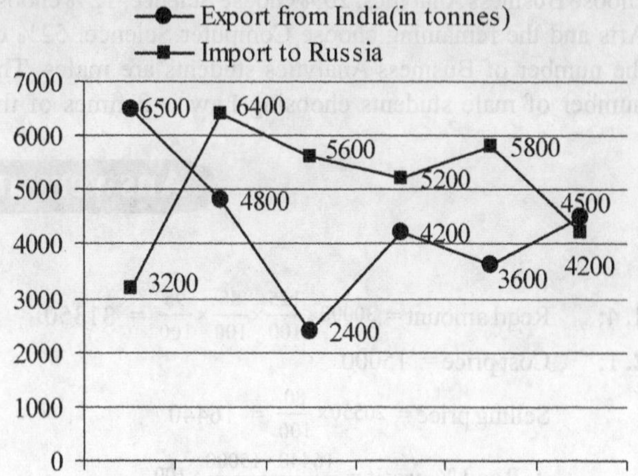

16. The ratio of import to export of tea in India in the year 2015 was 3 : 2 and the export of tea from Russia in 2015 was 20% more than the import of tea to Russia in 2018. Then the export of tea from Russia in 2015 is what per cent less/more than the import of tea to India in 2015?
1) 3.33% more 2) 3.33% less 3) 5.33% more
4) 6.33% less 5) 4.33% less

17. The average quantity of tea imported to Russia in the years 2014, 2015, 2017 and 2018 together is what per cent

of the average exports of tea from India in the years 2015, 2016 and 2017 together?
1) 118.52 2) 110 3) 125.52
4) 135.52 5) None of these

18. What is the difference between the export of tea from India in 2019 to the import of tea to Russia in 2018?
1) 1200 tonnes 2) 1080 tonnes 3) 1260 tonnes
4) 1300 tonnes 5) None of these

19. It is mentioned that the quantity of tea exported from India in the year 2013 is the same as the quantity of tea imported to Russia in 2013. If it is mentioned that the ratio of tea exported from India in the period 2013-15 to the tea imported to Russia in the same period is 141 : 124, then what is the value of tea exported from India in 2013?
1) 3400 tonnes 2) 2800 tonnes 3) 6400 tonnes
4) 5800 tonnes 5) 5700 tonnes

20. If it is mentioned that in the year 2015, the ratio of imports to exports for India is 7 : 6 and in the year 2017, exports of Russia are 25% more than imports in the same year, then the imports of India in 2015 is approximately what % of the exports of Russia in 2017?
1) 66 2) 56 3) 76 4) 86 5) 98

Directions (Q. 21-25): Study the following information carefully and answer the questions given below:

In a survey of 8500 students in a college, students choose different courses, viz Business Analytics, Science, Arts, Law and Computer Science. 25% students choose Law, 15% choose Business Analytics, 20% choose Science, 12% choose Arts and the remaining choose Computer Science. 52% of the number of Business Analytics students are males. The number of male students choosing Law is 2 times of the number of male students choosing Business Analytics. The number of female students choosing Arts is $\frac{1}{3}$ time of the number of male students choosing Law. The number of female students choosing Science is 2 times the number of male students choosing Arts. The number of female students choosing Computer Science is $\frac{3}{2}$ times of the number of male students choosing Science.

21. What is the difference between the total number of male students and the total number of female students from all the courses together?
1) 1260 2) 1450 3) 1350 4) 1050 5) 850

22. What is the ratio of the number of male students in Law and Science together to the number of female students in Computer Science ?
1) 29 : 53 2) 1121 : 619 3) 55 : 24
4) 123 : 623 5) 1122 : 517

23. The total number of students in Business Analytics is approximately what per cent of the total number of male students in all courses?
1) 27% 2) 23% 3) 37% 4) 30% 5) 36%

24. What is the average number of male students if we exclude Business Analytics course?
1) 1028 2) 1003 3) 1205 4) 785 5) 985

25. The total number of female students except those in Law is what per cent of the total number of students in the college?
1) 33.3% 2) 39.6% 3) 35.6% 4) 28.6% 5) 41.6%

Answers and explanations

1. 4; Reqd amount $= 30000\times\frac{125}{100}\times\frac{88}{100}\times\frac{95}{100}$ = `31350

2. 1; Cost price = `15000

Selling price $= 20550\times\frac{80}{100}$ = `16440

$\therefore$ Reqd % profit $=\frac{16440-15000}{15000}\times100$

$=\frac{1440}{15000}\times100=\frac{48}{5}=9.6\%$

3. 3; Marked price $=\frac{15640}{92}\times100$ = `17000

$\therefore$ Cost price $=\frac{17000}{136}\times100$ = `12500

$\because$ Selling price = `15640

$\therefore$ Actual profit % $=\frac{15640-12500}{12500}\times100$

$=\frac{3140}{12500}\times100=25.12\%$

4. 5; Reqd difference

$=\frac{25140}{120}\times100-\left(\frac{15500}{125}\times100+1450\right)$

= 20950 − 13850 = `7100

5. 2; Marked price of the mobile = `15500

$\therefore$ Selling price of the mobile before tax

$= 15500\times\frac{92}{100}$ = `14260

$\therefore$ Selling price of the mobile after tax

$= 14260\times\frac{110}{100}$ = `15686

(6-10):

Company	Officer			Clerk		
	Male	Female	Total	Male	Female	Total
P	140	160×90/100 = 144	284	1.3×100 = 130	160	290
Q	168+15 =183	26	209	140×120/100 = 168	168×3/4 = 126	294
R	97	160+2 = 162	259	168×125/100 = 210	140×5/7 = 100	310
S	210	210×2/3 = 140	350	210×2/3 = 140	700 −(160+126+100+100) = 214	354
T	210×1/3 = 70	70×2/5 = 28	98	900 −(130+168+210+140) = 252	140×5/7 = 100	352
Total	1200/12×7 = 700	500	1600/4×3 = 1200	900	900/9×7 = 700	1600

6. 4; Reqd difference $=(209+259)-(284+98)=468-382$ $=86$

7. 2; Reqd % $=\frac{26}{183}\times100=14.20 \approx 14\%$

8. 3; Reqd % $=\frac{900-700}{700}\times100$

$=\frac{200}{7}=28.57\approx29\%$

9. 1; Reqd ratio $=(160+126+214):(183+70)=500:253$

10. 5; Reqd average

$==\frac{284+290+209+294+259+310+350+354}{4}$

$=\frac{2350}{4}=587.5\approx588$

11. 2; Total distance covered by T

$=22\%$ of $3200=22\times32=704$ km

Reqd no. of days

$=\frac{704-(70\times2)}{70\times2}+2=\frac{141}{35}+2=\frac{141+70}{35}$

$=\frac{211}{35}=6\frac{1}{35}$ days

11. 1; Total distance covered by R

$=32\times18=576$ km

Total time $=\frac{576}{48}=12$ hours

$\therefore$ Remaining time $=12-1-1=10$ hours

After increasing the speed, the speed of R

$=\frac{576}{10}=57.6$ km/hr

$\therefore$ Increase in speed $=57.6-48=9.6$ km/hr

11. 4; Total distance covered by Q

$=14\%$ of $3200=448$ km

Distance covered by scooty = 200 km

Distance covered by auto $=448-200=248$ km

Let the speed of the auto be x km/hr.

Case I. Time taken

$=\frac{200}{40}+\frac{248}{x}=\left(5+\frac{248}{x}\right)$ hours

Case II. Time taken

$=\frac{200}{x}+\frac{248}{40}=\left(\frac{200}{x}+6.2\right)$ hours

According to the question,

$\left(\frac{200}{x}+6.2\right)-\left(5+\frac{248}{x}\right)=\frac{1}{4}$

$\Rightarrow \frac{200}{x}+1.2-\frac{248}{x}=\frac{1}{4}$

$\Rightarrow -\frac{48}{x}=\frac{1}{4}-1.2=\frac{1}{4}-\frac{6}{5}=\frac{5-24}{20}$

$\Rightarrow -\frac{48}{x}=-\frac{21}{20}$

$\therefore x=\frac{48\times20}{21}=\frac{320}{7}=45.71$ km/hr

14. 2; Distance covered by U $=32\times12=384$ km

Speed of U $=\frac{384\times\frac{5}{3}}{8}=\frac{128\times5}{8}=80$ km/hr

Speed of S $=80\times\frac{5}{8}=50$ km/hr

$\therefore$ Speed of R $=50+10=60$ km/hr

Distance covered by R $=32\times18=576$ km

$\therefore$ Time taken by R $=\frac{576}{60}=9.6$ hours

15. 2; Total distance covered by P $=32\times16=512$ km

$\because$ Distance covered by car

$=512-(212+240)=512-452=60$

	Air	Train	Car
Speed	4x	2x	x
Distance	212	240	60

Now, $\frac{212}{4x}+\frac{240}{2x}+\frac{60}{x}=8$

$\Rightarrow \frac{212+480+240}{4x}=8 \Rightarrow \frac{932}{4x}=8$

$4x=\frac{932}{8}=116.5$ km/hr

16. 2; Import of tea to India in 2015 $=\frac{4800\times3}{2}=7200$

Export of tea from Russia in 2015 $=\frac{5800\times120}{100}=6960$

$\therefore$ Required % less $=\frac{(7200-6960)}{7200}\times100$

$=\frac{240}{7200}\times100=\frac{240}{72}=3.33\%$ less

17. 4; Average imports to Russia in 2014, 2015, 2017 and 2018 together

$=\frac{3200+6400+5200+5800}{4}=\frac{20600}{4}=5150$

Average exports from India in 2015, 2016 and 2017

$=\frac{4800+2400+4200}{3}=\frac{11400}{3}=3800$

$\therefore$ Required % $=\frac{5150}{3800}\times100=\frac{5150}{38}=135.52\%$

18. 4; Required difference $=5800-4500=1300$ tonnes

19. 2; Let N = tea exported from India in 2013 = tea imported to Russia in 2013.

Now, according to the question,

$\frac{6500+4800+N}{3200+6400+N}=\frac{141}{124}$ $\therefore N=2800$

20. 4; Imports of India in 2015 $=\frac{4800}{6}\times7=5600$ tonnes

Exports of Russia in 2017 $=\frac{5200}{100}\times125=6500$ tonnes

Required % $=\frac{5600}{6500}\times100=86.15\% \approx 86\%$

(21-25):

Business Analytics:

Total students $=8500\times\frac{15}{100}=1275$

Male students $=1275\times\frac{52}{100}=663$

Female students $=1275-663=612$

Arts:

Total students $=8500\times\frac{12}{100}=1020$

Female students $=\frac{1}{3}\times1326=442$

Male students $=1020-442=578$

Science:

Total students $=8500\times\frac{20}{100}=1700$

Female students $=2\times578=1156$

Male students $=1700-1156=544$

Law:

Total students $=8500\times\frac{25}{100}=2125$

Male students $=2\times663=1326$

Female students $=2125-1326=799$

Computer science:

Percentage of students $=100-(25+15+20+12)=28\%$

Thus, total students $=8500\times\frac{28}{100}=2380$

Female students $=\frac{3}{2}\times544=816$

Male students $=2380-816=1564$

This information can be tabulised as:

Course	Total	Male	Female
Business Analytics	1275	663	612
Science	1700	544	1156
Art	1020	578	442
Law	2125	1326	799
Computer science	2380	1564	816

21. 5; Reqd difference $=(663+544+578+1326+1564)-(612+1156+442+799+816)=4675-3825=850$

22. 3; Required ratio $=1326+544:816$ $=1870:816=55:24$

23. 1; Reqd % $=1275\times\frac{100}{4675}=27.27\% \approx 27$

24. 2; Required average

$=\frac{544+578+1326+1564}{4}=\frac{4012}{4}=1003$

25. 3; Required percentage

$=(612+1156+442+816)\times\frac{100}{8500}=\frac{3026}{8500}\times100=35.6\%$

Practice Set 3

Directions (Q. 1-5): Study the following data carefully and answer the questions:

There are two cities A and B in a state. A bird flies from city A to city B in the morning for its food and comes back to city A in the evening on five different days of a week starting from Monday to Friday.

Note:

1. The flight speed (without wind) of the bird from city A to city B in the morning is different on all the five days while its flight speed (without wind) from city B to city A in the evening is also different on all the five days.
2. The direction of wind remains the same and is from city B to city A. The speed of wind in the morning is 100 km/hr while the speed of wind in the evening is 80 km/hr.

The first pie-chart given below shows the percentage distribution of the flight speed (without wind) of the bird from city A to city B in the morning on all the five days and the sum of the speeds is 2000 km/hr.

The second pie-chart given below shows the percentage distribution of the flight speed (without wind) of the bird from city B to city A in the evening on all the five days and the sum of the speeds is 1600 km/hr.

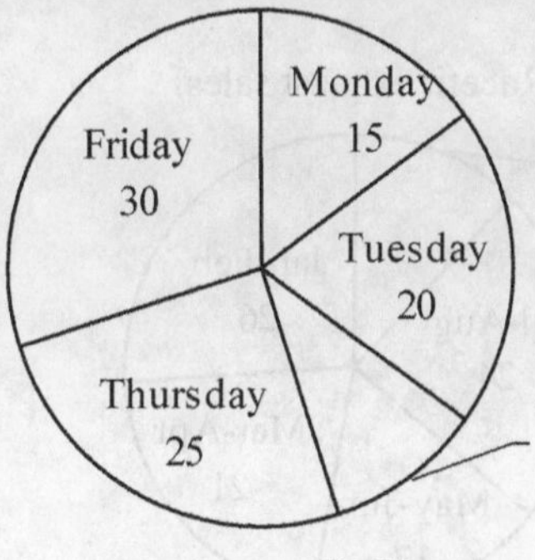

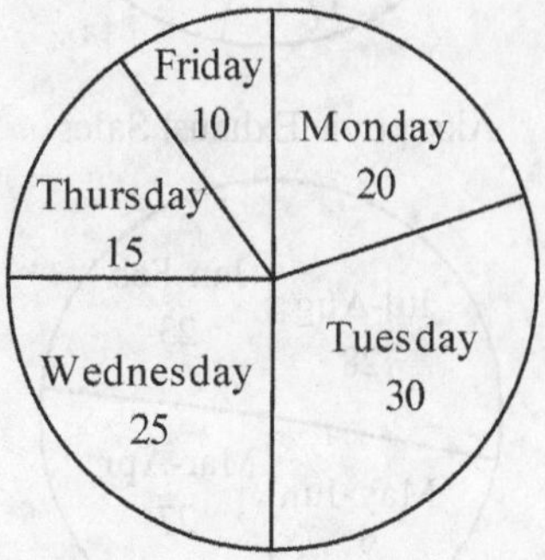

1. The bird starts flying from city A towards city B at 6:00 AM in the morning on Friday and searches for food in the city. In the process of searching food it spends 7 hours 9 minutes there and comes back to city A at 3:00 PM in the evening on the same day, then how far is city B from city A? Assume there is no other loss of time other than flight and searching.
   1) 175 km 2) 225 km 3) 150 km
   4) 250 km 5) 300 km
2. On Wednesday morning, the bird starts from city A towards city B and at the same time another bird with its flight speed (without wind) 240 km/hr starts from city B towards city A. If the difference between the total distances travelled by both the birds before meeting is 180 km, then what is the distance between city A and B?
   1) None of the given options 2) 370 km 3) 270 km
   4) 325 km 5) 330 km
3. The distance between city A and B is 196 km and on Tuesday evening the speed of wind increases by 40 km/hr from usual and the bird also increases its flight (without wind) speed while returning from city B towards city A. Now, if the time taken by the bird to reach city A from city B decreases by 4.2 minutes than the original calculated time, then what is the increment in the flight (without wind) speed of the bird?
   1) 80 km/hr 2) 120 km/hr 3) 100 km/hr
   4) 125 km/hr 5) 75 km/hr
4. If the distance between city A and B is 540 km, then what is the difference between the time taken by the bird to reach city B from city A on Monday morning and the time taken by the bird to reach city A from city B on Friday evening?
   1) 23 minutes 2) 33 minutes 3) 27 minutes
   4) 19 minutes 5) 42 minutes
5. If, on Thursday, the bird flies from city A to city B in the morning but with its flight (without wind) speed 20% more than its original flight (without wind) speed and comes back to the original point in the evening on the same day with the speed as mentioned in the charts, how much less time will the bird take than the original time in its flight if city A and B are 160 km apart?
   1) 4.2 minutes 2) 3.6 minutes 3) 4.8 minutes
   4) 6.2 minutes 5) None of the given options

Directions (Q. 6-10): Study the following information carefully and answer the questions given below:

Three friends Renuka, Priya and Rahul bought three items

P, Q and R respectively from a shopkeeper. The shopkeeper bought these items together from a salesman at ₹9000. He marked all three items at 30% above their cost price and after allowing 20%, 24% an 18% discount on marked price of item P, Q and R respectively, he sold all the three items to these three friends. The marked price of item Q was ₹3250, which was ₹650 less than the marked price of item P. Then, after some months, Renuka and Priya sold their items to the shopkeeper at 10% and 12% loss respectively and Rahul spent ₹350 in repairing the item R and then sold back to the shopkeeper at ₹3000.

6. What is the difference between the loss incurred when Priya and Rahul sold back the items Q and R to the shopkeeper?
1)₹966.3 2)₹654.5 3)₹786.4 4)₹784.6 5)₹814.2

7. What is the sum of discount (in ₹) given by shopkeeper on the marked price of item P and Q?
1)₹1650 2)₹1580 3)₹1320 4)₹1560 5)₹1413

8. What is the difference between the price of items P and R at which Renuka and Rahul bought them respectively?
1)₹465 2)₹654 3)₹621 4)₹611 5)₹512

9. The price at which Renuka sold back item P to shopkeeper is what per cent of the price at which the shopkeeper bought it from the salesman?
1)94.2% 2) 93.6% 3) 73.8% 4) 84.2 % 5) None of the given options

10. What is the ratio of the price of item Q at which the shopkeeper bought it from the salesman to that of R?
1) 5 : 8 2) 5 : 7 3) 3 : 7 4) 5 : 3 5) 7 : 4

Directions (Q. 11-15): Read the given data carefully and answer the questions that follow:

The table given below shows the difference between the selling price and the cost price for six shopkeepers and the mark-up percentage above the cost price.

Shopkeeper	Difference between selling price and cost price	Mark-up per cent above the cost price
Kalpana	300	60%
Srishti	500	80%
Divya	400	75%
Shikhar	600	$66\frac{2}{3}\%$
Deepti	200	50%
Abhilipsa	300	75%

11. Divya sells her article at a discount of ₹700 and incurs a loss. Then what is the price marked by Divya?
1) ₹600 2) ₹900 3) ₹700 4) ₹300 5) ₹400

12. For Srishti and Deepti, the cost prices of the articles are equal and the marked price for Srishti is ₹300 more than that for Deepti. What will be the ratio of the selling price of Deepti to the selling price of Srishti, if it is given that both of them sell their articles at profit?
1) 4 : 7 2) 7 : 5 3) 4 : 3 4) 4 : 5 5) 3 : 4

13. The ratio of the cost prices for Kalpana, Srishti and Abhilipsa is 3 : 2 : 4 and each shopkeeper sells her article at profit. Find that the selling price for Kalpana is what per cent of the selling price for Srishti if Abhilipsa sells her article at a discount of ₹600.
1) $109\frac{1}{11}\%$ 2) $94\frac{1}{7}\%$ 3) $112\frac{9}{11}\%$ 4) $122\frac{11}{23}\%$ 5) None of the given options

14. The ratio of the marked price for Divya to that for Deepti is 7 : 6. What is the difference of their selling prices if Divya sells her article at a profit and Deepti sells her articles at a loss?
1) ₹400 2) ₹600 3) ₹500 4) ₹300 5) ₹900

15. Shikhar makes the same profit as before by selling an article at successive discounts of 10% and 20%. Find the profit per cent of Shikhar if he sells the article at a discount of ₹1250.
1) 30% 2) 12% 3) 20% 4) None of the given options 5) 24%

Directions (Q. 16-20): Study the given data carefully and answer the questions that follow.

Two prime companies of custom exhausts — Akrapovic and Racefit — furnish their sales data on bi-monthly basis in 2019. Given pie charts show the sales data of both these companies in per cent of the total sales.

Note: Total sales of Racefit and Akrapovic exhausts during the given period are 3600 lakhs and 4800 lakhs respectively.

Racefit exhaust sales

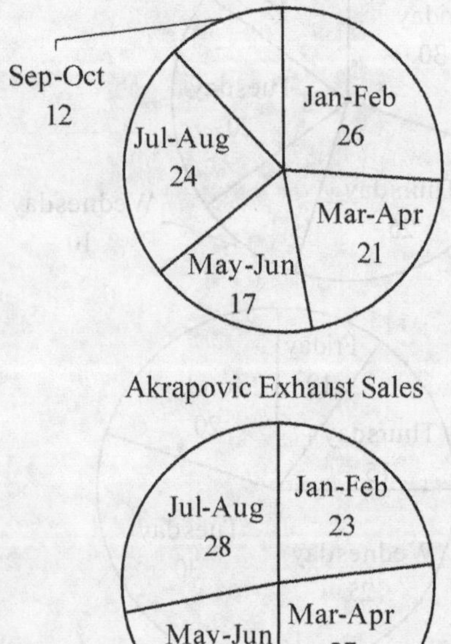

Akrapovic Exhaust Sales

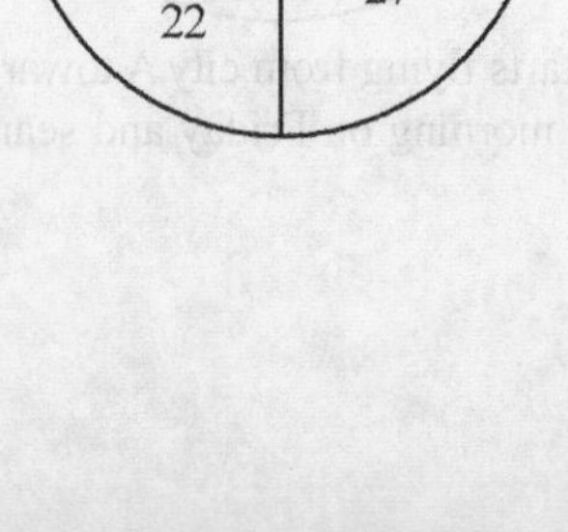

16. If the total sale of Akrapovic exhausts in 2019 is 5800 lakhs and the sale of Akrapovic exhausts in Sep-Oct is $81\frac{9}{11}\%$ of the sale of it in Nov-Dec, then what will be the average sale of Akrapovic exhaust in Jul-Aug and Sep-Oct?
1) 879 lakhs 2) 978 lakhs 3) 659 lakhs
4) 965 lakhs 5) 897 lakhs

17. Total sales of Racefit exhausts in the month of Mar-Apr and Sep-Oct together is approximately what per cent more or less than the sale of the same custom exhausts in the month of May-Jun?
1) None of the given options 2) 94 3) 82
4) 88 5) 97

18. If we include the sales of Nov-Dec in the first pie-chart for Racefit exhausts, the percentage of sales for Mar-Apr will become 15% of the total sales of Racefit in the year 2019. What is the sale (in lakhs) of Racefit exhausts in Nov-Dec?
1) 1540 2) 1210 3) 928
4) 1440 5) None of the given options

19. The average of sales (in lakhs) for Akrapovic exhausts in the month of Jan-Feb and May-June together is what per cent of total sale of Racefit exhausts in the month of Jul-Aug?
1) 125% 2) 95% 3) 120%
4) 75% 5) 145%

20. If the total sales of Racefit exhausts in the month of Nov-Dec is 180 lakhs more than the sale of Akrapovic in the month of Jul-Aug, then what will be the total sales of Racefit exhausts in the year 2019?
1) 5124 lakhs 2) 5214 lakhs 3) 4568 lakhs
4) 5862 lakhs 5) None of the given options

Directions (Q. 21–25) : Study the following information carefully and answer the given question.

The following bar graph shows the number of days taken by 5 different persons to complete a work and the table shows the ratio of total number of days taken by another five different persons to complete the work.

Number of days taken by different persons to complete the work

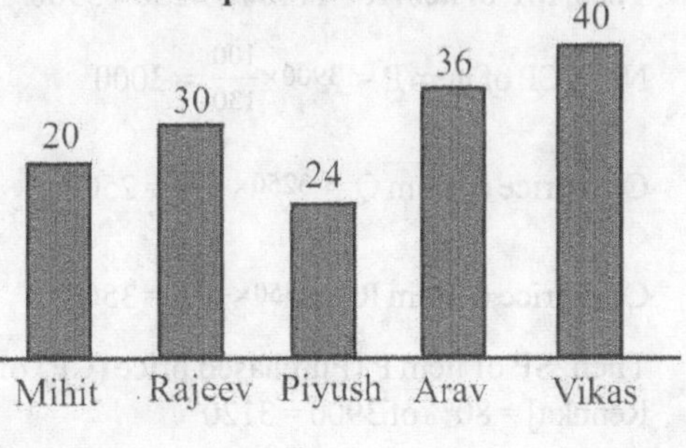

Persons	Ratio
Mohit : Pintu	5 : 08
Rajeev : Punit	3 : 04
Piyush : Rahul	1 : 02
Arav : Sanjeev	6 : 07
Vikas : Tinku	5 : 03

21. Mohit and Rahul started the work and after 10 days Mohit left the job, Rahul and Manoj complete the remaining work in $3\frac{1}{2}$ days. Find the total number of days taken by Manoj alone to complete the work?
1) 24 days 2) 20 days 3) 18 days
4) 16 days 5) None of these

22. Rajeev and Sanjeev started the work and after some days Rajeev left the job. Sanjeev completed the remaining work in 18 days. The number of days after which Rajeev left the job ?
1) 12 days 2) 20 days 3) 5 days
4) 10 days 5) 15 days

23. Rajeev and Rahul undertake to complete a piece of work for ₹7500. With the help of Santosh they complete the work in 16 days. Find the share of Santosh?
1) ₹1500 2) ₹1000 3) ₹1750
4) ₹1250 5) None of these

24. Mohit starts the work and works for 'x' days while Piyush and Vikas complete the remaining work in 9 days, then find the value of 'x' ?
1) 4 days 2) 5 days 3) 8 days
4) 6 days 5) None of these

25. Manish is 50% more efficient than Arav. After how many days one-third of the work is completed when both are working simultaneously ?
1) 20 days 2) 14 days 3) $\frac{24}{5}$ days
4) 10 days 5) None of these

Answers and explanations

(1-5): Flight speed of bird (without wind) in morning from A to B:

Monday = 15% of 2000 = 300 km/hr
Tuesday = 20% of 2000 = 400 km/hr
Wednesday = 10% of 2000 = 200 km/hr
Thursday = 25% of 2000 = 500 km/hr
Friday = 30% of 2000 = 600 km/hr

Flight speed of bird (without wind) in evening from B to A:

Monday = 20% of 1600 = 320 km/hr
Tuesday = 30% of 1600 = 480 km/hr
Wednesday = 25% of 1600 = 400 km/hr
Thursday = 15% of 1600 = 240 km/hr
Friday = 10% of 1600 = 160 km/hr

This information can be tabulised as:

Days	Speed in morning from A to B		Speed in evening from B to A	
	Without wind	With wind	Without wind	With wind
Monday	300	300 – 100 = 200	320	320 + 80 = 400
Tuesday	400	400 – 100 = 300	480	480 + 80 = 560
Wednesday	200	200 – 100 = 100	400	400 + 80 = 480
Thursday	500	500 – 100 = 400	240	240 + 80 = 320
Friday	600	600 – 100 = 500	160	160 + 80 = 240

1. 5; Time between 6:00 AM and 3:00 PM = 9 hours = 540 minutes
Time taken in search of food = 7 hours 9 minutes = 429 minutes
Time taken in flight = 540 – 429 = 111 minutes
Let distance between the cities be D km.

Then, as per information given, $\frac{D}{500}+\frac{D}{240}=\frac{111}{60}$

$\Rightarrow \frac{12D+25D}{6000}=\frac{111}{60} \Rightarrow D=300$

2. 5; Effective speed of both the birds = 100 + 240 + 100 = 440 km/hr
Let both the birds meet after travelling for 't' hours.
$\therefore$ Required difference = 340t – 100t = 180
$\Rightarrow 240t = 180 \Rightarrow t = 0.75$ hours
$\therefore$ Distance between both the cities = $440 \times 0.75 = 330$ km

3. 3; Let increment in flight speed of bird be x km/hr.
Effective speed of bird on Tuesday evening while returning from B to A
= (560 + 40 + x) = (600 + x) km/hr
Original calculated time taken by bird

$= \frac{196}{560} \times 60 = 21$ minutes

Actual time taken by bird (21 – 4.2) = 16.8 minutes

Thus, $\frac{196 \times 60}{600+x} = 16.8 \Rightarrow 600 + x = 700 \Rightarrow x = 100$

4. 3; Distance between A and B = 540 km
Time taken by bird to reach city B on Monday morning

$= \frac{540}{200} = 2.7$ hours

Time taken by bird to reach city A on Friday evening

$= \frac{540}{240} = 2.25$ hours

$\therefore$ Required difference = 2.7 – 2.25 = 0.45 hours = 27 minutes

5. 3; Changed flight speed (without wind) of bird = 120% of 500 = 600 km/hr
Changed flight speed (with wind) of bird = 600 – 100 = 500 km/hr
Original flight time of bird

$= \frac{160}{400}+\frac{160}{320} = (0.4 + 0.5)$ hour

= 0.9 hours = 54 minutes
Changed flight time of bird

$= \frac{160}{500}+\frac{160}{320} = (0.32 + 0.5)$ hour

= 0.82 hours = 49.2 minutes
$\therefore$ Required less time = 54 – 49.2 = 4.8 minutes

(6-10): For shopkeeper:

Total cost of item P, Q and R together = 9000
Total MP of item P, Q and R together = 130% of 9000 = 11700
Now, MP of item Q = 3250
MP of item P = 3250 + 650 = 3900
Then, MP of item R = 11700 – 3250 – 3900 = 4550

Now, CP of item P = $3900 \times \frac{100}{130} = 3000$

Cost price of item Q = $3250 \times \frac{100}{130} = 2500$

Cost price of item R = $4550 \times \frac{100}{130} = 3500$

Then, SP of item P [Purchased price (CP) of P by Renuka] = 80% of 3900 = 3120

SP of item Q [CP of Q by Priya]
= 76% of 3250 = 2470
SP of item R [CP of R by Rahul]
= 82% of 4550 = 3731

6. 4; **For Priya:** Loss on item Q = 12% of 2470 = 296.40
For Rahul: Total expenses on item R by Rahul = CP of R bought by Rahul + 350 = 3731 + 350 = 4081
Loss = 4081 – 3000 = 1081
∴ Difference = 1081 – 296.40 = ₹784.60

7. 4; Discount given on item P = 3900 – 3120 = 780
Discount given on item Q = 3250 – 2470 = 780
∴ Sum = 780 + 780 = ₹1560

8. 4; SP of P = `3120 SP of R = ₹3731
∴ Required difference = 3731 – 3120 = ₹611

9. 2; **For Renuka:** SP of shopkeeper = 90% of 3120 = 2808
For shopkeeper: CP of item P = 3000

∴ Required % = $\frac{2808}{3000}\times 100 = 93.6\%$

10. 2; **For shopkeeper:** CP of item Q = 2500
CP of item R = 3500
∴ Required ratio = 2500 : 3500 = 5 : 7

11. 3; Let CP of article be ₹T. SP = ₹(T – 400)
MP = T × 1.75 = 1.75T
As per information given, T – 400 = 1.75T – 700
⇒ 0.75T = 300 ⇒ T = 400 ∴ MP = 1.75T = ₹700

12. 4; Let CP for Srishti and Deepti be ₹N. Then,
MP for Srishti = ₹1.8N
MP for Deepti = ₹1.5N
As per information given, 1.8N – 1.5N = 300
⇒ N = ₹1000

∴ Required ratio = $\frac{1200}{1500} = 4:5$

13. 1; Let CP for Kalpana, Srishti and Abhilipsa be 3x, 2x and 4x respectively.
SP for Kalpana = 3x + 300
SP for Srishti = 2x + 500
SP for Abhilipsa = 4x + 300
MP of Abhilipsa = 4x × 1.75 = 7x
As per information given, 7x – (4x + 300) = 600
⇒ 3x – 300 = 600 ⇒ x = 300
SP for Kalpana = 3 × 300 + 300 = ₹1200
SP for Srishti = 2 × 300 + 500 = ₹1100

∴ Required % = $\frac{1200}{1100}\times 100 = 109\frac{1}{11}\%$

14. 2; Let the MP for Divya and Deepti be ₹700n and ₹600n respectively.

CP for Divya = $\frac{700n}{175}\times 100 = 400n$

CP for Deepti = $\frac{600n}{150}\times 100 = 400n$

So, required difference
= (400n + 400) – (400n – 200) = ₹600

15. 4; Let CP be ₹3t. MP will be ₹5t.

$SP = 5t\times\frac{90}{100}\times\frac{80}{100} = ₹3.6t$

As per information given,
0.6t = 600 ⇒ t = 1000
So, MP = ₹5000 and CP = ₹3000
New SP = 5000 – 1250 = ₹3750

∴ Required profit % = $\frac{750}{3000}\times 100 = 25\%$

16. 5; Total sales of Akrapovic in 2019 = 5800 lakhs
Total sales of Akrapovic in last 4 months
= 5800 – 4800 = 1000 lakhs
Let sales in Nov-Dec = x

So, $81\frac{9}{11}\%$ of x + x = 1000 lakhs

⇒ $\frac{900x}{1100} + x = 1000$ lakhs

⇒ x = 550 lakhs ⇒ Sales in Sep-Oct
= 1000 – 550 = 450 lakhs
Sales in Jul-Aug = 28% of 4800 lakhs = 1344 lakhs

Required average = $\frac{(1344+450)}{2} = \frac{1794}{2} = 897$ lakhs

17. 2; Required percentage = $\frac{(21+12)-17}{17}\times 100 = 94\frac{2}{17}\% \approx 94\%$

18. 4; Let total sales of Racefit in 2019 be P.
Now, as per information given,

$\frac{15P}{100} = \frac{21}{100}\times 3600 \Rightarrow P = 5040$ lakhs

⇒ Required sales = (5040 – 3600) = 1440 lakhs

19. 1; Required % = $\dfrac{\frac{1}{2}\left(\frac{23+22}{100}\right)4800}{\frac{24}{100}\times 3600}\times 100$

$= \frac{1080}{864}\times 100 = 125\%$

20. 1; Required sales = (28% of 4800 + 180) + 3600
= 1524 + 3600 = 5124 lakhs

21. 4; Mohit can complete the work in 20 days.
Now, Piyush : Rahul = 1 : 2 (given)
Piyush completes the work in 24 days
Rahul can complete the same work in (2 × 24) days = 48 days.
One day's work of Mohit and Rahul

$= \frac{1}{20} + \frac{1}{48} = \frac{12+5}{240} = \frac{17}{240}$

10 day's work of Mohit and Rahul $= \frac{17}{240}\times 10 = \frac{17}{24}$

Remaining work $= 1 - \left(\frac{17}{24}\right) = \frac{7}{24}$

$\left(\frac{17}{24}\right)$ (Rahul and Manoj) whole work $= \frac{7}{2}$

Rahul and Manoj whole work $= \left(\frac{7}{2}\right) \times \left(\frac{24}{7}\right) = 12$ days

Manoj's one day work $= \frac{1}{12} - \frac{1}{48} = \frac{4-1}{48} = \frac{3}{48} = \frac{1}{16}$

Manoj alone can complete the work in 16 days.

22. 4; Rajeev can complete the work in 30 days.
Arav : Sanjeev = 6 : 7 (given)
Arav's 6 days' work = 36
Arav's 1 day's work = 6
Sanjeev can complete the same work in = (7×6=)42 days
Let Rajeev left the job after x days.
Now, according to the question,

$$\left(\frac{1}{30} + \frac{1}{42}\right) \times x + \frac{18}{42} = 1$$

or, $\left(\frac{1}{30} + \frac{1}{42}\right) \times x = 1 - \frac{18}{42}$ or, $\left(\frac{1}{30} + \frac{1}{42}\right) \times x = 1 - \frac{3}{7}$

or, $\left(\frac{72}{30 \times 42}\right) \times x = \frac{4}{7}$ $\therefore x = \frac{4}{7} \times \frac{30 \times 42}{72} = 10$ days

Rajeev left the job after 10 days.

23. 2; Rajeev can complete the work in 30 days.
Now,
Piyush : Rahul = 1 : 2
Piyush can complete the work in 24 days.
Rahul can complete the same work in = 2 × 24 = 48 days.
Let Santosh can complete the work in x days.
Now, according to the question,

$$\frac{1}{30} + \frac{1}{48} + \frac{1}{x} = \frac{1}{16}$$

or, $\frac{1}{x} = \frac{1}{16} - \left(\frac{1}{30} + \frac{1}{48}\right) = \frac{1}{16} \left(\frac{8+5}{240}\right) = \frac{1}{16} - \frac{13}{240}$

or, $\frac{1}{x} = \frac{1}{120} \Rightarrow \frac{1}{30} : \frac{1}{48} : \frac{1}{120}$

Santosh can complete the work alone in 120 days.
The efficiency of Rajeev, Rahul and Santosh are in the ratio of

$$\left(\frac{1}{15}\right) : \left(\frac{1}{24}\right) : \left(\frac{1}{60}\right) \Rightarrow 8 : 5 : 2$$

$(8 + 5 + 2 =) 15 \equiv$ ₹7500

$\therefore 2 \equiv \frac{7500}{15} \times 2 =$ ₹1000

The share of Santosh = ₹1000

24. 3; Mohit's one day's work $= \frac{1}{20}$

Piyush's one day's work $= \frac{1}{24}$

Vikas's one day's work $= \frac{1}{40}$

(Piyush's + Vikas's) one day's work $= \frac{1}{24} + \frac{1}{40}$

Now, according to the question,

$$= \frac{5+3}{120} = \frac{8}{120} = \frac{1}{15}$$

Again, according to the question,

$$\frac{x}{20} + (9) \times \frac{1}{15} = 1 \Rightarrow \frac{x}{20} + \frac{3}{5} = 1$$

$$\Rightarrow \frac{x}{20} = \frac{2}{5} \Rightarrow x = 8 \text{ days}$$

25. 3; Arav can complete the work in 36 days.
Manish is 50% more efficient than Arav.
Efficiency ratio ⇒ Manish : Arav = 150 : 100 = 3 : 2
Day ratio = Manish : Arav = 2 : 3
Arav can complete the work in = 36 days.
∴ Manish can complete the work in

$= 36 \times \frac{2}{3} = 24$ days.

Now, $\left(\frac{1}{24} + \frac{1}{36}\right) \times x = \frac{1}{3}$

$\Rightarrow \left(\frac{3+2}{72}\right) x = \frac{1}{3} \Rightarrow \frac{5}{72} x = \frac{1}{3}$ $\therefore x = \frac{24}{5}$

One-third of the work can be completed in $\frac{24}{5}$ days.

Practice Set 4

Directions (Q. 1–5) : Study the following paragraph carefully and answer the following questions :

A women travels 200 km on three days (Monday, Tuesday and Sunday) each by bus, car and motorcycle. The fare of bus is ₹25 minimum up to 4 km and ₹12 per km for distance greater than 4 km. The fare of car is ₹10 per km. The fare of motocycle is ₹4 per 10 km.

Monday : The distance travelled by motorcycle on Monday is equal to the distance travelled by car on Sunday, the total fare on Monday is ₹961.

Tuesday : The distance travelled by motorcycle on Tuesday is equal to the distance travelled by car on Monday. The difference between the distance by car and bus on Tuesday is equal to the distance by motorcycle on Tuesday (Distance travelled by car is greater than the distance travelled by bus).

Sunday : Minimum ride only in bus. The fare on Sunday is ₹1159.40.

1. What is the ratio of distance travelled by motorcycle on Sunday and Monday?
1) 55 : 43 2) 47 : 55 3) 43 : 55
4) 55 : 47 5) None of these

2. The distance travelled by car on Sunday is how much per cent more/less than the distance travelled by car on Tuesday ?
1) 10% less 2) 15% less 3) 9.09% more
4) 10% more 5) 15% more

3. Find the total fare on Tuesday.
1) ₹1413 2) ₹1314 3) ₹1365
4) ₹1356 5) ₹1456

4. What is the approximate average amount spent on motorcycle on three days?
1) ₹36 2) ₹36.54 3) ₹35 4) ₹35.5 5) ₹35, 12

5. On Tuesday, the ride in bus is reduced to minimum distance such that the half of the remaining distance is covered by car and half by motorcycle. Find how much per cent **approximately** can he save in this way.
1) 8% 2) 13% 3) 24% 4) 5% 5) 10%

Directions (Q. 6–10) : Study the following information carefully and answer the questions given below.

There are three companies X, Y and Z. The number of vacancies released by Company X, Y and Z are 2, 4 and 1 respectively. The number of candidates who got an interview call for each post in X are 24, same for company Y are 2k and for company Z are k.

The total number of candidates who applied in Z is one-fourth of the total number of candidates applied in Y or three- fifths of the total number of candidates who applied in X. Difference between the number of candidates who get an interview call in Y and Z is 105.

6. Find the value of *k*.
1) 12 2) 10 3) 15
4) 20 5) 24

7. Total number of candidates who applied for Y is what percentage more or less than that of X ?
1) 120% 2) 140% 3) 150%
4) 110% 5) 160%

8. What is the average number of candidates who got interview calls for all the companies ?
1) 61 2) 62 3) 63
4) 59 5) 64

9. Out of the total number of candidates who got an interview call from X, 75% are females and after selection process company X allotted its posts to male and female equally, then find the number of females who did not get job in that company.
1) 33 2) 35 3) 36
4) 18 5) 27

10. What is the ratio of the number of candidates who got an interview call in Y and Z ?
1) 4 : 1 2) 8 : 1 3) 2 : 1
4) 5 : 1 5) 6 : 1

Directions (Q. 11–15) : Read the following data carefully and answer the following questions :

The pie chart shows the percentage distribution of six wings in a society who have fiber connection.

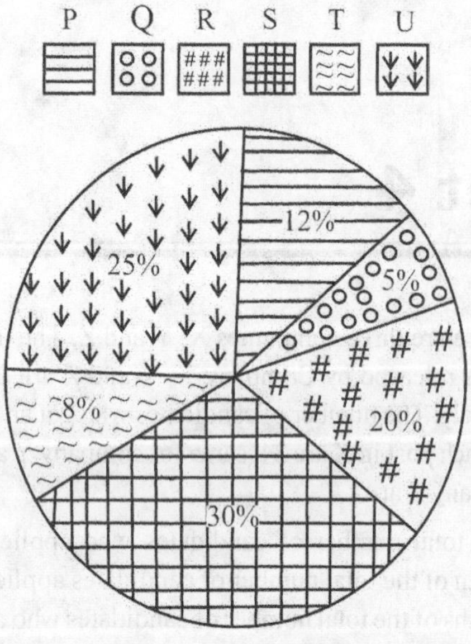

The total number of persons having fiber connection is 800.

11. In wing S people who have taken subscription of Airtel fiber are connection 25% more than that of wing U people. Number of people having Jio fiber connections is same in both wings. Find how much per cent people have Jio fiber subscription in wing S ?
1) $13\frac{3}{4}\%$ 2) $11\frac{1}{3}\%$ 3) $15\frac{1}{2}\%$
4) $16\frac{2}{3}\%$ 5) None of these

12. Ratio of subscribers of fiber connections Airtel, Jio and Vodafone in wing P is 5 : x : 1 respectively. 50% of people subscribed for Airtel fiber connection. Find the per cent of people who subscribed for platform Jio as compared to the total people of wing P.
1) 33.4% 2) 34.8% 3) 39.58%
4) 36.2% 5) None of these

13. Ratio of male who subscribed for fiber connection from wing P and R is 3 : 8. Females are 20% who have fiber connection from wing R. Find the percentage of females who subscribed from wing P.
1) 40% 2) 38% 3) 45%
4) 50% 5) None of these

14. If some people shifted in wing Q from wing T and number of people increased by 40% in wing Q, then find how much per cent people left in wing T.
1) 42% 2) 75% 3) 63%
4) 50% 5) None of the above

15. In wing Q people who have taken fiber connection is how much % less than the people who have taken fiber connection in wing R.
1) 72% 2) 24% 3) 75%
4) 86% 5) None of these

Directions (Q. 16–20) : Read the following data carefully and answer the following questions :

The table shows the total number of Bats (Ton + Kokabura) sold by three shops P, Q and R. It also shows the percentage of unsold Bats (Ton + Kokabura) and number of Ton Bats sold by shopkeepers.

Shopkeeper	Total Bats (Ton + Kokabura)	Per cent of unsold bat	Number of Ton Bats sold
P	200	50%	25
Q	300	30%	100
R	400	50%	80

16. Find the ratio of total number of Kokabura bats sold by Q and R to total Bats sold by P.
1) 31 : 18 2) 33 : 10 3) 24 : 19
4) 35 : 22 5) None of these

17. Ratio of price of Kokabura bat and Ton bat is 9 : 5 for shopkeeper P. Total amount received after selling both bats is ₹8000. Price of Ton bats sold by S is 2/3rd of price of Kokabura bats sold by P. If S sells Ton and Kukabura bat in the ratio 5 : 1 and his sale is equal to unsold Bats of Q, then find the total collection of S by selling Ton Bats.
1) ₹3750 2) ₹3420 3) ₹3600
4) ₹3840 5) None of these

18. Average of unsold bats of shops Q, R and T is 145. If Ton Bats of T which were unsold was 62, then find the number of Kokabura which were unsold.
1) 80 2) 85 3) 88
4) 83 5) None of these

19. Kokabura bats sold by all the shopkeepers are what per cent of the total bats of all three shops ?
1) 19% 2) 25% 3) 45%
4) 36% 5) None of these

20. Shopkeeper F sells is 60% more Kokabura bats than that of shopkeeper P. If F sold 2/3rd Ton bats out of his total sales then find the total bats sold.
1) 365 2) 385 3) 360
4) 345 5) None of these

Directions (Q. 21–25) : Read the following data carefully and answer the following questions :

A juicer shop prepares two types of makes- strawberry and butterscotch in the given four days.

Thursday : Total no. of glasses of strawberry shake is 25.

Friday : The no. of glasses of strawberry shake was X% more than as compare to Thursday.

Saturday : The no. of glasses of strawberry shake was 50% more than as compare to that Friday.

Sunday : The no. of glasses of strawberry shake was 100.

Total number of glasses of strawberry shakes in all four days was 250.

Butterscotch in these four days were Y% less than strawberry shake glasses on each day. Total butterscotch glasses were 50.

21. Find the ratio between the total no. of strawberry glasses on Thursday and Friday together to no. of butterscotch glasses on Friday and Saturday together.

1) 1 : 2 2) 3 : 1 3) 2 : 1
4) 1 : 3 5) None of these

22. Find the ratio between X and Y.

1) 3 : 5 2) 2 : 1 3) 3 : 4
4) 5 : 4 5) None of these

23. On Thursday, strawberry shake glasses sold are 8 times as compare to butterscotch shake glasses on same day. Sold butterscotch shake glasses are less than unsold butterscotch shake glass. If price of strawberry shake and butterscotch shake glasses was ₹20 and ₹10 respectively then find the total collection by selling shake glasses on Thursday.

1) 600 2) 554 3) 450
4) Cannot be determined 5) None of these

24. Find the average number of butterscotch shake glasses on Friday, Saturday and Sunday together.

1) 15 2) 12 3) 14
4) 12 5) None of these

25. The number of butterscotch shake glasses on Sunday is how much per cent of the total number of strawberry shake glasses on all days ?

1) 8% 2) 6% 3) 9%
4) 12% 5) 4%

Answers and explanations

(1–5) :

Sunday:

Distance by bus = 4 km (since minimum ride)

Let a be the distance travelled by car. Distance travelled by motorcycle = $200 - 4 - a = 196 - a$

Fare = 1159.40

Now, according to the question,

$$25 + 10 \times a + (196 - a) \times \left(\frac{4}{10}\right) = 1159.40$$

$$\Rightarrow 10a + 196 \times 0.4 - 0.4a = 1159.40 - 25$$

$$\Rightarrow 9.6a = 1134.40 - 196 \times 0.4$$

$$\Rightarrow 9.6a = 1134.40 - 78.4 = 1056$$

$$\Rightarrow a = \frac{10560}{96} = 110$$

Distance travelled by motorcycle = 196–110 = 86 km and by car = 110 km.

Monday:

Distance travelled by motorcycle = 110 km

Let y be the distance travelled by car.

Distance travelled by bus = $200 - 110 - y = 90 - y$

Bus fare = 25 + 12 × (Distance above 4 km)

= $25 + 12 \times (86 - y)$

Fare = 961

$$\therefore 25 + (86 - y) \times 12 + 10 \times y + 110 \times \left(\frac{4}{10}\right) = 961$$

$$\Rightarrow 25 + 86 \times 12 - 12a + 10a + 44 = 961$$

$$\Rightarrow 2y = 25 + 86 \times 12 + 44 - 961 = 140 \Rightarrow y = 70$$

By car = 70km; By bus = 200 – 110 – 70 = 20 km

Tuesday:

Distance travelled by motorcycle = Distance by car on Monday = 70 km

Also, difference between car and bus = 70

$C - A = 70 \Rightarrow C = A + 70$

Total distance = 200

$A + 70 + A + 70 = 200 \Rightarrow 2A = 60 \Rightarrow A = 30$

$\Rightarrow C = 30 + 70 = 100$

By car = 100km; By bus = 30km; By Motorcycle = 70km

	Monday	Tuesday	Sunday
Car	70	100	110
Motorcycle	110	70	86
Bus	20	30	4

1. 3; Ratio = 86 : 110 = 43 : 55

2. 4; Distance travelled by car on Sunday = 110 km

Distance travelled by car on Tuesday = 100 km

So, Sunday > Tuesday

Per cent increase = $\left(\frac{110-100}{100}\right) \times 100 = 10\%$

3. 3; **Tuesday:**
Distance travelled by bus = 30 km; Fare
= 25 + (26 × 12) = 337
Distance travelled by car = 100 km, Fare = 10 × 100
= 1000

Motorcycle = 70km; Fare = $\left(\frac{4}{10}\right) \times 70 = 28$

Total Fare = 337 + 1000 + 28 = ₹1365

4. 4; **Motorcycle:**
Monday = 110 km
Tuesday = 70 km
Sunday = 86 km
Total distance = 266 km

Total fare = $266 \times \frac{4}{10} = 106.4$

Average fare = $\frac{106.4}{3} = 35.467 = 35.5$

5. 2; **Tuesday:**
Distance travelled by bus = 30 km; Minimum ride = 4 km; Fare = ₹25

Distance travelled by car = 100 km (initially) + $\left(\frac{26}{2}\right)$
= 113 km
Distance travelled by fare = 10 × 113 = ₹1130
Distance travelled by Motorcycle = 70 km (initially)
+ $\left(\frac{26}{2}\right)$ = 83 km; Fare = $83 \times \frac{4}{10}$ = ₹33.2

Total fare initially = ₹1365
Total fare now = 25 + 1130 + 33.2 = ₹1188.2

% save = $\frac{1365-1188.2}{1365} \times 100 = \frac{176.8}{1365} \times 100$

= 12.95 ≈ 13%

6. 3; $4k \times 2k - k \times 1 = 105 \Rightarrow k = 15$

7. 2; $Z = \frac{Y}{4}$ $Z = \frac{3}{5} \times X$

Required percentage = [42 – (5z/3)]/(5z/3) × 100
= 140%

8. 1; $4k \times 2k - k \times 1 = 105 \Rightarrow k = 15$
Required average = (24 × 2 + (8 × 15) + 15)/3 = 61

9. 2; Total number of candidates who get interview call from X = 48
Female candidates = 48 × 75/100 = 36
Male candidates = 48 × 25/100 = 12
Number of vacancies from X = 2
i.e., The number of female candidates who did not get job in X = 36 – 1 = 35

10. 2; Required ratio = $4 \times 2k : k \times 1 = 8 : 1$

(11–15) :
Total no. of persons having fiber connection = 800

No. of persons in P having connection = $800 \times \frac{12}{100} = 96$

No. of persons in Q having connection = $800 \times \frac{5}{100} = 40$

No. of persons in R having connection = $800 \times \frac{20}{100} = 160$

No. of persons in S having connection = $800 \times \frac{30}{100}$
= 240

No. of persons in T having connection = $800 \times \frac{8}{100}$
= 64

No. of persons in U having connection = $800 \times \frac{25}{100}$
= 200

11. 4; People having Airtel fiber connection in S = $\frac{5}{4}$ (people having Airtel fiber in U) .... (1)
According to the question,
In wing S,
Airtel fiber connection + Jio fiber connection = 240 ....(2)
In wing U,
Airtel fiber connecton + Jio fiber connection = 200 ....(3)
Using (1) in (2),

$\frac{5}{4}$ (Airtel fiber connection in U) + Jio fiber connection
= 240
Airtel fiber connection in U + Jio fiber connection = 200
In both wing, Jio fiber connection is equal

240 – $\frac{5}{4}$ (Airtel fiber connection in U) = 200 – Airtel fiber connection in U.
4 × 40 = Airtel fiber connection in U
160 = Airtel fiber connection in U.

Jio fiber connection in S $= 240 - \frac{5}{4}(160) = 40$

Required percentage $= \frac{40}{240} \times 100 = \frac{50}{3} = 16\frac{2}{3}\%$

12. 3; Total no. of fiber connections in P = 96
50% of people having Airtel fiber connection = 48
S $\rightarrow$ 48 I $\rightarrow$ 9.6
The people having Jio fiber connection = 96 – (48 + 9.6) = 96 – 58
No. of people having Jio fiber connection = 38
$\because$ No. of people can't be taken in 9.6 so, 10 value is taken. Required percentage = 39.58%.

13. 4; Total no. of Females in R who have fiber connection

$= 160 \times \frac{20}{100} = 32$

Males in R = 160 – 32 = 128.
According to the question,

$8 \rightarrow 128 \qquad 1 \rightarrow \frac{128}{8} = 16 \qquad 3 \rightarrow 16 \times 3 = 48$

Males in wing P = 48
Females in wing P = 96 – 48 = 48

Required percentage $= \frac{48}{96} \times 100 = 50\%$

14. 2; Let the no. of people shifted from T to Q = X

Total no. of people in wing Q $= 40 \times \frac{140}{100} = 56$

No. of people shifted in wing Q = 56 – 40 = 16
No. of people left in T = 64 – 16 = 48

Required percentage $= \frac{48}{64} \times 100 = 75\%$

15. 3; Required percentage $= \frac{160-40}{160} \times 100 = \frac{120}{160} \times 100$

= 75%

(16–20) :

Shopkeeper	Total Bats (Ton + Kokabura)	No. of unsold Bats	Ton Bats sold	Kokabura Bats sold
P	200	100	25	75
Q	300	90	100	110
R	400	200	80	120

16. 2; Total no. of Kokabura bats sold by Q and R = 110 + 120 = 330
Total no. of bats sold by P = 100
Required ratio = 330 : 100 = 33 : 10

17. 5; Let the ratio of price of Kokabura Bat to Ton Bat = x
Therefore, price of Kokabura Bat = $9x$
Price of Ton Bat = $5x$
Total amount received after selling both bats = 8000
$9x + 5x = 8000$
No. of Ton Bats sold by P = 25
No. of Kokabura Bats sold by P = 75
Now, $75 \times 9x + 25 \times 5x = 8000$
$\Rightarrow 800x = 8000 \therefore x = 10$
Cost of 1 Kokabura Bat = 90
Cost of 1 Ton Bat = 50
Total Ton and Kokabura Bats sold by S = 90

Ton Bat sold by S $= 90 \times \frac{5}{6} = 75$

Kokabura Bat sold by S $= 90 \times \frac{1}{6} = 15$

Price at which Ton Bat is sold by S $= \frac{2}{3} \times 90 = 60$

Total collection of S by selling Ton Bat
= 75 × 60 = ₹4500.

18. 4; Total unsold bats by Q, R and T = 145 × 3 = 435
According to the question,
90 + 200 + T = 435 $\therefore$ T = 145
Unsold Ton Bats + Unsold Kokabura Bats = 145
Unsold Kokabura Bats = 145 – 62 = 83

19. 5; Required percentage $= \frac{305}{900} \times 100 = 33.88\%$

20. 3; No. of Kokabura Bats sold by F $= 75 \times \frac{160}{100} = 120$

F sells $\frac{2}{3}$rd, which means $\frac{1}{3}$ bats sold are Kokabura Bats.

$\therefore \frac{1}{3} \rightarrow 120 \therefore$ Total bats sold = 360

(21–25):

Days	Strawberry shake glasses	Butter scotch shake glasses
Thursday	25	5
Friday	50	10
Saturday	75	15
Sunday	100	20
Total	250	50

No. of strawberry shake glasses on Friday

$= 25\left(\frac{100+x}{100}\right) = 25+\frac{x}{4}$

No. of strawberry shake glasses on Saturday

$= \frac{3}{2}\left(25+\frac{x}{4}\right)$

Total no. of strawberry shake glasses = 250

$25+25+\frac{x}{4}+\frac{3}{2}\left[25+\frac{x}{4}\right]+100 = 250$

$\frac{400+2x+300+3x+800}{8} = 250$

$5x = 2000-1500 = 500 \therefore x = 100$

Strawberry shake glasses on Friday $= 25+\frac{100}{4} = 50$

Strawberry shake glasses on Saturday $= \frac{3}{2}(50) = 75$

According to the question,

Butter scotch shakes glasses are 200 less than strawberry shake glasses.

$\therefore$ Required percentage $= \frac{200}{250}\times 100 = 80\%$

Now, Butterscotch shake glasses on Thursday

$= 25\times\frac{20}{100} = 5$

Butterscotch shake glasses on Friday

$= 50\times\frac{20}{100} = 10$

Butterscotch shake glasses on Saturday

$= 75\times\frac{20}{100} = 15$

Butterscotch shake glasses on Sunday

$= 100\times\frac{20}{100} = 20$

21. 2; Required ratio = 75 : 25 = 3 : 1

22. 4; Required ratio = 100 : 80 = 5 : 4

23. 4; Cannot be determined, as sold and unsold ratio not mentioned.

24. 1; Avg. no. of glasses $= \frac{10+15+20}{3} = 15$

25. 1; No. of butterscotch shake glasses sold R = 20

No. of strawberry shake glasses sold on all 4 day = 250

Required percentage $= \frac{20}{250}\times 100 = 8\%$

Practice Set 5

Directions (Q. 1–6) : The given pie chart shows the percentage distribution of number of students (Boys + Girls) in five different colleges and the table given below shows the percentage of boys in each college out of total number of boys in all the colleges i.e. 80.

Boys + Girls = 200

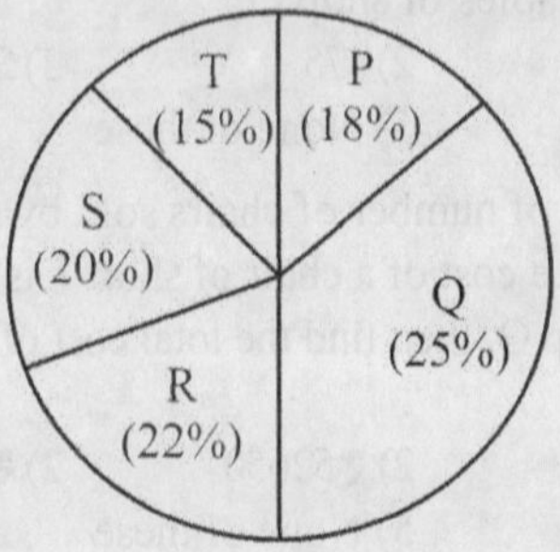

Colleges	% of Boys
P	30%
Q	10%
R	20%
S	25%
T	15%

1. In college P, total number of students studying in B. A. is 50% of the total students in that college and rest are in B.Sc. Out of the total students studying in B.A., 1/3rd are girls, then find the number of boys studying in B Sc.

1) 10 2) 12 3) 18
4) 16 5) None of these

2. If out of the total number of boys in college R, 1/4th are from cityA and rest are from city B and X of girls from college C are from city B and rest are form city A. If total number of students from college R who are from cityA is 18.18% of the total students in that college, then find the value of X.

1) 71.42% 2) 85.71% 3) 56.25%
4) 57.14% 5) 61.16%

3. If the monthly fees of a boy in college S is ₹2000 which is 25% more than that of a girl in the same college, then find the total monthly fees of all the girls in college S.

1) ₹35000 2) ₹34000 3) ₹38000
4) ₹32000 5) None of these

4. If the ratio of number of girls in college Q and U is 6 : 11 and out of the total girls in college U, 28.56% have opted for B. Com, then find the difference between the number of girls in college U who do not opted for B.com and the number of students in college T.

1) 30 2) 25 3) 20
4) 35 5) None of these

5. If 20% of the boys and 25% of the girls from college S travel by bus and the rest travels by family car, then find the ratio of number of students from college S, who travel by family car and the number of students from college P.

1) 45 : 41 2) 36 : 31 3) 41 : 45
4) 31 : 36 5) None of these

6. Find the average of number of girls in all the colleges together except P and T.

1) 25 2) 22 3) 32
4) 30 5) None of these

Directions (Q. 7–12) : The table given below shows the number of bikes manufacutred by four different companies and the number of bikes sold and the number of bikes unsold by each company.

Note : 1. Average of number of bikes manufactured by L and M is 985.

2. The number of bikes sold by L is 50% of that by M.

3. Total number of bikes manufactured by K = 1386.

Companies	Manufactured bikes	Sold	Unsold
J	1620	x	b
K	$1.65x$	$a + b$	506
L	810	—	$3.3a$
M	—	c	200

7. Find the ratio of number of bikes unsold by company L and M.
1) 20 : 31 2) 20 : 33 3) 30 : 23
4) 33 : 20 5) None of these

8. If out of the total unsold bikes of company J, 45% are TVS and the rest is Hero, then find the unsold Hero is what per cent of the total manufactured bikes by company J ?
1) 15.51% 2) 38.91% 3) 26.48%
4) 18.80% 5) None of these

9. If the ratio of number of sold bikes of companies K and N is 11 : 12, and 40% of the manufactured bikes by company N were sold, find the sum of total unsold bikes of companies N and M.
1) 1560 2) 1450 3) 1640
4) 1480 5) None of these

10. If company P manufactured 8*a* bikes out of which 0.5*b* bikes are unsold, then find the average of number of sold bikes of the companies P and J.
1) 625 2) 825 3) 515
4) 745 5) None of these

11. If the unsold bikes of company L are transferred to a third party for selling and the third party was able to sell only 2/6th of the bikes, then find the number of bikes still unsold of company L.
1) 330 2) 240 3) 220
4) 280 5) None of these

12. If the difference between the number of bikes manufactured by company K and O is *x* and company K manufactured more bikes than O and company O sold 33.33% of their bikes, then find the number of unsold bikes of company O.
1) 364 2) 268 3) 324
4) 296 5) None of these

Directions (Q. 13–16) : Study the following information carefully and answer the questions given below :

There are three shops P, Q and R. All the shops are selling furniture. The number of tables sold by shop P is 33.33% less than the number of chairs sold by it. The cost of a table and a chair of shop P is ₹240 and ₹200 respectively. The number of tables sold by shop Q is 5 more than that by P. The number of chairs sold by shop Q is 80. The cost of a table and a chair of shop Q is ₹260 and ₹210 respectively. The number of tables sold by shop R is 150. The number of tables sold by shop Q is 16.66% less than that by shop R. The total number of furniture sold by shop R is 270. The cost of a table of shop R is 50% more than that of Q.

Note : Total furniture = Tables + Chairs

13. Find the difference between the total cost of all the tables of shop P and the total cost of all the chairs of shop R.
1) ₹1250 2) ₹1440 3) ₹1560
4) ₹1380 5) ₹1620

14. If the number of tables sold by shop S is average of number of tables sold by P and R and the number of chairs sold by S is 1/3rd more than the number of tables sold by it, then find the ratio of number of chairs sold by Q and S.
1) 5 : 9 2) 3 : 5 3) 5 : 7
4) 4 : 9 5) None of these

15. If the number of tables sold by shop Q is 20% of the manufactured tables by the shop, then find the number of unsold tables of shop Q.
1) 500 2) 475 3) 525
4) 625 5) None of these

16. If the ratio of number of chairs sold by shop R and T is 4 : 7 and the cost of a chair of shop T is 40% more than that of shop Q, then find the total cost of all the chairs of shop T.
1) ₹60520 2) ₹52650 2) ₹52650
4) ₹61740 5) None of these

Directions (Q. 17–21) : Read the following information carefully and answer the questions given below :

The total number of flats in society A was 2.5*y* more than the number of unsold flats in that society. All the flats were sold in society C. The number of flats sold in society B is 36 which is 60% of the number of total flats (sold + unsold) in society C. The number of unsold flats in society is 64. If the total number of flats (sold + unsold) in society A is doubled, then the total number of flats (sold + unsold) in all three societies become 500.

17. If unsold number of flats in society A is 70, then find the value of *y*.
1) 16 2) 32 3) 48
4) 36 5) 12

18. If the number of flats sold in society B would have been 14 more and the number of flats sold in society C would have been 15 more, then find the ratio of sold flats in society B and C.
1) 5 : 8 2) 3 : 8 3) 4 : 5
4) 2 : 3 5) 1 : 3

19. Find the number of unsold flats in society B is how much less than the total flats in society A ?
1) 45 2) 78 3) 106
4) 102 5) None of these

20. If the number of flats sold in society D is 20% of the total number of fiats in society A, then find the difference between total number of flats sold in societies D and C ?
1) 72 2) 84 3) 96
4) 30 5) 26

21. If out of total number of flats sold in society C, 60% are AC types and rest are non-AC types, then find the number of non-AC types sold flats in society C.
1) 26 2) 28 3) 32
4) 38 5) 24

Directions (Q. 22–27) : Read the following information carefully and answer the questions given below :

The bar graph given below shows the quantity of coal extracted (in kg) by companies X and Y in 4 different years. The table shows the percentage of coal extracted by worker M in company X and quantity of coal extracted by worker M in company Y in each year.

Total quantity of coal extracted in any company in any year = Quantity of coal extracted by worker M + Quantity of coal extracted by worker N.

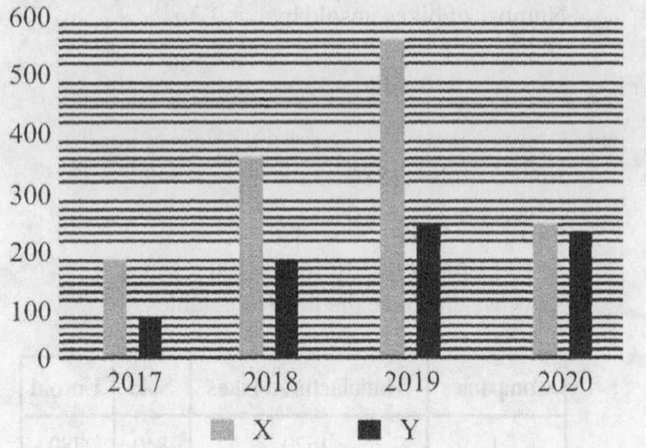

Year	% of Coal extracted by M in company X	Quantity of Coal extracted by M in company Y (in kg)
2017	60%	70
2018	42.84%	90
2019	40%	150
2020	45%	80

22. Find the sum of quantity of coal extracted by worker M in both the companies together in 2017 is approximately how much per cent more or less than the sum of quantity of coal extracted by worker N in both the companies together in 2020 ?
1) 14% 2) 8% 3) 6%
4) 21% 5) 9%

23. In 2021, the quantity of coal extracted by worker N in both the companies together is 40% of total quantity of coal extracted by M in both the companies in 2018. The ratio of quantity of coal extracted by N in companies X and Y in 2021 is 7 : 5 respectively, find the quantity of coal extracted by N in company Y in 2021.
1) 56 kg 2) 84 kg 3) 40 kg
4) 45 kg 5) None of these

24. If the quantity of coal extracted by worker R in company Y in 2019 is 30% more than the quantity of coal extracted by M in company Y in 2019 and the quantity of coal extracted by worker R in company X in 2019 is 12 kg less than the quantity of coal extracted by N in company X in 2019, then find the total quantity of coal extracted by R in 2019,
1) 339 kg 2) 469 kg 3) 459 kg
4) 519 kg 5) None of these

25. If 25% of the quantity of coal extracted by M in company X in 2020 went for purification and the quantity of coal extracted by worker N in company X in 2020 went for purification is 33.33% more than that by M find the total quantity of coal extracted by M and N in company X in 2020, which did not go for purification.
1) 123 kg 2) 147 kg 3) 117 kg
4) 177 kg 5) None of these

26. Find the ratio of total quantity of coal extracted by M and N in company X in 2019 and the total quantity of coal extracted by M and N in company Y in 2018.
1) 13 : 5 2) 12 : 5 3) 5 : 2
4) 14 : 5 5) None of these

27. If N was paid ₹240 for per kg extraction of coal in company Y in 2017 and ₹360 for per kg extraction of coal in company X in 2017, find the total amount earned by N in both the companies together in 2017.
1) 34500 2) 39700 3) 34900
4) 38400 5) None of these

Answers and explanations

(1–6) :

Colleges	Boys	Girls	Total
P	24	12	36
Q	8	42	50
R	16	28	44
S	20	20	40
T	12	18	30

1. 2; Students studying in B. A. in college P $= 36 \times \frac{50}{100} = 18$

$\therefore$ Students studying in B.Sc in college P = 36 – 18 = 18

Girls in B. A. $= 18 \times \frac{1}{3} = 6$

$\therefore$ Girls in B.Sc = 12 – 6 = 6

Hence, the number of boys studying in B.Sc. =18–6 = 12

2. 2; Boys from city A in college R $= 16 \times \frac{1}{4} = 4$

Boys from city B in college R = 16 – 4 = 12

Total students from City A in college R = 18.18% of 44 = (9.09 × 2)% of 44

$= \left(\frac{100}{11} \times 2\right)\%$ of $44 = 44 \times \frac{200}{11 \times 100} = 8$

$\therefore$ Girls from city A in college R = 8 – 4 = 4

Girls from city B in college R = 28 – 4 = 24

Hence, value of $x = \frac{24}{28} \times 100 = 85.71\%$

3. 4; Fees of a girl in college S $= 2000 \times \frac{100}{125} =$ ₹1600

Hence, total monthly fees of all the girls in college S = 1600 × 20 = ₹32000

4. 2; Number of girls in college U $= \frac{42}{6} \times 11 = 77$

Girls opted for B.com in college U $= 77 \times \frac{2}{7} = 22$

$\left[\because \frac{1}{7} = 14.28\% \text{ and therefore } 28.56\% = \frac{2}{7}\right]$

$\therefore$ Girls who do not opted for B.Com in college U = 77 –22 = 55

Number of students in college T = 30

Hence, required difference = 55 – 30 = 25

5. 4; Number of students who travel by family car in colleges $= 20 \times \frac{80}{100} + 20 \times \frac{75}{100} = 16 + 15 = 31$

Number of students from college P = 36

Hence, required ratio = 31 : 36

6. 4; Average number of girls in colleges Q, R and S

$= \frac{42 + 28 + 20}{3} = \frac{90}{3} = 30$

(7– 12) :

$\frac{L + M}{2} = 985 \Rightarrow L + M = 2 \times 985 = 1970$

Since, L = 810 therefore, M = 1970 – 810 = 1160

C = 1160–200 = 960

$\therefore$ Number of bikes sold by L $= \frac{960}{2} = 480$

Number of bikes unsold by L = $3.3a$

$\Rightarrow 3.3a = 810 - 480 = 330 \Rightarrow a = \frac{330}{3.3} = 100$

Again, $1.65x = 1386 \Rightarrow x = \frac{1386}{1.65} = 840$

$\Rightarrow a + b = 1386 - 506 = 880$

$\Rightarrow 100 + b = 880 \Rightarrow b = 880 - 100 = 780$

Now, we can have the following table :

Companies	Manufactured bikes	Sold	Unsold
J	1620	840	780
K	1386	880	506
L	810	480	330
M	1160	960	200

7. 4; Ratio of number of bikes unsold by the companies L and M = 330 : 200 = 33 : 20

8. 3; Number of unsold Hero bikes of company J $= 780 \times \frac{55}{100} = 429$

Hence, required percentage $= \frac{429}{1620} \times 100 = 26.48\%$

9. 3; Number of sold bikes of company N = $\frac{880}{11} \times 12 = 960$

$\therefore$ Unsold bikes of company N = $\frac{960}{40} \times 60 = 1440$

Hence, sum of total unsold bikes of companies N and M = 1440 + 200 = 1640

10. 1; Number of manufactured bikes by company P = 8 × 100 = 800

$\therefore$ Number of unsold bikes of company P = 0.5×780 = 390

So, Number of sold bikes of company P = 800 – 390 = 410

Number of sold bikes of company J = 840

Hence, required average = $\frac{410+840}{2} = \frac{1250}{2} = 625$

11. 3; Bikes sold by third party = $330 \times \frac{2}{6} = 110$

Hence, the number of bikes still unsold of company L = 330 – 110 = 220

12. 1; As $x = 840$

Bikes manufactured by company O = 1386 – 840 = 546

Hence, the number of unsold bikes of company O

$= 546 \times \frac{2}{3} = 364$

(13–16) :

Number of tables sold by shop Q = 150 – 16.66% of 150

$= 150 - \frac{1}{6} \times 150 = 125$

Hence, number of tables sold by shop P = 150 – 5 = 120

Number of chairs sold by shop P = $\frac{100}{\frac{200}{3}} \times 120 = 180$

Number of chairs sold by shop R = 270 – 150 = 120

Cost of table of shop R = 260 + 50% of 260 = 260 + 130 = 390

Now, we can have the following table:

Shops	Tables		Chairs	
	Sold	Cost	Sold	Cost
P	120	₹240	180	₹200
Q	125	₹260	80	₹210
R	150	₹390	120	₹252

13. 2; Required difference = 120 × 252 – 120 × 240 = 120 × 240 = ₹1440

14. 4; Number of tables sold by shop S = $\frac{120+150}{2}$

$= \frac{270}{2} = 135$

Number of chairs sold by S = $135 \times \frac{4}{3} = 180$

Hence, required ratio = 80 : 180 = 4 : 9

15. 1; Total manufactured tables by shop Q = $\frac{125}{20} \times 100 = 625$

Hence, the number of unsold tables by Q

$\Rightarrow 625 - 125 = 500$

16. 2; Number of chairs sold by shop T = $\frac{120}{4} \times 7 = 210$

Cost of a chair of shop T = $210 \times \frac{140}{100}$ = ₹294

Hence, the total cost of all chairs of shop = 210 × 294 = ₹61,740

(17–21) :

Flats	Sold	Unsold	Total
A	$x + 2.5y$	x	P = 170
B	36	64	100
C	60	0	60

$2p + 100 + 60 = 500$

$\Rightarrow 2p = 340 \Rightarrow \boldsymbol{p = 170}$

17. 5; If $x = 70$ Then, $x + 2.5y + x = 170$

$\Rightarrow 2.5y = 170 - 140 = 30 \Rightarrow y = \frac{300}{25} = 12$

18. 4; Number of flats sold in society B = 36 + 14 = 50

Number of flats sold in society C = 60 + 15 = 75

Required Ratio = 50 : 75 = 2 : 3

19. 3; Number of unsold flats in society B = 64

Total flats in society A = 170

Required difference = 170 – 64 = 106

20. 5; Number of flats sold in society D = $170 \times \frac{20}{100} = 34$

Number of flats sold in society C = 60

Required difference = 60 – 34 = 26

21. 5; Non AC types flats = 100 – 60 = 40%

Number of Non AC types sold flats in society C

$= 60 \times \frac{40}{100} = 24$

(22–27) :

Year	Quantity of Coal extracted in Company X		Quantity of Coal extracted in company Y	
	M	N	M	N
2017	120 kg	80 kg	70 kg	40 kg
2018	150 kg	200 kg	90 kg	110 kg
2019	224 kg	336 kg	150 kg	90 kg
2020	108 kg	132 kg	80 kg	70 kg

22. 3; Quantity of coal extracted by worker M in both the companies to gether in 2017 = 120 + 70 = 190 kg

Quantity of coal extracted by worker N in both the companies together in 2020 = 132 + 70 = 202 kg

$\therefore$ Required percentage $= \frac{202\text{-}190}{202} \times 100 = \frac{1200}{202}$

$= 5.94\% \approx 6\%$.

23. 3; Total quantity of coal extracted by M in both the companies in 2018 = 150 + 90 = 240 kg

In 2021, the quantity of coal extracted by worker N in both the companies together $= 240 \times \frac{40}{100} = 96$ kg

Quantity of coal extracted by N in company Y in 2021

$= \frac{96}{12} \times 5 = 40$ kg

24. 4; Quantity of coal extracted by M in company Y in 2019 = 150 kg

Quantity of coal extracted by R in company Y in 2019

$= 150 \times \frac{130}{100} = 195$ kg

Quantity of coal extracted by N in company X in 2019 = 336 kg

Quantity of coal extracted by R in company X in 2019 = 336 kg – 12 kg = 324 kg

Total quantity of coal extracted by R in 2019 = 195 + 324 = 519 kg

25. 4; Quantity of coal extracted for purification by M in company X in 2020 $= 108 \times \frac{25}{100} = 27$ kg

Quantity of coal extracted for purification by N in company X in 2020 $\Rightarrow 27 \times \frac{4}{3} = 36$ kg

The total quantity of coal extracted by M and N in company X in 2020, which did not go for purification = (108 + 132) – (27 + 36) = 240 – (27 + 36) = 177 kg

26. 4; Total quantity of coal extracted by M and N in company X in 2019 = 224 + 336 = 560 kg

Total quantity of coal extracted by M and N in company Y in 2018 = 90 + 110 = 200 kg

$\therefore$ Required ratio = 560 : 200 = 14 : 5

27. 4; Extraction of coal in company Y in 2017 by N = 40 kg

N was paid = 40 × 240 = ₹9600

Extraction of coal in company X in 2017 by N = 80 kg

N was paid = 80 × 360 = ₹28800

$\therefore$ Total amount = 9600 + 28800 = ₹38,400

Practice Set 6

Directions (Q. 1–6) : Read the following passage to answer the questions given below.

The first pie chart (top) given below shows the percentage distribution of the total products manufactured by shopkeepers Z, Y, X, W and V. **Total number of products manufactured by all five together is 20000.**

The second pie chart (bottom) given below shows the percentage distribution of products sold by these five shopkeepers. **Total products sold by all the shopkeepers is 12000.**

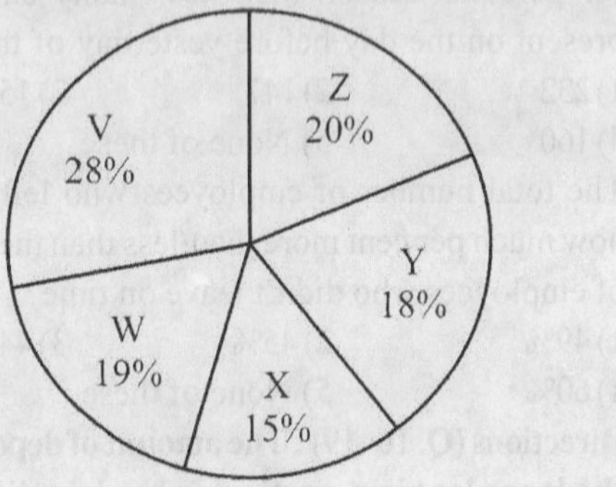

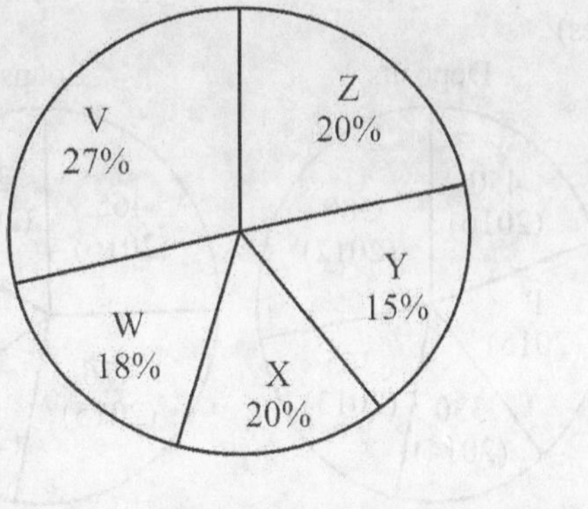

1. Find the average of the number of products unsold by Z, Y and X.
1) 1222.22 2) 1343.33 3) 1333.33
4) 1920.5 5) None of these

2. The total number of unsold products of shopkeepers W and V is **approximately** what percentage of total sold products of V ?
1) 128% 2) 123% 3) 120% 4) 105% 5) 119%

3. Find the ratio of total unsold products of X and V together to that of Y and W together.
1) 45 : 37 2) 37 : 43 3) 31 : 29
4) 32 : 43 5) None of these

4. If the ratio of number of unsold products of shopkeeper Z and U is 40x and the number of sold products of shopkeeper U is 30% more than that of X and the sold products of shopkeeper U is 40% of the total manufactured products by him, then find the value of x.
1) 123 2) 57 3) 117
4) 121 5) None of these

5. The number of manufactured products of shopkeeper I is average of total manufactured products of shopkeepers W and V. The difference between the number of sold products of I and X is 800, what is the number of unsold products of shopkeepers I ?
1) 1600 2) 1200 3) 1700 4) 1500 5) 3200

6. If *Z* sold his products at ₹20 each and Y sold his products at ₹40 each, then find the difference between the revenue earned by shopkeepers Z and Y by selling all their products.
1) ₹16000 2) ₹32000 3) ₹24000
4) ₹28000 5) None of these

Directions (Q. 7–10) : Study the paragraph and answer the questions that follow.

There were two similar tanks P and Q with five similar pipes A, B, C, D and E. Pipes A, B and C can fill the empty tank in 20 minutes, 30 minutes and 60 minutes respectively. While pipes D and E can empty the filled tank in 40 minutes and 60 minutes respectively. Tank P had no leaks but tank Q had a leak, such that when pipe A was opened in the empty tank Q it took 24 minutes to fill the tank.

7. Pipes A, B and C were simultaneously opened into the empty tank P such that pipes A and B were discharging milk and pipe C was discharging water into the tank. So, the tank will be 60% filled after ______ minutes and the mixture in the tank will contain ______ part of milk. Which of the following options satisfies the two blanks in the question?
1) 2, 3/4 2) 2, 4/5 3) 3, 3/20
4) 3, 6/7 5) 6, 5/6

8. When pipes A and B were simultaneously opened into a 30% filled tank P, it will be ______ % filled after 6 minutes, while if pipes B and C were simultaneously opened into a 30% filled tank P, it will be 70% after ______ minutes.
Which of the following options satisfies the two blanks in the question?
1) 60, 2 2) 60, 3 3) 70, 3
4) 70, 4 5) 80, 8

9. When pipes B and D were simultaneously opened in the empty tank P, 20 gallons of liquid was filled in the tank after 12 minutes. This means that the tank has a capacity of ______ gallons and pipe D can empty it at a rate of ______ gallons per minute.
Which of the following options satisfies the two blanks in the question?
1) 200, 5 2) 240, 12 3) 280, 15
4) 320, 20 5) None of these

10. All the five pipes A, B, C, D and E were simultaneously opened into the tank P which was initially $\frac{2}{5}$ part filled, and were closed one by one respectively after every minute, then the tank is ______ part filled when the pipe C was closed and ______ part filled when the pipe E was closed.
Which of the following options satisfies the two blanks in the question?
1) $\frac{23}{40}, \frac{53}{120}$ 2) $\frac{53}{120}, \frac{23}{60}$ 3) $\frac{23}{60}, \frac{23}{40}$
4) $\frac{25}{48}, \frac{23}{60}$ 5) $\frac{40}{7}, \frac{25}{8}$

Directions (Q. 11–15) : Study the following information carefully and answer the questions given below.

One day, in a BOB Branch the attendance of all the employees was 100% but all the employees were not punctual to the office and did not all the employees stayed till the end of the office time. On that day, of all the employees who arrived early at the office, 30% of them left early but 20% of them left late and rest of them left on time. Of the employees who arrived late at the office, 25% of them left late but 50% of them left on time and rest of them left early. Of the employees who arrived on time, 37.5% of them left early and an equal number of them left late but rest of them left on time. The number of employees who arrived early was equal to the number of employees who left early and the number of employees who left early was 84 more man the number of employees who arrived late at the office. The number of employees who didn't leave on time was 228.

11. What is the difference between the total number of employees who left late and the total number of employees who left early?
1) 12 2) 16 3) 20
4) 22 5) None of these

12. What is the total number of employees working in that branch?
1) 400 2) 432 3) 392
4) 356 5) None of these

13. Find the respective ratio of the number of employees who arrived early, the number of employees who arrived on time, and the number of employees who arrived late?
1) 15 : 28 : 6 2) 17 : 50 : 15 3) 15 : 51 : 16
4) 16 : 50 : 17 5) None of these

14. Suppose on the day before yesterday of that day 25% of the total number of employees was on leave on the medical ground and 50% of the ramaining was on leave for personal reason then how many employees was present on the day before yesterday of that day?
1) 232 2) 147 3) 157
4) 160 5) None of these

15. The total number of employees who left on time was how much per cent more than/less than the total number of employees who didn't leave on time?
1) 49% 2) 45% 3) 44.44%
4) 60% 5) None of these

Directions (Q. 16–19) : The amount of deposits received, and the loans lent in a particular bank in different years has been illustrated as the following pie-chart (Amount in crores)

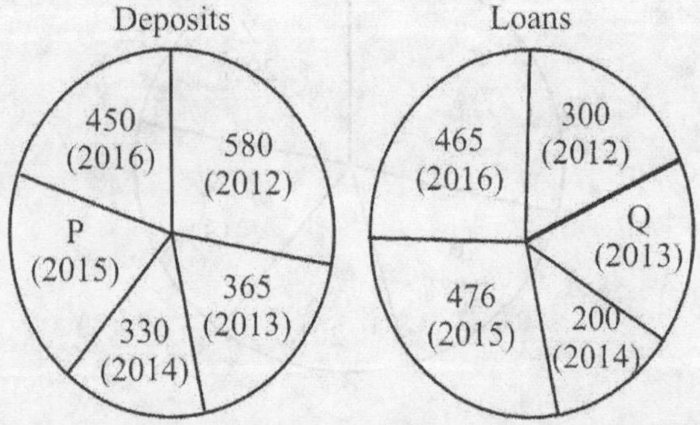

(Spread = Lending rate on loans - Borrowing rate on deposits)

16. The deposit in the year of 2015 is 20% less than that of 2012 and loans in the year of 2013 is 10% less than that of 2014. Then what is the probability that the bank gives loan in any of the year is more than the deposits received in any of the given year.
1) $\frac{3}{25}$ 2) $\frac{4}{7}$ 3) $\frac{11}{25}$

4) $\frac{7}{25}$ 5) None of these

17. If the borrowing rate of deposits is $9\frac{1}{11}\%$ and lending rate of loans is $14\frac{2}{7}\%$. In which year the bank got the highest spread, if P and Q are same as the loan and deposit respectively for the same year?
1) 2013 2) 2015 3) 2016
4) 2014 5) Can't be determined

18. What is the value of P?
I. In the year of 2015, the bank earns spread nil with the borrowing rate of $9\frac{1}{11}\%$.
II. Q is $5\frac{15}{17}\%$ more than that of P.
III. With borrowing rate is 25% less than the lending rate on the same year.
1) All three options are required
2) Data inadequate
3) Only options I and II are enough
4) Only options I and III are enough
5) None of these

19. In the year of 2016, if the total loan is paid back yearly in four equal instalments with the rate of interest at 11% compounded annually. What is amount of instalment? (all the values in crores)
1) 456.2 2) 146.41 3) 1300.1
4) 3214 5) None of these

Directions (Q. 20–24) : The bar graph given below shows the data of the production of mobile phones (in lakh tonnes) by three different companies α, β and γ over the years.

Production of Mobile phones (in lakh tonnes) by Three Companies α, β and γ over the years

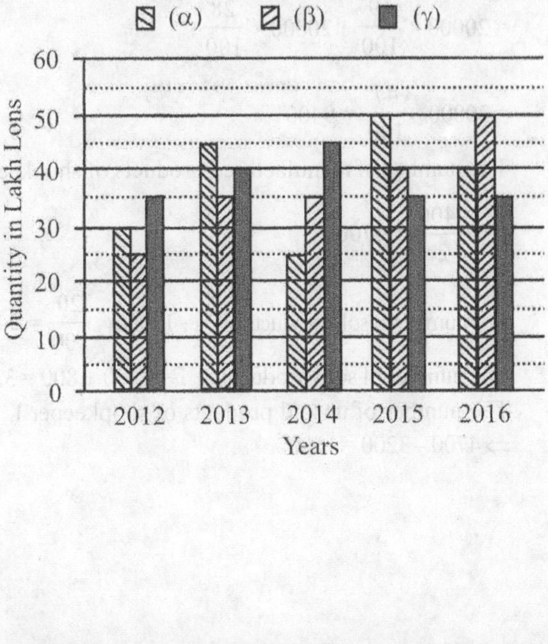

20. For which of the following years, the percentage rise or fall in production from the previous year is the maximum for Company β?
1) 2013 2) 2014 3) 2015
4) 2016 5) None of these

21. What is the ratio of the average production of company α in the period (2014–2016) to the average production of company β in the same period ?
1) 1 : 1 2) 15 : 17 3) 23 : 25
4) 27 : 29 5) None of these

22. The average production for five years was maximum for which company?
1) α 2) β 3) γ
4) α and γ 5) None of these

23. In which year was the percentage of production of Company γ to the production of company β the maximum ?
1) 2012 2) 2013 3) 2014
4) 2015 5) None of these

64. What is the percentage increase in the production of Company β from 2012 to 2015 ?
1) 30% 2) 45% 3) 50%
4) 60% 5) None of these

Directions (Q. 25–29) : Study the following table carefully and answer the questions given below:

In the following table, Data related to candidates appeared and qualifed from Ranchi in a competitive exam during 5 years.

Years	No. of appeard candidates	% of appeared candidates who qualified	Respective ratio of no. of qualified male & no. of qualified female candidates
2013	1050	–	2 : 2
2014	–	–	5 : 3
2015	720	60%	–
2016	–	42%	9 : 5
2017	1350	64%	–

25. In 2017, if the number of female qualified candidates was 264, what was the respective ratio of number of male qualified candidates and number of female qualified candidates?
1) 25 : 16 2) 5 : 4 3) 25 : 11
4) 21 : 16 5) 17 : 11

26. The number of appeared candidates was increased by 40% from 2013 to 2018. If 30% of the appeared candidates

qualified in 2018, what was the number of qualified candidates in 2018?
1) 400 2) 252 3) 552
4) 441 5) 320

27. In 2014, the respective ratio of number of appeared candidates to qualified candidates was 5 : 4. Number of female qualified candidates constitutes, what per cent of number of appeared candidates in the same year?
1) 20% 2) 25% 3) 30%
4) 15% 5) 40%

28. In 2016, if the difference between number of male qualified candidates and female qualified candidates was 108, what was the number of appeared candidates in 2016?
1) 800 2) 900 3) 850
4) 600 5) 950

29. If the average number of qualified candidates in 2013 and 2015 was 321, what per cent of appeared candidates qualified in the competitive exam in 2013?
1) 40% 2) 30% 3) 20%
4) 35% 5) 25%

Answers and explanations

(1–6) :

$$\text{Products unsold by Z} = 12000 \times \frac{80}{100} = 9600$$

$$\text{Products unsold by Y} = 12000 \times \frac{85}{100} = 10200$$

$$\text{Products unsold by X} = 12000 \times \frac{80}{100} = 9600$$

1. 3; Total number of products unsold by Z, Y and X

$$= 20000 \times \frac{53}{100}\ 12000 \times \frac{55}{100} = 4000$$

$$\therefore \text{Required average} = \frac{4000}{3} = 1333.33$$

2. 2; Total number of unsold products of W and V

$$= 20000 \times \frac{47}{100} - 12000 \times \frac{45}{100}$$

$$= 9400 - 5400 = 4000$$

Total sold products of V = 3240

$$\therefore \text{Required percentage} = \frac{4000}{3240} \times 100 \approx 123\%$$

3. 2; Unsold products of X and V

$$= 20000 \times \frac{43}{100} - 12000 \times \frac{47}{100} = 8600 - 5640 = 2960$$

Unsold products of Y and W

$$= 20000 \times \frac{37}{100} = -12000 \times \frac{33}{100} = 7400 - 3960 = 3440$$

$$\therefore \text{Required ratio} = 2960 : 3440 = 37 : 43$$

4. 3; Number of unsold products of shopkeeper Z

$$= 20000 \times \frac{20}{100} - 12000 \times \frac{20}{100}$$

$$= 4000 - 2400 = 1600$$

Let the number of unsold products of shopkeeper U be p.

According to the question,

$$\frac{1600}{p} = \frac{40}{x}$$

$$\Rightarrow p = 40x \quad \text{.............(i)}$$

$$\text{Number of sold products by X} = 12000 \times \frac{20}{100} = 2400$$

$$\text{Number of sold products by U} = 2400 \times \frac{130}{100} = 3120$$

Total manufactured products by U =

$$\frac{3120}{40} \times 100 = 7800$$

Number of unsold products of shopkeeper U

$$= 7800 - 3120 = 4680$$

Put the value in eqn. (i)

$$4680 = 40x$$

$$\therefore x = 117$$

5. 4; Total manufactured products of shopkeepers W and V

$$= 20000 \times \frac{19}{100} + 20000 \times \frac{28}{100}$$

$$= 20000 \times \frac{47}{100} = 9400$$

The number of manufactured products of shopkeeper

$$\text{I} = \frac{9400}{2} = 4700$$

$$\text{The number of sold products of X} = 12000 \times \frac{20}{100} = 2400$$

The number of sold products of I = 2400 + 800 = 3200

The number of unsold products of shopkeeper I

$$\Rightarrow 4700 - 3200 = 1500$$

6. 3; The number of products sold by Z = $12000 \times \frac{20}{100} = 2400$

Revenue earned by Z = 2400 × 20 = ₹48000

The number of products sold by Y = $12000 \times \frac{15}{100}$

= 1800

Revenue earned by Y = 1800 × 40 = ₹72000

Required difference = ₹72000 – ₹48000 = ₹24000

7. 5; Part of tank P filled by pipes A, B and C in 1 minute

$= \frac{1}{20} + \frac{1}{30} + \frac{1}{60} = \frac{3+2+1}{60} = \frac{6}{60} = \frac{1}{10}$

⇒ The tank will be completely filled in = 10 minutes

⇒ Tank will be 60% filled in = 60% of 10 = 6 minutes

Now, part of milk filled by pipes A and B in 1 minute

$= \frac{1}{20} + \frac{1}{30} = \frac{3+2}{60} = \frac{1}{12}$

⇒ Part of milk filled in 6 minutes = $6 \times \frac{1}{12} = \frac{1}{2}$

But, part of tank filled in 6 minutes = $\frac{3}{5}$

⇒ Part of milk in the mixture = $\left(\frac{1}{2} \div \frac{3}{5}\right) = \frac{5}{6}$

∴ Only option (5) satisfies the two blanks in the question.

8. 5; Part of tank filled by pipes A and B in 1 minute

$= \frac{1}{20} + \frac{1}{30} = \frac{3+2}{60} = \frac{5}{60} = \frac{1}{12}$

⇒ Part of tank filled in 6 minutes = $6 \times \frac{1}{12} = \frac{1}{2} = 50\%$

∵ The tank was initially 30% filled, it is 30 + 50 = 80% filled after 6 minutes.

Similarly,

Part of tank filled by pipes B and C in 1 minute

$= \frac{1}{30} + \frac{1}{60} = \frac{2+1}{60} = \frac{3}{60} = \frac{1}{20}$

∵ The tank was initially 30% filled, so part of tank to be filled = (70 – 30 =) 40% = $\frac{2}{5}$

⇒ Time taken to fill 40% of tank = $\frac{2}{5} \times 20 = 8$ minutes

∴ Only option (5) satisfies the two blanks in the question.

9. 1; When pipes B and D were simultaneously opened.

Part of tank filled in 1 minute = $\frac{1}{30} - \frac{1}{40} = \frac{4-3}{120} = \frac{1}{120}$

⇒ Part of tank filled in 12 minutes = $12 \times \frac{1}{120} = \frac{1}{10}$

⇒ $\frac{1}{10}$ × Capacity of tank = 20

⇒ Capacity of tank = 20 × 10 = 200 gallons.

∵ Pipe D can empty $\frac{1}{40}$ part of tank in 1 minute

⇒ Rate at which pipe D can empty the tank

$= \frac{1}{40} \times 200 = 5$ gallons/minute

∴ Only option (1) satisfies the two blanks in the question.

10. 2; Pipe A was closed after 1 minute, pipe B was closed after 2 minutes and pipe C was closed after 3 minutes. When the pipe C was closed, pipes D and E were also opened for 3 minutes each.

⇒ Part of tank filled in 3 minutes

$= \left(1 \times \frac{1}{20}\right) + \left(2 \times \frac{1}{30}\right) + \left(3 \times \frac{1}{60}\right)\left(3 \times \frac{1}{40}\right) - \left(3 \times \frac{1}{60}\right)$

$= \frac{1}{24}$

∵ The pipe was initially $\frac{2}{5}$ part filled.

⇒ When pipe C was closed, part of tank filled

$= \frac{2}{5} + \frac{1}{24} = \frac{48+5}{120} = \frac{53}{120}$

Similarly,

When pipe E was closed, pipe D was opened for 4 minutes and pipe E for 5 minutes

⇒ Part of tank filled in 5 minutes

$= \left(1 \times \frac{1}{20}\right) + \left(2 \times \frac{1}{30}\right) + \left(3 \times \frac{1}{60}\right) - \left(4 \times \frac{1}{40}\right) - \left(5 \times \frac{1}{60}\right) = -\frac{1}{60}$

This means that in 5 minutes $\frac{1}{60}$ part of the tank is emptied.

$\because$ The pipe was initially $\frac{2}{5}$ part filled.

$\Rightarrow$ When pipe E was closed, part of the tank filled

$= \frac{2}{5} - \frac{1}{60} = \frac{23}{60}$

$\therefore$ Only option (2) satisfies the two blanks in the question.

(11–15) :

Let the number of employees who arrived early $= 10x$

The number of employees who left early $= 30\%$ of $10x = 3x$

The number of employees who left late $= 20\%$ of $10x = 2x$

The number of employees who left on time $= 10x - 5x = 5x$

Let the number of employees who arrived late at the office $= 8z$

The number of employees who left late $= 25\%$ of $8z = 2z$

The number of employees who left on time $= 50\%$ of $8z = 4z$

The number of employees who left early $= 8z - 6z = 2z$

Let the number of employees who arrived on time $= 16y$

The number of employees who left early $= 37.5\%$ of $16y = 6y$

The number of employees who left late $= 6y$

The number of employees who left on time $= 16y - 12y = 4y$

	Early	On time	Late
Arrived	10x (assume)	16y (assume)	8z (assume)
Left	3x + 6y +2z	5x + 4z + 4y	2x + 2z + 6y

According to the question, $10x = 3x + 6y + 2z$

$7x = 2z + 6y$ ...(i)

The number of employees who didn't leave on time

$3x + 6y + 2z + 2x + 2z + 6y = 228$

$\Rightarrow 5x + 12y + 4z = 228$ ...(ii)

From the equation (i)

$[7x = 2z + 6y] \times 2$

$14x = 4z + 12y$ ...(iii)

Now, from equations (ii) and (iii) we get,

$5x + 14x = 228 \therefore x = \frac{228}{19} = 12$

$3x + 6y + 2z = 8z + 84$

or, $36 + 6y + 2z = 8z + 84$

or, $6y - 6z = 84 - 36$

or, $6y - 6z = 48$ ...(iv)

Adding equation (iii) and equation (iv),

$12y - 12z = 96$

$$\frac{42x - 36y - 12z = 0}{48y - 42x = 96}$$

$48y = 96 + 48 \times 12$ ($\because x = 12$)

$\Rightarrow y = \frac{672}{48} = 14$

From the equation (iv), we have, $6y - 6z = 48$

or, $14 \times 6 - 6z = 48$ or, $-6z = 48 - 84$

or, $6z = 36 \therefore z = 6$

11. 1; The total number of employees who left early

$= 3x + 6y + 2z = 36 + 84 + 12 = 132$

The total number of employees who left late

$= 2x + 2z + 6y = 24 + 12 + 84 = 120$

The required difference $= 132 - 120 = 12$

12. 3; The total number of employees working in that branch $= 10x + 16y + 8z = 120 + 224 + 48 = 392$

13. 1; The respective ratio $= 10x : 16y : 8z$

$= 120 : 224 : 48 = 15 : 28 : 6$

14. 2; The total number of employees working in that branch $= 10x + 16y + 8z = 120 + 224 + 48 = 392$

Of the total number of employees was on leave on the medical ground $= 25\%$ of $392 = 98$

Remaining $= 392 - 98 = 294$

The number of employees who was on leave for personal reason $= 50\%$ of $294 = 147$

The number of employees present on the day before yesterday of that day $= 294 - 147 = 147$

15. 3; The number of employees who left on time

$5x + 4z + 4y = 60 + 56 + 24 = 140$

The number of employees who didn't leave on time

$= 3x + 6y + 2z + 2x + 2z + 6y$

$= 5x + 12y + 4z = 60 + 168 + 24 = 252$

The reqd. % $= \frac{(252 - 140)}{252} \times 100 = \frac{112}{252} \times 100$

$= 44.44\%$

16. 3; $P = 80\%$ of $580 = 464$

$Q = 90\%$ of $200 = 180$

Probability of loan being more than deposits

$\Rightarrow$ Total number of chances $= 5$ years of loan $\times$ 5 years of deposits

$\therefore$ Total number of chances are 25

$\Rightarrow$ Number of chances that loan is more than deposits

$\Rightarrow 576 > 365, 330, 464, 450 = 4$ chances
$\Rightarrow 465 > 365, 330, 450, 464 = 4$ chances
$\Rightarrow$ Total 8 chances

$\therefore$ Probability of loan being more than deposit is $\frac{8}{25}$.

17. 2; P = 576   Q = 365

Spread of 2012 $= \frac{300}{7} - \frac{580}{11} = 42.85 - 52.72 = -9.87$

Spread of 2013 $= \frac{365}{7} - \frac{365}{11} = 52.142 - 33.18$
$= 18.062$

Spread of 2014 $= \frac{200}{7} - \frac{330}{11} = 28.57 - 30 = -1.43$

Spread of 2015 $= \frac{576}{7} - \frac{576}{11} = 82.28 - 52.36 = 29.92$

Spread of 2016 $= \frac{465}{7} - \frac{450}{11} = 66.42 - 40.90 = 25.52$

In 2015, Bank got highest spread.

18. 4; There is no relation between P and Q, so option II is of no use.

By option III, lending rate is $\frac{4}{3}rd$ of $9\frac{4}{11}\%$.

Lending rate is $12\frac{4}{33}\%$.

By option 1, No spread
$\because$ Interest on loan = Interest on deposits

$12\frac{4}{33}\%$ of $576 = 9\frac{1}{11}\%$ of P

or, $\frac{400}{33} \times 576 = \frac{100}{11}$ P or, $\frac{4}{33}$ of $576 = \frac{1}{11}$P

$\therefore$ P = 767.99 ≈ 768

19. 2; Sum of money compounded for 4 years $= 1 + \frac{r}{100}$

$\Rightarrow$ Instalments $= S_1 = S_2 = S_3 = S_4$

$= \left(1+\frac{r}{100}\right)^1, \left(1+\frac{r}{100}\right)^2, \left(1+\frac{r}{100}\right)^3, \left(1+\frac{r}{100}\right)^4$

Principal or compounded sum

$= \frac{10}{11}, \frac{100}{121}, \frac{1000}{1331}, \frac{10000}{14641}$

Make the instalments equal as given below.

$= \frac{13310}{14641}, \frac{12100}{14641}, \frac{21000}{14641}, \frac{10000}{14641}$

Sum is $13310 + 12100 + 21000 + 10000 = 46410$

Given sum is 464.1

Instalment is 146.41.

20. 1; Percentage change (rise or fall) in the production of Company β in comparison to the previous year, for different years are:

For 2013 $= \left[\frac{(35-25)}{25} \times 100\right]\% = 40\%$

For 2014 $= \left[\frac{(35-25)}{35} \times 100\right]\% = 0\%$

For 2015 $= \left[\frac{(40-35)}{35} \times 100\right]\% = 14.29\%$

For 2016 $= \left[\frac{(50-40)}{40} \times 100\right]\% = 25\%$

Hence, the maximum percentage rise or fall in the production of Company β is for 2013.

21. 3; Average production of Company α in the period 2014–2016

$= \left[\frac{1}{3} \times (25 + 50 + 40)\right] = \left(\frac{115}{3}\right)$ lakh tons

Average production of Company β in the period 2014–2016

$= \left[\frac{1}{3} \times (35 + 40 + 50\right] = \left(\frac{125}{3}\right)$ lakh tons

$\therefore$ Required ratio $= \frac{\left(\frac{115}{3}\right)}{\left(\frac{125}{3}\right)} = \frac{115}{125} = \frac{23}{25}$

22. 4; Average production (in lakh tons) in five years for the three companies are :

For Company (α)

$= \left[\frac{1}{5} \times (30 + 45 + 25 + 50 + 40)\right] = \frac{190}{5} = 38$

For Company (β)

$= \left[\frac{1}{5} \times (25 + 35 + 35 + 40 + 50)\right] = \frac{185}{5} = 37$

For company (γ)

$= \left[\frac{1}{5} \times (35 + 40 + 45 + 35 + 35)\right] = \frac{190}{5} = 38$

$\therefore$ Average production of five years is maximum for both the Companies α and γ.

23. 1; The percentages of production of Company (γ) to the production of Company β for various years are :

For 2012 $= \left(\frac{35}{25} \times 100\right)\% = 140\%$

For 2013 $= \left(\frac{40}{35} \times 100\right)\% = 114.29\%$

For 2014 $= \left(\frac{45}{35} \times 100\right)\% = 128.57\%$

For 2015 $= \left(\frac{35}{40} \times 100\right)\% = 87.5\%$

For 2016 $= \left(\frac{35}{50} \times 100\right)\% = 70\%$

Clearly, this percentage is highest for 2012.

24. 4; Percentage increase in the production of Company β from 2012 to 2015.

$= \left[\frac{(40-25)}{25} \times 100\right]\% = \left[\frac{15}{25} \times 100\right]\% = 60\%$

25. 3; Number of qualified candidates in 2017 = (1350 × 64)/100 = 864

Number of qualified male candidates = 864 – 264 = 600

So, required ratio = 600 : 264 = 25 : 11

26. 4; Number of appeared candidates in 2018 = (1050 × 140)/100 = 1470

Total number of qualified candidates in 2018 = (1470 × 30)/100 = 441

27. 3; Suppose the number of appeared candidates = $5x$

Qualified candidates = $4x$

Qualified female candidates $= \frac{3}{8} \times 4x = \frac{3x}{2}$

Required percentage $= \frac{(3x \times 100)}{(2 \times 5x)} = 30\%$

28. 2; According to the question,

$9x - 5x = 108 \Rightarrow 4x = 108 \therefore x = 27$

The number of qualified candidates $= 9x + 5x = 14 \times 27 = 378$

Let the number of appeared candidates in year 2016 = y

So, $y \times (42/100) = 378$

$\therefore y = 900$

29. 3; Let the number of qualified candidates in year 2013 be x.

The number of qualified candidates in year 2015

$= \frac{(720 \times 60)}{100} = 432$

According to the question, $x + 432 = 2 \times 321$

$\therefore x = 210$

Percentage of appeared candidates who qualified in 2013 = (210 × 100)/1050 = 20%

Practice Set 7

Directions (Q. 1–5) : Study the following line-chart carefully and answer the questions given below.

The following line-graph shows the information about the percentage increase in turnover of four software companies (HCL, TCS, IBM and Accenture) during the year 2013 to 2018 with respect to previous year.

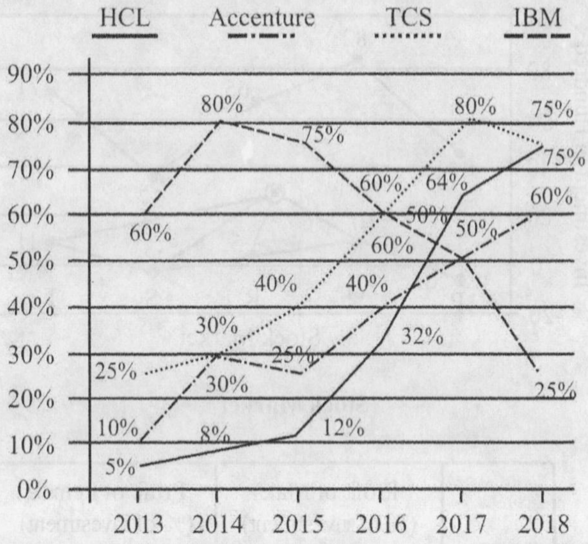

1. If at the end of year 2012, the turnover of HCL was 25% less than the turnover of IBM, then at the end of 2015, the turnover of HCL was how much per cent less than the turnover of IBM **(approximately)**?
   1) 40% 2) 60% 3) 51%
   4) 81% 5) 85%
2. If at the end of 2016, the turnover of HCL was 75% of the turnover of IBM, turnover of IBM was 60% of the turnover of Accenture and the turnover of Accenture was 80% of the turnover of TCS. If it is given that the turnover of TCS at the end of 2016 was $1.75 billion, then what was the sum of the total turnover of all the companies together at the end of 2018 ? (round off upto two decimals)
   1) $ 12.25 billion 2) $ 14.21 billion 3) $ 7.48 billion
   4) $ 9.64 billion 5) $ 6.14 billion
3. If the total turnover of HCL at the end of 2013 was $ 1 billion then find the total turnover of HCL at the end of 2018 ? (round off upto two decimals)
   1) $ 6.21 billion 2) $ 7.21 billion 3) $ 4.58 billion
   4) $ 3.21 billion 5) $ 2.24 billion
4. At the end of 2013, the respective ratio of the turnover of HCL, TCS, IBM and Accenture was 2 : 7 : 4 : 5, then what was the respective ratio of the turnover of all the companies at the end of 2012 ?
   1) $\frac{40}{21} : \frac{28}{5} : \frac{7}{2} : \frac{50}{11}$ 2) $\frac{40}{21} : \frac{27}{5} : \frac{5}{2} : \frac{50}{11}$
   3) $\frac{40}{21} : \frac{28}{5} : \frac{5}{2} : \frac{40}{11}$ 4) $\frac{20}{21} : \frac{14}{5} : \frac{5}{4} : \frac{25}{11}$
   5) None of these
5. Which of the following shows the approximate percentage increase in the turnover of Accenture during the six years ?
   1) 450% 2) 500% 3) 600%
   4) 550% 5) 300%

Directions (Q. 6–10) : Read the data given below carefully and answer the following questions :

The line-graph indicates the number of days taken by six boys to complete a work.

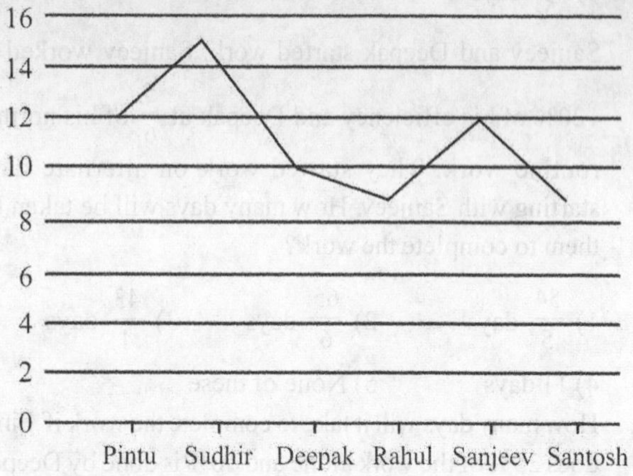

The chart below shows the number of days taken by six girls to complete a work.

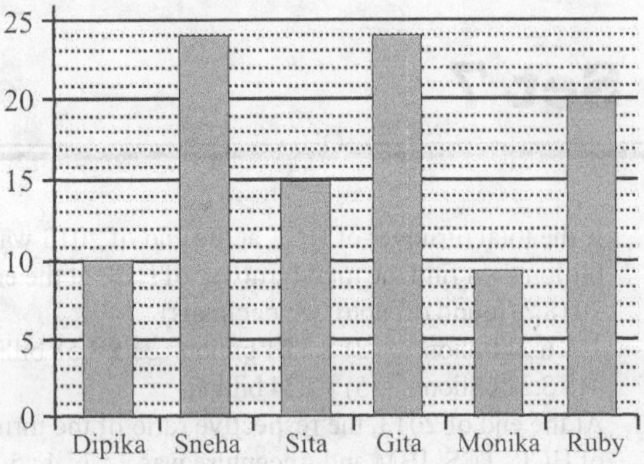

6. If Pintu and Santosh started to work and after 2 days, they were replaced by Sneha, Monika and Gita, then they stopped. How much work is still left? (Sneha, Monika and Gita worked for 2 days together)

1) $\frac{1}{10}$ 2) $\frac{2}{9}$ 3) $\frac{1}{9}$

4) $\frac{1}{12}$ 5) $\frac{1}{18}$

7. If all the boys work together then time taken by them will be how much less than the time taken by Dipika, Sita, Sneha and Gita together to do the work ?

1) $\frac{12}{5}$ days 2) $\frac{13}{2}$ days 3) $\frac{11}{5}$ days

4) $\frac{14}{5}$ days 5) None of these

8. Sanjeev and Deepak started work. Sanjeev worked at 120% of his efficiency and Deepak at $\frac{5}{6}$ of his normal routine work. They started work on alternate days starting with Sanjeev. How many days will be taken by them to complete the work?

1) $\frac{54}{5}$ days 2) $\frac{65}{6}$ days 3) $\frac{43}{4}$ days

4) 11 days 5) None of these

9. How many days will it take to complete the work if Pintu does 25% of the work alone and 10% is done by Deepak alone and the remaining is done by Ruby ?

1) 19 days 2) 16 days 3) 13 days

4) 17 days 5) None of these

10. Sudhir started working alone at his normal efficiency but after 5 days of starting he found that he has done only 25% work so to complete the remaining work on time by how much percentage he should increase his efficiency ?

1) 12.5% 2) 15% 3) 10%

4) 20% 5) None of these

Directions (Q. 11–15) : Read the given information carefully and answer the questions given below :

One Male and one Female invest in 5 Stock Markets as shown in the graph below. Profit earned by them is shown in the table below.

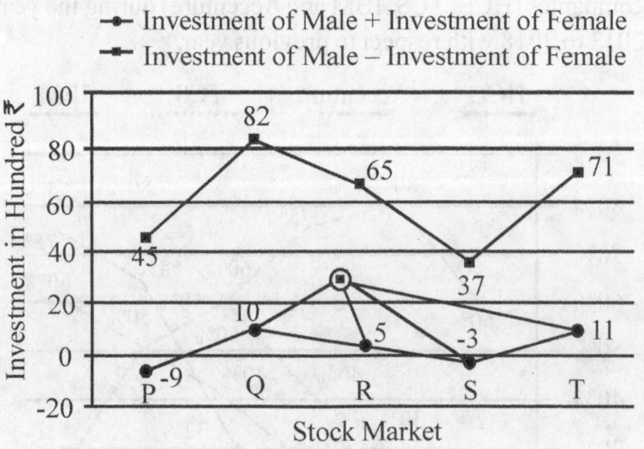

Stock Market

	Profit of Male (% of investment)	Profit of Female (% of investment)
P	15	5
Q	7	11
R	9	7
S	13	5
T	19	20

11. What is the average investment of Male in all stock markets?

1) ₹2950 2) ₹3140 3) ₹3350

4) ₹3170 5) None of these

12. What Stock Markets will be the total profit of Female in those Stock Markets where Male invests less than Female?

1) ₹475 2) ₹230 3) ₹240

4) ₹425 5) None of these

13. If profit percentage of each in Stock market T got interchange then what will be the new profit of (Male + Female) in Stock Market T ?
1) ₹1390 2) ₹1379 3) ₹1410
4) ₹1411 5) ₹1399

14. What is the difference of total investment of Male in all Stock Markets and overall profit of Female in all Stock Markets?
1) ₹14359 2) ₹14859 3) ₹13459
4) ₹14259 5) None of these

15. Profit of Male in Stock Market T is how much percentage more than profit of Female in Stock Market T ?
1) 55% 2) 50% 3) 60%
4) 52% 5) 53%

Directions (Q. 16–20) : Study the following table chart carefully and answer the questions given below:

The Franchise of a Company are classified into six categories, F1 to F6, based on their customers. The following table gives the number of Franchise of the company belonging to different categories in the years 2009 and 2019.

Category	Customers	No. of Franchises in 2009	No. of Franchises in 2019	Ratio of no. of males to females	Number of regular customers	Literacy rate among regular customers
F1	<200	104	92	5 : 3	60%	60%
F2	200-500	141	127	2 : 5	50%	50%
F3	501-1000	145	144	5 : 3	60%	40%
F4	1001-2000	110	129	3 : 2	60%	40%
F5	2001-5000	62	80	6 : 7	40%	80%
F6	>5000	13	18	8 : 7	64%	50%

The ratio of literacy for regular males to regular females in every category is the same as the ratio of customers of males to females given in the table.

16. Find the customer of category F6 franchises if 25% of regular female literates are doctors, 20% of rest of regular female literates are engineers, 25% of rest of regular female literates are teachers and remaining 1008 of regular female literates are CA.
1) 12500 2) 13000 3) 16275
4) 15000 5) 15050

17. Find the average customers of franchises of category F4 in 2009, if 15840 regular females are literate in category F4 from all the franchises combined.
1) 1600 2) 1475 3) 1500
4) 1565 5) 1400

18. In 2019, the total customers in category F2 franchises was at least what percentage of the total customers in category F5 franchises?
1) 5% 2) 6% 3) 7%
4) 8% 5) 4%

19. If the total customers in category F4 franchises in 2019 was less than that in 2009, find what could be the least possible average customers of category F4 franchises in 2009 ? (approx.)
1) 1773 2) 1772 3) 1771
4) 1174 5) 1734

20. In franchises of category F1 consider all the franchises have equal customers. Find what could be the maximum number of employed females in percentage among all regular customers if only literate females can have jobs.
1) 7% 2) 6.2% 3) 5.6%
4) 5% 5) 5.2%

Directions (Q. 21–24) : Study the following information carefully and answer the questions that follow:

In a school there are 800 students who have visited five different cities viz. Delhi, Ajmer, Goa, Mumbai and Dehradun. Fifty four per cent of the total students are boys. One-fourth of the total number of girls visited Mumbai. Twenty five per cent of the total number of girls visited Delhi. The number of girls who visited Dehradun is half the number of girls who visited Delhi. Five-sixths of the remaining girls visited Ajmer. The total number of students who visited Mumbai is 192. One-fourth of the total number of boys visited Goa. 101 boys have visited Ajmer. Two-thirds of the remaining number of boys have visited Delhi.

21. What is the total number of students who visited Goa?
1) 123 2) 133 3) 142
4) 131 5) None of these

22. Total number of students who visited Dehradun is approximately what per cent of number of girls who visited Delhi?
1) 90% 2) 81% 3) 95%
4) 93% 5) 97%

23. What is the average number of boys who visited Delhi, Goa and Dehradun together?
1) 82 2) 72 3) 77
4) 85 5) 75

24. If 7 boys did not go to Ajmer then what is the approximate per cent of the girls who went to Goa to that of the boys who went to Ajmer?
1) 23% 2) 21% 3) 22%
4) 24% 5) 25%

Directions (Q. 25–27) : Study the following information carefully and answer the questions that follow :

A milkman goes to a city by bicycle and travels the distance of 10 km to reach the city in 50 minutes. He buys a cylinder whose volume of 4620 m^3 and also buys a conical container. The volume of the container is (1/7) times the volume of a cylinder and the height of the container is 10 m. During returning from the city he takes 20 minutes less time than coming to city.

25. What is the slant height of a conical container?
1) $\sqrt{163}\ m$ 2) $\sqrt{171}\ m$ 3) $\sqrt{168}\ m$
4) $\sqrt{173}\ m$ 5) None of these

26. What is the curved surface area of cylinder if the height of cylinder is 30 metres?
1) 1310 m^2 2) 1300 m^2 3) 1320 m^2
4) 1340 m^2 5) None of these

27. How much speed did he increase during returning from the city?
1) 3 km/hr 2) 2 km/hr 3) 4 km/hr
4) 5 km/hr 5) $2\frac{1}{2}$ km/hr

Answers and explanations

1. 4; At the end of 2012, the respective ratio of the turnover of HCL and IBM = 3 : 4 (the turnover of HCL was 25% less than the turnover of IBM)

Let us assume that the turnover of HCL at the end of 2012 = 3x and the turnover of IBM at the end of 2012 = 4x

Then, the turnover of HCL at the end of 2015

$$= 3x \times \frac{105}{100} \times \frac{108}{100} \times \frac{112}{100} = \text{approximately } 3.81x$$

The turnover of IBM at the end of 2015

$$= 4x \times \frac{160}{100} \times \frac{108}{100} \times \frac{175}{100} = 20.16x$$

$$\text{The required \%} = \frac{(20.16x - 3.81x) \times 100}{20.16x}$$

= 81% **(Approximately)**

2. 1; At the end of 2016, let the turnover of IBM = 4x, then the turnover of HCL = 75% of 4x = 3x.

Turnover of IBM was 60% of the turnover of Accenture, 60% of Accenture's turnover = 4x

$$\text{Accenture's turnover} = 4x \times \frac{100}{60} = \frac{20x}{3}$$

Similarly,

$$\text{TCS's turnover} = \frac{\left(\frac{20x}{3}\right) \times 100}{80} = \frac{25x}{3}$$

According to the question, $\frac{25x}{3} = 1.75$

$\Rightarrow x = 0.21$

At the end of 2018,

$$\text{The turnover of IBM} = 4x \times \frac{150}{100} \times \frac{125}{100} = 7.5x$$

$$\text{The turnover of HCL} = 3x \times \frac{164}{100} \times \frac{175}{100} = 8.61x$$

$$\text{The turnover of Accenture} = \frac{20x}{3} \times \frac{150}{100} \times \frac{160}{100} = 16x$$

$$\text{The turnover of TCS} = \frac{25x}{3} \times \frac{180}{100} \times \frac{175}{100} = 26.25x$$

Required sum = 7.5x + 8.61x + 16x + 26.25x = 58.36x
= 58.36 × 0.21 = 12.2556 billion

3. 3; The total turnover of HCL at the end of 2018

$$= 1 \times \frac{108}{100} \times \frac{112}{100} \times \frac{132}{100} \times \frac{164}{100} \times \frac{175}{100}$$

= $ 4.58 billion **(Approximately)**

4. 4; Let at the end of 2012, the respective ratio of the turnover of HCL, TCS, IBM and Accenture = A : B : C : D

Then, 105% of A = 2x ⇒ $A = \frac{40x}{21}$

For TCS, 125% of B = $7x \Rightarrow B = \frac{28x}{5}$

For IBM 160% of C = $4x \Rightarrow C = \frac{5x}{2}$

For Accenture, 110% of D = $5x \Rightarrow D = \frac{50x}{11}$

The required ratio = $\frac{40x}{21} : \frac{28x}{5} : \frac{5x}{2} : \frac{50x}{11}$

$= \frac{40}{21} : \frac{28}{5} : \frac{5}{2} : \frac{50}{11} = \frac{20}{21} : \frac{14}{5} : \frac{5}{4} : \frac{25}{11}$

5. 2; Let the turnover of Acccnture at the end of 2012 = 1 then the turnover of Accenture at the end of 2018

$= 1 \times \frac{110}{100} \times \frac{130}{100} \times \frac{125}{100} \times \frac{140}{100} \times \frac{150}{100} \times \frac{160}{100} = 6.006$

Required % = $\frac{(6-1) \times 100}{1}$ = 500% **(Approximately)**

6. 2; Let the work be 180 units (LCM of 12,15,10,9,12,9).
Pintu's 1 day's work = 15 units
Santosh's 1 day's work = 20 units
Sneha's 1 day's work = 7.5 units
Gita's 1 day's work = 7.5 units
Monika's 1 day's work = 20 units
Santosh and Pintu worked for 2 days = (15+20) × 2 = 70
Remaining work = 110 units
Now Sneha, Gita and Monika worked for 2 days = (7.5 + 7.5 + 20) × 2 = 70 units
Remaining work = 40 units

So, $\frac{40}{180} = \frac{2}{9}$ part of work is still left.

7. 3; Total days taken by boys to do the work

$= \frac{180}{100} = \frac{9}{5}$ days

Days taken by 4 girls = $\frac{180}{45}$ = 4 days

Difference = $4 - \frac{9}{5} = \frac{11}{5}$ days

8. 2; Sanjeev's one day's work = $\frac{180}{12}$ = 15 units

Deepak's one day's work $\frac{180}{10}$ = 18 units

Now, Sanjeev works at 12% of 15 = 18 units

Deepak at $\frac{5}{6}$ of 18 = 15 units

(Sanjeev + Deepak)'s 2 day's work = 33
In 10 days work done = (33 × 5 =) 165 units
Remaining work = (180 - 165 =) 15 units
Sanjeev's one day's work = 18 units.

So to do 15 units. He will take $\frac{5}{6}$ days.

Therefore, total time taken = $10\frac{5}{6}$ days = $\frac{65}{6}$ days.

9. 4; Pintu's 1 day's work = 15 units so to do 25% work (assumed total work = 180) = 45, he will take 3 days. Now, to do 10% work i.e., 18 units, Deepak will take 1 day.
Now, remaining work = 180 – 63 = 117 units

To do 117 units of work, Ruby will take $\frac{117}{9}$ = 13 days (Ruby's 1 day's work = $\frac{180}{20}$ = 9 units)

Total days = 3 + 1 + 13 = 17 days

10. 1; Sudhir's 1 day's work = $\frac{180}{15}$ = 12 units

In 5 days, he should have done = 60 units

But he did = $\frac{180}{4}$ = 45 units

So, the remaining work = 135 units.

Sudhir completes it in 10 days, he should do $\frac{135}{10}$ = 13.5 units per day
Therefore, increased efficiency = 13.5 – 12 = 1.5

Per cent increase = $\frac{1.5 \times 100}{12}$ = 12.5%

11. 2; **For Stock Market P :**
Investment by Male + Investment by Female = ₹4500
Investment by Male – Investment by Female = –₹900 or
Investment by Female – Investment by Male = ₹900
Then,
₹ 2 × Investment by Female = ₹5400
∴ Investment of Female = ₹2700
and Investment of Male = ₹2700 – ₹900
= ₹1800 ... (1)

For Stock Market Q :
Investment by Male + Investment by Female = ₹8200
Investment by Male – Investment by Female = ₹1000

Then,

$\Rightarrow 2 \times$ Investment by Male = 9200

$\therefore$ Investment of Male = 9200 ÷ 2 = ₹4600 ... (2)

For Stock Market R :

Investment by Male + Investment by Female = ₹6500

Investment by Male – Investment by Female = ₹500

Then,

$\Rightarrow 2 \times$ Investment by Male = 7000

$\therefore$ Investment of Male = 7000 ÷ 2 = ₹3500 ... (3)

For Stock Market S :

Investment by Male + Investment by Female = ₹3700

Investment by Male – Investment by Female = –₹300

or

Investment by Female – Investment by Male = ₹300

Then,

$\Rightarrow 2 \times$ Investment by Female = ₹4000

$\therefore$ Investment of Female = ₹2000 ... (4)

For Stock Market T :

Investment by Male + Investment by Female = ₹7100

Investment by Male – Investment by Female = ₹1100

Then,

$\Rightarrow 2 \times$ Investment by Male = ₹8200

$\therefore$ Investment of Male = 8200 ÷ 2 = ₹4100 ... (5)

$\therefore$ From equations (2), (3), (1), (4) and (5), we can calculate total investment of Male

= 1800 + 4600 + 3500 + 1700 + 4100

= 6400 + 5200 + 4100

= 11600 + 4100 = ₹15700

$\therefore$ Average investment by Male in all schemes

$= \frac{15700}{5} =$ ₹3140

12. 5; Two such stock markets i.e. P and S exist where Male invests less than Female because (Male – Female) is negative there.

For Stock Market P :

Investment by Male + Investment by Female = ₹4500

Investment by Male – Investment by Female = –₹900

or

Investment by Female – Investment by Male = ₹900

Then,

$\Rightarrow 2 \times$ Investment by Female = ₹5400

$\therefore$ Investment of Female = ₹2700

Profit of Female = 5% of ₹2700

$= 5 \times \frac{2700}{100} = 5 \times 27 = 135$ ... (1)

For Stock Market S :

Investment by Male + Investment by Female = ₹3700

Investment by Male – Investment by Female = –₹300

or

Investment by Female – Investment by Male = ₹300

Then,

$\Rightarrow 2 \times$ Investment by Female = ₹4000

$\therefore$ Investment of Female = ₹2000

Profit of Female = 5% of 2000

$= 5 \times \frac{2000}{100} = 4 \times 20 = 100$ ... (2)

$\therefore$ Total profit = 135 + 100 = ₹235

13. 1; **For Stock Market T :**

New profit percentage of Male = 20%

New profit percentage of Female = 19%

Investment of Male + Investment of Female = ₹7100

Investment of Male – Investment of Female = ₹1100

Then,

$\Rightarrow 2 \times$ Investment of Male = ₹8200

$\therefore$ Investment of Male $= \frac{8200}{2} =$ ₹4100

Profit of Male = 20% of 4100

$= 20 \times \frac{4100}{100} = 20 \times 41 =$ ₹820

And investment of Female = 4100 – 1100 = ₹3000

Profit of Female = 19% of 3000

$= 19 \times \frac{3000}{100} = 19 \times 30 =$ ₹570

$\therefore$ Total profit of (Male + Female) = 820 + 570 = ₹1390

14. 4; **For Stock Market P :**

Investment by Male + Investment by Female = ₹4500

Investment by Male – Investment by Female = –₹900

or

Investment by Female – Investment by Male = ₹900

Then,

$\Rightarrow 2 \times$ Investment by Female = ₹5400

$\therefore$ Investment of Female = ₹2700

Profit of Female = 5% of ₹2700

$= 5 \times \frac{2700}{100} = 5 \times 27 = 135$ ... (1)

And investment of Male

= 2700 – 900 = ₹1800 ... (2)

For Stock Market Q :

Investment by Male + Investment by Female = ₹8200

Investment by Male – Investment by Female = ₹1000

Then,

$\Rightarrow 2 \times$ Investment by Male = ₹9200

$\therefore$ Investment of Male = 9200 ÷ 2 = ₹4600 ... (3)

and investment of Female = 4600 – 1000 = ₹3600

Profit of Female = 11% of ₹3600

$= 11 \times \frac{3600}{100} = 11 \times 36 = ₹396$ ... (4)

For Stock Market R :

Investment by Male + Investment by Female = ₹6500

Investment by Male – Investment by Female = ₹500

Then,

⇒ 2 × Investment by Male = 7000

∴ Investment of Male = 7000 ÷ 2 = ₹3500 ... (5)

And Investment of Female = 3500 – 500 = ₹3000

Profit of Female = 7% of ₹3000

$= 7 \times \frac{3000}{100} = 7 \times 30 = ₹210$ ... (6)

For Stock Market S :

Investment by Male + Investment by Female = ₹3700

Investment by Male – Investment by Female = –₹300

or

Investment by Female – Investment by Male = ₹300

Then, 2 × Investment by Female = ₹4000

∴ Investment of Female = ₹2000

Profit of Female = 5% of 2000 $= 5 \times \frac{2000}{100} = 5 \times 20$

= ₹100 ... (7)

And investment of Male = 2000 – 300 = ₹1700 ... (8)

For Stock Market T :

Investment by Male + Investment by Female = ₹7100

Investment by Male – Investment by Female = ₹1100

Then,

⇒ 2 × Investment by Male = 8200

∴ Investment of Male = 8200 ÷ 2 = ₹4100 ... (9)

And investment of Female = 4100 – 1100 = ₹3000

Profit of Female = 20% of 3000

$= 20 \times \frac{3000}{100} = 20 \times 30 = 600$ ... (10)

∴ From equations (2), (3), (5), (8) and (9) we can calculate total investment of Male

= 1800 + 4600 + 3500 + 1700 + 4100

= 6400 + 5200 + 4100 = 11600 + 4100 = ₹15700

And from equations (1), (4), (6), (7) and (10) we can calculate profit of Female

= 135 + 396 + 210 + 100 + 600 = 841 + 600 = ₹1441

∴ Required difference = 15700 – 1441 = ₹14259

15. 2; Investment of Male in stock market R + Investment of Female in Stock Market R = ₹6500

Investment of Male in Stock Market R – Investment of Female in Slock Market R = ₹500

Therefore,

2 × Investment of Male in Stock Market R

= 6500 + 500 = ₹7000

∴ Investment of Male = 7000 ÷ 2 = ₹3500 and investment of Female = 3500 – 500 = ₹3000

Profit of Male in Stock Market R = 9% of 3500

$= 3500 \times \frac{9}{100} = 35 \times 9 = ₹315$

Profit of Female in Stock Market R = 7% of 3000

$= 3000 \times \frac{7}{100} = 30 \times 7 = ₹210$

∴ We need to find out that 315 is how much percentage more than 210

$= (315–210) \times \frac{100}{210} = 105 \times \frac{100}{210} = \frac{1050}{21} = \frac{350}{7} = 50\%$

∴ Profit of Male in Stock Market R is 50% more than the profit of Female in Stock Market R.

16. 4; Let there be 1000y regular customer literate females.

Then, 0.75 × 0.8 × 0.75 × 1000y = 1008 ∴ y = 2.24

So, regular customer literate female = 2240

Now, total regular customer literate

$= \frac{8+7}{7} \times 2240 = 4800$

We have,

50% of total regular customer (literate + illiterate) = 4800

So, total regular customer (literate + illiterate)

= 4800 × 2 = 9600

Then we have, 64% of total customer = Number of regular customer (literate + illiterate) = 9600

Total customer $= \frac{100}{64} \times 9600 = 15000$

17. 3; Number of literate regular customers

$= \frac{5}{2} \times 15840 = 39600$

40% of total regular customer (literate + illeterate) = 39600

Hence, total regular customer (literate + illeterate)

$= \frac{100}{40} \times 39600 = 99000$

Then, we have 60% of the total customer = Number of regular customer (literate + illetracte) = 99000

∴ Total customer $= \frac{100}{60} \times 99000 = 165000$

Average customer of Franchises = $= \frac{165000}{110} = 1500$

18. 2; Here we have to take the least possible customers of category F2 and the highest possible customers of category F5 Franchises.
In 2019, the least possible customers of category F2 franchises $= 127 \times 200$
The highest possible customers of category F5 franchises $= 80 \times 5000$

The required per cent $= \frac{127 \times 200}{80 \times 5000} \times 100 = 6.35\%$.

19. 4; To find the least possible customers of F4 in 2009, we must start with least possible customers of F4 category franchises in 2019.
So,
Total population of F4 type Franchises in 2019 $= 1001 \times 129$
Since, it is less than what the customers was in 2009, the customers in 2009 must be in the form $= 1001 \times 129 + y$, where $y = 1, 2, 3$, and so on.
But we have to tell the minimum possible customers, we must choose $y = 1$
So, total customers in 2009 $= 1001 \times 129 + 1 = 129130$

Average customers $= \frac{129130}{110} = 1173.9$

$= 1174$ (approx.)

20. 3; Let the customers of any Franchise of category F1 be $800y$, then
Number of regular customers (literate + illiterate) $= 60\%$ of $800y = 480y$
Number of literate regular customers $= 60\%$ of $480y = 288y$

Number of literate females $= \frac{3}{8} \times 288y = 108y$ ... (1)

Now, according to the question, $800y < 200 \Rightarrow y < \frac{1}{4}$

Therefore, we have from (1),
Number of literate females $= 108y < 27$ (max.)
To find the maximum number of employed women, it is possible that all are employed, so

Perentage $= \frac{\text{number of employed females}}{\text{all regular customers}} \times 100$

$= \frac{27Y}{480y} \times 100 = 5.625\%$

So, less than 5.625% literate women among the regular customers are employed.

21. 4; Total number of students who visited Goa $= 23 + 108 = 131$
Total no. of students $= 800$
Number of boys $= 54\%$ of $800 = 432$
Number of girls $= 800 - 432 = 368$

	Boys	Girls
Delhi	82	92
Mumbai	100	92
Goa	108	23
Ajmer	101	115
Dehradun	41	46

22. 3; Total number of students who visited Dehradun $= 46 + 41 = 87$
Number of girls who visited Delhi $= 92$
Percentage = (Total number of students who visited Dehradun × 100) / Number of girls who visited Delhi $= (87 \times 1\,00)/92 = 95\%$

23. 3; Average = (Total number of boys who visited Delhi, Goa and Dehradun)/3 $= (82 + 108 + 41)/3 = 77$

24. 4; If 7 boys did not go to Ajmer, then number of boys who went to Ajmer $= 101 - 7 = 94$
Number of girls who went to Goa $= 23$

Required percentage $= \frac{23}{94} \times 100 = 24.46\% \approx 24\%$

25. 1; The curved surface area of a cylinder $= 2\pi rh$, where r is the radius of a cylinder and h is the height of the cylider.

The volume of the conical container $= \frac{1}{3}\pi R^2 H$,

where R is the radius of the conical container. H is the height of the conical container and π is $\frac{22}{7}$.

The slant height of a container$= \sqrt{(\text{height}^2 + \text{radius}^2)}$

The volume of a conical container $= \frac{1}{7} \times 4620 = 660\ m^3$

The volume of a conical container $= \frac{1}{3}\pi R^2 \times 10$

$\Rightarrow 660 = \frac{10}{3} \times \frac{22}{7} \times R^2$

$\Rightarrow R^2 = \frac{660 \times 3 \times 7}{10 \times 22} \Rightarrow R^2 = 3 \times 3 \times 7$

$\Rightarrow R = \sqrt{3 \times 3 \times 7} = 3\sqrt{7}m$

The slant height of the conical container

$= \sqrt{(10)^2 - (3\sqrt{7})^{\frac{2}{3}}} = \sqrt{100+63} = \sqrt{163}\ m$

The slant height of the conical container is $\sqrt{163}\ m.$

26. 3; The volume of cylinder $= \frac{22}{7} \times r^2 \times 30$

$\Rightarrow 4620 = \frac{22}{7} r^2 \times 30 \Rightarrow r^2 = \frac{4620 \times 7}{30 \times 22} = 49$

$\Rightarrow r = \sqrt{49} = 7\,m$

The curved surface area of a cylinder

$= 2 \times \frac{22}{7} \times 7 \times 30 = 1320\ m^2$

27. 1; The distance travelled by him = 10 km

Reaching time = 50 minutes = $\frac{5}{6}$ hours

The volume of the cylinder = 4620 m^2

The volume of the container

$= \frac{1}{7} \times$ the volume of the cylinder

And the height of the container = 10 m

Reduced time = 50 – 20 = 30 minutes

$= \frac{30}{60}$ hours $= \frac{1}{2}$ hr

The speed when he went city = $= \frac{10}{5/6} = 12$ km/hr

And the speed during returning = $= \frac{10}{1/2} = 20$ km/hr

Increased speed = 20 – 15 = 5 km/hr

Therefore, his increased speed was 3 km/hr

Practice Set 8

Directions (Q. 1–5) : Given data is about track record of car racing game, where 4 cars P, Q, R and S are competing to reach finishing line which is at a distance of 3000 m from their initial starting point.

A. Drift refers to over starting intentionally done by driver

B. While calculating average speed, do not consider time taken in drift /crash.

C. Points = 50 × drifts – 20 × crashes

Cars	Drift	Times to reach finishing line (in Sec)	Crash
P	5	180	3
Q	7	120	5
R	6	150	4
S	8	100	6

1. Which car earned maximum points at the end of the race?
   1) P 2) R 3) S
   4) Q 5) More than one of the above
2. In order to gain 10 more points than car S, how many total drifts should car P have made, if car P's time and number of crashes remain same?
   1) 5 2) 8 3) 7
   4) 9 5) None of the above
3. Another car named T, makes total number of drifts same as that of car R and it still receives 0 points at the end. How many crashes must car T have suffered ?
   1) 12 2) 15 3) 18
   4) 20 5) None of the above
4. Speed of car S is what percentage more than that of car Q ?
   1) 15% 2) 20% 3) 25%
   4) 12.5% 5) None of the above
5. How much speed does car R need to gain in order to cover twice the distance in 5/3 of the original time taken?
   1) 25 2) 20 3) 18
   4) 24 5) None of the above

Directions (Q. 6–11) : Given data is regarding volume and height of 4 right circular cylindrical tanks P, Q, R and S. The given data also depicts time taken to fill or empty the tank by inlet pipe A, B and outlet pipe C.

Tank	Volume	Height	Time taken by pipe A to fill blank (in hrs)	Ratio of Time taken by pipe B to fill and pipe C to empty the tank
P	38808	28	10	02 : 03
Q	____	10	12	03 : 02
R	5390	35	18	01 : 03
S	19250	____	____	02 : 05

1. Ratio between time taken by pipe B and that by pipe C is different because pipes were used by the operator in different ways for different tanks.
2. Radius of tank S is 10.5 m

6. How much volume of initially empty tank P was filled in 1 hour, when all 3 pipes were opened simultaneously (Time taken by pipe C is 30 hours)
   1) 4527.6 2) 5511.6 3) 5544.6
   4) 4500 5) None of these
7. In tank R, pipe A was opened for 9 hrs, and then closed. Pipe B and C were then opened together for 3 hrs and then, both pipes were closed. After a total of 12 hrs, approximately, what volume of tank remained empty (in cubic metres). (If both pipesA and C were opened together, tank will always be empty.)
   1) 780 2) 898 3) 924
   4) 856 5) None of these
8. Pipe B can alone fill the tank Q in 36 hours. When all three pipes were opened for 1 hr, then volume of tank Q filled was approximately 428 cubic metres/hour. What is the approximated radius of tank Q ?
   1) 21 2) 11 3) 14
   4) 16 5) None of these
9. When all 3 pipes were opened simultaneously, volume of tank S filled in 1 hr is 3575 cubic metres/hr. Pipe B alone can fill 25% of tank in 3.5 hrs. In how much time

can pipe A fill 40% of the tank alone?
1) 7 2) 35 3) 4
4) 18 5) None of these

10. Another tank Z has its height as 20% more than that of tank R and radius as 20% more than that of P. What is the sum of total curved surface area of tanks P and Z together (approximately).
1) 10720 m^2 2) 17325 m^2 3) 11273 m^2
4) 10270 m^2 5) None of these

11. Find the respective ratio of curved surface area of tank P and that of tank R.
1) 5 : 3 2) 12 : 7 3) 14 : 11
4) 14 : 5 5) None of these

Directions (Q. 12–14) : Read the following data carefully and the questions that follow:

1) Market Value is equal to price per share multiplied by total number of shares.
2) Gross profit is equal to (Market Value - Liability - Other Expenses)
3) Cost of share increases by 20% in 2002 from 2001 and decreases by 5% in the next year.
4) Number of shares increases by 20% in 2002 from 2001
5) Cost of share decreases by 12% in 2006 as compared to 2005 and increases by 20% in next year

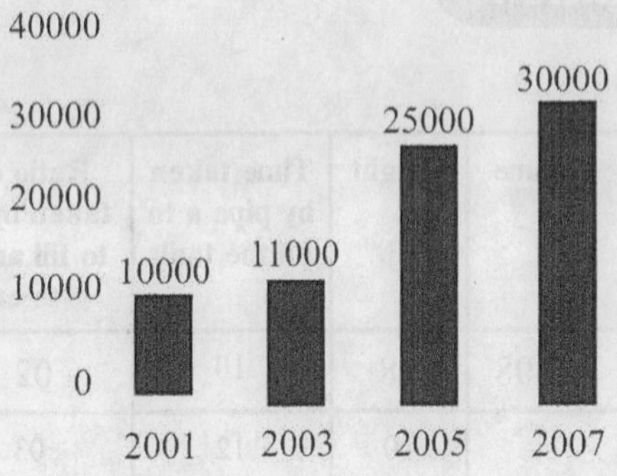

● Number of Shares

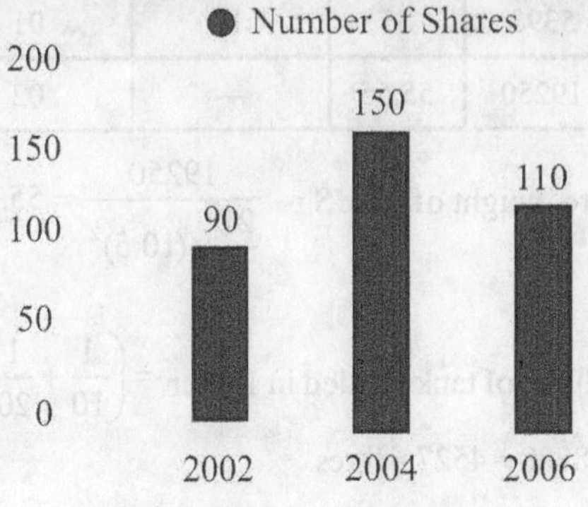

■ Price per share

12. If liability in year 2004 is 1.5 times the expenses, which is ₹30000 and gross profit in 2004 was ₹1800000. Then, find total number of shares in the same year.
1) 12500 2) 12000 3) 13500
4) 13000 5) None of these

13. What is the average number of shares (approximately) in all the years if in 2004, market value is ₹1500000 and number of shares in 2006 is 25% more than that of 2004?
1) 17100 2) 19700 3) 16800
4) 19900 5) None of these

14. Find the difference between market value in 2003 and average market value in 2001 and 2002 together.
1) 22500 2) 24000 3) 25500
4) 23000 5) None of these

Directions (Q. 15–18) : In the paragraph some information is given about some different trains. Study the paragraph carefully and answer the questions that follow.

Train A starts at 10 AM on Monday and completes its journey at 8 AM on Tuesday. Train D covers 25% less distance than train A and it takes 50% less time than train A. Respective ratio of speed of train D and that of train E is 4 : 5. Respective ratio of speed of trains A, C and B is 5 : 6 : 8. Speed of train A is 60 km/hr on first day and it runs with $\frac{5}{6}$ th of its original speed on second day. Running time of train A is 10% more than that of B. Respective ratio of time taken by D and that of E is 1 : 2. Respective ratio of distance covered by train C and train D is 4 : 3.

15. What is average speed of all the trains together ?
1) 80.79 km/hr 2) 79.80 km/hr 3) 97.80 km/hr
4) 89.07 km/h 5) None of these

16. Average speed of train A is what per cent more/less than that of E ?
1) 526% 2) 46.6% 3) 54.7%
4) 58.6% 5) None of these

17. If train B crosses a 200 m platform in 20 sec and train D crosses a person standing on platform in 18 sec then what is respective ratio of length of train B and that of train D ?
1) 6 : 5 2) 7 : 8 3) 11 : 17
4) 42 : 55 5) None of these

18. If destination of train A and C is interchanged then what is difference between their running time ?
1) 4 hrs 2) 2.7 hrs 3) 4.5 hrs
4) 3.7 hrs 5) None of these

Directions (Q. 19–21) : Given table shows the per cent range of commission earned on all sold books and commission earned by five shops in rupees.

Shop	Range of commission (%)	Commission earned in Rupees
PP	0-16	3200
QQ	16-32	—
RR	—	3500
SS	—	—
TT	0-20	400

Note : Commission per cent is on selling price.

Note : Some values are missing, you have to calculate them according to the question.

Note : Range of commission are in integral values.

19. Shop PP sells 480 books and only 3 types of books it has, their number are in ratio 1 : 2 : 3 and their selling prices are 200, 300 and 100 respectively and commission charged on them have difference of 1 per cent in sequence (least number of articles sold have least commission per cent) respectively, then find the highest commission per cent of books.

1) 14.375% 2) 12.375% 3) 15.45%
4) 16.375% 5) None of these

20. Shop RR sells 3 products in equal numbers (105) and equal commission per cent. If their selling price (in Rupees) are 20, 30 and 40, then what is the commission per cent?

1) $\frac{1200}{27}\%$ 2) $\frac{900}{27}\%$ 3) $\frac{1150}{27}\%$
4) $\frac{1000}{27}\%$ 5) $\frac{1040}{27}\%$

21. Shop SS sold 3 books each in number 100 and each have S.P. of ₹80 and commission per cent for each is in A.P. with common difference of 5. If total commission earned by Shop SS is $14\frac{2}{7}\%$ more than that of Shop RR, find the minimum range of commission per cent.

1) (11–22) 2) (16–23) 3) (05–08)
4) (14–24) 5) (07–10)

Answers and explanations

1. 3; Maximum points at end of race by S = 50 × 8 – 20 × 6 = 400 – 120 = 280

2. 3; $P = 50 \times x - 20 \times 3$

$S = 290$

$\Rightarrow 290 = 50 \times x - 60$

$\Rightarrow 350 = 50x \Rightarrow x = 7$

3. 2; Points = 0

$0 = 50 \times 6 - 20 \times c$

$\Rightarrow 20c = 300 \quad \Rightarrow c - 15$

4. 2; Speed of car S = $\frac{300}{100} = 30$ m/s

Speed of car Q = $\frac{300}{120} = 25$ m/s

Required per cent = $\frac{5}{25} \times 100 = 20\%$

5. 4; Speed of car R initially = $\frac{3000}{150} = 20$ m/s

Speed of car R now = $\frac{6000 \times 3}{150 \times 5} = 24$ m/s

(6–11) :

Tank	Volume	Height	Time taken by pipe a to fill the tank	Ratio of time taken by pipe B to fill and pie C to empty
P	38808	28	10	02 : 03
Q	—	10	12	03 : 02
R	5390	35	18	01 : 03
S	19250	55.55	—	02 : 05

Here, height of tank S = $\frac{19250}{\frac{22}{7} \times (10.5)^2} = 55.55$ m

6. 1; Volume of tank P filled in 1 hour = $\left(\frac{1}{10} + \frac{1}{20} - \frac{1}{30}\right) \times 38808 = 4527.6$ litres.

7. 2; Time to fill the tank R by pipe A = Time to empty the tank R by pipe C = 18 hr

$\therefore$ Time to fill tank R by B = $\frac{18}{3} = 6$ hr

Portion of tank R emptied after first 9 hr $= \frac{5390}{7}$

$= 2695$ litres

Portion of tank R emptied after next 3 hr

$= 2695 \times 3 \times \left(\frac{1}{6} - \frac{1}{18}\right) = 898$ litres

8. 3; Pipe B can fill the tank Q in 36 hrs.

$\therefore$ Pipe C can empty the tank Q in $36 \times \frac{2}{3} = 24$ hrs.

Portion of the tank filled in 1 hr when all the three pipes are opened $= \left(\frac{1}{12} + \frac{1}{36} - \frac{1}{24}\right) = \frac{6+2-3}{72} = \frac{5}{72}$ tank

Now, $\left(\frac{5}{72}\right)$ tank $= 428$

$\therefore$ Capacity of the tank $= \frac{428 \times 72}{5} = 6163.2$ litres

$\therefore$ Radius of the tank Q $= \sqrt{\frac{6163.2 \times 7}{22 \times 10}} = 14$ m

9. 4; Pipe B fills 25% of tank S in 3.5 hr.

$\therefore$ Pipe B fills full tank in $3.5 \times 4 = 14$ hrs

and pipe C empties the tank in $\frac{14 \times 5}{2} = 35$ hrs

Let pipe A fill the tank in t hr.

Then, $19250\left[\frac{1}{t} + \frac{1}{14} - \frac{1}{35}\right] = 3575$

$\frac{1}{t} + \frac{3}{70} = \frac{3575}{19250} = \frac{13}{70}$

$\therefore \frac{1}{t} = \frac{13-3}{70} \Rightarrow t = 7$ hr

Time to fill 40% of the tank $= 7 \times \frac{40}{100} = 2.8$ hr

10. 3; Height of tank Z $= 35 \times \frac{120}{100} = 42$ m

$\therefore$ Radius of tank Z $= \sqrt{\frac{38808}{\frac{22}{7} \times 28}} \times \frac{120}{100} = 25.2$ m

Total surface area of tank P and Z

$= 2 \times \frac{22}{7} \times [28 \times 21 + 42 \times 25.2] = 10348.88\ m^2$

$= 1049\ m^2$

11. 3; Curved surface area of the tank P $= 2 \times \frac{22}{7} \times 28 \times 21$

Curved surface area of the tank R $= 2 \times \frac{22}{7} \times 35 \times 7$

Ratio $= 28 \times 21 : 35 \times 7 = 12 : 5$

12. 1; Expenses in 2004 = 30000

Liability in 2004 = 1.5 × 3000 = 45000

Gross profit in 2004 = 1800000

$\Rightarrow$ Market value in 2004 = 1800000 + 30000 + 45000 = 1875000

$\Rightarrow$ Total number of shares in 2004

$= \frac{1875000}{150} = 12500$

13. 5; Number of shares in 2002 $= 10000 \times \frac{120}{100} = 12000$

Number of shares in 2004 $= \frac{1500000}{150} = 10000$

Number of shares in 2006 $= 10000 \times \frac{125}{100} = 12500$

$\therefore$ Average number of shares in all the years

$= \frac{10000 + 12000 + 11000 + 10000 + 25000 + 12500 + 30000}{7} \approx 15785$

14. 3; Cost of share in 2003 $= 90 \times \frac{95}{100} = 85.5$

$\therefore$ Market value in 2003 = 85.5 × 11000 = 940500

Cost of share in 2001 $= 90 \times \frac{100}{120} = 75$

Number of shares in 2002 $= 10000 \times \frac{120}{100} = 12000$

Average market value in 2001 and 2002

$= \frac{1}{2}[75 \times 10000 + 90 \times 12000] = 915000$

Difference = 940500 − 915000 = 25500

(15–18) :

Trains	Speed	Time	Distance	Notes
A	$\frac{1240}{22}$ $= 56.36$ km/hr	22 hrs	$60 \times 14 - 50 \times 8 = 840 + 400$ $= 1240$ km	Speed of train A is 60 km/hr on first day and it runs with $\frac{5}{6}$ th of its orginal speed on second day. Train A starts at 10 am on Monday and completes its journey at 8 am on Tuesday.
B	$\frac{1240}{22} \times \frac{8}{5}$ $= 90.18$ km/hr	$22 \times \frac{100}{110}$ $= 20$ hrs	$\frac{1240 \times 8}{110} \times 20 = 1803.6$ km	Respective ratio of speed of trains A, C and B is 5 : 6 : 8. Running time of train A is 10% more than that of B.
C	$\frac{1240}{22} \times \frac{6}{5}$ $= 67.6$ km/hr	$\frac{1240 \times 110}{1240 \times 6}$ $= 18.3$ hr	$930 \times \frac{4}{3} = 1240$ km	Respective ratio of speed of trains A, C and B is 5 : 6 : 8. Respective ratio of distance covered by train C and train D is 4 : 3.
D	$\frac{930}{11}$ $= 84.5$ km/hr	$22 \times \frac{50}{100}$ $= 11$ hrs	$1240 \times \frac{75}{100} = 930$ km	Train D covers 25% less distance than train A. Train D takes 50% less time than A.
E	$\frac{930}{11} \times \frac{5}{4}$ $= 105.68$ km/hr	$\frac{11 \times 2}{1}$ $= 22$ hr	$\frac{930 \times 5}{44} \times 22 = 2325$ km	Respective ratio of speed of train D and that of train E is 4 : 5. Respective ratio of time taken by D and that of E is 1 : 2.

15. 1; Total distance covered by all trains together
$= 1240 + 1803.6 + 1240 + 930 + 2325 = 7538.6$ km
Total time taken by all trains together
$= 22 + 20 + 18.3 + 11 + 22 = 93.3$ hrs

Required average speed $= \frac{7538.6}{93.3} = 80.79$ km/hr

16. 2; Average speed of train A = 56.36 km/hr
Average speed of train E = 105.68 km/hr
Difference = $105.68 - 56.36 = 49.32$ km/hr

Required % $= \frac{49.32}{105.68} \times 100 = 46.6\%$

17. 3; Distance covered by train B in 20 sec

$= 90.18 \times \frac{5}{18} \times 20 = 501$ m

Length of train B = 501 – 200 = 301 m

Length of train D $= 84.5 \times \frac{5}{18} \times 18 = 422.5$ m

Required ratio = 301 : 422.5 = 602 : 845

18. 4; According to the question,
Distance covered by train A = 1240 km
Time = 22 hrs
Distance covered by train C = 1240 km
Time = 18.3 hrs
Since distance covered by train A and train B is same, therefore, required difference = 22 – 18.3 = 3.7 hrs

19. 3; Selling price of book I = 20 × 200 = ₹4000
Selling price of book II = 40 × 300 = ₹12000
Selling price of book III = 60 × 100 = ₹6000
Let the commission per cent be $(a-1)$, a and $(a+1)$ respectively.
Now, according to the question,

$$4000\frac{(a-1)}{100} + \frac{12000(a)}{100} + \frac{6000(a+1)}{100} = 3200$$

$\Rightarrow a = 14.45\%$

$\Rightarrow$ highest commission = 15.45%

20. 4; Total commission earned by shop RR = ₹3500
Total selling price of Book I = 105 × 20 = ₹2100
Total selling price of Book II = 105 × 30 = ₹3150

Total selling price of Book III = 105 × 40 = ₹4200

Let the commission per cent be $x\%$.

Now, according to the question,

$$(2100+3150+4200)\times\frac{x}{100}=3500$$

$$\Rightarrow x=\frac{1000}{27}\%$$

21. 1; Total commission of SS = $\frac{3500\times 8}{7}$ = ₹4000

SP of each product = 100 × 80 = ₹8000

Let commission per cent charged on 3 products be $(x-5)\%$, $x\%$ and $(x+5)\%$.

Now, according to the questions,

$$8000\frac{(x-5)}{100}+8000\frac{(x)}{100}+8000=\frac{(x+5)}{100}4000$$

$$\Rightarrow 240x=4000$$

$$\Rightarrow x=\frac{400}{24}=\frac{100}{6}\%=16\frac{2}{3}\%$$

Least range could be = (16 − 5 =) 11%

and 16 + 6 = 22% = (11 − 22)

Practice Set 9

Directions (Q. 1–3) : Study the given information carefully and answer the questions that follow.

Given below the data about three employees of e-commerce centre named Alibaba. In the given table, data about calls received by them, calls selected for further lead and calls finally received is given:

	P	Q	R
Initial calls (% out of total calls)	40%	30%	30%
Lead calls (% out of initial calls)	80%	x%	88%
Final received calls (% out of lead calls)	90%	80%	y%

1. Total number of initial calls in the compny is 24000 and total number of calls not received by R is 4464 less than the total number of calls received by P. Find the value of y.
1) 70 2) 75 3) 85
4) 90 5) None of these
2. If the total number of calls not received by P and received by Q is 224 and 432 respectively. Find the value of x.
1) 80 2) 75 3) 90
4) 85 5) None of these
3. Find the ratio of number of lead calls made by P to the number of initial calls by Q.
1) 15 : 13 2) 16 : 13 3) 16 : 15
4) 17 : 13 5) None of these

Directions (Q. 4–7) : Study the given information carefully and answer the following questions.

A person who was watching 4 films on Amazon. Each film has some parts (not equal necessarily). Time length of each part of these films is 20 minutes. Given bar graph shows percentage distribution of number of parts of each film out of total number of parts of all 4 films and percentage of watched contents of given films by person.

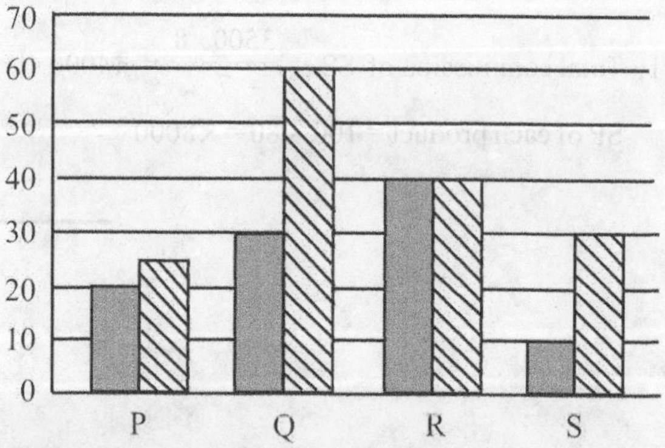

Note :

i. Total number of parts of all 4 films is x.
ii. Average of total watched content of film P and film S by given person is x -192.
iii. Daily watch time for this person is 35 minutes, 25 minutes, 18 minutes, 21 minutes for films P, Q, R, S respectively.
iv. Everyday, the person watches each part in numerical order. For example, person watches 1st part of film P, then he will start 2nd part of film P on same day only after watching 1st part of each film or complete his quota of watch time of other films, whichever is earlier. Same applies for other films as well.

4. Find the number of complete parts watched by person in first 2 days ?
1) 9 2) 8 3) 10
4) 7 5) None of these
5. Which parts of film S are watched by person on day 3?
1) 2, 3 2) 3, 4 3) 4, 5
4) 5, 6 5) Cannot be determined
6. Find the difference between number of days taken by person for watching 25 parts of films Q and 20 parts of film R ?
1) 3 2) 4 3) 2
4) 6 5) None of these

7. In how many days, person completes his quota of watching film P ?
1) 4　2) 5　3) 6
4) 9　5) None of these

Directions (Q. 8–12) : The data given below shows the information of total students in class P, Q and R which is divided in three groups A, B and C.

Class P : Total no. of students are 180. 60 students are in group A. Ratio of number of students in group B and C is 1:2.

Class Q : Total no. of students are 160. The ratio of no. of students in group A, B and C is 3 : 5 : 8.

Class R : The no. of students in group B are half of that in group A. The no. of students in group A of class R are 20 more than that in group A of class P. The number of students in group C of class R are 20% less than that in group A of same class.

8. No. of students in group A of class Q are what percentage of no. of students in group B of class R.
1) 90%　4) 100%　3) 85%
4) 75%　5) 120%

9. Find the respective ratio between average students in group A in class P and Q to total students in class R.
1) 7 : 32　2) 7 : 12　3) 7 : 23
4) 35 : 184　5) 45 : 184

10. There is total 34 girls in class P. If 12 girls are in group A, then find the no. of boys in group B and C together in class A.
1) 108　2) 50　3) 60
4) 98　5) 118

11. What are the total no. of students in group B of all the classes?
1) 85　2) 80　3) 70
4) 130　5) 100

12. Total no. of students in group A is how much more or less than that in group C.
1) 44　2) 54　3) 64　4) 84　5) 74

Directions (Q. 13–16) : Refer the table given below and answer the following questions with the help of actual work done by persons P, Q and R with the maximum time required by each to complete the work.

Data about three persons P, Q, and R is given in the table below :

Persons	Actual work done	Maximum time (in hrs)
P	50 units	5
Q	60 units	6
R		15

13. If Q works with 60% more than his minimum efficiency, then find the ratio of total units of work by Q and total units of rest by Q.
1) 5 : 3　2) 2.1 : 1.2　3) 43 : 2.5
4) 1.7 : 5.2　5) None of the above

14. If R works for 1 hour and then rests for next 10 mins. In similar manner, he completes his entire duration of work. If efficiency of R is 20% more than average of minimum efficiency of P and Q, then find the total work done by R (in units).
1) 180　2) 128　3) 164
4) 156　5) None of the above

15. If Q works with 60% more than his minimum efficiency, then find the total time of rest of Q in his entire duration of work.
1) 2.75　2) 2.25　3) 3.75
4) 1.25　5) None of the above

16. P worked for 1 hour then he took rest for next 15 minutes. In similar pattern, he completed his entire duration of work. Then, find the net efficiency of P in units per hour.
1) $\frac{30}{4}$　2) $\frac{100}{7}$　3) $\frac{75}{4}$
4) $\frac{50}{4}$　5) None of the above

Directions (Q. 17–21) : Study the following information carefully and answer the given questions:

The following table shows the total number of students studied in 3 different colleges and the total number of students in class B.Tech also given.

College	Total No. of Students (Male + Female)	Total No. of Students (Male + Female) in Class B.Tech	Total No. of Female Students in Class B.Tech
X	500	96	24
Y	960	128	20
Z	720	160	50

17. In college Z, the number of female students in class other than class twelve is 202. What per cent of student in college Z are female ?
1) 45%　2) 50%　3) 40%
4) 35%　5) None of these

18. Find the difference between the number of male students in class B. Tech of college X to that of college Y ?

1) 36 2) 40 3) 26
4) 42 5) 34

19. Find the respective ratio between the total number of students (Male+Female) in class B.Tcch of college Z and the total number of students (Male + Female) in all the classes together in college Y ?
1) 1 : 12 2) 1 : 16 3) 1 : 6
4) 1 : 8 5) None of these

20. In the given college's standard MBA, MCA and B.Tech are there. The ratio of number of students in standard MBA to that of standard MCA in college X and Y together is 55 : 48. Then find the total number of students in standard MBA in college X and Y together ?
1) 600 2) 660 3) 670
4) 700 5) 760

21. The total number of students in B.Tech of college Y is what per cent less than the total number of students in college X ?
1) 68.5% 2) 70.8% 3) 66.2%
4) 74.4% 5) 82.6%

Directions (Q. 22–24) : Given below is information about two trains X and Y.

Train X : It starts from station P and after travelling 40 km, it reduces its speed by 20%. Hence, it reaches station Q at 10 am.

Train Y : It starts from station P at same time when train X starts and after travelling 50 km, it reduces its speed by 20%. Hence it reaches station Q at 9 : 45 am.

Had both travelled at their original speeds, then they would have reached Q at 8 : 30 am.

22. Find the ratio of time taken by X and Y to cover half of the distance PQ.
1) 16 : 15 2) 18 : 5 3) 21 : 20
4) 7 : 2 5) None of these

23. If speed of train Z is 200% more than the speed of train X. Then, find the time taken by it to cover distance PQ.
1) 3.1 2) 4 3) 3.3
4) 1.9 5) None of these

24. Find the distance between P and Q stations.
1) 150 km 2) 180 km 3) 210 km
4) 100 km 5) None of these

Answers and explanations

(1–3) :

Let the total number of calls be 1000z

Initial calls (% out of total calls) of P

$= 1000z \times \frac{40}{100} = 400z$

Initial calls (% out of total calls) of Q

$= 1000z \times \frac{30}{100} = 300z$

Initial calls (% out of total calls) of R

$= 1000z \times \frac{30}{100} = 300z$

Lead calls (% out of initial calls) of P

$= 400z \times \frac{80}{100} = 320z$

Lead calls (% out of initial calls) of Q

$= 300z \times \frac{x}{100} = 3zx$

Lead calls (% out of initial calls) of R

$= 300z \times \frac{88}{100} = 264z$

Final received calls (% out of lead calls) of P

$= 320z \times \frac{90}{100} = 288z$

Final received calls (% out of lead calls) of Q

$= 3zx \times \frac{80}{100} = 3zx \times \frac{4}{5}$

Final received calls (% out of lead calls) of R

$= 264z \times \frac{y}{100}$

Total number of initial calls in the company

$\Rightarrow (400z + 300z + 300z) = 24000$

$\Rightarrow 1000z = 240000 \Rightarrow z = \frac{24000}{1000} \Rightarrow z = 24$

Total number of calls not received by R

$= 300 \times 24 - 264z \times \frac{y}{100} = 7200 - 264 \times \frac{y}{100}$

1. 2; Total number of calls not received by R is 4464 less than the total number of calls received by P.

$\Rightarrow \left(7200 - 264z \times \frac{y}{100}\right) + 4464 = 288z$

$\Rightarrow \left(7200 - 264 \times 24 \times \frac{y}{100}\right) + 4464 = 288 \times 24$

$$\Rightarrow 7200 - \frac{6336y}{100} + 4464 = 6912$$

$$\Rightarrow \frac{720000 - 6336y + 446400}{100} = 6912$$

$\Rightarrow (720000 - 6336y + 446400) = 6912 \times 100$

$\Rightarrow 1166400 - 6336y = 691200$

$\Rightarrow -6336y = 691200 - 1166400$

$$\Rightarrow -6336y = -475200 \Rightarrow y = \frac{-475200}{-6336} \Leftrightarrow y = 75$$

2. 3; The total calls not received by P

= (Initial calls by P – Final received calls by P)

$= (400z - 288z) = 112z$

Now, according to the question,

$112z = 224 \Rightarrow r = 2$

Now, the total calls received by Q,

$$3zx \times \frac{4}{5} = 432 \Rightarrow 3 \times 2 \times x \times \frac{4}{5} = 432$$

$$\Rightarrow 6x \times \frac{4}{5} = 432 \Rightarrow \frac{24x}{5} = 432 \Rightarrow x = \frac{432 \times 5}{24} = 90$$

∴ The value of x is 90.

3. 3; The ratio of number of lead calls made by P to the number of initial calls by $Q = (320z : 300z) = 16 : 15$

∴ The required ratio is 16 : 15.

(4–7) :

Let the total number of parts of all 4 films be 100 h.

Films of P = 20% of 100 h = 20 h

Films of Q = 30% of 100 h = 30 h

Films of R = 40% of 100 h = 40 h

Films of S = 10% of 100 h = 40 h

Watched content of P = 20 h × 25% = 5 h

Watched content of Q = 30 h × 60% = 18 h

Watched content of R = 40 h × 40% = 16 h

Watched content of S = 10 h × 30% = 3 h

Now, as we have taken total number of parts of all 4 Films = 100 h = x (as given in the note)

Average of total watched content of Films P and Films Q by given person = 100 h – 192 (As given in the note)

So, (5 h + 3 h) ÷ 2 = 100 h – 192

⇒ 4 h = 100 h – 192 ⇒ – 96 h = – 1 92 ⇒ h = 2

So, x = 100 h ⇒ 100 × 2 = 200

Daily watch time for this person for P = 35 minutes

Daily watch time for this person for Q = 25 minutes

Daily watch time for this person for R = 18 minutes

Daily watch time for this person for S = 21 minutes

Everyday, the person watches each show in numerical order.

So, time left after watching 1st part of P and will start 2nd part on the same day = (35 – 20) min = 15 mins

Time left after watching 1st part of Q and will start 2nd part on the same day = (25 – 20) mins = 5 mins

Time left after watching 1st part of R and will start 2nd part on the same day = (18 – 20) mins = 2 mins

Time left after watching 1st part of S and will start 2nd part on the same day = (21 – 20) min = 1 min

4. 2;

	P	Q	R	S
Day 1	20 min 1st 15 min 2nd	20 min 1st 15 min 2nd	18 min 1st	20 min 1st 1 min 2nd
Day 2	5 min 2nd 20 min 3rd 10 min 4th	15 min 2nd 10 min 3rd	2 min 1st 16 min 2nd	19 min 2nd 2 min 3rd

On Day 1 and Day 2 number of complete parts by P = 3

On Day 1 and Day 2 number of complete parts by Q = 2

On Day 1 and Day 2 number of complete parts by R = 1

On Day 1 and Day 2 number of complete parts by S = 2

The number of complete parts watched by person in first 2 days = (3 + 2 + 1 + 2) = 8

∴ The required number of complete parts watched by person in first 2 days is 8.

5. 2; According to the question,

Day 1	20 min 1st part	1 min 2nd part
Day 2	19 min 2nd part	2 min 3rd part
Day 3	18 min 3rd part	3 min 4th part

On Day 3, person watched 3 or 4 parts.

∴ Required answer is 3, 4.

6. 1; Number of days taken by person for watching 25 parts of Film Q = $\frac{25 \times 20}{25} = 20$ days

Number of days taken by person for watching 20 parts of Film R = $\frac{20 \times 20}{18} = \frac{400}{18} = 22.22$ days $\approx$ 23 days

The difference between number of days taken by person for watching 25 parts of Film Q and 20 parts of Film R = (23 – 20) = 3 days

∴ Required difference is 3 days.

7. 3; Total parts of Film P = 5 h = 5 × 2 = 10 parts
Total length of 10 parts of P = 10 × 20 = 200 mins
Total length watched in 5 days = 35 × 5 = 175 mins
Time to complete remaining 25 mins = 1 day
Total time taken in 5 + 1 = 6 days
∴ Person completes his quota of watching Film P in 6 days.

(8–12) :

	Group A	Group B	Group C	Total
P	60	40	80	180
Q	30	50	80	160
R	80	40	64	184
Total	170	130	224	524

8. 4; Required percentage = $\frac{30}{40}\times 100\% = 75\%$

9. 3; Average students in group A of class P and Q
$= \frac{60+30}{2} = 45$
Required ratio = $\frac{45}{184}$

10. 4; Total girls in group B and C together = 34 – 12 = 22
Total boys in group B and C together of class P
= (180 – 60) – 22 = 98

11. 4; Total students in group B of all the classes = 130

12. 2; Required difference = 224 – 170 = 54

(13–16) :

13. 1; Maximum time taken by Q = 6 hours
Maximum efficiency of Q = $\frac{60}{6} = 10$
Q works with 60% more than his minimum efficiency
$= 10\times\frac{60}{100} = 6$
Efficiency of Q = (10 + 6) = 16
Total units of work done by Q = $\frac{60}{16} = \frac{15}{4}$ hrs
Time taken by Q to rest = $\left(6 - \frac{15}{4}\right) = \frac{9}{4}$ hrs
Total ratio of total units of work by Q and total units of rest by Q = $\left(\frac{15}{4}:\frac{9}{4}\right)$
The required ratio = 5 : 3

14. 4; Maximum time taken by R = 15 hrs
Time taken by R to work = 1 hour
Time taken by R to rest = 10 mins
According to the question,
1 hour work = 10 min rest
× 12 × 12
12 hours work = 2 hours rest
Total working hours of R = (12 + 1) = 13 hours
Now,
Average of minimum efficiency of P and Q
$= \frac{(10+10)}{2} = 10$
Efficiency of R is 20% more than the average of minimum efficiency of P and Q = (20% of 10) = 2
Efficiency of R = (10 + 2) = 12
Total work done by R (in units) = (13 × 12) = 156 units

15. 2; Maximum time taken by Q = 6 hours
Minimum efficiency of Q = $\frac{60}{6} = 10$
Q works with 60% more than his minimum efficiency = (60% of 10) = 6
Efficiency of Q = (10 + 6) = 16
Total units of work dony by Q = $\frac{60}{16} = \frac{15}{4}$ hrs
Time taken by Q to rest = $6 - \frac{15}{4} = \frac{9}{4}$ hrs = 2.25 hrs

16. 4; Actual work done by P = 50 units
Maximum time taken by P = 10 hours
According to the question,
1 hour work = 15 min rest
Then, 4 hour work = 1 hour rest
Now, net efficiency of P in units per hour = $\frac{50}{4} = 12.5$

17. 4; The number of female students in class other than B. Tech in college Z = 202
The number of female students in class B.Tech in college Z = 50
Required % = $\frac{252}{720}\times 100 = 35\%$

18. 1; The number of male students in class B.Tech of college X = 72

The number of male students in class B.Tech of college Y = 108

Required difference = 108 – 72 = 36

19. 3; The total number of students in B.Tech in college Z = 160

The total number of students in all the classes together in college Y = 960

Required ratio = 160 : 960 = 1 : 6

20. 2; The ratio of number of students in standard MBA to that of standard MCA in college X and Y together = 55 : 48

The total number of student in class B. Tech in college X and Y together = (500 – 96) + (960 – 128)

= 404 + 832 = 1236

Given, (55 + 48 =) 103 ≡ 1236

1 ≡ 12

The total number of students in standard MBA in college X and Y together = 12 × 55 = 660

21. 4; The total number of students in class B.Tech of college Y = 128

The total number of students in class B.Tech of college X = 500

$$\text{Required \%} = \frac{(500-128)}{500} \times 100 = 74.4\%$$

(78–80) :

22. 3;

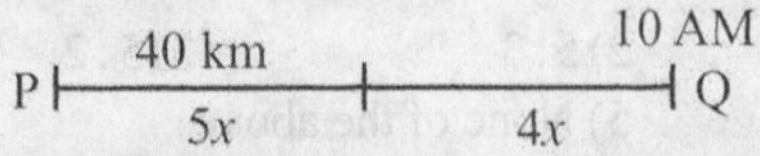

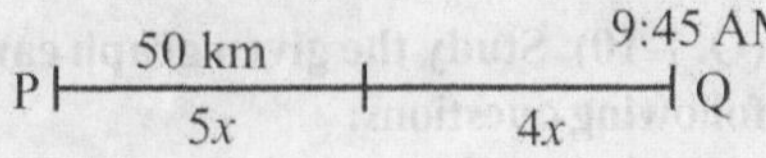

Train X :

$$\frac{D}{4x} - \frac{D}{5x} = \frac{3}{2} \Rightarrow D\left[\frac{x}{20x^2}\right] = \frac{3}{2} \Rightarrow D = 30x$$

Train Y :

$$\frac{D}{4x} - \frac{D}{5x} = \frac{5}{4} \Rightarrow D\left(\frac{x}{20x^2}\right) = \frac{5}{4} \Rightarrow D = 25x$$

$40 + 30x = 50 + 285x$

$\Rightarrow 5x = 10$

$\Rightarrow x = 2$

Initial speed of trains X and Y = 5 × 2 = 10 km/hr

After reducing, speed = 8 km/hr

Total distance = (40 + 30x) = (40 + 30 × 2) = 100 km

The time taken by X to cover half of distance PQ

$$= \frac{40}{10} + \frac{10}{8} = \frac{21}{4}$$

The time taken by Y to cover half of the distance PQ

$$= \frac{50}{10} = 5$$

The ratio of time taken by X and Y to cover half of the distance

$$PQ = \frac{21}{4} : \frac{5}{1} = 21 : 20$$

23. 3; According to the question,

Speed of train X = 10 km/hr

Speed of train Z is 200% more than the speed of train

$$X = 10 \times \frac{300}{100} = 30$$

Distance between P and Q = 100 km

$$\text{Time taken by it to cover distance PQ} = \frac{100}{30} = 3.3$$

24. 4; Distance between P and Q

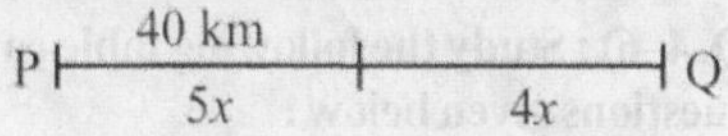

D = (40 + 30x) = 40 + 60 = 100 km

Practice Set 10

Directions (Q. 1-3): Study the given information carefully and answer the questions that follow:

Rolly and Dolly earned different amounts of salaries. After a year, Rolly received a hike of N% and Dolly received a hike of 12% in their respective salaries. Rolly invested 70% of her salary after the hike in a scheme X, for two years, which offers compound interest at the rate of 10% per annum. She earned an interest of ₹4226.25. Dolly, on the other hand, invested 65% of her salary after the hike in a scheme X that offers simple interest at the rate of 15% per annum. She earned an interest of ₹12230.40 in 4 years.

1. Which of the following can be determined using the above given information?
(A) Value of N (B) Rolly's salary after hike
(C) Dolly's initial salary (D) Rolly's salary before hike
1) Only (B) and (D) 2) All (A), (B), (C) and (D)
3) Only (C) 4) Only (A) and (C)
5) Nothing can be determined

2. If it is given that Rolly's salary increased by ₹3750 after N% hike, then what is the value of N?
1) 23% 2) 20% 3) 10% 4) 12% 5) 15%

3. If N is the same as given in the above question, then the salary of Dolly is approximately what per cent of the salary of Rolly?
1) 140 2) 70 3) 112
4) 120 5) None of these

Directions (Q. 4–6) : Study the following table carefully and answer the questions given below :

The table grtaph given below shows the data about goods sold by five seller on three different days of a week.

Seller	Mon : Tue	Tue	Wed % out of total goods sold on three days
P	——	12.5m	x%
Q	7 : m	——	——
R	4 : 05	10m	20%
S	——	——	(x-5)%
T	3 : 04	15m	30%

Note :

1. Difference between total goods sold on all three days by R and T is 120.
2. Total goods sold by S on all three days is 120.

4. If the average number of goods sold by seller Q on all three days is 200 and on Tuesday if seller Q sold 20% of the goods out of all goods S sold by it on all the three days then find the number of goods sold by seller Q on Wednesday.
1) 300 2) 350 3) 325 4) 375 5) 400

5. If seller P sold 60% more goods on Monday than it was sold on Tuesday and the number of goods sold by seller P on Monday and Wednesday is in the ratio of 8 : 7, then find the number of goods sold by S on Tuesday, if S sold a total of 360 goods on all three days and 40% of the total goods sold by it was on Monday.
1) 136 2) 108 3) 90 4) 110 5) 120

6. Find the ratio of total goods sold by T on Tuesday and the total goods sold by R on Wednesday.
1) 10 : 3 2) 5 : 3 3) 5 : 2
4) 12 : 5 5) None of the above

Directions (Q. 7-10): Study the given graph carefully and answer the following questions:

The graph given below shows the percentage of boys out of the total number of students in three different classes during three different years, ie 2018, 2019 and 2020, of Angels Public Senior Secondary School.

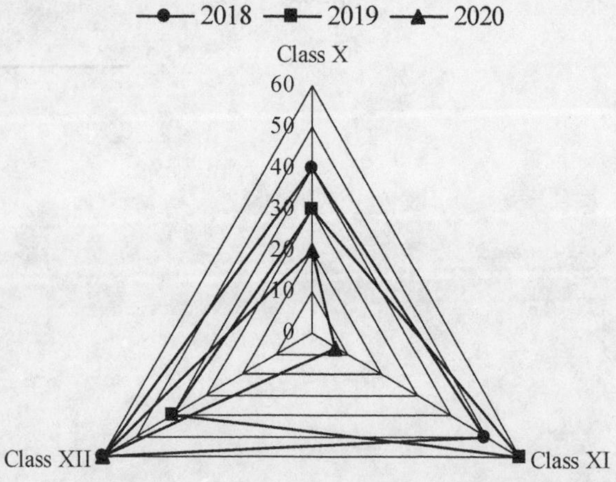

7. It is mentioned that in class XI the number of boys who like cricket in 2018 is 13 less than the number of girls who like cricket in the same year and the total number of boys who study in class XI in 2018 is 160. The number of girls who like cricket in 2019 is $\frac{5}{16}$ of the total number of girls in 2018. The number of boys in class XI who do not like cricket in 2019 is 272% more than the number of girls who like cricket in 2019. The number of boys who like cricket in 2019 is 5 less than the number of girls who do not like cricket in 2018. The number of girls who do not like cricket in 2019 is 94, which is 46 more than number of boys who do not like cricket in 2018. What is the sum of the total number of students studying in class XI in 2018 and 2019 together?
[Note: All data given in this question pertain to class XI students only.]
1) 720 2) 360 3) 650
4) 680 5) 540

8. The total number of boys who studied in 2018 in all the classes is the same. If it is mentioned that in 2018, the difference between the total number of students in class X and class XI is the same as the difference between total number of students between class XI and class XII, then the number of students in class XII is what per cent more or less than the number of students in class X?
[Note: The number of students in class X is greater than the number of students in class XI, which in turn is greater than the number of students in class XII.]
1) 50 2) 60 3) 40 4) 20 5) None of these

9. The total number of students in class XI decreases from 2018 to 2020 continuously. It decreases by the same number in both the years. If it is mentioned that the number of boys in class XI remains the same in all the three years, then by what per cent is the total number of students in class XI in 2020 less than that in 2018?
1) $66\frac{2}{3}\%$ 2) 50% 3) $33\frac{1}{3}\%$
4) $14\frac{2}{3}\%$ 5) Cannot be determined

10. The sum of class X students in 2018 and 2019 is 380 and the sum of class X students in 2019 and 2020 is 530. If the sum of class X students in all the three years together is 660, then find the number of girls in class X in 2019.
1) 75 2) 150 3) 175 4) 250 5) 130

Directions (Q. 11–14) : Study the given information carefully and answer the following questions :

The table shows data about distance (km) about one point to another point by the vehicles used in each point and the speed of each vehicle (km/hr).

Example : If one person wants to travel from P to S then he/she can only use the vehicle available at point P or *vice versa.*

X means there is no direct connection between points.

	P	Q	R	S	Transport vehicle	Speed
P	0	120	X	260	Train	40
Q	180	0	X	200	Auto	25
R	140	240	0	X	E-Rickshaw	30
S	320	X	420	0	Cycle	12

11. If one person travels from P to Q and another person travels from S to R, then find the difference between distance travelled by them.
1) 280 km 2) 300 km 3) 340 km
4) 320 km 5) None of the above

12. If one person wants to travel from P to R, then find the minimum time required to cover this distance.
1) 55 hrs 2) 45.5 hrs 3) 36 hrs
4) 41.5 hrs 5) 30.5 hrs

13. If a person travels P to S via Q and the fair of vehicle per km from point Q is 20% more than that from point P, and the total fare to cover from P to S via Q is ₹37800, then find the per km cost of Auto.
1) ₹20 2) ₹100 3) ₹105
4) ₹126 5) None of the above

14. Find the minimum possible sum of time taken to cover distances from P to S and from R to S.
1) 43/3 hrs 2) 53/3 hrs 3) 40/3 hrs
4) 10 hrs 5) None of the above

Directions (Q. 15–18) : Following bar graph shows working efficiency of four people to complete the work.

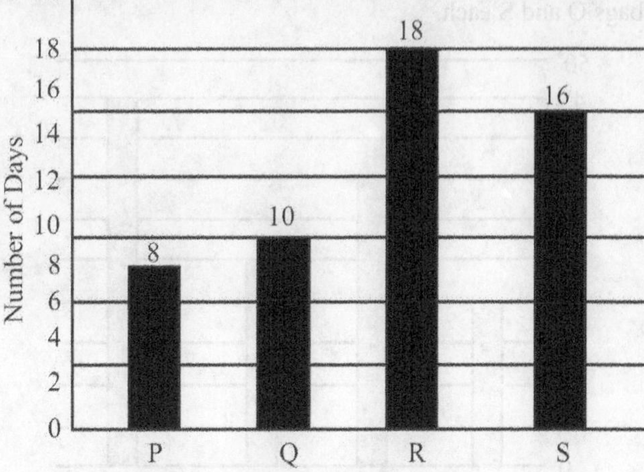

15. P and Q starts working together and alter 2 days, both of them left the work. Then in how many days the remaining work will be completed by S ?

1) $\frac{13}{6}$ days 2) $\frac{41}{5}$ days 3) $\frac{44}{5}$ days
4) $\frac{47}{5}$ days 5) $\frac{49}{5}$ days

16. In how many days the total work will be completed, if all the four persons start working together ?

1) $\frac{720}{247}$ days 2) $\frac{947}{734}$ days 3) $\frac{780}{249}$ days
4) $\frac{698}{233}$ days 5) $\frac{587}{144}$ days

17. If S and P starts working together and after 2 days, they both left the work and Q alone works on third day, then find the remaining portion of the work after 3 days.

1) $\frac{1}{10}$ 2) $\frac{21}{40}$ 3) $\frac{1}{12}$
4) $\frac{11}{25}$ 5) $\frac{2}{5}$

18. If at the place of Q, T joins the work with P, R and S, then work will be completed in $\frac{48}{13}$ days. Working efficiency of T is

1) 12 2) 30 3) 27
4) 36 5) 36

Directions (Q. 19–21) : Study the following information carefully and answer the questions given below.

The bar graph shows the total number of balls (White + Yellow + Black) in 4 different bags. The line graph given below shows the probability of picking a white ball from bag P and R each and probability of picking a yellow ball from bags Q and S each.

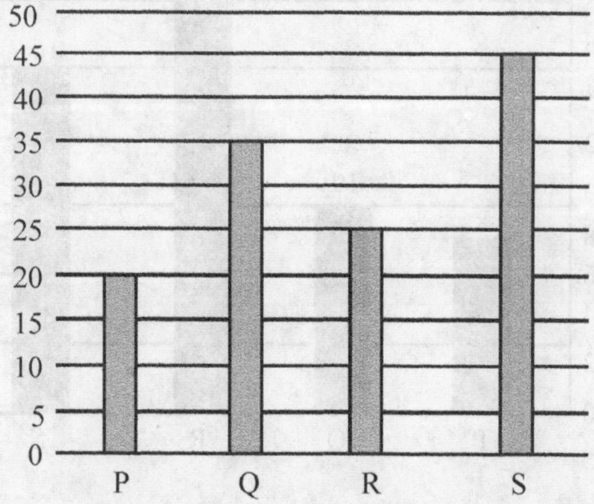

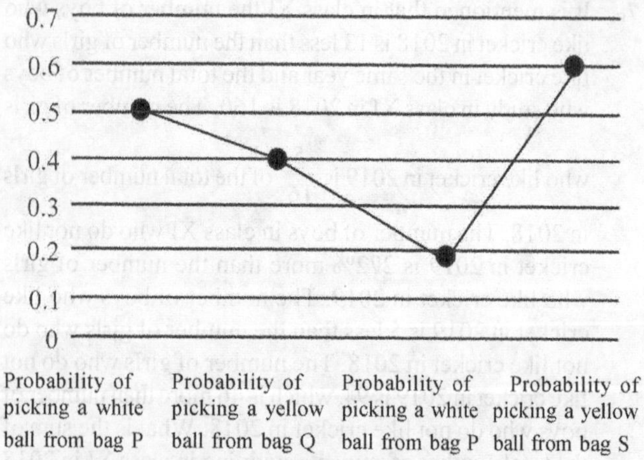

19. If the number of white balls in bag P would have been 20% more and the number of yellow balls in bag P would have been $\frac{1}{7}$th of the number of yellow balls in bag Q, then the number of black balls in bag P and Q is equal. Which one of the following is/are true ?

I. The difference between probability of picking a white ball from bag Q and the probability of picking a black ball from bag P is more than 0.1.

II. The difference between the number of yellow balls in bag P and the number of yellow balls in bag S is a perfect square.

III. The average of number of white balls in bag Q and R is 8.

1) Only I and III 2) Only I and II 3) Only II and III
4) Only III 5) All I, II and III

20. If the number of black balls in bag Ris more than 8 and the number of black balls in bag R is more than the number of yellow balls in that bag. The number of yellow balls in bag R is a prime number. Which one of the following/s is/are true?

I. The probability of picking a black ball from bag R is less than 0.74.

II. The sum of probability of picking a yellow ball from bag Q and the probability of picking a black ball from bag R is always greater than 1.

III. The total number of white and black balls in bag S can be equal to the number of black balls in bag R.

1) Only I and III 2) Only I and II 3) Only II and III
4) Only III 5) All I, II and III

21. In bag T, the total number of balls (white + black + yellow) is 30. The probability of picking a black ball from bag T is 0.1. The number of white balls in bag S is 4 times the number of black balls in bag T. Which one of the following is/are true?

I. The probability of picking a black ball from bag S is not more than 0.2.

II. If the ratio of number of black balls in bag P and S is 2 : 3, then the probability of picking two yellow balls from bag Pis 3/38.

III. The difference between the probability of picking two black balls from bag S and the probability of picking two balls from bag Q, which are not yellow is 379/1122.

1) Only I and III 2) Only I and II 3) Only II and III 4) Only III 5) All I, II and III

Answers and explanations

1. 3; Let the salaries (initial) of Rolly and Dolly be R and D respectively. Rolly's salary after the hike $= R\left(1+\frac{N}{100}\right)$

$\because$ Dolly's salary after the hike $= \frac{D\times 112}{100} = \frac{28D}{25}$

For Dolly: Investment in scheme X

$= \frac{65}{100}\times\frac{28D}{25} = \frac{91}{125}D$

Now, $\frac{91D\times 15\times 4}{125\times 100} = 12230.4$

$\Rightarrow D = \frac{12230.4\times 100\times 125}{91\times 15\times 4} = ₹28000$; which is the inital salary of Dolly. Hence option (C) is correct.

For Rolly: Principal $= \frac{70}{100}\times R\left(\frac{100+N}{100}\right) = \frac{7R}{10}\left(\frac{100+N}{100}\right)$

So, $\frac{7R}{10}\left(\frac{100+N}{100}\right)\frac{21}{100} = 4226.25$

$\Rightarrow \frac{147R}{1000}\left(\frac{1+N}{100}\right) = 4226.25$ ... (1)

Now, (A) and (B) cannot be determined as values of R and N cannot be found from this equation.
Similarly, (D) can't be found as R can't be determined.

2. 5; As per information given,
N% of R = 3750

$\Rightarrow NR = 3750\times 100 \Rightarrow R = \frac{375000}{N}$

Putting the value of R in (1),

$\frac{147}{1000}\times\frac{375000}{N}\left(\frac{100+N}{100}\right) = 4226.25$

$\Rightarrow N = \frac{147\times 375}{3675} \Rightarrow N = 15\%$

3. 3; Putting, N = 15%, we get

Now, $\frac{147R}{1000}\left(\frac{115}{100}\right) = 4226.25$

$\Rightarrow R = \frac{4226.25\times 100\times 1000}{115\times 147} = 25000$

And Dolly's salary = 28000

$\therefore$ Required % $= \frac{28000}{25000}\times 100 \approx 112$

(4–6) :

Seller	Mon : Tue	Tue	Wed % out of total Products Sold on three days
P	8 : 5	100	35%
Q	7 : 8	120	62.5%
R	4 : 5	80	20%
S	4 : 3	108	30%
T	3 : 4	120	30%

Wednesday % out of total products sold on three days by seller T = 30%

Remaining percentage = 100 − 30 = 70%

Product sold on Monday $= \frac{70}{7}\times 3 = 30\%$

Product sold on Tuesday $= \frac{70}{7}\times 4 = 40\%$

$T\times\frac{40}{100} = 15m \Rightarrow T = \frac{75m}{2}$

Wednesday % out of total goods sold on three days by sellers R = 20%

Remaining percentage = 100 − 20 = 80%

Product sold on Monday $= \frac{80}{9}\times 4 = \frac{320}{9}\%$

Product sold on Tuesday $= \frac{80}{9}\times 5 = \frac{400}{9}\%$

$R\times\frac{400}{900} = 10m \Rightarrow = \frac{45}{2}m = \frac{45}{2}m$

Again, T − R = 120

$\Rightarrow \frac{75m}{2} - \frac{45m}{2} = 120 \Rightarrow m = \frac{120}{15} = 8$

4. 4; Total number of goods sold by seller Q on all the three days = 200 × 3 = 600

Goods sold by seller Q on Tuesday $= 600 \times \frac{20}{100} = 120$

Goods sold by seller Q on Monday $= \frac{120}{8} \times 7 = 105$

Goods sold by seller Q on Wednesday = 600 (120 + 105) = 375

5. 2; Goods sold by seller P on Tuesday $= 12.5 \times 8 = 100$

Goods sold by seller P on Monday $= 100 \times \frac{160}{100} = 160$

Goods sold by seller P on Monday and Wednesday is in the ratio of = 8 : 7

Goods sold by seller P on Wednesday $= \frac{160}{8} \times 7 = 140$

The value of $x = \frac{140}{400} \times 100 = 35\%$

Goods sold by Seller S on Wednesday $= 35 - 5 = 30\%$

Goods sold by Seller S on Monday = 40%

Goods sold by Seller S on Tuesday $= 100 - (30 + 40) = 30\%$

Goods sold by Seller S on Tuesday $= 360 \times \frac{30}{100} = 108$

6. 1; Goods sold by T on Tuesday = 120

Goods sold by R on Wednesday $= \frac{45}{2} \times 8 \times \frac{20}{100}$

$= \frac{180}{5} = 36$

Required Ratio = 120 : 36 ≡ 10 : 3

7. 4; From the data given in the question, we can make a table as given below:

2018	Boys	Girls	2019	Boys	Girls
Like cricket	112	125	Like cricket	30	50
Do not like cricket	48	35	Do not like cricket	186	94
Total	160	160	Total	216	144

Hence, total number of students = 160 + 160 + 216 + 144 = 680

8. 3; Let the number of students in class X, Class XI and Class XII in 2018 be M, (M – D) and (M – 2D) respectively. Then, as per information given,

$$\frac{40M}{100} = \frac{50}{100}(M - D)$$

$$\Rightarrow 4M = 5M - 5D \Rightarrow 5D = M \Rightarrow D = \frac{M}{5}$$

Number of students in class XII $= M - 2\left(\frac{M}{5}\right) = \frac{3M}{5}$

$\therefore$ Required percentage $= \frac{M - \frac{3M}{5}}{M} \times 100 = 40\%$

9. 3; Let the total number of students in class XI in 2018 be N. And, let the total number of students decrease by T every year.

Then, number of students in class XI in 2019 = N – T

And, number of students in class XI in 2020 = N – 2T

As per information given,

$$\frac{50N}{100} = \frac{60(N - T)}{100}$$

$$\Rightarrow \frac{N}{N - T} = \frac{6}{5} \quad \Rightarrow T = \frac{N}{6} \quad ...(i)$$

Thus, number of students in class XI in 2020

$= N - 2T = N - 2\left(\frac{N}{6}\right) = \frac{2N}{3}$

$\therefore$ Required percentage $= \frac{N - \frac{2N}{3}}{N} \times 100 = 33\frac{1}{3}\%$

10. 3; Number of students in class X in 2019 $= (380 + 530) - 660 = 250$

Number of girls $= \frac{70}{100} \times 250 = 175$

11. 2; The distance between P and Q = 120 km

The distance between S and R = 420 km

Required difference = 420 – 120 = 300 km

12. 4; There are two ways to go from P to R.

P 120km Q 200 km S 420 km R

or

P 260 km S 420 km R

The minimum time to cover this distance $= \frac{260}{40} + \frac{420}{12}$

$= 6.5 + 35 = 41.5$ hrs

13. 4; The distance between P and Q = 120 km

The distance between Q and S = 200 km

Let the fair of vehicle per km from Q be $6x$ and the fair of vehicle per km from P be $5x$.

Now, according to the question,

$120 \times 5x + 200 \times 6x = 37{,}800$

$\Rightarrow 600x + 1200x = 37{,}800 \Rightarrow x = 21$

The per km cost of Auto is = 6 × 21 = ₹126

14. 2; The distance between P and S = 260 km

The distance between R and S = R **140 km** P **260 km**S

or

R **240 km** Q **200 km** S

The minimum time required $= \frac{260}{40} + \frac{140}{30} + \frac{260}{40}$

$= 13 + \frac{14}{3} = \frac{39+14}{3} = \frac{53}{3}$ hrs

15. 3; P can complete the work in = 8 days

Q can complete the work in = 10 days

R can complete the work in = 18 days

S can complete the work in = 16 days

(90, 72, 40, 45 → 720)

Let the total work be 720 units (LCM of 8, 10, 18, 16).
And the efficiency of P, Q, R and S be 90, 72, 40 and 45 respectively.
P and Q complete the work in 2 days = 2 (90 + 72)
= 2 × 162 = 324 units
Remaining work = 720 – 324 = 296 units

Remaining work will be completed by S in $= \frac{396}{45}$

$= \frac{44}{5}$ days

16. 1; The total work will be comleted in $= \frac{720}{90+72+40+45}$

$= \frac{720}{247}$ days

17. 2; S and P completed the work in 2 days = 2 (90 + 45)
= 2 × 135 = 270 units
Q completed the work on third day = 72 units
Remaining work = 720 – (270 + 72) = 720 –342 = 378 units

Remaining part of the work $= \frac{378}{720} = \frac{42}{80} = \frac{21}{40}$

18. 5; P, R, S and T complete the work in $\frac{48}{13}$ days

Working efficiency of P, R, S and T together

$= \frac{720}{48} \times 13 = \frac{60}{4} \times 13 = 15 \times 13 = 195$

Working efficiency of T = 195 – (90 + 40 + 45)
= 195 – 175 = 20

19. 2;

Bags	White	Yellow	Black	Total
P	12	2	6	20
Q	15	14	6	35

I. Probability of picking a white ball from bag

$Q = \frac{15}{35} = \frac{3}{7} = 0.42$

Probability of picking a black ball from bag

$P = \frac{6}{20} = 0.3$

Required difference = 0.42 – 0.3 = 0.12
0.12 > 0.10 (true)

II. Yellow balls in bag P = 2
Yellow balls in bag S = 27
Required difference = 27 – 2 = 25
$(5)^2 = 25$ (Perfect Square) (true)

III. Number of white balls in bag Q = 15
Number of white balls in bag R = 5

Required average $= \frac{15+5}{2} = 10$ (false)

Hence, Only I and II follow.

20. 1;

Bag	White	Yellow	Black	Total
R	5	$20 - x$	$x > 8$	25

$x > 20 - x \Rightarrow x > 10$
Possible values of x = 18, 17, 15 and 13
Number of yellow balls = 2, 3, 5 and 7

I. Probability of picking a back ball from bag R in all cases :

$\frac{18}{25} = 0.72$, $\frac{17}{25} = 0.68$, $\frac{15}{25} = 0.6$ and $\frac{13}{25} = 0.52$

Probability of picking a black ball is less then 0.75 in all cases. So, (I) is true.

II. Probability of picking a yellow ball from bag

$Q = \frac{14}{35} = 0.4$

Probability of picking a black ball from bag R in all cases :

$\frac{18}{25} = 0.72$, $\frac{17}{25} = 0.68$, $\frac{15}{25} = 0.6$ and $\frac{13}{25} = 0.52$

Sum of the probabilities = 0.4 + 0.52 = 0.92 < 1
This is not always greater than 1. So, (II) is not true.

III. The total number of white and black balls in bag $S = 45 - 27 = 18$

The number of black balls in bag R can be 18.

Hence, III is true.

21. 5;

Bags	White	Yellow	Black	Total
T			3	30

I. The probability of picking a black ball from bag

$S = \frac{6}{45} = 0.13$

Here, $0.13 < 0.2$. So, (I) is true.

II. The number of black balls in bag $S = 6$

The number of black balls in bag $P = \frac{6}{3} \times 2 = 4$

The number of yellow balls in bag $P = 20-(10+4) = 6$

The probability of picking two yellow balls from bag

$P = \frac{6}{20} \times \frac{5}{19} = \frac{30}{380} = \frac{3}{38}$

So, (II) is true

III. The probability of picking two black balls from bag

$S = \frac{6}{45} \times \frac{5}{44} = \frac{30}{45 \times 44} = \frac{1}{66}$

The probability of picking two balls (which are not yellow)

From bag $Q = \frac{21}{35} \times \frac{20}{34} = \frac{6}{17}$

Reqmred difference $= \frac{6}{17} - \frac{1}{66} = \frac{396-17}{1122} = \frac{379}{1122}$

So, III is true.

Hence, All I, II and III are true is the correct answer.

Practice Set 11

Directions (Q. 1–5) : Study the following information carefully and answer the questions given below.

The bar graphs given below shows the discount percentage given on marked price of four different items in 2023 and 2024.

Note : The marked price of an item can be same or different in both the years.

The cost price of an item can be same or different in both the years.

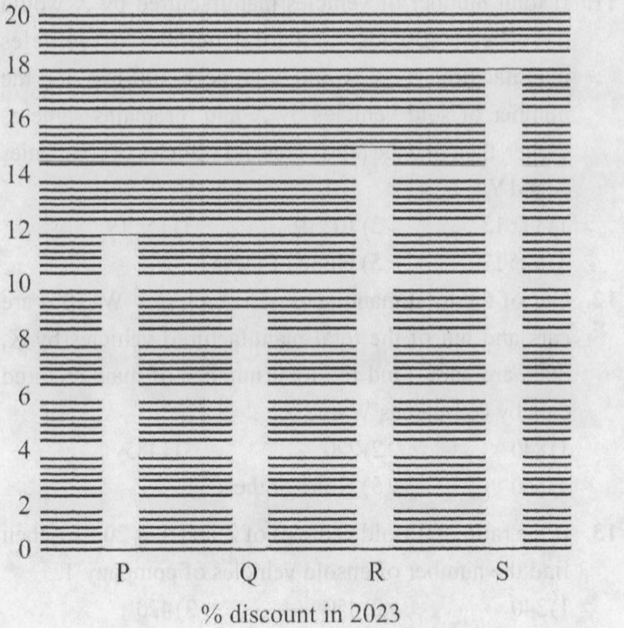

% discount in 2023

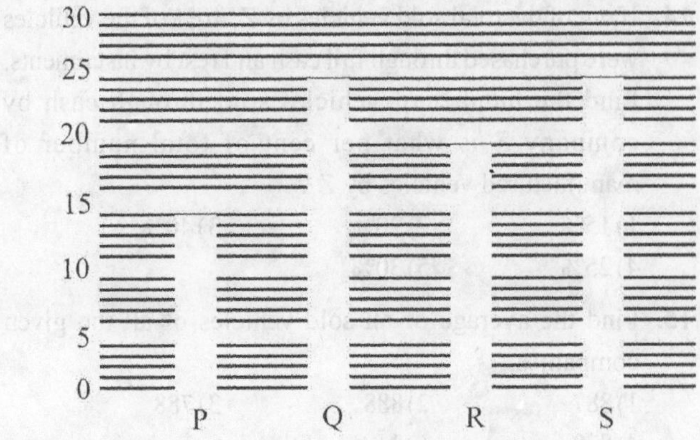

% discount in 2024

1. The marked price of item S in 2023 is ₹418 more than the profit earned by selling this item in 2023; whereas the profit percentage on selling article S in 2023 is 25%, then find the marked price of article S in 2023.
1) 400 2) 450 3) 500 4) 950 5) 550

2. The marked price of item Q is twice the marked price of item P in 2023. Find the ratio of the selling prices of item P and Q in 2023.
1) 43 : 91 2) 53 : 93 3) 54 : 97 4) 44 : 91 5) 45 : 93

3. The ratio of selling price of item R and S in 2024 is 2 : 5 and the profit per cent on selling items R and S in 2024 is 20% and 25% respectively, find the cost price of item R is what per cent of the cost price of item S in 2024?
1) 43.66% 2) 36.5% 3) 41.66% 4) 44.6% 5) 46.4%

4. If the ratio of marked price of item Q and R in 2024 is 3 : 4 and item R is sold at a profit of 60% and the difference between cost price and selling price of item R in 2024 is ₹480. If the marked price of item Q in 2023 and 2024 is same, then find the selling price of item Q in 2023.
1) 1194 2) 1232 3) 1436
4) 1092 5) 1096

5. If the cost price of item P in 2023 and 2024 is same, then find the ratio of selling price of item P in 2023 and 2024.
1) 21 : 20 2) 15 : 13 3) 43 : 42
4) Cannot be determined 5) None of these

Directions (Q. 6–10) : Study the following information carefully and answer the questions given below.

The line graph given below shows the profit percentage and discount percentage of five different articles. The table given shows the cost price of each items.

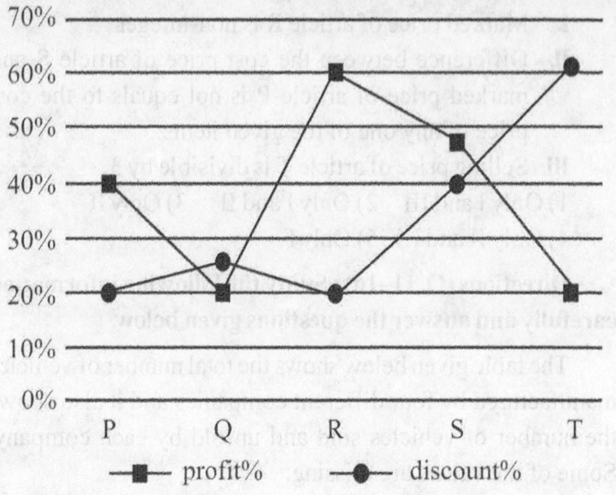

Articles	Cost price (in ₹)
P	1050
Q	1600
R	1720
S	1800
T	900

6. Find the average of selling prices of articles P and Q.
1) 2092 2) 2312 3) 2111
4) 2331 5) None of these

7. If article S would have been sold at 20% profit but the marked price remains the same as earlier, then find the difference between the profit earned earlier and the new profit
1) 340 2) 350 3) 420
4) 450 5) None of these

8. If the cost price of article M is

$\sqrt{\text{If article Q is marked 20\% above its Cost price)} + 105}$ and the selling price of article M is ₹$(9^2 - 4^2)$. Then find the profit percentage earned by selling article M.
1) 37.5% 2) 48.21% 3) 66.66%
4) 44.44 % 5) None of these

9. If the marked price of article Q is 25% more than that of article M, then find the difference between the marked prices of articles Q and M.
1) 578 2) 688 3) 672
4) 498 5) 512

10. Find which of the following/s is/are false.
I. Marked price of article R is non-integer
II. Difference between the cost price of article S and marked price of article P is not equals to the cost price of any one of the given items.
III. Selling price of article T is divisible by 3.
1) Only I and III 2) Only I and II 3) Only II
4) Only II and III 5) Only I

Directions (Q. 11–16) : Study the following information carefully and answer the questions given below.

The table given below shows the total number of vehicles manufactured by four different companies and it also shows the number of vehicles sold and unsold by each company. Some of the values are missing.

Note 1. Total number of vehicels sold by all companies together is 3442.
2. In company Z, the number of vehicles unsold is 1/3rd of the vehicles sold by them.

	Manufactured	Sold	Unsold
W	A	C	——
X	A + 150	$8\frac{4}{7}$ B	—
Y	900	648	3B
Z	——	2 C + 132	(A/3) + 150

11. If total number of vehicles manufactured by X would have been 400 less and total number of vehicles manufactured by Y would have been 100 less and the number of sold vehicles by X and Yremains same as earlier, then find the ratio of unsold vehicles of companies X and Y.
1) 11 : 13 2) 10 : 19 3) 15 : 19
4) 12 : 17 5) None of these

12. Out of the total manufactured vehicles by W, 50% are cars and out of the total manufactured vehicles by X, 80% are cars. Find the total number of manufactured cars by companies W and X.
1) 840 2) 720 3) 1485
4) 560 5) None of these

13. If the ratio of unsold vehicles of Z and T is 20 : 13, then find the number of unsold vehicles of company T.
1) 340 2) 450 3) 420
4) 325 5) None of these

14. If out of the total sold vehicles by Z, 40% of the vehicles were purchased through full cash and rest by instalments. Find the number of vehicles sold through cash by company Z is what per cent of total number of manufactured vehicles by Z ?
1) 15% 2) 20% 3) 40%
4) 25% 5) 30%

15. Find the average of all sold vehicles of all the given companies.
1) 887 2) 888 3) 788
4) 878 5) None of these

16. The number of vehicles sold by company M is equal to the average of number of vehicles sold by X and Y, and the total number of vehicles manufactured by company M is 300 more than that by company Z. Find the number of unsold vehicles by company M.

1) 1336 2) 1416 3) 1316
4) 1616 5) None of these

Directions (Q. 17-21): Study the following information carefully and answer the questions given below.

Given below is the line graph showing the percentage profit of two IT firms, TCS and HCL, from the year 2016 to 2020. The pie charts show the percentage distribution of the total income of each company in different years. Study the data carefully and answer the following questions.

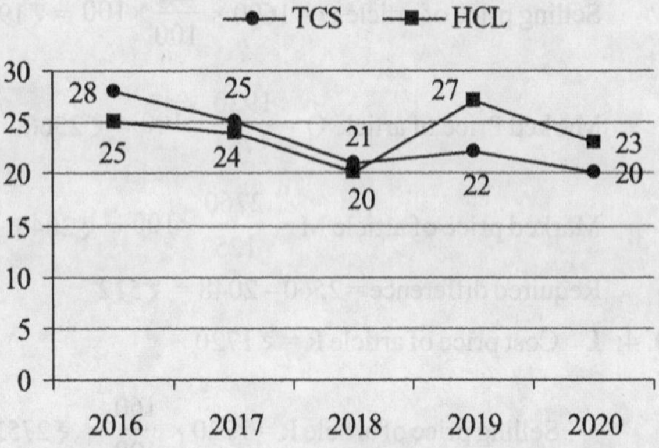

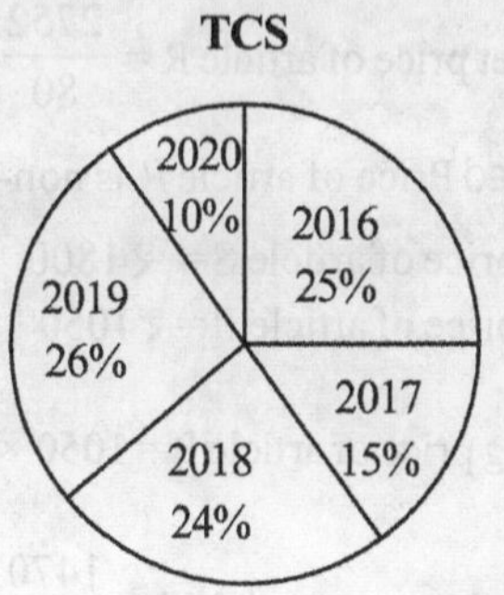

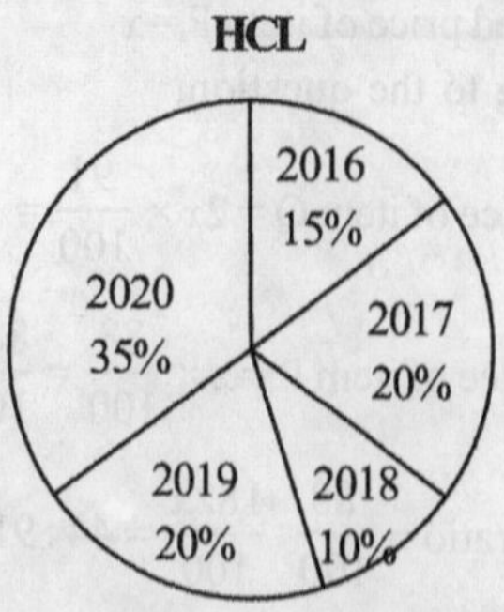

Note:

- Per cent profit = $\frac{\text{Income} - \text{Expenditure}}{\text{Expenditure}} \times 100$
- Total income of TCS over the given years = ₹1500 crore.
- Total income of HCL over the given years = ₹1800 crore.

17. The expenditure of TCS in 2018 is approximately how much per cent less/more than that of HCL in 2017?
1) 8 2) 3 3) 6
4) 5 5) 12

18. The total income of TCS in the year 2016, 2017 and 2018 together is how much per cent more than the total income of HCL for the same years?
1) 15.51% 2) 23.14% 3) 19.96%
4) 16.54% 5) 18.51%

19. The income of HCL in 2020 is approximately how much per cent less/more than the average expenditure of TCS for the years 2019, 2020 and 2017?
1) 289 2) 275 3) 313
4) 307 5) None of the given options

20. What approximately is the collective profit of TCS and HCL for years 2019 and 2020? (in crore rupees)
1) 226 2) 212 3) 290
4) 344 5) 121

21. Calculate the difference between the expenditures of TCS and HCL in 2021 if their expenditures in 2021 are 80% and 90% of their incomes in 2020 respectively.
1) ₹354 crores 2) ₹454 crores 3) ₹447 crores
4) ₹462 crores 5) ₹554 crores

Answers and explanations

(1–5):

1. 3; Let the marked price of item be ₹x.

Now, according to the question,

Market Price - Profit = ₹418 .... (i)

$$SP = x \times \frac{82}{100}$$

$$CP = \frac{x \times 82 \times 100}{100 \times 125} = \frac{328x}{500}$$

$$SP - CP = \frac{410x}{500} - \frac{328x}{500} = \frac{82x}{500}$$

$$\Rightarrow \text{Profit} = \frac{82x}{500}$$

On putting the value in equ. (i), we get,

$$x - \frac{82x}{500} = 418 \Rightarrow x = ₹500$$

2. 4; Let the marked price of item Q be $2x$.

The marked price of item P = x
According to the question,

Selling price of item Q = $2x \times \frac{91}{100} = \frac{182x}{100}$

Selling price of item P = $x \times \frac{88}{100} = \frac{88x}{100}$

Required ratio = $\frac{88}{100} : \frac{182x}{100} = 44:91$

3. 3; Let the selling price of item R in 2024 be $2x$.
The selling price of item S in 2024 = $5x$

Cost price of item R in 2024 = $\frac{2x}{120} \times 100 = \frac{5x}{3}$

Cost price of item R in 2024 = $\frac{5x}{125} \times 100 = 4x$

Required percentage = $\frac{\frac{5x}{3}}{4x} \times 100 = \frac{125}{3} = 41.66\%$

4. 4; Let the marked price of item Q in 2024 be $3x$.
The marked price of item R in 2024 = $4x$

Selling price of item R= $4x \times \frac{80}{100} = \frac{16x}{5}$

Cost price of item R = $\frac{16x}{5} \times \frac{100}{160} = 2x$

Now, according to the question,

$\frac{16x}{5} - 2x = 480$

$\Rightarrow \frac{6x}{5} = 480 \Rightarrow x = 400$

The marked price of item Q in 2024 = 400 × 3 = ₹1200
The marked price of item Q in 2023 = ₹1200
The selling price of item Q in 2023 = $1200 \times \frac{91}{100}$
= ₹1092

5. 4; As the cost price and discount is given.
Therefore, we cannot calculate the selling price of the items.

6. 3; Selling price of article P = $1050 \times \frac{140}{100}$ = ₹1470

Selling price of article R= $1720 \times \frac{160}{100}$ = ₹2752

Required average = $\frac{1470 + 2752}{2}$ = ₹2111

7. 4; Required difference = 1800 × (45% – 20%)
= $1800 \times \frac{25}{100}$ = ₹450

8. 4; Cost price of Q = ₹1600

Market price of Q = $1600 \times \frac{120}{100}$ = ₹1920

Cost price of article M = $\sqrt{1920 + 105} = \sqrt{2025} = 45$
Selling price of article M = (81 – 16) = 65

Profit percentage = $\frac{65 - 45}{45} \times 100 = \frac{400}{9} = 44,44\%$

9. 5; Cost price of article Q = ₹1600

Selling price of article Q = $1600 \times \frac{120}{100} \times 100$ = ₹1920

Marked Price of article Q = $\frac{1920}{75} \times 100$ = ₹2560

Marked price of article M = $\frac{2760}{125} \times 100$ = ₹2048

Required difference = 2560 – 2048 = ₹512

10. 4; **I.** Cost price of article R = ₹1720

Selling price of article R = $1720 \times \frac{160}{100}$ = ₹2752

Market price of article R = $\frac{2752}{80} \times 100$ = ₹3440

Marked Price of article R is non-integer is false.

II. Cost price of article S = ₹1800
Cost price of article P = ₹1050

Selling price of article P = $1050 \times \frac{140}{100}$ = ₹1470

Marked price of article P = $\frac{1470}{80} \times 100$ = ₹1837.5

Ruired difference = 1837.5 – 1470 = ₹367 5
Difference between the cost price of article S and marked price of article P is not equal to cost price of any one of the given items is true.

III. Cost price of article T = ₹900

Selling price of article T = $900 \times \frac{120}{100}$ = ₹1080

Selling price of article T is divisible by 3 is true.

(11–16) :

In Company Y :

Unsold vehicles = 900 – 648 = 252
$\Rightarrow 3B = 252 \Rightarrow B = 84$

Sold vehicles = $18\frac{4}{7}B = \frac{60}{7} \times 84 = 720$

Total number of vehicles sold by all companies = 3552
Now, according to the question,

$C + \frac{60}{7} \times 84 + 648 + 2C + 132 = 3552$

$\Rightarrow 3C + 720 + 648 + 132 = 3552 \Rightarrow C = \frac{2052}{3} = 684$

In Company Z:
Sold vehicles = 2C + 132 = 2 × 684 + 132 = 1500

Unsold vehicles = $\frac{1500}{3} = 500$

In Company Z:
Total manufactured vehicles = 1500 + 500 = 2000

Unsold vehicles = $\frac{A}{3} + 150$

According to the question,

$500 = \frac{A}{3} + 150 \Rightarrow A = 1050$

Companies	Manufactured	Sold	Unsold
W	1050	684	366
X	1200	720	480
Y	900	648	252
Z	2000	1500	500

11. 2; Total number of vehicles manufactured by X = 800
Total number of vehicles manufactured byY = 800
Unsold vehicles of company X = 800 – 720 = 80
Unsold vehicles of company Y = 800 – 648 = 152
Required ratio = 80 : 152 = 10 : 19

12. 3; Cars manufactured by company W = $1050 \times \frac{50}{100} = 525$

Cars manufactured by company X = $1200 \times \frac{80}{100} = 960$

Total number of manufactured cars = 525 + 960 = 1485

13. 4; Unsold vehicles of company T = $\frac{500}{20} \times 13 = 325$

14. 5; Thc number of vehicles sold through cash by company

$Z = 1500 \times \frac{40}{100} = 600$

Total number of manufactured vehicles by Z = 2000

Required percentage = $\frac{600}{2000} \times 100 = 30\%$

15. 2; Average of all sold vehicles = $\frac{684 + 720 + 648 + 1500}{4}$

= 888

16. 4; Average of number of vehicles sold by X and Y

$= \frac{720 + 648}{2} = \frac{1368}{2} = 684$

The number of vehicles sold by comapny M = 684
The number of vehicles manufactured by company M = 2300
The number of unsold vehicles by company M = 2300 – 684 = 1616

17. 2; Expenditure of TCS in 2018

$= \frac{24}{100} \times 1500 \times \frac{100}{121}$ » `298 crore

Expenditure of HCL in 2017

$= \frac{20}{100} \times 1800 \times \frac{100}{124} \approx$ ₹290 crore

$\therefore$ Required percentage = $\frac{298 - 290}{290} \times 100 \approx 3\%$

18. 5; Total income of TCS in years 2016, 2017 and 2018

$= \frac{25 + 15 + 24}{100} \times 1500 = 64 \times 15 = 960$

Total income of HCL in years 2016, 2017 and 2018 =

$\frac{15 + 20 + 10}{100} \times 1800 = 45 \times 18 = 810$

$\therefore$ Required percentage = $\frac{960 - 810}{810} \times 100 = \frac{1500}{81}$

= 18.51%

19. 5; Average expenditure of TCS in 2017, 2019 and 2020

$= \frac{\frac{15}{100} \times 1500 \times \frac{100}{125} + \frac{26}{100} \times 1500 \times \frac{100}{122} + \frac{10}{100} \times 1500 \times \frac{100}{120}}{3}$

$= \frac{180 + 319.67 + 125}{3} = \frac{624.67}{3} = 208.22 \approx 208$

$\therefore$ Required percentage $= \frac{\frac{35}{100} \times 1800 - 208}{208} \times 100$

$= \frac{630 - 208}{208} \times 100 = \frac{422}{208} \times 100 = 202.88\%$

20. 3; Profit of TCS in 2019 = $\frac{26}{100} \times 1500 \times \frac{22}{122} = 70.32$

Profit of TCS in 2020 $= \frac{10}{100} \times 1500 \times \frac{20}{120} = 25$

Profit of HCL in 2019 $= \frac{20}{100} \times 1800 \times \frac{27}{127} = 76.53$

Profit of HCL in 2020 $= \frac{35}{100} \times 1800 \times \frac{23}{123} = 117.80$

Total profit $= 70.32 + 25 + 76.53 + 117.80$

$= 289.65$ cr ≈ 290 crore

21. 3; Expenditure of TCS in 2021

$= \frac{80}{100} \times \frac{10}{100} \times 1500 =$ ₹120 cr

Expenditure of HCL in 2021

$= \frac{90}{100} \times \frac{35}{100} \times 1800 =$ ₹567 cr

$\therefore$ Required difference $= 567 - 120 =$ ₹447 cr

Practice Set 12

Directions (Q. 1-6): Study the following information carefully and answer the questions given below.

A milkman has X litres of mixture of milk and water in the ratio of 5 : 1. He sells milk to Asma, Bano and Chandni in the same order. And after selling milk, he adds a certain amount of milk or water or both to the mixture. The information regarding this is given below. All amounts are in litres. Read the following information carefully and answer the questions that follow. Some values are missing in the table. Candidates are expected to find those values as and when required.

Persons	Mixture given	Amount of milk added	Amount of water added	Remaining quantity of mixture
Asma	120	80	NIL	560
Bano	Y	60	10	M
Chandani	70	3R	R	Z

1. Find the value of X.

1) 600 2) 720 3) 850
4) 910 5) None of the given options

2. If the difference between milk and water in mixture M is 250 litres, then find the value of Y.

1) 560 2) 260 3) 280
4) 210 5) 140

3. If it is given that in mixture Z, the ratio of milk to that of water is 9 : 2, then what is the value of R?

1) 40 litres 2) 20 litres 3) 30 litres
4) 50 litres 5) Cannot be determined

4. The value of Y is what per cent more or less than the value of R?

1) 700% 2) 450% 3) 600%
4) 250% 5) 500%

5. What is the average of the values of M, Y, X and R?

1) 325.5 2) 317.5 3) 335
4) 323.5 5) None of the given options

6. What is the value of Z?

1) 560 litres 2) 420 litres 3) 440 litres
4) 625 litres 5) Cannot be determined

Directions (Q. 7-11): Study the following bar graph and table carefully and answer the questions given below.

Total production under various heads (in tonnes) in six different years

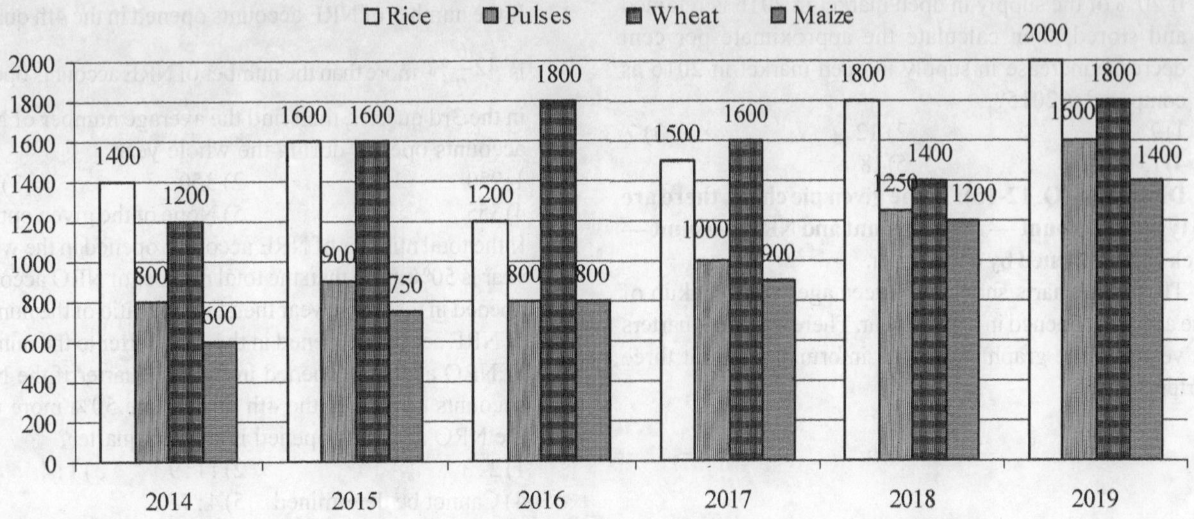

Per cent of the total production used only under these three heads as given below:

Year	Export	PDS supply	Supply in open market
2014	42%	38%	__%
2015	55%	__%	25%
2016	48%	22%	__%
2017	__%	20%	18%
2018	__%	33%	32%
2019	40%	__%	35%

7. The average production of Wheat and Maize in 2016 is what per cent of the supply in open market in the year 2014?
1) 162.5 2) 132.5 3) 172
4) 165.5 5) None of the given options

8. What is the ratio of export in 2017 to PDS supply in 2019?
1) 17 : 13 2) 31 : 29 3) 31 : 17
4) 31 : 23 5) 17 : 23

9. What is the difference between the overall production of Maize in years 2014 to 2019 and production that was exported in 2017?
1) 2750 tonnes 2) 2265 tonnes 3) 2350 tonnes
4) 2550 tonnes 5) None of the given options

10. The average production of all four crops in 2017 is what per cent less than the average export in the years 2014 and 2019?
1) 41.32 2) 52.65 3) 43.18
4) 54.55 5) 37.46

11. If 20% of the supply in open market in 2016 is retained and stored, then calculate the approximate per cent decrease/increase in supply in open market in 2016 as compared to 2015?
1) 9 2) 12 3) 7
4) 13 5) 18

Directions (Q. 12-15): In the given pie chart, there are two types of account — NRE account and NRO account — which can be opened by a foreigner.

These pie charts show the percentage-wise breakup of these accounts opened in a given year. There are four quarters in a year and the graph shows the information about three quarters.

NRE Accounts (750)

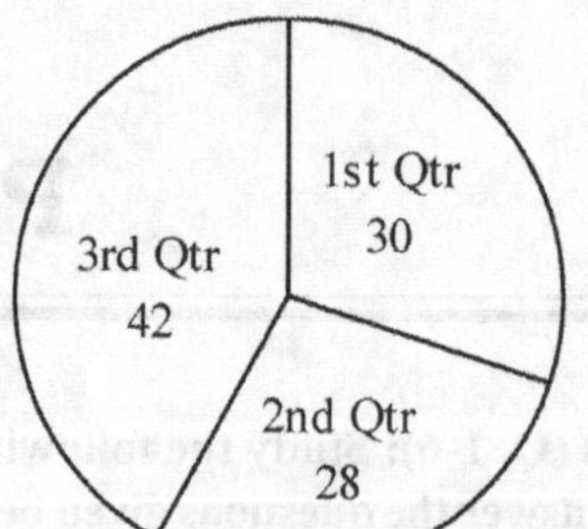

NRO Accounts (500)

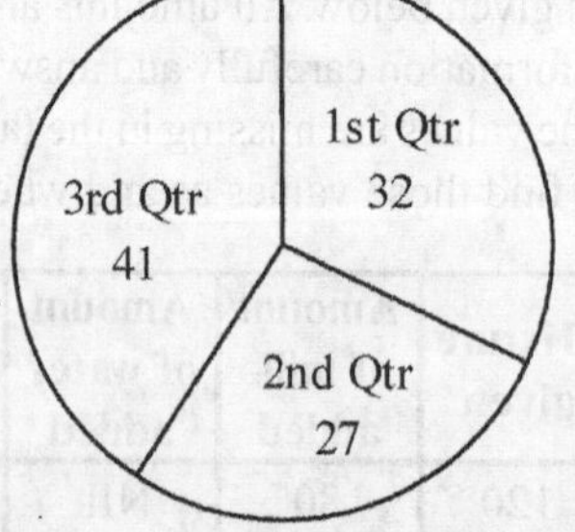

12. If we include the 4th quarter in the given year, the percentage of NRO accounts opened in the 2nd quarter will become $16\frac{7}{8}\%$ of the total NRO accounts opened during the whole year. Then what is the number of NRO accounts opened in the 4th quarter?
1) 1200 2) 400 3) 300
4) 350 5) 250

13. If the number of NRE accounts opened in the 4th quarter is $42\frac{6}{7}\%$ more than the number of NRE accounts opened in the 3rd quarter, then find the average number of NRE accounts opened during the whole year.
1) 250 2) 350 3) 300
4) 555 5) None of the given options

14. If the total number of NRE accounts opened in the whole year is 50% more than the total number of NRO accounts opened in the whole year then find the ratio of the number of NRE accounts opened in the 4th quarter to the number of NRO accounts opened in the 4th quarter if the NRE accounts opened in the 4th quarter are 50% more than the NRO accounts opened in the 4th quarter?
1) 2 : 3 2) 11 : 9 3) 1 : 4
4) Cannot be determined 5) 4 : 7

15. If the number of NRE accounts opened in the 4th quarter is 240 more than the number of NRE accounts opened in the 2nd quarter, then the number of NRE accounts opened in the 4th quarter is what per cent of the total

number of NRE accounts opened in the whole year?
1) 42.5% 2) 35% 3) 32.5%
4) 37.5% 5) 45%

Directions (Q. 16-20): The given bar graph shows the percentage of questions solved by three students Parul, Bhavya and Chinar out of the total questions attempted by them from two tests, ie Test-1 and Test-2.

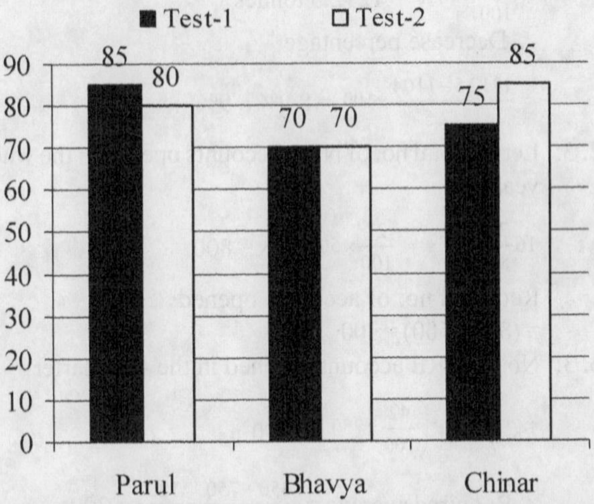

Note: Total number of questions attempted from each test need not be the same for each of the students, ie the number of questions attempted from Test-1 by Parul need not be the same as the number of questions attempted from Test-1 by Bhavya or Chinar.

16. If the number of questions attempted by Parul and Chinar each from Test-2 exceeds that from their respective Test-1 by 6.25% and the average number of questions solved by them from Test-2 is 245 more than that solved from Test-1, find the difference between the number of questions attempted by Chinar from Test-1 and that from Test-2.
1) Cannot be determined 2) 185 3) 255
4) 250 5) 200

17. If the number of questions solved by Parul from Test-1 and Chinar from Test-2 is 510, what could be maximum number of questions that were not solved by Parul from Test-1?
1) 89 2) Cannot be determined
3) 45 4) 93 5) 87

18. What is the ratio of the number of questions attempted by Parul, Bhavya and Chinar from Test-1, if the number of questions solved by them from Test-1 is in the ratio of 5 : 5 : 6?
1) 1050 : 1275 : 1211 2) 350 : 425 : 476
3) 1428 : 1275 : 1050 4) Cannot be determined
5) 1858 : 1275 : 1429

19. The number of questions solved by Bhavya from Test-2 is 175 and the total number of questions attempted from Test-2 by her is 50 less than the number of questions solved by Chinar from Test-1. Find the number of questions attempted from Test-1 by Chinar.
1) 300 2) 400 3) 250
4) 325 5) 450

20. The number of questions solved by Chinar from Test-1 is 75% of the number of questions solved by him from Test-2. The number of questions solved by Bhavya from Test-2 is equal to the sum of the numbers of questions solved by Chinar from either of the tests. What will be the ratio of the number of questions attempted by Bhavya from Test-2 to that by Chinar?
1) 23 : 21 2) 85 : 28 3) 64 : 23
4) 28 : 85 5) None of these

Answers and explanations

1. 1; Here, $X - 120 + 80 = 560$
$\Rightarrow X = 560 + 120 - 80$
$\therefore X = 600$ litres

2. 3; From the above solution, we know that the milkman had 600 litres of mixture initially. Since milk : water = 5 : 1, this means he had 500 litres of milk and 100 litres of water initially.
After selling milk to Asma, remaining milk
$= 500 - \frac{120}{6} \times 5 + 80 = 480$ litres
Remaining water = 560 − 480 = 80 litres
So, ratio = 480 : 80 = 6 : 1
Now, after selling milk to Bano and adding milk and water, we have
Milk $= 480 - \frac{Y}{7} \times 6 + 60 = 540 - \frac{6Y}{7}$
Water $= 80 - \frac{Y}{7} + 10 = 90 - \frac{Y}{7}$
As per information given, $540 - \frac{6Y}{7} - \left[90 - \frac{Y}{7}\right] = 250$
$\Rightarrow 450 - \frac{5Y}{7} = 250 \Rightarrow 200 = \frac{5Y}{7} \Rightarrow Y = \frac{1400}{5} = 280$

3. 1; In mixture M,
Milk $= \frac{280}{7} \times 6 + 60 = 300$
Water $= \frac{280}{7} + 10 = 50$
Ratio = 300 : 50 = 6 : 1
Now, after selling to Chandni, mixture left = 350 − 70 = 280 litres
So, after adding milk and water, we have

$$\frac{300-\frac{70}{7}\times 6+3R}{50-\frac{70}{7}\times 1+R}=\frac{9}{2}$$

$\Rightarrow \frac{240+3R}{40+R}=\frac{9}{2}\Rightarrow 480+6R=360+9R\Rightarrow 120=3R$

$\therefore R=40$ litres

4. 3; Here, Y = 280 and R = 40

So, required percentage $=\frac{280-40}{40}\times 100$

$=\frac{240}{40}\times 100=600\%$

5. 2; Here, M = 350, Y = 280, X = 600 and R = 40

So, required average $=\frac{350+280+600+40}{4}$

$=\frac{1270}{4}=317.5$

6. 3; Here, M = 350 and R = 40

So, value of Z = 350 – 70 + 3(40) + 40

= 350 – 70 + 120 + 40 = 440

7. 1; Supply in open market in 2014

$=\frac{20}{100}\times 4000=800$ tonnes

Average production of wheat and maize in 2016

$=\frac{1800+800}{2}=\frac{2600}{2}=1300$ tonnes

$\therefore$ Required percentage $=\frac{1300}{800}\times 100=162.5\%$

8. 3; Export in 2019 $=\frac{62}{100}\times[1600+1500+1000+900]$

$=62\times 50=3100$ tons

PDS supply in 2017 $=\frac{25}{100}\times[2000+1800+1400+1600]$

$=25\times 68=1700$ tonnes

$\therefore$ Required ratio = 3100 : 1700 = 31 : 17

9. 4; Export in 2017 = 3100 tonnes

(From solution of Q. No. 8)

Overall production of maize in given years

= 600 + 750 + 800 + 900 + 1200 + 1400 = 5650 tonnes

$\therefore$ Difference = 5650 – 3100 = 2550 tonnes

10. 3; Average production in 2017

$=\frac{1600+1500+1000+900}{4}=1250$ tonnes

Average export in 2014 and 2019

$$=\frac{\left(\frac{42}{100}\times 4000+\frac{40}{100}\times 6800\right)}{2}=\frac{1680+2720}{2}=\frac{4400}{2}$$

= 2200 tonnes

$\therefore$ Required percentage

$=\frac{2200-1250}{2200}\times 100=\frac{950}{2200}\times 100=43.18\%$

11. 1; Actual amount of crop supplied in open market in 2016 $=\frac{80}{100}\times\frac{30}{100}\times 4600=1104$ tonnes

Amount supplied in open market in 2015

$=\frac{25}{100}\times 4850=1212.5$ tonnes

$\therefore$ Decrease percentage

$=\frac{1212.5-1104}{1212.5}\times 100=8.9\%\approx 9\%$

12. 3; Let the total no. of NRO accounts opened in the whole year be x.

$16\frac{7}{8}\%$ of $x=\frac{27}{100}\times 500\ \therefore x=800$

Required no. of accounts opened

= (800 – 500) = 300

13. 3; No. of NRE accounts opened in the 4th quarter =

$142\frac{6}{7}\%$ of $\left(\frac{42}{100}\times 750\right)=450$

$\therefore$ Required average $=\frac{450+750}{4}=\frac{1200}{4}=300$

14. 4; No. of NRE accounts = 3x (let)

No. of NRO accounts = 2x

(3x – 750) = (2x – 500) 1.5x

We cannot determine the value of x.

15. 4; No. of NRE accounts opened in 4th quarter =

$240+\frac{28}{100}\times 750=240+210=450$

$\therefore$ Required percentage $=\frac{450}{750+450}\times 100=37.5\%$

16. 5; Let the total no. of questions attempted by Parul and Chinar from Test-1 be 100p and 100q respectively.

No. of questions solved by Parul and Chinar from Test-1 will be 85p and 75q respectively.

Total questions attempted by Parul and Chinar from Test-2 will be 106.25p and 106.25q respectively.

As per information given,

$$\frac{\frac{80}{100}\times 106.25p+\frac{85}{100}\times 106.25q}{2}-\frac{85p+75q}{2}=245$$

$\Rightarrow \frac{90.3125q-75q}{2}=245\Rightarrow q=32$

$\therefore$ Required difference = 106.25q – 100q = 6.25q

= 6.25 × 32 = 200

17. 5; Let the total number of questions from Test-1 attempted by Parul and that from Test-2 attempted by Chinar be 100p and 100q respectively.

It is given that, 85p + 85q = 510 $\Rightarrow$ p + q = 6

$\Rightarrow$ 100p + 100q = 600

Now, for the maximum number of questions attempted

by Parul from Test-1, we need the least integral value for the number of questions solved by Chinar.
Now, Chinar solved 85% of questions attempted from Test-2. Thus, Chinar attempted 20 questions from Test-2, out of which she solved 85%, ie 17 questions.
So, maximum number of questions attempted by Parul from Test-1 = 600 – 20 = 580
∴ Maximum number of unsolved questions by Parul from Test-1 will be $\frac{15}{100} \times 580 = 87$

18. 2; Let the total no. of questions solved by Parul, Bhavya and Chinar in Test-1 be 500n, 500n and 600n respectively.

∴ Required ratio $= \frac{500n}{85} \times 100 : \frac{500n}{70} \times 100 : \frac{600n}{75} \times 100$

$= 1050 : 1275 : 1428 = 350 : 425 : 476$

19. 2; Let the total number of questions attempted by Bhavya from Test-2 be N.

Then, $\frac{70N}{100} = 175 \Rightarrow N = \frac{175 \times 100}{70} = 250$

So, number of questions solved by Chinar from Test-1 = 250 + 50 = 300
∴ Total number of questions attempted by Chinar from Test-1 $= \frac{300}{75} \times 100 = 400$

20. 5; Let the total number of questions attempted by Chinar from Test-1 be 100n
⇒ Number of questions solved by him from Test-1 = 75n
⇒ Number of questions solved by him from Test-2

$= \frac{75n}{75} \times 100 = 100n$

As per information given,
Questions solved by Bhavya from Test-2 = 175n
Questions attempted by Bhavya from Test-2 $= \frac{175n}{70} \times 100$

∴ Required ratio $= \frac{175n}{70} \times 100 : \frac{100n}{85} \times 100 = 17 : 8$

Practice Set 13

Directions (Q. 1-4): Study the graphs given below and answer the questions based on the given information.

The table given below gives the information about the number of runs scored by eight different teams in IPL 2020 held recently.

Teams	Number of runs scored by the teams
Mumbai Indians	$26\frac{25}{28}\%$
Delhi Capitals	$22\frac{1}{7}\%$
Sunrisers Hyderabad	$7\frac{3}{14}\%$
Kings XI Punjab	700
Kolkata Knight Riders	$11\frac{9}{28}\%$
Chennai Super Kings	7%
Royal Challengers Bangalore	$14\frac{3}{7}\%$
Rajasthan Royals	840

Note: Runs scored by some teams are given as percentage of the total runs scored and runs scored by other teams are given in absolute values.

The pie-chart given below gives information (in degrees) about the number of balls played by different players in IPL 2020.

Number of balls (in degrees) played by different players

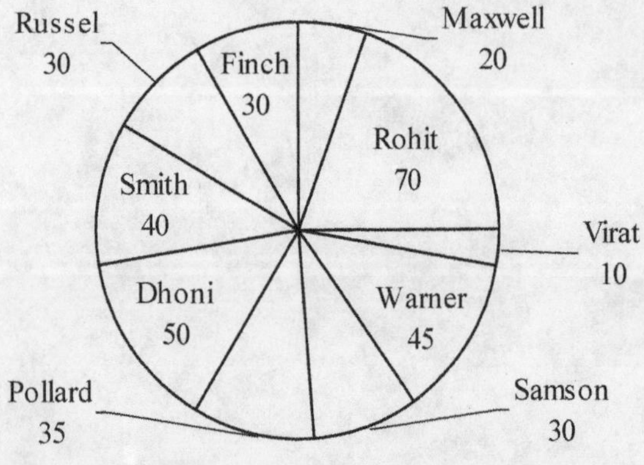

Note: The number of balls played by Virat is 200 less than the number of balls played by Russel.

$$\text{Strike Rate} = \frac{\text{Runs scored}}{\text{Balls faced}} \times 100$$

1. If all the runs scored by Rajasthan Royals are scored by Dhoni, and 30% of the runs scored by Delhi Capitals are scored by Samson, then find the difference between the strike rate of these two batsmen.
1) 147 2) 133 3) 142
4) None of the given options 5) 154

2. Pollard and Rohit collectively score 40% of the runs scored by Mumbai Indians. If both of them hit a six for every 10 balls they face, then find the ratio of runs scored by them in sixes to the ratio of total runs scored by them.
1) 105 : 113 2) 105 : 251 3) 233 : 251
4) 13 : 29 5) Cannot be determined

3. The number of balls faced by Smith, Dhoni, Warner and Maxwell is approximately what per cent more/less than the average number of runs scored by Royal Challengers Banglore, Sunrisers Hyderabad and Delhi Capitals together?
1) 19 2) 32 3) 28
4) 24 5) 18

4. The strike rate of Finch in IPL 2020 was 180. If the ratio of sixes hit to that of fours hit by him was 7 : 11, and runs scored by him in boundaries were 66.66% of the total runs scored by him, then find the runs scored by him in sixes as an approximate percentage of total runs scored by him.
1) 37 2) 18 3) 24
4) 28 5) 26

Directions (Q. 5-10): The bar graph given below shows the number of people who used mobile banking applications of six different banks. The radar graph given below it depicts the percentage of those first-time users who got cashback as a reward for their first transactions.

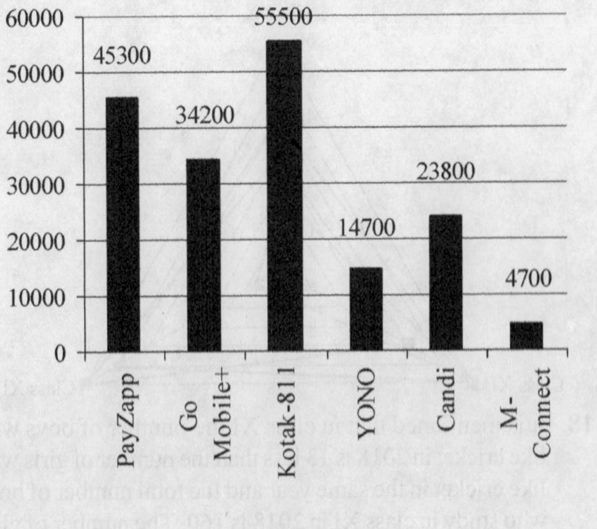

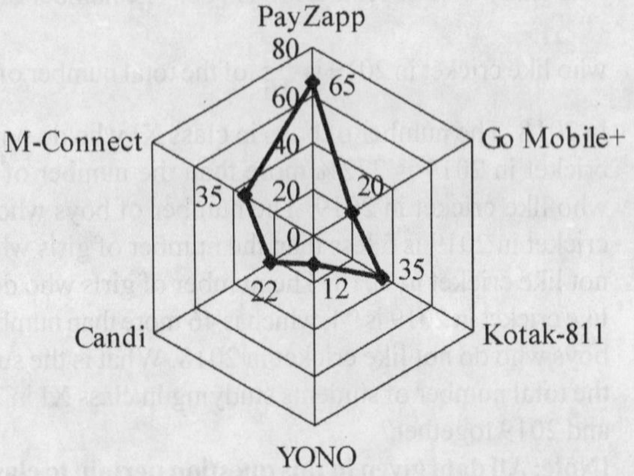

It is mentioned to us that all of these six platforms of digital transactions give only two kinds of cashback, ie ₹10 and ₹25. The table given below shows the ratio of the first-time users getting these two kinds of cashbacks.

Platforms of Digital Transactions	Ratio of first time users getting ₹10 cash back to the first time users getting ₹25 as cash back
PayZapp	8 : 7
Go Mobile+	11 : 8
Kotak-811	21 : 16
YONO	4 : 3
Candi	13 : 15
M-Connect	4 : 3

5. What will be the sum of the average number of people getting ₹25 as cashback from PayZapp and CANDI together and the average number of people getting ₹10 as cashback from YONO, M-Connect and Kotak-811 together?

1) $33362\frac{3}{4}$ 2) $12597\frac{1}{3}$ 3) $45697\frac{1}{3}$ 4) $12337\frac{2}{3}$ 5) None of these

6. What is the difference between the number of the first-time users of Kotak-811, Go Mobile+ and PayZapp not getting cashbacks and the number of the first-time users of YONO, CANDI and M-Connect not getting cashbacks?

1) 79290 2) 34555 3) 46982 4) 44735 5) None of these

7. Those first time users getting ₹25 as cashback from CANDI and M-Connect together are approximately what per cent more or less than the number of people getting ₹10 as cashback from PayZapp?

1) 62 2) 78 3) 74 4) 87 5) None of these

8. The amount given by CANDI and YONO in cashback is what per cent more or less than the amount given by PayZapp in cashback?

1) 75.34 2) 73.89 3) 64.89 4) 92.29 5) Cannot be determined

9. If 60% and 40% of the users getting ₹25 as cashback from Go Mobile+ and Kotak-811 respectively are females, then the average male first-time users getting ₹25 as cashback from Kotak-811 and Go Mobile+ is what per cent of the first-time users of CANDI getting cashback?

1) 59.13% 2) 36.13% 3) 44.59% 4) 95.36% 5) 55.55%

10. Find the ratio of the number of people getting ₹25 as cashback from PayZapp and YONO together to the number of people who get ₹10 as cashback from Go Mobile+, Kotak-811 and M-Connect together.

1) 2071 : 4849 2) 2071 : 2275 3) 2283 : 2071 4) 2275 : 2071 5) None of these

Directions (Q. 11-17): Study the given information carefully and answer the questions that follows:

The table given below shows the sum of the length of five trains, ie V, W, X, Y and Z, taken two at a time and the time taken by those two trains to completely cross each other when they are both running in opposite directions.

Two trains taken	V + W	W + X	X + Y	Y + Z	Z + V
Sum of length of two trains (in metres)	84	108	120	156	156
Time taken by two trains to cross each other (in seconds)	3.5	9	12	13	7.8

11. There is another train M, whose length is three-fourths

the length of the sum of the length of trains X and Y, and whose speed is equal to average speed of all the given five trains. In how much time will it completely cross a man running in opposite direction at the rate of 2.2 m/s?
1) 18 seconds 2) 5 seconds 3) 10 seconds
4) 13 seconds 5) 9 seconds

12. What will be the sum of the time difference for all the five pairs when the difference is calculated between the time taken by the trains to cross each other in the given pair if they travel in the same direction and the time taken by them to cross each other travelling in opposite directions as given above?
1) 78.6 seconds 2) 144.6 seconds
3) 115.4 seconds 4) 110.3 seconds
5) Cannot be determined

13. What is the ratio of the time taken by V and Y to cross each other to the time taken by X and Z to cross each other if it is given that V and Y are running in the same direction and X and Z are running in opposite directions?
1) 45 : 24 2) Cannot be determined
3) 39 : 23 4) 24 : 39 5) 24 : 45

14. What will be the time taken by train W and Z to cross each other if they travel in the same direction?
1) 32 seconds 2) 44 seconds
3) 36 seconds 4) 28 seconds
5) Cannot be determined

15. The length of which of the following trains is more than the average length of all the five trains?
1) Z and X only 2) Z, W and V only
3) V, W and Y only 4) Y and V only
5) Cannot be determined

16. The sum of the speeds of V, Y and X is what per cent more than the sum of the speeds of W and Z?
1) 82.67% 2) 78.57% 3) 64.56%
4) 57.59% 5) Cannot be determined

17. The average speed of train V and W is approximately what per cent of the average speed of all the given trains?
1) 154% 2) 105% 3) 144%
4) 124% 5) None of the given options

Directions (Q. 18-22): Study the given graph carefully and answer the following questions:

The graph given below shows the percentage of boys out of the total number of students in three different classes during three different years, ie 2018, 2019 and 2020, of Angels Public Senior Secondary School.

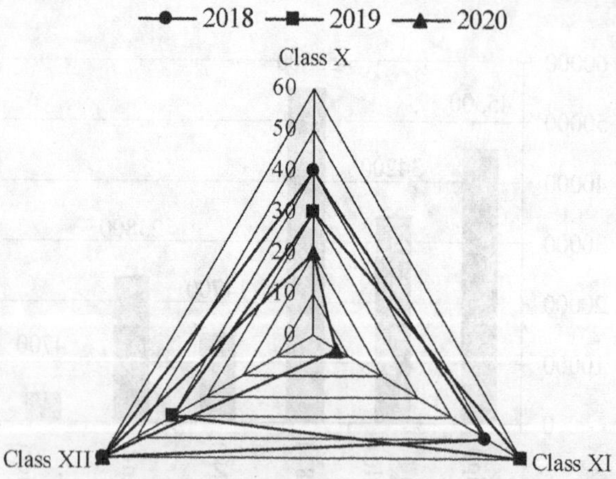

18. It is mentioned that in class XI the number of boys who like cricket in 2018 is 13 less than the number of girls who like cricket in the same year and the total number of boys who study in class XI in 2018 is 160. The number of girls who like cricket in 2019 is $\frac{5}{16}$ of the total number of girls in 2018. The number of boys in class XI who do not like cricket in 2019 is 272% more than the number of girls who like cricket in 2019. The number of boys who like cricket in 2019 is 5 less than the number of girls who do not like cricket in 2018. The number of girls who do not like cricket in 2019 is 94, which is 46 more than number of boys who do not like cricket in 2018. What is the sum of the total number of students studying in class XI in 2018 and 2019 together?
[Note: All data given in this question pertain to class XI students only.]
1) 720 2) 360 3) 650
4) 680 5) 540

19. The total number of boys who studied in 2018 in all the classes is the same. If it is mentioned that in 2018, the difference between the total number of students in class X and class XI is the same as the difference between total number of students between class XI and class XII, then the number of students in class XII is what per cent more or less than the number of students in class X?
[Note: The number of students in class X is greater than the number of students in class XI, which in turn is greater than the number of students in class XII.]
1) 50 2) 60 3) 40 4) 20 5) None of these

20. The total number of students in class XI decreases from 2018 to 2020 continuously. It decreases by the same number in both the years. If it is mentioned that the number of boys in class XI remains the same in all the three years, then by what per cent is the total number of students in class XI in 2020 less than that in 2018?

1) $66\frac{2}{3}\%$ 2) 50% 3) $33\frac{1}{3}\%$

4) $14\frac{2}{3}\%$ 5) Cannot be determined

21. The sum of class X students in 2018 and 2019 is 380 and the sum of class X students in 2019 and 2020 is 530. If the sum of class X students in all the three years together is 660, then find the number of girls in class X in 2019.

1) 75 2) 150 3) 175 4) 250 5) 130

22. The total number of students studying in class XII in the year 2018, 2019 and 2020 are in the ratio of 2 : 3 : 4. If the average number of boys studying in class XII in all three years is 96, then find the total number of students studying in class XII in 2019.

1) 240 2) 180 3) 120 4) 60 5) 150

Answers and explanations

1. 3; Let the total number of balls faced by the given batsmen be x.

Then, $\frac{(30-10)x}{360} = 200 \Rightarrow x = 18 \times 200 = 3600$

Ball faced by Dhoni = $\frac{50}{360} \times 3600 = 500$

Ball faced by Samson = $\frac{30}{360} \times 3600 = 300$

Total runs scored by Kings XI Punjab + Rajasthan Royal = 700 + 840 = 1540

Percentage of runs scored by Kings XI Punjab + Rajasthan Royals = 100 – 89 = 11%

Total runs scored = $1540\left(\frac{100}{11}\right) = 140000$

Run scored by Delhi Capital = $\frac{155}{700} \times 14000 = 3100$

Runs scored by Samson = 30% of 3100 = 930

Strike rate of Samson = $\frac{930}{300} \times 100 = 310$

Strike rate of Dhoni = $\frac{840}{500} \times 100 = 168$

∴ Difference = 310 – 168 = 142

2. 2; Runs scored by Mumbai Indians

$= \frac{753}{2800} \times 14000 = 3765$

Runs scored by Rohit and Pollard

$= \frac{40}{100} \times 3765 = 1506$

Balls faced by Rohit and Pollard

$= \frac{105}{360} \times 3600 = 1050$

Number of sixes scored by them

$= \frac{1050}{10} = 105$

∴ Required ratio = $\frac{105 \times 6}{1506} = \frac{105}{251} = 105 : 251$

3. 4; Number of balls faced by them

$= \frac{155}{360} \times 3600 = 1550$

Average runs scored by three teams

$= \frac{1}{3}\left[\frac{101}{700} \times 14000 + \frac{101}{1400} \times 14000 \times + \frac{155}{700} \times 14000\right]$

$= \frac{1}{3}[2020 + 1010 + 3100] = \frac{1}{3} \times 6130 \approx 2043$

∴ Required percentage = $\frac{2043 - 1550}{2043} \times 100$

$= \frac{493}{2043} \times 100 = 24.14\% \approx 24\%$

4. 5; Balls faced by Finch

$= \frac{30}{360} \times 3600 = 300$

Runs scored by him = $\frac{180 \times 300}{100} = 540$

Runs scored by him in boundaries

$= \frac{2}{3} \times 540 = 360$

Runs scored by him in sixes

$= \frac{7}{18} \times 360 = 140$

∴ Required percentage

$= \frac{140}{540} \times 100 = 25.92 \approx 26\%$

(5-10):

Number of 1st-time users getting cashback from

PayZapp = $\frac{65}{100} \times 45300 = 29445$

from Go Mobile+ = $\frac{20}{100} \times 34200 = 6840$

from Kotak-811 = $\frac{35}{100} \times 55500 = 19425$

from YONO = $\frac{12}{100} \times 14700 = 1764$

from Candi = $\frac{22}{100} \times 23800 = 5236$

from M-Connect = $\frac{35}{100} \times 4700 = 1645$

This information can be tabulised as:

Platforms of Digital Transactions	1st time users	1st time users getting cashback	Users getting ₹10 as cashback	Users getting ₹25 as cashback
PayZapp	45300	29445	$\frac{29445}{15}\times 8 = 15704$	$\frac{29445}{15}\times 7 = 13741$
Go Mobile+	34200	6840	$\frac{6840}{19}\times 11 = 3960$	$\frac{6840}{19}\times 8 = 2880$
Kotak-811	55500	19425	$\frac{19425}{37}\times 21 = 11025$	$\frac{19425}{37}\times 16 = 8400$
YONO	14700	1764	$\frac{1764}{12}\times 4 = 1008$	$\frac{1764}{12}\times 3 = 756$
Candi	23800	5236	$\frac{5236}{28}\times 13 = 2431$	$\frac{5236}{28}\times 15 = 2805$
M-Connect	4700	1645	$\frac{1645}{12}\times 4 = 940$	$\frac{1645}{12}\times 3 = 705$

5. 2; Required sum $= \frac{13741+2805}{2} + \frac{11025+1008+940}{3}$

$= 12597\frac{1}{3}$

6. 4; First time users of Kotak-811, Go Mobile+ and PayZapp not getting cashbacks

$= \frac{35}{100}\times 45300 + \frac{80}{100}\times 34200 + \frac{65}{100}\times 55500$

$= 15855 + 27360 + 36075 = 79290$

First time users of YONO, CANDI and M-Connect not getting cashback

$= \frac{88}{100}\times 14700 + \frac{78}{100}\times 23800 + \frac{65}{100}\times 4700$

$= 12936 + 18564 + 3055 = 34555$

$\therefore$ Required difference $= 79290 - 34555 = 44735$

7. 2; Required percentage $= \frac{15704 - (2805 + 705)}{15704}\times 100$

$\approx 78\%$ (approx.)

8. 1; Amount given as cashback by Candi

$= 10\times 2431 + 25\times 2805 = 24310 + 70125 = 94435$

Amount given as cashback by YONO

$= 10\times 1008 + 25\times 756 = 10080 + 18900 = 28980$

Amount given as cashback by PayZapp

$= 10\times 15704 + 25\times 13741 = 157040 + 343525 = 500565$

$\therefore$ Required percentage

$= \frac{500565 - [94435 + 28980]}{500565}\times 100$

$= \frac{500565 - 123415}{500565}\times 100 = 75.34\%$

9. 1; Male users of Go Mobile+ getting ₹25 as cashback

$= \frac{40\times 2880}{100} = 1152$

Male users of Kotak-811 getting ₹25 as cashback

$= \frac{60\times 8400}{100} = 5040$

$\therefore$ Average $= \frac{1152 + 5040}{2} = \frac{6192}{2} = 3096$

$\therefore$ Required percentage $= \frac{3096}{5236}\times 100 = 59.13\%$

10. 2; Required ratio $= 13741 + 756 : 3960 + 11025 + 940 = 2071 : 2275$

(11-17):

Let the speed of trains V, W, X, Y and Z be v, w, x, y and z m/s respectively and the length of V, W, X, Y and Z be p, q, r, s and t metres respectively.

Then, $p + q + q + r + r + s + s + t + t + p = 84 + 108 + 120 + 156 + 156 \Rightarrow p + q + r + s + t = \frac{624}{2} = 312$ m

Since, $p + q = 84$ m and $r + s = 120$ m

$\Rightarrow 84 + 120 + t = 312 \text{ m} \Rightarrow t = 108$ m

$t + p = 156 \text{ m} \Rightarrow p = 156 - 108 = 48$ m

$p + q = 84 \text{ m} \Rightarrow q = 84 - 48 = 36$ m

$q + r = 108 \text{ m} \Rightarrow r = 108 - 36 = 72$ m

$r + s = 120 \text{ m} \Rightarrow s = 120 - 72 = 48$ m

Now, when trains V and W cross each other moving in opposite directions:

$\frac{p+q}{v+w} = 3.5;\ \frac{q+r}{w+x} = 9;\ \frac{r+s}{x+y} = 12;\ \frac{s+t}{y+z} = 13;\ \frac{t+p}{z+v} = 7.8$

$\Rightarrow \frac{84}{v+w} = 3.5;\ \frac{108}{w+x} = 9;\ \frac{120}{x+y} = 12;\ \frac{156}{y+z} = 13;$

$\frac{156}{z+v} = 7.8$

$\Rightarrow v + w = 24 \text{ m/s} \Rightarrow w + x = 12$ m/s

$\Rightarrow x + y = 10$ m/s

$\Rightarrow y + z = 12 \text{ m/s} \Rightarrow z + v = 20$ m/s

Solving further, we get

v = 15 m/s

w = 9 m/s

x = 3 m/s

y = 7 m/s

z = 5 m/s

The above solved information can be tabulised as:

Trains	Length (in m)	Speed in (m/s)
V	48	15
W	36	9
X	72	3
Y	48	7
Z	108	5

11. 5; Length of M $= \frac{3}{4}(72+48) = 90\text{m}$

Speed of M $= \frac{15+9+3+7+5}{5} = \frac{39}{5}$ m/s $= 7.8$ m/s

Time taken $= \frac{90}{7.8+2.2} = 9$ seconds

12. 4; **For trains V & W (same direction):**

Time $= \frac{48+36}{15-9} = 14$ seconds

Difference $= 14 - 3.5 = 10.5$ seconds

For trains W & X (same direction):

Time $= \frac{108}{9-3} = 18$ seconds

Difference $= 18 - 9 = 9$ seconds

For trains X & Y (same direction):

Time $= \frac{120}{7-3} = 30$ seconds

Difference $= 30 - 12 = 18$ seconds

For trains Y & Z (same direction):

Time $= \frac{156}{7-5} = 78$ seconds

Difference $= 78 - 13 = 65$ seconds

For trains Z & V (same direction):

Time $= \frac{156}{15-5} = 15.6$ seconds

Difference $= 15.6 - 7.8 = 7.8$ seconds

$\therefore$ Required sum $= 10.5 + 9 + 18 + 65 + 7.8$
$= 110.3$ seconds

13. 5; Required ratio $= \frac{48+48}{15-7} : \frac{72+108}{5+3} = 24:45$

14. 3; Relative speed $= (9-5) = 4$ m/s

Distance to cover $= 36 + 108 = 144$ minutes

Required time $= \frac{144}{4} = 36$ seconds

15. 1; Average length

$= \frac{48+36+72+48+108}{5} = \frac{312}{5} = 62.4$ m

Hence, only the length of X and Z is more than 62.4m.

16. 2; Required percentage $= \frac{(15+7+3)-(9+5)}{(9+5)} \times 100$

$= \frac{25-14}{14} \times 100 = \frac{11}{14} \times 100 = 78.57\%$

17. 1; Average speed of train V and W $= \frac{15+9}{2} = 12$ m/s

Average speed of all the given trains

$\frac{15+9+3+7+5}{5} = \frac{39}{5} = 7.8$ m/s

Reqd percentage $= \frac{12}{7.8} \times 100 = 153.84\% \approx 154\%$

18. 4; From the data given in the question, we can make a table as given below:

2018	Boys	Girls	2019	Boys	Girls
Like cricket	112	125	Like cricket	30	50
Do not like cricket	48	35	Do not like cricket	186	94
Total	160	160	Total	216	144

Hence, total number of students
$= 160 + 160 + 216 + 144 = 680$

19. 3; Let the number of students in class X, Class XI and Class XII in 2018 be M, (M – D) and (M – 2D) respectively.

Then, as per information given, $\frac{40M}{100} = \frac{50}{100}(M-D)$

$\Rightarrow 4M = 5M - 5D \Rightarrow 5D = M \Rightarrow D = \frac{M}{5}$

Number of students in class XII $= M - 2\left(\frac{M}{5}\right) = \frac{3M}{5}$

$\therefore$ Required percentage $= \frac{M - \frac{3M}{5}}{M} \times 100 = 40\%$

20. 3; Let the total number of students in class XI in 2018 be N.

And, let the total number of students decrease by T every year.

Then, number of students in class XI in 2019 = N – T

And, number of students in class XI in 2020 = N – 2T

As per information given, $\frac{50N}{100} = \frac{60(N-T)}{100}$

$\Rightarrow \frac{N}{N-T} = \frac{6}{5} \Rightarrow T = \frac{N}{6}$ ...(i)

Thus, number of students in class XI in 2020

$= N - 2T = N - 2\left(\frac{N}{6}\right) = \frac{2N}{3}$

$\therefore$ Required percentage $= \dfrac{N - \dfrac{2N}{3}}{N} \times 100 = 33\dfrac{1}{3}\%$

21. 3; Number of students in class X in 2019 = (380 + 530) − 660 = 250

Number of girls = $\dfrac{70}{100} \times 250 = 175$

22. 2; Let the number of students in class XII in 2018, 2019 and 2020 be 2n, 3n and 4n respectively.

Then, as per information given,

$$\frac{60(2n)}{100} + \frac{40(3n)}{100} + \frac{60(4n)}{100} = 96 \times 3$$

$$\Rightarrow \frac{120n + 120n + 240n}{100} = 288$$

$$\Rightarrow 480n = 288 \times 100 \Rightarrow n = \frac{280 \times 100}{480} = 60$$

So, number of students in class XII in 2019 = 3n = 3 × 60 = 180

Practice Set 14

Directions (Q. 1-6): The following information is about the number of officers and clerks posted in six different states, viz Kerala, Haryana, Karnataka, Odisha, Bengal and Delhi. Study it carefully and answer the following questions:

The ratio of the total number of Officers to that of Clerks is 73 : 105. The total number of Clerks is 320 more than the total number of Officers posted. 110 Officers are available in Kerala, which is 85 less than the number of Clerks posted in Haryana. Total 320 posts are available in Karnataka, where the number of Clerks available is 20 more than that of Officers.

The number of Officers in Odisha is $23\frac{1}{3}\%$ of that posted in Karnataka. Also, the number of Officers posted in Odisha is $17\frac{1}{2}\%$ of the number of Clerks posted in the same state. 149 Officers are posted in Bengal, which is 4 less than the number of Clerks posted in Delhi. There are a total of 321 bank employees (Officers and Clerks) in Bengal, which is 52 more than the total number of bank employees posted in Delhi.

1. What is the ratio of the average number of Officers posted in Delhi, Haryana and Kerala to the average number of Clerks posted in the same states?
   1) 123 : 91 2) 127 : 99
   3) None of the given options 4) 121 : 123
   5) 99 : 127
2. The number of bank employees posted in which of the following states is more than the average number of bank employees posted in all the states together?
   1) Karnataka, Odisha and Delhi
   2) Haryana and Delhi
   3) Kerala and Bengal
   4) None of the given options
   5) Haryana, Bengal and Karnataka
3. What is the total number of bank employees posted in Delhi?
   1) 272 2) 256 3) 269 4) 359 5) None of these
4. The total number of Clerks posted in Bengal, Haryana and Odisha is what per cent of the total number of Officers posted in all the six states together?
   1) 66.67 2) 77.67 3) 45.55 4) 73.76 5) 82.67
5. What is the average number of Clerks posted in Haryana, Kerala, Odisha and Bengal?
   1) 181.75 2) 185.75 3) 145.55
   4) 223.25 5) 185.50
6. The total number of bank employees posted in Haryana is how much per cent more or less than the total number of bank employees posted in Karnataka?
   1) 14.0625 2) 23.0625 3) 12.6025
   4) 16.2565 5) 8.0925

Directions (Q. 7-11): Study the following graph carefully and answer the given questions.

Rashika, Ashutosh, Deepti, Tushar and Lokesh were collecting money for a charity. They collected notes in denominations of ₹10, ₹20, ₹50 and ₹100.

The table gives partial information about the number of notes of each denomination collected by them:

	₹10	₹20	₹50	₹100
Rashika	10	4	—	2
Ashutosh	—	8	—	#
Deepti	12	10	#	—
Tushar	—	—	4	2
Lokesh	—	6	—	4

Note: (#) denotes they did not collect that denomination notes.

The following information is also known:

- No one collected more than 26 notes.
- The amount collected by each of them was less than ₹800.
- Rashika collected ₹680 while Deepti collected ₹720.
- Ashutosh and Tushar collected equal number of ₹50 notes. One of them collected more than ₹600.
- Lokesh collected 18 notes and the highest amount.
- The total number of ₹50 notes collected was 18.

7. How many ₹10 notes were collected by Ashutosh? Which of the following statements is/are sufficient to answer the above question?
   Statement I: The ratio of the amount collected by Ashutosh to that of Deepti is 25: 36.
   Statement II: The number of notes collected by Ashutosh is equal to the number of notes collected by Deepti.
   1) Only I 2) Only II 3) Neither I nor II
   4) Either I or II 5) Both I and II
8. Which of the following statements is/are definitely true?
   Statement I: The total money collected by them was ₹3340.
   Statement II: Lokesh collected more than ₹600.

Statement III: Ashutosh collected the least amount.
1) Only I and II 2) Only III 3) Only II and III
4) Only II 5) All the three

9. Find the number of ₹10 notes collected by Tushar if the total amount collected by him is equal to the total amount collected by Rashika. Assume that he has the maximum possible number of notes.
1) 12 2) 9 3) 6 4) 10 5) 11

10. Which of the following statements is/are true?
I. The difference between the total amount collected by Lokesh and Rashika is ₹180.
II. The ratio of the total amount collected by Deepti to that by Rashika is 1 : 1.
III. The total amount collected by Rashika is 5.55% less than the total amount collected by Deepti.
1) Only III 2) Both I and II 3) All the three
4) None 5) Only II

11. **Quantity I:** If a person takes one note from Ashutosh's collected notes, the probability of his getting a ₹10 note is $\frac{7}{13}$. The total amount collected by Ashutosh is what per cent of the total amount collected by Deepti?
Quantity II: The total amount collected by Rashika is what per cent of the total amount collected by Lokesh?
1) Quantity I > Quantity II
2) Quantity I ≥ Quantity II
3) Quantity I ≤ Quantity II
4) Quantity I < Quantity II
5) Quantity I = Quantity II or relationship cannot be determined

Directions (Q. 12-15): Study the given information carefully and answer the questions given below.

There are some employees (male + female) in company P and Q. In company P, females are 45% of the total number of employees and in company Q, the number of female employees and the number of male employees are the same.

Female employees of company Q are $\frac{7}{5}$ times the number of male employees of company P.

12. The number of male employees in company P is approximately how much per cent of the total number of employees in both the companies together?
1) 32 2) 28 3) 22
4) Cannot be determined 5) 18

13. The number of females in company Q is how much per cent of the number of males in company P?
1) 160 2) 75 3) 120
4) 140 5) None of the above

14. The number of male employees in both the companies together is how much per cent of the number of female employees in company Q?
1) 171.42 2) 154.36 3) 185.56
4) Cannot be determined 5) 145.45

15. What is the ratio of the total number of employees in company P to the total number of employees in company Q?
1) 55 : 77 2) 77 : 45 3) 50 : 77
4) None of the given options 5) 50 : 63

Directions (Q. 16-21): Read the following paragraph carefully and answer the following questions.

Unitech Limited has ______ **(A)** men and ______ **(B)** women. Each man takes ______ **(x)** hours to manufacture a soap while each woman takes one more hour. Working 8 hours per day, they manufacture 200 soaps. The daily wages of one man and one woman are ₹400 and ₹320 respectively.

Unitech Limited has 110 workers manufacturing soaps. There is an agreement between Unitech Limited and Subhash Gupta, a retail shop owner, that Unitech Limited has to supply ______ **(n)** products per trip at ₹ ______ **(C)** per soap. The transportation fee per trip is ₹10,000 which should be taken care by Subhash Gupta.

In one trip, Unitech Limited gains 25%. Subhash Gupta marks the soap at 10% profit. Selling all the manufactured soaps in one month at the marked price, the total profit earned by Subhash Gupta is ₹162000.

Note: 1. Assume material cost in manufacturing soap to be nil.

2. Also, all the soaps manufactured by Unitech is sold only to Subhash Gupta.

16. What is the total profit of Unitech per month (in ₹)?
1) 300000 2) 1200000 3) 800000
4) 120000 5) 462000

17. If B men and A women work for 10 hours in a day and the daily wages of the workers are unchanged, then what will be the price (in ₹) at which the soap is sold by Unitech Limited to keep the profit per cent the same?
1) 170 2) 190 3) 200 4) 215 5) 230

18. If due to improved efficiency the number of trips is halved and the transportation fee is also halved, then how much profit will Subhash Gupta get if he gives a discount of 10%?
1) 10.60 2) 12.30 3) 15.50 4) 20.60 5) 7.30

19. If the transportation fee is paid by Unitech Limited itself, then find the profit percentage of Unitech Limited and Subhash Gupta if he sells at the same price as before.
1) 12%, 18% 2) 15%, 18%
3) 15.8%, 18.8% 4) 12.5%, 18%
5) 15%, 18.8%

20. If the shop owner provides an offer of giving one soap free to those who are buying 20 soaps, what is the approximate profit percent in this case?
1) 5.76% 2) 4.16% 3) 4.76%
4) 4.5% 5) 5.5%

21. A is how much per cent more or less than B?
1) None of the given options
2) 30 3) 10 4) 25 5) 20

Answers and explanations

(1-6):

Officers : Clerks = 73 : 105

Difference = 320 ≡ (105 – 73) ⇒ 32 ≡ 320 ∴ 1 ≡ 10

⇒ Total Officers = 730 ⇒ Total Clerks = 1050

Officers in Kerala = 110

Clerks in Haryana = 110 + 85 = 195

Total bank staff in Karnataka = 320

Clerks in Karnataka = 20 + Officers in Karnataka

⇒ Clerks in Karnataka = 170

And, Officers in Karnataka = 150

Officers in Odisha = $\frac{70}{300} \times 150 = 35$

Clerks in Odisha = $\frac{200}{35} \times 35 = 200$

Officers in Bengal = 149

Clerks in Delhi = 153

Clerks in Bengal = 321 – 149 = 172

Total bank staff in Delhi = 321 – 52 = 269

Officers in Delhi = 269 – 153 = 116

Officers in Haryana

= 730 – [110 + 150 + 35 + 149 + 116] = 170

Clerks in Kerala = 1050 – [195 + 170 + 200 + 172 + 153]

= 160

The above information can be tabulised as:

	Officers (730)	Clerks (1050)	Total bank employees
Kerala	110	160	270
Haryana	170	195	365
Karnataka	150	170	320
Odisha	35	200	235
Bengal	149	172	321
Delhi	116	153	269

1. 5; Average number of Officers posted in Delhi, Haryana and Kerala

$= \frac{116+170+110}{3} = \frac{396}{3}$

Average number of Clerks posted here

$= \frac{153+195+160}{3} = \frac{508}{3}$

∴ Required ratio = $\frac{396}{3} : \frac{508}{3} = 99 : 127$

2. 5; Average no. of bank employees posted in all cities

$= \frac{270+360+320+235+321+269}{6} = \frac{1775}{6} = 295\frac{5}{6}$

Hence, in Haryana, Karnataka and Bengal no. of employees posted is more than the average.

3. 3; Total bank employees posted in Delhi

= 116 + 153 = 269

4. 2; No. of Clerks posted in Bengal, Haryana and Odisha

= 172 + 195 + 200 = 567

∴ Required percentage = $\frac{567}{730} \times 100 = 77.67\%$

5. 1; Required average = $\frac{195+160+200+172}{4} = 181.75$

6. 1; Required percentage = $\frac{365-320}{320} \times 100 = \frac{4500}{320}$

= 14.0625%

7. 4; **From I:** Total amount collected by Ashutosh

$= \frac{720}{36} \times 25 =$ ₹500

Total amount = 500 = 10a + 20 × 8 + 50 × 4 ⇒ a = 14

From II: No. of notes collected by Ashutosh = No. of notes collected by Deepti = 26

Then, a + 8 + 4 = 26 ⇒ a = 26 – 12 = 14

Hence, either of these statements are sufficient to answer the question.

8. 3; **Statement I:** We do not know Ashutosh and Tushar's total amount.

Statement II: Lokesh collected ₹760, which is more than ₹600. Hence statement II is true.

Statement III: We do not know Ashutosh's total amount.

But we know Ashutosh's amount is less than 600. All other except him have amount more than 600, so Ashutosh has the least amount.

Thus, statement II and III are true.

9. 1; Total number of notes = 26

Total no. of ₹10 and ₹20 notes = 26 – 6 = 20

Total amount collected by Rashika = ₹680

Hence, 4 × 50 + 10 × (20 – a) + 20a + 100 × 2 = 680

⇒ a = 8

∴ No. of ₹10 notes collected by Tushar

= 20 – 8 = 12

10. 1; **From I:**

Total amount collected by Lokesh = ₹760

Total amount collected by Rashika = ₹680

∴ Difference = 760 – 680 = 80 ≠ 180

So, this statement is not true.

From II:

Total amount collected by Rashika = ₹680

Total amount collected by Deepti = ₹720

∴ Ratio = 720 : 680 = 18 : 17 ≠ 1 : 1

So, this statement is not true.

From III:

Total amount collected by Rashika = ₹680

Total amount collected by Deepti = ₹720

$\therefore$ Required % = $\frac{40}{720}\times100 = 5.55\%$

$\therefore$ Only statement III is true.

11. 4; **Quantity I:** Total no. of notes collected by Ashutosh $= 8+4+x = 12+x$

Probability $= \frac{7}{13} = \frac{^{x}C_1}{^{12+x}C_1} \Rightarrow \frac{7}{13} = \frac{x}{12+x}$

$\Rightarrow 84+7x = 13x \Rightarrow x = 14$

So, total amount collected by Ashutosh $= 14\times10+8\times20+4\times50 =$ ₹500

Reqd % $= \frac{500}{720}\times100 = 69.44\%$

Quantity II: Required % $= \frac{680}{760}\times100 = 89.47\%$

Hence, Quantity I < Quantity II

(12-15):

Let total no. of employees in company P be 100n.

Then, No. of males in P = 55n

No. of females in P = 45n

No. of females in Q $= \frac{7}{5}\times55n = 77n$, which is equal to no. of males in Q.

Total no. of employees in Q = 77n + 77n = 154n

12. 3; Required % $= \frac{55n}{154n+100n}\times100 = \frac{55n}{254n}\times100 = 21.65\% \approx 22$

13. 4; Required % $= \frac{77n}{55n}\times100 = 140\%$

14. 1; Required % $= \frac{55n+77n}{77n}\times100 = \frac{132n}{77n}\times100 = 171.42\%$

15. 3; Required ratio = 100n : 154n = 50 : 77

16. 1; Given

$A+B = 110$ ...(i)

Now, $A\left(\frac{8}{x}\right)+B\left(\frac{8}{x+1}\right) = 200$ ...(ii)

Daily wages will be according to the efficiency. Thus,

$\left(\frac{8}{x}\right):\left(\frac{8}{x+1}\right) = \frac{400}{320} \Rightarrow \left(\frac{x+1}{x}\right) = \frac{5}{4} \Rightarrow x = 4$

So, 2A + 1.6B = 200 [Putting x = 4 in (ii)]

Multiplying (i) by 2, we get

2A + 2B = 220

$\Rightarrow 0.4B = 20 \Rightarrow$ **B** = 50 and **A** = 60

Total wages for one day

$= 400\times60+320\times50$

$= 24000+16000 = 40000$

No. of soaps manufactured in one day = 200

So, CP of 1 soap for Unitech $= \frac{40000}{200} = 200$

Profit % for Unitech Limited = 25%

SP of soap (C) $= \frac{125}{100}\times200 = 250$

Profit per soap (250 – 200 =) 50

Total profit of Unitech per month

$= 50\times200\times30 =$ ₹300000

17. 3; No. of men = 50 **(from solution Q. No. 16)**

No. of women = 60

No. of products manufactured in 10 hours

$= \left(\frac{50\times10}{4}\right)+\left(\frac{60\times10}{5}\right) = 245$

Total wages $= 50\times400+60\times320$

$= 20000+19200 = 39200$

Cost price for Unitech Limited per soap

$= \frac{39200}{245} = 160$

$\therefore$ SP for 25% profit $= 1.25\times160 = 200$

Hence the selling price of a soap = ₹200

18. 1; Profit of Subhash Gupta = 10%

Total profit per month = 162000

No. of soaps manufactured per month

$= 200\times30 = 6000$

Total SP of Subhash Gupta

$= \frac{162000}{10}\times110 = 1782000$

SP of Subhash Gupta for one soap

$= \frac{1782000}{200\times30} = 297$

Now, $\frac{10}{100}\times CP\times200\times30 = 162000$

$\Rightarrow$ CP = 270 (Cost price for Subhash Gupta)

CP is equal to buying of soap and transportation per trip.

If n is no. of soaps transported per trip. **(From given information and solution Q. No. 16.)**

Then, $C+\frac{10000}{n} = 270 \Rightarrow 250+\frac{10000}{n} = 270$

$\Rightarrow \frac{10000}{n} = 20 \Rightarrow n = 500$

Total no. of trips in 1 month $= \frac{200\times30}{500} = 12$

On being halved, total no. of trips = 6 and transportation fee = 5000

Now, No. of soaps per trip = 1000

CP for Subhash Gupta $= 250+\frac{5000}{1000} = 255$

SP of 1 soap $= \frac{90}{100}\times297 =$ ₹267.30

$\therefore$ Profit = 267.30 – 255 = ₹12.30

19. 5; In a trip, 500 products are transported at ₹250 per soap.

Total amount = 500 × 250 = ₹125000

Wages for 500 products = 200 × 500 = ₹100000

Transportation fee = ₹10000

Total expense of Unitech limited = 110000

$\therefore$ Profit = 125000 – 110000 = ₹15000

$\therefore$ Required % profit $= \frac{15000}{100000}\times100 = 15\%$

For Subhash Gupta;

CP = 250

MP = 297, Profit = 297 − 250 = 47

$\therefore$ Profit % = $\frac{47}{250} \times 100$ = **18.8%**

20. 3; CP of 21 soaps for Subhash Gupta = 270 × 21

SP of 20 soaps = 297 × 20

SP : CP = 297 × 20 : 297 × 21 = 22 : 21

$\therefore$ % Profit = $\frac{1}{21} \times 100$ = 4.76%

21. 5; We have, A = 60, B = 50

So, reqd % = $\frac{60-50}{50} \times 100 = \frac{10}{50} \times 100$ = 20% more

Practice Set 15

Directions (Q. 1-6): In a company ABC, a recruitment drive is going on. In this drive, applicants have applied for recruitment in five departments.

Given below is the data and information about the applications received during this recruitment drive in a tabulised form. Read the given information carefully and answer the questions that follow.

Departments	Total number of applications received	Number of duplicate applicants	Average number of duplicate applications received from duplicate applicants
Finance	612	28	5
R&D	398	—	2
Marketing	999	43	—
HR	—	61	—
IT	961	—	—

Note: A duplicate applicant is an applicant who has submitted additional application after submitting his/her original application. All applications received (original + duplicate) from duplicate applicants, are rejected. None of the applicants applied for more than one department.

1. For recruitment in Finance department, if the ratio of accepted male applications to that of rejected male applications is 5 : 2 and the ratio of accepted female applications to that of rejected female applications is 14 : 5, then what is the number of rejected male applications from Finance department?
1) 120 2) 100 3) 80 4) 88 5) 66

2. For recruitment in IT department, the number of accepted applications from males, the number of accepted applications from females and the number of rejected applications (from both males and females) are 22X, (8X+8Y) and (X+23Y) respectively. Considering that the average number of duplicate applications received from duplicate applicants is a positive integer, which of the following is true?
(A) The number of accepted applications from females is 252.
(B) The number of male applications from males is more than 704.
(C) The number of accepted applications from females is 248.
1) Only (B) 2) Only (A) and (C)
3) Only (C) 4) All (A), (B) and (C)
5) None of the given statements is true

3. If the average number of accepted applications for Finance and R&D department is 383.5, then what is the number of duplicate applicants for R&D department?
1) 25 2) 26 3) 31 4) 19 5) 23

4. For recruitment in Marketing department, the number of accepted male applications ranges between 400 and 450 and the number of accepted female applications ranges between 300 and 350. Then which of the following can be the value of the average number of duplicate applications received in Marketing department?
1) 2 2) 4 3) 9 4) 11 5) 15

5. If in the IT department, the average number of duplicate applications received 6, then what is the total number of applications accepted in that department if it is given that number of duplicate applicants in IT department is 7 less than the number of duplicate applicants in HR department?
1) 223 2) 648 3) 545 4) 378 5) 583

6. The ratio of the total number of applications received for recruitment in Marketing department to that in HR department is 333 : 302. What will be the average number of duplicate applications received from duplicate applicants in HR department if the number of accepted applications in the HR department is 662?
1) 7 2) 2 3) 6 4) 4 5) 3

Directions (Q. 7-12): Study the following information carefully and answer the questions given below.

There are four men, namely Qasim, Arhaan, Rajat and Dinesh, and four women, namely Sunita, Shivangi, Srishti and Huma in a group. Each man can complete a piece of work in different number of days. Similarly, each woman can complete it in a different mumber of days.

Shivangi can complete the piece of work in 20 days. The number of days taken by Shivangi to complete the work is 25% more than the number of days taken by Rajat to complete the work. The ratio of the number of days taken by Rajat and Qasim to complete the work is 4 : 3. The number of days taken by Qasim to complete the work is 20% less than the number of days taken by Sunita to complete the work. The efficiency of Huma is 50% more than the efficiency of Sunita. The ratio of the number of days taken by Qasim, Arhaan, and Srishti is 4 : 3 : 6. The number of days taken by Srishti to complete the work is 10% less than the number of days taken by Dinesh to complete the work.

7. Bhuwan can complete the work in half the time taken by Qasim to finish the work. Find the time taken by Bhuwan and Swati together to finish the work.
Statement I: The number of days taken by Swati alone to finish the work is a prime number which is more than the number of days taken by Qasim alone and less than the number of days taken by Srishti alone to finish the work.
Statement II: The number of days taken by Swati is 120% of the number of days taken by Dinesh and Huma together to finish the work.
1) Only statement I is sufficient to answer the question.
2) Only statement II is sufficient to answer the question.
3) Either statement I or statement II is sufficient to answer the question.
4) Neither statement I nor statement II is sufficient to answer the question.
5) Both statement I and II are necessary to answer the question.

8. Who is the most efficient among Srishti, Arhaan, Huma and Minku?
Statement I: The efficiency of Minku is 40% of the sum of efficiency of Arhaan and Qasim.
Statement II: The efficiency of Minku is more than the efficiency of Rajat.
1) Only statement I is sufficient to answer the question.
2) Only statement II is sufficient to answer the question.
3) Either statement I or statement II is sufficient to answer the question.
4) Neither statement I nor statement II is sufficient to answer the question.
5) Both statement I and II are necessary to answer the question.

9. Find the number of days taken by Vinay alone to finish the work.
Statement I: The ratio of the number of days taken by Prabhat alone to the days taken by Vinay alone to finish the work is 2 : 3.
Statement II: The number of days taken by Prabhat alone to finish the work is 60% more than the number of days taken by Huma alone to finish the work.
1) Only statement I is sufficient to answer the question.
2) Only statement II is sufficient to answer the question.
3) Either statement I or statement II is sufficient to answer the question.
4) Neither statement I nor statement II is sufficient to answer the question.
5) Both statement I and II are necessary to answer the question.

10. Sunita and Shivangi together worked for 4 days and then both were replaced by Dinesh and Suresh. Find the number of days taken by Dinesh and Suresh together to complete the remaining work.
Statement I: The efficiency of Suresh is 20% less than the efficiency of Rajat.
Statement II: Suresh and Prem together can complete the work in 10 days.
1) Only statement I is sufficient to answer the question.
2) Only statement II is sufficient to answer the question.
3) Either statement I or statement II is sufficient to answer the question.
4) Neither statement I nor statement II is sufficient to answer the question.
5) Both statement I and II are necessary to answer the question.

11. If Qasim left the work after working for 2 days then find the number of days taken by Dheeraj to finish the remaining work.
Statement I: The efficiency of Dheeraj is 90% of the efficiency of Siddharth and the ratio of the number of days taken by Siddharth and Arhaan alone to finish the work is 2: 1.
Statement II: The number of days taken by Dheeraj alone to finish the work is 2 more than the number of days taken by Srishti alone to finish the work.
1) Only statement I is sufficient to answer the question.
2) Only statement II is sufficient to answer the question.
3) Either statement I or statement II is sufficient to answer the question.
4) Neither statement I nor statement II is sufficient to answer the question.
5) Both statement I and II are necessary to answer the question.

12. What is the difference between the number of days taken by Shivangi and Srishti to complete the work alone?
1) 2 2) 3 3) 5
4) 7 5) None of the given options

Directions (Q. 13-17): Study the following information carefully and answer the questions given below.

There are six manufacturing companies in a city. Each company has borrowed some percentage of their first-year expenditure from a bank at the beginning of 2018 and the remaining is invested by the company itself. The interest on the borrowed amount is 10% per annum. Each company pays the interest from its annual income and invests the remaining in next year's expenditure. The following pie-chart shows the percentage of amount borrowed from the bank (total amount borrowed by all companies = ₹2 lakhs) by six companies. The following bar graph represents the profit per cent of the company for two years 2018 and 2019, respectively and also the percentage of first-year expenditure amount borrowed from the bank.

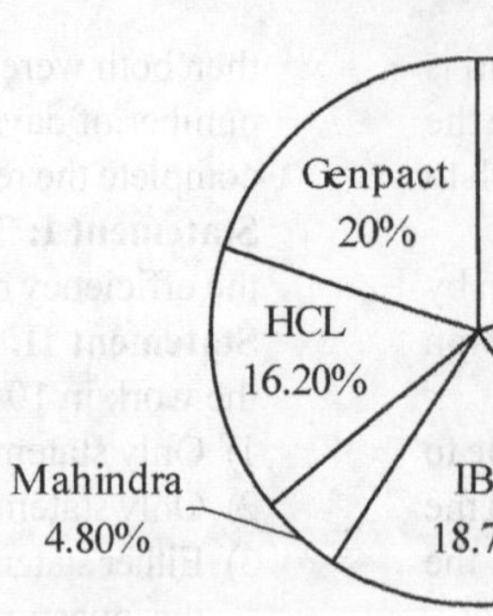

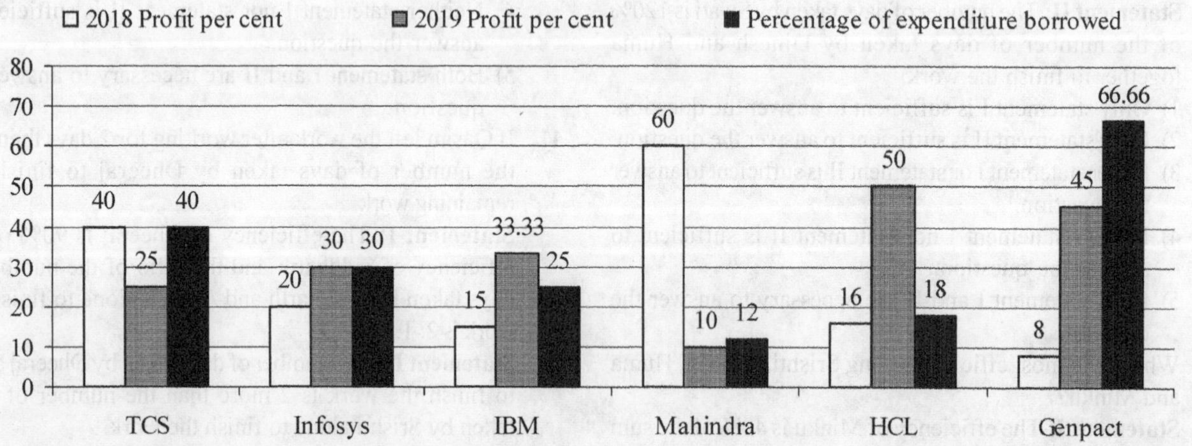

Note: Total expenditure = Investment by company + Amount from bank

13. At the end of 2019, what was the percentage profit of TCS on its initial investment after paying back the borrowed amount to the bank at the end of 2nd year?
1) 119 2) 125 3) 78 4) 110 5) 94

14. At the end of 2019, Infosys and IBM collaborated and started a business. Both invested their remaining amount after paying the amount to the bank. The annual profit of that business is 20%. What is the profit (in ₹) in that business?
1) 70689 2) 96807 3) 68907
4) 83750 5) None of the given options

15. Quantity I: The total profit amount of Genpact in two years.
Quantity II: The total profit amount of Mahindra in two years.
After solving for the two quantities given above, what will be the relation between these quantities?
1) Quantity I < Quantity II
2) Quantity II < Quantity I
3) Quantity I = Quantity II or No relation can be established.
4) Quantity I ≥ Quantity II
5) Quantity II ≥ Quantity I

16. What is the average (in ₹) of all six companies' investment?
1) None of the given options 2) $85000\frac{1}{3}$ 3) $95000\frac{2}{3}$
4) $90000\frac{2}{3}$ 5) $84166\frac{2}{3}$

17. If HCL decides to pay back the amount to the bank at the end of 1st year itself, how much more/less (in ₹) will it get when compared to paying back the amount at the end of 2nd year?
1) 13260 more 2) 12960 less 3) 16236 less
4) 13620 more 5) 13266 less

Directions (Q. 18-22): The following table shows different items sold by shopkeeper, cost price per kg of items, percentage mark-up on cost price, marked price per kg and percentage discount offered on marked price. Some of the values are missing, students are expected to calculate them as and when required.

Items	Cost price per kg	% mark-up on cost price	Marked price per kg	% discount
P	—	—	—	9%
Q	1000	20%	—	—
R	—	10%	550	—
S	—	—	1600	18%
T	1500			

18. The shopkeeper gives two successive discounts of 12% and 13% instead of a single discount of 18% on item S. If the percentage mark-up price for the item is $33\frac{1}{3}\%$, then his profit decrease by what per cent approximately as compared to his previous profit?
1) 72 2) 75 3) 78
4) 82 5) 65

19. How much quantity of item P is sold by the shopkeeper if the cost price of item P is ₹300 less than twice of the marked price of item R and the marked price of item P is $\frac{5}{8}$ times of the marked price of item S and the total profit earned by selling item P is ₹1320?
1) 10 kg 2) 12 kg 3) 24 kg
4) 20 kg 5) None of the given options

20. To earn more profit the shopkeeper mixes 5 kg of cheaper quality of item R (cost ₹240/kg) with 15 kg of pure item R and sells the mixture at a discount which is 10% more than the original discount offered on item R. If the original discount offered on item R is 14%, then find the **approximate** new profit per cent on selling the whole quantity of item R.
1) 7 2) 5 3) 8 4) 12 5) 10

21. If 4 kg of item Q is spoiled out of total 40 kg, then what is the total profit or loss (in ₹) made by the shopkeeper on selling the remaining quantity of the item, if a discount of 8% is given on the marked price of the item.
1) 225 loss 2) 256 loss 3) 325 profit
4) 256 profit 5) 325 loss

22. Find the profit or loss percentage of item T, if it is mark-up 20% above the cost price and 20% discount is allowed.
1) 4% profit 2) 0.5% profit 3) 0.4% loss
4) 4% loss 5) None of the given options

Answers and explanations

1. 4; $\because$ 5 are average duplicate applications and 1 is original which will be rejected.
$\therefore$ No. of rejected applications from finance department $= (5+1) \times 28 = 168$
No. of accepted applications total $= 612 - 168 = 444$
Let no. of male accepted and rejected applications be 5n and 2n respectively.
Then, as per information given, $\frac{444-5n}{168-2n} = \frac{14}{5}$
$\Rightarrow 2220 - 25n = 2352 - 28n \Rightarrow 3n = 132 \Rightarrow n = 44$
So, rejected male applications $= 2n = 2 \times 44 = 88$

2. 3; Male accepted applications $= 22x$
Female accepted applications $= 8x + 8y = 8(x+y)$
Total no. of applications rejected $= x + 23y$
Total no. of applications received $= 961$
$\Rightarrow 22x + 8x + 8y + x + 23y = 961 \Rightarrow x + y = 31$
So, $8(x+y) = 31 \times 8 = 248$
So, (C) is true and (A) is false.
Now, if no. of accepted male applications is more than 704, then $22x > 704$
$\Rightarrow x > 32$, which cannot be true as $x + y = 31$.
Hence, only (C) is true.

3. 1; Toal no. of accepted applications for R&D and Finance department $= 383.5 \times 2 = 767$
As no. of accepted applications for Finance department $= 444$ **(from solution of Q. No. 1)**
No. of accepted applications for R&D $= 767 - 444 = 323$
No. of duplicate applications for R&D = L (let)
No. of rejected applications $= 398 - 323 = 75$
So, $L(2+1) = 75 \Rightarrow L = 25$

4. 2; Accepted male applications $= 400$ to 450
Accepted female applications $= 300$ to 350
Accepted applications $= 700$ to 800
Rejected applications $= (999-700)$ to $(999-800)$ $= 299$ to 199
Since, rejected applications $= 43n$ (where n is any integer)
From **choice (1)**, let average = 2.
Then, $43(2+1) = 43 \times 3 = 129$, which is not in range of 199 to 299.
From **choice (2)**, let average = 4. Then, $43(4+1) = 43 \times 5 = 215$, which can be the answer as it belongs to 199 to 299.

5. 5; Total applications = 961
Average = 6
No. of duplicate applicants $= 61 - 7 = 54$
No. of rejected applications $= (6+1) \times 54 = 378$
$\therefore$ No. of accepted applications $= 961 - 378 = 583$

6. 5; No. of applications received for HR department
$= \frac{999}{333} \times 302 = 906$
Let average be K. Then,
$(K+1)61 = 906 - 662 = 244$
$\Rightarrow K + 1 = 4 \therefore K = 3$

(7-12):
No. of days taken by Shivangi = 20
No. of days taken by Rajat $= 20 \times \frac{100}{125} = 16$
No. of days taken by Qasim $= 16 \times \frac{3}{4} = 12$
No. of days taken by Sunita $= 12 \times \frac{100}{80} = 15$
Let efficiency of Sunita $= 10x$
and efficiency of Huma $= 10x\left(\frac{150}{100}\right) = 15x$

So,
No. of days taken by Huma = 10

No. of days taken by Arhaan = $12\times\frac{3}{4}=9$

No. of days taken by Srishti = $12\times\frac{6}{4}=18$

No. of days taken by Dinesh = $18\times\frac{100}{90}=20$

This can be tabulised as:

Person	No. of days	Person	No. of days
Qasim	12	Sunita	15
Arhaan	9	Shivangi	20
Rajat	16	Srishti	18
Dinesh	20	Huma	10

7. 2; No. of days taken by Bhuwan alone = $\frac{12}{2}=6$

Statement I: No. of days taken by Swati alone = 13 or 17 (Exact value is not obtained)

Statement II: Work done by Dinesh and Huma together in 1 day = $\frac{1}{20}+\frac{1}{10}=\frac{3}{20}$

No. of days taken by them to finish the work = $\frac{20}{3}$

No. of days taken by Swati alone = $\frac{20}{3}\times\frac{120}{100}=8$

Per day work of Bhuwan and Swati = $\frac{1}{6}+\frac{1}{8}=\frac{7}{24}$

$\therefore$ No. of days taken = $\frac{24}{7}$ days

Thus, statement II alone is sufficient.

8. 1; **Statement I:** Per day work of Minku

$=\left(\frac{1}{9}+\frac{1}{12}\right)\frac{40}{100}=\frac{7}{90}$

Hence, efficiency of Arhaan is the maximum.
This statement is sufficient to answer the question.

Statement II: Efficiency of Minku > $\frac{1}{16}$

Exact efficiency cannot be obtained.
Hence only (I) is sufficient to answer the question.

9. 5; **Statement I:**
Let no. of days taken by Prabhat alone = 2x
And no. of days taken by Vinay alone = 3x
This statement is not enough to answer the question.

Statement II:

No. of days taken by Prabhat alone = $10\left(\frac{160}{100}\right)=16$

Again, this statement is not sufficient.

From I and II: No. of days taken by Vinay $=16\times\frac{3}{2}=24$

Hence, both the statements are required.

10. 1; Work done by Sunita and Shivangi together for 4 days = $4\left(\frac{1}{15}+\frac{1}{20}\right)=\frac{7}{15}$

Work left = $1-\frac{7}{15}=\frac{8}{15}$

Statement I: Let efficiency of Rajat = 100x

Efficiency of Suresh = $100x\left(\frac{80}{100}\right)=80x$

$\Rightarrow$ No. of days taken by Suresh = 20

Dinesh + Suresh's 1 day's work = $\left(\frac{1}{20}+\frac{1}{20}\right)=\frac{8}{15}$

No. of days taken by Dinesh and Suresh together to complete the remaining work = $\frac{8}{15}\div\frac{8}{15}=1$

Thus, this statement is sufficient to answer the question.

Statement II: Suresh + Prem = 10 days
From this we can't find the anwer.
Thus only (I) is sufficient to answer the question.

11. 3; Work completed by Qasim in 2 days = $\frac{2}{12}=\frac{1}{6}$

$\therefore$ Work left = $1-\frac{1}{6}=\frac{5}{6}$

Statement I: No. of days taken by Siddharth alone $=9\times\frac{2}{1}=18$

Let efficiency of Siddharth = 10x and efficiency of Dheeraj = $10x\left(\frac{90}{100}\right)=9x$

$\Rightarrow$ No. of days taken by Dheeraj alone = 20
No. of days taken by Dheeraj to finish the remaining work = $20\times\frac{5}{6}=\frac{50}{3}$

Statement II:
No. of days taken by Dheeraj alone = 18 + 2 = 20
No. of days taken by Dheeraj to finish remaining work $=20\times\frac{5}{6}=\frac{50}{3}$

Thus, either of the statements alone is sufficient.

12. 1; Required difference = 20 – 18 = 2 days

13. 4; Profit at the end of first year = $100000\times\frac{40}{100}=40000$

Income of first year = 100000 + 40000 = 140000

Interest of first year $= 40000 \times \frac{10}{100} = 4000$

Remaining amount $= 140000 - 4000 = 136000$, which is investment in the year 2019.

Profit at the end of 2019

$= 136000 \times \frac{25}{100} = 136000 \times \frac{1}{4} = 34000$

Income for second year $= 136000 + 34000$
$= 170000$

Interest of the second year

$= 40000 \times \frac{10}{100} = 4000$

Since TCS pays back the total amount to bank, Remaining amount with him
$= 170000 - 4000 - 40000 = ₹126000$

$\therefore$ Reqd % $= \frac{126000 - 60000}{60000} \times 100$

$= \frac{66000}{60000} \times 100 = 110\%$

14. 3; Profit at the end of first year $= 135000 \times \frac{20}{100} = 27000$

Income of 2018 $= 135000 + 27000 = 162000$

Interest of 2018 $= \frac{40500 \times 10}{100} = 4050$

$\therefore$ Remaining amount in 2018 $= 162000 - 4050 = 157950$

Profit at the end of 2019 $= 157950 \times \frac{30}{100} = 47385$

Income for 2019 $= 157950 + 47385 = 205335$

Payable amount to bank $= 40500 + 4050 = 44550$

Remaining amount for Infosys $= 205335 - 44550$
$= 160785$

Similarly, calculating for IBM, remaining amount with IBM $= 183750$

Total amount $= 160785 + 183750 = 344535$

$\therefore$ Profit $= 344535 \times \frac{20}{100} = 68907$

15. 1; **Quantity I:** Genpact:

Amount borrowed from bank $= 40000$

Total expenditure $= 60000$

So, amount invested by Genpact $= 20000$

Profit at the end of 2018 $= 60000 \times \frac{8}{100} = 4800$

Income for 2018 $= 60000 + 4800 = 64800$

Interest $= 40000 \times \frac{10}{100} = 4000$

Remaining amount $= 64800 - 4000 = 60800$, which is investment of second year.

Profit at the end of second year

$= 60800 \times \frac{45}{100} = 27360$

$\therefore$ Total profit $= 4800 + 27360 = 32160$

Quantity II: Similarly, calculating for Mahindra, as in **Quantity I**, we have

Profit $= 48000 + 12704 = 60704$

Hence, Quantity I < Quantity II.

16. 5; Total $= 60000 + 94500 + 112500 + 70400 + 147600 + 20000 = 505000$

$\therefore$ Average $= \frac{505000}{6} = 84166\frac{2}{3}$

17. 2; Profit at the end of first year

$= 180000 \times \frac{16}{100} = 28800$ (For HCL)

Income for 2018 $= 180000 + 28800 = 208800$

Interest $= 32400 \times \frac{10}{100} = 3240$

Case I: Paying amount fully at the end of first year itself.

Amount at the end of first year
$= 32400 + 3240 = 35640$

Remaining amount with HCL
$= 208800 - 35640 = 173160$ (investment for 2019).

Profit of 2019 $= 173160 \times \frac{50}{100} = 86580$

Amount with HCL $= 173160 + 86580 = 259740$

Case II: Paying amount at the end of second year.

Amount with at the end of 2018
$= 208800 - 3240 = 205560$

Profit at the end of second year

$= 205560 \times \frac{50}{100} = 102780$

Amount payable to bank $= 32400 + 3240 = 35640$

Amount with HCL $= 205560 + 102780 - 35640 = 272700$

Case I < Case II

$\therefore$ Difference $= 272700 - 259740 = 12960$

18. 3; CP of item S $= \frac{MP \times 100}{(100 + \%\text{ mark up})}$

$= \frac{1600 \times 100}{100 + 33\frac{1}{3}} = \frac{1600 \times 100}{400} \times 3 = ₹1200$

Original SP $= MP \times \frac{(100 - \%\text{ discount})}{100}$

$= 1600 \times \frac{(100 - 18)}{100} = 16 \times 82 = ₹1312$

Original profit $= SP - CP = 1312 - 1200 = 112$

New SP $= 1600 \times \frac{88}{100} \times \frac{87}{100} = 1224.96$

New profit $= SP - CP = 1224.96 - 1200 = 24.96$

Required % decrease in profit

$= \frac{112-24.96}{112} \times 100 = 78\%$ (approx)

19. 2; CP of item P = 2 × MP of R − 300

$= 2 \times 550 - 300 = 800$

MP of item P = $\frac{5}{8}$ × MP of S = $1600 \times \frac{5}{8} = 1000$

SP of item P = $1000 \times \frac{91}{100} = ₹910$

Profit/kg = 910 − 800 = ₹110

Quantity sold = $\frac{1320}{110} = 12$ kg

20. 1; CP of pure item R = $550 \times \frac{100}{100+10} = ₹500$

CP/kg of the mixture

$= \frac{5 \times 240 + 15 \times 500}{5+15} = \frac{8700}{20} = ₹435$

New discount = $14\% \times \frac{110}{100} = 15.4\%$

New SP = $550 \times \frac{(100-15.4)}{100} = ₹465.3$

New profit % = $\frac{(465.3-435)}{435} \times 100$

$= 6.9\% \approx 7\%$ (approx)

21. 2; SP of Q = $1000 \times \frac{120}{100} \times \frac{92}{100} = ₹1104$

4 kg of item Q is spoiled out of total 40 kg. So only 36 kg is available for sale.

Total profit/loss = Total SP – Total CP

= 36 × 1104 − 40 × 1000 = 39744 − 40000 = −₹256 (loss)

22. 4; SP of tiem T = $1500 \times \frac{120}{100} \times \frac{80}{100} = ₹1440$

Loss = CP − SP = 1500 − 1440 = ₹60

$\therefore$ Loss % = $\frac{60}{1500} \times 100 = 4\%$

Practice Set 16

Directions (Q. 1-6): Read the following passage carefully and answer the given questions.

A certain number of students applied for UG (undergraduation) from two universities, namely ABC and PQR universities.

In ABC, males and females who applied for UG are 75% of the total males and 25% of the total females in the university respectively. Total number of students who applied for UG from ABC is 550. Total number of males in PQR is twice that of males in ABC. The number of females who applied for UG from ABC is 100. In PQR, $\frac{3}{5}$ of the total number of students are males. Half of the total females and half of the total males in PQR applied for UG.

1. The number of female students who did not apply for UG from PQR is what per cent of the number of males who applied for UG from ABC?
   1) 54.45 2) 88.89 3) 66.67
   4) 94.26 5) None of the given options
2. What is the ratio of the number of females who did not apply for UG from ABC to the number of males who applied for UG from PQR?
   1) 3 : 2 2) 2 : 1 3) 5 : 6
   4) 6 : 5 5) None of the given options
3. What is the difference between the number of students in both the universities?
   1) 1000 2) 1200 3) 1500
   4) 800 5) 600
4. The number of males in ABC is what percentage less than the number of females in PQR?
   1) 30 2) 25 3) 50 4) 75 5) 15
5. Find the total number of students who did not apply for UG in both the universities.
   1) 1200 2) 1250 3) 1450 4) 1050 5) 950
6. What is the average number of students who took admission in both the universities?
   1) 2500 2) 1200 3) 2000
   4) 1500 5) None of the given options

Directions (Q. 7-12): Study the following information carefully and answer the questions given below.

There is a Bajaj dealer which sells three models of Bajaj motorcycles, ie Avenger, Pulsar and Dominaar. The bikes are sold in three time slots, ie 12 pm-2 pm, 4 pm-6 pm and 8 pm-10 pm. The price per bike for Avenger, Pulsar and Dominaar variant is ₹72000, ₹84000 and ₹90000 respectively. The total number of bikes of all three variants sold in all three slots in a day is 64000.

12 pm - 2 pm: 25% of the bikes are sold in this time slot. The ratio of the number of Avenger variants sold to the number of Dominaar variants sold is 2: 3. The number of Pulsar variants sold is 4000. Hence the number of Avenger variants sold is **(A)** times the number of Pulsar variants sold. The total revenue generated by selling Dominaar variants is ₹**(B)** crore.

4 pm - 6 pm: The number of bikes sold in this time slot is 175% of the number of bikes sold during 12 pm - 2 pm. The number of Dominaar variants sold is 60% more than the number of Avenger variants sold and the number of Avenger variants sold is $\frac{5}{12}$ of the number of Pulsar variants sold. The revenue generated by selling Pulsar variants is **(C)** % of the revenue generated by selling Avenger variants.

8 pm - 10 pm: The remaining bikes are sold in this time slot and the ratio of number of Avenger, Pulsar and Dominaar variants sold is 3: 5: 2 respectively. The total revenue generated by selling Dominaar variants is ₹**(D)** crore less than the revenue generated by selling Avenger variants.

7. What value will come in place of 'A'?
   1) 1.1 2) 1.3 3) 1.5 4) 1.4 5) 1.2
8. What value will come in place of 'B'?
   1) 46.4 2) 68.5 3) 64.8
   4) 36.2 5) None of the given options
9. What value will come in place of 'C'?
   1) 180 2) 320 3) 225 4) 280 5) 332
10. What value will come in place of 'D'?
    1) 7.2 2) 6.4 3) 3.5
    4) 8.6 5) None of the given options
11. Ravi purchases a bike in time slot 4pm-6pm. If 5% of the Dominaar variants sold during 4pm-6pm are defective and other variants are not defective then what is the probability that the bike purchased by Ravi is defective?
    1) $\frac{4}{123}$ 2) $\frac{2}{15}$ 3) $\frac{2}{125}$
    4) $\frac{3}{119}$ 5) Cannot be determined

12. Rudra, a bike seller, purchased 50% Dominaars and 25% Pulsars from 12pm-2pm slot from the Bajaj dealer and sold them at 12% profit. What will be the total profit earned by him (in ₹ Crore)?
1) 4.562 2) 2.325 3) 6.665
4) 5.635 5) 4.896

Directions (Q. 13-17): Study the following data carefully and answer the questions:

There are total five trains M, J, L, S and T. The bar graph given below shows the percentage distribution of length (in metres) of five trains respectively while the pie-chart given below shows the distribution (in degrees) of speed (km/h) of those five trains respectively.

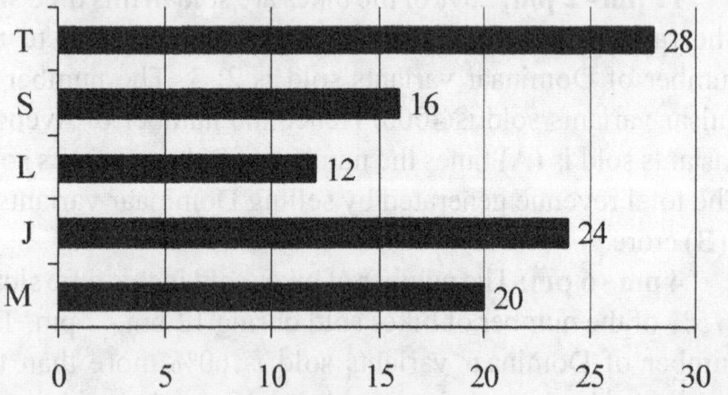

Percentage of length

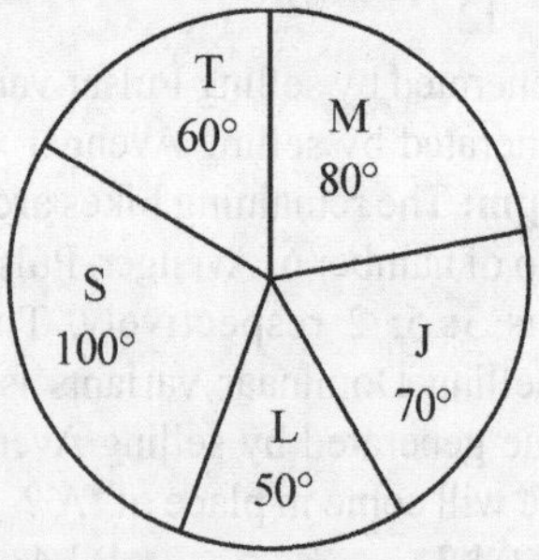

Speed of train

The sum of length of all trains is 2500 metres while the sum of speed of all trains is 360 km/h.

13. Train P can cross a pole in 72 seconds. What is the time taken by train M to cross train P when both the trains are travelling in opposite directions if time taken by train M to cross train P when both the trains are travelling in the same direction is 79.2 seconds?
1) 24 sec 2) 36 sec 3) 12 sec
4) 45 sec 5) Cannot be determined

14. If a car can cross train L in 27 seconds when travelling in the same direction, then what is the total distance covered by the car in 2.5 hours if it travels at a speed 20% less than its original speed and also if the length of car is negligible and the speed of the car is more than that of the train?
1) 120 km 2) 220 km 3) 175 km 4) 150 km 5) 180 km

15. Train J can cross a platform in 72 seconds. What is the time taken by another train Q of length equal to that of platform to cross train J if both the trains are travelling in the same direction and the speed of train Q is 126 kmph?
1) 60 sec 2) 75 sec 3) 45 sec
4) 90 sec 5) 110 sec

16. Train S can cross a platform of certain length in 36 seconds. If a person boarded the train and started running inside the train at a speed of 20 km/hr in the opposite direction as that of train, then what is the time taken by the person to cross the platform?
1) 24 sec 2) 25 sec 3) 27 sec
4) 32 sec 5) None of the given options

17. Train L can cross a person travelling in opposite direction of train in 13.5 seconds. What is the time taken by train T to cross that person when he is travelling in opposite direction of the train at a speed one-third of his original speed?
1) 36 sec 2) 24 sec 3) 18 sec
4) 42 sec 5) 62 sec

Directions (Q. 18-22): Given below is the table which shows six different bank schemes and rate of simple interest (SI) and rate of compound interest (CI) offered on these schemes. Study the following information carefully and answer the questions that follow.

Scheme	Compound Interest	Simple Interest
A	10	
B	—	14
C	40	—
D		15
E	20	10
F	30	25

Note: All rates of interest are calculated annually.

18. An amount was invested in Scheme F for the first year on SI but then the entire amount was switched to CI and back again to SI. This switching went on every year. What is the approximate interest earned after 5 years?
1) ₹56421 2) ₹75740 3) ₹57520
4) ₹57250 5) ₹65430

19. Dilbagh invested ₹12000 in Scheme D at SI for 6 years. The interest that Dilbagh obtained is divided into two equal parts and invested in two different schemes, ie Scheme B and Scheme C, for 4 years each at SI. If the ratio of interest obtained in both the schemes is 4 : 5 find out the rate of interest in Scheme C.
1) 17.5% 2) 20% 3) 15.5%
4) 22.5% 5) 12%

20. If a sum is invested in Scheme B at CI the amount obtained after 2 years from this scheme is 1.44 times the sum invested. The rate of SI for Scheme A is half of the rate of CI for Scheme B. Find out the total interest earned when ₹10000 was invested for 2 years in Scheme A at SI and in

Scheme B for 2 years at CI.

1) ₹4600 2) ₹6400 3) ₹2300
4) ₹6200 5) ₹7300

21. A sum is invested in Scheme C for 5 years at SI and then the amount received from it is invested in the same scheme for 2 years at CI. The total amount received after 7 years is 194% more than the sum invested initially. Find out the rate of interest in Scheme C for SI.

1) 20 2) 8 3) 15
4) 12 5) 10

22. **Quantity I:** If the amount invested in Scheme D at CI is ₹25000 and the rate of interest in this scheme is half of the interest rate (CI) in Scheme C find the amount received after 4 years.

Quantity II: If the amount invested in Scheme F is ₹30000 for a period of 7 years at simple rate of interest find the amount received at the end of 7 years.

Solve for the given two quantities and compare them.

1) Quantity I > Quantity II
2) Quantity I < Quantity II
3) Quantity I ≤ Quantity II
4) Quantity I ≥ Quantity II
5) Quantity I = Quantity II or relation cannot be established

Answers and explanations

(1-6):

University ABC:

Number of females who applied for UG = 100 = 25% of total females.

$\therefore$ Total females = $\frac{100}{25} \times 100 = 400$

Total number of males who applied for UG = 550 – 100 = 450 = 75% of total males

Total number of males = 600

University PQR:

Total males = 2 × 600 = 1200

Total students = $\frac{1200}{3} \times 5 = 2000$

Total females = $2000 \times \frac{2}{5} = 800$

Number of males who applied for UG = $\frac{1200}{2} = 600$

Number of females who applied for UG = $\frac{800}{2} = 400$

This information can be tabulised:

	ABC		PQR	
	Males	Females	Males	Females
Applied	450	100	600	400
Not applied	150	300	600	400
Total	600	400	1200	800

1. 2; Reqd % = $\frac{400}{450} \times 100 = 88.89\%$

2. 5; Reqd ratio = 300 : 600 = 1 : 2

3. 1; Reqd difference = 2000 – 1000 = 1000

4. 2; Reqd % = $\left(\frac{800-600}{800}\right) \times 100 = 25\%$

5. 3; Reqd total = 150 + 300 + 600 + 400 = 1450

6. 4; Reqd average = $\frac{600+400+1200+800}{2} = \frac{3000}{2} = 1500$

(7-12):

12 pm-2 pm: Total number of bikes sold

$= 64000 \times \frac{25}{100} = 64000 \times \frac{1}{4} = 16000$

Number of Pulsar variants sold = 4000

Sum of number of Avengers and Dominaars sold = 16000 – 4000 = 12000

Number of Avengers sold = $12000 \times \frac{2}{5} = 4800$

Then, A = $\frac{4800}{4000} = 1.2$**(A)**

Number of Dominaars sold = 12000 – 4800 = 7200

Revenue generated by selling Dominaars **(B)** = 7200 × 90000 = 64.8 crore

4 pm - 6 pm: Number of bikes sold

$= 16000 \times \frac{175}{100} = 16000 \times \frac{7}{4} = 28000$

Let number of Avengers sold be 10x.

Then, number of Dominaars sold = $10x \times \frac{160}{100} = 16x$

Number of Pulsars sold = $10x \times \frac{12}{5} = 24x$

Now, 10x + 16x + 24x = 28000

⇒ 50x = 28000 ⇒ x = 560

$\therefore$ Number of Avengers sold = 560 × 10 = 5600

Revenue generated by selling Avengers = 5600 × 72000

Revenue generated by selling Pulsars = 24 × 560 × 84000

Reqd % = $\frac{24 \times 560 \times 8400}{5600 \times 72000} = 280\%$**(C)**

No. of Dominaars sold = 16x = 16 × 560 = 8960

8 pm - 10 pm:

Number of bikes sold = 64000 – (16000 + 28000) = 64000 – 44000 = 20000

Number of Avengers variant sold $= 20000 \times \frac{3}{10} = 6000$

Similarly, Pulsar variants sold $= 20000 \times \frac{5}{10} = 10000$

Dominaars = 4000

Revenue generated by selling Avengers
$= 6000 \times 72000 = 43.2$ crore
Revenue generated by selling Dominaars
$= 4000 \times 90000 = 36$ crores
Reqd difference $= 43.2 - 36 = 7.2$ crore **(D)**
This information can be tabulised as:

Time slot	Avenger	Pulsar	Dominaar	Total
12 pm - 2 pm	4800	4000	7200	16000
4 pm - 6 pm	5600	13440	8960	28000
8 pm - 10 pm	6000	10000	4000	20000

7. 5; A = 1.2
8. 3; B = 64.8 crore
9. 4; C = 280%
10. 1
11. 3; Total bikes sold = 28000
Dominaars sold = 8960

Number of defective variants $= 8960 \times \frac{5}{100} = 448$

Reqd probability $= \frac{^{448}C_1}{^{28000}C_1} = \frac{448}{28000} = \frac{2}{125}$

12. 5; Dominaars purchased by Rudra $= \frac{50}{100} \times 7200 = 3600$

Pulsar purchased by Rudra $= \frac{25}{100} \times 4000 = 1000$

Required profit = 12% of $(36 \times 9000 + 10 \times 84000)$
$= 12 \times (3240000 + 840000) = 4.896$ crore

(13-17):
Length of train M = 20% of 2500 = 500 m

Speed of train M $= 360 \times \frac{80}{360} = 80$ kmph

Length of train J = 24% of 2500 = 600 m

Speed of train J $= 360 \times \frac{70}{360} = 70$ kmph

Length of train L = 12% of 2500 = 300 m

Speed of train L $= 360 \times \frac{50}{360} = 50$ kmph

Length of train S = 16% of 2500 = 400 m

Speed of train S $= 360 \times \frac{100}{360} = 100$ kmph

Length of train T = 28% of 2500 = 700 m

Speed of train T $= 360 \times \frac{60}{360} = 60$ kmph

This can be tabulised as:

Trains	Length (m)	Speed (kmph)
M	500	80
J	600	70
L	300	50
S	400	100
T	700	60

13. 2; Let the length and the speed of train P be xm and y kmph respectively.

Then, as per given information, $x = y \times 72 \times \frac{5}{18}$
$= 20y$ ...(i)

Now, $(x + 500) = (80 - y)\, 79.2 \times \frac{5}{18}$

From (i), we get, $[20y + 500] = 22(80 - y)$
$20y + 500 = 1760 - 22y \Rightarrow 42y = 1260 \Rightarrow y = 30$ kmph
$\therefore x = 20 \times 30 = 600$ m
Let time taken by train M to cross P when both trains are travelling in opposite directions be t seconds.

Then, $(500 + 600) = (80 + 30)t\left(\frac{5}{18}\right) \Rightarrow t = 36$ seconds

14. 5; Let the speed of the car be v kmph.

Then, as per given information, $300 = (v - 50)\, 27 \times \frac{5}{18}$

$\Rightarrow (v - 50) = 40 \Rightarrow v = 90$ kmph
Reduced speed of car = 80% of 90 = 72 kmph
Total distance travelled by car in 2.5 hours
$= 72 \times 2.5 = 180$ km

15. 4; Let the length of the platform and traiin Q be x metres.

According to the question, $(600 + x) = 70 \times 72 \times \frac{5}{18}$

$\Rightarrow 600 + x = 1400 \Rightarrow x = 800$ m

Now, $(600 + 800) = (126 - 70)t \times \frac{5}{18}$

$\Rightarrow 1400 = 56 \times t \times \frac{5}{18} \Rightarrow t = 90$ seconds

16. 3; Let the length of the platform be x metres.

As per information given, $(400 + x) = 100 \times 36 \times \frac{5}{18}$

$\Rightarrow x = 600$ m
The persons is running inside the train at speed 20 kmph in opposite direction as that of train. Then effective speed of person inside train $= 100 - 20 = 80$ kmph

Time taken by person to cross the train

$= \frac{600}{80} \times \frac{18}{5} = 27$ seconds

17. 1; Let the speed of the person be x kmph.
Then, as per information given,

$300 = (50 + x)\, 13.5 \left(\frac{5}{18}\right) \Rightarrow 50 + x = 80 \Rightarrow x = 30$ kmph

Reduced speed of the person $= \frac{x}{3} = 10$ kmph

Now, $700 = (60 + 10)t\left(\frac{5}{18}\right) \Rightarrow t = 36$ seconds

18. 3; Principal = ₹25000; SI = 25%, and CI = 30%

So, total amount $= 25000 \times \frac{125}{100} \times \frac{130}{100} \times \frac{125}{100} \times \frac{130}{100} \times \frac{125}{100}$

$= 82519.53$

Total interest earned $= 82519.53 - 25000$

$= 57519.53 \approx$ ₹57520

19. 1; Interest received in Scheme D

$= \frac{12000 \times 6 \times 15}{100} =$ ₹10800

Amount invested in Scheme B for 4 years with SI

$= \frac{10800}{2} = 5400$

Interest $= \frac{5400 \times 14 \times 4}{100} =$ ₹3024

Now, ratio of interest received = 4 : 5

So, interest in Scheme C $= \frac{3024}{4} \times 5 =$ ₹3780

Hence, rate of interest in C $= \frac{3780 \times 100}{5400 \times 4} = 17.5\%$

20. 2; Let the sum invested in B at CI be ₹x.

Now, $1.44x = x\left(1 + \frac{r}{100}\right)^2 \Rightarrow 120 = 100 + r \Rightarrow r = 20\%$

Then, rate of SI in A $= \frac{20}{2}\% = 10\%$

Interest received from A at SI $= \frac{10000 \times 2 \times 10}{100} =$ ₹2000

Similarly, interest received from B at 20% per annum for 2 years equivalent to CI $= 20 + 20 + \frac{20 \times 20}{100} = 44\%$

Si, CI = 44% of 10000 = 4400

And, total interest earned = 2000 + 4400 = ₹6400

21. 5; Let the initial sum be 100n.

After 7 years, amount $= 100n + \frac{194}{100} \times 100n = 294n$

Let b = sum invested in scheme C with CI.

Now, $294n = b\left(1 + \frac{40}{100}\right)^2 \Rightarrow b = 150n$

Interest on SI for 5 years = 150n – 100n = 50n

So, $50n = 100n \times \frac{r}{100} \times 5 \Rightarrow r = 10\%$

22. 2; **Quantity I:** Amount invested in D at SI is ₹25000.

Rate of interest $= \frac{40}{2} = 20\%$

So, amount received in scheme D after 4 years.

$= 25000 \times \left(1 + \frac{20}{100}\right)^4 =$ ₹51840

Quantity II: Amount invested in scheme F = ₹30000

Rate of interest = 25%

Then, SI after 7 years will be $\frac{30000 \times 7 \times 25}{100} =$ ₹52500

Hence, Quantity I < Quantity II

Practice Set 17

Directions (Q. 1-5): Study the following table carefully and answer the given questions. The table shows the number of students in different sections of five different schools.

School	Total	Section A	Section B	Section C
P	—	—	—	15
Q	20	6	—	—
R	—	8	12	—
S	24	—	—	8
T	—	12	18	—

1. A group of two students has to be formed from School T such that the group contains at least one student from Section C. The number of ways in which this can be possible is 195. A committee of five students is to be formed from School T such that the committee contains 2 students from Section A, 1 student from Section B and 2 students from Section C. Find the number of ways in which this can be possible.
1) 12870 2) 17820 3) 18720
4) 15640 5) 14560

2. A group of four students has to be formed from School R such that the group contains one student from each section and the remaining one from any of the sections. The number of ways in which this can be possible is 25920. Find the number of students in Section C from school R.
1) 6 2) 18 3) 12
4) 10 5) None of the given options

3. In school Q, the number of students in Section C is 75% of the number of students in Section B.
Quantity I: In Committee N, five students are to be chosen from School Q such that the committee contains at least one student from each section. Find the number of ways in which Committee N can be formed.
Quantity II: In Committee M, five students are to be chosen from School Q such that the committee contains at least one student from section A. Find the number of ways in which Committee M can be formed.
Solve for the given quantities and compare these values and mark the answer accordingly.
1) Quantity I > Quantity II
2) Quantity I < Quantity II
3) Quantity I ≤ Quantity II
4) Quantity I ≥ Quantity II
5) Quantity I = Quantity II or the relation cannot be established

4. Find the total number of students in School P.
Statement I: All the students in Section B from school P are shaking hands with each other and the total number of handshakes is 105.
Statement II: All the students in School P are shaking hands with each other and the total number of handshakes is 780.
The above question can be answered using which of the following statements?
1) Statement (I) only 2) Statement (II) only
3) Both the given statements together
4) Either of the given two statements
5) None of the given statements

5. Committees of three members each are to be formed in School Q and School S. The number of possible ways the committee contains three students from Section C in School S is what per cent of the number of possible ways the committee contains three students from Section A in School Q?
1) 250 2) 140 3) 180
4) None of the given options 5) 280

Directions (Q. 6-7): Read the given information and data carefully and answer the questions given below.

Kritika and Tulika invested ₹3000 together. Kritika invested her amount at compound interest for $\frac{a}{10}$ years at a% rate of interest and Tulika invested half of her amount at compound interest and the remaining half at simple interest at the same rate of interest for the same time period.

[It is given that $\frac{a}{10}$ is a natural number.]

6. What is the value of 'a'?
Statement I: The ratio of investments of Kritika and Tulika is 1 : 2 and the total sum received by them together after a particular time at a% rate of interest is ₹4280.
Statement II: The simple interest received by Tulika is ₹40 less than the compound interest received by her.
Statement III: The sum of the simple interest and the compound interest received by Tulika after a certain time

at a% rate of interest is ₹2500.

Which of the above statements is/are redundant to find the answer to the given question?

1) Only statement III alone
2) Only statement II alone
3) All statements I, II and III even together are not sufficient
4) Only either statements I and II or statements II and III
5) Only statement I alone

7. What amount is received by Tulika after $\frac{a}{10}$ years?

Statement I: The value of 'a' can be determined by the equation: $3a^2 - 55a - 100 = 0$.
Statement II: Kritika invested ₹1000 less than the amount invested by Tulika.
Statement III: The interest received by Kritika and Tulika together after $\frac{a}{10}$ years is ₹1280.

Which of the following statements is/are necessary to find the answer?

1) Only statements I and II together are sufficient
2) Either statement I alone or III alone is sufficient
3) Only statements I and III together are sufficient.
4) Statement I and either statement II or III together are sufficient
5) Only statements II and III together are sufficient

Directions (Q. 8-13): Study the following graph carefully and answer the given questions.

Vineet, Kushagra, Shobit, Garvit and Rudra were collecting money for a charity. They collected notes in denominations of ₹10, ₹20, ₹50 and ₹100.

The table gives partial information about the number of notes of each denomination collected by them.

	₹10	**₹20**	**₹50**	**₹100**
Vineet	10	4		2
Kushagra	—	8	—	#
Shobit	12	10	#	—
Garvit	—	—	4	2
Rudra	—	6	—	4

Some of the fields are empty. Candidates are required to calculate and fill those fields as and when required.

Note: (#) denotes they did not collect notes of that denomination.

The following additional information is also given:

- Kushagra and Garvit collected equal number of ₹50 notes. Only one of the two collected more than ₹600.
- Rudra collected 18 notes and the highest amount.
- The total number of ₹50 notes collected was 18.
- Vineet collected ₹680 while Shobit collected ₹720.
- No one collected more than 26 notes.
- The amount collected by each of them was less than ₹800.

8. Which of the following statements is/are true?

Statement I: The difference between the total amount collected by Rudra and Vineet is ₹180.
Statement II: The ratio of the total amount collected by Shobit to that by Vineet is 1 : 1.
Statement III: Total amount collected by Vineet is 5.55% less than the total amount collected by Shobit.

1) All the three
2) Only III
3) None is true
4) Both I and II
5) None of these

9. **Quantity I:** If a person takes one note from Kushagra's collected notes, the probability of getting a ₹10 note is $\frac{7}{13}$. Total amount collected by Kushagra is what percentage of the total amount collected by Shobit?

Quantity II: Total amount collected by Vineet is what percentage of the total amount collected by Rudra?

Solve for the given quantities and compare these values and mark the answer accordingly.

1) Quantity I > Quantity II
2) Quantity I < Quantity II
3) Quantity I ≤ Quantity II
4) Quantity I ≥ Quantity II
5) Quantity I = Quantity II or the relation cannot be established

10. Find the maximum possible number of ₹10 notes collected by Garvit if the total amount collected by him is equal to the total amount collected by Vineet.

1) 6
2) 16
3) 10
4) 8
5) 12

11. Which of the following statements is/are definitely true?

Statement I: The total money collected by all of them was ₹3340.
Statement II: Rudra collected more than ₹600.
Statement III: Kushagra collected the least amount.

1) Statement I and III only
2) None of the given statements is true
3) Statement II only
4) Statement II and III only
5) Statement I only

12. How many ₹10 notes were collected by Kushagra?

Statement I: The amount collected by Kushagra was ₹500.
Statement II: The number of notes collected by Kushagra is equal to that collected by Shobit.

Which of the following statements is/are necessary to find the answer?

1) Only I
2) Only II
3) Either I or II
4) Both I and II together
5) Neither I nor II

13. The average number of notes collected by Vineet of all

denominations is **approximately** what per cent more or less than the average number of notes collected by Rudra of all denominations?

1) 30 2) 22 3) 28
4) 12 5) None of the given options

Directions (Q. 14-18): Given below are four statements (I), (II), (III) and (IV). In these statements four values are given. Solve these values from the statements. Put these values further into the paragraph given below and solve the questions further. Read the given data carefully and answer the questions given below.

(I): Solve the numeric series:
472 497 272 **(A)** –328

(II): Solve the numeric series:
(A), 299, 74.75, **(B),** 2.49

(III): Solve the equation:
$(\sim B)^2 - 5^3 + 99 - 42 + 132 = (C)$; **where (~B) denotes the approximate value of (B)**

(IV): Solve the equation: $(\sqrt{C}) + \frac{A+3}{(\sim B)} - 17 = (D)$

Rochak invested ₹5000, which is $\frac{1}{4}$ of his monthly salary, in the Scheme 'My Money' for **(D)** months at **(~B)%** interest and gained an interest **(X)**. After investing in the scheme he bought five different types of books at different prices. The price of the first book is ₹200. The price of the third book is 20% more than the second book, which is 25% more than the first book. The fourth book costs ₹[10% of {(X) – 25}], which is 30% less than the fifth book. He spent 10 times the average of all five books as his medical allowance. With 50% of the remaining salary he entered into a business partnership with Rovil for 12 months whereas Rovil invested 100 times of **(D)** for 12 months. At the end of the year the difference between their total investments is **₹(Y).**

14. If the value of (C) is decreased by 120 and accordingly the value of (D) also changes and if Rochak invests the same amount of money on SI for (D) months at (~B)% per annum, what will be the amount received by Rochak?

1) ₹4200 2) ₹2800 3) ₹3200
4) ₹3500 5) ₹2100

15. If Rovil has invested 90 times of (D), what will be the the ratio of profit of Rovil to that of Rochak at the end of the year?

1) 18 : 17 2) 18 : 19 3) 17 : 14
4) 13 : 9 5) None of the given options

16. The value of (Y) is what per cent of the quarterly salary earned by Rochak?

1) 16 2) 28 3) 18 4) 12 5) 20

17. If Rochak got 10% and 15% discount on the first and fifth book respectively, what is the percentage of money he spent in buying all the books with respect to his monthly salary? Note that prices of some other books will also change as they are inter-related.

1) 12.5 2) 7.25 3) 4.25
4) 6.75 5) None of the given options

18. If Rochak has bought the third book at 40% less than the second book, what is the average value (in rupees) of all the five books?

1) Cannot be determined 2) 250 3) 190
4) 270 5) 290

Directions (Q. 19-21): Study the following information carefully and answer the questions given below.

Kalpana and Khyati are best friends. They both own two versions of KTM Duke bike. Kalpana owns a KTM Duke 250cc bike which uses A-type petrol, whereas Khyati owns a KTM Duke 390cc bike which uses B-type petrol. Kalpana's bike's average is 25% lesser than Khyati's bike. Here, average is given in terms of litres of fuel per kilometre (not in terms of kilometre per litre), which means Kalpana's bike consumes lesser petrol for a given distance. It is known that B-type petrol price is 40% lesser than A-type petrol.

19. The expense of cost per kilometre of Kalpana's bike to that of Khyati's bike is in the ratio of

1) 5 : 4 2) 4 : 5 3) 5 : 3 4) 2 : 7 5) 9 : 1

20. If it has been found out that Khyati's bike gave an average of 25 kilometres per litre and the price of one litre of A-type petrol is ₹70, then the difference in the travelling cost per kilometre of both the bikes is (in ₹)

1) 0.21 2) 0.42 3) 4.21 4) 0.40 5) 1.20

21. Kalpana purchased the bike at a cost of ₹5,00,000. If the conditions given in the above question hold good and she sold the bike at a cost of ₹4,56,000 after incurring additional expenditure on the bike equivalent to a journey of 20,000 km by that bike, then the approximate loss per cent incurred by her in the transaction is

1) 12% 2) 20% 3) 19%
4) 16% 5) None of the above

Answers and explanations

1. 2; Number of students in Section C from School T = y
Total number of students in T
= y + 12 + 18 = y + 30
Number of ways = ${}^{y}C_1 \times {}^{30}C_1 + {}^{y}C_2 = 195$

$\Rightarrow y(30) + \frac{y(y-1)}{1 \times 2} = 195$

$\Rightarrow (y + 65)(y - 6) = 0 \Rightarrow y = 6, -65$

Total number of students in school T
= 30 + 6 = 36 (eliminating negative value)
Required number of ways = ${}^{12}C_2 \times {}^{18}C_1 \times {}^{6}C_2$
= 6 × 11 × 18 × 3 × 5 = 17820

2. 4; Let the number of students in Section C of School R be x.

Total number of students in school R
$= x + 8 + 12 = 20 + x$
Number of possible ways
$= {}^{8}C_1 \times {}^{12}C_1 \times {}^{x}C_1 \times ({}^{20+x-3}C_1) = 25920$
$\Rightarrow 8 \times 12 \times x \times (17 + x) = 25920$
$\Rightarrow x(17 + x) = 270 \Rightarrow x = 10$

3. 1; Number of students in Section B of School Q = x
Number of students in Section C of School Q

$= \frac{75}{100} \times x = \frac{3x}{4}$

Total number of students in Section B and C from

School Q $= 20 - 6 = 14 = x + \frac{3x}{4} \Rightarrow x = 8$

So, $\frac{3x}{4} = 6$

Quantity I: Number of ways

$= {}^{6}C_1 \times {}^{8}C_1 \times {}^{6}C_1 \times {}^{(20-3)}C_2 = 6 \times 8 \times 6 \times \frac{17 \times 16}{1 \times 2} = 39168$

Quantity II: In Committee M, five students are to be formed from School Q such that there is at least one student from Section A.

Number of ways $= {}^{6}C_1 \times {}^{14}C_4 + {}^{6}C_2 \times {}^{14}C_3 + {}^{6}C_3 \times {}^{14}C_2 + {}^{6}C_4 \times {}^{14}C_1 + {}^{6}C_5$
$= 6006 + 5460 + 1820 + 210 + 6 = 13502$

Hence, Quantity I > Quantity II

4. 2; **From I:** Number of students in Section B from School P = n

No. of handshakes $= {}^{n}C_2 = 105$

$\Rightarrow n(n - 1) = 210 \Rightarrow n = 15 \therefore n = 15$

But from this we cannot find the total number of students in School P.

From II: Total number of students in P = x

No. of handshakes $= {}^{x}C_2 = 780 \Rightarrow \frac{x(x-1)}{1 \times 2} = 780$

$\Rightarrow x(x - 1) = 780 \times 2 = 1560 \Rightarrow x = 40$

So, statement II alone is sufficient to answer the question.

5. 5; Desired number of ways in School S

$= {}^{8}C_3 = \frac{8 \times 7 \times 6}{3 \times 2 \times 1} = 56$

Desired number of ways in School Q $= {}^{6}C_3 = 20$

Required % $= \frac{56}{20} \times 100 = 280\%$

6. 3; Let investment of Tulika be P.
$\therefore$ Investment of Kritika = 3000 – P

For Kritika:

$$CI = (3000 - P)\left[\left(1 + \frac{a}{100}\right)^{\frac{a}{10}} - 1\right]$$

For Tulika:

$$CI = \frac{P}{2}\left[\left(1 + \frac{a}{100}\right)^{\frac{a}{10}} - 1\right]$$

$$SI = \frac{P \times a \times a}{2 \times 100 \times 10} = \frac{a^2 P}{2000}$$

Statement I: Let time be 't' years.

Investment of Tulika $= P = \frac{2}{3} \times 3000 = 2000$

Investment of Kritika $= 3000 - P$
$= 3000 - 2000 = 1000$

For Kritika:

$$CI = 1000 \times \left[\left(1 + \frac{a}{100}\right)^{t} - 1\right]$$

For Tulika:

$$CI = 1000 \times \left[\left(1 + \frac{a}{100}\right)^{t} - 1\right]$$

$$SI = \frac{100 \times a \times t}{10 \times 1000} = at$$

Total sum received by them together after given years (t) = ₹4280

$$4280 - 3000 = 1000 \times \left[\left(1 + \frac{a}{100}\right)^{t} - 1\right] + 1000 \times \left[\left(1 + \frac{a}{100}\right)^{t} - 1\right] + at$$

From the above equation, the value of 'a' can't be determined.

Statement II:

$$SI = \frac{P \times a \times a}{2 \times 100 \times 10},\quad CI = \frac{P}{2}\left[\left(1 + \frac{a}{100}\right)^{\frac{a}{10}} - 1\right]$$

$$40 = \left[\frac{P}{2}\left\{\left(1 + \frac{a}{100}\right)^{\frac{a}{10}} - 1\right\} - \left(\frac{a^2}{1000}\right)\right]$$

Again, the value of 'a' can't be determined.

Statement III: For Tulika, let time be 'n' years.
SI + CI = 2500

$$\Rightarrow \frac{P \times a \times n}{2 \times 1000} + \frac{P}{2}\left[\left(1 + \frac{a}{100}\right)^{n} - 1\right] = 2500$$

So, the value of 'a' can't be determined.
Even on combining all three equations, we have four variables but only three equations. So, the value of 'a' can't be determined.

7. 4; **Statement I:** $3a^2 - 55a - 100 = 0 \Rightarrow a = 20, -1.67$

For Tulika: $CI = \frac{P}{2}\left[\left(1+\frac{20}{100}\right)^{\frac{20}{10}} - 1\right] = \frac{11P}{50}$

And, $\frac{a^2P}{2000} = \frac{20 \times 20 \times P}{2000} = \frac{P}{5}$

Statement II: $P - 3000 + P = 1000 \Rightarrow P = 2000$

Statement III: $1280 = (3000 - P)\left[\left(1+\frac{a}{100}\right)^{\frac{a}{10}} - 1\right] + \frac{P}{2}\left[\left(1+\frac{a}{100}\right)^{\frac{a}{10}} - 1\right] + \frac{a^2P}{2000}$

From I and II: $SI = \frac{P}{5} = \frac{2000}{5} = ₹400$

$CI = \frac{11P}{50} = ₹440$

Total amount received by Tulika after $\frac{a}{10}$ years

$= 2000 + 400 + 440 = ₹2840$

From II and III: $1280 = 2000\left[\left(1+\frac{a}{100}\right)^{\frac{a}{10}} - 1\right] + a^2$

So, these two statements are not sufficient.

From I and III: For Kritika:

$CI = (3000 - P)\left[\left(1+\frac{20}{100}\right)^{\frac{20}{10}} - 1\right]$

$= (3000 - P)\left(\frac{11}{25}\right)$

For Kritika and Tulika:

$1280 = (3000 - P)\left(\frac{11}{25}\right) + \frac{11P}{50} + \frac{P}{5}$

$\therefore P = 2000$

$SI = \frac{P}{5} = \frac{2000}{5} = 400;$

$CI = \frac{11P}{50} = 440$

Total amount received $= 2000 + 400 + 440 = ₹2840$

Hence, either statement II or III and statement I is required.

(8-13):

Vineet: Total amount

$= 10 \times 10 + 20 \times 4 + 50 \times x + 100 \times 2 = 680$

$\Rightarrow 50x = 300 \Rightarrow x = 6$

Shobit: Total amount

$= 10 \times 12 + 20 \times 10 + 100 \times y = 720$

$\Rightarrow 120 + 200 + 100y = 720 \Rightarrow 100y = 400$

$\Rightarrow y = \frac{400}{100} = 4$

Total number of ₹50 notes is 18.

Kushagra and Garvit collected equal number of ₹50 notes = 4

z → Remaining number of ₹50 notes collected by Rudra.

$18 = 6 + 4 + 4 + z \Rightarrow z = 4$

Rudra: Total amount

$= 10(18 - 6 - 4 - 4) + 20 \times 6 + 50 \times 4 + 100 \times 4$

$= 40 + 120 + 200 + 400 = 760$

The above calculation can be tabulised as below:

	₹10	₹20	₹50	₹100	Total amount	No. of notes
Vineet	10	4	6	2	680	22
Kushagra	—	8	4	#	—	—
Shobit	12	10	#	4	720	26
Garvit	—	—	4	2	—	—
Rudra	4	6	4	4	760	18
Total			18	12		

8. 2; **From I:** Total amount collected by Rudra = ₹760

Total amount collected by Vineet = ₹680

$\therefore$ Difference $= 760 - 680 = 80 \neq 180$

So, statement I is false.

From II: Total amount collected by Vineet = ₹680

Total amount collected by Shobit = ₹720

$\therefore$ Required ratio $= 720 : 680 \neq 1 : 1$

So, statement II is false.

From III: Total amount collected by Vineet = ₹680

Total amount collected by Shobit = ₹720

$\therefore$ Required % $= \frac{720 - 680}{720} \times 100 = 5.55\%$

Hence, statement III is true.

9. 2; **Quantity I:** Total number of notes collected by Kushagra $= 8 + 4 + x = x + 12$

Probability of a ₹10 note $= \frac{7}{13} = \frac{^{x}C_1}{^{12+x}C_1}$

$\Rightarrow \frac{7}{13}=\frac{x}{12+x} \Rightarrow 84=6x \Rightarrow x=14$

Now, total amount collected by him
$=14\times10+8\times20+4\times50$
$=140+160+200=₹500$

$\therefore$ Required % $=\frac{500}{720}\times100=69.44\%$

Quantity II: Required % $=\frac{680}{760}\times100=89.47\%$

Hence, Quantity I < Quantity II

10. 5; Max possible number of notes = 26
Max number of ₹10 and ₹20 notes = 26 – 6 = 20
Let the number of ₹20 notes be a and ₹10 notes be (20 – a).
Total amount collected by Garvit = ₹680
$\Rightarrow 680=4\times50+10(20-a)+20\times a+100\times2$
$\Rightarrow 10a=80 \Rightarrow a=8$
Max number of ₹10 notes collected by Garvit
$=20-8=12$

11. 4; **Statement I:** We do not know Kushagra and Garvit's total amount. Hence, this statement is not true.
Statement II: Rudra collected ₹760, which is more than ₹600. Hence, this statement is true.
Statement III: We do not know Kushagra's total amount. But since no one collected more than 26 notes, he can possibly have at most 26 – (8 + 4) = 14 notes of ₹10 denomination. So he can have maximum ₹500. Which means Garvit collected more than ₹600. So, this statement is definitely true.
Hence, statement II and III are true.

12. 3; **From statement I:** Total amount $=500=20\times8+10\times a+50\times4 \Rightarrow a=14$
From that we can answer the question.
From statement II: Number of notes collected by Kushagra = Number of notes collected by Shobit = 26
$\therefore$ Number of ₹10 notes = 26 – 8 – 4 = 14
From that we can answer the question.
Hence, either statement I alone or statement II alone is sufficient to answer the question.

13. 2; Average number of notes collected by Vineet

$=\frac{10+4+6+2}{4}=\frac{22}{4}=5.5$

Average number of notes collected by Rudra

$=\frac{4+6+4+4}{4}=\frac{18}{4}=4.5$

$\therefore$ Required % $=\frac{5.5-4.5}{4.5}\times100=\frac{1}{4.5}\times100$

$=22.22\%\approx22\%$

14. 4; $\sqrt{169}+\frac{(897+3)}{15}-17=(D) \Rightarrow 13+\frac{900}{15}-17=D$

$\Rightarrow D=13+60-17=56$

So, SI $=\frac{5000\times56\times15}{12\times100}=\frac{42000}{12}=₹3500$

15. 1; Rovil's investment $=90\times60=₹5400$
Rochak's investment = ₹5100
$\therefore$ Reqd ratio = 5400 : 5100 = 18 : 17

16. 3; Monthly salary = ₹20000
Quarterly salary $=20000\times3=₹60000$

$\therefore$ Required % $=\frac{10800}{60000}\times100=18\%$

17. 2; First book with discount = 200 – 20 = ₹180

Second book $=180\times\frac{125}{100}=₹225$

Third book $=225\times\frac{120}{100}=₹270$

Fourth book $=\left(\frac{10}{100}\times3750\right)-25=₹350$

Fifth book $=350\times\frac{100}{70}=₹500$

With discount of 15% = 500 – 75 = ₹425
Total money spent = 180 + 225 + 270 + 350 + 425 = ₹1450

$\therefore$ Required % of money spent $=\frac{1450}{20000}\times100=7.25\%$

18. 5; First book = ₹200

Second book $=200\times\frac{125}{100}=₹250$

Third book $=250\times\frac{60}{100}=₹150$

Fourth book $=\left(\frac{10}{100}\times3750\right)-25=₹350$

Fifth book $=350\times\frac{100}{70}=₹500$

So, required average $=\frac{200+250+150+350+500}{5}$

= ₹290

19. 1; It is given that Kalpana's bike's average (litres per km) is 25% lesser than Khyati's bike.
Means, Kalpana's bike consumes 25% less of A-type petrol per km than Khyati's bike's consumption of B-type petrol per km.
Let Khyati's bike consume N litres of B-type petrol.

$\Rightarrow$ Kalpana's bike consumes $\frac{3N}{4}$ litres of A-type petrol.

Also, $\frac{3}{5}$ (cost per litre A-type petrol)
= Cost per litre B-type petrol

$\Rightarrow \frac{\text{Cost of A-type petrol}}{\text{Cost of B-type petrol}} = \frac{5}{3}$

Now, $\frac{\text{Cost per km (Kalpana)}}{\text{Cost per km (Khyati)}} = \frac{5 \times \frac{3N}{4}}{3N} = \frac{5}{4}$

$\therefore$ Required ratio = 5 : 4

20. 2; Khyati's bike travels 25 km in 1 litre of B-type petrol.

$\Rightarrow$ In 1 km, it consumes $\frac{1}{25}$ = 0.04 litre of B-type petrol.

So, consumption per km of Kalpana's bike

$= \frac{3}{4} \times 0.04 = 0.03$ litre

Now, let price of 1 litre of B-type petrol = ₹N

$\Rightarrow \frac{70}{N} = \frac{5}{3}$ (from above question) $\Rightarrow$ N = ₹42

Per km travelling cost of Khyati

$= 42 \times 0.04 =$ ₹1.68

And, per km travelling cost of Kalpana

$= 70 \times 0.03 =$ ₹2.10

$\therefore$ Required difference = 2.10 – 1.68 = ₹0.42

21. 4; From above question, cost of travelling per km = ₹2.10

So, in 20000 km, it will cost = 2.1 × 20000 = ₹42000

$\therefore$ Total expense of Kalpana = ₹(500000 + 42000) = ₹542000

Hence, loss % = $\frac{542000 - 456000}{542000} \times 100$

= 15.86% ≈ 16% (approx)

Practice Set 18

Directions (Q. 1-6): Study the following data carefully and answer the questions:

The information given below shows the method by which electricity bill is generated. There are two categories—Domestic and Commercial—and parameters to calculate the bill are different for both the categories.

For both categories there are three ranges P, Q and R and the table given below shows the fixed charge (rupees) and per unit charge (rupees) of those three ranges for the two categories:

Categories	Range P		Range Q		Range R	
	Fixed charge	Per unit charge	Fixed charge	Per unit charge	Fixed charge	Per unit charge
Domestic	200	5	400	8	800	10
Commercial	250	7.5	600	10	1250	15

Formula to calculate electricity bill is given below:

- Net amount = Fixed charges + Energy charges + Electricity Duty – Rebate
- Energy charges = Charged units (KW) × Per unit charge
- Rebate = 10% of fixed charge + 25% of energy charges

Note: If not specified the number of days in a month should be taken as 30.

1. A family (domestic) comes under range R of the connection and the total monthly electricity bill amount paid by the family is ₹2400 while the average consumption per day of electricity in the family is 5 KW, then what is the electricity duty fee of the family in a month?
   1) ₹500 2) ₹555 3) ₹635 4) ₹545 5) ₹440
2. There are two shops M and N (both commercial) - M comes under connection range P while N comes under connection range Q. If the average consumption per day of both the shops is 2.5 KW and electricity duty fee for the shops is ₹497.50, then the monthly electricity bill for shop M is what per cent of the monthly electricity bill for shop N? (up to two decimal places)
   1) 85.40 2) 71.52 3) 96.45
   4) 62.25 5) None of the given options
3. What is the difference between the monthly electricity bill for a family (domestic) and for a shopkeeper (commercial) if the average consumption per day of electricity in the family is 3 KW while the average consumption per day of electricity in the shop is 4 KW? The connection range for family and shop are Q and P respectively and the monthly electricity duty for family and shop are ₹600 and ₹500 respectively.
   1) ₹120 2) ₹125 3) ₹100 4) ₹85 5) ₹80
4. A business (commercial) comes under connection range R and electricity duty for the business is ₹325. If the total monthly electricity bill amount paid by the business is ₹2800, then what is the average consumption per day of electricity in that business?
   1) 2 kW 2) 8 kW 3) 5 kW 4) 6 kW 5) 4 kW
5. If in present month, the connection range of a family (domestic) is P while in previous month, it becomes range Q. If the electricity duty and the average consumption per day of electricity of the family for both the months are ₹450 and 2 KW respectively, then what will be the ratio of the monthly electricity bill of the family in present month to that in previous month?
   1) 11 : 14 2) 17 : 23 3) 14 : 11 4) 19 : 17 5) 19 : 26
6. Ankit and Arijit are two friends who live with their families having houses in range Q and R respectively. In the month of October, electricity duty that is charged from Ankit and Arijit is ₹325 for both whereas the consumption of electricity for both of them are 125 KW and 80KW respectively. The difference between the monthly electricity bills of Arijit and Ankit is what per cent of the Ankit electricity bill?
   1) 155 2) 164 3) 124 4) 168 5) 94

Directions (Q. 7-11): Study the following information carefully and answer the questions given below.

In a company three kinds of grains - rice, wheat and corn - are liked by the employees. The total number of employees working in the company is 800, and 42.5% employees do not like any of these three grains.

The number of employees who like rice is 10 less than the number of employees who like corn, and the number of employees who like all the three kinds of grains is 5% of the number of total employees. The number of employees who like rice and wheat but not corn is half of the number of employees who like all the three kinds of grains, and the number of employees who like rice and corn but not wheat is 10 less than the number of employees who like wheat only. The number of employees who like wheat and corn but not rice is 10 more than the number of employees who like rice and wheat but not corn. The number of employees who like only rice is 10 more than twice the number of employees who like wheat only.

7. What is the difference between the numbers of employees who like wheat and rice?
1) 82 2) 75 3) 90 4) 120 5) 65

8. What is the number of employees who like exactly two kinds of grains?
1) 80 2) 95 3) 100 4) 125 5) 112

9. The number of employees who like only wheat is what per cent of the number of employees who like rice and corn but not wheat?
1) 100 2) 75 3) 120 4) 125 5) 150

10. The number of employees who like all the three grains together is what per cent of the average number of employees who like only two of the three grains mentioned above?
1) 125 2) 80 3) 75 4) 110 5) 120

11. What is the ratio of the number of employees who like at least two out of the three grains mentioned to the number of employees who do not like any of the three grains mentioned?
1) 17 : 5 2) 5 : 17
3) None of the given options
4) 13 : 17 5) 7 : 17

Directions (Q. 12-16): Study the following data carefully and answer the questions:

In a factory, labour productivity is calculated on a yearly basis. There are total two types of productivity: Labour productivity per hour and Labour productivity per worker. The formula to calculate labour productivity is given below:

Labour productivity per hour

$$= \frac{\text{Worth of output produced}}{\text{Total input hours}}$$

Labour productivity per worker

$$= \frac{\text{Worth of output produced}}{\text{Total input workers}}$$

Also, there is one more term called efficiency.
Formula to calculate efficiency is given below:

$$\% \text{Efficiency} = \frac{\text{Standard labour hours}}{\text{Number of hours worked}} \times 100$$

The table given below shows the standard labour hours and the total number of workers allotted for the work in five different years in the company:

Years	Standard Labour Hours	Total Workers Input
2015	160	80
2016	120	120
2017	240	100
2018	300	160
2019	250	150

12. If the labour productivity per hour and the labour productivity per worker of the company in 2017 is ₹90 per hour and ₹180 per worker, then what will be the percentage efficiency of the company in 2017?
1) 120% 2) 80% 3) 115% 4) 125% 5) 90%

13. If the labour productivity per worker and the efficiency of the company in 2016 are ₹175 per worker and 120% respectively, then what is the labour productivity per hour of the company in 2016?
1) ₹210 2) ₹223 3) ₹175 4) ₹140 5) ₹340

14. If the efficiency of the company in 2019 is 62.5% and the total worth of output produced by the company in 2019 is ₹18600, then what is the difference between the labour productivity per hour and the labour productivity per worker of the company in 2019?
1) 84.6 2) 77.5 3) 78
4) 72.25 5) None of the given options

15. If in 2015, the efficiency of the workforce of the company is $66\frac{2}{3}\%$ and the labour productivity per hour is ₹105 per hour, then what is the total worth of the output produced by the company in 2015?
1) ₹54200 2) ₹25200 3) ₹36800
4) ₹22500 5) ₹18900

16. If the efficiency of the company in 2018 is 125% and the labour productivity per hour of the company in 2018 is ₹75 per hour, then what is the labour productivity per worker (of the company in 2018)?
1) ₹112.50 2) ₹96.75 3) ₹125.75
4) ₹145.25 5) ₹115.50

Directions (Q. 17-22): Study the following data carefully and answer the questions:

In a location there are five families P, Q, R, S and T who consume water. The table given below shows the number of members in their family and the ratio of the number of adults to that of kids in those families.

Families	Total Members	Ratio (Adults : Kids)
P	24	3 : 1
Q	16	5 : 3
R	20	3 : 2
S	12	2 : 1
T	18	1 : 2

Total expense on water of a family is given by the formula below:

- Expense on water = (10 × total consumption of water by adults) + (5 × total consumption of water by kids)
- Average consumption of water by an adult = (Total consumption by adults)/number of adults
- Average consumption of water by a kid = (Total consumption by kids)/number of kids.

Note: Consumption of water is in litres.

17. If the total expenses on water by family S is ₹1040 and the total consumption of water by adults is 80 litres more than that by kids, then the average consumption of water by a kid is what per cent of the average consumption of water by an adult?
1) 25 2) 66.66 3) 33.33
4) 50 5) None of the given options

18. The ratio of the average consumption of water by an adult to that by a kid is 4: 3 and the income of family Q is ₹30625, out of which 4% is spent on water. What is the total consumption of water (in litres) of family Q?
1) 125 2) 150 3) 145 4) 95 5) 160

19. The average consumption of water by adults of family P is 16 litres and the ratio of the total consumption of water by an adult to that by a kid is 24 : 5. If out of its total income, family P spent 6% on water, then what is the income of family P?
1) ₹53000 2) ₹52800 3) ₹5250 4) ₹5300 5) ₹64000

20. Total expenditure on electricity by family T is ₹112 and the ratio of expenses on electricity to that on water is 8: 5. If the ratio of total consumption of water by adults to that by kids is 2 : 3, then what is the difference between the average consumption of water (in litres) by an adult to that by a kid?

1) $\frac{2}{5}$ 2) $\frac{1}{4}$ 3) $\frac{1}{3}$ 4) $\frac{1}{2}$ 5) $\frac{1}{6}$

21. The difference between the average consumption of water by an adult and that by a kid is 12 litres and the ratio of the total consumption of water by adults to thet by kids is 9: 4. What is the total expense of water consumed by family R?
1) ₹2580 2) ₹5250 3) ₹6340 4) ₹6240 5) ₹5280

22. There is another family Z in which the number of members is the average of the total number of members from all the given families together and the ratio of the number of adults to that of kids in that family is 5 : 1. Out of the total monthly salary of family Z, they spend half of it on food and rent, and half of what they spent on food and rent is spent on clothing. Rest of their family income is spent in the ratio of 1 : 2 on water bill and savings respectively. If it is given that each adult and each kid from family Z uses 25 and 22 litres of water respectively in the month and the water is charged at ₹5 per unit of usage, then what is the annual income of family Z?
1) ₹26460 2) ₹35640 3) ₹28540
4) ₹317520 5) None of the given options

Directions (Q. 23-25): Study the following information carefully and answer the questions given below.

Kalpana and Khyati are best friends. They both own two versions of KTM Duke bike. Kalpana owns a KTM Duke 250cc bike which uses A-type petrol, whereas Khyati owns a KTM Duke 390cc bike which uses B-type petrol. Kalpana's bike's average is 25% lesser than Khyati's bike. Here, average is given in terms of litres of fuel per kilometre (not in terms of kilometre per litre), which means Kalpana's bike consumes lesser petrol for a given distance. It is known that B-type petrol price is 40% lesser than A-type petrol.

23. The expense of cost per kilometre of Kalpana's bike to that of Khyati's bike is in the ratio of
1) 5 : 4 2) 4 : 5 3) 5 : 3 4) 2 : 7 5) 9 : 1

24. If it has been found out that Khyati's bike gave an average of 25 kilometres per litre and the price of one litre of A-type petrol is ₹70, then the difference in the travelling cost per kilometre of both the bikes is (in ₹)
1) 0.21 2) 0.42 3) 4.21 4) 0.40 5) 1.20

25. Kalpana purchased the bike at a cost of ₹5,00,000. If the conditions given in the above question hold good and she sold the bike at a cost of ₹4,56,000 after incurring additional expenditure on the bike equivalent to a journey of 20,000 km by that bike, then the approximate loss per cent incurred by her in the transaction is
1) 12% 2) 20% 3) 19%
4) 16% 5) None of the above

Answers and explanations

1. 2; Let electricity duty be x.
Fixed charges = ₹800
Energy charges = (30 × 5) × 10 = ₹1500
Rebate = 10% of 800 + 25% of 1500
= 80 + 375 = ₹455
Net bill amount = 800 + 1500 + x – 455 = 2400
⇒ x = 2400 – 1845 = 555
So, electricty duty fee = ₹555

2. 2; **For shop M:**
Energy charges = (30 × 2.5) × 7.5 = ₹562.50
Rebate = 10% of 250 + 25% of 562.50
= 25 + 140.625 = ₹165.625
Net bill amount = 250 + 562.50 + 497.5 – 165.625
= ₹1144.375
For shop N:
Energy charges = (30 × 2.5) × 10 = ₹750
Rebate = 10% of 600 + 25% of 750
= 60 + 187.50 = ₹247.50

Net bill amount = 600 + 750 + 497.50 – 247.50 = ₹1600

∴ Required percentage = $\frac{1144.375}{1600} \times 100$ = 71.52%

3. 3; **For family:** Energy charges = (30 × 3) × 8 = ₹720

Rebate = 10% of 400 + 25% of 720

= 40 + 180 = ₹220

Net bill amount = 400 + 720 + 600 – 220 = ₹1500

For shop: Energy charges = (30 × 4) × 7.5 = ₹900

Rebate = 10% of 250 + 25% of 900 = 25 + 225 = ₹250

Net bill amount = 250 + 900 + 500 – 250 = ₹1400

∴ Required difference = 1500 – 1400 = ₹100

4. 5; Fixed charges = ₹1250

Let the average consumption per day of electricity be x.

Energy charges = 30x × 15 = ₹450x

Rebate = 10% of 1250 + 25% of 450x = 125 + 112.5x

Net bill amount = 1250 + 450x + 325 – (125 + 112.5x) = 2800 ⇒ 337.5x = 1350 ⇒ x = 4

So, average consumption of electricity per day = 4 kw

5. 5; **In present month:**

Energy charges = (30 × 2) × 5 = ₹300

Rebate = 10% of 200 + 25% of 300 = 20 + 75 = ₹95

Net bill amount = 200 + 300 + 450 – 95 = ₹855

In previous month:

Energy charges = (30 × 2) × 8 = ₹480

Rebate = 10% of 400 + 25% of 480 = 40 + 120 = ₹160

Net bill amount = 400 + 480 + 450 – 160 = ₹1170

∴ Required ratio = 855 : 1170 = 19 : 26

6. 4; **For Ankit:** Energy charges = 125 × 8 = ₹1000

Rebate = 10% of 400 + 25% of 1000

= 40 + 250 = ₹290

Net bill amount = 400 + 1000 + 325 – 290 = ₹1435

For Arijit: Energy charges = 80 × 10 = ₹800

Rebate = 10% of 800 + 25% of 800 = 80 + 200 = ₹280

Net bill amount = 800 + 800 + 325 – 280 = ₹1645

∴ Difference = 1645 – 1435 = 210

∴ Required percentage = 210 × 100/1435 = 14.63%

(7-11): Let the areas in the Venn-diagram be a, b, c, d, e, f, g and h.

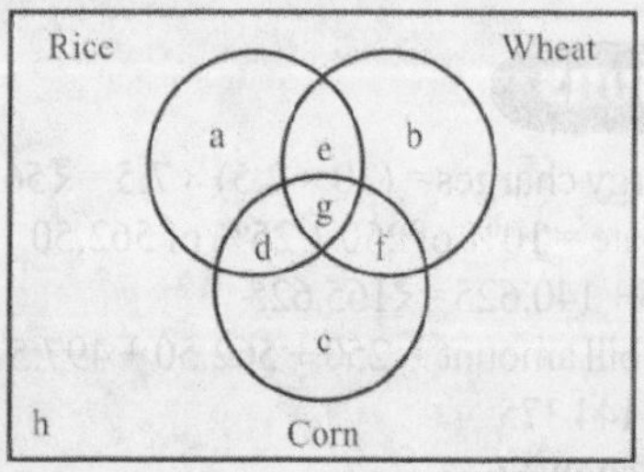

Total number of employees working in the company = 800

Number of employees who do not like grains = h

$= \frac{800 \times 42.5}{100} = 340$

Number of employees who like grains = 800 – 340 = 460

So, a + b + c + d + e + f + g = 460 ...(i)

Now, g = $800 \times \frac{5}{100} = 40$

Also, (a + d + e + g) = (c + d + g + f) – 10

⇒ a + e = c + f – 10 ...(ii)

And, e = $\frac{1}{2} \times g = \frac{1}{2} \times 40 = 20$

d = b – 10 ⇒ b – d = 10 ...(iii)

Also, it is given that f = 10 + e = 30

From (ii), we get that a + 20 = c + 30 – 10 ⇒ a = c

And, a = 10 + 2b ...(iv)

Fom (i), we get 2(10 + 2b) + b + d = 370

⇒ 5b + d = 350 ...(v)

Adding (iii) and (v), we get b = 60 and d = 50

So, a = c = 130

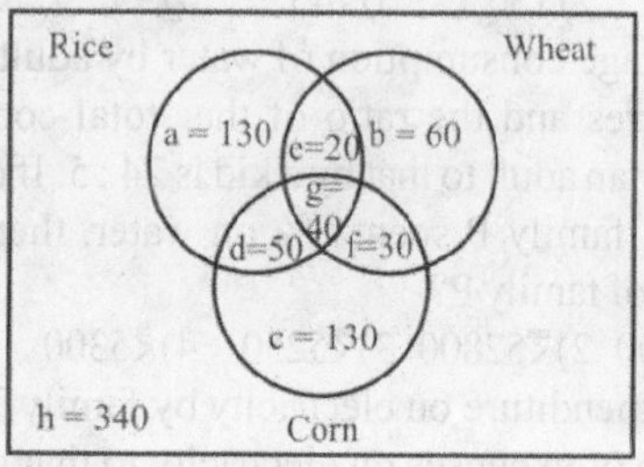

7. 3; Required difference

= (130 + 20 + 40 + 50) – (60 + 30 + 40 + 20)

= 240 – 150 = 90

8. 3; Required total = 20 + 50 + 30 = 100

9. 3; Required percentage = $\frac{60}{50} \times 100$ = 120%

10. 5; Average number of employees who like two out of three grains = $\frac{20 + 50 + 30}{3} = \frac{100}{3}$

∴ Required percentage

$= \frac{40}{\frac{100}{3}} \times 100 = \frac{40 \times 3}{100} \times 100 = 120\%$

11. 5; Required ratio = (20 + 50 + 30 + 40) : 340

= 140 : 340 = 7 : 17

12. 1; Labour productivity per worker

$= \frac{\text{Worth of output produced}}{\text{Total input workers}}$

⇒ Worth of output produced

= 180 × 100 = 18000

Total hours input = $\frac{18000}{90}$ = 200 hours

$\therefore$ Required efficiency $= \frac{240}{200} \times 100 = 120\%$

13. 1; $\frac{\text{Worth of output produced}}{120} = 175$

$\Rightarrow$ Worth of output produced

$= 175 \times 120 = 21000$

$\text{Efficiency} = \frac{\text{Standard labour hours}}{\text{Number of hours worked}} \times 100$

$\therefore$ Amount of time worked = 100 hours

$\therefore$ Labour productivity per hour

$= \frac{\text{Worth of output produced}}{\text{Total input hours}} = \frac{21000}{100} = ₹210$

14. 2; $62.5 = \frac{250}{\text{Amount of time worked}} \times 100$

$\Rightarrow$ Amount of time worked

$= \frac{250}{62.5} \times 100 = 400$ hours

Total worth of output produced by the company in 2019 = ₹18600

Labour productivity per hour $= \frac{18600}{400} = 46.5$

Labour productivity per worker $= \frac{18600}{150} = ₹124$

$\therefore$ Required difference $= 124 - 46.5 = ₹77.50$

15. 2; $66\frac{2}{3} = \frac{160}{\text{Amount of time worked}} \times 100$

$\Rightarrow$ Amount of time worked $= \frac{160 \times 3}{2} = 240$ hours

Worth of output produced $= 105 \times 240 = ₹25200$

16. 1; $125 = \frac{300}{\text{Amount of time worked}} \times 100$

$\Rightarrow$ Amount of time worked $= \frac{300 \times 100}{125} = 240$ hours

Worth of output produced $= 240 \times 75 = ₹18000$

Labour productivity per hour

$= \frac{18000}{160} = ₹112.50$

(17-22):

Calculating and tabulising the data, we get

Family	Total members	Adults	Kids
P	24	$\frac{24}{4} \times 3 = 18$	$24 - 18 = 6$
Q	16	$\frac{16}{8} \times 5 = 10$	$16 - 10 = 6$
R	20	$\frac{20}{5} \times 3 = 12$	$20 - 12 = 8$
S	12	$\frac{12}{3} \times 2 = 8$	$12 - 8 = 4$
T	18	$\frac{18}{3} \times 1 = 6$	$18 - 6 = 12$

17. 3; Let the average consumption of water by an adult and a kid in family S be x and y respectively.

Total consumption by adults $= 8 \times x = 8x$

Total consumption by kids = 4y

Now, $8x - 4y = 80 \Rightarrow 2x - y = 20$ ...(i)

Total expenses of water $= 8x \times 10 + 4y \times 5 = 1040$

$\Rightarrow 80x + 20y = 1040$

$\Rightarrow 4x + y = 52$ ...(ii)

From (i) and (ii), we get $6x = 72$

$\Rightarrow x = 12$ and $y = 4$

So, required percentage $= \frac{4}{12} \times 100 = 33.33\%$

18. 3; Let the average consumption of water by a adult and kid of family Q be 4x and 3x respectively.

Total consumption of water by adults of family Q $= 4x \times 5 = 20x$

Total consumption of water by kids of family Q $= 3x \times 3 = 9x$

Total expenses $= [40x(10)] + [18x(5)] = 30625 \times \frac{4}{100}$

$\Rightarrow 490x = 1225 \Rightarrow x = 2.5$

$\therefore$ Total expenses of water by family Q

$= 40x + 18x = 100 + 45 = 145$ litres

19. 1; Total consumption of water by adults of family P $= 16 \times 18 = 288$ litres

Total consumption of water by kids of family P

$= 288 \times \frac{5}{24} = 60$ litres

Expenses of water $= (288 \times 10) + (60 \times 5) = 3180$

Total income of family $= 3180 \times \frac{100}{6} = ₹53000$

20. 5; Total expenditure on electricity by family T = ₹112

Total expenditure on water by family T

$= 112 \times \frac{5}{8} = ₹70$

Let total consumption of water by adult and kids be 2x and 3x respectively.
According to the question,
$(2x \times 10) + (3x \times 5) = 70 \Rightarrow x = 2$

Average consumption by adult $= \frac{2x}{6} = \frac{2}{3}$ litres

Average consumption by kid $= \frac{3x}{12} = \frac{1}{2}$ litres

So, required difference $= \frac{2}{3} - \frac{1}{2} = \frac{1}{6}$ litres

21. 5; Let total consumption of water by adult and kids of family R be 9x and 4x respectively.
Average consumption of water by adult

$= \frac{9x}{12} = 0.75x$

Average consumption of water by kid $= \frac{4x}{8} = \frac{x}{2}$

According to the question, $0.75x - \frac{x}{2} = 12 \Rightarrow x = 48$

So, total expenses = [9x(10)] + [4x(5)]
= 110x = 110 × 48 = ₹5280

22. 4; Number of members in family Z

$= \frac{24+16+20+12+18}{5} = \frac{90}{5} = 18$

Number of adults $= \frac{18}{6} \times 5 = 15$

Number of kids $= \frac{18}{6} \times 1 = 3$

Water bill $= (15 \times 25 + 22 \times 3) \times 5 = 2205$
Amount saved $= 2205 \times 2 = 4410$
Let N = Total salary of Z (monthly)

Amount spent on food and rent $= \frac{N}{2}$

Amount spent on clothing $= \frac{N}{4}$

Remaining $= N - \left(\frac{N}{2} + \frac{N}{4}\right) = N - \frac{3N}{4} = \frac{N}{4} = 4410 + 2205$

$\Rightarrow N = 6615 \times 4 = 26460$
∴ Total annual salary = 26460 × 12 = ₹317520

23. 1; It is given that Kalpana's bike's average (litres per km) is 25% lesser than Khyati's bike.
Means, Kalpana's bike consumes 25% less of A-type petrol per km than Khyati's bike's consumption of B-type petrol per km.
Let Khyati's bike consume N litres of B-type petrol.

⇒ Kalpana's bike consumes $\frac{3N}{4}$ litres of A-type petrol.

Also, $\frac{3}{5}$ (cost per litre A-type petrol)
= Cost per litre B-type petrol

$\Rightarrow \frac{\text{Cost of A-type petrol}}{\text{Cost of B-type petrol}} = \frac{5}{3}$

Now, $\frac{\text{Cost per km (Kalpana)}}{\text{Cost per km (Khyati)}} = \frac{5 \times \frac{3N}{4}}{3N} = \frac{5}{4}$

∴ Required ratio = 5 : 4

24. 2; Khyati's bike travels 25 km in 1 litre of B-type petrol.

⇒ In 1 km, it consumes $\frac{1}{25} = 0.04$ litre of B-type petrol.
So, consumption per km of Kalpana's bike

$= \frac{3}{4} \times 0.04 = 0.03$ litre

Now, let price of 1 litre of B-type petrol = ₹N

$\Rightarrow \frac{70}{N} = \frac{5}{3}$ (from above question) ⇒ N = ₹42

Per km travelling cost of Khyati
= 42 × 0.04 = ₹1.68
And, per km travelling cost of Kalpana
= 70 × 0.03 = ₹2.10
∴ Required difference = 2.10 – 1.68 = ₹0.42

25. 4; From above question, cost of travelling per km = ₹2.10
So, in 20000 km, it will cost = 2.1 × 20000 = ₹42000
∴ Total expense of Kalpana = ₹(500000 + 42000)
= ₹542000

Hence, loss % $= \frac{542000 - 456000}{542000} \times 100$

$= 15.86\% \approx 16\%$ (approx)

Practice Set 19

Direction (Q. 1-5): Study the following information carefully and answer the given questions:

The line graph represents the number of students in four different schools P, Q, R and S in the year 2018.

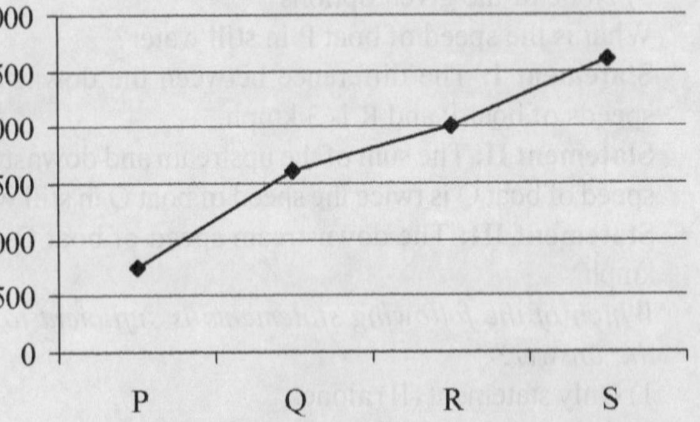

1. The ratio of the male to female students in each of the schools is 3 : 2 and 40% of the female students from each of the schools like Football. The total number of students who like football from each school is 60%. What is the number of male students who like football from each school?

1) 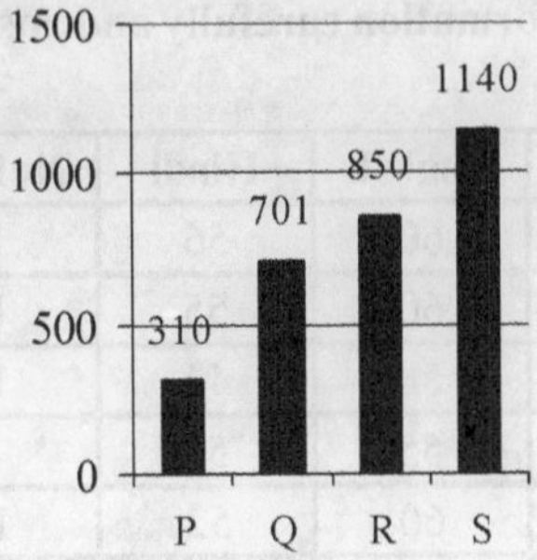

2) 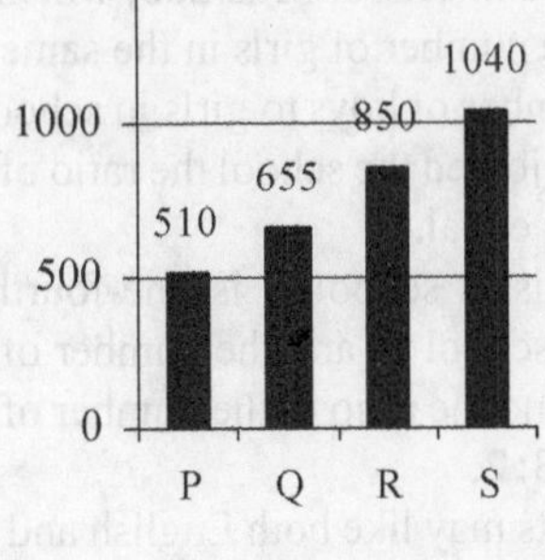

3) 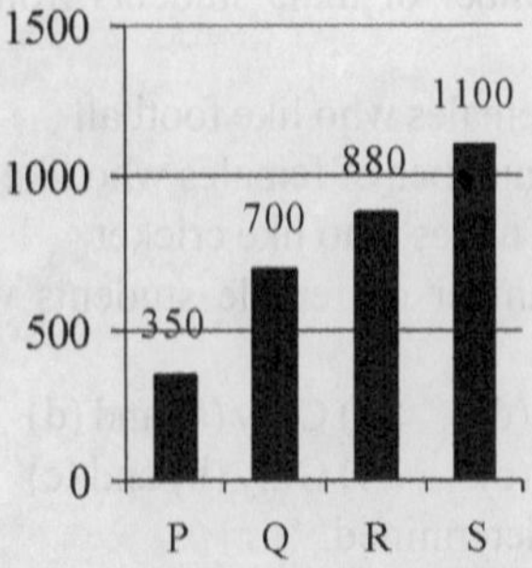

4) 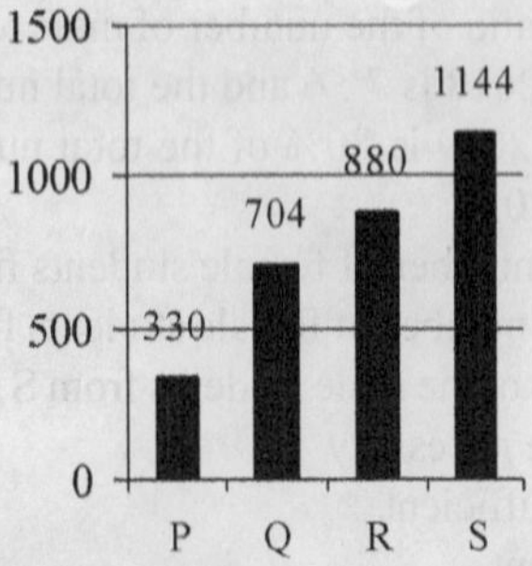

5) None of these

2. The ratio of the number of male to female students from P is 3 : 2 and 40% of the students like cricket. 40% of the female students like cricket.
Which of the following statements is correct?
(i) The ratio of the number of male students from P who like cricket to the number of female students from Q who like cricket is 5 : 4 if the number of female students from Q who like cricket is 120.
(ii) Half of the students from Q are males and half of the males like cricket, which is equal to the number of male students who like cricket from P.
(iii) 40% of the students from R are females and 15% of the male students from R like cricket, which is equal to the number of male students who like cricket from P.
(iv) The number of male students from T is three times the number of female students from P and 50% of the female students from T like cricket, which is equal to the number of female students from P like cricket.

1) Only (i) and (ii) 2) None is correct
3) All are correct 4) Only (iii) and (iv)
5) Only (iii)

3. 20% of the students left from each of the schools and among those leaving 80% are females. The ratio of the number of students who like cricket to that of those who like football from each of the schools is 3 : 2. 80% of the boys from each school like football and 60% of the female students like cricket.
From the statement given in the above question, which of the following can be determined?
(a) The average number of male students from all the schools
(b) The number of females who like football
(c) The ratio of the number of females who like football to the number of males who like cricket
(d) The average number of female students who like cricket
1) Only (a), (b) and (d) 2) Only (a) and (d)
3) Only (a), (b) and (c) 4) Only (b) and (c)
5) Nothing can be determined

4. Find the number of male students from S in 2019.
Statement I: The ratio of the number of male to female students from S in 2018 is 7 : 6 and the total number of students from S in 2019 is 80% of the total number of students from S in 2018.
Statement II: The number of female students from S in 2019 is equal to the number of female students from P in 2018, which is 50% of the male students from S in 2018.
1) Both I and II are necessary
2) Either I or II is sufficient
3) Only I is sufficient
4) The question can't be answered even with both I and II
5) Only II is sufficient

5. The ratio of the male to female students in each of the schools is 7 : 3.
Quantity I: The difference between the number of female students from Q and the number of male students from S
Quantity II: The sum of the female students from P and R.
Solve for these two quantities and compare them and thus mark the answer correctly.
1) Quantity I > Quantity II
2) Quantity I < Quantity II
3) Quantity I ≤ Quantity II
4) Quantity I ≥ Quantity II
5) Quantity I = Quantity II or the relation cannot be established

Directions (Q. 6-7): Study the following information carefully and answer the questions given below:

Two boats P and R have speeds in still water in the ratio 7 : 6. Water is flowing with a speed 7 kmph less than that of the speed of boat Q in still water. The time taken by boat P and boat Q to travel a certain distance D downstream are 3 hours and 4 hours respectively.

6. Find the distance D.
Statement I: The average of the speeds of boats P, Q and R in still water is 18 kmph.
Statement II: The time taken by boat R to travel a distance N km downstream is 5 hours.
Statement III: The time taken by boat P to travel D km downstream is 2 hours more than the time taken by boat Q to travel 'D+N' km downstream.
Which of the above statements is redundant to find the answer to the given question?
1) Only statement (II) 2) Only statement (I)
3) Only statements (II) and (III)
4) Only statements (I) and (III)
5) None of the given options

7. What is the speed of boat P in still water?
Statement I: The difference between the downstream speeds of boat P and R is 3 kmph.
Statement II: The sum of the upstream and downstream speed of boat Q is twice the speed of boat Q in still water.
Statement III: The downstream speed of boat Q is 21 kmph.
Which of the following statements is sufficient to find the answer?
1) Only statement (II) alone
2) Only statement (I) alone
3) Either statement (I) or (III)
4) Only statements (II) and (III)
5) None of the given options

Directions (Q. 8-13): The following table gives the percentage distribution of the number of boys and girls who like Hindi, English or neither in three schools M, N and O. Study the following information carefully and answer the given questions.

Schools		English	Hindi	Neither
M	Boys	60	56	4
	Girls	60	55	10
N	Boys	58	44	14
	Girls	55	55	5
O	Boys	60	52	16
	Girls	68	46	10

- The number of boys in school M is 200, which is one-ninth more than the number of girls in the same school.
- The ratio of the number of boys to girls in school N is 5 : 4. If 50 more girls joined the school the ratio of boys to girls would become equal.
- The number of girls in school O is one-fourth of the number of boys in school M and the number of girls in school N together and the ratio of the number of boys to girls in school O is 3: 2.

Note: Some students may like both English and Hindi.

8. In which of the following schools, the difference between

the number of boys and the number of girls who like at least one subject, is the maximum?
1) School M 2) School N
3) Schools O and M 4) School O
5) None of the given options

9. Find the ratio of the total number of students who like neither English nor Hindi to the total number of students who like both English and Hindi..
1) 17 : 19 2) 221 : 223
3) 105 : 221 4) None of the given options
5) 105 : 119

10. What is the difference between the total number of boys who like only one subject and the total number of girls who like neither English nor Hindi?
1) 272 2) 454 3) 119 4) 273 5) 373

11. Find the total number of girls who like only one subject in all the three schools.
1) 373 2) 273 3) 243
4) 343 5) None of the given options

12. **Quantity I:** The total number of boys who like only one subject in school O is what percentage more than the total number of girls who like only Hindi in school M?
Quantity II: The number of boys who like both English and Hindi in school M, the number of girls who like both English and Hindi in school N and the number of boys who like both English and Hindi in school O together is what per cent more/less than the number of girls who like only English in School N?
Quantity III: The number of girls who like both English and Hindi in school O is what percentage of the number of boys who like only English in the same school?
1) Quantity I > Quantity II > Quantity III
2) Quantity I > Quantity II < Quantity III
3) Quantity I ≤ Quantity II < Quantity III
4) Quantity I ≥ Quantity II ≥ Quantity III
5) Quantity I > Quantity II = Quantity III

13. The average number of students who like both the subjects from all the given three schools is **approximately** what per cent more or less than the average number of students who do not like either of the given subjects from all the given three schools?
1) 115 2) 110 3) 134 4) 123 5) 106

Directions (Q. 14-18): Study the following information carefully and answer the questions given below.

There are six companies in a city. Each company has two types of employees, viz Temporary and Permanent. The salary differs for both types of employees. The following pie-chart represents the average salary of an employee in each company. The sum of the average salaries of employees in all six companies is 1 lakh rupees.

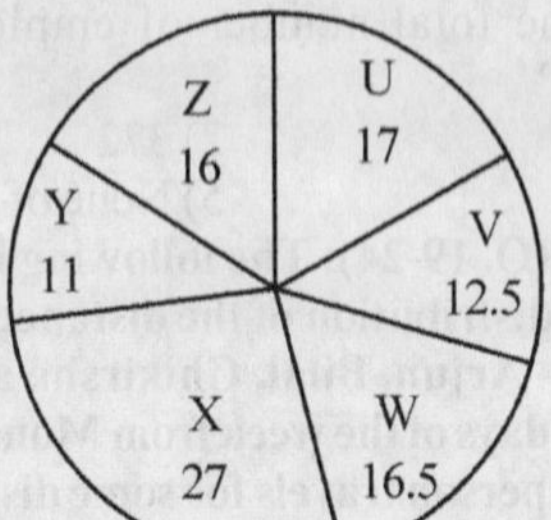

The following table gives the details of ratio of the salary of a temporary employee to that of a permanent employee and also the number of temporary employees as percentage with respect to the number of permanent employees.

Company	Ratio of salary of Temporary to Permanent Employee	Percentage of temporary employee more/less with respect to permanent employee	Difference between the total salary of temporary and permanent employees (Temporary – Permanent)
U	3 : 4	50% more	50000
V	5 : 8	40% more	–50000
W	2 : 3	$66\frac{2}{3}\%$ less	–504000
X	1 : 2	30% less	–884000
Y	17 : 28	20% more	–114000
Z	20 : 23	25% more	60000

14. **Quantity I:** The combined salary of a permanent employee in company U and that in V
Quantity II: The combined salary of a temporary employee in company V, that in W and that in Y
Solve for these two quantities and compare them and thus mark the answer correctly.
1) Quantity I ≥ Quantity II 2) Quantity I < Quantity II
3) Quantity I ≤ Quantity II 4) Quantity I > Quantity II
5) Quantity I = Quantity II or the relation cannot be established

15. The number of permanent employees in company U and X together is what per cent of the number of permanent employees in company Y?
1) 100 2) 200 3) 150 4) 250 5) 275

16. What is the total salary of all employees in company Z?
1) ₹750000 2) ₹1120000 3) ₹1320000
4) ₹1650000 5) ₹1440000

17. What is the total number of male permanent employees in company V?
Statement I: The percentage of males is 60%.
Statement II: The total salary of male employees is 50% more than that of female ones.
Statement III: The number of female temporary employees is one less than the number of male permanent employees.
The above question can be answered using which of the given statements?
1) Any of the two statements 2) Only II and III together
3) Only I and II together 4) Both options 2) and 3)
5) All the statements are not sufficient

18. What is the total number of employees in all six companies?
1) 415 2) 372 3) 382
4) 423 5) None of the given options

Directions (Q. 19-24): The following bar graph shows the percentage distribution of the distance (in km) covered by four people - Arjun, Bilal, Chikirsha and Dhwani - on each of the four days of the week from Monday to Thursday. Every day each person travels for some distance by bus and some distance by train. Total distance travelled by all of them together on Monday, Tuesday, Wednesday and Thursday is 120 km, 80 km, 60 km and 100 km respectively. Study the given information and data carefully and answer the questions that follow.

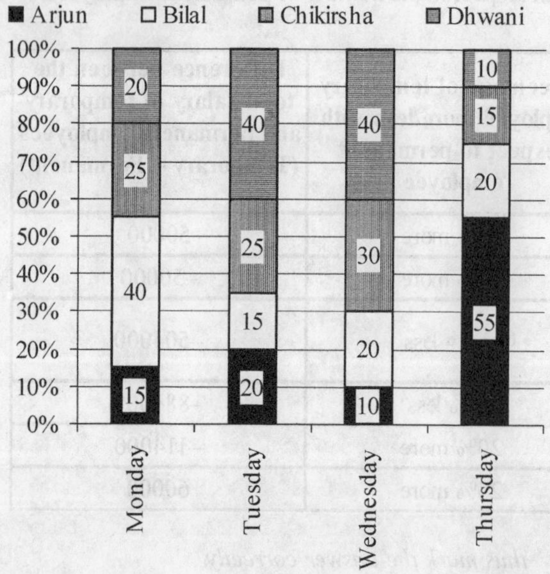

19. On Monday Bilal travelled 8 km by bus and the remaining by train. On Monday he travelled for 30 minutes by train and the speed of the bus is 25% of the speed of the train. If his average speed Tuesday was $\frac{3}{8}$ of the average speed on Monday, and the time travelled by him by bus and train are in the ratio 1 : 2 then what is the distance travelled by him by bus on Tuesday when the speed of the train is 25 km/hr?
1) 1 km 2) 2 km 3) 1.5 km
4) 2.5 km 5) None of the given options

20. The length of Train A is 30% of the difference between the distance travelled by Arjun on Monday and Tuesday and the length of Train B is 5% of the average of the distance travelled by Bilal on Wednesday and Thursday. If a train of length 400 m with speed 56 m/s can cross a platform in 25 seconds, the ratio of the speed of Train A to that of Train B is 4 : 5 and Train B can cross that platform in 4 seconds less time than Train A, then what is the average speed of Train A and Train B?
1) 60 m/s 2) 45 m/s 3) 42 m/s 4) 36 m/s 5) 54 m/s

21. Chikirsha travels by train 75% of the distance she travels on Monday and 60% of the distance she travels on Wednesday. The length of a platform is 14 km less than the sum of the distance travelled by Chikirsha by bus on Monday and Wednesday. The speed of a train of length 500 m is 20% more than Chikirsha's average speed on Tuesday and Chikirsha travelled for $\frac{1}{3}$ hour on Tuesday to cover the distance. In how much time can the train cross the platform?
1) 1 minute 2) 2 minutes 3) 1.5 minutes
4) 3 minutes 5) None of the given options

22. On Wednesday Dhwani travelled 16 km by bus and the remaining by train. On Wednesday, she travelled for 20 minutes by train and the speed of the train is 60% of the speed of the bus. What is the total time taken by her to cover the distance on Wednesday?
1) 48.5 minutes 2) 24.25 minutes 3) 45 minutes
4) 44 minutes 5) 32.5 minutes

23. The average distance travelled by Arjun and Chikirsha on all the days together is what per cent more or less than the distance travelled by Dhwani on all the days together?
1) $1\frac{5}{9}$% more 2) $7\frac{1}{7}$% less 3) $2\frac{1}{9}$% more
4) $1\frac{1}{9}$% less 5) None of the given options

24. What is the ratio of the total distance travelled by Dhwani on Monday, Bilal on Monday and Chikirsha on Tuesday together to the total distance travelled by Bilal on Thursday, Dhwani on Thursday and Arjun on Wednesday together?
1) 23 : 9 2) 17 : 12 3) 19 : 17
4) 17 : 19 5) None of the given options

Answers and explanations

1. 4; **For school P:**

Number of male students $= \frac{3}{5} \times 750 = 450$

Number of female students $= \frac{2}{5} \times 750 = 300$

Total number of students who like football

$= \frac{60}{100} \times 750 = 450$

Number of female students who like football

$= 300 \times \frac{40}{100} = 120$

Number of male students who like football

$= 450 - 120 = 330$

For school Q:

Number of male students $= \frac{3}{5} \times 1600 = 960$

Number of female students $= \frac{2}{5} \times 1600 = 640$

Total number of students who like football

$= \frac{60}{100} \times 1600 = 960$

Number of female students who like football

$= \frac{40}{100} \times 640 = 256$

Number of male students who like football

$= 960 - 256 = 704$

For school R:

Number of male students $= \frac{3}{5} \times 2000 = 1200$

Number of female students $= \frac{2}{5} \times 2000 = 800$

Total number of students who like football

$= \frac{60}{100} \times 2000 = 1200$

Number of female students who like football

$= \frac{40}{100} \times 800 = 320$

Number of male students who like football

$= 1200 - 320 = 880$

For school S:

Number of male students $= \frac{3}{5} \times 2600 = 1560$

Number of female students $= \frac{2}{5} \times 2600 = 1040$

Total number of students who like football

$= \frac{60}{100} \times 2600 = 1560$

Number of female students who like football

$= \frac{40}{100} \times 1040 = 416$

Number of male students who like football

$= 1560 - 416 = 1144$

1. 5; Number of male students from P $= \frac{3}{5} \times 750 = 450$

Number of female students from P $= \frac{2}{5} \times 750 = 300$

Number of students who like cricket

$= \frac{40}{100} \times 750 = 300$

Number of female students who like cricket

$= \frac{40}{100} \times 300 = 120$

Number of male students who like cricket

$= 300 - 120 = 180$

From (i): Number of male students from P who like cricket $= \frac{5}{4} \times 120 = 150$

So, this statement is not correct.

From (ii): Number of male students from Q

$= \frac{1600}{2} = 800$

Number of male students from Q who like cricket

$= \frac{800}{2} = 400$

So, this statement is not correct.

From (iii): Number of male students from R

$= \frac{60}{100} \times 2000 = 1200$

Number of male students who like cricket

$= \frac{15}{100} \times 1200 = 180$

So, this statement is correct.

From (iv): Number of male students from T

$= 3 \times 300 = 900$

Number of female students from T

$= 2600 - 900 = 1700$

Number of female students from T who like cricket

$= \frac{50}{100} \times 1700 = 850$

So, this statement is not correct.

3. 5; We need number of females and males in all the schools.

4. 1; **From Statement I:**

Number of male students from S in 2018

$= \frac{7}{13} \times 2600 = 1400$

Number of female students from S in 2018

$= \frac{6}{13} \times 2600 = 1200$

Total number of students from S in 2019

$= \frac{80}{100} \times 2600 = 2080$

So, this statement alone is not sufficient to answer the question.

From Statement II: Total number of students from P in 2018 = 750

So, this statement alone is not sufficient to answer the question.

From Statement I and II:

Number of female students from P in 2018

$= \frac{50}{100} \times 1400 = 700$

Number of female students from S in 2019 = 700

Number of male students from S in 2019

$= 2080 - 700 = 1380$

5. 1; **Quantity I:**

Number of male students from S $= \frac{7}{10} \times 2600 = 1820$

Number of female students from Q $= \frac{3}{10} \times 1600 = 480$

$\therefore$ Difference $= 1820 - 480 = 1340$

Quantity II:

Number of female students from P $= \frac{3}{10} \times 750 = 225$

Number of female students from R $= \frac{3}{10} \times 2000 = 600$

$\therefore$ Sum $= 225 + 600 = 825$

Hence, Quantity I > Quantity II.

6. 3; Let the speed of P and R in still water be 7a and 6a respectively.

Let the speed of Q in still water be y kmph.

For P: Upstream speed $= 7a - y + 7$

Downstream speed $= 7a + y - 7$

For Q: Upstream speed = 7 kmph

Downstream speed $= (2y - 7)$ kmph

For R: Upstream speed $= 6a - y + 7$

Downstream speed $= 6a + y - 7$

Now, $\frac{D}{7a + y - 7} = 3$ ...(i)

And, $\frac{D}{2y - 7} = 4$ ...(ii)

Equating (i) and (ii), we get

$\Rightarrow 3(7a + y - 7) = 4(2y - 7)$

$\Rightarrow 21a - 5y = -7$ ...(iii)

From I: Total speed $= 18 \times 3 = 54$ kmph

So, $7a + y + 6a = 54$

$\Rightarrow y + 13a = 54$ ...(iv)

Solving (iii) and (iv), we can get the value of y and a.

Using the value of y in (ii), we can get the value of D.

From II: Downstream speed of R

$= (6a + y - 7)$ kmph $\Rightarrow \frac{N}{6a + y - 7} = 5$

We can't get value of either N, a or y with the help of this statement.

From III: $\frac{D}{7a + y - 7} - \frac{N + D}{2y - 7} = 2$

We have 4 variables and 3 equations. So, we can't find D.

Thus, only statement I alone is necessary to answer the question. II and III are redundant.

7. 3; **From I:**

$(7a + y - 7) - (6a + y - 7) = 3 \Rightarrow a = 3$ kmph

So, speed of boat P in still water

$= 7 \times 3 = 21$ kmph

So, this statement is sufficient to answer the question.

From II: Given data is superfluous and hence not sufficient to answer the question.

From III: $2y - 7 = 21$

$y = 14$ kmph and $a = 3$ kmph

So, speed of P $= 7 \times 3 = 21$ kmph

So, this statement alone is sufficient to answer the question.

(8-13):

School M:

Number of boys = 200

Number of girls $= 200 \times \frac{900}{1000} = 180$

Boys who like English $= \frac{60}{100} \times 200 = 120$

Boys who like Hindi $= \frac{56}{100} \times 200 = 112$

Boys who like Neither $= \frac{4}{100} \times 200 = 8$

Total = English + Hindi + Neither − Both

$\Rightarrow$ Boys who like both $= 120 + 112 + 8 - 200$

$= 240 - 200 = 40$

Boys who like only English $= 120 - 40 = 80$

Boys who like only Hindi $= 112 - 40 = 72$

Girls who like English $= \frac{60}{100} \times 180 = 108$

Girls who like Hindi $= \frac{55}{100} \times 180 = 99$

Girls who like Neither $= \frac{10}{100} \times 180 = 18$

So, girls who like both the subjects

$= 108 + 99 + 18 - 180 = 45$

Girls who like only English $= 108 - 45 = 63$

Girls who like only Hindi $= 99 - 45 = 54$

School N: Let the number of boys and girls be 5x

and 4x respectively.
As per given information,

$\frac{5x}{4x+50}=\frac{1}{1} \Rightarrow x=50$

So, number of boys = 250
Number of girls = 200

School O: Total number of girls $=\frac{200+200}{4}=100$

Number of boys $=\frac{3}{2}\times 100=150$

Now, calculating the values similarly as for school M and tabulising, we get

Schools		English	Hindi	Neither	Only English	Only Hindi	Both English & Hindi	Total
M	Boys	120	112	8	80	72	40	200
	Girls	108	99	18	63	54	45	180
N	Boys	145	110	35	105	70	40	250
	Girls	110	110	10	80	80	30	200
O	Boys	90	78	24	48	36	42	150
	Girls	68	46	10	44	22	24	100

8. 4; **School M:**
Total number of boys that like at least one subject $=200-8=192$
Total number of girls that like at least one subject $=180-18=162$
$\therefore$ Required difference $=192-162=30$
School N:
Total number of boys that like at least one subject $=250-35=215$
Total number of girls that like at least one subject $=200-10=190$
$\therefore$ Required difference $=215-190=25$
School O:
Total number of boys that like at least one subject $=150-24=126$
Total number of girls that like at least one subject $=100-10=90$
$\therefore$ Required difference $=126-90=36$
Hence, school O has the maximum difference.

9. 3; Number of students that like neither English nor Hindi $=8+18+35+10+24+10=105$
Students who likes both the subjects $=40+45+40+30+42+24=221$
$\therefore$ Required $=105:221$

10. 5; Boys who like only one subject $=80+72+105+70+48+36=411$
Number of girls who like neither of the subjects $=18+10+10=38$
$\therefore$ Required difference $=411-38=373$

11. 4; Required total $=(63+54+80+80+44+22)=343$

12. 2; **Quantity I:** Required %

$=\frac{(36+48)-54}{54}\times 100=55.56\%$

Quantity II: Required %

$=\frac{(40+30+42)-80}{80}\times 100=\frac{32}{80}\times 100=40\%$

Quantity III: Required % $=\frac{24}{48}\times 100=50\%$

Hence, Quantity I > Quantity II < Quantity III.

13. 2; Avg of students who like both subjects

$=\frac{40+45+40+30+42+24}{3}=\frac{221}{3}=73.66$

Average of students who do not like either subject

$=\frac{8+18+35+10+24+10}{3}=\frac{105}{3}=35$

$\therefore$ Required % $=\frac{73.66-35}{35}\times 100=\frac{38.66}{35}\times 100$

$=110.45\%\approx 110\%$

(14-18):

Company U:
Average salary of employees $=0.17\times 100000=17000$
Let salary of temporary and permanent employee be 3x and 4x respectively.
Let the no. of temporary employees be T and that of permanent employees be P.

Now, $T=\frac{150}{100}P \Rightarrow T=1.5P$

So, $3x(1.5P)+4xP=17000(1.5P+P)$
$\Rightarrow x=2000\times 2.5=5000$
Salary of permanent employee $=4\times 5000=20000$
Salary of temporary employee $=3\times 5000=15000$
Difference between total salary of temporary and permanent employees = 50000
$\Rightarrow 1.5P\times 15000-20000P=50000$
$\Rightarrow 22500P-20000P=50000 \Rightarrow P=20$ and $T=30$

Company V:
Average salary of employees $=0.125\times 100000=12500$
Ratio of salary of temporary to permanent employee $=5:8$
Let the salary of temporary and permanent employee be 5x and 8x respectively.
Number of temporary employees

$= \frac{140}{100} \times$ Number of permanent employees

or, T = 1.4 P

$\Rightarrow 5x(T) + 8x(P) = 12500(T + P)$

$\Rightarrow x = 2500 \times 0.8 = 2000$

Salary of permanent employee $= 8 \times 2000 = 16000$

Salary of temporary employee $= 5 \times 2000 = 10000$

Difference between temporary and permanent $= -50000$

Now, $1.4P(10000) - 16000P = -50000$

$\Rightarrow P = 25$ and $T = 35$

Company W:

Average salary $= 0.165 \times 100000 = 16500$

Let salary of temporary and permanent employee be 2x and 3x respectively.

Number of temporary employees

$= \frac{33.33}{100} \times$ Number of permanent employees

$T = \frac{P}{3}$

So, $2x(T) + 3x(P) = 16500(T + P)$

$\Rightarrow 2x\left(\frac{P}{3}\right) + 3xP = 16500\left(\frac{P}{3} + P\right)$

$\Rightarrow x = 1500 \times 4 = 6000$

Salary of permanent employee $= 3 \times 6000 = 18000$

Salary of temporary employee $= 2 \times 6000 = 12000$

Difference $= -504000$

Now, $\frac{P}{3} \times 12000 - 18000P = -504000$

$\Rightarrow P = 36$ and $T = 12$

Company X:

Average salary of employees $= 0.27 \times 100000 = 27000$

Let salary of temporary and permanent employee be x and 2x respectively.

$T = 0.7 \times P$

So, $x(T) + 2xP = 27000(P + T)$

$\Rightarrow x(0.7P) + 2xP = 27000(0.7P + P)$

$\Rightarrow x = 10000 \times 1.7 = 17000$

Salary of permanent employee $= 2 \times 17000 = 34000$

Salary of temporary employee = 17000

$\therefore$ Difference $= -884000$

Then, $0.7P(17000) - 34000P = -884000$

$\Rightarrow P = 40$ and $T = 0.7 \times 40 = 28$

Company Y: Average salary of employees $= 0.11 \times 100000 = 11000$

Let salary of temporary and permanent employee be 17x and 28x respectively.

$T = 1.2P$

So, $17x(T) + 28xP = 11000(T + P)$

$\Rightarrow 17x(1.2P) + 28xP = 11000(1.2P + P) \Rightarrow x = 500$

Salary of permanent employee $= 28 \times 500 = 14000$

Salary of temporary employee $= 17 \times 500 = 8500$

Difference $= -114000$

Now, $1.2P \times 8500 - 14000P = -114000$

$\Rightarrow 3800P = 114000 \Rightarrow P = 30$ and $T = 36$

Company Z:

Average salary of employee $= 0.16 \times 100000 = 16000$

Let salary of temporary and permanent employee be 20x and 23x respectively.

$T = 1.25P$

So, $20xT + 23xP = 16000(T + P)$

or, $20x(1.25P) + 23xP = 16000(1.25P + P)$

or, $48xP = 16000(2.25P) \Rightarrow x = 750$

Salary of permanent employee $= 23 \times 750 = 17250$

Salary of temporary employee $= 20 \times 750 = 15000$

Difference = 60000

Now, $1.25P(15000) - 17250P = 60000$

$\Rightarrow P = 40$ and $T = 40 \times 1.25 = 50$

14. 4; **Quantity I:** Combined salary of permanent employee in company U and V $= 20000 + 16000 = 36000$

Quantity II: Combined salary of temporary employee in company V, W and Y $= 10000 + 12000 + 8500 = 30500$

Hence, Quantity I > Quantity II.

15. 2; Number of permanent employees in U and X $= 20 + 40 = 60$

Number of permanent employees in Y = 30

$\therefore$ Required % $= \frac{60}{30} \times 100 = 200\%$

16. 5; Total salary $= (40 + 50) \times 16000 = 1440000$

17. 4; **Statement I:**

Let number of temporary and permanent male employees be x and y respectively.

Number of male employees $= \frac{60}{100} \times 60 = 36$

$\Rightarrow x + y = 36$

Statement II:

$10000(x) + 16000(y) = \frac{150}{100} \times [10000(35 - x) + 16000(25 - y)]$

Statement III: $35 - x = y - 1 \Rightarrow x + y = 36$

Hence, statement II with either statement I or III can be used to answer the question.

18. 3; Required sum $= 20 + 30 + 25 + 35 + 36 + 12 + 40 + 28 + 30 + 36 + 40 + 50 = 382$

(19-24): Given data can be tabulised as

	Monday	Tuesday	Wednesday	Thursday	Total
Arjun	$\frac{15}{100}\times120=18$	$\frac{20}{100}\times80=16$	$\frac{10}{100}\times60=6$	$\frac{55}{100}\times100=55$	95
Bilal	$\frac{40}{100}\times120=48$	$\frac{15}{100}\times80=12$	$\frac{20}{100}\times60=12$	$\frac{20}{100}\times100=20$	92
Chikirsha	$\frac{25}{100}\times120=30$	$\frac{25}{100}\times80=20$	$\frac{30}{100}\times60=18$	$\frac{15}{100}\times100=15$	83
Dhwani	$\frac{20}{100}\times120=24$	$\frac{40}{100}\times80=32$	$\frac{40}{100}\times60=24$	$\frac{10}{100}\times100=10$	90
Total	120	80	60	100	360

19. 2; Distance travelled by Bilal on Monday by train

$=48-8=40$ km

Speed of train $=40\times2=80$ km/hr

Speed of bus $=\frac{25}{100}\times80=20$ km/hr

Time taken by bus $=\frac{8}{20}=0.4$ hour

Time taken by train = 0.5 hour

Average speed of Bilal on Monday

$=\frac{48}{0.5+0.4}=\frac{160}{3}$ km/hr

Average speed of Bilal on Tuesday

$=\frac{160}{3}\times\frac{3}{8}=20$ km/hr

Time for which he travelled on Tuesday

$=\frac{12}{20}\times60=36$ minutes

Time for which he travelled by train on Tuesday

$=\frac{2}{3}\times36=24$ minutes

The distance travelled by Bilal on Tuesday by train

$=25\times\frac{24}{60}=10$ km

The distance travelled by Bilal on Tuesday by bus

$=12-10=2$ km

20. 2; Length of Train A $=\frac{30}{100}\times(18-16)=0.6$ km $=600$m

Length of Train B

$=\frac{5}{100}\times\frac{(12+20)}{2}=0.8$ km $=800$m

Length of platform $=56\times25-400=1000$ m

Let the speeds of train A and B be 4n km/hr and 5n km/hr respectively.

$\frac{1000+600}{4n}-\frac{1000+800}{5n}=4$

$\Rightarrow \frac{400}{n}-\frac{360}{n}=4 \Rightarrow 4n=40 \Rightarrow n=10$

$\therefore$ Required average speed

$=\frac{4n+5n}{2}=\frac{40+50}{2}=45$ m/s

21. 1; Sum of distance travelled by Chikirsha by bus on Monday and Wednesday $=\frac{25}{100}\times30+\frac{40}{100}\times18$

$=7.5+7.2=14.7$ km $=14700$m

Length of platform $=(14.7-14)$ km

$=14700-14000=700$m

Average speed of Chikirsha on Tuesday

$=\frac{20}{\frac{1}{3}}=60$ km/hr

Speed of train $=\frac{120}{100}\times60=72$ km/hr $=72\times\frac{5}{18}$

$=20$ m/s

Time taken by train to cross platform

$=\frac{500+700}{20}=60$ seconds $=1$ minute

22. 4; Distance travelled by Dhwani on Wednesday by train $=24-16=8$ km

Speed of train on Wednesday $=\frac{8}{20}\times60=24$ km/hr

Speed of bus on Wednesday $=24\times\frac{100}{60}=40$ km/hr

Time travlled by bus on Wednesday

$=\frac{16}{40}\times60=0.4\times60=24$ minutes

Total time $=20+24=44$ minutes

23. 4; Average distance travelled by Arjun and Chikirsha

$=\frac{95+83}{2}=\frac{178}{2}=89$ km

$\therefore$ Required percentage less

$=\frac{90-89}{90}\times100=\frac{10}{9}\%=1\frac{1}{9}\%$ less

24. 1; Required ratio $=(24+48+20):(20+10+6)$

$=92:36=23:9$

Practice Set 20

Directions (Q. 1-5): Study the following information carefully and answer the questions given below.

A company consists of 21 employees. The employees of the company work in five different departments. 7 employees work in IT department, 5 in Sales, 3 in R&D, 4 in Accounts and 2 employees work in HRM department. A team of 11 employees needs to be chosen for different projects run by the company. The team will include employees of all the five departments. The minimum and maximum number of employees that can be chosen from different departments is given as under:

Employees	Number of employees	
	Minimum	Maximum
IT	3	6
Sales	2	4
R&D	1	1
Accounts	1	2
HRM	1	2

1. What is the difference between the number of ways in which maximum number of IT department employees are included in a team for a project and the number of ways in which the maximum number of Sales department employees are included in the project?
1) 16820 2) 12600 3) 10980 4) 8830 5) None of these

2. Dilshad and Gaumukh are two best IT guys available in the company and it is necessary for them to be part of the team for a project. Similarly, Kritika is the best Sales executive in the company and it is necessary for her to be a part of the team. If it is given that the maximum possible number of Accounts and HRM section employees have to be part of the project and the number of IT employees in the team should be more than the number of Sales employees in the team, then in how many ways can the team be selected?
1) 3120 2) 720 3) 5040 4) 1080 5) None of these

3. The number of IT department employees to be included in a team is 2 more than the number of Sales department employees to be included in the team. If it is given that the maximum possible number of HRM department employees are to be included in the team, then in how many ways can the team be formed?
1) 6300 2) 5250 3) 3012 4) 7200 5) None of these

4. If the number of HRM and Accounts section employees needed to be included in the project team are equal and the number of Sales and IT department employees are three and five times respectively of the number of Accounts department employees to be included, then in how many ways can the project team be formed?
1) 10050 2) 1250 3) 5040
4) 5850 5) Cannot be determined

5. If the number of IT department employees to be included in a team is not less than the number of Sales employees in the team and the number of Sales employees in the team is more than the number of Accounts and HRM department employees together in the team, then in how many ways can the project team be formed?
1) 4200 2) 5040 3) 8460
4) 9240 5) Cannot be determined

Directions (Q. 6-8): Study the following information carefully and answer the questions given below.

Shikhar and Deepak are two friends. They are travelling towards each other. Shikhar is travelling from Alianagar and Deepak from Katrinanagar. Shikhar left Alianagar at 9:00 am at the speed of 50 kmph. After 2 hours, Deepak starts at speed of 90 kmph from Katrinanagar towards Alianagar. Alianagar and Katrinanagar are situated at a distance of D km from each other and both the friends meet each other at 6:30 pm on the same day.

6. What is the value of D?
1) 850 km 2) 1050 km
3) 1275 km 4) None of the given options
5) 1150 km

7. If both Shikhar and Deepak start at the same time and travel in the same direction, then the time taken for them to meet is T hours. What is the difference between T and the time taken by them to meet as per the above information?
1) 19 hours 15 minutes 2) 28 hours 45 minutes
3) 23 hours 30 minutes 4) None of the given options
5) 13 hours 15 minutes

8. If after travelling for 1 hour from their respective starts, Shikhar and Deepak increase their speed by 15 kmph and 5 kmph respectively, then what will be the time at which they meet?
1) 6:30 pm 2) 5:45 pm 3) 5:30 pm
4) 3:15 pm 5) None of the given options

Directions (Q. 9-14): Study the data carefully and answer the following questions:

Five companies manufacture two kinds of pen - Gel and Ball - of three colours Black, Blue and Red. The table given below shows the total number of pens manufactured, the percentage of Gel pens manufactured, the percentage of black Ball pens among Ball pens manufactured and the ratio of blue Ball pens to red Ball pens manufactured by five companies.

Companies	Total number of pens manufactured	Per cent of gel pens manufactured	Per cent of black ball pens manufactured	Ratio of blue ball pens to red ball pens manufactured
Pilot	—	60%	—	4 : 5
Amazonbasics	12000	—	30%	—
Uniball	16000	55%	—	4 : 3
Linc		45%	20%	—
Montex	15000	—	25%	3 : 2

9. If the number of black Ball pens manufactured by Pilot and Uniball are 1440 and 900 respectively and the number of Gel pens manufactured by Pilot is 10800, then how many red Ball pens are manufactured by Pilot and Uniball together?

1) 5400 2) 8200 3) 5900
4) 4700 5) None of the given options

10. If the ratio of black Gel, blue Gel and red Gel pens manufactured by Uniball is 3 : 4 : 4 and 30% black Ball pens are manufactured by Uniball, then what is the ratio of black, blue and red pens manufactured by Uniball?

1) 49 : 47 : 52 2) 37 : 39 : 47
3) 57 : 76 : 67 4) None of the given options
5) 57 : 67 : 76

11. If the total number of pens manufactured by all five companies is 70000 and Ball pens manufactured by Linc, Amazonbasics and Montex are 7150, 50% and 40% respectively, then what is the average number of Gel pens manufactured by all five companies?

1) 7480 2) 7610 3) 8540 4) 7160 5) 9660

12. If the total number of pens manufactured by Pilot is 15000 and 40% of the total pens manufactured by Amazonbasics are Gel pens, then what is the average number of Ball pens manufactured by Pilot, Amazonbasics and Uniball together?

1) 6800 2) 6500 3) 7250
4) 5430 5) Cannot be determined

13. The total number of pens manufactured by Pilot and Linc are 20000 and 25000 respectively. 45% and 60% black Ball pens are manufactured by Pilot and Uniball respectively. What is the total number of blue Ball pens and red Ball pens manufactured by Pilot, Uniball and Linc together?

1) 12850 2) 18280 3) 17540 4) 18220 5) 22180

14. If the number of blue Ball pens manufactured by Montex is 4050, and the number of Ball pens manufactured by Amazonbasics is 45% of its total pens then what is the difference between the number of Gel pens manufactured by Montex and that by Amazonbasics?

1) 6600 2) 600 3) 1250
4) 1175 5) None of the given options

Directions (Q. 15-19): Study the data carefully and answer the following questions:

There are six different containers P, Q, R, S, T and U containing mixtures of Refined oil, Mustard oil and Groundnut oil.

The pie chart below shows the distribution (in degrees) of the quantity of Mustard oil and Refined oil together in these six containers.

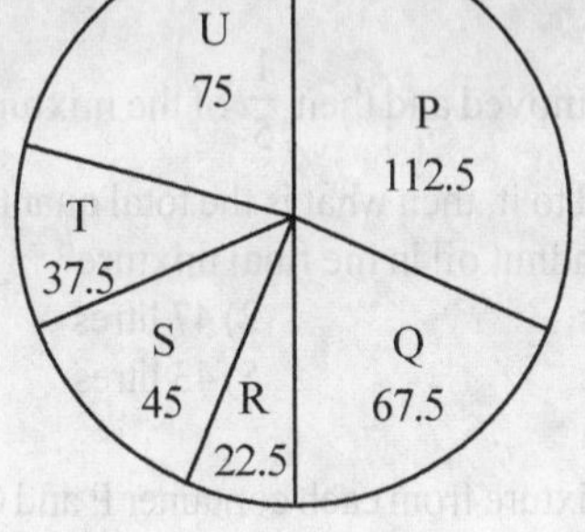

The line graph below shows the ratio of Refined oil to Groundnut oil in these six containers.

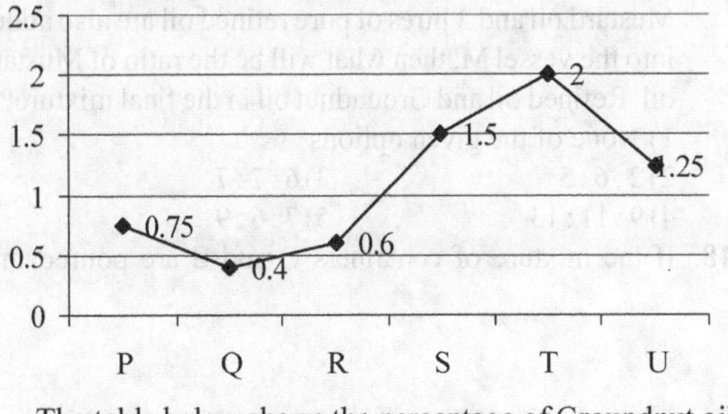

The table below shows the percentage of Groundnut oil in these six containers.

Container	Per Cent of Groundnut Oil
P	$44\frac{4}{9}\%$
Q	$52\frac{12}{19}\%$
R	50%
S	25%
T	$16\frac{2}{3}\%$
U	$27\frac{4}{7}\%$

The amount of Mustard and Refined oil in the container T is 10 litres more than the amount of Mustard and Refined oil in container R.

15. If 38 litres of mixture of container Q, 12 litres of mixture of container T and 14 litres of mixture of container U are poured into another container X and 4 litres of Refined oil and 2 litres of Groundnut oil is also added into the container X, then what will be the ratio of Mustard oil, Refined oil and Groundnut oil in the mixture of container X?

1) 3 : 4 : 4 2) 5 : 3 : 4 3) 4 : 3 : 3
4) None of the given options 5) 3 : 3 : 4

16. If 40% of the mixture of container P is mixed with 60% of the mixture of container S and from the final mixture 26 litres is removed and then $\frac{1}{5}$ of the mixture of container U is added to it, then what is the total quantity of Mustard and Groundnut oil in the final mixture?

1) 67 litres 2) 47 litres 3) 39 litres
4) 41 litres 5) 43 litres

17. If $\frac{2}{5}$ of mixture from each container P and Q and $\frac{2}{3}$ from container R is poured into another vessel M and 56 litres of mixture from vessel M is removed and 8 litres of pure Mustard oil and 2 litres of pure refined oil are also added into the vessel M, then what will be the ratio of Mustard oil, Refined oil and Groundnut oil in the final mixture?

1) None of the given options
2) 2 : 6 : 5 3) 6 : 7 : 7
4) 9 : 11 : 13 5) 7 : 6 : 9

18. If the mixture of containers Q and S are poured into another container L and 54 litres of mixture from container L is removed and one-third of the mixture of container R is added to container L, then what part of Mustard oil is there in container L?

1) $\frac{7}{13}$ 2) $\frac{4}{5}$ 3) $\frac{2}{7}$ 4) $\frac{4}{9}$ 5) $\frac{1}{7}$

19. The average of Mustard oil in all the given vessels except R is what per cent more or less than the average of Refined oil in all the given containers except R?

1) 4.34 2) 3.25 3) 5.62 4) 6.21 5) 3.44

Directions (Q. 20-25): Study the following information carefully and answer the questions given below.

The time taken by Karun, Reena and Lakshya to complete 20% of the work is **(A)** less than the time taken by Meenal and James to complete 30% of the work and the efficiency of Reena is 40% less than Soni while the efficiency of James is 40% more than Karun. Karun alone can complete the whole work in **(B)** while Meenal and Reena together can complete **(C)** of the work in 6 days. The part of work done by Lakshya and Karun in 12 days is **(D)** and James and Karun together can complete 80% of the work in 14 days. Reena, Meenal and James together can complete the whole work in **(E)** while Soni, Lakshya and Meenal alone can complete the whole work in 24 days, 56 days and 60 days respectively.

20. What should come in place of **(A)**?

1) 6 days 2) 3 days 3) 2 days
4) 4 days 5) None of the given options

21. What should come in place of **(B)**?

1) 21 days 2) 42 days 3) 65 days
4) 36 days 5) 40 days

22. What should come in place of **(C)**?

1) 25% 2) 30% 3) 15%
4) 50% 5) Cannot be determined

23. What should come in place of **(D)**?

1) $\frac{4}{5}$ 2) $\frac{1}{2}$ 3) $\frac{1}{7}$ 4) $\frac{4}{9}$ 5) $\frac{1}{3}$

24. What should come in place of **(E)**?

1) $17\frac{3}{4}$ days 2) $15\frac{1}{4}$ days 3) $13\frac{1}{3}$ days
4) $9\frac{1}{2}$ days 5) None of the given options

25. The numerical values of A and B together is what per cent of the numerical value of E?

1) 337.5% 2) 242.6% 3) 184.5%
4) None of the given options 5) 344.5%

Answers and explanations

1. 5; Employees' distribution when maximum IT employees are working will be IT = 6, Sales = 2, R&D = 1, Accounts = 1 and HRM = 1.

So, number of ways $= {}^7C_6 \times {}^5C_2 \times {}^3C_1 \times {}^4C_1 \times {}^2C_1$
$= 7 \times 10 \times 3 \times 4 \times 2 = 1680$

Employees distribution when maximum. Sales employees are working will be, Sales = 4, R&D = 1.

Now, three cases arise:

(i) IT = 4, Accounts = 1, HRM = 1
Number of ways $= {}^5C_4 \times {}^3C_1 \times {}^7C_4 \times {}^4C_1 \times {}^2C_1$
$= 5 \times 3 \times 35 \times 4 \times 2 = 4200$

(ii) IT = 3, Accounts = 2, HRM = 1
Number of ways $= {}^5C_4 \times {}^3C_1 \times {}^7C_3 \times {}^4C_2 \times {}^2C_1$
$= 5 \times 3 \times 35 \times 6 \times 2 = 6300$

(iii) IT = 3, Accounts = 1, HRM = 2
Number of ways $= {}^5C_4 \times {}^3C_1 \times {}^7C_3 \times {}^4C_1 \times {}^2C_2$
$= 5 \times 3 \times 35 \times 4 \times 1 = 2100$

So, total number of ways $= 2100 + 6300 + 4200 = 12600$

$\therefore$ Required difference $= 12600 - 1680 = 10920$

2. 2; As per information given, employees' distribution can be done from the departments in the following way:
IT = 4 (of which 2 are fixed)
Sales = 2 (of which 1 is fixed)
R&D = 1
Accounts = 2
HRM = 2
Hence, number of ways $= {}^5C_2 \times {}^4C_1 \times {}^3C_1 \times {}^4C_2 \times {}^2C_2$
$= 10 \times 4 \times 3 \times 6 \times 1 = 720$ ways

3. 1; **Case I:** Number of Sales employees = 4
Number of IT employees = 6
Number of HRM employees = 2
Total 6 + 4 + 2 = 12 not possible.
There won't be any place for Accounts and R&D employees. So, this is not possible.

Case II: Number of Sales employees = 3
Number of IT employees = 5
Number of R&D employees = 1
Number of HRM employees = 2
Which leaves no place for Accounts employees. So, this is not possible.

Case III: Number of Sales employees = 2
Number of IT employees = 4
Number of R&D employees = 1
Number of Accounts employees = 2
Number of HRM employees = 2
So, required number of ways
$= {}^5C_2 \times {}^7C_4 \times {}^3C_1 \times {}^4C_2 \times {}^2C_2$
$= 10 \times 35 \times 3 \times 6 \times 1 = 6300$

4. 3; Let the number of Accounts department employees included in the project team = x = Number of HRM employees.
Number of IT employees = 5x
Number of sales employees = 3x
According to the question,
$x + x + 3x + 5x + 1 = 11 \Rightarrow 10x = 10 \therefore x = 1$
Thus, required number of ways
$= {}^2C_1 \times {}^4C_1 \times {}^3C_1 \times {}^5C_3 \times {}^7C_5$
$= 2 \times 4 \times 3 \times 10 \times 21 = 5040$

5. 4; As per information given, 4 cases arise:
Case I: When Accounts employees = HRM employees = 2, R&D employees = 1
Now, Sales employees must be greater than 2 + 2 = 4 (which is not possible)
Case II: When Accounts employees = 2, HR employees = 1, R&D = 1,
Sales > 2 + 1 $\Rightarrow$ Sales = 4 $\Rightarrow$ IT = 3
This is also not possible as IT employees < Sales employees.
Case III: When, number of employees in Accounts = 1, HRM = 2, R&D = 1,
Sales > 2 + 1 $\Rightarrow$ Sales = 4
$\Rightarrow$ IT employees = 3
Again, this is not possible.
Case IV: When, number of employees in HRM = 1, Accounts = 1 and R&D = 1, again 2 cases arise:
(i) Number of employees in Sales = 3 and number of employees in IT = 5
$\Rightarrow$ Number of ways
$= {}^4C_1 \times {}^2C_1 \times {}^3C_1 \times {}^5C_3 \times {}^7C_5 = 4 \times 2 \times 3 \times 10 \times 21$
$= 5040$
(ii) Number of employees in Sales = 4 and number of employees in IT = 4
$\Rightarrow$ Number of ways $= {}^4C_1 \times {}^2C_1 \times {}^3C_1 \times {}^5C_4 \times {}^7C_4$
$= 4 \times 2 \times 3 \times 5 \times 35 = 4200$
$\therefore$ Total number of ways $= 5040 + 4200 = 9240$

6. 5; Distance covered by Shikhar in 2 hours
$= 50 \times 2 = 100$ km
Time of travel (for both)
$= 11{:}00$ am to $6{:}30$ pm $= 7\frac{1}{2}$ hours
Relative speed $= (50 + 90) = 140$ km/hr
Distance covered in $7\frac{1}{2}$ hours $= \frac{15}{2} \times 140 = 1050$ km
$\therefore$ Total distance between Alianagar and Katrinanagar $= 1050 + 100 = 1150$ km $=$ D

7. 1; Time taken by them to meet as per given information
$= \left(\frac{15}{2} + 2\right) = 9\frac{1}{2}$ hours
If they travel in the same direction, then
Distance = D = 1150 km **(from solution of Q. No. 6)**
Relative speed $= 90 - 50 = 40$ km/hr

So, time taken = $\frac{1150}{40}$ = 28 hours 45 minutes

∴ Required difference

= 28 hours 45 minutes – 9 hours 30 minutes

= 19 hours 15 minutes

8. 3; Shikhar starts at 9:00 am and travels at 50 km/hr. In 1 hour he travels 50 km.

From 10 am to 11 am, he travels at (50 + 15) = 65 km/hr

From 11 am to 12:00 noon, relative speed

= (65 + 90) = 155 km/hr

From 12:00 noon onwards, relative speed

= 65 + 95 = 160 km/hr

Distance to be covered after 12:00 noon

= 1150 – (50 + 65 + 155) = 880 km

Time taken = $\frac{880}{160}$ = 5.5 hours = 5:30 hours

∴ Time at which they meet = (12+5:30) = 5:30 pm

9. 3; Total number of pens manufactured by Pilot

$= 10800 \times \frac{100}{60} = 18000$

Total number of balls pens manufactured by Pilot

= 18000 – 10800 = 7200

Number of red ball pens manufactured by Pilot = $(7200 - 1440) \times \frac{5}{9} = 3200$

Number of ball pens manufactured by Uniball

$= 16000 \times \frac{45}{100} = 7200$

Number of red ball pens manufactured by Uniball

$= (7200 - 900) \times \frac{3}{7} = 2700$

So, required total = 3200 + 2700 = 5900

10. 3; Manufactured by Uniball

Gel pens = $16000 \times \frac{55}{100} = 8800$

Black gel pens = $8800 \times \frac{3}{11} = 2400$

Blue gel pens = $8800 \times \frac{4}{11} = 3200$

Red gel pens = $8800 \times \frac{4}{11} = 3200$

Ball Pens = 16000 – 8800 = 7200

Black ball Pens = $7200 \times \frac{30}{100} = 2160$

Blue ball Pens = $7200 \times \frac{70}{100} \times \frac{4}{7} = 2880$

Red ball Pens = $7200 \times \frac{70}{100} \times \frac{3}{7} = 2160$

So, required ratio

= (2400 + 2160) : (3200 + 2880) : (3200 + 2160)

= 4560 : 6080 : 5360 = 57 : 76 : 67

11. 2; Number of pens manufactured by Link = $7150 \times \frac{100}{55}$

= 13000

Number of pens manufactured by Pilot

= 70000 – (12000 + 16000 + 13000 + 15000) = 14000

Number of gel pens manufactured by Pilot

= 60% of 14000 = 8400

Number of gel pens manufactured by Amazonbasics

$= 12000 \times \frac{50}{100} = 6000$

Number of gel pens manufactured by Uniball

$= 16000 \times \frac{55}{100} = 8800$

Number of gel pens manufactured by Linc

$= 13000 \times \frac{45}{100} = 5850$

Number of gel pens manufactured by Montex

$= 15000 \times \frac{60}{100} = 9000$

So, required average = $\frac{8400 + 6000 + 8800 + 5850 + 9000}{5}$

$= \frac{38050}{5} = 7610$

12. 1; Total number of pens manufactured by Pilot = 15000

So, total number of Ball pens manufactured by Pilot

$= 15000 \times \frac{40}{100} = 6000$

And, the total number of Ball pens manufactured by Amazonbasics = $12000 \times \frac{60}{100} = 7200$

Total number of Ball pens manufactured by Uniball

$= 16000 \times \frac{45}{100} = 7200$

So, required average = $\frac{6000 + 7200 + 7200}{3} = \frac{20400}{3}$

= 6800

13. 2; Number of red Ball and blue Ball pens manufactured by Pilot = $20000 \times \frac{40}{100} \times \frac{55}{100} = 4400$

Number of red and blue Ball pens manufactured by Uniball = $16000 \times \frac{45}{100} \times \frac{40}{100} = 2880$

Number of red and blue ball pens manufactured by Linc = $25000 \times \frac{55}{100} \times \frac{80}{100} = 11000$

∴ Required total = 4400 + 2880 + 11000 = 18280

14. 2; Let per cent of Ball pens manufactured by Montex be n%.

So, $15000\times\frac{n}{100}\times\frac{75}{100}\times\frac{3}{5}=4050$

$\Rightarrow n=4050\times\frac{5}{3}\times\frac{100}{75}\times\frac{100}{15000}=60\%$

So, number of Gel pens manufactured by Montex

$=15000\times\frac{40}{100}=6000$

And number of Gel pens manufactured by

Amazonbasics $=12000\times\frac{55}{100}=6600$

$\therefore$ Required difference = 6600 – 6000 = 600

(15-19):

Let total amount of Mustard oil and Refined oil in six containers be N litres.

So, $N\times\frac{37.5}{360}-N\times\frac{22.5}{360}=10\Rightarrow N\times\frac{15}{360}=10$

$\Rightarrow N=240$ litres

Container P: Amount of Mustard oil and Refined oil

$=240\times\frac{112.5}{360}=75$

Let total amount of mixture in container P be x litres. Then, the amount of Groundnut oil

$=44\frac{4}{9}\%$ of $x=x-75=x\times\frac{4}{9}=x-75\Rightarrow x=135$ litres

So, amount of Groundnut oil $=135\times\frac{4}{9}=60$ litres

Amount of Refined oil = 30 × 0.75

$=30\times\frac{3}{4}=45$ litres

Amount of Mustard oil = 75 – 45 = 30 litres

Calculating remaining data:

Container	Amount of mustard and refined oil (in litres)	Ratio of refined and groundnut oil	Amount of groundnut oil (in litres)	Amount of mustard oil (in litres)	Amount of refined oil (in litres)	Total amount of mixture (in litres)
P	75	0.75 : 1 = 3 : 4	60	30	45	135
Q	45	0.4 : 1 = 2 : 5	50	25	20	95
R	15	0.6 : 1 = 3 : 5	15	6	9	30
S	30	1.5 : 1 = 3 : 2	10	15	15	40
T	25	2 : 1	5	15	10	30
U	50	1.25 : 1 = 5 : 4	20	25	25	70

15. 5; Ratio of mustard oil, refined oil and groundnut oil in mixture of container Q

= 25 : 20 : 50 = 5 : 4 : 10

Ratio of mustard oil, refined oil and groundnut oil in mixture of container T = 15 : 10 : 5 = 3 : 2 : 1

Ratio of mustard oil, refined oil and groundnut oil in mixture of container U = 25 : 25 : 20 = 5 : 5 : 4

So, amount of mustard oil in container X

$=38\times\frac{5}{19}+12\times\frac{3}{6}+14\times\frac{5}{14}=21$ litres

Amount of refined oil in container X

$=38\times\frac{4}{19}+12\times\frac{2}{6}+14\times\frac{5}{14}+4=21$ litres

Amount of groundnut oil in container X

$=38\times\frac{10}{19}+12\times\frac{1}{6}+14\times\frac{4}{14}+2=28$ litres

So, required ratio = 21 : 21 : 28 = 3 : 3 : 4

16. 5; Amount of mustard oil in final mixture

$=30\times\frac{2}{5}+15\times\frac{3}{5}=21$ litres

Amount of refined oil in final mixture

$=45\times\frac{2}{5}+15\times\frac{3}{5}=27$ litres

Amount of groundnut oil in final mixture

$=60\times\frac{2}{5}+10\times\frac{3}{5}=30$ litres

Now, ratio becomes 21 : 27 : 30 = 7 : 9 : 10

In $\frac{1}{5}$ of mixture of container U, amount of

refined oil $=\frac{25}{5}=5$ litres

groundnut oil $=\frac{20}{5}=4$ litres

and mustard oil = 5 litres

Now, from the final mixture 26 litres of mixture is removed and $\frac{1}{5}$ of the mixture of container U is added to it.

Then, amount of mustard oil in final mixture

= 21 – 7 + 5 = 19 litres

Amount of refined oil in final mixture

= 27 – 9 + 5 = 23 litres

Amount of groundnut oil in final mixture

= 30 – 10 + 4 = 24 litres

So, total amount of mustard and groundnut oil in final mixture = 19 + 24 = 43 litres

17. 5; Amount of mustard oil in container M

$=30\times\frac{2}{5}+25\times\frac{2}{5}+6\times\frac{2}{3}=26$ litres

Amount of refined oil in container M

$=45\times\frac{2}{5}+20\times\frac{2}{5}+9\times\frac{2}{3}=32$ litres

Amount of groundnut oil in container M

$= 60\times\frac{2}{5}+50\times\frac{2}{5}15\times\frac{2}{3}=54$ litres

So, ratio becomes 26 : 32 : 54 = 13 : 16 : 27

Now, after replacement, ratio of mustard, refined and groundnut oil in final mixture

$=(26-13+8):(32-16+2):(54-27)=7:6:9$

18. 3; Amount of mustard oil in vessel L

$=25+15=40$ litres

Amount of refined oil in vessel L $=20+15=35$ litres

Amount of groundnut oil in vessel L

$=50+10=60$ litres

So, ratio becomes 40 : 35 : 60 = 8 : 7 : 12

In 54 litres in vessel L:

Mustard oil = $54\times\frac{8}{27}=16$ litres

Refined oil = $54\times\frac{7}{27}=14$ litres

Groundnut oil = $54\times\frac{12}{27}=24$ litres

In $\frac{1}{3}$ mixture of container R, mustard oil = $\frac{6}{3}=2$ litres

In $\frac{1}{3}$ mixture of container R, refined oil = $\frac{9}{3}=3$ litres

In $\frac{1}{3}$ mixture of container R, groundnut oil = $\frac{15}{3}$

= 5 litres

So, in final mixture of vessel L:

mustard oil = 40 – 16 + 2 = 26 litres

refined oil = 35 – 14 + 3 = 24 litres

groundnut oil = 60 – 24 + 5 = 41 litres

total = 26 + 24 + 41 = 91 litres

So, part of mustard oil in vessel L is 26 litres out of 91 litres, or 2 : 7.

19. 1; Average of mustard oil $=\frac{30+25+15+15+25}{5}=\frac{110}{5}$

= 22

Average of refined oil $=\frac{45+20+15+10+25}{5}=\frac{115}{5}=23$

$\therefore$ Required percentage $=\frac{1}{23}\times100=4.34\%$

(20-25):

Suppose Karun, Reena, Lakshya, Meenal, James and Soni alone can complete the work in K days, R days, L days, M days, J days and S days respectively.

Ratio of efficiency of Reena to Soni = 60 : 100 = 3 : 5

$\Rightarrow R:S=5:3$

Ratio of efficiency of James to Karun

$=140:100=7:5\Rightarrow J:K=5:7$

Let R = 5x days and S = 3x days; J = 5y days and K = 7y days.

Soni and Meenal alone can complete whole work in 24 days and 60 days respectively.

So, $S=24$ days $\Rightarrow 3x=24\Rightarrow x=8$

Thus, R = 5 × 8 = 40 days

Similarly, $\frac{1}{5y}+\frac{1}{7y}=\frac{80}{100}\times\frac{1}{14}=\frac{2}{35}\Rightarrow\frac{12}{35y}=\frac{2}{35}\Rightarrow y=6$

J = 5 × 6 = 30 days and K = 7 × 6 = 42 days **(B)**

M = 60 days, L = 56days

20. 2; Required difference **(A)** $=\frac{\frac{30}{100}\times1}{\left(\frac{1}{60}+\frac{1}{30}\right)}-\frac{\frac{20}{100}\times1}{\left(\frac{1}{42}+\frac{1}{40}+\frac{1}{56}\right)}$

$=\frac{3}{10}\times\frac{60}{(1+2)}-\frac{1}{5}\times\frac{840}{(20+21+15)}$

$=6-\frac{1}{5}\times\frac{840}{56}=6-3=3$ days

21. 2; Karun alone can complete the whole work in 7 × 6 = 42 days.

22. 1; % of work done by Meenal and Reena together in 6 days $=\left(\frac{6}{60}+\frac{6}{40}\right)\times100=\left(\frac{1}{10}+\frac{3}{20}\right)\times100$

$=\frac{5}{20}\times100=25\%$

23. 2; The part of work done by Lakshya and Karun in 12 days $=12\times\left(\frac{1}{56}+\frac{1}{42}\right)=12\times\frac{(3+4)}{168}$

$=12\times\frac{7}{168}=12\times\frac{1}{24}=\frac{1}{2}$

24. 3; Reena, Meenal and James together can complete the work in $\frac{1}{\frac{1}{40}+\frac{1}{60}+\frac{1}{30}}=\frac{40}{3}=13\frac{1}{3}$ days

Another approach:

LCM of 40, 60 and 30 is 120 (Total work).

Reena can do $\frac{120}{40}=3$ units/day

Meenal can do $\frac{120}{60}=2$ units/day

James can do $\frac{120}{30}=4$ units/day

Total work done by all three together in 1 day = 3 + 2 + 4 = 9 units

Thus 120 units work is done in $\frac{120}{9}=\frac{40}{3}=13\frac{1}{3}$ days

25. 1; The number of days = 3 + 42 = 45

The number of days (E) $=\frac{40}{3}$

$\therefore$ Required percentage $=\frac{45\times3\times100}{40}=337.5\%$

Practice Set 21

Directions (Q. 1-5): Study the following information carefully and answer the questions given below.

There are five persons Aniket, Bikram, Chetna, Dheeraj and Elon that are travelling from their home to office by three vehicles - car, bus and train . The table given below shows the distance (km) travelled by all the five persons by car and the line graph given below shows the distance travelled by those five persons by bus and train respectively as a percentage of the distance travelled by car.

Persons	Distance travelled by car (in km)
Aniket	30
Bikram	10
Chetna	20
Dheeraj	40
Elon	50

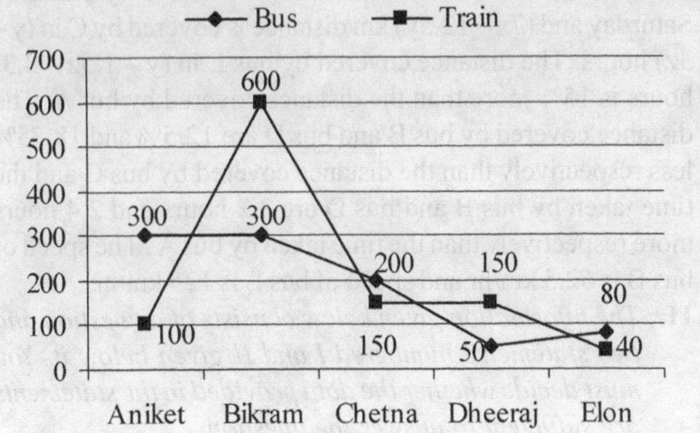

Note: It is not necessary that the distance between their home and office is the sum of the distances travelled by all three vehicles together. They may take another vehicle or travel by foot to reach office.

1. Chetna goes to her office from home by these three vehicles only and travels for 12 minutes by car. The ratio of the speed of the car, bus and train for Chetna is 5 : 4 : 6. She takes rest for a while and completes her journey in 1 hour. For how long does she take rest?
   1) 6 minutes 2) 4 minutes 3) 5 minutes
   4) 3 minutes 5) 12 minutes

2. Bikram starts from his house by car and travels for 6 minutes. He then walks for 'x' km. After that he takes the train and then the bus to reach his office. The total time of his travelling is 3 hours and the speed of the bus and the train are 40 km per hour and 70 km per hour less than the speed of the car respectively. If his walking speed is 30 km/hr, then what is the value of 'x'?
   1) 18km 2) 9 km 3) 15 km 4) 12 km 5) 24 km

3. It is given that Elon covers the distance between his office and home with these three vehicles only and the ratio of the speed of the car, bus and train is 8 : 10 : 5. If the speed of the car increases by 25% while the speeds of the bus and the train decrease by 20% each, then the total time taken to cover the distance between home and office by Elon increases by 4.5 minutes. What is the original speed of the bus for Elon?
   1) 150 kmph 2) 80 kmph 3) 120 kmph
   4) 100 kmph 5) None of the given options

4. If the ratio of speeds of the car, bus and train for Aniket is 3 : 2 : 2 and the difference between the time taken to reach office from home travelling all the distance by car and the time taken when he takes all the three vehicles is 30 minutes, then what is the speed of the train for Aniket? (He didn't opt for any other vehicle or walk.)
   1) 60 kmph 2) 90 kmph 3) 95 kmph
   4) 75 kmph 5) 80 kmph

5. Dheeraj first takes the car, then the bus and then the train and finally to reach office he walks for 36 minutes. The distance travelled by walking is 20% of the total distance from home to office. If the ratio of the speed of walking to that of the car is 5 : 8, then for how long did Dheeraj travel by car?
   1) 40 minutes 2) 45 minutes 3) 35 minutes
   4) 30 minutes 5) 15 minutes

Directions (Q. 6-10): Given below is the bar graph which shows the time taken by five pipes P, Q, R, S and T to fill a tank individually in minutes. The table shows the pipes which remain open to fill the same tank on different dates of a month.

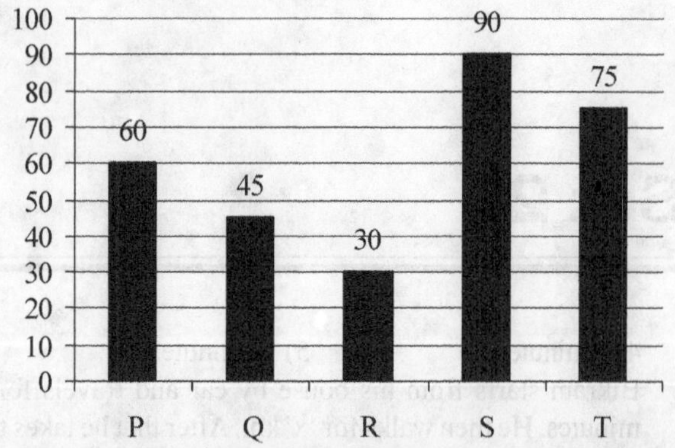

Days	Pipes which remain open on different days
23rd	P, S
24th	Q, R, S
25th	P, R
26th	Q, R, S
27th	P, T

6. On the 23rd, pipe P works with an efficiency of 120% and both pipe P and S remained open for 7 minutes in all that day but alternately for each minute, starting with P. The remaining part of the tank is filled the next day. What is the total time for which pipe S remained open on both days if next day all the pipes filled the tank together?

1) 12 min 15 sec 2) 16 min 18 sec 3) 20 min 10 sec 4) 18 min 15 sec 5) 17 min 12 sec

7. On the 25th, the tank is filled by both pipes working simultaneously but on the 26th all pipes work alternately for each minute starting from pipe Q, then R and then S. Find the difference in the time taken to fill the tank on the 25th and the time taken to fill it on the 26th.

1) 28 min 2) 30 min 3) 34 min 4) 15 min 5) 25 min

8. If on the 27th, 135 litres of water per minute is filled by both the pipes, then the amount of water filled by pipe S on the 23rd is what per cent of the amount of water filled by pipe T on the 27th?

1) 85% 2) 95% 3) 90% 4) 75% 5) None of the given options

9. On the 27th, P works with 120% of its efficiency and T with 75% of its efficiency and they together fill 162 litres of water in 12 minutes. On the 23rd, if the pipes (P and S) are working with a different efficiency then both pipes working together can fill $\frac{7}{30}$ part of the tank in 8 minutes and if P is opened for 8 minutes and S for 15 minutes then they can fill $\frac{7}{20}$ part of the tank. Find the ratio of the time taken by P alone and the time taken by S alone to fill the tank according to the new efficiency on the 23rd.

1) 3 : 4 2) 4 : 3 3) 4 : 7 4) 5 : 6 5) 1 : 3

10. If the rate of flow of pipe Q is 18 litres/min, and the cost incurred in filling 1 litre of water in the tank by pipe Q, R and S is ₹12 per litre, ₹15 per litre and ₹10 per litre respectively, then find the total cost incurred in filling the tank on the 24th if all the pipes fill the tank simultaneously.

1) ₹10665 2) ₹15365 3) ₹11665 4) ₹12065 5) None of the given options

Directions (Q. 11-14): Study the following information carefully and answer the questions given below.

Below data is given regarding the distance travelled by five buses (A, B, C, D and E) on two days (Saturday and Sunday).

On Saturday: $(4x + 15y)$ km distance is travelled by bus A in $(y - z - 3)$ hours and $(5x + 25y)$ km distance is travelled by bus E in $(2y - 5.5z)$ hours. Bus D travelled x km more than bus A in $\frac{(y-z)}{2}$ hours and the time taken by bus C to cover $(3x + 15y)$ km distance is equal to the time taken by bus E. The distance covered by bus B in $(3z - 5.4)$ hours is 60% more than the distance covered by bus C and the speed of bus A is 75 km/hr.

On Sunday: The distance covered by bus A in $(y - 2z - 2)$ hours is 20% less than the distance covered by bus E on Saturday and $(7x - 12.5y)$ km distance is covered by C in $(y - 3z)$ hours. The distance covered by bus E in $(y - 1.5z - 3.3)$ hours is 15% more than the distance covered by bus A. The distance covered by bus B and bus D are 12.5% and 18.75% less respectively than the distance covered by bus C and the time taken by bus B and bus D are 3.2 hours and 2.4 hours more respectively than the time taken by bus A. The speed of bus B is 62.5 km/hr and speed of bus E is 125 km/hr.

11. *The information given below consists of a question and two statements numbered I and II given below it. You must decide whether the data provided in the statements are sufficient to answer the question.*

If bus X is travelling at $(2y + 4z)$ km/hr on Saturday and on Sunday its speed is $16\frac{2}{3}\%$ less than its speed on the previous day, then what is the ratio of the value of 'a' to that of 'b'?

Statement I: On Saturday, bus B is $(2x + 1.2y)$ km behind the bus X but in $(5a - 2b)$ hours bus B will be $(x + 4y - 8)$ km ahead of bus X.

Statement II: On Sunday, bus B is $(x - 2y)$ km behind bus X but in $(7b - 6a + 2)$ hours bus B will be $(3y + z)$ km ahead of bus X.

1) Only (II) is required
2) Either (I) or (II) is required

3) Only (I) is required
4) Both statement (I) and (II) together are necessary
5) None of the given options

12. On Friday, the speed of bus A and bus E are 5y km/hr and x km/hr respectively and bus E starts at 6:40 am from Delhi towards Mathura and bus A starts at 7:20 am from Mathura towards Delhi. The distance between Mathura and Delhi is $(11x + 6y + 6z)$ km.
Quantity I: How much time will bus A take to cover the remaining distance after meeting bus E?
Quantity II: How much time will bus E take to cover the remaining distance after meeting bus A?
Quantity III: In how much time will both the buses meet each other?
Which of the following statements is/are true?
(A) $5 \times$ Quantity I $+ 3 \times$ Quantity II $< (3y + 2z)$
(B) $2 \times$ Quantity I $> 3 \times$ Quantity II $< 1.2 \times$ Quantity III
(C) 120% of (Quantity I – Quantity II) > Quantity III
(D) $12 \times$ Quantity I $- 6 \times$ Quantity II $- 15 \times$ Quantity III $>$ 4% of $(x - y - z)$
1) B and D are correct 2) A, C and D are correct
3) A, B and C are correct 4) C and D are correct
5) A and C are correct

13. If on Monday, the speed of bus D is increases by 47.5 km/hr from the previous day and the speed of bus C decreases by 60 km/hr from the previous day, then the distance covered by bus D in _______ hours is _______ km more than the distance covered by bus C in the same time?
Which of the following options satisfies the given blanks in the question?
(A) $(y - 2.3z)$ hours and $(x - 3y - z)$ km
(B) $(2y + z)$ hours and $(3x)$ km
(C) $(1.2y - 3z)$ hours and $(4y - z)$ km
1) Both (A) and (C) 2) Only (C)
3) Both (A) and (B) 4) All (A), (B) and (C)
5) Both (C) and (B)

14. Two places Aligarh and Patna are $(8x + 5y)$ km apart. On Sunday, bus D starts travelling at 5:00 am and bus A starts travelling at 9:00 am from the same place, viz Aligarh, and for the same destination, viz Patna. What is the difference between the time taken by bus D and that by bus A to cover the remaining distance after they meet?
1) None of the given options
2) 9.6 hours 3) 4.5 hours
4) 5.8 hours 5) 6.4 hours

Directions (Q. 15-19): Study the following information carefully and answer the questions given below.

There are five sellers Somesh, Sarthak, Varun, Dimpy and Kalpana. They are selling four different items.

The discount (as per cent) is given on the marked price of these four items by different sellers.

Sellers	M	N	O	P
Somesh	12%	30%	34%	—
Sarthak	25%	—	32%	50%
Varun	—	15%	14%	10%
Dimpy	33%	40%	25%	—
Kalpana	—	11%	—	7%

(**Note: 1.** Some values are missing. You have to calculate these values as per data given in the questions.

2. The marked price of a particular item is the same for all the sellers.)

15. The profit percentage of Somesh after selling item N is m% and that of Varun for the same item is (2m – 5)%. If the ratio of the cost price of item N of seller Somesh to that of Varun is 14 : 17, then find the value of 'm'.
1) 2 2) 3 3) 1 4) 5 5) 4

16. For seller Dimpy, the difference between the selling price of item N and that of item O is ₹465. If the sum of the marked price of item N and that of item O is ₹430300, then the marked price (in ₹) of item N is what per cent more/ less than that of item O? (The selling price of item N is greater than that of item O.)
1) 32.32 2) 25.55 3) 23.56
4) 26.40 5) 25.40

17. The average selling price of item N of sellers Somesh and Sarthak is ₹3225, and that of sellers Sarthak and Varun is ₹3870. Find the selling price (in ₹) of item N of Varun.
1) 7150 2) 8530
3) Cannot be determined 4) 7310
5) 3710

18. The selling price of item M and item O of seller Kalpana are in the ratio of 2 : 3. If the seller earns a profit of 25%, which is ₹280, on Item M and 20% on Item O then find the total profit (in ₹) by selling item M and item O together by the same seller.
1) 630 2) 450 3) 730
4) 540 5) 840

19. The cost price of item O is ₹50 for all of the sellers and all of them mark the same item at 64% higher than the cost price, then to get a total combined profit of ₹70 by all of the five sellers after selling item O, what is the discount that should be allowed by seller Kalpana on item O?
1) None of the given options
2) 5.65 3) 2.50
4) 3.25 5) 4.75

Answers and explanations

(1-5):

Persons	Distance travelled by car (in km)	Distance travelled by bus (in km)	Distance travelled by train (in km)
Aniket	30	300% of 30 = 90	100% of 30 = 30
Bikram	10	300% of 10 = 30	600% of 10 = 60
Chetna	20	200% of 20 = 40	150% of 20 = 30
Dheeraj	40	50% of 40 = 20	150% of 40 = 60
Elon	50	80% of 50 = 40	40% of 50 =20

1. 4; **For Chetna:**

Speed of car $= \frac{20}{12} \times 60 = 100$ km/hr

Speed of bus $= 100 \times \frac{4}{5} = 80$ km/hr

Speed of train $= 100 \times \frac{6}{5} = 120$ km/hr

Total time of travelling $= \frac{20}{100} + \frac{40}{80} + \frac{30}{120}$

$= \frac{1}{5} + \frac{1}{2} + \frac{1}{4} = \frac{19}{20} = \frac{19}{20} \times 60 = 57$ minutes

1 hour = 60 minutes

Time for which she takes rest $= 60 - 57 = 3$ minutes

2. 4; **For Bikram:**

Speed of car $= \frac{10 \times 60}{6} = 100$ km/hr

Speed of bus $= 100 - 40 = 60$ km/hr

Speed of train $= 100 - 70 = 30$ km/hr

Total time for which Bikram travels by car, bus and train $= \frac{10}{100} + \frac{30}{60} + \frac{60}{30} = \frac{1}{10} + \frac{1}{2} + 2$

$= 0.1 + 0.5 + 2 = 2.6$ hours

Time for which he walked $= 3 - 2.6 = 0.4$ hours

Distance $= x = 0.4 \times 30 = 12$ km

3. 4; **For Elon:**

Let the original speed of car, bus and train be 8x, 10x and 5x respectively.

Changed speed of car = 125% of 8x = 10x

Changed speed of bus = 80% of 10x = 8x

Changed speed of train = 80% of 5x = 4x

Original time taken $= \frac{50}{8x} + \frac{40}{10x} + \frac{20}{5x} = \frac{14.25}{x}$

Again, time taken with changed speed

$= \frac{50}{10x} + \frac{40}{8x} + \frac{20}{4x} = \frac{15}{x}$

According to the question, we get

$\frac{15}{x} - \frac{14.25}{x} = \frac{4.5}{60}$

$\Rightarrow x = \frac{0.75 \times 60}{4.5} \Rightarrow x = 5 \times 2 = 10$

So, original speed of bus for Elon

$= 10x = 10 \times 10 = 100$ km/hr

4. 5; **For Aniket:**

Let the speed of car, bus and train be 3x, 2x and 2x respectively.

Time taken to reach office from home when travelling by car only $= \frac{30 + 90 + 30}{3x} = \frac{50}{x}$

Time taken to reach office from home when using all these vehicles $= \frac{30}{3x} + \frac{90}{2x} + \frac{30}{2x} = \frac{70}{x}$

As per information given, $\frac{70}{x} - \frac{50}{x} = \frac{30}{60}$

$\Rightarrow \frac{20}{x} = \frac{1}{2} \Rightarrow x = 20 \times 2 = 40$

Speed of train for Aniket $= 2x = 2 \times 40 = 80$ km/hr

5. 4; **For Dheeraj:**

Let the walking distance be D km

As per information given,

D = 20% of (40 + 20 + 60 + D)

$\Rightarrow D = \frac{1}{5} \times (120 + D) \Rightarrow 4D = 120 \Rightarrow D = 30$

Walking speed of D $= \frac{30}{36} \times 60 = 50$ km/hr

Speed of car $= 50 \times \frac{8}{5} = 80$ km/hr

Time for which D travelled by car

$= \frac{40}{80} \times 60 = 30$ minutes

6. 2; With 120% efficiency pipe P alone will fill the tank in $\frac{60}{6} \times 5 = 50$ minutes

Part of tank filled in 7 minutes working alternately

$= \frac{4}{50} + \frac{3}{90} = \frac{4}{50} + \frac{1}{30} = \frac{17}{150}$

Part of tank filled in 1 minute on the 24th

$= \frac{1}{45} + \frac{1}{30} + \frac{1}{90} = \frac{2+3+1}{90} = \frac{1}{15}$

So, remaining part of tank will be filled in

$= 15 \times \left(1 - \frac{17}{150}\right) = 15 \times \frac{133}{150}$ = 13 minutes 18 seconds

Here on the 23rd, pipe S is open for (7 – 4 =) 3 minutes.

Required time = (3 + 13) minutes 18 seconds = 16 minutes 18 seconds

7. 5; Time taken to fill the tank on the 25th

$= \frac{30 \times 60}{90}$ = 20 minutes

Part of tank filled in 3 minutes on the 26th

$= \frac{1}{45} + \frac{1}{30} + \frac{1}{90} = \frac{2+3+1}{90} = \frac{1}{15}$

Total time to fill the tank on the 26th = 15 × 3 = 45 minutes

∴ Required difference = 45 – 20 = 25 minutes

Another approach:

On the 25th:

LCM of 30 and 60 is 60 units (total work).

Pipe P can fill $\frac{60}{60}$ = 1 unit/min

Pipe R can fill $\frac{60}{30}$ = 2 units/min

Both pipe can fill in $\frac{60}{3}$ = 20 min

On the 26th:

LCM of 45, 30 and 90 = 90 units (total work)

Pipe Q can fill $\frac{90}{45}$ = 2 units/min

Pipe R can fill $\frac{90}{30}$ = 3 units/min

Pipe S can fill $\frac{90}{90}$ = 1 unit/min

All three pipe can fill in 3 minutes = 3 + 2 + 1 = 6 units

So, in (3 × 15 =) 45 minutes they can fill 6 × 15 = 90 units

Hence difference = 45 – 20 = 25 minutes

8. 3; Total time taken on the 27th to fill the tank

$= \frac{60 \times 75}{135} = \frac{100}{3}$ minutes

Total capacity of the tank $= \frac{100}{3} \times 135$ = 4500 litres

Ratio of time for P to T = 60 : 75 = 4 : 5

Ratio of efficiency of P to T = 5 : 4

Amount of water filled by T and Q on the 27th

$= 4500\left(\frac{4}{9}\right)$ = 2000 litres

On the 23rd, ratio of time taken by P to S = 60 : 90 = 2 : 3

Ratio of efficiency = 3 : 2

Amount of water filled on the 23rd by S

$= \frac{2}{5} \times 4500$ = 1800 litres

∴ Required percentage $= \frac{1800}{2000} \times 100$ = 90%

9. 2; Time taken to fill the tank by P alone with increased efficiency $= \frac{60 \times 5}{6}$ = 50 minutes

Time taken to fill the tank by T with increased efficiency $= \frac{75 \times 100}{75}$ = 100 minutes

Together they can fill tank in $\frac{100 \times 50}{150} = \frac{100}{3}$ minutes.

Capacity of tank $= \frac{162}{12} \times \frac{100}{3}$ = 450 litres

Suppose P and S can fill the tank alone with a different efficiency in x minutes and y minutes respectively.

So, $\frac{8}{x} + \frac{8}{y} = \frac{7}{30}$ ...(i)

And, $\frac{8}{x} + \frac{15}{y} = \frac{7}{20}$ ...(ii)

Solving (i) and (ii), $\frac{7}{y} = \frac{7}{20} - \frac{7}{30}$

⇒ y = 60 minutes and x = 80 minutes

∴ Required ratio = 80 : 60 = 4 : 3

10. 1; Rate of flow in Pipe Q = 18 *l*/m

Capacity of tank = 18 × 45 = 810 *l*

Rate of flow in Pipe R $= \frac{810}{30}$ = 27 *l*/m

Rate of flow in Pipe S $= \frac{810}{90}$ = 9 *l*/m

Part of tank filled in one minute

$= \frac{1}{45} + \frac{1}{30} + \frac{1}{90} = \frac{1}{15}$

Time taken to fill tank by all = 15 minutes

Total cost incurred in filling the tank

= (15 × 18 × 12) + (15 × 27 × 15) + (15 × 9 × 10)

= 15 (216 + 405 + 90) = 15 × 711 = ₹10665

(11-14): On Saturday:

Distance covered by A = (4x + 15y) km and time taken = (y – z – 3) hours

Distance covered by E = (5x + 25y) km and time taken = (2y – 5.5z) hours

Distance covered by C = (3x + 15y) km and time taken = (2y – 5.5z) hours
Distance covered by D = (5x + 15y) km and time taken $= \frac{(y-z)}{2}$

Distance covered by B

$= \frac{160}{100} \times (3x + 15y) = \frac{8(3x+15y)}{5}$ km

and time taken = (3z – 5.4) hours

Thus, $\frac{(4x+15y)}{y-z-3} = 75$

$\Rightarrow z = \frac{-4x}{75} + \frac{4y}{5} - 3$ ...(i)

On Sunday:

Distance covered by A = 80% of (5x + 25y) = 4(x + 5y) km and time taken = (y – 2z – 2) hours
Distance covered by C = (7x – 12.5y) km and time taken = (y – 3z) hours

Distance covered by E $= \frac{23(x+5y)}{5}$ km and time taken = (y – 1.5z – 3.3) hours

Distance covered by D $= \frac{13}{16}(7x - 12.5y)$ km and time taken by D = (y – 2z + 0.4) hours

Distance covered by B $= \frac{7}{8}(7x + 12.5y)$ km and time taken = (y – 2z + 1.2) hours

Speed of bus B is 62.5 km/hr $\Rightarrow \frac{\left[\frac{7}{8}(7x-12.5y)\right]}{y-2z+1.2} = 62.5$

$\Rightarrow z = \frac{-49x}{1000} + \frac{47y}{80} + 0.6$ ...(ii)

Similarly,

For bus E:

$z = \frac{-46x}{1875} + \frac{68y}{125} - 2.2$ ...(iii)

From (ii) and (iii), we get

$\frac{-49x}{1000} + \frac{47y}{80} + 0.6 = \frac{-46x}{1875} + \frac{68y}{125} - 2.2$

$\Rightarrow \frac{-367x}{15000} + \frac{87y}{2000} + 2.8 = 0$ ...(iv)

From (i) and (iii), we get

$\frac{-4x}{75} + \frac{4y}{5} - 3 = \frac{-46x}{1875} + \frac{68y}{125} - 2.2$

$\Rightarrow \frac{-18x}{625} + \frac{32y}{125} - 0.8 = 0$ ...(v)

Solving (iv) and (v), we get x = 150 and y = 20
Putting in (i), we get

$z = \frac{-(4\times150)}{75} + \frac{4\times20}{5} - 3 \Rightarrow z = 5$

11. 4; Speed of bus X on Saturday = (2y + 4z) = 60 km/hr

Speed of bus X on Sunday $= 60 \times \frac{5}{6} = 50$ km/hr

From I: On Saturday:

Speed of bus B $= \frac{\frac{[8(3\times150+15\times20)]}{5}}{3\times5-5.4} = 125$ km/hr

Relative speed of bus B and bus X = 125 – 60 = 65 km/hr
Total distance covered with the relative speed = (2x + 1.2y) + (x + 4y – 8) = 546 km

Time taken = (5a – 2b) $= \frac{546}{65} = 8.4$ hours

⇒ 5a – 2b = 8.4 ...(i)
This data is not sufficient to answer the question.

From II: On Sunday:

Speed of bus B = 62.5 km/hr
Relative speed of bus B and bus X = 62.5 – 50 = 12.5 km/hr
Total distance covered = (150 – 2 × 20) + (3 × 20 + 5) = 175 km

So, time taken = (7a – 6a + 2) $= \frac{175}{12.5} = 14$ hours

⇒ 7b – 6a = 12 ...(ii)
This data is not sufficient to answer the question.

From statement I and II:

Solving (i) and (ii), we get, a = 3.6 and b = 4.8
So, required ratio = 3.6 : 4.8 = 3 : 4
Hence, both the statements are required to answer.

12. 2; **On Friday:**

Speed of bus A and E are 5y = 100 km/hr and x = 150 km/hr respectively.
Distance between Delhi and Mathura is (11x + 6y + 6z) = 1800 km

Quantity III: In 40 minutes, distance travelled by E

$= \frac{40}{60} \times 150 = 100$ km

So, time taken by both buses to meet

$= \frac{(1800-100)}{150+100} = \frac{1700}{250} = 6.8$ hours

Quantity I: Distance covered by A in 6.8 hours = 6.8 × 100 = 680 km
Time taken by A to cover remaining distance

$= \frac{1800-680}{100} = 11.2$ hours

Quantity II: Distance covered by E in 6.8 hours = 6.8 × 150 = 1020 km
Time taken by E to cover remaining distance

$= \frac{1700-1020}{150}$ hours $= \frac{68}{15}$ hours

Statement A: $5 \times 11.2 + 3 \times \frac{68}{15} = 69.6$

$= 3 \times 20 + 2 \times 5 = 70$

So, 5 × Quantity I + 3 × Quantity II $< (3y + 2z)$

Hence, statement A is correct.

Statement B:

$2 \times 11.2 = 22.4$

$3 \times \frac{68}{15} = 13.6$

$1.2 \times 6.8 = 8.16$

Hence, statement B is not correct.

Statement C: $\frac{120}{100} \times \left(11.2 - \frac{68}{15}\right) = 8 > 6.8$

Hence, statement C is correct.

Statement D:

$12 \times 11.2 - 6 \times \frac{68}{15} - 15 \times 6.8 = 5.2$

4% of $(x - y - z) = \frac{4}{100} \times 125 = 5$

Hence, statement D is correct.

13. 3; **On Monday:**

Speed of D = 110 km/hr

Speec of C $= \frac{7 \times 150 - 12.5 \times 20}{20 - 3 \times 5} - 60 = 100$ km/hr

Option A: Distance travelled by D in $(y - 2.3z)$ hours

$= 110(20 - 2.3 \times 5) = 110 \times 8.5 = 935$ km

Distance covered by C in $(y - 2.3z)$ hours

$= 100(20 - 2.3 \times 5) = 100 \times \times 8.5 = 850$ km

So, required difference $= 935 - 850$

$= 85$ km $= (x - 3y - z)$ km

Option B: Calculating similarly as above,

Required difference $= 4950 - 4500 = 450$ km $= 3x$ km

Option C: Calculating similarly as above,

Required difference $= 990 - 900 = 90$ km

$(4y - z) = 4 \times 20 - 5 = 75$ km $\neq 90$ km

14. 5; **On Sunday:**

Distance between Aligarh and Patna

$= 8 \times 150 + 5 \times 20 = 1300$ km

Speed of D $= \frac{\frac{13}{16}(7 \times 150 - 12.5 \times 20)}{20 - 2 \times 5 + 0.4} = 62.5$ km/hr

And speed of bus A $= \frac{4(150 + 5 \times 20)}{20 - 2 \times 5 - 2} = 125$ km/hr

In 4 hours, distance covered by D

$= 4 \times 62.5 = 250$ km

Relative speed of A and D $= 125 - 62.5 = 62.5$ km/hr

So, time taken $= \frac{250}{62.5} = 4$ hours

Meeting point from Aligarh $= 4 \times 125 = 500$ km

Remaining distance $= 1300 - 500 = 800$ km

Time taken by D to cover remaining distance

$= \frac{800}{62.5} = 12.8$ hours

Time taken by A to cover remaining distance

$= \frac{800}{125} = 6.4$ hours

So, required difference $= 12.8 - 6.4 = 6.4$ hours

15. 4; Let MP of item N of Somesh and that of item N of seller Varun be x each.

Then, CP of N of Somesh $= \frac{100}{100+m} \times \frac{70x}{100}$

CP of N of Varun $= \frac{100}{100+2m-5} \times \frac{85x}{100}$

As per information given, $\frac{\left(\frac{100}{100+m}\right) \times \left(\frac{70x}{100}\right)}{\left(\frac{100}{100+2m-5}\right) \times \frac{85x}{100}} = \frac{14}{17}$

$\Rightarrow m = 5$

16. 5; Let MP of N be 100x and that of O be 100y.

$100x + 100y =$ ₹430300

$\therefore x + y =$ ₹4303 ...(i)

As per information given,

$100 \times \frac{60x}{100} - 100y \times \frac{75}{100} = 465 \Rightarrow 4x - 5y = 31$

Putting the value of y from (i), we get

$4x - 5(4303 - x) = 31$

$\Rightarrow x = 2394$ and $y = 1909$

MP of N = 239400

MP of O = 190900

$\therefore$ Required percentage

$= \frac{239400 - 190900}{190900} \times 100 = 25.40\%$

17. 4; Let MP of N be 100a.

$\therefore$ SP of N of Somesh $= \frac{70 \times 100a}{100} = 70a$

Similarly, SP of N of Sarthak $= (100 - y)a$

According to the question,

$\frac{70a + (100 - y)a}{2} = 3225$

$\Rightarrow (170 - y)a = 3225 \times 2$ ...(i)

SP of N of Varun $= 85 \times \frac{100a}{100} = 85a$

According to the question,

$\frac{85a + (100 - y)a}{2} = 3870$

$\Rightarrow (185 - y)a = 3870 \times 2$ ...(ii)

Dividing (i) by (ii), $\frac{170 - y}{185 - y} = \frac{3225}{3870} \Rightarrow y = 95$

So, $(170 - 95)a = 3225 \times 2 \Rightarrow a = 86$

SP of N by Varun $= 100 \times 86 \times \frac{85}{100} =$ ₹7310

18. 1; Let SP of M be ₹200.

$\therefore$ SP of item Q = ₹300

CP of M $= 200 \times \frac{100}{125} =$ ₹160

CP of O $= 300 \times \frac{100}{120} =$ ₹250

Profit of M $= (200 - 160) = 40$

Profit of O $= (300 - 250) = 50$

Now, $4 \equiv 280$ (given) $\Rightarrow 50 \equiv 350$

Hence, total profit for Kalpana

$= 280 + 350 =$ ₹630

19. 5; CP = ₹50

MP $= 50 \times \frac{64}{100} + 50 =$ ₹82

Total CP $= 5 \times 50 =$ ₹250

Total SP $= 250 + 70 =$ ₹320

SP of O for Kalpana

$= 320 - 82 \times \frac{66}{100} - 82 \times \frac{68}{100} - 82 \times \frac{86}{100} - 82 \times \frac{75}{100} =$ ₹78.1

So, minimum required discount

$= \frac{82 - 78.1}{82} \times 100 = \frac{3.9}{82} \times 100 = 4.75$

Practice Set 22

Directions (Q. 1-5): Read the following line graph carefully and answer the questions given below:

Different places, viz A, B, C, D, E and F, are connected to each other through a waterway on the same riverfront. The following line graph shows the distance from place S to another place.

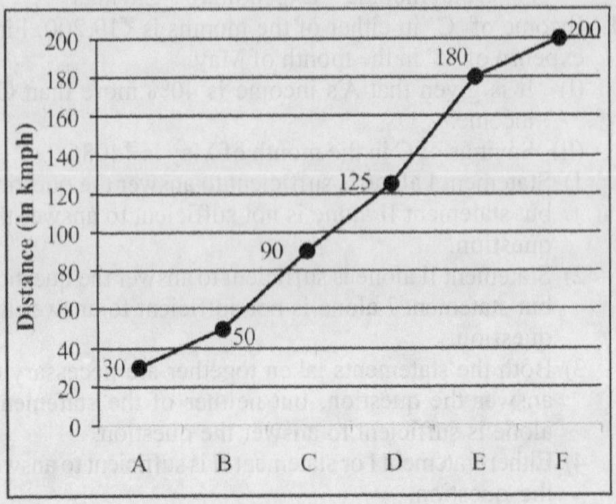

Note:

I. The velocity of the river is 3 kmph.

II. The river is running from place S to other places. For example, if a person travels from S to A then the speed of the boat is downstream and if the person travels from A to S then the speed of boat is upstream.

III. Assume all the places are in a straight line one after another on the riverfront.

IV. If a person wants to go from place A to E, he has to go through place B, C, D and then reach the place E.

1. Ravi travels from place S to M, which is 275 km away from place D. He travels place S to D downstream by a boat whose speed in still water is 22 kmph and then he hires a car for place M. If his average speed from place S to M is 40 kmph, what is the speed of the car? Assume that that car also has to cover the same distance as on the boat route.

   1) 75 kmph 2) 65 kmph 3) 80 kmph
   4) 48 kmph 5) None of these

2. Two boats X and Y run ferry services between two places, namely B and F. Boat X starts from place B, while boat Y starts from place F at the same time at 9 a.m. When will the two boats meet? (The speeds of boat X and boat Y in still water are 18 kmph and 12 kmph respectively.)

   1) 1 : 00 p.m. 2) 2 : 00 p.m 3) 12 : 30 a.m
   4) 11 : 30 p.m. 5) None of these

3. Find which of the following statements is/are true based on the given information. (The speed of Boat Q in still water is 15.5 kmph.)

   I. If Boat P takes 3 hours more than Boat Q to travel from place D to S, then the speed of Boat P in still water is 15 kmph.

   II. Boat Q can row a distance from place S to D and return to the same place in 9 hours.

   III. If the Boat P takes 2.8 hours more than Boat Q to travel from place C to S then the ratio of the upstream speed of Boat P to that of Boat Q is 5 : 4.

   1) Only statement I
   2) Both statements I and II
   3) All the three statements are true
   4) Only statement III
   5) None of these

4. A motorboat goes from place S to place X and returns to place B immediately. The place X is 40 km ahead of place F. What must be the least speed of the motorboat in still water during the entire journey if it is to be completed in not more than 18 hours? (Assume that the motorboat does not stop at any place)

   1) 20 kmph 2) 25 kmph 3) 27 kmph
   4) 30 kmph 5) 22 kmph

5. A motorboat started travelling from place S to C. After travelling 40% of the total distance, the engine develops some sort of issues due to which the speed became $\frac{3}{5}$th of the initial speed, As a result, the boat reached place C 2 hours late. What is the speed of the motorboat in still water?

   1) 17 kmph 2) 20 kmph 3) 15 kmph
   4) 22 kmph 5) None of these

Directions (Q. 6-10): Study the following information carefully and answer the given questions.

The bar graph shows the number of days required by different people to finish the percentage of work.

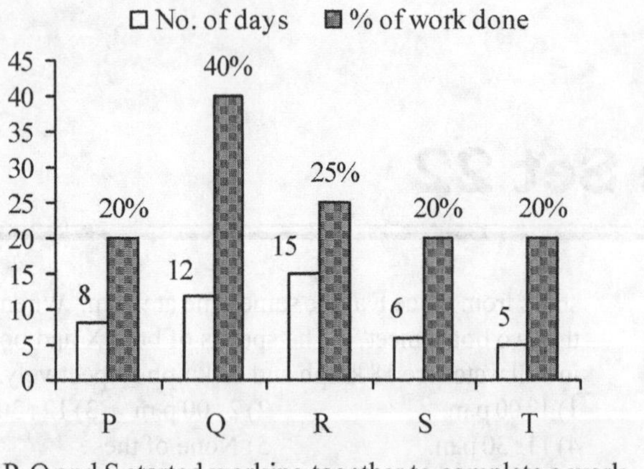

6. P, Q and S started working together to complete a work. After 4 days, Q left the work and T joined P and S to finish the work. After next ____ days P and T both left the work. Now S worked for ____ days and finished the remaining work.
Which of the following options are possible for the blanks in the same order?
1) 5, 3 2) 5, 2 3) 4, 3.5
4) 6, 1 5) None of these

7. P, Q and R together started working. After 7 days 'R' left and again 3 days after 'P' and 'Q' left. The remaining work is completed by S in '*n*' days. What is the value of '*n*'?
1) 10 2) 12 3) 9
4) 6 5) None of these

8. Find which of the following pair takes the minimum number of days to finish the work (working together).
1) P and Q 2) P and T 3) R and S
4) Q and T 5) Q and S

9. P and S together started working, but after 8 days P left and S alone finished the remaining work. If P takes ₹300 per day and S takes ₹200 per day, find the total money they earned.
1) ₹5000 2) ₹5700 3) ₹7200
4) ₹5500 5) None of these

10. P, Q and R started working together to complete a work. After some days, Q and R left the work (not necessarily on the same day). Work done by Q is double of the work done by R. P worked for 't' days and completed the work. Find the value of 't' if Q worked for only 12 days.
1) 12 days 2) 16 days 3) 20 days
4) 24 days 5) None of these

Directions (Q. 11-14): The chart given below shows the ratio of expense to savings of five persons in two months. The income of a person remains the same in either month.

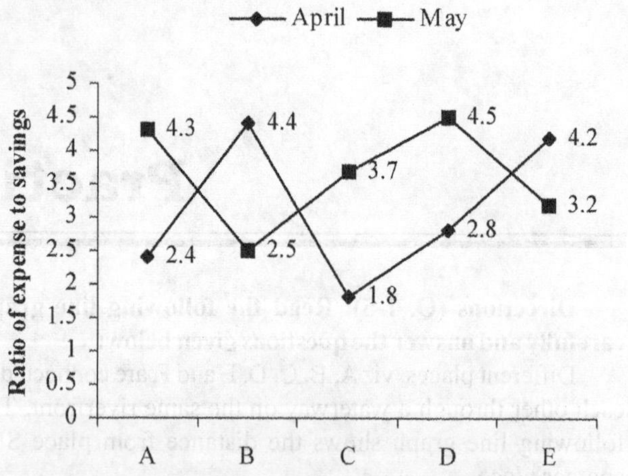

Total Income = Expenditure + Savings

11. Income of 'C' in either of the months is ₹19,200. Find expense of 'A' in the month of May.
(I) It is given that A's income is 40% more than C's income.
(II) Savings of C in the month of May is ₹4085.
1) Statement I alone is sufficient to answer the question but statement II alone is not sufficient to answer the question.
2) Statement II alone is sufficient to answer the question but statement I alone is not sufficient to answer the question.
3) Both the statements taken together are necessary to answer the question, but neither of the statements alone is sufficient to answer the question.
4) Either statement I or statement II is sufficient to answer the question.
5) Statements I and II taken together are not sufficient to answer the question.

12. 'B' invested some amount of his income in his friend's business in April. Find the amount invested by 'B' in his friend's business.
(I) The income of B in the month of April is ₹10800.
(II) The ratio of expense of B to the total income of B in the month of April is 22 : 27.
(III) The savings of B in the month of April is 37.5% of the amount invested in the business.
The above question can be answered by the information given in which of the following statements?
1) (I) only 2) (I) and (III) only
3) (II) and (III) only 4) All (I), (II) and (III)
5) Can't be answered

13. It is given that D's income is ₹7700 for the month of May. If D invested twice of his savings in May in a scheme that offered him simple interest at the rate of 12% per annum for 3 years. The amount received by him is invested in another scheme which gives compound interest of 15% per annum for 2 years. What will be the approximate amount received by him at the end of the maturity period of the second scheme?
1) ₹1008 2) ₹5302 3) ₹5000 4) ₹3808 5) ₹5036

14. It is given that B's income for the month of May is ₹5264.

The savings of E in the month of April is 5 times the savings of B in the month of May and it is known that E invested his total income in the month of April in Baua's business, which offers a return of 18% per annum. Then find out the profit earned by E by investing in the business for one year.
1) ₹7038.72 2) ₹7100.89 3) ₹7000
4) ₹7025.46 5) None of these

Directions (Q. 15-17): Study the following information carefully and answer the questions that follow:

Salman and Karan are best friends. They both own two versions of Maruti Suzuki Swift car. Karan owns petrol version of the car while Salman owns its diesel version. Karan's car gives an average that is 25% lesser than Salman's car. Here, average is given in terms of litres of fuel per kilometre. It is known that petrol costs per litre 40% higher than diesel per litre.

15. The expense of cost per kilometre of Karan's car and Salman's car are in the ratio of
1) 21 : 20 2) 14 : 15 3) 15 : 13 4) 12 : 17 5) 19 : 11

16. It has been found that Salman's car ran 25 kilometres per litre and the price of one litre of petrol is ₹70. The difference in the travelling cost per kilometre of both the cars is
1) ₹0.1 2) ₹0.42 3) ₹0.21 4) ₹0.40 5) ₹1.20

17. Karan purchased the car at a cost of ₹5,00,000. If the conditions given in above question are true and he sold the car at a cost of ₹4,56,000 after travelling a total of 20,000 km by that car, then the approximate loss per cent incurred by him in the transaction is
Note: Assume his travelling expenditure to be part of the total cost.
1) 12% 2) 20% 3) 19%
4) 16% 5) None of the above

Directions (Q. 18-21): Study the given graph given below and answer the following questions:

The graph given below shows the percentage of postgraduate employees in three different MNCs in three different years.

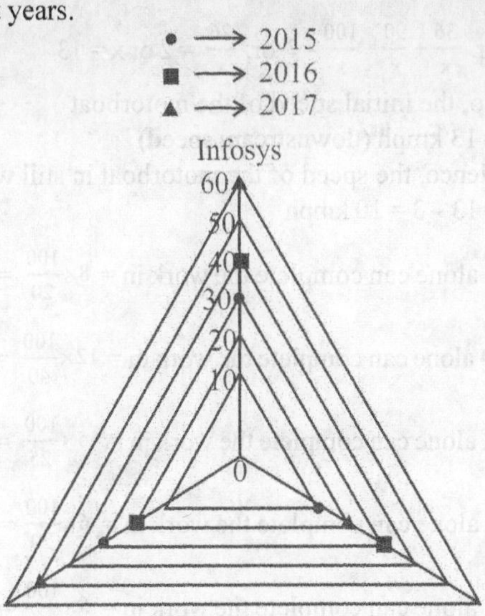

18. The number of employees of Infosys continuously decreases from 2015 to 2017. It decreases by the same number in both the years. If it is mentioned that the number of postgraduate employees in Infosys is the same in all the three years then by what per cent is the number of employees of Infosys in 2017 less than that in 2015?
1) 70% 2) 30% 3) 50%
4) 40% 5) Cannot be determined

19. If the sum of the number of postgraduate employees in HCL in 2015 and 2016 is 1550 and sum of the number of postgraduate employees in 2016 and 2017 is 2480. If the total sum of postgraduate employees in HCL in all the years together is 3400, then find the number of non-postgraduate employees in HCL in 2016.
1) 1420 2) 1400 3) 630 4) 1470 5) None of these

20. The number of employees working in TCS in the year 2015, 2016 and 2017 are in the ratio of 1 : 6 : 13. If the average of postgraduate employees of TCS in all three years is 800 then find the total number of employees working in TCS in 2017.
1) 3900 2) 1950 3) 300 4) 1800 5) 2250

21. It is given that the number of male postgraduate employees working in Infosys in the year 2015 is 60 and $\frac{10}{3}$ of the number of postgraduate male employees is the number of non-postgraduate male employees in the same year. The number of female postgraduate employees in twice the number of male postgraduate employees is the same year. Female postgraduate employees as well as non-postgraduate employees are equal in the following year. Also, ratio of non-postgraduate male employees in 2016 to postgraduate male employees in 2015 is 21 : 2. Non-postgraduate female employees in 2016 is $\frac{1}{3}$ of their male counterparts. Find the total number of employees working in Infosys in 2015 and 2016 together.
Note: All data given in this question pertain to Infosys.
1) 2200 2) 2000 3) 2500
4) 4200 5) Data insufficient

Answers and explanations

1. 3; ∵ Boat travels from place S to D downstream,

∴ Downstream speed = 22 + 3 = 25 kmph

Time taken by Ravi to travel from place S to D

$= \frac{125}{25} = 5$ hours.

Let the time taken by the Car to travel from place D to M be x hours.

Now, according to the question, $40(5 + x) = 275$

$\Rightarrow 40x = 75 \therefore x = \frac{75}{40} = \frac{15}{8}$ hours.

∴ Speed of the car $= \frac{275 - 125}{15} \times 8 = 80$ kmph

2. 2; The following diagram shows the distance and direction of Boat X and Boat Y.

B 200 – 50 = 150 km F

Boat X-> <-Boat Y

Given, the speed of Boat X from place B to F is downstream and the speed of Boat Y from place F to B is upstream. Then,

Upstream speed of Boat Y = 12 – 3 = 9 kmph

Downstream speed of Boat X = 18 + 3 = 21 kmph

Relative speed = 21 + 9 = 30 kmph

Required time $= \frac{150}{30} = 5$ hours

Hence, they meet each other at 9 am + 5 hours = 2 pm.

3. 5; Distance between place D and S = 125 km

As, the boat travels from place D to S its speed will be upstream.

Then, Upstream speed of Boat Q = 15.5 – 3 = 12.5 kmph

Time required by Boat Q to row a distance of 125 km

$= \frac{125}{12.5} = 10$ hours

Thus, time required by Boat P = 10 + 3 = 13 hours

So, the upstream speed of Boat P $= \frac{125}{13}$ kmph

Speed of Boat P in still water

$= \frac{125}{13} - 3 = \frac{125 - 39}{13} = \frac{86}{13} = 6\frac{8}{13}$ kmph

Statement II.

Required time $= \frac{125}{18.5} + \frac{125}{12.5} = 6\frac{28}{37} + 10 = 16\frac{28}{37}$ hours

Statement III. Let the speed of Boat P be x.

Distance between C to S = 90 km

Then, $\frac{90}{x-3} = \frac{90}{15.5-3} + 2.8 \Rightarrow \frac{90}{x} - \frac{90}{12.5} = 2.8 \Rightarrow x = 9$

∴ Upstream speed of Boat P = 9 – 3 = 6 kmph

Upstream speed of Boat Q = 15.5 – 3 = 12.5 kmph

∴ Reqd ratio $= \frac{6}{12.5} = \frac{60}{125} = \frac{12}{25} = 12 : 25$

Hence statement III is not true.

4. 3; Distance between place S and X = Distance between place S and F + 40 km = 200 + 40 = 240 km

Let the least speed of motorboat in still water = v kmph

Upstream speed of motorboat = (v – 3) kmph

Downstream speed of motorboat = (v + 3) kmph

According to the question, $\Rightarrow \frac{240}{v+3} + \frac{240}{v-3} \le 18$ hour

$\Rightarrow \frac{240(v - 3 + v + 3)}{(v+3)(v-3)} \le 18$

$\frac{240v}{v^2 - 9} \le 9$

$\Rightarrow 240v \le 9v^2 = 81 \Rightarrow 9v^2 - 240v - 81 \ge 0$

$\Rightarrow 3v^2 - 80v - 27 \ge 0 \Rightarrow 3v^2 - 81v + v - 27 \ge 0$

$\Rightarrow 3v(v - 27) + (v - 27) \ge 0 \Rightarrow (v - 27)(3v + 1) \ge 0$

$\Rightarrow$ v is either $\le -\frac{1}{3}$ or ≥ 27

Neglect the –ve value.

⇒ The least value of v is 27 km/hr.

5. 5; Distance between place S and C = 90 km

Let the initial speed of the motorboat be x kmph

According to the question,

$\left(\frac{40\% \text{ of } 90}{x} + \frac{60\% \text{ of } 90}{x \times \frac{3}{5}} - \frac{90}{x} = 2\right)$

or, $\frac{36}{x} + \frac{90}{x} - \frac{100}{x} = 2$ or, $\frac{26}{x} = 2$ or $x = 13$

So, the initial speed of the motorboat = 13 kmph (downstream speed)

Hence, the speed of the motorboat in still water = 13 – 3 = 10 kmph

6. 5; P alone can complete the work in $= 8 \times \frac{100}{20} = 40$ days

Q alone can complete the work in $= 12 \times \frac{100}{40} = 30$ days

R alone can complete the work in $= 15 \times \frac{100}{25} = 60$ days

S alone can complete the work in $= 6 \times \frac{100}{20} = 30$ days

T alone can complete the work in $= 5 \times \frac{100}{20} = 25$ days

Let total work = 600 units (LCM of total number of days required by all individually)

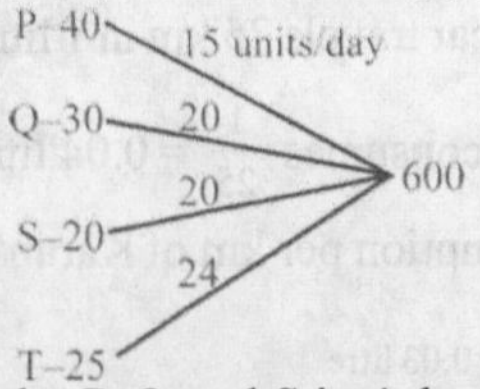

Work done by P, Q and S in 4 days
$= (15 + 20 + 20) \times 4 = 220$ units
Remaining work $= 600 - 220 = 380$ units
Now, let after next x days P and T both left the work and S worked for a total of y days and finished the remaining work.
Then, $(15 + 20 + 24) \times x + 20 \times y = 380$
$\Rightarrow 59x + 20y = 380$
None of the given option satisfies the equation, hence (5) will be the answer.

7. 3; Let the total work = 120 units (LCM of number of days required by P, Q, R and S)

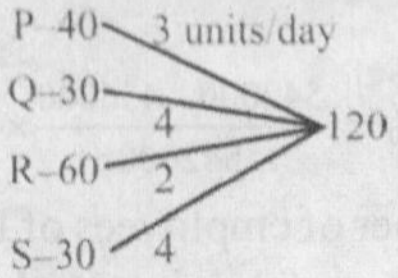

Work done by R in 7 days $= 7 \times 2 = 14$ units
Work done by P and Q in 10 days $= 10 \times 7 = 70$ units
Remaining work $= 120 - (70 + 14) = 36$ units
Number of days required by S to finish the remaining

work $= \frac{36}{4} = 9$ days

8. 4; Let the total work = 600 units

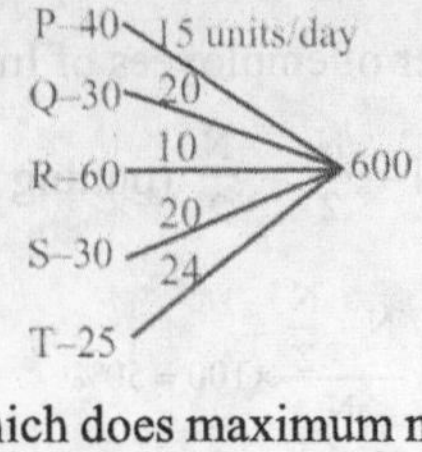

The pair which does maximum number of units per day will take minimum no. of days.
$P + Q \rightarrow 35$ units/day
$P + T \rightarrow 39$ units/day
$R + S \rightarrow 30$ units/day
$Q + T \rightarrow 44$ units/day
$Q + S \rightarrow 40$ units/day
Hence, Q and T will take the minimum time to finish the work.

9. 3; P alone can complete the whole work in $8 \times \frac{100}{20}$
$= 40$ days
S alone can complete the whole work in

$6 \times \frac{100}{20} = 30$ days

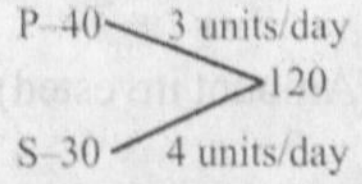

$\because$ (P + S)'s 8 days' work $= 7 \times 8 = 56$ units
Remaining work $= 120 - 56 = 64$ units

S alone finished 64 units work in $= \frac{64}{4} = 16$ days

Total money earned by P $= 8 \times 300 = ₹2400$
Total money earned by S $= (16 + 8) \times 200 = ₹4800$
Total $= 2400 + 4800 = ₹7200$

10. 2; Let the total work = 120 units

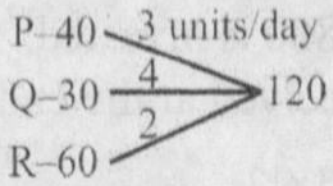

Q's 12 days' work $= 4 \times 12 = 48$ units
As given, Q does double the work done by R.
Then, R does 24 units of the work
Remaining work $= 120 - (48 + 24)$
$= 120 - 72 = 48$ units

48 unit works is done by P in t $= \frac{48}{3} = 16$ days

11. 1; **From I.** Income of C = ₹19200

Income of A $= \frac{140}{100} \times 19200 = 26880$

Now, it is given that in May,

$\frac{\text{Expense of A}}{\text{Saving of A}} = 4.3 = \frac{43}{10}$

Let saving of A be 10x
Expense of A be 43x
Now, $43x + 10x = 26880$
$\Rightarrow 53x = 26880 \Rightarrow x = 507.16$
$\therefore 10x = 5071.69 \Rightarrow 43x = 21808.267$
From II. It is given that, savings of C in May is ₹4085.
Which does not give any relation with A's income.
$\therefore$ We can't find A's expense from II.
Hence only I is sufficient.

12. 2; **From I.** Income of B is ₹10800.
This information is not sufficient to find B's investment.
From II. Ratio of expense to income is given as 22 : 27.
Which is also not sufficient alone.
From III. Savings is 37.5% less than the amount invested. Since we do not know amount of savings, we can't find investment from III alone.
From I and III.
Total income = 10800

We know that in the month of April $\frac{\text{Expense}}{\text{Savings}} = 4.4$

Let Savings = x ⇒ Expense = 4.4x

Now, 4.4x + x = 5.4x = 10800 ∴ x = 2000

Since, savings = 37.5% of amount invested

∴ $2000 = \frac{3}{8}$ (Amount invested)

⇒ Amount invested = $\frac{8 \times 2000}{3}$ = ₹5333.33

Hence I and III are required to answer the question.

13. 5; It is given that income of D in May = ₹7700

Let his savings in that month be x.

∴ Expenses = 4.5x

Now, x + 4.5x = 7700 ⇒ x = 1400

According to the question,

2x is invested in scheme I

∴ Amount ₹2800 is invested.

⇒ Amount received at the end of 3 years

$= 2800 + \frac{2800 \times 3 \times 12}{100} = 2800 + 1008 = 3808$

∴ Amount received at maturity of 2nd scheme

$= 3808\left(1 + \frac{15}{100}\right)^2$ = ₹5036 (approx)

14. 1; It is given that B's income (May) = ₹5264

Let his savings be S

∴ Expense = 2.5S

Now, S + 2.5S = 5264 ⇒ S = $\frac{5264}{3.5}$ = ₹1504

So, savings of E in April = 5 × 1504 = 7520

Expense of E in April = 4.2 × 7520 = 31584

So, total income = 31584 + 7520 = ₹39104

This amount is invested in a business offering 18% return.

So, profit = 18% of 39104 = ₹7038.72

15. 1; It is given that Karan's car gives an average of 25% lesser than Salman's car.

It means Karan's car consumers 25% less petrol per km than Salman's car's consumption of diesel.

Let Salman's car consume N litres diesel per km.

∴ Karan's car consumes $\frac{3}{4}$ N litres petrol per km

Also, Cost per litre of petrol = cost per litre diesel + 40% cost per litre diesel.

⇒ Cost per litre petrol = $\frac{7}{5}$ per litre cost of diesel

$\Rightarrow \frac{\text{Cost per litre petrol}}{\text{Cost per litre diesel}} = \frac{7}{5}$

Now, $\frac{\text{Cost per km (Karun)}}{\text{Cost per km(Salman)}} = \frac{7 \times \left(\frac{3}{4}\right)N}{5 \times N}$

$= \frac{7 \times 3}{4} \times \frac{1}{5} = 21:20$ ∴ Reqd ratio = 21 : 20

16. 1; Salman's car travels 25 km in 1 litre of diesel.

In 1 km, it consumes $\frac{1}{25}$ = 0.04 litre of diesel

So, consumption per km of Karan's car

$= \frac{3}{4} \times 0.04 = 0.03$ litre

Now, let price of 1 litre of diesel = ₹N

$\Rightarrow \frac{70}{N} = \frac{7}{5}$ (From above question) ⇒ N = ₹50

∴ Per km travelling cost of Salman = 50 × 0.4 = ₹2 and per km travelling cost of Karan = 70 × 0.03 = ₹2.1

∴ Reqd difference = ₹(2.1 − 2) = ₹0.1

17. 4; From the above question Karan's cost of travelling per km = ₹2.1

So, in 20000 km travel, it will cost him

= ₹(2.1 × 20000) = ₹42000

∴ Total expense of Karan = ₹(500000 + 42000)

= ₹542000

Hence loss % = $\frac{542000 - 456000}{542000} \times 100 = 15.86\% \approx 16\%$

18. 3; Let the number of employees of Infosys in 2015 be N.

Let the number of employees decrease by P. Infosys in 2016 = N − P

Number of employees of Infosys in 2017 = N − 2P

According to the question,

$\frac{30}{100}N = \frac{40}{100}(N - P)$

or, N = 4P ∴ $P = \left(\frac{N}{4}\right)$

Thus, number of employees of Infosys in 2017

$= N - 2P = N - \frac{N}{2} = \frac{N}{2}$ (putting the value of P)

∴ Reqd % = $\frac{N - \frac{N}{2}}{N} \times 100 = 50\%$

19. 4; Postgraduate employees in 2015 and 2016 = 1550 and in 2016 and 2017 = 2480

Number of postgraduate employees in 2016 = (1550 + 2480) − 3400 = 630

Now, the number of non-postgraduate employees in HCL in 2016 = $\frac{630}{30} \times 70 = 1470$

20. 1; Let number of employees working in TCS in 2015 be x.

Let number of employees working in TCS in 2016 be 6x.

Let number of employees working in TCS in 2017 be 13x.

Then, according to the question,

$$\frac{30}{100}\times(x)+\frac{20}{100}\times(6x)+\frac{50}{100}\times(13x)=800\times3 \Rightarrow x=300$$

Total number of employees working in TCS in 2017 $=300\times13=3900$

21. 2; From the data given in the question we can make a table for Infosys:

2015	Non PG	PG	2016	Non PG	PG
Males	200	60	Males	630	350
Females	220	120	Females	210	210
Total	180(70/30) = 420	180	Total	840	(40/60) ×840 =560

Hence total number of employees $=420+180+840+560=2000$

Practice Set 23

Directions (Q. 1-3): Study the following information carefully and answer the questions that follow:

There are two jugglers – Raman and Raghav. They both have one box each which consists of balls of three colours – White, Orange and Green. Each one of them has different number of balls of different colours and also the numbers of balls of each colour are different integers for both the jugglers. The total number of balls that Raman and Raghav have are in the ratio of 4 : 11. The probability of Raman taking out an Orange ball out of the box is $\left(\frac{1}{12}\right)$ greater than his taking White ball out of the box. The number of Green balls in Raghav's box is 11 more than the number of Green balls in Raman's box. The probability of Raghav taking out a White ball out of the box is $\left(\frac{2}{33}\right)$ greater than his taking a Green ball out of the box. The number of Green balls in Raman's box is 8. The number of Orange balls in Raghav's box is 5 more than Green balls in his box. The number of White balls in Raman's box is 12 less than number of Green balls in Raghav's box. The number of Orange balls in Raman's box is 14 less than the number of White balls in Raghav's box.

1. The total number of balls in Raman's box differs from the total number of balls in Raghav's box by

1) 42 2) 36 3) 25 4) 24 5) 48

2. Raghav chooses 3 balls for juggling. What is the probability that all the balls chosen by Raghav are of different colours?

1) Cannot be determined 2) None of the give options

3) $\frac{2622}{5720}$ 4) $\frac{1229}{5720}$ 5) $\frac{1311}{5720}$

3. Raman steals 8 Orange balls from Raghav and keeps them in his box. Then the probability of Raman taking out a Green ball out of the box now differs from taking out one White ball previously by

1) $\frac{1}{12}$ 2) $\frac{3}{17}$ 3) $\frac{1}{24}$ 4) $\frac{8}{11}$ 5) $\frac{5}{24}$

Directions (Q. 4-7): Study the graph given below and answer the following questions:

The graph given below shows the percentage of males in three different towns (ABC, PQR and XYZ) in three different years.

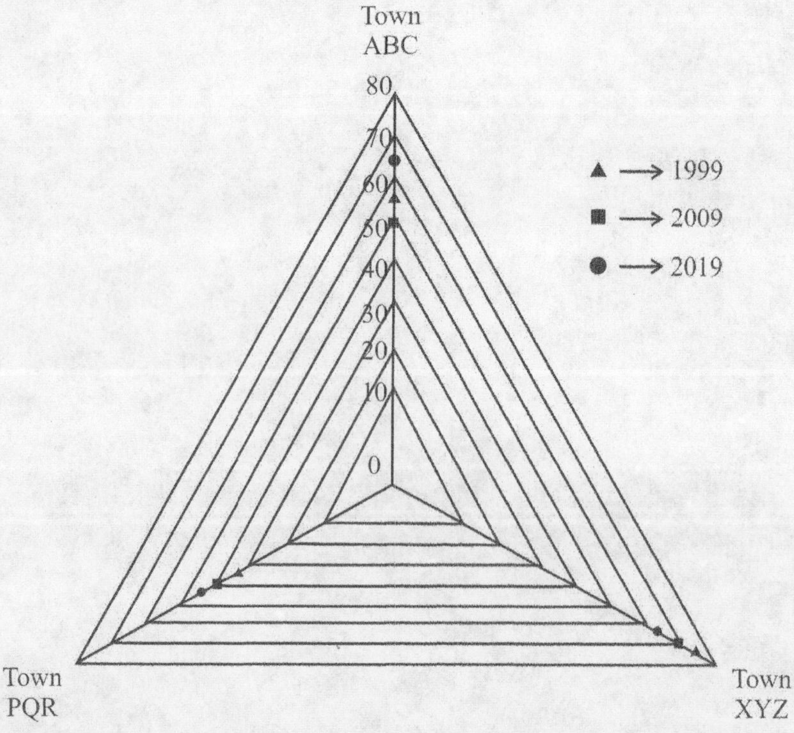

4. If the population of Town ABC in 1999, 2009 and 2019 are in the ratio 90 : 115 : 128 and the average number of males in 1999, 2009 and 2019 is 12680, then find the population of Town ABC in 1999.
1) 18000 2) 9000 3) 11500
4) 16640 5) 1800

5. The sum of males from Town PQR in 1999 and 2009 is 19840 and the sum of males from Town PQR in 2009 and 2019 is 25670. If the sum of males from Town PQR in all the given years is 33790 then find the total population of Town PQR in 2009.
1) 23200 2) 17580 3) 11720
4) 29300 5) None of the above.

6. What is the total population of Town XYZ in the year 2019?
(I) It is given that the population of Town ABC in 2009 is 23000.
(II) The population of Town ABC and Town PQR in the year 2009 are in the ratio 230 : 293.
(III) The population of Town PQR is 8284 more than the population of Town XYZ in the year 2009. This difference is 218% of the difference between the population of town XYZ in the years 2009 and 2019 respectively (population being more in 2019 as compared to 2009).
The abovementioned question can be answered by the information given in which of the following statements?
1) All the three statements 2) Only (I)
3) Both (III) and (I) 4) Either (II) and (I) or (III)
5) Cannot be answered using any of the statements

7. It is given that the male population of Town ABC and the female population of the Town XYZ in the year 2019 are in the ratio of 416 : 217. If the total population of Town ABC is 800 more than the total population of Town XYZ in 2019, then find the average female population of Town ABC and PQR in the year 2019.
1) 8680 2) 8820 3) 8960
4) 25600 5) Cannot be determined

Directions (Q. 8-12): Study the following information carefully and answer the questions that follow:

At 11 : 00 am, Lokesh started riding his bike towards Barood Nagar which is **(P)** km away, with a speed **(Q)** km/hr and at l/5th of the way, at 12 : 12 p.m. his bike ran out of fuel. So, he dragged his bike on foot at a speed of 6 km/hr and reached a petrol station 3 km away. Refuelling took 10 mins and he rode his bike at 25% more speed than earlier and was just 60 km before Barood Nagar that he met his friend Kamlesh at 3 : 52 p.m, who was just eating at a roadside dhaba. They talked for 20 minutes after which they decided to have a race to see who reaches Barood Nagar first. Kamlesh was riding at speed **(R)** km/hr and reached there 20 minutes before Lokesh, who was riding with his initial speed. Lokesh and Kamlesh, after reaching Barood Nagar, started working on an assignment. Normally Lokesh can complete the assignment in 3 hrs and Kamlesh can complete it in 33.33% more time than Lokesh while both of them are working alone. But they were working together with Lokesh working at 20% more than his efficiency and Kamlesh working at 80% of his efficiency. They completed the task in **(S)** minutes. After finishing the task, they decided to order food from Zomato. Lokesh ordered veg food and Kamlesh ordered non-veg food. The marked price of non-veg food is twice that of veg food and the discount percentage offered on veg and non-veg food is 10% and 30% respectively. The delivery charge is 10% applied on the total marked price of the food ordered. The delivery boy, Gulshan, asked for ₹50 as tip and the final amount they had to pay came out to be ₹570. The cost price of veg food was ₹(T) and it was marked up by 25%.

8. The value of Q, according to the given information, is
1) 60 2) 50
3) Cannot be determined 4) 40
5) 120

9. The value of P, according to the given information, is
1) Cannot be determined 2) 240 3) 300
4) 360 5) 120

10. The value of R, according to the given information, is
1) 100 2) 60 3) 90
4) 200 5) Cannot be determined

11. The value of T, according to the given information, is
1) 150 2) 640 3) 100
4) Cannot be determined 5) 160

12. The value of S, according to the given information, is
1) 100 2) 150 3) 160
4) 90 5) Cannot be determined

Directions (Q. 13-16): The graph given below shows the per cent increase/decrease in the total number of bikes sold by five different bike companies.

□ In 2017 from 2016 ▨ In 2018 from 2017

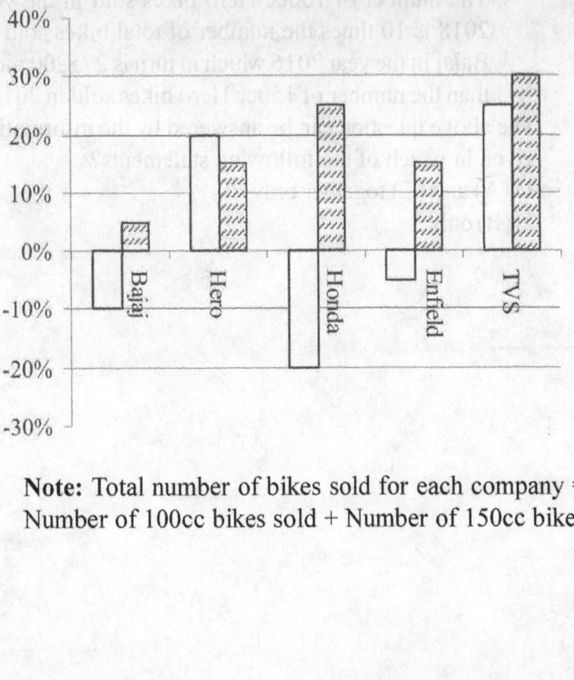

Note: Total number of bikes sold for each company = Number of 100cc bikes sold + Number of 150cc bikes sold + Number of 200cc bikes sold

13. The total number of Honda bikes sold in 2018 is 4350 and the number of Honda 150cc bikes sold in 2018 is 34% of the total Honda bikes sold that year. It is also given that the number of 150cc Honda bikes sold in 2016 is 79 less than that in 2018. Then the number of 150cc Honda bikes sold is what per cent of the total number of Honda bikes sold in 2016?
1) 35.68 2) 38.09 3) 37.41
4) Cannot be determined 5) 32.18

14. The ratio of total number of 100cc bikes sold to the total number of 150cc bikes sold to the total number of 200cc bikes sold by TVS company in the years 2016, 2017 and 2018 are 11 : 6 : 5, 10 : 5 : 7 and 60 : 50 : 33 respectively. Find the total number of 200cc bikes sold by TVS in all these three years if the total number of TVS bikes sold in 2018 is 14300.
1) 8500 2) 3300 3) 11000
4) 8800 5) 8400

15. If the total number of bikes sold by Enfield in 2016, Bajaj in 2018 and Hero in 2016 are 60,000, 66,150 and 1,30,000 respectively, then find the average of the total number of bikes sold by Enfield, Hero and Bajaj in the year 2017.
1) Cannot be determined 2) None of the given options
3) 89833 4) 90000 5) 92000

16. What is the number of Hero 150cc bikes sold in the year 2017?
(A) The number of 200cc Hero bikes sold in the year 2018 is half the number of 100cc bikes sold in the same year. Also, in the year 2017, the ratio of 100cc bikes sold to 200cc bikes sold of Hero is 3 : 2 and the difference between them is 59000.
(B) The ratio of 150cc bikes sold by Hero in the year 2017 to 2016 is in the ratio of 197 : 100.
(C) The number of 100cc Bajaj bikes sold in 2016 is 13456, which is 40% of the total bikes sold in 2016 by Bajaj. The number of 100cc Hero bikes sold in the year 2018 is 10 times the number of total bikes sold by Bajaj in the year 2016 which in turn is 275200 more than the number of 150cc Hero bikes sold in 2018.

The above question can be answered by the information given in which of the following statements?
1) (A) and (C) together only
2) (B) only
3) All the given statements are required
4) (A) and (B) together only
5) (B) and (C) together only

Directions (Q. 17-19): Study the following information carefully and answer the questions given below:

There are total 6000 employees in an MNC. Each one of them likes one or more among the three superbikes, viz Suzuki Hayabusa, Harley Davidson Fat Boy and Honda CBR 1000RR. 50% of the total number of employees like only two superbikes. The number of employees who like Honda CBR 1000RR but not Suzuki Hayabusa is 35% of the total number of employees. 15% of the total number of employees like only Suzuki Hayabusa and Harley Davidson Fat Boy both but not Honda CBR 1000RR. 20% of the total number of employees like only Harley Davidson Fat Boy and Honda CBR 1000RR both but not Suzuki Hayabusa. 55% of the total number of employees like Honda CBR 1000RR. 10% of the total number of employees like only Suzuki Hayabusa.

17. Under a promotion campaign, Harley Davidson Fat Boy is giving free test ride to female employees of the MNC who like that superbike and each female employee is allowed a free ride of maximum 10 km. If it is given that the ratio of males to females who like Harley Davidson Fat Boy in the MNC is 2 : 1 and the rate of petrol is ₹75 per litre, then find the maximum expenditure that Harley Davidson can incur in conducting the promotion campaign (given that the bike gives an average of 15 kmph).
1) ₹85000 2) ₹50000 3) ₹65000
4) ₹45000 5) ₹60000

18. Find the ratio of the number of employees who like at most two superbikes to the number of employees who like at least two superbikes.
1) 19 : 11 2) 11 : 13 3) 19 : 15
4) 11 : 19 5) None of these.

19. If there is a new superbike launched in the market, namely Kawasaki ZX-10R SE, and 65% of the employees in the MNC who liked only one superbike and 35% of the employees who liked two or more superbikes prior to the launch changed their liking to Kawasaki ZX-10R SE, then how many employees like Kawasaki ZX-10R SE now?
1) 1755 2) 2580 3) 2910 4) 3020 5) 1150

Answers and explanations

(1-3):

Let Raman have 4x and Raghav have 11x balls

Green (Raman) = 8

Green (Raghav) = 11 + 8 = 19

Orange (Raghav) = 5 + 19 = 24

White (Raman) = 19 – 12 = 7

Let the number of Orange balls in Raman's box be P

Then, $\frac{P}{4x} - \frac{7}{4x} = \frac{1}{12} \Rightarrow \frac{P-7}{4x} = \frac{1}{12}$

$\Rightarrow 3P - 21 = x$ ... (i)

Orange (Raman) = P

$\Rightarrow$ White (Raghav) = P + 14

Then, $\frac{P+14}{11x} - \frac{19}{11x} = \frac{2}{33} \Rightarrow \frac{P+14-19}{11x} = \frac{2}{33}$

$\Rightarrow \frac{P-5}{11x} = \frac{2}{33} \Rightarrow 3P - 15 = 2x$ ... (ii)

Solving (i) and (ii), we get P = 9 and x = 6

	Raman	Raghav
White	7	23
Orange	9	24
Green	8	19
Total	24	66

1. 1; Total balls in Raman's box = 4x = 4 × 6 = 24

Total balls in Raghav's box = 11x = 66

$\therefore$ Reqd difference = 66 – 24 = 42

2. 5; Reqd probability $= \frac{^{23}C_1 \times {^{24}C_1} \times {^{19}C_1}}{^{66}C_3} = \frac{23 \times 24 \times 19}{65 \times 64 \times 11}$

$= \frac{1311}{5720}$

3. 3; Previously, probability of Raman taking out one White ball $= \frac{7}{24}$

Raman's bag consists of White balls = 7

After stealing the number of Orange balls = 9 + 8 = 17

Green = 8

Total = 7 + 17 + 8 = 32

Probability of taking out a Green ball $= \frac{8}{32} = \frac{1}{4}$

$\therefore$ Reqd difference $= \frac{7}{24} - \frac{1}{4} = \frac{7-6}{24} = \frac{1}{24}$

4. 1; Let total population of Town ABC in 1999, 2009 and 2019 be 90N, 115N and 128N respectively.

Then, according to the question,

$= \frac{55}{100} \times 90N + \frac{50}{100} \times 115N + \frac{65}{100} \times 128N = 12680 \times 3$

$\Rightarrow \frac{99N}{2} + \frac{115N}{2} + \frac{416N}{5} = 12680 \times 3$

or, $\frac{1902N}{10} = 12680 \times 3 \Rightarrow N = 200$

$\therefore$ Population of Town ABC in 1999 = 90N = 18000

5. 4; Sum of males from Town PQR in 2009 and 1999 = 19840

Sum of males from Town PQR in 2009 and 2019 = 25670

Total number of males = 33790

So, males in 2009 = 19840 + 25670 – 33790 = 11720

Now, in 2009, 40% of the total population are males.

So, 40% ≡ 11720

$\therefore 100\% \equiv \frac{11720}{40} \times 100$

$\therefore$ Total population $= \frac{11720}{40} \times 100 = 29300$

6. 1; **From statement I.** It is given that population of ABC in 2009 is 23000. We can't find population of XYZ in 2019 from this.

From statement II. Ratio of population is given, which is again insufficient.

From statement III. Difference in population of towns PQR and XYZ in 2009 = 8300

Difference between population of Town XYZ in 2009 and 2019 $= \frac{8284}{218} \times 100 = 3800$ ... (i)

So, this is again not sufficient.

From (I), (II) and (III), we have

Population of ABC (in 2009) = 23000

Ratio of population of ABC and PQR (in 2009) = 230 : 293

$\Rightarrow$ Population of PQR in 2009 = 29300

Now, difference in population of PQR and XYZ in 2009 = 8284

Population of XYZ in 2009 = 29300 – 8284 = 21016

From (i), we have

Population of XYZ in 2019 = 21016 + 3800 = 24816

Hence all three statements are required.

7. 2; Let total population of Town XYZ in 2019 = N

Then, population of town ABC in 2019 = N + 800

According to the question

$$\frac{\frac{65}{100}(N+800)}{\frac{35}{100}(N)} = \frac{416}{217}$$

$\Rightarrow \frac{13(N+800)}{7N} = \frac{416}{217} \Rightarrow N = 24800$

Population of ABC in 2019 = 24800 + 800 = 25600

Female population of Town ABC in 2019

$= \frac{35}{100} \times 25600 = 8960$

Female population of Town XYZ in 2019

$= \frac{35}{100} \times 24800 = 8680$

$\therefore$ Average required $= \frac{8960+8680}{2} = 8820$

(8-12):

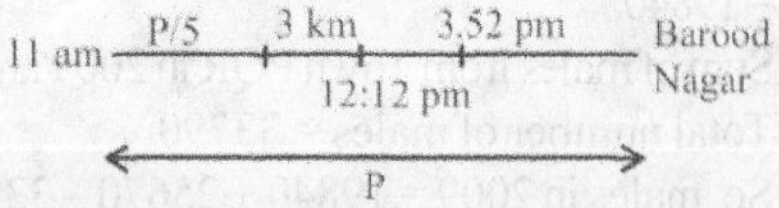

According to the question,

To travel the distance of $\frac{P}{5}$ km $= (12:12 \text{ pm} - 11 \text{ am})$

$= 1$ hour 12 minutes $= 72$ minutes $= \frac{6}{5}$ hours

$\therefore \frac{P}{5} = Q\left(\frac{6}{5}\right)$

$P = 6Q$ ... (i)

Now, time taken to reach petrol station

$= \frac{3}{6}$ hours $= 30$ minutes and refuelling took 10 minutes more. Hence after refuelling time is $(12:12+30+10=)$ 12:52 pm.

Now, he increases his speed by 25%. So, by speed of 1.25Q he travels $\left(P - \frac{P}{5}\right) - 3 - 60$ km $= \left(\frac{4P}{5} - 63\right)$ km

Time taken to travel this distance = 12 : 52 pm to 3 : 52 pm = 3 hours

$\therefore \frac{4P}{5} - 63 = 1.25Q \times (3) \Rightarrow \frac{4P}{5} - 63 = 3.75\,Q$

$\Rightarrow 4P - 315 = 18.75Q \Rightarrow 24Q - 18.75Q = 315$ (Using (i))

$\therefore$ **Q = 60**

$\therefore P = 6 \times 60 =$ **360 km**

Now, as Barood Nagar is 60 km away,

time taken by Lokesh to reach there $= \frac{60}{60} = 1$ hour

Time taken by Kamlesh to reach there $= 60 - 20 = 40$ min

In 40 min covers 60 km

$\therefore$ In 60 min $= \frac{60}{40} \times 60 = 3 \times 30 = 90$ km

$\Rightarrow$ **R = 90 kmph**

Time taken by Lokesh to complete assignment alone

$= 3$ hours and Kamlesh completes it alone in $3 + \frac{1}{3} \times (3)$

$= 4$ hours

New efficiency of Lokesh

$= \frac{3 \times 100}{120} = \frac{5}{2}$ hours for the work

$\therefore$ Lokesh can do $\frac{2}{5}$ work per hour

Again, Kamlesh's new efficiency $= 4 \times \frac{100}{80}$

$= 5$ hours for the work

$\therefore$ Kamlesh can do $\frac{1}{5}$ work per hours

Work done by them in 1 hour $= \frac{2}{5} + \frac{1}{5} = \frac{3}{5}$

So, total time in which assignment will be completed

$= \frac{5}{3}$ hours $= \left(\frac{5}{3} \times 60 = \right)$ 100 minutes.

Thus, S = **100 minutes**

Suppose market price of veg and non-veg food be ₹100N and ₹200N respectively.

Then, $100N\frac{90}{100} + 200N\frac{70}{100} + \left(\frac{10}{100}\right) \times (300N) + 50 = 570$

$\Rightarrow 90N + 140N + 30N = 520$

$\therefore$ **N = 2**

MP of Veg food = ₹200

CP of Veg food $= \frac{200}{1.25} =$ ₹160

So, T = ₹160

So, finally the values are as follows:

P = 360 km

Q = 60 kmph

R = 90 kmph

S = 100 minutes

T = ₹160

8. 1 **9.** 4 **10.** 3 **11.** 5 **12.** 1

13. 5; Total number of Honda bikes sold in 2018 = 4350

Number of 150cc Honda bikes sold in 2018

$= \frac{34}{100} \times 4350 = 1479$

Number of 150cc Honda bikes sold in 2016

$= 1479 - 79 = 1400$

Also, let the total number of bikes sold in 2016 by Honda be N.

Then, $N \times \frac{80}{100} \times \frac{125}{100} = 4350 \therefore N = 4350$

$\therefore$ Reqd % $= \frac{1400}{4350} \times 100 = 32.18\%$

14. 4; It is given that in the year 2018, total no. of TVS bikes sold = 14300

Total no. of TVS bikes sold in 2017 $= 14300 \times \frac{100}{130} = 11000$

Total no. of TVS bikes sold in 2016 $= 11000 \times \frac{100}{125} = 8800$

Now, 200cc TVS bikes sold in 2018

$= \frac{14300 \times 33}{(60+50+33)} = \frac{14300 \times 33}{143} = 3300$

200cc TVS bikes sold in 2017

$= \frac{11000}{(10+5+7)} \times 7 = \frac{11000}{22} \times 7 = 3500$

200cc TVS bikes sold in 2016

$= \frac{8800}{(11+6+5)} \times 5 = \frac{8800}{22} \times 5 = 2000$

$\therefore$ Total 200CC TVS bikes sold $= 2000 + 3500 + 3300 = 8800$

15. 5; Bikes sold by Enfield in 2017 $= 60000 \times \frac{95}{100} = 57000$

Bikes sold by Bajaj in 2017 $= 66150 \times \frac{100}{105} = 63000$

Bikes sold by Hero in 2017 $= 130000 \times \frac{120}{100} = 156000$

Hence, required average $= \frac{57000 + 63000 + 156000}{3}$

$= 92000$

16. 1; **From statement (A):** We can't find the number of 150cc bikes sold in 2017 as there is no mention of the number of bikes – only the ratio is given.

From statement (B): Again, only ratio is given, so it is insufficient as well.

From statement (C): 100cc Bajaj bikes sold in 2016 $= 13456$

Total Bajaj bikes sold in 2016 $= \frac{13456}{40} \times 100 = 33640$

100cc Hero bikes sold in 2018 $= 10 \times 33640 = 336400$

150cc Hero bikes sold in 2018 $= 336400 - 275200 = 61200$

This information is insufficient.

From statement (A) and (C):

200cc Hero bikes sold in 2018 $= \frac{336400}{2} = 168200$

Thus, total Hero bikes sold in 2018 $= 168200 + 336400 + 61200 = 565800$

Total Hero bikes sold in 2017 $= 565800 \times \frac{100}{115} = 492000$

Now, 100cc hero bikes sold (in 2017) : 200cc Hero bikes sold (in 2017) $= 3 : 2$ and difference in them is 59000.

Thus, 100cc and 200cc Hero bikes sold in 2017 $= 59000 \times 5 = 295000$

150cc hero bikes sold in 2017 $= 492000 - 295000 = 197000$

Hence, statement (A) and (C) are required.

(17-19):

Let us analyse the given information and represent it as follows:

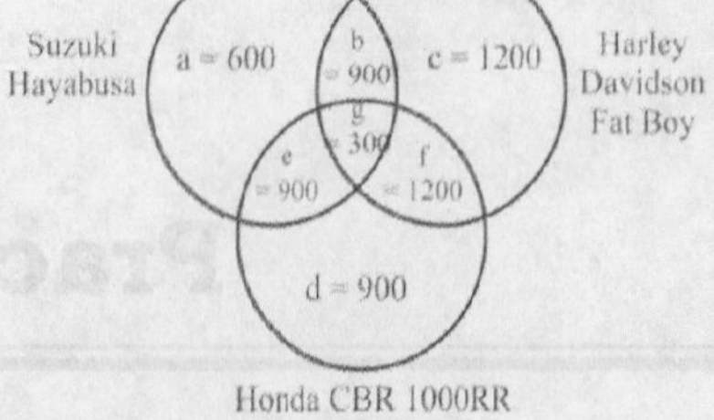

$b + e + f = 50\%$ of $6000 = \frac{1}{2} \times 6000 = 3000$ ... (i)

$d + f = 35\%$ of $6000 = \frac{7}{20} \times 6000 = 2100$ ... (ii)

$b = 15\%$ of $6000 = 900$ ... (iii)

$f = 20\%$ of $6000 = 1200$ ... (iv)

$d + e + f + g = 55\%$ of $6000 = 55 \times 60 = 3300$ ... (v)

$a = 10\%$ of $6000 = 600$ ... (vi)

From (i), (iii) and (iv), we get

$900 + e + 1200 = 3000$

$\therefore e = 3000 - 2100 = 900$ ... (vii)

From (ii) and (iv), we get

$d = f = 2100$

$d = 2100 - 1200 = 900$ ... (viii)

$\therefore d + 1200 = 2100 \Rightarrow d = 2100 - 1200 = 900$

From (v), (ii) and (vii), we get

$2100 + 900 + g = 3300$

$\therefore g = 3300 - 3000 = 300$ ... (ix)

Now, $a + b + c + d + e + f + g = 6000$

$\Rightarrow 600 + 900 + C + 900 + 900 + 300 + 1200 = 6000$

$\Rightarrow c = 6000 - 4800 = 1200$ ... (x)

17. 5; Total number of employees who like Harley Davidson Fat Boy $= b + c + g + f = 900 + 1200 + 1200 + 300 = 3600$

Ratio of males to females $= 2 : 1$

Female employees who like bike $= \frac{3600}{3} = 1200$

Maximum ride that can happen $= 1200 \times 10 = 12000$ km

Now, litres of petrol consumed $= \frac{12000}{15} = 800$ litres

Total maximum expenditure $= 800 \times 75 =$ ₹60000

18. 1; Number of employees who like at most two superbikes $= a + c + d + b + e + f = 600 + 1200 + 900 + 900 + 900 + 1200 = 5700$

Nubmer of employees who like at least two superbikes $= b + e + f + g = 900 + 900 + 1200 + 300 = 3300$

$\therefore$ Reqd ratio $= 5700 : 3300 = 19 : 11$

19. 3; Employees who liked only one superbike earlier $= a + c + d = 600 + 1200 + 900 = 2700$

Employees who liked two or more superbikes earlier $= b + e + g + f = 900 + 900 + 300 + 1200 = 3300$

According to the question,

Number of employees who like Kawaskaki ZX–10RSE

$= \frac{65}{100} \times 2700 + \frac{35}{100} \times 3300 = 1755 + 1155 = 2910$

Practice Set 24

Directions (Q. 1-3): The bar graph given below shows the per cent profit earned on five different articles by a shopkeeper Sachin in two years (2018 and 2019).

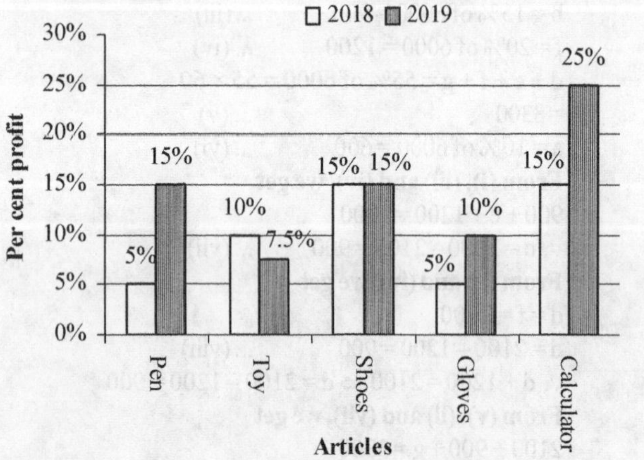

And the table below shows the marked price as a per cent of cost price of those articles. This remains the same in both the given years.

Articles	MP/CP × 100
Pen	125
Toy	112.5
Shoes	160
Gloves	200
Calculator	150

1. It is given that marked price of pen in the year 2019 is ₹175 more than the cost price, and marked price of shoes in the same year is ₹10 more than twice the marked price of pen. Then find the ratio of selling price of pen to that of shoes in the year 2019.
   1) 11 : 7   2) 85 : 87   3) 23 : 11
   4) 7 : 11   5) None of the above
2. What will be the difference between the marked price of calculator in the year 2018 and 2019?
   (I) The selling price of calculator in 2018 is ₹675 less than the selling price of gloves in 2018.
   (II) The cost price of calculator in both the years is the same.
   (III) The ratio of cost price of shoe in 2018 to that of calculator in 2019 is 5 : 6.
   (IV) The marked price of calculator in 2019 is ₹100 more than mark price of shoes in 2018 and the marked price of calculator in 2018 is ₹100 more than the marked price of shoes in the same year.
   The above question can be answered by the information given in which of the following statements?
   1) Either (II) or (IV) alone   2) Only (III)
   3) Both (II) and (IV)   4) Cannot be answered
   5) All (I), (II), (III) and (IV)
3. Kritika, a businesswoman, purchased 888 toys from Sachin in 2018 and thrice the number in 2019. The ratio of the cost price of a toy in 2018 to that in 2019 is 3 : 5 and the difference in their selling prices for Sachin is ₹622.5. If it is given that Kritika made a profit of 20% in both the years then find the total profit earned by Kritika in both the years.
   1) ₹925000   2) ₹959040   3) ₹1034964
   4) ₹859964   5) ₹956964

Directions (Q. 4-9): The line graph given below shows the export of wheat (in tonnes) from India and the import of wheat (in tonnes) to Australia in six different years. Study the graph carefully and answer the questions that follow:

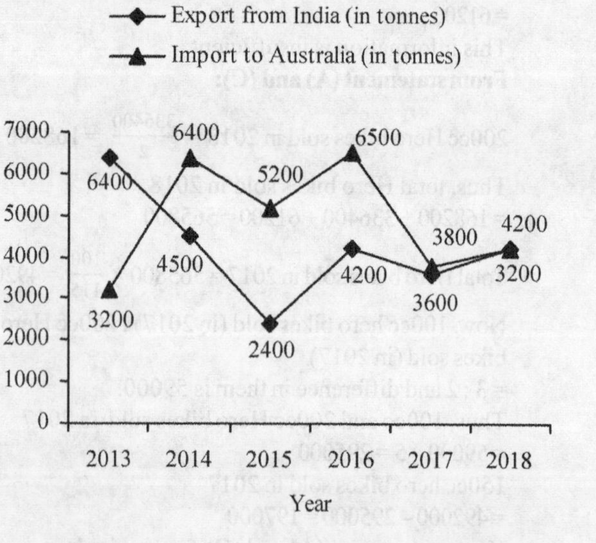

4. The ratio of import to export of wheat in India in the year 2015 was 3 : 2 and the export of wheat from Australia in 2015 was $33\frac{1}{3}$% more than that of the import of wheat

to Australia in 2018. Then the export of wheat from Australia in 2015 is what per cent more than the import of wheat to India in 2015?

1) $44\frac{2}{7}$ 2) $31\frac{1}{9}$ 3) $33\frac{1}{3}$
4) $55\frac{5}{9}$ 5) $66\frac{2}{3}$

5. The average quantity of wheat imported to Australia in the years 2013, 2015, 2017 and 2018 together is what per cent of the average exports of wheat from India in the years 2014, 2016 and 2017 together?
1) Zero 2) 10 3) 100
4) 50 5) None of these

6. It is mentioned that the cost incurred in importing 1 tonne of wheat by India in the year 2013 was ₹62 and the sum of the total cost incurred in exporting wheat from India and the cost incurred in importing wheat to India in 2013 was ₹616000. What is ratio of the cost incurred per tonne in importing wheat by India to the cost incurred per tonne exporting wheat in 2013 from India if it is given that ratio of quantity of wheat exported to quantity of wheat imported is 8 : 7 in that year?
1) 62 : 41 2) 31 : 22 3) 31 : 21
4) 62 : 39 5) None of these

7. It is mentioned that the quantity of wheat exported from India in the year 2012 is the same as the quantity of wheat imported to Australia in 2012. If it is mentioned that the ratio of wheat exported from India in the period 2012-15 to the wheat imported to Australia in the same period is 38:41, then what is the value of wheat exported from India in 2012?
1) 3400 tonnes 2) 2800 tonnes 3) 6400 tonnes
4) 5800 tonnes 5) 5700 tonnes

8. If it is mentioned that in the year 2015, the ratio of imports to exports for India is 7 : 6 and in the year 2017, exports of Australia are $5\frac{5}{19}$% more than imports in the same year, then the imports of India in 2015 is what % of the exports of Australia in 2017?

1) $142\frac{6}{7}$ 2) 70 3) $123\frac{6}{7}$
4) 75 5) None of these

9. If $14\frac{2}{7}$%, $12\frac{1}{2}$% and 25% of the exports of wheat from India in the years 2016, 2017 and 2018 respectively were to Australia, then what is the average (in tonnes) of imports of Australia from other countries in these three years?

1) $4216\frac{2}{3}$ 2) $4568\frac{1}{3}$ 3) $5866\frac{17}{22}$
4) $4466\frac{4}{9}$ 5) None of these

Directions (Q. 10-15): Study the given information carefully and answer the questions that follow.

A product M is sold in all three stores (ie Big Bazaar, Reliance and Walmart). The table given below shows the selling price of product M in three different stores in five different cities.

Days	Big Bazaar	Reliance	Walmart
Faridabad	3150	3220	2975
Kolkata	2975	2905	3010
Pune	2800	3150	2695
Bengaluru	3325	2625	2730
Ludhiana	3150	3115	2800

NOTE: The marked price of product M is the same in all three stores across all five cities.

10. If the cost price of the product M at Big Bazaar in Faridabad is 10% less than the cost price of the product M at Reliance in the same city and the percentage profit on selling the product M in Big Bazaar in Faridabad is $16\frac{2}{3}$%, then what is the percentage profit on the product M in Reliance in Faridabad?

1) $7\frac{1}{3}$ 2) $5\frac{2}{3}$ 3) 10
4) 12 5) None of these

11. If the discount on product M at Big Bazaar in Pune is ₹700, then what is the total percentage discount offered on product M in Bengaluru and Ludhiana in Walmart?
1) 28 2) 24 3) 15 4) 21 5) 12

12. In Bengaluru, the discount percentage offered on product M in Reliance is 25%. If the discount offered on the product M in Reliance had been 60% more than the present discount amount, there would have been a profit of 5%. What is the present percentage profit on product M at Reliance in Bengaluru?
1) 33.33 2) 27.50 3) 31.25
4) 37.25 5) 12.25

13. If the discount offered on product M at Big Bazaar in Kolkata is ₹525, then what is average discount offered on product M at Walmart in all the cities together?
1) ₹446 2) ₹658 3) ₹758
4) ₹568 5) None of these

14. If the discount offered on product M at Reliance in Ludhiana is 11%, then what is the ratio of the sum of percentage discount offered on product M at Reliance and Walmart in Pune to the sum of percentage discount

offered on product M at Big Bazaar and Reliance in Bengaluru?
1) 13:12 2) 11:10 3) 14:9
4) 10:11 5) Cannot be determined

15. If the discount offered on product M in Ludhiana at Big Bazaar is increased by 24% of the discounted price, the discount price obtained is ₹204 more than the original discount price. What is the marked price of product M?
1) ₹4000 2) ₹3750 3) ₹3500
4) ₹4500 5) Cannot be determined

Directions (Q. 16-18): Study the given information carefully and answer the questions that follow:

Rolly and Dolly earned different amounts of salaries. After a year, Rolly received a hike of N% and Dolly received a hike of 12% in their respective salaries. Rolly invested 70% of her salary after the hike in a scheme X, for two years, which offers compound interest at the rate of 10% per annum. She earned an interest of ₹4226.25. Dolly, on the other hand, invested 65% of her salary after the hike in a scheme X that offers simple interest at the rate of 15% per annum. She earned an interest of ₹12230.40 in 4 years.

16. Which of the following can be determined using the above given information?
(A) Value of N
(B) Rolly's salary after hike
(C) Dolly's initial salary
(D) Rolly's salary before hike
1) Only (B) and (D) 2) All (A), (B), (C) and (D)
3) Only (C) 4) Only (A) and (C)
5) Nothing can be determined

17. If it is given that Rolly's salary increased by ₹3750 after N% hike, then what is the value of N?
1) 23% 2) 20% 3) 10% 4) 12% 5) 15%

18. If N is the same as given in the above question, then the salary of Dolly is approximately what per cent of the salary of Rolly?
1) 140 2) 70 3) 112
4) 120 5) None of these

Directions (Q. 19-21): Study the following information carefully to answer the given questions.

In an organisation there are 3400 employees. The organisation has five departments – Publishing, Education, Accounts, Transportation and Courier Service. Out of the total number of female employees in the organisation, 34% work in Publishing, 20% in Accounts, 18% in Education and remaining 448 female employees work in the Transporation department. The Courier department has no female employee. Out of the total number of male employees in the organisation, 12% work in Publishing, 35% in Accounts, 30% in Education and 10% work in the Transport department and the remaining employees work in the Courier department.

(Note: The ratio of male to female employees in the organisation is 9 : 8.)

19. What is the average number of employees (male and female) who work in Publishing, Education and Accounts department together?
1) 856 2) 846 3) 836
4) 896 5) None of these

20. If the male employees in Transportation increase by 10%, 36 male employees decrease in Publishing, 20% male employees increase in Accounts and in other two departments the number of male employees remains the same, then find the total number of male employees in the organisation.
1) 1918 2) 1928 3) 1888
4) 1908 5) None of these

21. If 28 male employees from the Publishing department are transferred to the Education department and 38 female employees from the Education department are transferred to the Accounts department then what is the ratio of the number of male employees to the number of female employees in the Education department after the transfer of employees?
1) 125 : 284 2) 184 : 125 3) 284 : 125
4) 282 : 125 5) None of these

Answers and explanations

1. 4; Let CP of pen in 2019 = ₹N ⇒ MP = $\frac{125}{100}N = \frac{5N}{4}$

According to the question,

$\frac{5N}{4} - N = 175$

$\Rightarrow \frac{N}{4} = 175 \Rightarrow N = ₹700$

Now, marked price of pen in 2019 = 700 + 175 = ₹875

MP of shoes in 2019 = 2 × 875 + 10 = ₹1760

So, CP of shoes in 2019 = $\frac{1760}{160} \times 100$ = ₹1100

SP of shoes in 2019 = $1100 \times \frac{115}{100}$ = ₹1265

SP of pen in 2019 = $700 \times \frac{115}{100}$ = ₹805

∴ Reqd ratio = 805 : 1265 = 7 : 11

2. 1; **From statement I.** We can't find marked price or difference between them as no relationship between prices of calculator in both years in given.

From statement II. Let CP of calculator in both years be ₹N.

MP in 2018 = $\frac{150}{100}$N = MP in 2019 of calculator.

Difference = ₹0. Hence from II we get the answer.
From statement III. Again, we can't find difference.
From statement IV. Let the marked price of shoes in 2018 = N
MP of calculator in 2019 = N + 100
MP of calculator in 2018 = N + 100
∴ Difference = 0
Hence, either statement II or IV can give answer.

3. 3; Let CP of a toy in 2018 and 2019 be 3x and 5x respectively for Sachin.

Then, SP of a toy in 2018 = $\frac{110}{100}\times(3x)$

SP of a toy in 2019 = $\frac{107.5}{100}\times(5x)$

According to the question

$\frac{537.5x}{100}-\frac{330x}{100}=622.5$

$\Rightarrow 207.5x = 622.5\times 100 \therefore x=\frac{622.5\times 100}{207.5}=300$

$\Rightarrow x = 300$

Now, CP of Kritika in 2018 for a toy

= SP fo Sachin = $\frac{110}{100}\times 900 = 990$

And CP of Kritika in 2019 = $\frac{107.5}{100}\times 5\times 300 = 1612.5$

Thus, total CP of toys for Kritika in 2018
= 888 × 990 = ₹879120
Total CP of toys for Kritika in 2019
= 3 × 888 × 1612.5 = ₹4295700
Total CP = 879120 + 4295700 = 5174820

∴ Profit earned = $\frac{20}{100}\times 5174820$ = ₹1034964

4. 4; Import of wheat to India in 2015

$=\frac{2400}{2}\times 3 = 3600$ tonnes

Export of wheat from Australia in 2015

$= 4200\times\frac{4}{3} = 5600$ tonnes

∴ Required % = $\frac{5600-3600}{3600}\times 100$

$=\frac{2000}{3600}\times 100=\frac{20}{36}\times 100=\frac{500}{9}=55\frac{5}{9}\%$

5. 3; The average imports to Australia in 2013, 2015, 2017 and 2018 together

$=\frac{3200+5200+3800+4200}{4}=\frac{16400}{4}=4100$

The average exports from India in 2014, 2016 and 2017

together = $\frac{4500+4200+3600}{3}=\frac{12300}{3}=4100$

∴ Required % = $\frac{4100}{4100}\times 100 = 100\%$

6. 3; Quantity of wheat imported in 2013

$=\frac{6400}{8}\times 7 = 5600$ tonnes

Cost incurred in importing wheat
= 5600 × 62 = ₹347200
Cost incurred in exporting wheat
= ₹(616000 − 347200) = ₹268800
Cost per tonne incurred to exporting wheat

$=\frac{268800}{6400}$ = ₹42

Reqd ratio = 62 : 42 = 31 : 21

7. 5; Let N = wheat exported from India in 2012 = Wheat imported to Australia in 2012. According to the question,

$=\frac{6400+4500+2400+N}{3200+6400+5200+N}=\frac{38}{41}\Rightarrow\frac{13300+N}{14800+N}=\frac{38}{41}$

$\Rightarrow 545300+41N=562400+38N\Rightarrow 3N=17100$

∴ N = 5700 tonnes

8. 4; Imports of India in 2015 = $\frac{2400}{6}\times 7 = 2800$ tonnes

Exports of Australia in 2017

$= 3800+\frac{1}{19}\times 3800 = 3800+200 = 4000$ tonnes

∴ Required % = $\frac{2800}{4000}\times 100 = 70$

9. 1; Reqd average

$=\frac{\left(6500-\frac{4200}{7}\right)+\left(3800-\frac{3600}{8}\right)+\left(4200-\frac{3200}{4}\right)}{3}$

$=\frac{1}{3}[5900+3350+3400]=\frac{12650}{3}=4216\frac{2}{3}$

10. 1; CP at Big Bazaar

$= 3150\frac{100}{\left(100+\frac{50}{3}\right)}=3150\left(\frac{300}{350}\right)=2700$

CP at Reliance = $2700\left(\frac{100}{90}\right)=3000$

Reqd % profit = $\frac{3220-3000}{3000}\times 100$

$=\frac{220}{3000}\times 100=\frac{22}{3}=7\frac{1}{3}$

11. 4; MP of product M = 2800 + 700 = ₹3500
Total MP of product M at Walmart in Bengaluru and Ludhiana = ₹(3500 + 3500) = ₹7000
Total SP = 2730 + 2800 = ₹5530
∴ Reqd % discount offered

$= \frac{7000-5530}{7000} \times 100 = \frac{1470}{70} = 21\%$

12. 3; MP of product M $= \frac{2625}{75} \times 100 =$ ₹3500

Discount amount $= 3500 - 2625 = 875$

If this discount had been 60% more,

ie $875 \times \frac{160}{100} = 1400$

$SP = 3500 - 1400 = 2100.$

Then there is 5% profit. $CP = 2100 \times \frac{100}{105} =$ ₹2000

$\therefore$ Reqd % profit $= \frac{2625-2000}{2000} \times 100$

$= \frac{62500}{2000} = 31.25\%$

13. 2; MP of product M $= 2975 + 525 = 3500$

Discount offered at Walmart in Faridabad

$= 3500 - 2975 = 525$

Kolkata $= 3500 - 3010 = 490$

Pune $= 3500 - 2695 = 805$

Bengaluru $= 3500 - 2730 = 770$

Ludhiana $= 3500 - 2800 = 700$

$\therefore$ Required average

$= \frac{525+490+805+770+700}{5} = \frac{3290}{5} =$ ₹658

14. 2; MP of product M $= \frac{3115}{89} \times 100 =$ ₹3500

Reqd % discount offered at Reliance (Pune)

$= \frac{3500-3150}{3500} \times 100 = 10\%$

Reqd % discount offered at Walmart (Pune)

$= \frac{3500-2695}{3500} \times 100 = 23\%$

Reqd % discount offered at Big Bazaar (Bengaluru)

$= \frac{3500-3325}{3500} \times 100 = 5\%$

Reqd % discount offered at Reliance (Bengaluru)

$= \frac{3500-2625}{3500} \times 100 = 25\%$

$\therefore$ Required ratio $= (10+23) : (5+25) = 33 : 30 = 11 : 10$

15. 1; Let discount price offered initially on product M be D.

As per given information, $\frac{24}{100} D = 204 \therefore D = 850$

$\therefore$ MP of product M $= 3150 + 850 =$ ₹4000

16. 3; Let the salaries (initial) of Rolly and Dolly be R and D respectively. Rolly's salary after the hike $= R\left(1 + \frac{N}{100}\right)$

$\because$ Dolly's salary after the hike $= \frac{D \times 112}{100} = \frac{28D}{25}$

For Dolly: Investment in scheme X

$= \frac{65}{100} \times \frac{28D}{25} = \frac{91}{125} D$

Now, $\frac{91D \times 15 \times 4}{125 \times 100} = 12230.4$

$\Rightarrow D = \frac{12230.4 \times 100 \times 125}{91 \times 15 \times 4} =$ ₹28000; which is the inital salary of Dolly. Hence option (C) is correct.

For Rolly: Principal $= \frac{70}{100} \times R\left(\frac{100+N}{100}\right) = \frac{7R}{10}\left(\frac{100+N}{100}\right)$

So, $\frac{7R}{10}\left(\frac{100+N}{100}\right)\frac{21}{100} = 4226.25$

$\Rightarrow \frac{147R}{1000}\left(\frac{1+N}{100}\right) = 4226.25 \ldots (1)$

Now, (A) and (B) cannot be determined as values of R and N cannot be found from this equation. Similarly, (D) can't be found as R can't be determined.

17. 5; As per information given,

N% of $R = 3750 \Rightarrow NR = 3750 \times 100 \Rightarrow R = \frac{375000}{N}$

Putting the value of R in (1),

$\frac{147}{1000} \times \frac{375000}{N}\left(\frac{100+N}{100}\right) = 4226.25$

$\Rightarrow N = \frac{147 \times 375}{3675} \Rightarrow N = 15\%$

18. 3; Putting, N = 15%, we get

Now, $\frac{147R}{1000}\left(\frac{115}{100}\right) = 4226.25$

$\Rightarrow R = \frac{4226.25 \times 100 \times 1000}{115 \times 147} = 25000$

And Dolly's salary = 28000

$\therefore$ Required % $= \frac{28000}{25000} \times 100 \approx 112$

(19-21):

	Male employees 3400×9/17=1800	Female employees 3400×8/17 =1600
Department	Male	Female
Education	1800×30/100=540	1600×18/100 =288
Accounts	1800×35/100=630	1600×20/100 =320
Publishing	1800×12/100=216	1600×34/100 =544
Transportation	1800×10/100=180	448
Courier	234	0

19. 2; Reqd average

$= \frac{(216+544)+(540+288)+(630+320)}{3} = \frac{2538}{3} = 846$

20. 4; Number of employees (male) in the organisation

$= 180\times\frac{110}{100}+(216-36)+630\times\frac{120}{100}+540$

$+234 = 198+180+756+540+234 = 1908$

21. 3; Number of male employees in Education department $= 540+28 = 568$

Number of female employees in Education Department $= 288-38 = 250$

So, reqd ratio $= 568 : 250 = 284 : 125$

Practice Set 25

Directions (Q. 1-3): Study the following information carefully and answer the questions given below:

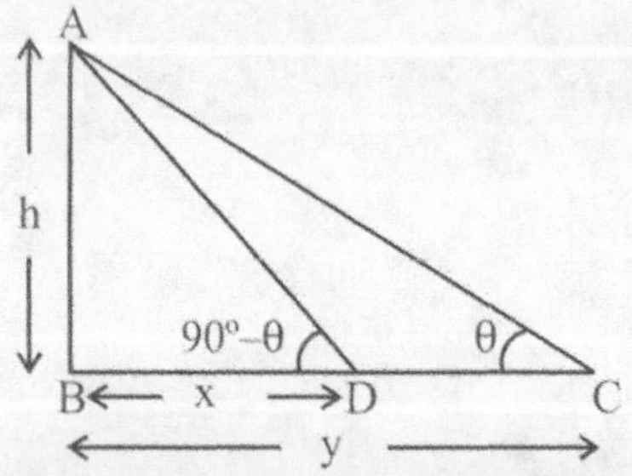

Some values are missing in the table given below. You have to calculate these values if requried.

Cases	x (in m)	y (in m)	h (in m)
Case I	9	25	–
Case II	–	49	28
Case III	25	–	30

1. Find the ratio of the value of h in Case I to the value of x in Case III.
   1) 5 : 6 2) 4 : 5 3) 3 : 5
   4) 6 : 5 5) None of these
2. Find the average value of x in all three cases, ie I, II and III, together.
   1) $16\frac{2}{3}$m 2) $17\frac{1}{3}$m 3) $18\frac{2}{3}$m
   4) 25m 5) None of these
3. Find the difference between the value of y in case III and the value of x in case II. (in m)
   1) 9 2) 16 3) 17
   4) 20 5) None of these

Directions (Q. 4-8): Study the table to answer the given questions.

Percentage of people (males and females) who watch the movies of different categories out of the total population of the city

City	Total population of the city	Horror		Romantic		Comedy		Scientific	
		M	F	M	F	M	F	M	F
P	50000	12	16	16	21	13	16	15	16
Q	30000	22	15	18	24	19	17	17	18
R	60000	16	15	20	25	15	18	16	15
S	40000	22	30	19	15	23	16	14	13
T	20000	21	28	30	12	24	14	12	11

Note: For example, 12% of 50000 = 6000 males (M) and 16% of 50000 = 8000 females (F) watch horror movies.

4. The ratio of the total number of males to the total number of females in City R is 7 : 5. What per cent of the female population watches Romantic movies in City R?
   1) 48% 2) 24% 3) 30%
   4) 60% 5) None of these
5. The total population (male and female) of City P watching Scientific movies is what per cent more than the total population (male and female) of City S watching the same type of movies?
   1) 43.38% 2) 54.51% 3) 52.51%
   4) 46.43% 5) 43.51%
6. What is the ratio of the number of females who watch Horror movies in City Q and City T together to the number of females who watch Comedy movies in the same city together?
   1) 102 : 79 2) 79 : 101 3) 83 : 105
   4) 101 : 79 5) None of these
7. What is the average number of males who watch Comedy movies in all the cities together?
   1) 7140 2) 7040 3) 7180
   4) 7240 5) None of these
8. What is the difference between the total population of cities R, S and T together that does not watch Romantic movies and the total population living in these three cities together that watches Romantic movies?
   1) 22000 2) 24000 3) 26000
   4) 23000 5) None of these

Directions (Q. 9-11): Study the bar-graph to answer the given questions.

The bar-graph shows the sales of six different cars in 2016 (in thousand). The following pie-chart shows the break-up of sales of each type of car .

Global sales of different cars (in thousand) in year 2016

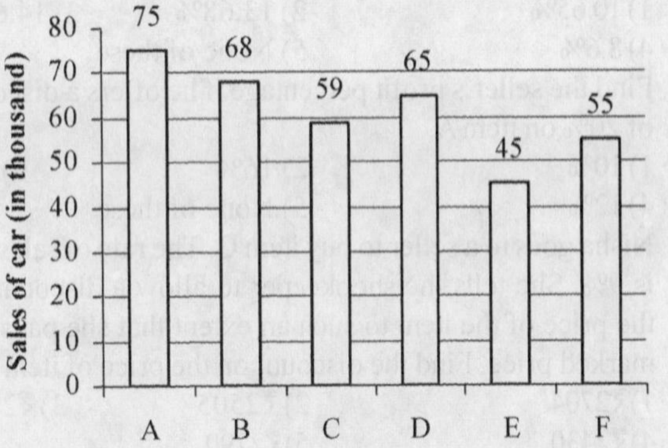

Countrywise sales of each type of car in year 2016

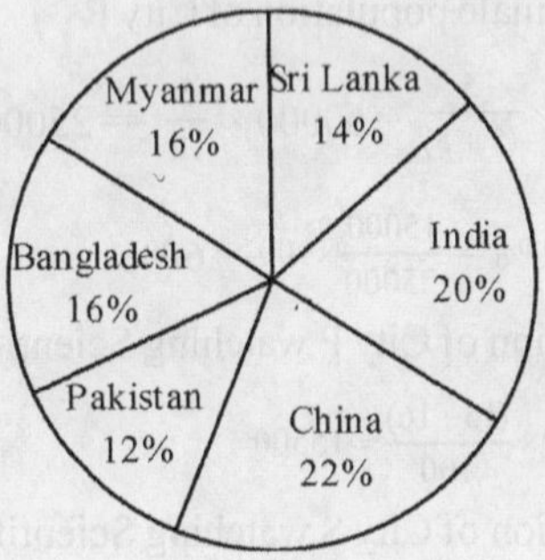

9. What is the difference between the volume of sales of Car A in India and that in Myanmar?
1) 5000 2) 3000 3) 4000
4) 25000 5) None of these

10. In year 2017, the global sales of Car A increases by 20% while its sale in India increases by 30% and in China by 40%, what is the approximate percentage sales increase in the rest of the countries taken together?
1) 8.97% 2) 12.13% 3) 15.97%
4) 6.27% 5) 3.33%

11. If the sale of cars in 2017 registers a uniform 25% growth across all brands and all countries, then what would be the combined sales volume of cars in India, Pakistan and Myanmar taken together in that year?
1) 210200 2) 230200 3) 220200
4) 222200 5) None of these

Directions (Q. 12-15): Study the following information carefully and answer the questions given below:

The graph below shows the number of Graduates (in thousand) in different streams, from six different districts (A, B, C, D, E and F).

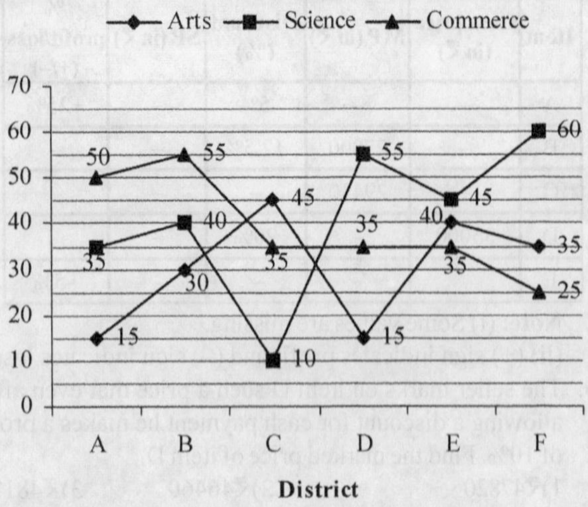

12. What is the ratio of the total number of Graduates from District B and the total number of Graduates from District E?
1) 24 : 25 2) 25 : 24 3) 26 : 25 4) 13 : 12 5) 12 : 13

13. The number of Graduates from district B, C, D and E in Science stream in approximately what per cent of the total number of Graduates in Commerce stream from all districts together?
1) 58% 2) 105% 3) 85%
4) 64% 5) 90%

14. The number of Graduates in all streams together from district F increases by 50 per cent after one year. After one year if the numbers of Graduates in Arts and Commerce stream are 45000 and 32000 respectively, then find the number of Science Graduates from district F after one year.
1) 103000 2) 105000 3) 95000
4) 110000 5) None of these

15. The number of Graduates in all streams from district A is what per cent less than the number of Graduates from district E?
1) $16\frac{2}{3}\%$ 2) $13\frac{1}{3}\%$ 3) $14\frac{1}{5}\%$
4) $17\frac{1}{3}\%$ 5) None of these

Directions (Q. 16-20): Study the following table and answer the questions given below:

The table shows the cost price, marked price, discount offered, selling price and the profit/loss percentage on different types of items.

Item	Cost price (in ₹)	MP (in ₹)	Discount (%)	SP (in ₹)	% profit/loss (+/–)
A	–	–	5%	–	+25%
B	–	27000	12.5%	–	–
C	–	29430	–	–	–
D	35000	–	20%	–	–
E	–	–	–	–	–5%

Note: (i) Some values are missing.
(ii) (+) sign indicates profit and (–) sign indicates loss.

16. The seller marks on item D such a price that even after allowing a discount for cash payment he makes a profit of 10%. Find the marked price of item D.
1) ₹47820 2) ₹46460 3) ₹48125
4) ₹49340 5) None of these

17. Had the seller sold the item E for ₹1500 more than earlier, he would have gained 10%. For what value should he sell the item to gain 20%?
1) ₹12000 2) ₹18000 3) ₹17000
4) ₹15000 5) None of these

18. The seller supplies item B to a customer after allowing discount on the marked price. If the seller sells item B at the list price and his expenses on freight is ₹125, determine his % profit.
1) 10.65% 2) 13.68% 3) 14.62%
4) 8.6% 5) None of these

19. Find the seller's profit percentage if he offers a discount of 20% on item A.
1) 10% 2) 16% 3) 8%
4) 12% 5) None of these

20. Nisha goes to a seller to buy item C. The rate of sales tax is 9%. She tells the shopkeeper to allow a discount on the price of the item to such an extent that she pays the marked price. Find the discount on the price of item C.
1) ₹2704 2) ₹2505 3) ₹2840
4) ₹2430 5) ₹2790

Answers and explanations

(1-3):

In ΔABC, $\tan\theta = \frac{AB}{BC}$

$\Rightarrow \tan\theta = \frac{h}{y}$ ... (i)

In ΔABD, $\tan(90° - \theta) = \frac{AB}{BD}$

$\Rightarrow \cot\theta = \frac{h}{x}$ ... (ii)

By multiplying both equations, we get

$\tan\theta.\cot\theta = \frac{h}{y} \times \frac{h}{x}$ or, $1 = \frac{h^2}{xy}$ $\therefore h = \sqrt{xy}$

1. 3; Value of h in Case I = $\sqrt{9 \times 25} = 15$m
Value of x in Case III = 25m
So, required ratio = 15 : 25 = 3 : 5

2. 1; Value of x in Case II. $h = \sqrt{xy}$
Then, $28 = \sqrt{x \times 49} \Rightarrow 28 = 7\sqrt{x}$ $\therefore x = 16$
$\therefore$ Reqd average $= \frac{9+16+25}{3} = \frac{50}{3} = 16\frac{2}{3}$ m

3. 4; Value of y in Case III
$h = \sqrt{xy} \Rightarrow 30 = \sqrt{25 \times y} \Rightarrow \sqrt{y} = 6 \therefore y = 36$m
Value of x in Case II = 16m (Calculated in above question)
So, reqd difference = 36 – 16 = 20m

4. 4; Total number of females who watch Romantic movies in City R = $60000 \times \frac{25}{100} = 60000 \times \frac{1}{4} = 15000$

Total female population of City R

$= 60000 \times \frac{5}{(7+5)} = 60000 \times \frac{5}{12} = 25000$

$\therefore$ Reqd % $= \frac{15000}{25000} \times 100 = 60\%$

5. 5; Population of City P watching Scientific movies

$= 50000 \times \frac{(15+16)}{100} = 15500$

Population of City S watching Scientific movies

$= 40000 \times \frac{(14+13)}{100} = 10800$

Reqd % $= \frac{4700}{10800} \times 100 = \frac{4700}{108} \approx 43.51\%$

6. 4; Reqd ratio $= \left(30000 \times \frac{15}{100} + 20000 \times \frac{28}{100}\right) : \left(30000 \times \frac{17}{100} + 20000 \times \frac{14}{100}\right)$

$= (4500 + 5600) : (5100 + 2800)$
$= 10100 : 7900 = 101 : 79$

7. 2; Reqd average

$= \frac{50000 \times \frac{13}{100} + 30000 \times \frac{19}{100} + 60000 \times \frac{15}{100} + 40000 \times \frac{23}{100} + 20000 \times \frac{24}{100}}{5}$

$= \frac{6500 + 5700 + 9000 + 9200 + 4800}{5} = \frac{35200}{5} = 7040$

8. 1; Population that watches Romantic movies in City R,

S and T together

$= 60000\times\frac{45}{100}+40000\times\frac{34}{100}+20000\times\frac{42}{100}$

$=27000+13600+8400=49000$

Population that does not watch romantic movies in City R, S and T together

$=(60000+40000+20000)-49000$

$=120000-49000=71000$

So, reqd difference $= 71000-49000 = 22000$

Quicker Approach:

$(55-45)\%$ of $60000+(66-34)\%$ of $40000+(58-42)\%$ of $20000=6000+12800+3200=22000$

9. 2; Reqd difference $= 75000\times\frac{(20-16)}{100} = 75000\times\frac{4}{100} = 3000$

10. 1; Sales of Car A in the year 2017

$75000\times\frac{120}{100}=90000$

Sales of Car A in India in 2016 $= 75000\times\frac{20}{100} = 15000$

Sales of Car A in China in 2016 $= 75000\times\frac{22}{100} = 16500$

Sales of Car A (in 2016) in rest of the countries $= 75000-(15000+16500)=75000-31500=43500$

Now, in year 2017

Sales of Car A in India $= 15000\times\frac{130}{100} = 19500$

Sales of Car A in China $= 16500\times\frac{140}{100} = 23100$

Sales of Car A in the rest of the countries in 2017 $=90000-(19500+23100)=90000-42600=47400$

Reqd % $= \frac{47400-43500}{43500}\times100 = \frac{3900}{43500}\times100 \approx 8.97\%$

11. 3; Total sales of cars in 2016 $= 75+68+59+65+45+55 = 367$ thousand

Sale of car in India, Pakistan and Myanmar in 2016

$= 367000\times\frac{(20+12+16)}{100} = 176160$

So, sale of cars in India, Pakistan and Myanmar in year 2017 $= 176160\times\frac{125}{100} = 220200$

12. 2; Reqd ratio $=(30+40+55):(40+45+35)=125:120 =25:24$

13. 4; Reqd per cent $= \frac{(40+10+55+45)}{(50+55+35+35+35+25)}\times100$

$= \frac{150}{235}\times100 \approx 64\%$

14. 1; Total number of graduates after one year in district F

$= 120\times\frac{150}{100} = 180$ thousand

$\therefore$ Number of Science graduates

$=180000-(45000+32000)=180000-77000=103000$

15. 1; Reqd % $= \frac{(120-100)}{120}\times100 = \frac{100}{6} = \frac{50}{3} = 16\frac{2}{3}\%$

16. 3; Reqd marked price $= 35000\times\frac{110}{100}\times\frac{100}{80} = ₹48125$

17. 1; Suppose the seller bought item E for ₹x.

The selling price at 5% loss $= 0.95x$

And the selling price at 10% profit $= 1.1x$

According to the question, $1.1x-0.95x=1500$

or, $0.15x=1500$ or, $x=\frac{1500}{0.15}=₹10000$

Selling price at 20% profit $= 10000\times\frac{120}{100} = ₹12000$

18. 2; Marked price $= 27000$

Discount $= 27000\times\frac{12.5}{100} = 3375$

$\therefore$ CP of item B of the seller

$=27000-3375+125=₹23750$

$\therefore$ Profit earned by the seller

$=27000-23750=3250$

$\therefore$ Reqd % profit $= \frac{3250}{23750}\times100 = 13.68\%$

19. 5; Reqd % profit $=(100+25)\left[\frac{100-20}{100-5}\right]-100$

$= 125\times\frac{80}{95}-100 = \frac{10000}{95}-100 = \frac{500}{95} = \frac{100}{19} = 5\frac{5}{19}\%$

20. 4; Let the reduced price of the item after discount be ₹x.

Then, sales tax = 9% of $x = \frac{9x}{100}$

$\therefore SP = x+\frac{9x}{100} = \frac{109x}{100}$ Now, $\frac{109x}{100} = 29430$

$\therefore x = \frac{29430\times100}{109} = ₹27000$

$\therefore$ Discount $= 29430-27000 = ₹2430$

Practice Set 26

Directions (Q. 1-5): Study the following table to answer the given questions.

The table shows the quantity of milk and water in different types of vessels.

Vessel	Quantity of mixture (in litres)	Ratio of milk to water	Quantity of milk (in litres)	Quantity of water (in litres)
P	–	–	–	–
Q	60	–	48	–
R	–	–	–	20
S	75	–	–	0
T	–	7 : 3	–	–

Note: Some values are missing. You have to calculate as per data given in the questions.

1. Vessel P, R and T have equal quantities and in Vessel P and R the ratios of milk to water are 7 : 5 and 5 : 3 respectively. The contents of all three vessels are emptied into another vessel. What is the proportion of milk and water in it?
1) 132 : 139 2) 137 : 229 3) 229 : 147
4) 229 : 131 5) None of these

2. From Vessel S, 15 litres of mixture is replaced with water. If the same process is repeated two more times, what will be the proportion of milk to water in the final mixture?
1) 62 : 63 2) 64 : 61 3) 61 : 63
4) 63 : 64 5) None of these

3. If the ratio of milk to water in Vessel R is 8 : 5, then how much water is to be added in Vessel R to get a new mixture containing milk and water in the ratio of 4 : 3?
1) 4 litres 2) 6 litres 3) 7 litres
4) 5 litres 5) None of these

4. From Vessel T, if 16 litres of mixture is replaced with 16 litres of water then the ratio becomes 7 : 4. How many litres of mixture does the vessel initially hold?
1) 165 2) 250 3) 176 4) 156 5) None of these

5. In Vessel P the mixture of milk and water is 20% more than that in Vessel Q. In what proportion should the quantities be taken out from the two vessels so as to make a mixture in which milk and water be in the proportion of 9 : 4 if the quantity of water in Vessel P is 18 litres?
1) 15 : 17 2) 17 : 19 3) 21 : 23
4) 28 : 15 5) 19 : 21

Directions (Q. 6-10): Study the following information carefully and answer the questions given below:

In a bag there are a certain number of mobiles of three different companies, viz Redmi, Samsung and Apple. The probability of selecting one Apple mobile out of all the mobiles is $\frac{1}{3}$ and the probability of selecting one Redmi mobile is $\frac{5}{12}$. The number of Samsung mobiles in the bag is 6.

6. If each company's mobiles are numbered starting from 1, 2, 3, ... and so on, then what is the probability of selecting one mobile which is numbered 2 of one company and 5 of another?
1) $\frac{7}{12}$ 2) $\frac{1}{4}$ 3) $\frac{3}{4}$ 4) $\frac{12}{19}$ 5) $\frac{5}{12}$

7. What is the total number of mobiles in the bag?
1) 26 2) 28 3) 30 4) 24 5) 20

8. In how many ways can six mobiles be chosen so as to include at least three Apple mobiles?
1) 41343 2) 36450 3) 35644
4) 42650 5) None of these

9. Among all the mobiles, 3 Apple mobiles, 4 Redmi mobiles and 3 Samsung mobiles are defective. Find the probability of selecting 4 defective mobiles out of which 3 are Redmi mobiles.
1) $\frac{5}{1258}$ 2) $\frac{3}{574}$ 3) $\frac{6}{1857}$
4) $\frac{4}{1771}$ 5) None of these

10. In how many different ways can 4 mobiles be chosen so as to include at most 3 Redmi mobiles?
1) 11517 2) 13413 3) 9857
4) 12312 5) 10416

Directions (Q. 11-15): The pie-chart given below shows the percentage breakup of books published by six different publishers A, B, C, D, E and F.

Total number of books published = 2.45 lakh

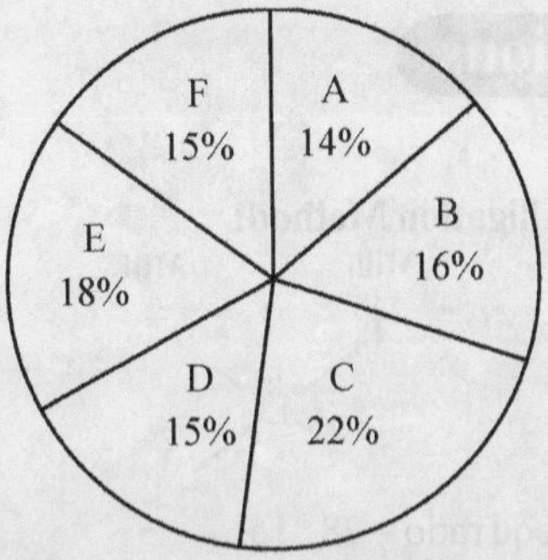

The line graph shows the percentage of books in different languages published by the six different publishers A, B, C, D, E and F.

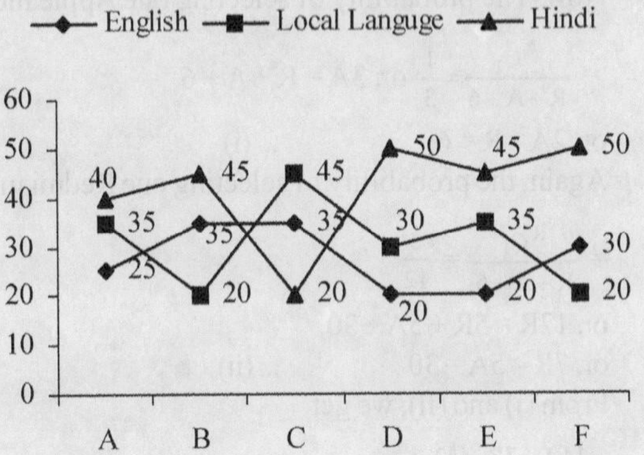

11. What is the approximate average number of Hindi books published by all six publishers?
1) 16456 2) 16885 3) 16346
4) 16876 5) 16495

12. What is the ratio of the total books published by A and B to that published by C and E?
1) 5 : 9 2) 4 : 9 3) 8 : 9
4) 3 : 4 5) 7 : 4

13. What is the angle for the share of books (in the pie-chart) published by A, B and D taken together?
1) 165° 2) 162° 3) 168°
4) 175° 5) 160°

14. If each book costs ₹4 and ₹5 for Hindi and English language respectively, then what is the total amount (in ₹) earned by the sales of Hindi and English books by Publisher A?
1) 97755 2) 85850 3) 95780
4) 94825 5) 96875

15. The English books published by Publisher B and F is what per cent more than that published by Publisher D and E together?
1) 56% 2) 48% 3) 52%
4) 55% 5) 53%

Directions (Q. 16-20): Study the following information carefully and answer the given questions:

Funnel chart given below shows percentage distribution of five different age groups people from Kolkata.

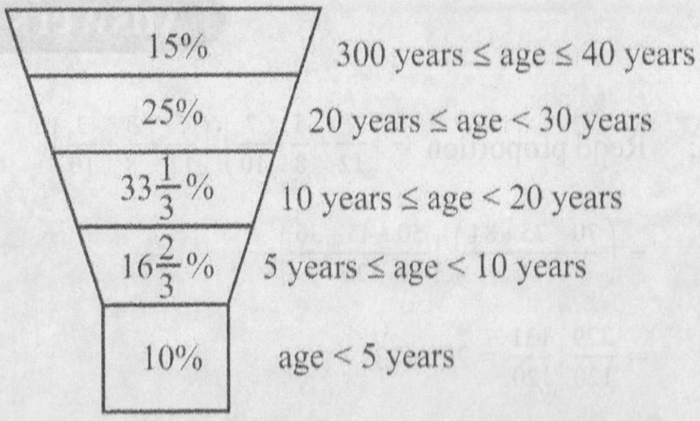

16. If the ratio of male to female whose age is greater than or equal to 30 yrs and below or equal to 40 yrs and greater than or equal to 20 yrs and below 30 yrs are 3 : 2 and 8 : 7 respectively. Number of males whose age is greater than or equal to 30 yrs and below or equal to 40 yrs is how much per cent more or less than number of females whose age is greater or equal to 20 yrs and below to 30 yrs?
1) 22(6/7)% 2) 12.5% 3) 33((1/3)%
4) 21(6/7)% 5) None of these

17. If the difference between persons whose age group is greater than equal to 10 yrs or less than 20 yrs and persons with age group greater than or equal to 5 yrs but less than 10 yrs is 15000, then find the number of persons with age group less than 5 yrs.
1) 2700 2) 4500 3) 90000
4) 9000 5) 27000

18. If the total population increases at the rate of 10% pa and the total population previously known as 60,000. Then find the population of age group of $5 \leq X < 10$ and $10 \leq x < 20$ after 3 yrs? [If percentage distribution remains the same]
1) 33030 2) 39930 3) 38930
4) 42080 5) 37990

19. If the difference between persons whose age group is greater than equal to 20 yrs or less than 30 yrs and persons with age group less than 5 years is 9000, then find the number of persons with age group greater than or equal to 5 yrs but less than 10 yrs.
1) 2700 2) 4500 3) 10000
4) 9000 5) 27000

20. If total population is 144000 and persons having age of 25 yrs, 35 yrs and 16 yrs are 33 (1/3)%, 80% and 75% respectively of their respective age group, then what is the total population having age of 25 yrs, 35 yrs and 16 yrs together?
1) 36280 2) 57280 3) 65280
4) 53280 5) None of these

Answers and explanations

1. 4; Reqd proportion $= \left(\frac{7}{12}+\frac{5}{8}+\frac{7}{10}\right):\left(\frac{5}{12}+\frac{3}{8}+\frac{3}{10}\right)$

$= \left(\frac{70+75+84}{120}\right):\left(\frac{50+45+36}{120}\right)$

$= \frac{229}{120}:\frac{131}{120} = 229:131$

2. 2; Amount of milk left $= 75\left(\frac{75-15}{75}\right)^3$

$= 75\left(\frac{60}{75}\right)^3 = 75\times\frac{64}{125} = 38.4$ litres

Reqd proportion $= \frac{38.4}{75-38.4} = \frac{38.4}{36.6} = \frac{64}{61} = 64:61$

3. 1; **Logical approach:**

$5 \equiv 20$

$8 \equiv \frac{20}{5}\times 8 = 32$ litres

Let x litres of water be added.

Then, $\frac{32}{20+x} = \frac{4}{3}$

$\Rightarrow 20 + x = 24 \Rightarrow x = 24 - 20 = 4$ litres

4. 3; Let Vessel T have 7x litres of milk and 3x litres of water.

Total quantity = 10x litres

Now, $\frac{7x-16\times\frac{7}{10}}{3x-16\times\frac{3}{10}+16} = \frac{7}{4}$

or, $4\left(7x-\frac{56}{5}\right) = 7\left(3x-\frac{24}{5}+16\right)$

or, $28x - \frac{224}{5} = 21x - \frac{168}{5} + 112$

or, $7x = \frac{224}{5} - \frac{168}{5} + 112 = \frac{224-168+560}{5} = \frac{616}{5}$

or, $x = \frac{616}{5\times 7} = \frac{88}{5}$

$\therefore$ Total quantity $= \frac{88}{5}\times 10 = 176$ litres

5. 4; Total quantity in Vessel P $= 60\times\frac{120}{100} = 72$ litres

		Milk	Water
Vessel	P(72)	54	18 (3:1)
	Q(60)	48	12 (4:1)

By Alligation Method:

Milk $\frac{3}{4}$ Milk $\frac{4}{5}$

$\frac{9}{13}$

$\frac{7}{65}$: $\frac{3}{52} = \frac{7}{5}:\frac{3}{4}$

$\therefore$ Reqd ratio = 28 : 15

(6-10):

Let the number of Redmi and Apple mobiles be R and A respectively.

Now, The probability of selecting one Apple mobile

$= \frac{{}^{A}C_1}{R+A+6} = \frac{1}{3}$ or, $3A = R + A + 6$

or, $2A - R = 6$ ... (i)

Again, the probability of selecting one Redmi mobile

$= \frac{{}^{R}C_1}{R+A+6} = \frac{5}{12}$

or, $12R = 5R + 5A + 30$

or, $7R - 5A = 30$ ... (ii)

From (i) and (ii), we get

$14A - 7R = 42$

$-5A + 7R = 30$

$9A = 72$

$\therefore A = \frac{72}{9} = 8$

Putting the value of A in eqn (i) or (ii), we get

$\therefore R = 10$

Hence Apple = 8, Samsung = 6, Redmi = 10

6. 2; The number of favourable cases of selecting mobiles starting with 2 and 5

	Apple	Samsung	Redmi
(1)	2	5	
(2)	2		5
(3)	5	2	
(4)	5		2
(5)		5	2
(6)		2	5

$\therefore n(E) = 6$

And $n(S) = 24$

$\therefore P(E) = \frac{n(E)}{n(S)} = \frac{6}{24} = \frac{1}{4}$

7. 4

8. 5; Reqd number of ways $= {}^{8}C_3 \times {}^{16}C_3 + {}^{8}C_4 \times {}^{16}C_2 + {}^{8}C_5 \times {}^{16}C_1 + {}^{8}C_6 \times {}^{16}C_0$

$= 56 \times 560 + 70 \times 120 + 56 \times 16 + 28 \times 1$

$= 31360 + 8400 + 896 + 28 = 40684$

9. 5; Reqd probability $= \frac{{}^{4}C_3}{{}^{10}C_3} \times \frac{{}^{6}C_1}{{}^{14}C_1}$

$= \frac{4}{120} \times \frac{6}{14} = \frac{24}{120 \times 14} = \frac{1}{70}$

10. 5; Reqd number of ways $= {}^{10}C_1 \times {}^{14}C_3 + {}^{10}C_2 \times {}^{14}C_2 + {}^{10}C_3 \times {}^{14}C_1 + {}^{10}C_0 \times {}^{14}C_4$

$= 10 \times 364 + 45 \times 91 + 120 \times 14 + 1 \times 1001$

$= 3640 + 4095 + 1680 + 1001 = 10416$

(11-15):

Publisher	English	Local	Hindi	Total
A	8575	12005	13720	34300
B	13720	7840	17640	39200
C	18865	24255	10780	53900
D	7350	11025	18375	36750
E	8820	15435	19845	44100
F	11025	7350	18375	36750
Total	68355	77910	98735	245000

11. 1; Hindi books = 98735

Reqd average $= \frac{98735}{6} = 16456$

12. 4; Books from A and B = (34300 + 39200) = 73500

Books from C and E = (53900 + 44100) = 98000

Reqd ratio $= \frac{73500}{98000} = 3:4$

13. 2; Total percentage of A and B and D = (14 + 16 + 15) = 45%

$\therefore$ Reqd degree $= \frac{45}{100} \times 360° = 162°$

14. 1; Amount from Hindi books sold by A

$= 13720 \times 4 = 54880$

Amount from English books sold by A

$= 8575 \times 5 = 42875$

Reqd amount = (54880 + 42875) = ₹97755

15. 5; English books published by B and F

= (13720 + 11025) = 24745

English books published by D and E

= (7350 + 8820) = 16170

$\therefore$ Reqd % $= \frac{24745 - 16170}{16170} \times 100 = 53\%$

16. 1; Ratio of male (M) to female (F) for age group

$30 \le \text{age} \le 40: \frac{M}{F} = \frac{3}{2} \quad 20 \le \text{age} < 30: \frac{M}{F} = \frac{8}{7}$

Number of males in age the group 30 to 40

$= \frac{15}{100} \times \frac{3x}{(3+2)} = \frac{9x}{100}$

Number of females in the age group 20 to 30

$= \frac{25}{100} \times \frac{7x}{(8+7)} = \frac{35x}{300}$

$\therefore \text{Reqd \%} = \left(\frac{\frac{35x}{300} - \frac{9x}{100}}{\frac{35x}{300}} \right) \times 100 = 22\frac{6}{7}\%$

17. 4; Let the total number of persons be x.

Then, $x \times \frac{100}{300} - x \times \frac{50}{300} = 15000$

$\Rightarrow \frac{x}{3} - \frac{x}{6} = 15000 \Rightarrow \frac{x}{6} = 15000 \Rightarrow x = 90000$

Number of persons of age group less than 5 years

$= 90000 \times \frac{10}{100} = 9000$

18. 2; Population of age group of 5 to 10 and 10 to 20 after three years

$= 60000 \times \left(\frac{100}{300} + \frac{50}{300} \right) \times \frac{110}{100} \times \frac{110}{100} \times \frac{140}{100} = 39930$

19. 3; Let the total number of persons be x.

Then, according to the question,

$x \times \frac{25}{100} - x \times \frac{10}{10} = 9000$

$\Rightarrow x\left(\frac{1}{4} - \frac{1}{10} \right) = 9000$

$\Rightarrow x = 60000$

Number of persons with the age group 5 to 10 years

$= 60000 \times \frac{50}{300} = 10000$

20. 4; 25 years $= \frac{1}{4} \times \frac{1}{3} \times 144000 = 12000$

35 years $= \frac{3}{20} \times \frac{4}{5} \times 144000 = 17280$

16 years $= \frac{1}{3} \times \frac{3}{4} \times 144000 = 36000$

Total = 12000 + 17280 + 36000 = 65280

Practice Set 27

Directions (Q. 1-3): Scattered line graph shows the data regarding the age and weight of nine children.

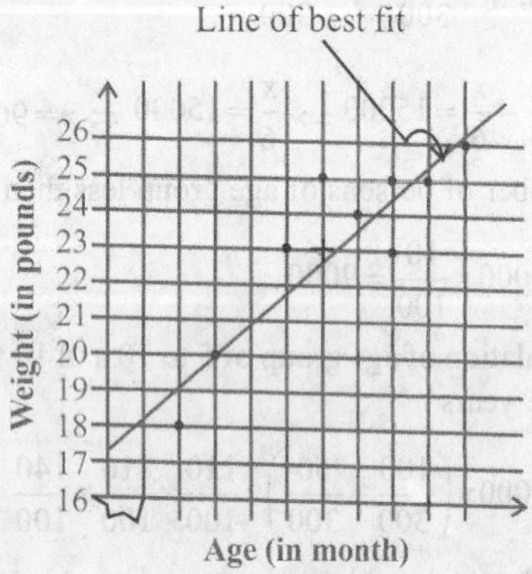

A group of nine male children was weighed, and the individual ages and weights were plotted as shown above. (The weights are rounded to the nearest whole number).

1. What is the average weight of the 9 children?

1) 22.3 2) 23.2 3) 24.6
4) 24 5) None of these

2. Find the slope of the line of best fit.

1) $\frac{2}{3}$ 2) $\frac{3}{4}$ 3) $\frac{4}{7}$
4) $\frac{6}{7}$ 5) None of these

3. Use the slope of the line to approximate the weight of a 30-month-old boy.

1) 24 2) 18 3) 31
4) 27 5) None of these

Directions (Q. 4-6): Amort, Divya, Nikhil, Gitanshi and Mona, are persons employed to complete a job X. Line graph shows the data regarding the time taken by these persons to complete the job. Table graph shows the actual time for which everyone of him worked on the job.

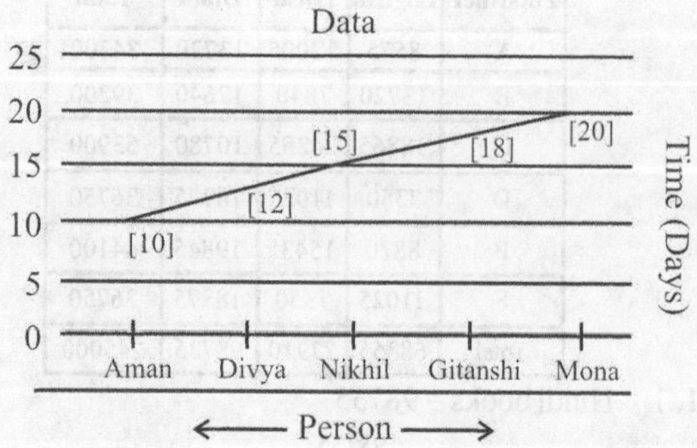

Person	Time (Days)
Aman	2
Divya	–
Nikhil	3
Gitanshi	–
Mona	2

Note 1: All the persons worked on the job X for whole number days.

Note 2: Two jobs Y and Z are similar to job X and required same effort as required by job X.

4. If Aman, Nikhil and Mona worked on job Z for 2 days each and the remaining job was done by Divya and Gitanshi. If the ratio of number of days for which Divya and Gitanshi worked is 20 : 21, then find the number of days for which Divya worked?

1) 50 days 2) 4.5 days 3) 5.5 days
4) 4 days 5) None of these

5. Mona worked on job Z for 5 days and the remaining job was completed by Aman, Divya and Gitanshi who worked on alternate days starting with Aman and followed by Divya and Gitanshi in that order. Find the number of days Divya worked for?

1) 2 days 2) 4 days 3) 9 days
4) 3 days 5) None of these

6. Aman and Nikhil worked on job Y working alternately for 10 days, then Divya and Gitanshi worked together for X days. If 1/36th of the jobs was still remained, then find the value of X?

1) 2 days 2) 1.25 days 3) 1 day
4) 1.33 days 5) 1.2 days

Directions (Q. 7-11): Study the fallowing information carefully and answer the questions given below.

The census officers provided the data regarding changes in population of three major towns for three years. Population of town A was 180600 in the third year and it increased 5% and 7.5% in second and third year respectively. Population of town B increased by 25% in second year and in the second years it was equal to 150% of the population of town A in first year. After taking population control measures, town B succeeds in controlling population as growth rate in third year was half of that of previous year. The area of town C is 1250 km^2 and population density for second year was 250. Growth rate for town C was 11.11 % and 10% for second and third years respectively.

Note: Population density is calculated as Total population ÷ Total area

7. Population of town B in third year exceeds by how much compare to population of town A in second year?
1) 110000 2) 107500 3) 102000
4) 105250 5) None of these

8. The average population of town B for three years forms what percentage of average population of town C for three years?
1) 73.15% 2) 74.88% 3) 78.44%
4) 76.28% 5) None of these

9. For town B, male to female ratio for the last two years was 7 : 5 and literate male and illiterate male are in the ratio of 4 : 1 for same years. Find the ratio between illiterate male in second year and literate male in third year.
1) 8 : 9 2) 4 : 9 3) 9 : 2
4) 2 : 9 5) 7 : 2

10. Refer the data provided in previous question, by what percentage the number of illiterate male in third year for town B less than female in third year for town B?
1) 72% 2) 75% 3) 69%
4) 70.50% 5) 74.25%

11. For the third year, if $\frac{3}{8}$th part of population of town A are not above 20 years old, 33% of population of town B are below 20 years old and 70% of population of town C are above 20 years old, how much population of three towns are above 20 years for third year?
1) 530440 2) 545.400 3) 543300
4) 534400 5) Can't be determined

Directions (Q. 12-15): Answer the questions based on the following information.

Deepak distributed 10-acre land to Janak and Ritesh who paid him the total amount in the ratio 2 : 3. Janak invested a further ₹2 lakh in the land and planted Mango and Ashoka trees in the ratio 1 : 5 on equal areas of land. There were a total of 100 Ashoka trees. The cost of one Mango was Rs 5. The trees took 7 yrs to mature and when the tree was reaped in 2017, the total revenue generated was 25% of the total amount put in by Janak and Ritesh together. The revenue generated from the Mango and Ashoka trees was in the ratio 3 : 2 and it was shared equally by Janak and Ritesh as the initial amounts spent by them were equal.

12. What was the ratio of yield per acre of land for Mango and Ashoka (in terms of number of Ashoka and Mango)?
1) 3 : 2 2) 2 : 3 3) 1 : 1
4) Cannot be detennincd 5) None of these

13. What was the value of output per tree for Mango?
1) ₹36 2) ₹360 3) ₹3,600
4) ₹240 3) None of these

14. What was the amount received by Janak in 2017?
1) ₹1.5 lakh 2) ₹3 lakh 3) ₹6 lakh
4) Cannot be determined 5) None of these

15. What was the value of output per acre of the Ashoka tree planted?
1) 0.24 lakh/acre 2) 2.4 lakh/acre 3) 24 lakh/acres
4) Cannot be determined 5) None of these

Directions (Q. 16–20) : Read the following information and answer the questions that follow :

There are a total of 5 different manufacturers A, B, C, D and E. They manufacture their articles and distribute them among their friends. It is also known that none of these friends are mutual with respect to each other. Also the following information are available:

(i) A has a total of 7 friends. Each of his friends has 4 friends.
(ii) B has a total of 5 friends. Each of his friends has 3 friends.
(iii) C has a total of 4 friends. Each of his friends has 5 friends.
(iv) D has a total of 6 friends. Each of his friends has 2 friends.
(v) E has a total of 3 friends. Each of his friends has 5 friends.

16. If E has manufactured 300 articles, these articles are distributed equally among his respective friends by him. Each of his friends further distributes equal amount of articles to his/her friends. Also it is known that among his friends, 1 is male and the remaining are females. Now,

if the male friend of E can distribute a maximum of 60 articles to his female friends, find the maximum possible number of female friends of the male friend of E.
1) 1 2) 5 3) 2 4) 3 5) 4

17. If E has manufactured 300 articles, these articles are distributed equally among his respective friends by him. Each of his friends further distributes equal amount of articles to his/her friends. Also it is known that among his friends, 1 is male and the remaining are females. In how many ways female friends of E can distribute 1 article to their friends more than that by the male friends?
1) 100 2) 120 3) 130
4) 125 5) 115

18. If C has manufactured 400 articles and D has manufactured 600 articles. These articles are distributed equally among their respective friends by both of them. The friends of C do not distribute these articles to their respective friends but the friends of D distributed the articles they received among their respective friends. What will be the average of the number of articles received by each of the friends of C and those received by each of the friends of the friends of D ?
1) 75 2) 80 3) 60
4) 65 5) 85

19. If A has manufactured 700 articles and B has manufactured 450 articles. These articles are distributed equally among their respective friends by both of them. Then their friends also distributed the articles they received among their respective friends. By how much percentage the number of articles received by the friends of the friends of B more than those received by the friends of the friends of A ?
1) 10% 2) 17% 3) 20%
4) 15% 5) 25%

20. In how many ways the friends of A exchange their 1 article with each other ?
1) 20 2) 32 3) 30
4) 28 5) None of these

Answers and explanations

1. 2; Average $= \dfrac{18+20+23+25+24+23+25+25+26}{9}$

$= 23.2$

2. 4; Choose the two points that are closest to the line of best fit : (17, 20) and (24, 26). The slope of the line passing through these points is

$$m = \frac{y_2 - y_1}{x_2 - x_1} = \frac{26-20}{24-17} = \frac{6}{7}$$

3. 3; Let y = the weight of a 30-month old boy
The slope of the line passing through the points (17, 20) and (30, y) should approximate $\frac{6}{7}$.

$$m = \frac{y-20}{30-17} = \frac{6}{7} \Rightarrow y = 31$$

4. 4; $2\,\text{Aman} + 2\,\text{Nikhil} + 2\,\text{Mona} = 2\left[\frac{1}{10} + \frac{1}{15} + \frac{1}{20}\right] = \frac{13}{30}$

Remaining work $= \frac{17}{30}$

Divya + Gitanshi $= \frac{20x}{12} + \frac{21x}{18} = \frac{17}{30} \quad \therefore x = \frac{1}{5}$

Divya $= 20x = \frac{20}{5} = 4$ days

5. 4; Work done by Mona in 5 days $= \frac{5}{20} = \frac{1}{4}$ units

Remaining work $= 1 - \frac{1}{4} = \frac{3}{4}$ units

Work done by Aman, Divya and Gitanshi in three consecutive days $= \frac{1}{10} + \frac{1}{12} + \frac{1}{18} = \frac{18+15+10}{180}$

$= \frac{43}{180}$ units

Work done by them in 9 days $= \frac{3 \times 43}{180} = \frac{129}{180}$ units

Remaining work $= \frac{3}{4} - \frac{129}{180} = \frac{6}{180} = \frac{1}{30}$ units

Aman done the remaining $\frac{1}{30}$ unit in $\frac{10}{30} = \frac{1}{3}$ days

Hence, Divya worked for 3 days.

6. 5; Aman + Nikhil's 5 days work $= \frac{5}{10} + \frac{5}{15} = \frac{5}{6}$ units

Remaining work $= 1 - \frac{5}{6} = \frac{1}{6}$ units

Work done by Divya and Gitanish in x days

$= \frac{x}{12} + \frac{x}{18} = \frac{5x}{36}$ units

Remaining work $= \frac{1}{6} - \frac{5x}{36} = \frac{1}{36} \Rightarrow \frac{6-5x}{36} = \frac{1}{36}$

$\therefore x = \frac{6}{5} = 1.2$ days

7. 3; Let the population of Town A in first year be 100.

Thus, population of town A in third year = 105% of 107.50% of 100 = 112.875

∴ Population of Town A in first year

$= \frac{180600 \times 100}{112.875} = 160000$

Thus, population of town A in second year = 105% of 160000 = 168000

Population of town B in second year = 150% of 160000 = 240000

As given, growth rate of population for town B in the second year was 25% thus population in first year =

$\frac{240000 \times 100}{125} = 192000$

As growth year became half of previous years' grwoth rate, population of town B in third year

= 240000 + [240000 × [12.50% (half of 25%)]]

= 240000 + 30000 = 270000

For town C, population in second year = Population density × Area = 250 × 1250 = 312500

As growth rate for town C was 11.11% and 10% for second and third year respectively, population of C

in first year $= \frac{312500 \times 100}{111.11} = 281250$

Population of C in third year = 110% of 312500 = 343750.

Thus, we can present above data in tabular form as follows:

Towns	Population		
	Frist year	Second year	Third year
A	160000	168000	180600
B	192000	240000	270000
C	281250	312500	343750

Reqd. difference = Population of town B in third year – Population of town A in second year = 270000 – 168000 = 102000

8. 2; Average population of town B

$= \frac{192000 + 240000 + 270000}{3} = \frac{702000}{3} = 234000$

Average population of twon C

$= \frac{281250 + 312500 + 343750}{3} = \frac{937500}{3} = 312500$

$\therefore$ Reqd % $= \frac{234000}{312500} \times 100 = 74.88\%$

9. 4; Number of males in town B for second year

$= \frac{7 \times 240000}{12} = 140000$

Number of males in town B for third year

$= \frac{7 \times 270000}{12} = 157500$

Number of illiterate males in second year

$= \frac{1 \times 140000}{5} = 28000$

Number of literate males in third year

$= \frac{7 \times 157500}{5} = 126000$

Thus, the required ratio = 28000 : 126000 = 2 : 9

10. 1; Number of illiterate males in third year for town B

$= \frac{1 \times 157500}{5} = 31500$

Number of female in third year for town B

$= \frac{5 \times 270000}{12} = 112500$

$\therefore$ Reqd % $= \frac{112500 - 31500}{112500} \times 100 = 72\%$

11. 4; Population above 20 years in town A

$= 180600 - \frac{180600 \times 3}{8} = 112875$

Population above 20 years in town B = (100 – 33)% of 270000 = 180900

Population above 20 years in town C = 70% of 343750 = 240625

Thus, the required total = 112875 + 180900 + 240625 = 534400

12. 4; Data are insufficient to determine the required ratio.

13. 2; Ratio of number of Mango trees and Ashoka trees. = 1 : 5, therefore number of Mango trees is 500, since revenue generated from Mango trees is ₹180000

Hence value per tree $= \frac{180000}{500} =$ ₹360

14. 1; Since revenue of ₹300000 is equally divided by Janak and Ritesh. Hence amount reeived by Janak in 2017

$= \frac{1}{2} \times 300000 = `150000$

15. 1; The value of Ashoka output per acre of land

$= \frac{120000}{5} = 0.24$ lakh/acre

16. 4; Number of articles distributed to each friend of E

$= \frac{300}{3} = 100$

Hence, number of articles received by the only male friend of E = 100

Also, it is given that,

Male friend of E can equally distribute a maximum of 60 articles to his female friends.

Number of articles received by each friend of male friend of E $= \frac{100}{5} = 20$. So, females friends $= \frac{60}{20} = 3$

Hence, the maximum possible number of female friends of the male friend of E = 3.

∴ The maximum possible number of female friends of the male friend of E is 3.

17. 2; Number of ways in which 1 female can distribute the articles to her 5 friends = 5!

So, number of ways in which 2 females can distribute the articles to their friends = 2 × 5!

Number of ways in which male can distribute 1 article to his 5 friends = 5!

Difference between number of ways = (2 × 5!) – 5! = 5!

$\Rightarrow 5 \times 4 \times 3 \times 2 \times 1 = 120$ ways

∴ In 120 ways female friends of E can distribute 1 article to their friends more.

18. 1; Number of articles received by each friend of C

$= \frac{400}{4} = 100$

Number of articles received by each friend of D

$= \frac{600}{6} = 100$

When each friend of D distributes the article equally to their respective friends.

Number of articles received by each friend of the friends of D $= \frac{100}{2} = 50$

So, the required average $= \frac{100 + 50}{2} = 75$

∴ The average of the number of articles received by each of the friends of C and those received by each of the friends of D is 75.

19. 3; Number of articles received by each friend of A

$= \frac{700}{7} = 100$

Number of articles received by each friend of the friend of A $= \frac{100}{4} = 25$

Number of articles received by each friend of B

$= \frac{450}{5} = 90$

Number of articles received by each friend of the friends of B $= \frac{90}{3} = 30$

Hence, the required percentage

$= \frac{30 - 25}{25} \times 100 = 20\%$

∴ The number of articles received by the friends of the friends of B is more than those received by the friends of the friends of A by 20%.

20. 4; Number of friends of A = 7

Number of friends of each of the friends of A = 4

So, the required number of ways = 7 × 4 = 28

Therefore, the number of ways in which the friends of A exchange their 1 article with each other is 28.

Practice Set 28

Directions (Q. 1–4) : Read the following information carefully and answer the questions given below :

In a Game's item workshop, there work five carpenters namely A, B, C, D and E. They use to manufacture Bat, Hockey and Carrom Board.

Carpenter A can make 4 Bats, 2 Hockeys and 1 Carrom Board in 84 days. Carpenter B can make 4 Hockeys and 2 Carrom Boards in 100 days.

A, C and E together can make one Hockey in 4(92/157) days.

Carpenters A, B and C can make one Hockey together in 4(4/11) days.

For D, the ratio of number of days to manufacture 4 Bats, 3 Hockeys and 5 Carrom Boards respectively is 1:1:1. E and D can make one Carrom Board together in 6(6/7) days. E needs 9 more days for manufacturing a Bat than D needs for manufacturing a Bat.

Carpenter, C and D can make two Carrom Boards in 14.4 days.

Note: All the Bat, Hockey and Carrom Board that they make are identical.

1. If carpenter A can make 2 Bats and 2 Hockeys in 52 days, then find the sum of number of days for A to make 2 Bats and 1 Carrom Board; and number of days for B to make 2 Hockeys and 1 Carrom Board.
   1) 76 2) 80 3) 82
   4) 84 5) Can't be determined
2. For constructing a Hockey, all the carpenters except D are given the work to do together. Carpenters A and C work at double their efficiency while B and E works at normal efficiency. Find in how many days the Hockey will be constructed?
   1) $2\frac{38}{111}$ days 2) $2\frac{38}{161}$ days 3) $1\frac{28}{161}$ days
   4) $2\frac{38}{116}$ days 5) $1\frac{33}{149}$ days
3. If D constructs table at 66.67% more efficiency, he can construct it in 12 days. Find in how many days E can construct one Bat and one Carrom Board.
   1) 36 days 2) 56 days 3) 40 days
   4) 48 days 5) 50 days
4. Carpenter E needs six more days in the constructon of a Bat than C needs in the construction of a Carrom Board. Find the ratio of number of days for D in constructing a Hockey to the number of days for C in constructing a Carrom Board.
   1) 9 : 10 2) 7 : 9 3) 2 : 5 4) 10 : 9 5) 5 : 2

Directions (Q. 5–9) : Read the given pie chart and table carefully and answer the following questions.

There are three types of coaching classes Basic, Advance and Targeted are of duration 1 hour, 2 hours and 3 hours respectively.

In the given pie chart the percentage of coaching classes (in hours) taken by four Math teachers (Rakesh, Abhinay, Gagan and Rohit) are given.

Total time for classes (in a month) = 450 hours

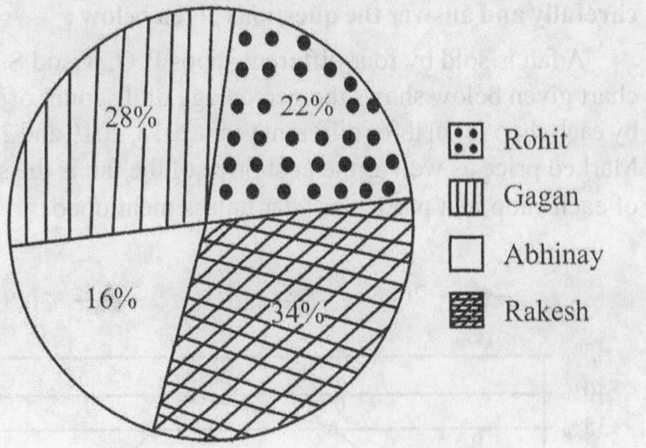

In the following table, the ratio of time spent on the different types of classes taken by a different teacher is given.

Teacher Name	1 Hour Class	2 Hours Class	3 Hours Class
Rohit	5	4	2
Gagan	2	7	5
Abhinay	1	2	6
Rakesh	6	8	3

5. What is the percentage of number of basic classes taken by Gagan to the number of advance classes taken by Rakesh?
1) 200% 2) 75% 3) 100%
4) 150% 5) 50%

6. How many more advance classes taken by Rohit than the Target classes taken by Gagan ?
1) 5 2) 3 3) 9
4) 6 3) 8

7. What is the ratio of time spent by Rakesh and Abhinay together in basic level classes to that of the advance level classes through the month ?
1) 13 : 19 2) 23 : 33 3) 31 : 36
4) 31 : 44 3) 39 : 44

8. Find the ratio of the number of basic classes of Gagan to the number of target classes taken by Abhinay in the given period of time.
1) 8 : 9 2) 3 : 4 3) 9 : 8
4) 5 : 6 3) 9 : 2

9. What is the sum of the number of basic classes of Gagan and the number of target classes taken by Abhinay in the given period of time ?
1) 32 2) 33 3) 34
4) 31 5) 35

Directions (Q. 10–15) : Study the following line chart carefully and answer the questions given below :

A fan is sold by four different shops P, Q, R and S. The chart given below shows the percentage of discount offered by each shop for in three different years 2018, 2019 and 2020. Marked price as well as the cost price of the fan is the same of each shop in a particular year unless mentioned.

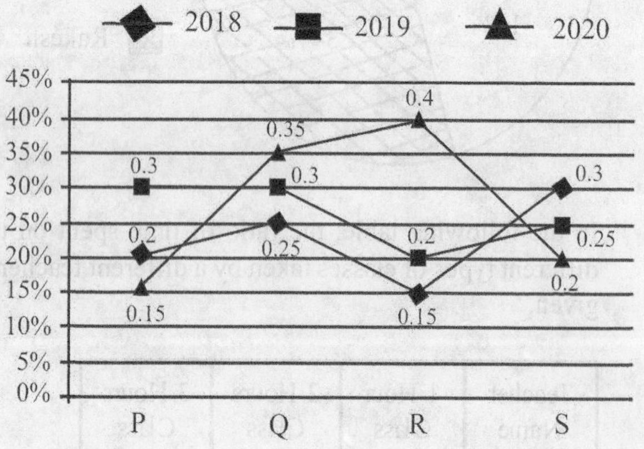

10. Marked price of fan increases by 20% every year with respect to previous year. Average of marked price of fan for the year 2017, 2018 and 2019 is ₹1820. Profit per cent earned by shop S on selling fan in 2020 was 38.24%. Find the differencc between profit percentage of shop Q and R in 2018, if cost price of fan increases by ₹150 with respect to the previous year.
1) 12% 2) 10% 3) 15%
4) 20% 5) 16%

11. Profit earned by shop R each year was same. Increase in marked price of fan from 2019 to 2020 was twice the increase in marked price of fan from 2018 to 2019. Both selling price and cost price for shop R increased by ₹100 from 2019 to 2020. Fan is marked up ₹700 and ₹1600 above the cost price in 2019 and 2020 respectively. What is the profit earned by shop P in 2018 ?
1) ₹120 2) ₹100 3) ₹140
4) ₹50 5) ₹200

12. Ratio of cost price of fan in 2018 : 2019 : 2020 was 2 : 4 : 5. Ratio of selling price at shop S in 2018 : 2019 : 2020 was 7 : 12 : 16. Average of profit earned by P and R in 2019 was ₹400 and total profit earned by Q in three years is ₹970. Find the difference of discount offered by R in 2018 and 2020.
1) ₹450 2) ₹650 3) ₹750
4) ₹700 5) ₹550

13. Marked price in 2020 was ₹8000 and marked price in 2019 was same as the selling price at shop P in 2020. Cost price in 2019 was same as the selling price at shop S in 2018. Profit per cent earned by P in 2019 was 36%. If cost price in 2018 was ₹2295, then find the ratio of profit earned by shop Q in 2018 to shop R in 2019.
1) 5 : 8 2) 2 : 3 3) 3 : 4
4) 4 : 3 5) 1 : 3

14. Selling price at shop Q in 2018 and 2019 was ₹2400 and ₹2800 respectively and selling price at shop S in 2020 was ₹3840. Ratio of profit earned by P and R in 2019 was 2 : 3. If cost prices were in an increasing AP with passing years with a common difference of ₹400, find the difference between profit earned by P in 2018 and in 2020.
1) ₹840 2) ₹800 3) ₹780
4) ₹720 5) ₹700

15. Marked price in 2020 was ₹8000 and marked price in 2019 was same as the selling price at shop P in 2020. Cost price in 2019 was same as the selling price at shop S in 2018. Profit per cent earned by P in 2019 was 36%. If cost price in 2018 was ₹2295 then find the sum of profit by shop Q in 2018 and shop R in 2019.
1) 3200 2) 3395 3) 3375
4) 3437 5) None of these

Directions (Q. 16–20) : Study the following information carefully and answer the related questions.

Three buses i.e. Fast, Super Fast and City run from place A to place B. The number of passengers who travelled on these buses in a particular week is given in the table. Some of the data is given in the table while some are missing.

	Fast Bus	Super Fast Bus	City Bus	Total no. of Passengers
Monday	204	—	172	614
Tuesday	—	214	226	630
Wednesday	244	—	216	—
Thursday	180	194	—	524
Friday	170	190	248	—
Saturday	236	—	—	698
Sunday	—	192	200	604
Total	—	1424	1464	—

16. Find the total fare earned from Fast bus in the whole week if the fare per person in the Fast bus is ₹15.
1) ₹22,760 2) ₹21,540 3) ₹23.720
4) ₹22,640 5) ₹21,300

17. Find the total number of passengers who travelled by all the three buses in the whole week.
1) 4134 2) 4524 3) 4422
4) 4200 5) 4324

18. Find the difference between the total number of passengers who travelled by all the three buses on Wednesday and the total number of passengers who travelled by all the three buses on Friday.
1) 38 2) 34 3) 44
4) 58 5) 22

19. The fare for each passenger in the Super Fast bus and in the City bus is ₹13 and ₹17 respectively. Find the difference between the amount earned by the Super Fast bus and the amount earned by the City bus in the whole week.
1) ₹6276 2) ₹6425 3) ₹6500
4) ₹6100 5) ₹6376

20. Find the difference between the number of passengers who travelled by Super Fast bus on Monday and Wednesday.
1) 62 2) 42 3) 52
4) 70 5) 44

Answers and explanations

(1–4) :

We assume the number of days needed by each carpenter for each of the products as given in the table below :

Carpenters	Number of Days for		
	Bat	Hockey	Carrom Board
A	A_b	A_h	A_c
B	B_b	B_h	B_c
C	C_b	C_h	C_c
D	D_b	D_h	D_c
E	E_b	E_h	E_c

Carpenter A can make 4 Bats, 2 Hockeys and 1 Carrom Board in 84 days.

$\Rightarrow 4A_b + 2A_h + 1A_C = 84$ ....(i)

Carpenter B can make 4 Hockeys, and 2 Carrom Boards in 100 days.

$\Rightarrow 4B_h + 2B_c = 100$ .... (ii)

A, C and E together can make one Hockey in 4(92/157) days.

$$\Rightarrow \frac{1}{A_h} + \frac{1}{C_h} + \frac{1}{E_h} = \frac{1}{\left[4\left(\frac{92}{157}\right)\right]} = \frac{157}{720} \text{ .... (iii)}$$

Carpenter A, B and C can make one Hockey together in 4(4/11) days.

$$\Rightarrow \frac{1}{A_h} + \frac{1}{B_h} + \frac{1}{C_h} = \frac{1}{\left[4\left(\frac{4}{11}\right)\right]} = \frac{11}{48} \text{ ....(iv)}$$

For D, the ratio of number of days to manufacture 4 Bats, 3 Hockeys and 5 Carrom Boards respectively is 1 : 1 : 1.

$\Rightarrow 4D_b : 3D_h : 5D_c = 1 : 1 : 1$ .... (v)

E and D can make one Carrom Board together in 6(6/7) days.

$$\Rightarrow \frac{1}{D_c} + \frac{1}{E_c} = \frac{7}{48} \text{ .... (vi)}$$

E needs 9 more days for manufacturing a Bat than D needs for manufacturing a Bat.

$\Rightarrow E_b = D_b + 9$ ....(vii)

Carpenter C and D together can make two Carrom Boards in 14.4 days.

Means, they can make one Carrom Board in 7.2 days. So,

$\frac{1}{C_c} + \frac{1}{D_c} = \frac{5}{36}$ .... (viii)

1. 3; From common explanation, we have

$4A_h + 2A_b + 1A_c = 84$ ....(i)

$4B_h + 2B_c = 100$ ....(ii)

From the question, we have

$2A_b + 2A_h = 52$ ....(iii)

Subtracting (iii) from (i), we get

$2A_h + 1A_c = 32$

From (ii), we have

The number of days for B to make 2 Hockeys and 1 Carrom Board

$= 2B_h + 1B_c = \frac{1}{2} \times (4B_h + 2B_c) = \frac{1}{2} \times 100 = 50$

Total number of days = 32 + 50 = 82

2. 2; From conmon explanation, we have

$\frac{1}{A_h} + \frac{1}{C_h} + \frac{1}{E_h} = \frac{1}{[4(92/157)]} = \frac{157}{720}$ .... (iii)

$\frac{1}{A_h} + \frac{1}{B_h} + \frac{1}{C_h} = \frac{1}{[4(4/11)]} = \frac{11}{48}$ .... (iv)

Adding these two, we get

$\frac{2}{A_h} + \frac{1}{B_h} + \frac{2}{C_h} + \frac{1}{E_h} = \frac{157}{720} + \frac{11}{48} = \frac{322}{720}$

Number of days = $\frac{720}{322} = 2\frac{38}{161}$ days

3. 3; $4D_b : 3D_h : 5D_c = 1 : 1 : 1$ .... (v)

$\Rightarrow \frac{1}{D_c} + \frac{1}{E_c} = \frac{7}{48}$ .... (vi)

$\Rightarrow E_b = D_b + 9$ .... (vii)

Now,

$\frac{1}{D_h} + 66.67 \text{ of } \left(\frac{1}{D_h}\right) = \frac{1}{12}$

$\Rightarrow \frac{5}{3}\left(\frac{1}{D_h}\right) = \frac{1}{12} \Rightarrow \frac{1}{D_h} = \frac{1}{20} \Rightarrow D = 20$

From (v), we have

$4D_b : 3 \times 20 : 5D_c = 1 : 1 : 1$

$\therefore D_c = 12$ amd $D_b = 15$

From (vi), we get

$\frac{1}{12} + \frac{1}{E_c} = \frac{7}{48} \Rightarrow E_c = 16$

From (vii), we get

$E_b = D_b + 9 = 15 + 9 = 24$

Number of days in which E construct one Bat and one Carrom Board = 16 + 24 = 40 days.

4. 4; From question, we have

$E_b = C_c + 6$ .... (1)

From common explanation, we get from (v) and (vii)

$4D_b : 5D_c = 1 : 1 \Rightarrow D_c = 1.25D_c$

$E_b = D_b + 9 \Rightarrow D_b = E_b - 9 \Rightarrow 1.25D_c = E_b - 9$

$\Rightarrow D_c = 0.8\,(E_b - 9)$

$\frac{1}{C_c} + \frac{1}{D_c} = \frac{5}{36}$

$\Rightarrow \frac{1}{(E_b - 6)} + \frac{1}{0.8(E_b - 9)} = \frac{5}{36} \Rightarrow E_b = 24$

So, from (1), we get $C_c = 18$.

$D_h = \frac{5}{3} D_c = \frac{5}{3} \times 0.8\,(E_b - 9) = 20$

$D_h : C_c = 20 : 18 = 10 : 9.$

5. 3; Total class hour taken by Gagan is

$\left(\frac{28}{100}\right) \times 450 = 126$ hours

Hours spent on the basic class by Gagan is

$\left(\frac{2}{14}\right) \times 126 = 18$ hours

Number of basic classes taken by Gagan is

$\left(\frac{18}{1}\right) = 18$

Total class hour taken by Rakesh is

$\left(\frac{34}{100}\right) \times 18 = 153$ hours

Hours spent on the advance class by Rakesh is

$\left(\frac{8}{17}\right) \times 153 = 72$ hours

Number of advance classes taken by Rakesh is

$\left(\frac{72}{2}\right) = 36$

Percentage of the number of basic class taken by Gagan to the number of advance classes taken by Rakesh $= \left(\frac{18}{36}\right) \times 100 = 50\%$

Therefore, required percentage is 50%.

6. 2; The total class hours taken by Gagan is

$\left(\frac{28}{100}\right) \times 450 = 126$ hours

Hours spent on the target class by Gagan is

$\left(\frac{5}{14}\right) \times 126 = 45$ hours

The number of target classes taken by Gagan is

$\left(\frac{45}{3}\right) = 15$

The total class hour taken by Rohit is

$\left(\frac{22}{100}\right) \times 450 = 99$ hours

Hours spent on the advance class by Rohit is

$\left(\frac{4}{11}\right) \times 99 = 36$ hours

Number of advance classes taken by Rohit is

$\frac{36}{2} = 18$

The number of more advance classes taken by Rohit than the number of target classes taken by Gagan $= 18 - 15 = 3$.

Therefore, 3 more advance classes taken by Rohit than the target classes taken by Gagan.

7. 4; Overall time spent by Rakesh is

$\left(\frac{34}{100}\right) \times 450 = 153$ hours

Time spent on the basic level classes by Rakesh

$= \left(\frac{6}{17}\right) \times 153 = 54$ hours

Time spent on the advance classes by Rakesh

$= \left(\frac{8}{17}\right) \times 153 = 72$ hours

Overall lime spent by Abhinay is $\left(\frac{16}{100}\right) \times 4500$

$= 72$ hours

Time spent on the basic level classes by Abhinay

$= \left(\frac{1}{9} \times 72\right) = 8$ hours

Time spent on the advance level classes by Abhinay

$= \left(\frac{2}{9} \times 72\right) = 16$ hours

Time spent by Rakesh and Abhinay in basic level class together is $(54 + 8) = 62$ hours

Time spent by Rakesh and Abhinay in advance level class together is $(72 + 16) = 88$ hours

The required ratio is $62 : 88 = 31 : 44$

The required ratio of time spent by Rakesh and Abhinay together in basic level classes to that of the advance level class through the month is 31 : 44.

8. 3; The total class was taken by Gagan is

$\left(\frac{28}{100}\right) \times 450 = 126$ hours

The ratio of 1 hour, 2 hours and 3 hours class taken by Gagan is 2 : 7 : 5.

Time spent on the basic classe by Gagan is

$\left(\frac{2}{14}\right) \times 126 = 18$

Number of basic classes taken by Gagan is

$\frac{18}{1} = 18$

The total class was taken by Abhinay

$\left(\frac{16}{100}\right) \times 450 = 72$ hours

The ratio of 1 hour, 2 hours and 3 hours class taken by Abhinay is 1 : 2 : 6.

Time spent on the target class by Abhinay is

$\left(\frac{6}{9}\right) \times 72 = 48$ hours

Number of target classes by Abhinay is $\frac{48}{3} = 16$

The ratio of the number of the basic classes of Gagan to the number of target classes taken by Abhinay is $18 : 16 = 9 : 8$.

The ratio of the number of the basic classes of Gagan to the number of target classes taken by Abhinay is 9 : 8.

9. 3; From the solution of **Q. No. 8,**

Number of basic classes taken by Gagan = 18

Number of target classes taken by Abhinay = 16

Required sum = 18 + 16 = 34.

10. 3; Let marked price of fan in 2017 be ₹x

Marked price of fan in 2018 was 120% of x = ₹$1.2x$

Marked price of fan in 2019 was 120% of $1.2x$ = ₹$1.44x$

So, $\frac{x+1.2x+1.44x}{3} = 1820$

$\Rightarrow 3.64x = 5460 \Rightarrow x = 1500$

Marked price of Fan in 2020 = 120% of $1.44x$ $= 1.728x$ = ₹2592

Selling price of Fan at shop 5 in 2020 = 80% of 2592 = ₹2073.6

Let cost price of fan in 2020 be ₹y.

So, $y + 38.24\%$ of $y = 2073.6$

$y = \frac{2073.6}{138.24} \times 100$ = ₹1500

Cost price of fan in 2018 = 1500 – 150 – 150 = ₹1200

Marked price of fan in 2018 = $1.2x$ = ₹1800

For shop Q in 2018,

Selling price = 75% of 1800 = ₹1350

Profit% $= \frac{1350-1200}{1200} \times 100 = 12.5\%$

For shop R in 2018,

Selling price = 85% of 1800 = ₹1530

Profit % $= \frac{1350-1200}{1200} \times 100 = 27.5\%$

Difference in profit percentage = 27.5 – 12.5 = 15%

11. 2; Let the marked price of fan in 2018 be ₹x.

Increase in marked price of fan in 2019 from 2018 was ₹y.

Marked price of fan in 2019 = ₹$(x + y)$

According to the question,

Increase in marked price of fan in 2020 from 2019 was ₹$2y$.

Marked price of fan in 2020 = ₹$(x + y + 2y)$ = ₹$(x + 3y)$

Let selling price of fan in 2019 be ₹b

Selling price of fan in 2020 was ₹$(b + 100)$

Selling price of fan in 2019 = 80% of $(x + y)$

Selling price of fan in 2020 = 60% of $(x + 3y)$

So, 80% of $(x + y) = 6$ ....(1)

And 60% of $(x + 3y) = b + 100$

60% of $(x + 3y) - 100 = b$ ....(2)

From (1) and (2),

$0.8x + 0.8y = 0.6x + 1.8y - 100 \Rightarrow y - 0.2x = 100$

Let cost price of fan in 2019 be ₹a.

Cost price of fan in 2020 = ₹$(a + 100)$

Marked cost price of fan in 2019 = ₹$(a + 700)$

Marked cost price of fan in 2020 = ₹$(a + 100 + 1600)$ = ₹$(a + 1700)$

So, $x + y = a + 700$

$\Rightarrow x + y - 700 = a$ ....(3)

And, $x + 3y = a + 1700 \Rightarrow x + 3y - 1700 = a$ ....(4)

From (3) and (4), $x + y - 700 = x + 3y - 1700$

$\Rightarrow 2y = 1000$

$\Rightarrow y = 500$

$\therefore x = \frac{y-100}{0.2} = 2000$; $a = x + y - 700 = 1800$

b = 80% of $(x + y) = 2000$

Profit earned by shop R in 2020 = 2000 – 1800 = ₹200

Marked price of Fan in 2018 = ₹2000

Selling price of Fan at shop R in 2018 = 85% of 2000 = ₹1700

Cost price of Fan in 2018 = 1700 – 200 = ₹1500

Selling price of Fan at shop P in 2018 = 80% of 2000 = ₹1600.

Profit earned by shop P in 2018 = 1600 – 1500 = ₹100.

12. 2; Let cost price of Fan in 2018, 2019 and 2020 was ₹$2z$, ₹$4z$; and ₹$5z$ respectively and selling price of fan at shop S in 2018, 2019 and 2020 was ₹$7y$, ₹$12y$ and ₹$16y$ respectively.

70% of marked price of Fan in 2018 = ₹$7y$

Marked price of fan in 2018 = ₹$10y$

Similarly,

Marked price of fan in 2019 = ₹$16y$

Marked price of fan in 2020 = ₹$20y$

Selling price of fan at shop P in 2019 = 70% of $16y$ $= 11.2y$

Selling price of fan at shop R in 2019 = 80% of $16y$ $= 12.8y$

Profit of shop P in 2019 = $11.2y - 4z$

Profit of shop R in 2019 = $12.8y - 4z$

So, $11.2y - 4z + 12.8y - 4z = 400 \times 2$

$\Rightarrow 24y - 8z = 800 \Rightarrow 3y - z = 100$ ....(1)

Selling price of fan at shop Q in 2018 = 75% of $10y$ $= 7.5y$

Selling price of fan at shop Q in 2019 = 70% of $16y$ $= 11.2y$

Selling price of fan at shop Q in 2020 = 65% of $20y$ $= 13y$

So, $7.5y + 11.2y + 13y - 2z - 4z - 5z = 970$

$31.7y - 11z = 970$

$31.7y - 11 \times (3y - 100) = 970$ [from (1)]

$31.7y - 33y = 970 - 1100$

$1.3y = 130$

$y = 100$

$z = 200$

Discount offered by P in 2018 = 15% of $10y$ = ₹150

Discount offered by R in 2020 = 40% of $20y$ = ₹800
Difference = 800 – 150 = ₹650

13. 3; Marked price in 2019 = 85% of 8000 = ₹6800
Selling price at shop P in 2019 = 70% of 6800 = ₹4760
Let the cost price in 2019 was ₹a
So, $a + 36\%$ of $a = 4760$

$$a = \frac{4760}{1.36} = ₹3500$$

Selling price at shop S in 2018 = ₹3500
70% of marked price in 2018 = 3500

$$\text{Marked price in 2018} = \frac{3500}{70} \times 100 = ₹5000$$

Selling price at shop Q in 2018 = 75% of 5000 = ₹3750
Profit earned by shop Q in 2018 = 3750 – 2295 = ₹1455
Selling price at shop R in 2019 = 80% of 6800 = ₹5440
Profit earned by shop P in 2019 = 5440 – 3500 = ₹1940
Ratio = 1455 : 1940 = 3 : 4.

14. 4; 75% of marked price in 2018 = 2400

$$\text{Marked price in 2018} = \frac{2400}{0.75} = ₹3200$$

70% of marked price in 2019 = 2800

$$\text{Marked price in 2019} = \frac{2800}{0.7} = ₹4000$$

80% of marked price in 2020 = ₹3840

$$\text{Marked price in 2020} = \frac{3840}{0.8} = ₹4800$$

Selling price at shop P in 2019 = 70% of 4000 = ₹2800
Selling price at shop R in 2019 = 80% of 4000 = ₹3200
Let profit earned by P and R in 2019 was $2x$ and $3x$ respectively.
Let cost price in 2019 was ₹y.
So, $2800 - 2x = y$ ....(1)
And, $3200 - 3x = y$ ....(2)
From (1) and (2),
$2800 - 2x = 3200 - 3x$
$x = 400$
$y = 2800 - 800 = 2000$
For P in 2018 :
Cost price = ₹1600
Selling price = 80% of 3200 = ₹2560
Profit earned = 2560 – 1600 = ₹960
For P in 2020 :
Cost price = ₹2400
Selling price = 85% of 4800 = ₹4080
Profit earned = 4080 – 2400 = ₹1680
Difference = 1680 – 960 = ₹720

15. 2; From the solution of **Q. No. 13**,
Profit earned by Q in 2018 = ₹1455
Profit earned by R in 2019 = ₹1940
Required sum = 1455 + 1940 = ₹3395.

16. 2; Total number of passengers travelled by Fast bus on Tuesday = [630 – (214 + 226)] = 190
Total number of passengers travelled by Fast bus on Sunday = [604 – (192 + 200)] = 212
Total number of passengers travelled by Fast bus in the whole week = (204 + 190 + 244 + 180 + 170 + 236 + 212) = 1436
So, required amount = 1436 × 15 = ₹21540.

17. 5; Total number of passengers travelled by Fast bus on Tuesday = [630– (214 + 226)] = 190
Total number of passengers travelled by Fast bus on Sunday = [604 – (192 + 200)] = 212
Total number of passengers travelled by Fast bus in the whole week = (204 + 00 +244 + 180 + 170 + 236 + 212) = 1436
Total number of passengers travelled by Super Fast bus in the whole week = 1424
Total number of passengers travelled by City bus in the whole week = 1464
Total number of passengers travelled by all the three buses in the whole week = (1436 + 1424 + 1464) = 4324.

18. 1; Total number of passengers travelled by Fast bus on Tuessday = [630 – (214 + 226)] = 190
Total number of passengers travelled by Fast bus on Sunday = [604 – (192 + 200)] = 212
Total number of passengers travelled by Fast bus in the whole week = (204 + 190 + 244 + 180 + 170 + 236 + 212) = 1436
Total number of passengers travelled by Super Fast bus in the whole week = 1424
Total number of passengers travelled by City bus in the whole week = 1464
Total number of passengers travelled by all the three buses in the whole week = (1436 + 1424 + 1464) = 4324
Total number of passengers travelled by all the three buses on Friday = (170 + 190 + 248) = 608.
Total number of passengers travelled by all the three buses on Wednesday = [4324 – (614 + 630 + 524 + 608 + 698 + 604)] = 646
Required difference = (646 – 608) = 38.

19. 5; Total number of passengers travelled by Super Fast bus in the whole week = 1424
Total amount earned by the Super Fast bus in the whole week = ₹1424 × 13 = ₹18512
Total number of passengers travelled by City bus in the whole week = 1464
Total amount earned by the City bus in the whole

week = ₹1464 × 17 = ₹24888
Therefore, required difference = ₹(24888 – 18512) = ₹6376.

20. 3; Total number of passengers travelled by City bus on Thursday = [524 – (180 +194)] = 150
Total number of passengers travelled by City bus on Saturday
= [1464 – (172+ 226 + 216 + 150 + 248 + 200)] = 252
Total number of passengers who travelled by Super Fast bus on Saturday = [698 – (236 + 252)] = 210
Total number of passengers who travelled by Super Fast bus on Monday = {614 – (204 + 172)} = 238
Total number of passengers who travelled by Super Fast bus on Wednesday
= [1424 – (238 + 214 + 194 + 190 + 210 + 192)] = 186
Therefore, required difference = 238 –186 = 52

Practice Set 29

Directions (Q. 1–6) : These questions are based on the following information. Study the information carefully and answer the questions.

Two companies A and B have some employees in three departments Marketing, Finance and HR.

Company A : There are 64 existing employees in company A and 2 employees in each department were added. Ratio of total employees of HR and Marketing department together (existing and added) to existing and added employees of Finance department is 4 : 3.

Company B : HR department has B employees and no new employee added in HR department. Marketing department has 10 existing employees. Employees join Marketing department are half of that in Finance. Total employees, existing and new employees including in company B is 36.

* Total Marketing employees (Existing and Added) of Company A are 6 more than that of Company B.
* Sum of existing employees of HR department in Company A and existing marketing department employees of company B is 28.

1. What is the difference between existing employees of Marketing and finance department in company A ?
   1) 9 2) 11 3) 14
   4) 10 5) None of these
2. What is the percentage of existing employees of HR department in company A to the existing employees of HR department in company B ?
   1) 2500% 2) 300% 3) 190%
   4) 160% 5) None of these
3. What is the ratio of total employees added in company B to company A ?
   1) 1 : 2 b) 3 : 2 3) 2 : 1
   4) 2 : 3 5) None of these
4. How many existing employees are there in finance department in company B ?
   1) 8 2) 16 3) 10
   4) 12 5) None of these
5. What is the average number of existing employees in all departments in company A and company B? (Approx.)
   1) 13 2) 15 3) 17
   4) 11 5) None of these
6. What is the ratio of total employees of finance department in company B to the total employees of HR department in company A ?
   1) 5 : 4 2) 2 : 5 3) 5 : 7
   4) 4 : 5 5) None of these

Directions (Q. 7–9) : Study the following information carefully and answer the given questions.

Two trains X and Y starting at same time from Station A to Station B with same speed.

(i) Train X travels 60 km then reduced speed by 25% and reached at station B at 10.00 am.

(ii) Train Y travels 90 km then reduced its speed by 25% and reached at 9 : 45 am.

(iii) With their original speeds they are supposed to reach at 8 : 30 am.

7. What is the distance between station A and station B?
   1) 180 km 2) 210 km 3) 270 km
   4) 240 km 5) None of these
8. What is the initial speed of train X ?
   1) 30 km/hr 2) 60 km/hr 3) 40 km/hr
   4) 45 kn/hr 5) None of these
9. If train Z's speed is 25% more than initial speed of train X, then how much time train Z will take to cover 150 km ?
   1) 2 hrs 2) 3 hrs 3) 4 hrs 4) 1.5 hrs 5) 4 hrs

Directions (Q. 10–15) : Study the following bar graph carefully to answer the questions given below.

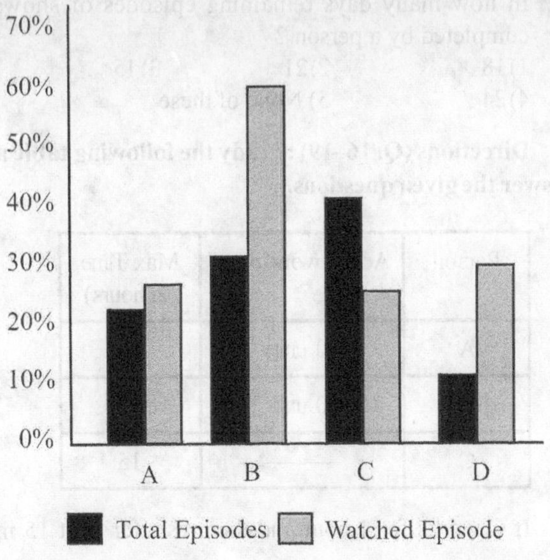

Bar 1: Percentage of episodes for Every Show out of Total Episodes of all four shows.

Bar 2 : Percentage of Watched Episodes out of Total Episodes for each show.

Total Episode = Watched Episodes + Remaining to watch Episodes

NOTE:

(i) Average of watched episodes for shows A and D is 192 less than total episodes of all four shows.

(ii) Each episode timing is 20 min.

(iii) Any episode which is not watched complete on next day.

(iv) Average time spend by person to watch shows A, B, C and D is 30 min/day, 24 min/day, 8 min/day, 35 min/day

10. How many days person will take to complete remaining episodes of shows D ?

1) 9 2) 10 3) 8
4) 11 5) None of these

11. On 12th day, how much remaining part of particular episode of show C completed by person which he continued from previous day ?

1) 16 min 2) 8 min 3) 4 mm
4) 12 min 5) None of these

12. What is the difference between remaining episode shows B and C ?

1) 20 2) 25 3) 32
4) 36 5) None of these

13. What is the ratio of total episodes of shows A and C together to the total episodes of shows B and D together?

1) 3 : 2 2) 4 : 3 3) 2 : 3
4) 5 : 4 5) None of these

14. How many days taken by a person to watch the watched episodes of shows B ?

1) 27 2) 30 3) 24
4) 32 5) None of these

15. In how many days remaining episodes of shows A completed by a person ?

1) 18 2) 21 3) 15
4) 24 5) None of these

Directions (Q. 16–19) : Study the following table and answer the given questions.

Person	Acutal work done	Max Time (in hours)
A	50 units	10
B	60 units	12
C	———	15

16. If C works for 1 hour and then rests for next 15 min. If efficiency of C is 20% of total efficiency of A and B then find the work done by C, if he completes his entire duration of work.

1) 28 2) 24 3) 32
4) 25 5) None of these

17. How much time taken by A and B to complete the work when they work together ?

1) 10.5 2) 9 3) 11
4) 7.5 5) None of these

18. If the total work is 200 units, then what will be the efficiency of C ?

1) 5 2) 4.5 3) 4
4) 6 5) None of these

19. If the total work is 170 units and A, B and C start working together and after some times C left the work. Remaining work completed by A and B in 10 hours, then after how many hours C left the work ?

1) 5 2) 7 3) 6
4) 4 5) None of these

Directions (Q. 20–24) : Study the following table and answer the given questions.

Schemes	Rate	Time
A	$x^2 - 2x - 15 = 0$	30 years
B	20%	$y^2 + 2y - 8 = 0$
C	———	40 years

* If time > rate, then consider SI.

* If time < rate, then consider CI.

* Rate in scheme C > rate in Scheme A

* J and K invested their amount in Scheme A and B respectively, K invested ₹10000.

* Amount invested by J = profit earned by J

* J also invested some amount in scheme C at SI and interest earned by him is equal to the profit earned by him from scheme A.

20. If the ratio of investment of J and K in schemes A and B is 4 : 5, then find the rate at which J invested in scheme A is what per cent of actual SI percentage of scheme A, it also given that J invested his sum for entire duration of schemes A?

1) 15% 2) $\frac{20}{7}$% 3) $\frac{20}{9}$%
4) $\frac{20}{3}$% 5) None of these

21. Rate of interest $z^2 - 9z + 18 = 0$ at which J invested in scheme C. The profit earned by him in scheme A is 150%

of the amount invested by K in scheme B. Then find the profit earned by J in scheme C ?
1) ₹15,000 2) ₹24,000 3) ₹18,000
4) ₹12,000 5) None of these

22. What is the ratio of the interest of J and K from their respective schemes A and B ?
1) 13 : 51 2) 17 : 68 3) 12 : 60
4) 22 : 55 5) None of these

23. If J invested same amount as K in their respective schemes A and B, then what is difference between their interest earned ?
1) ₹8800 2) ₹10000 3) ₹9400
4) ₹10600 5) None of these

24. If J invested ₹20000 in scheme A, then find the amount invested by J in scheme C, where rate of interest in scheme C is 40% of rate of interest in scheme B ?
1) ₹18,000 2) ₹15,000 3) ₹12,000
4) ₹14,000 5) None Of these

Answers and explanations

(1–6) :

Company	A		B	
Department	Existing	Added	Existing	Added
Marketing	18	2	10	4
Finance	28	2	8	8
HR	18	2	6	0
Total	64	6	24	12

1. 4; Required difference
= Existing employees of Finance department
– Existing employees of Marketing department
= 28 – 18 = 10

2. 2; Required percentage = $\frac{18}{6} \times 100 = 300\%$

3. 3; Fmployees added in company A = 6
Employees added in company B = 12
Hence, required ratio = 12 : 6 = 2 : 1

4. 1; Existing employees of Finance department in company B = 8

5. 2; Total number of existing employees in company A and Company B = 64 + 24 = 88
Hence, required average = $\frac{88}{6} = 14.67 = 15$

6. 4; Total employees of finance department in company B = 8 + 8 = 16
Total employees of HR department in company A = 18 + 2 = 20
Hence, required ratio = 16 : 20 = 4 : 5

(7–9) :

Let the initial speed of train X and train Y be x km/hr.

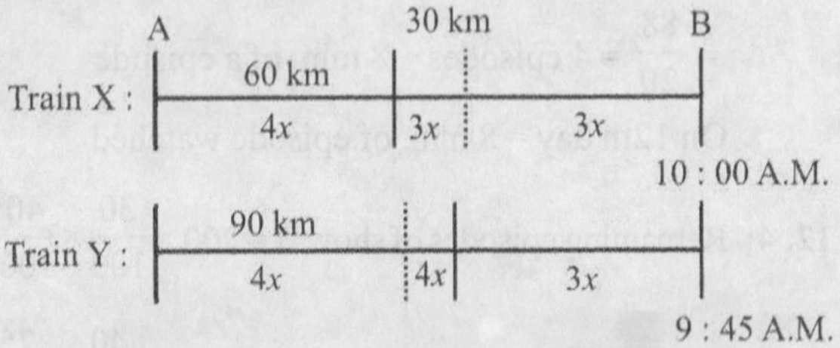

Time difference = 15 min.
Ratio of time = $4x : 3x = 4 : 3 = 60$ min : 45 mm

Initial speed of train X = $\frac{30\text{ km}}{45\text{ min}} = \frac{30}{3} \times 4 = 40$ km/hr

Time difference = 10 : 00 A.M. – 8 : 30 A.M. = 1.5 hrs
∴ Time ratio = 4 : 3 = 4 × 1.5 : 3 × 1.5 = 6hr : 4.5 hr

7. 4; Distance between station A and station B
= 40 km/hr × 6 hr = 240 km

8. 3; Initial speed of train X = 40 km/hr

9. 2; Train Z's speed = $40 \times \frac{125}{100} = 50$ km/hr

Hence, required time taken by train Z = $\frac{150}{50} = 3$ hrs

(10–15) :

Let the total episodes be 100 a.

Watched episodes for show A = $100a \times \frac{20}{100} \times \frac{25}{100} = 5a$

Watched episodes for show D = $100a \times \frac{10}{100} \times \frac{30}{100} = 3a$

∴ Average watched episodes for shows A and D

$= \frac{5a + 3a}{2} = 4a$

Now, according to the question,
$100a - 4a = 192$
$\Rightarrow 96a = 192 \Rightarrow a = 2$
Total episodes = 100 × 2 = 200

10. 3; Remaining episodes of show D = $200 \times \frac{10}{100} \times \frac{70}{100}$ $= 14$

Total remaining episodes timing = 14 × 20 = 280 minutes

Average time spent by a person to watch show D = 35 min/day

Hence, required number of days = $\frac{280}{35}$ = 8 days

11. 2; Show C watched episodes in 11 days = $\frac{8 \times 11}{20}$

$= \frac{88}{20}$ = 4 episodes + 8 min. of a episode

On 12th day = 8 min. of episode watched

12. 4; Remaining episodes of show B = $200 \times \frac{30}{100} \times \frac{40}{100} = 24$

Remaining episodes of show C = $200 \times \frac{40}{100} \times \frac{75}{100} = 60$

Hence, required difference = 60 – 24 = 36 episodes

13. 1; Total episodes of shows A and C = $200\left(\frac{20}{100} + \frac{40}{100}\right)$ $= 120$

Total episodes of shows B and D = $200 \times \frac{40}{100} = 80$

Hence, required ratio = 120 : 80 = 3 : 2

14. 2; Watched episodes of show B = $200 \times \frac{30}{100} \times \frac{60}{100} = 36$

Total timing of watched episodes = 36 × 20 = 720 minutes

Hence, required number of days = $\frac{720}{24}$ = 30 days

15. 3; Remaining episodes of show A = $200 \times \frac{20}{100} \times \frac{75}{100}$ $= 30$

Total timing for remaining episodes = 30 × 20 = 600 min.

Hence, required number of days = $\frac{600}{30}$ = 20 days

(16–19) :

Efficiency of A = $\frac{50}{10} = 5$ Efficiency of B = $\frac{60}{12} = 5$

∴ Efficiency of C = $(5+5) \times \frac{20}{100} = 2$

Actual work done by C in 15 hrs = 15 × 2 = 30 units

16. 2; Cs work time — Rest time

1 hr × 4 — 15 min × 4

↓ ↓

4 hrs × 3 — 1 hr × 3

↓ ↓

12 hrs — 3 hrs

Hence, work completed by C in his entire duration = 2 × 12 = 24 units

17. 3; Total work = 50 + 60 = 110 units

Total efficiency of A and B = 5 + 5 = 10

Hence, required time = $\frac{110}{10}$ = 11 hours

18. 4; Work done by C = 200 – (50 + 60) = 90 units.

Time taken by C = 15 hours

Hence, efficiency of C = $\frac{90}{15}$ = 6 units/hour

19. 1; C's acutal work done = 170 – (50 + 60) = 60 units.

Efficiency of C = $\frac{60}{15}$ = 4 units/hr

Total efficiency of A and B = $\frac{50}{10} + \frac{60}{12}$ = 10units/hr

∴ Work completed by A and B in 10 days = 10 × 10 = 100 units

∴ Remaining work = 170 – 100 = 70 units

Total efficiency of A, B and C = 10 + 4 = 14 units/hr

Hence, C left the work after = $\frac{70}{14}$ = 5 hours

(20–24) :

Rate for scheme A :

$x^2 - 2x - 15 = 0$

$\Rightarrow x^2 - 5x + 3x - 15 = 0$

$\Rightarrow (x-5)(x+3) = 0 \Rightarrow x = 5, -3$

∴ Rate = 5%

Time for scheme B : $y^2 + 2y - 8 = 0$

$\Rightarrow y^2 + 4y - 2y - 8 = 0 \Rightarrow (y+4)(y-2) = 0$

$\Rightarrow$ y = –4, 2 ∴ Time = 2 years

Scheme	Rate	Time
A	SI-5%	30 years
B	CI-20%	2 years
C	R%>5%	40 years

20. 3; K's investment = ₹10,000

$\therefore$ J's investment $= \frac{10,000}{5} =$ ₹8000

$\Rightarrow \frac{8000 \times 30 \times R}{100} = 8000 \Rightarrow R = \frac{100}{30} = \frac{10}{3}\%$

Hence, required percentage $= \frac{\frac{10}{3}}{150} \times 100 = \frac{20}{9}\%$

21. 1; $z^2 - 9z + 18 = 0 \Rightarrow z^2 - 6z - 3z + 18 = 0$

$\Rightarrow (z-6)(z-3) = 0 \Rightarrow z = 6, 3$

$\therefore$ Rate in scheme C > Rate in scheme A

$\therefore$ Rate = 6% in scheme C

Now, according to the question,

$\frac{\text{Amount} \times 5 \times 30}{100} = 10,000 \times \frac{150}{100} = 15,000$

$\therefore$ Amount invested by J $= \frac{15,000}{150} \times 100 =$ ₹10,000

For Scheme C : $\frac{\text{Amount} \times 6 \times 40}{100} = \frac{10,000 \times 5 \times 30}{100}$

$\Rightarrow$ Amount in scheme C $= \frac{10,000 \times 150}{240} =$ ₹6250

Hence, profit earned in scheme C $= \frac{6250 \times 6 \times 40}{100}$

= ₹15,000

22. 2; Required ratio = 5 : 20 = 1 : 4

In option (2) = 17 : 68 = 1 : 4

Hence, option (2) is the correct answer.

23. 4; Interest earned by J $= \frac{10000 \times 5 \times 30}{100} =$ ₹15,000

Interest earned by K $= 10000\left(1 + \frac{20}{100}\right)^2 - 10,000$

$= 10,000 \times \frac{36}{25} - 10,000 =$ ₹4400

Hence, required difference = 15000 − 4400 = ₹10,600

24. 3; Profit earned in scheme A $= \frac{20,000 \times 5 \times 30}{100} =$ ₹30,000

Rate of interest in scheme C $= 20 \times \frac{40}{100} = 8\%$

Now, according to the question,

Let the amount invested in scheme C be x.

Now, $\frac{x \times 8 \times 40}{100} = 30,000$

$\Rightarrow x = \frac{30000 \times 100}{8 \times 40} =$ ₹9375

Hence, J invested in scheme in C is ₹9375.

Practice Set 30

Directions (Q. 1–3): The scatter graph shows the number of boys (Y–Axis) and the number of girls (X– axis) In three different classes A, B and C.

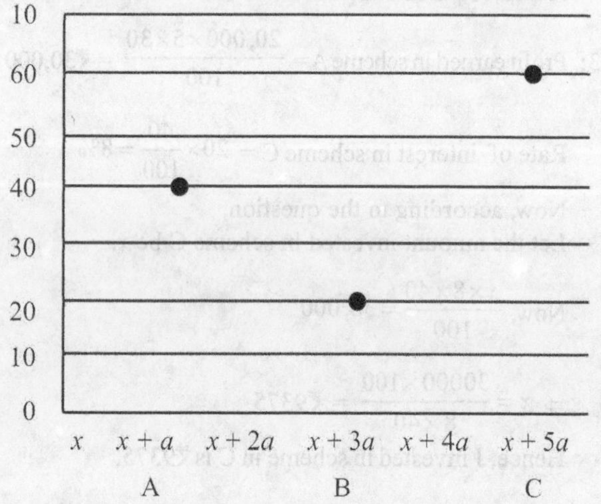

Note : If there were 10 more girls in class C then the probability of selecting a girl from class C would have been 40%.

1. If the number of girls in class D is 20% more than that in class B and the boys in class D are equal to that in class A, then find the probability of choosing 2 boys from class D. It is given that the number of girls in class B is half the number of girls in class C.

1) $\frac{260}{551}$ 2) $\frac{40}{58}$ 3) $\frac{39}{57}$

4) $\frac{240}{469}$ 5) None of the above

2. Find the difference between the total students of class A and B if the number of boys in class A are 4 times the number of girls in the same class.

1) 15 2) 18 3) 10
4) 20 5) None of these

3. Total number of girls in all the three classes are what per cent more/less than the total number of boys in all the three classes?

1) 37.5% 2) 25.48% 3) 75%
4) 50% 5) None of these

Directions (Q. 4–6) : Read the following information carefully and answer the questions that follow.

Amy and Brij have sold some wooden and plastic toys. Selling price of each wooden toy sold by Amy is equal to selling price of each wooden toy sold by Brij. Selling price of each plastic toy sold by Amy is equal to selling price of each plastic toy sold by Brij. The total units sale of plastic toys to wooden toys by Amy are in the ratio 3 : 8. Ratio of total wooden toys sold by Amy to that by Brij is 2 : 3. The total number of toys sold by Brij is 100. The number of plastic toys sold by Brij is equal to number of wooden toys sold by Amy. The selling price of each wooden toy is double the selling price of each plastic toy and it is applicable for both.

4. The number of plastic toys sold by Brij is what per cent more or less than the number of wooden toys sold by Amy.

1) 23% 2) 12% 2) 0%
4) 5.7% 5) None of these

5. Total selling amount of Brij is what per cent more/less than that of Amy.

1) 50% 2) 67.5% 3) 100%
4) 25% 5) None of these

6. Amy profit per cent on wooden toy is 60% and Brij's profit per cent on plastic toy is 25%. Find the square root ratio of cost price of wooden toy sold by Amy to plastic toy sold by Brij.

1) 8 : 5 2) 5 : 8 3) 8 : 13
4) 5 : 13 5) None of these

Directions (Q. 7–9) : Given below are two rows, in the first row some numbers are given and in the 2nd row the probability of picking that number is given.

4	a	b	$2b - 1$	$3(b + 1)$	38.5
1/3	1/6	1/3	1/6	1/6	1/6

7. If the series 4, a, b, $2b-1$, $3(b+1)$, 38.5 follows a certain pattern then find the value of a.
1) 3   2) 4   3) 5
4) 6   5) None of the above

8. If $c = 3b + 1$, then find the value of c.
1) 37   2) 13   3) 10
4) 16   5) None of the above

9. In the given question 'a' and 'b' are two independent events, then find P $(a \cup b)$.
1) $\frac{1}{6}$ 2) $\frac{1}{2}$ 3) $\frac{1}{3}$
4) $\frac{2}{3}$ 5) None of these

Directions (Q. 10–12) : Read the given information carefully and answer the questions that follow.

A right circular cylindrical vessel was filled with a mixture of milk and water, the quantity of which were in the respective ratio of 5 : 3. x ml mixture was sold and replaced with x ml of pure milk. The ratio between quantities of milk and water in the resultant mixture was 75 : 13. The quantity of mixture sold was 104 ml less than the original quantity of mixture in the vessel.

10. Had $0.25x$ ml of the initial mixture been sold and $0.75x$ ml pure milk and $0.05x$ ml water been added to the vessel, what solution be the volume of vessel that would have been filled in cm cube ?
1) 352 cm³   2) 268 cm³   3) 264 cm³
4) 165 cm³   5) None of these

11. What was the initial quantity of mixture in the vessel ?
1) 264 cm³   2) 104 cm³   3) 204 cm³
4) 352 cm³   5) None of these

12. Had the radius and height of the vessel been 3.5 cm and 10 cm respectively what portion of the vessel would have been empty at the end ?
1) 52 cm³   2) 33 cm³   3) 48.3 cm³
4) 18.5 cm³   5) None of these

Directions (Q. 13–16) : Read the given information carefully and answer the questions that follow.

Mita had total stock value of ₹240000. The bar graph given below shows the percentage of stocks sold by her to five different persons. The table shows the percentage increase in price of stocks in two years and the overall increase (in percentage) in price of stocks. With the increased price Mita earned some return amount from each of the persons.

Note: % increase in price = % of returns

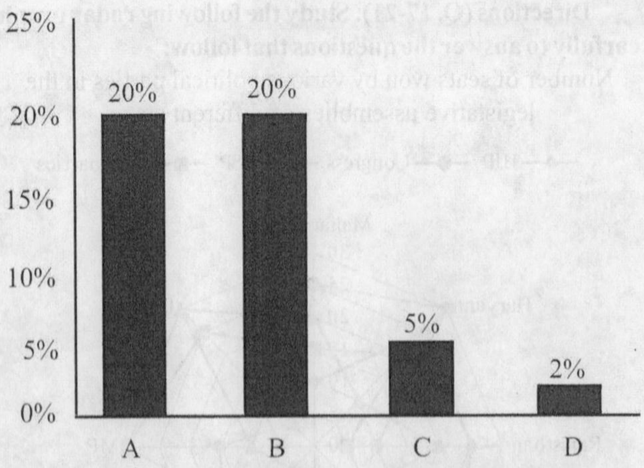

Person	% increment 1st year	& increment	Overall increment %
A	——	——	44%
B	10	——	21%
C	——	——	56.25%
D	——	——	32.25%
E	——	——	69%

13. If rate of increment for both the years are equal for both persons A and C, then find the difference in returned amount from both, if they are calculated just after a year.
1) 24800   2) 42600   3) 33750
4) 32665   5) None of these

14. If the returned amount earned by Mita from the person E is invested at a scheme at SI at the rate of 10% for 3 years, then find the amount earned by Mita from the scheme.
1) 21498806   2) 706974   3) 279458.4
4) 235547.4   5) None of these

15. If the returned amount earned by Mita from the person B is again used by her to purchase 8 shares of equal price, then find the value (in ₹) of each share.
1) 58080   2) 5264   3) 6460
4) 7260   5) None of these

16. The amount earned by Mita from the person D is how much more/less than the amount earned by her from person A and C together?
1) 83522   2) 81624   3) 78336
4) 81522   5) None of these

Directions (Q. 17-21): Study the following radar graph carfully to answer the questions that follow:

Number of seats won by various political parties in the legislative assemblies of different states

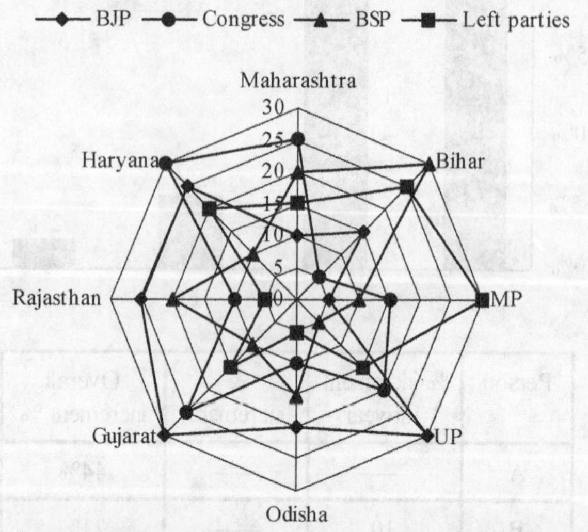

17. The total number of seats won by the BSP is what per cent more or less than that by the Left parties in all states together?
1) 8.21% more 2) 7.69% less 3) 6.56% more
4) 9.71% less 5) 10% less

18. What is the ratio of the total number of seats won by the BJP to the total number of seats won by the Congress in all states together?
1) 3 : 2 2) 4 : 5 3) 5 : 6 4) 6 : 7 5) 8 : 7

19. If 30% seats of the Maharashtra legislative assembly are won by the females and 40% seats of the Gujarat legislative assembly are won by the females, then the male members of the Maharashtra legislative assembly are what per cent more or less than the male members of the Gujarat legislative assembly?
1) 2.08% more 2) 3.18% less 3) 4.28% more
4) 5.38% more 5) 6.48% less

20. 40% members of the Haryana legislative assembly and 50% members of the UP legislative assembly are chargesheeted for involvement in crimes. Among these, 50% and 20% are females in the Haryana and UP legislative assembly respectively. Then the number of male members of the Haryana legislative assembly who are chargesheeted is what percentage more or less than the number of female members of the UP legislative assembly who are chargesheeted?
1) 250% more 2) 300% more
3) 142.85% more 4) 230% less
5) 220.45% less

21. Which political party won the highest number of seats in the given eight states?
1) BSP 2) Left parties 3) Congress
4) BJP 5) Either BJP or BSP

Answers and explanations

(1–3) :

If there were 10 more girls, total students from class C

$= x + 5a + 10 + 60 = (x + 5a + 70)$

According to the question,

Probability of selecting a girl from class C

$$\frac{(x+5a+10)}{(x+5a+70)} = \frac{40}{100} = 0.4$$

$$\Rightarrow (x+5a)(1-0.4) = 28 - 10 = 18$$

$$\Rightarrow (x+5a) = \frac{18}{0.6} = 30$$

1. 1; Boys in class D = Boys in class A = 40

Girls in class B $= \frac{1}{2} \times$ Girls in class C $= \frac{1}{2} \times 30 = 15$

$\therefore$ Girls in class D $= \left(1 + \frac{20}{100}\right) \times$ Girls in class B

$$= \frac{6}{5} \times 15 = 18$$

Total students in class D = 40 + 18 = 58

Now, required probability $= \frac{^{40}C_2}{^{58}C_2} = \frac{40 \times 39}{58 \times 57} = \frac{260}{551}$

2. 3; Number of boys in class A = 40

Girls in class A $= \frac{40}{4} = 10$

$\therefore$ Number of students in class A = 40 + 10 = 50

Now, girls in class A $= (x + a) = 10$ .... (i)

Girls in class C $= x + 5a = 30$ .... (ii)

$\therefore 4a = 20 \Rightarrow a = 5$ and $x = 5$

Now, girls in class B $= x + 3a = 5 + 3 \times 5 = 20$

Boys in class B = 20

Total students in class B = 20 + 20 = 40

Required difference = 50 − 40 = 10

3. 4; Required (%) difference

$$= \frac{(40+20+60)-(10+20+30)}{(40+20+60)} \times 100 = 50\%$$

(4–6) :

Selling price of each wooden toy by Amy
= S.P. of each wooden toy by Brij = X
S.P. of each plastic toy by Amy
= S.P. of each plastic toy by Brij = Y
Total toy sold by Amy = Plastic toy + Wooden toy
$= 3z + 8z = 11z$

$$\frac{\text{Wooden toy sold by Amy}}{\text{Wooden toy sold by Brij}} = \frac{2}{3}$$

$$\frac{8z}{\text{Wooden toy sold by Brij}} = \frac{2}{3}$$

$\Rightarrow$ Wooden toy sold by Brij = $12z$
Total toy sold by Brij = 100
Plastic toy sold by Brij = $100 - 12z$
According to the question,
$100 - 12z = 8z \Rightarrow 20z = 100, z = 5$
S.P. of a wooden toys $(x) = 2 \times$ S.P. of a plastic toy (y)
$\Rightarrow x = 2y$
Total toy sold by Amy $= 3 \times 5 + 8 \times 5 = 15 + 40 = 55$

	Plastic toy	Wooden toy	Total
Amy	15	40	55
Brij	40	100 – 40 = 60	100

4. 3; Required % $= \left(\frac{40-40}{40}\right) \times 100 = 0\%$

5. 3; Total selling amount obtained by Brij
$= 40 \times 2y + 60 \times y = 140y$
Total selling amount obtained by Amy
$= 15 \times 2y + 40 \times y = 70y$

$$\therefore \text{Required } \% = \frac{140y - 70y}{70y} \times 100 = 100\%$$

6. 2; Amy's profit per cent on total wooden toys = $60y$

Cost price of each wooden toy $= \frac{140y \times 100}{40 \times 160} = \frac{5y}{8}$

Brij's profit per cent on plastic toy = 25%
Cost price of each plastic toy sold by Brij

$$= \frac{15 \times 2y \times 100}{15 \times 125} = \frac{8y}{5}$$

$$\therefore \text{Required ratio} = \frac{\frac{5y}{8}}{\frac{8y}{5}} = \frac{25}{64}$$

7. 1; Given series :
$4, a, b, 2b-1, 3(b+1), 38.5$

Pattern of the series is : $\times\frac{1}{2}+1, \times\frac{2}{2}+1, \times\frac{3}{2}+1, ...$

Here,

$$a = 4 \times \frac{1}{2} + 1 = 3$$

$$b = 3 \times \frac{2}{2} + 1 = 4$$

$2b - 1 = 2 \times 4 - 1 = 7$
$3(b+1) = 3(4+1) = 15$

Last term $= 15 \times \frac{5}{2} + 1 = 38.5$

8. 2; $c = 3b + 1 = 3 \times 4 + 1 = 13$

9. 4; $P(a \cup b) = P(a) + P(b) - P(a \cap b)$
As a and b are independent events.
$\therefore P(a \cap b) = 0$
$P(a \cup b) = P(a) + P(b) - 0$

$$= \frac{1}{6} + \frac{1}{3} = \frac{1+2}{6} = \frac{1}{2}$$

(10–12) :

	Milk	:	Water
Initial :	5K	:	3K

After first removal :

$$\left\{5K - \frac{5}{(5+3)}X\right\} : \left\{3K - \frac{3}{5+3}X\right\}$$

After adding X ml pure milk :

$$\left\{5K - \frac{5X}{8} + X\right\} : \left\{3K - \frac{3X}{8}\right\}$$

$\Rightarrow \{40K + 3X\} : (24K - 3X)$
According to the question,

$$\left(\frac{40K + 3X}{24K - 3X}\right) = \frac{75}{13}$$

$520K + 39X = 1800K - 225X$
$1280K = 264X$

$$160K = 33X \Rightarrow X = \left(\frac{160}{33}\right)K$$

Again,
$8K - X = 104$

$$8K - \left(\frac{160}{33}\right)K = 104$$

$\Rightarrow (264 - 160)K = 104 \times 33$

$\therefore$ K = 33 and X = $\frac{160}{33} \times 33 = 160\,ml$

Now,

	Milk	Water	Mixture
Initial	$5 \times 33 = 165$	$3 \times 33 = 99$	$165 + 99 = 264$
After first removal	$165 - \frac{5}{8} \times 160 = 65$	$99 - \frac{3}{8} \times 160 = 39$	$65 + 39 = 104$
After adding Pure milk	$65 + 160 = 225$	39	264

10. 1; Total initial mixture = 264 ml
Volume removed = $0.25 \times 160 = 40$ ml
Volume added = $0.75x + 0.05x = 0.8x = 0.8 \times 160 = 128$ ml
Volume of resultant mixture = $264 - 40 + 128$
$= 352$ ml $= 352\ cm^3$

11. 2; Initial quantity = 264 ml
After X ml sold out = $264 - (65 + 39) = 104$ ml

12. 2; Radius (r) = 3.5 cm, Height (h) = 10 cm

Volume = $\pi (r)^2 h = \frac{22}{7} \times 3.5 \times 3.5 \times 10 = 385\ cm^3$

Portion of the vessel would have been empty
$= 385 - 352 = 33\ cm^3$

(13–16) :

For person B, 1st year increment = 10%
Second year increment = x%

$\therefore 10 + x + \frac{10 \times x}{100} = 21$

$\Rightarrow 10 + x + \frac{x}{10} = 21 \Rightarrow x + \frac{x}{10} = 21 - 10 = 11$

$\Rightarrow \frac{11}{10}x = 11 \Rightarrow x = 10\%$

13. 3; For A, $x + x + \frac{x.x}{100} = 44 \Rightarrow 2x + \frac{x^2}{100} = 44$

$\Rightarrow 200x + x^2 = 4400 \Rightarrow x^2 + 200x - 4400 = 0$
$\Rightarrow (x + 220)(x - 20) = 0 \therefore x = 20\%$

Now C, $y + y + \frac{y.y}{100} = 56.25$

$200y + y^2 = 5625$
$y^2 + 200y - 5625 = 0$
$(y + 225)(y - 25) = 0$
$\therefore y = 25\%$

Now, stocks given to A = $240000 \times \frac{20}{100} = 48000$

Stocks given to C = $240000 \times \frac{5}{100} = 12000$

Now, difference of return amount of A and C calculated after first year

$= 48000 \times \frac{120}{100} - 12000 \times \frac{125}{100}$

$= 12000 \times \left[\frac{4 \times 6}{5} - \frac{5}{4}\right] = 12000 \times \frac{71}{20} = 42600$

14. 3; Per cent of stock sold to E
$= 100 - 20 - 20 - 5 - 2 = 53\%$
Return amount earned from person E

$= 240000 \times \frac{53}{100} \times \frac{169}{100} = 214968$

Amount earned by Mita after getting returns from S.I.

$\left(214968 + \frac{214968 \times 10 \times 3}{100}\right) = 279458.4$

15. 4; Return amount earned by Mita from person B

$= 240000 \times \frac{121}{100} \times \frac{20}{100} = 58080$

Price of each share = $\frac{58080}{8} = 7260$

16. 4; Amount earned from person D

$= 240000 \times \frac{2}{100} \times \frac{132.25}{100} = 6348$

Amount earned from A and C together

$= 240000\left[\frac{20}{100} \times \frac{144}{100} + \frac{5}{100} \times \frac{156.25}{100}\right] = 87870$

Required difference = $87870 - 6348 - 81522$

17. 2; Total number of seats won by BSP in all states = $5 + 10 + 30 + 20 + 10 + 20 + 10 + 15 = 120$
Total number of seats won by Left Parties in all states $= 15 + 30 + 25 + 15 + 20 + 5 + 15 + 5 = 130$

$\therefore$ Reqd % = $\frac{130 - 120}{130} \times 100 = \frac{10}{130} \times 100 \approx 7.69$ % less

18. 5; Total number of seats won by BJP in all states = $30 + 5 + 15 + 10 + 25 + 25 + 30 + 20 = 160$
Total number of seats won by Congress in all states

$= 20 + 15 + 5 + 25 + 30 + 10 + 25 + 10 = 140$

$\therefore$ Reqd ratio $= 160 : 140 = 8 : 7$

19. 1; Total seats in Maharashtra assembly
$= 10 + 15 + 20 + 25 = 70$

Total male members of Maharashtra asembly $= 70 \times \frac{70}{100}$

$= 49$

Total seats in Gujarat assembly $= 30 + 25 + 15 + 10$
$= 80$

Total male members of Gujarat assembly

$= 80 \times \frac{60}{100} = 48$

$\therefore$ Reqd % $= \frac{49-48}{48} \times 100 = 2.08\%$ more

20. 3; The number of members in Haryana assembly

chargesheeted for involvement in crimes $= 85 \times \frac{40}{100}$

$= 34$

$\therefore$ Number of male members in Haryana assembly

chargesheeted for involvement in crimes $= 34 \times \frac{50}{100}$

$= 17$

Number of female members in UP assembly chargesheeted for involvement in crimes

$= 70 \times \frac{50}{100} \times \frac{20}{100} = 7$

$\therefore$ Reqd percentage $= \left(\frac{17-7}{7} \times 100\right) \approx 142.85\%$ more

21. 4; Total number of seats won by BJP in all states = 160
Total number of seats won by Congress in all states
$= 140$
Total number of seats won by BSP in all states = 120
Total number of seats won by Left Parties in all states
$= 130$
Hence, BJP won the highest number of seats.

Practice Set 31

Directions (Q. 1-5): Study the following graphs carefully to answer the questions that follow:

The line graph shows the number of students in various departments in different cities. The pie-chart shows the percentage of faculty members in different cities.

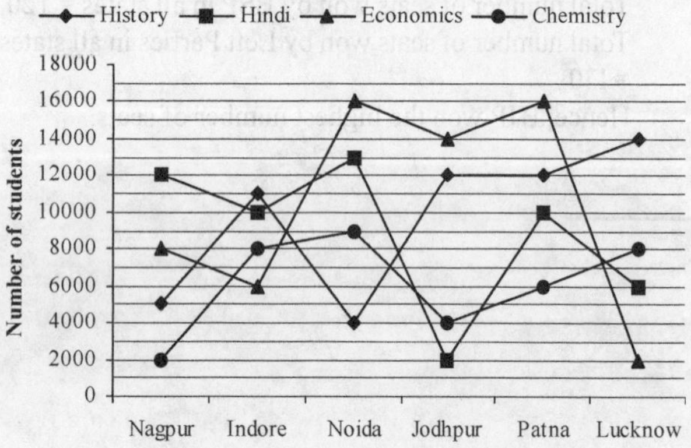

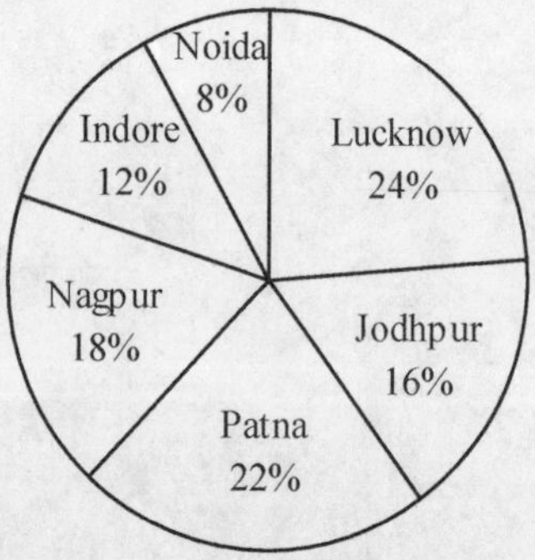

Total number of faculty members = 10000

1. The number of students studying History in Nagpur is what per cent less than the number of students studying Economics in Jodhpur?
   1) 34.28% 2) 44.28% 3) 54.28% 4) 64.28% 5) 74.28%
2. The number of faculty members in Noida is what per cent of the number of students in Economics in Indore?
   1) 13.33% 2) 16.66% 3) 17.77% 4) 18.88% 5) 19.99%
3. What is the ratio of the total number of students in all departments together to the number of faculty members in Patna?
   1) 18 : 5 2) 19 : 2 3) 20 : 1 4) 17 : 3 5) 16 : 7
4. In which city is the number of students per faculty member the maximum?
   1) Jodhpur 2) Noida 3) Patna
   4) Lucknow 5) Nagpur
5. In which department is the number of students the minimum?
   1) Hindi 2) History
   3) Either Hindi or Chemistry 4) Economics
   5) Chemistry

Directions (Q. 6-10): Study the given pie-charts carefully and answer the questions given below:

The graph shows the expenditure of School A and School B in 2012 under various heads.

Total expenditure of School A = ₹10 lakh

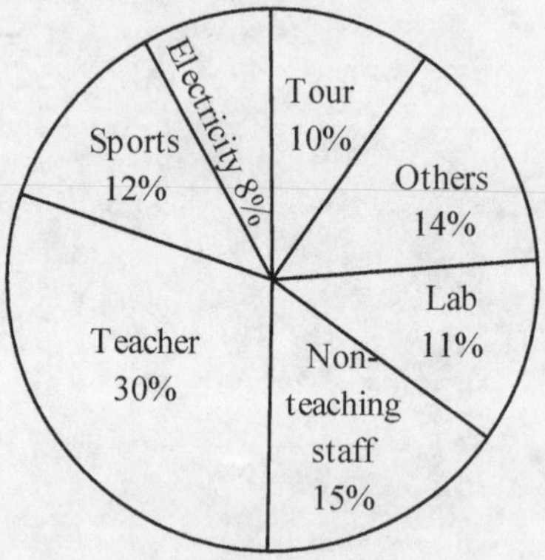

School A

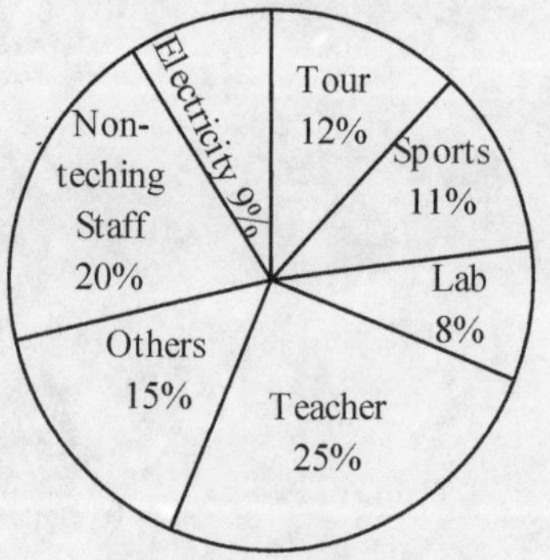

School B

6. If the total expenditure of School B is 95% of the total expenditure of School A, then what is the difference between the expenditure on teachers of School A and that on non-teaching staff of School B?
   1) ₹1.5 lakh 2) ₹1.1 lakh 3) ₹2 lakh
   4) ₹2.5 lakh 5) ₹1.97 lakh
7. If the total expenditure of School A is 20% less than the expenditure of School B, then what is the ratio of the

expenditure on tour of School B to that of School A?
1) 9 : 7 2) 7 : 5 3) 5 : 3 4) 3 : 2 5) 2 : 5

8. There are 60 teachers (including the principal) in School A of these 30% are new teachers who get 40% less salary than the old ones and the Principal gets 10% more salary than an old teacher. What is the salary of a new teacher?
1) ₹3212.57 2) ₹3658.53 3) ₹2835.75
4) ₹3789.47 5) ₹2312.91

9. In the summer vaccation, when sports, tour, electricity and labs are closed, the expenditure of School A reduces by what per cent?
1) 47% 2) 35% 3) 32% 4) 40% 5) 41%

10. The total expenditure of School B is ₹12 lakh and the number of non-teaching staff is 50. If 30% of the non-teaching staff are removed, then the total expenditure reduces by what per cent?
1) 12% 2) 4% 3) 6% 4) 8% 5) 13%

Directions (Q. 11-15): Study the following table carefully to answer the questions given below:

Name	Nature of Interest	Principal	Amount	Year	Rate (%)
M	Compound	₹10000			4
N	Simple		₹29500	3	
O	Compound	₹20000		2	3
P	Simple			4	
Q	Compound			5	2

11. What is the principal of N if the ratio of interest rate of M to that of N is 2 : 3?
1) ₹10449 2) ₹20230 3) ₹25000
4) ₹17121 5) ₹25423

12. What is the amount of O, if the interest is compounded yearly for 2 years?
1) ₹19165.7 2) ₹20320.9 3) ₹21218
4) ₹22418 5) ₹25300.5

13. If the ratio of principal of O to that of P is 4 : 5 and the rate of interest of P is 10% more than that of O, then what is the interest of P?
1) ₹3300 2) ₹3142 3) ₹3201 4) ₹2890 5) ₹2750

14. At what rate of interest the amount of N becomes five times that of his principal?
1) 63.58% 2) 69.96% 3) 60% 4) 133.33% 5) 162.58%

15. What is the amount of Q when the principal of Q is 20% more than that of M?
1) ₹32321.5 2) ₹13248.97 3) ₹54974.19
4) ₹32863.24 5) ₹17952.35

Directions (Q. 16-20): Study the following pie-chart and line graph and answer the questions given below:

The pie-chart shows the percentage of foreign currencies present in the Indian Economy in various years.

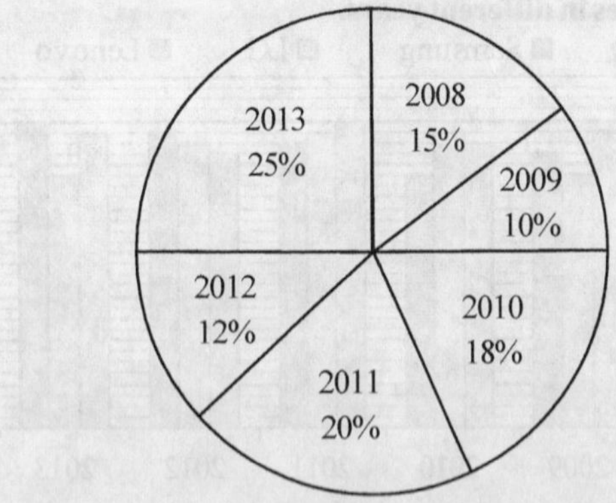

The line graph shows the value of ₹ with respect to other currencies – ¥ (yen), $ (dollar), £ (pound) and € (euro).

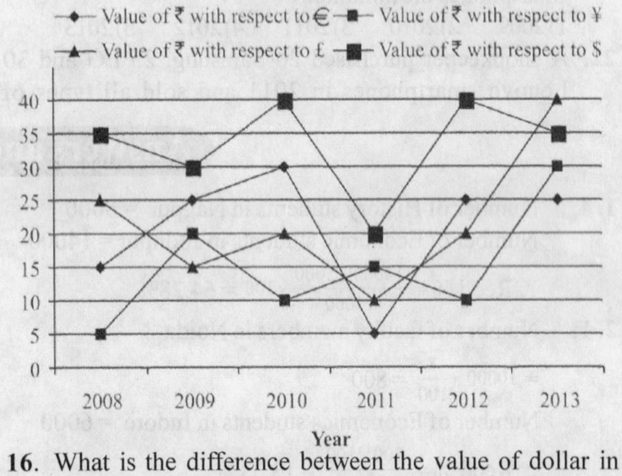

16. What is the difference between the value of dollar in 2013 and that of yen in 2010?
1) ₹25 2) ₹28 3) ₹30 4) ₹32 5) ₹39

17. Which currency has the maximum average value (in terms of ₹) for the given six years?
1) ¥ 2) $ 3) £
4) € 5) Either ¥ or $

18. If the total Indian Economy in 2008 was $300 billion and that in 2013 was $700 billion, then what is the ratio of the value of Indian currency in Indian Economy in 2008 to that in 2013?
1) 51 : 45 2) 7 : 3 3) 51 : 125 4) 4 : 5 5) 1 : 3

19. The total Indian Economy in 2011 was ₹9000 billion. If the value of dollar in foreign currency was 25% and the value of euro in foreign currency was 30% then what is the difference between their values in that year in terms of rupee?
1) ₹65.5 billion 2) ₹80 billion 3) ₹70 billion
4) ₹90 billion 5) ₹95 billion

20. What is the average value of all four currencies in 2010 in terms of rupee?
1) ₹30 2) ₹32 3) ₹31 4) ₹33 5) ₹25

Directions (Q. 21-25): Study the following bar-graph carefully to answer the given questions.

The graph shows the prices of three different types of

smartphones in different years.

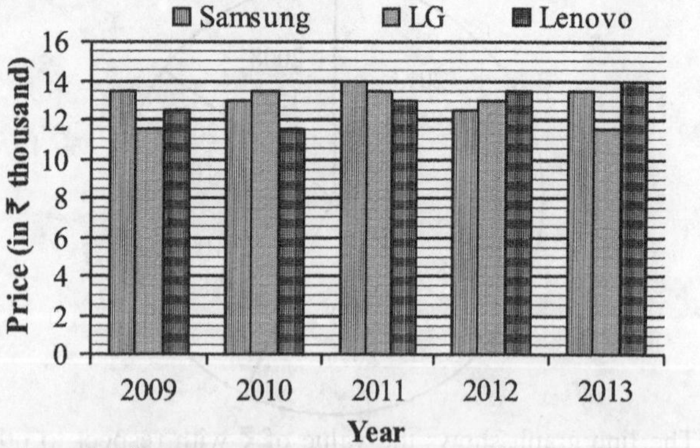

21. In which year was the average price of all three smartphones the minimum?
1) 2009 2) 2010 3) 2011 4) 2012 5) 2013

22. A shopkeeper purchased 20 Samsung, 25 LG and 30 Lenovo smartphones in 2011 and sold all types of smartphones at the rate of ₹13300. What is his percentage loss or profit?
1) 89% 2) 0.99% 3) 0.71% 4) 71% 5) 0.56%

23. The price of LG smartphones in 2012 was what per cent of its price in 2013?
1) 104.5% 2) 107.68% 3) 110.9% 4) 113.04% 5) 115.06%

24. If the total number of sales of Lenovo was 20000 in 2010 and the total number of sales of Samsung was 18500 in that year, then what was the difference of income of Samsung and Lenovo?
1) ₹10500000 2) ₹10700000 3) ₹10900000 4) ₹10300000 5) ₹10200000

25. Which smartphone has the minimum average price during the given five years?
1) Samsung 2) LG 3) Either Samsung or LG 4) Either LG or Lenovo 5) Lenovo

Answers and explanations

1. 4; Number of History students in Nagpur = 5000
Number of Economic students in Jodhpur = 14000

$\therefore$ Reqd % = $\frac{14000-5000}{14000}\times 100 = 64.28\%$

2. 1; Number of faculty members in Noida

$= 10000\times\frac{8}{100} = 800$

Number of Economics students in Indore = 6000

$\therefore$ Reqd % = $\frac{800\times 100}{6000} = 13.33\%$

3. 3; Reqd ratio = 44000 : 2200 = 20 : 1

4. 2; In Nagpur → $\frac{\text{Number of students}}{\text{Number of faculty members}}$

$= \frac{2000+5000+8000+12000}{10000\times\frac{18}{100}} = 15$

Indore → $\frac{6000+8000+10000+11000}{10000\times\frac{12}{100}} = 29.16 \approx 29$

In Noida → $\frac{4000+9000+13000+16000}{10000\times\frac{8}{100}} = 52.5 \approx 53$

In Jodhpur → $\frac{2000+4000+12000+14000}{10000\times\frac{16}{100}} = 20$

In Patna → $\frac{6000+10000+12000+16000}{10000\times\frac{22}{10}} = 20$

In Lucknow → $\frac{2000+6000+8000+14000}{10000\times\frac{24}{100}} = 12.5 \approx 13$

faculty members

In Noida the number of students per teacher is the maximum.

5. 5; Number of students in History = 5000 + 11000 + 4000 + 12000 + 12000 + 14000 = 58000
Number of students in Hindi = 12000 + 10000 + 13000 + 2000 + 10000 + 6000 = 53000
Number of students in Economics = 8000 + 6000 + 16000 + 14000 + 16000 + 2000 = 62000
Number of students in Chemistry = 2000 + 8000 + 9000 + 4000 + 6000 + 8000 = 37000
In Chemistry the number of students is the minimum.

6. 2; Total expenditure of School B

$= 1000000\times\frac{95}{100} =$ ₹950000 = ₹9.5 lakh

$\therefore$ Expenditure on teachers of School A

$= 1000000\times\frac{30}{100} =$ ₹300000 = ₹3 lakh

Expenditure on non-teaching staff of School B

$= 950000\times\frac{20}{100} =$ ₹190000 = ₹1.9 lakh

$\therefore$ Reqd difference = (3 lakh − 1.9 lakh) = ₹1.1 lakh

7. 4; Given total expenditure of School A = ₹10 lakh
Total expenditure of School B

$= \frac{1000000\times 100}{80} =$ ₹1250000 = 12.5 lakh

$\therefore$ Expenditure of School B on tour

$= 1250000\times\frac{12}{100} = 150000 = 1.5$ lakh

Expenditure of School A on tour

$= 1000000\times\frac{10}{100} =$ ₹1 lakh

$\therefore$ Reqd ratio = 150000 : 100000 = 3 : 2

8. 3; Salary of all the teachers in School A

$= 1000000 \times \frac{30}{100} = ₹300000$

Number of new teachers $= 60 \times \frac{30}{100} = 18$

Number of old teachers $= (60 - 18) = 42$

Let the salary of an old teacher be ₹x.

$\therefore$ Salary of a new teacher $= \frac{x \times 60}{100} = \frac{3x}{5}$

Now, salary of Principal $= ₹\frac{11x}{10}$

So, $x \times 41 + \frac{11x}{10} + \frac{3x \times 18}{5} = 300000$

or, $\frac{410x + 11x + 54x}{10} = 300000$ or, $475x = 300000 \times 10$

$\therefore x = \frac{300000 \times 10}{475} = ₹6315.78$

Salary of a new teacher $= 6315.78 \times \frac{3}{5} = 3789.47$

9. 5; In summer vacation there is no expenditure on sports, tour, electricity and lab.

The remaining expenditure = expenditure on teacher + non-teaching staff + others $= 30 + 15 + 14 = 59\%$

$\therefore$ Expenditure reduces by $(100 - 59 =) 41\%$

10. 3; In School B, the expenditure on non-teaching staff

$= 12 \times \frac{20}{100} = 2.4$ lakh

Expenditure on each non-teaching staff

$= \frac{240000}{50} = ₹4800$

After removing 30% the number of non-teaching staff

$= 50 \times \frac{70}{100} = 35$

Salary of 35 non-teaching staff $= 35 \times 4800 = ₹168000$ $= 1.68$ lakh

$\therefore$ Reduction in expenditure $= 2.4$ lakh $- 1.68$ lakh $= 0.72$ lakh $= ₹72000$

$\therefore$ Percentage reduction in total expenditure

$= \frac{72000}{1200000} \times 100 = 6\%$

11. 3; Interest rate of N $= \frac{4 \times 3}{2} = 6\%$

Amount = 29500. Time = 3 years

Let the principal be ₹x

Then, $x + \frac{x \times 3 \times 6}{100} = 29500$

or, $x = ₹25000$

12. 3; Amount $= P\left(1 + \frac{R}{100}\right)^T$

$= 20000 \times 1.03 \times 1.03 = ₹21218$

13. 1; Principal of P $= \frac{5}{4} \times 20000 = 25000$

New rate of interest $= 3 + \frac{3 \times 10}{100} = 3.3$

Now, interest of P $= \frac{25000 \times 3.3 \times 4}{100} = ₹3300$

14. 4; Amount of N = ₹29500

$\therefore$ Prinicipal $= \frac{29500}{5} = ₹5900$

Time = 3 years

$\therefore$ Interest = Amount – Principal $= 29500 - 5900 = 23600$

$\therefore$ Reqd rate $= \frac{\text{Interest} \times 100}{\text{Principal} \times \text{time}}$

$= \frac{23600 \times 100}{5900 \times 3} = \frac{400}{3} = 133.33\%$

15. 2; Principal of Q $= 10000 \times \frac{120}{100} = ₹12000$

$\therefore$ Amount of Q $= 12000\left(1 + \frac{2}{100}\right)^5$

$= \frac{12000 \times 102 \times 102 \times 102 \times 102 \times 102}{10000000000} = ₹13248.97$

16. 1; Value of yen in 2010 = ₹10

Value of dollar in 2013 = ₹35

$\therefore$ Reqd difference $= 35 - 10 = ₹25$

17. 2; Average value of euro in the given six years $= \frac{1}{6} \times (15 + 25 + 30 + 5 + 25 + 25) = ₹20.834$

Average value of yen in given six years

$= \frac{1}{6} \times (5 + 20 + 10 + 15 + 10 + 30) = ₹15$

Average value of dollar in the given six years

$= \frac{1}{6} \times (35 + 30 + 40 + 20 + 40 + 35) = ₹33.34$

Average value of pound in the given six years

$= \frac{1}{6} \times (25 + 15 + 20 + 10 + 20 + 40) = ₹21.67$

Hence, dollar has the maximum average value.

18. 3; Value of foreign currency in Indian Economy in 2008

$= 300 \times \frac{15}{100} = \$45$ bn

Value of Indian currency in Indian Economy in 2008 $= \$(300 - 45)$ bn $= \$255$ bn

Value of Indian currency in Indian economy in 2013

$= 700$ bn $- 700 \times \frac{25}{100}$ bn $= \$(700 - 175)$bn $= \$525$ bn

$\therefore$ Reqd ratio $= 255 : 525 = 51 : 105$

19. 4; In 2011, total Indian Economy was ₹9000 bn.

Amount of foreign currency $= 9000 \times \frac{20}{100} = ₹1800$ bn

$\therefore$ Amount of dollar $= 1800 \times \frac{25}{100} = ₹450$ bn

Amount of Euro $= 1800 \times \frac{30}{100} = ₹540$ bn

∴ Difference between them = 540 – 450 = ₹90 bn

20. 5; Average value of four currencies in 2010 = $\frac{1}{4}(10+20+30+40)$ = ₹25

21. 3; Average price of all three smartphones in 2009 = $\frac{1}{3}\times(13500+11500+12500)$ = ₹12500

In 2010 = $\frac{1}{3}\times(13000+13500+11500)$ = ₹12666.7

In 2011 = $\frac{1}{3}\times(14000+13500+13000)$ = ₹13500

In 2012 = $\frac{1}{3}\times(12500+13000+13500)$ = ₹13000

In 2013 = $\frac{1}{3}\times(13500+11500+14000)$ = ₹13000

Hence, in 2011 the average price is the maximum for all the three smartphones.

22. 2; Cost price of 20 Samsung, 25 LG and 30 Lenovo smartphones in 2011
= 20 × 14000 + 25 × 13500 + 30 × 13000 = ₹1007500
∴ Selling price = 13300 × (20 + 25 + 30) = ₹997500

∴ % loss = $\frac{1007500-997500}{1007500}\times100\%$ = 0.99%

23. 4; Price of LG smartphones in 2012
= ₹13000 and in 2013 = ₹11500

Price of LG smartphones in 2012 is $\left(\frac{13000\times100}{11500}\right)\%$
= 113.04% of its price in 2013

24. 1; Income of Lenovo in 2010
= 20000 × 11500 = ₹230000000 = 23 crore
Income of Samsung in 2010
= 18500 × 13000 = 240500000 = 24.05 crore
∴ Reqd difference = 240600000 – 230000000
= ₹10500000 = 1.05 cr

25. 2; Average price of Samsung = $\frac{1}{5}\times(13500+13000+14000+12500+13500)$ = ₹$\frac{66500}{5}$ = ₹13300

Average price of LG = $\frac{1}{5}\times(11500+13500+13500+13000+11500)$ = ₹$\frac{63000}{5}$ = ₹12600

Average price of Lenovo = $\frac{1}{5}\times(12500+11500+13000+13500+14000)$ = ₹$\frac{64500}{5}$ = ₹12900

LG has the minimum average price during the given years.

Practice Set 32

Directions (Q. 1-5): Study the following bar-graph and pie-chart carefully to answer the following questions.

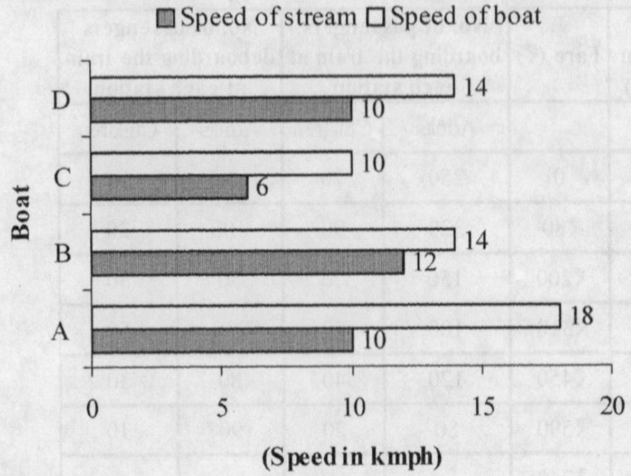

Percentage of distance travelled by Shyam by the four different boats

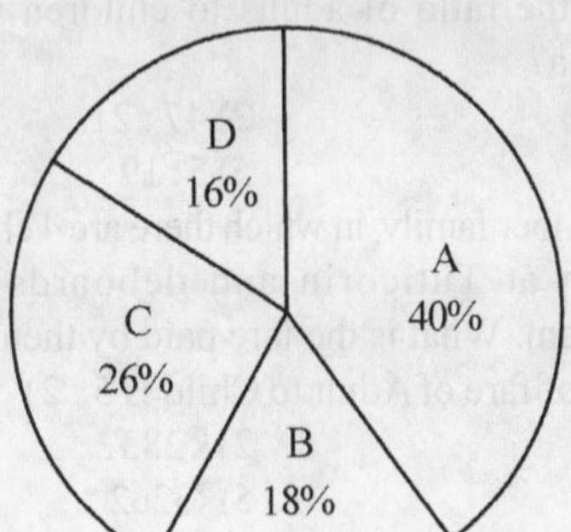

Total distance travelled = 1000 km

1. What is the difference of time taken by boat A and boat B to travel 200 km upstream?
   1) 68 hours 2) 72 hours 3) 71 hours
   4) 75 hours 5) 84 hours
2. What is the time taken by Shyam to reach his destination upstream?
   1) 272 hours 2) 245 hours 3) 240 hours
   4) 232 hours 5) 268 hours
3. If the speed of boat C is increased by 40% and the speed of stream decreases by 20% then what is the difference between the time taken by the boat now and that taken previously to travel 200 km? (Assume opposite direction of stream)
   1) $28\frac{6}{23}$ hours 2) $22\frac{4}{5}$ hours 3) $20\frac{4}{5}$ hours
   4) $18\frac{5}{6}$ hours 5) $35\frac{5}{6}$ hours
4. If the speed of boat D increases by 10% then what is the approximate time taken by Shyam to reach 500 km by boat D? (Assume opposite direction of stream)
   1) 88 hours 2) 92.6 hours 3) 68 hours
   4) 78 hours 5) 44 hours
5. What is the ratio of the time taken by boat C to that taken by boat D? (Assume same direction of stream)
   1) 9 : 7 2) 7 : 5 3) 5 : 3
   4) 4 : 3 5) 3 : 2

Directions (Q. 6-10): Study the given table carefully to answer the following questions.

The table shows the time (in days) taken by five men who do different types of work.

Types of work → Name ↓	Building construction	Road construction	Bridge construction	Tower installation
Rituraj	20	18	24	26
Amarkant	22	24	20	28
Vishwamohan	18	26	28	24
Prithusen	24	22	30	20
Laliteshwar	26	20	26	30

6. How many days would Rituraj, Amarkant and Prithusen take to construct a building when they work together?
   1) $5\frac{4}{5}$ days 2) $4\frac{1}{3}$ days 3) $8\frac{1}{2}$ days
   4) $\frac{53}{181}$ days 5) $6\frac{2}{3}$ days
7. How many days would Vishwamohan, Laliteshwar and Rituraj take to instal 10 towers when they work together?
   1) 90 days 2) 88.13 days 3) 92.92 days
   4) 87 days 5) 85.41 days
8. The bridge construction work is initiated by Rituraj, Prithusen and Laliteshwar together. After four days

Laliteshwar leaves the work and Amarkant joins them. In how many days will the work be completed?

1) $7\frac{13}{25}$ days 2) $5\frac{72}{143}$ days

3) $10\frac{68}{138}$ days 4) $4\frac{24}{65}$ days

5) $12\frac{12}{65}$ days

9. What would be the time taken to construct 5 buildings and 4 different roads when Rituraj, Prithusen and Vihwamohan work together?

1) 65.61 days 2) 61.53 days 3) 64.45 days
4) 62.63 days 5) 68.32 days

10. Rituraj and Amarkant got ₹50000 for building construction. What is the share of Rituraj?

1) ₹25000 2) ₹26190.47 3) ₹24130.5
4) ₹22990.7 5) ₹28970.5

Directions (Q. 11-15): Study the table carefully to answer the following questions.

Station	Arrival time	Departure time	Distance travelled from origin (in km)	Fare (₹)	No. of passengers boarding the train at each station		No. of pasengers deboarding the train at each station	
					Adults	Children	Adults	Children
Kanyakumari	Starting	01:00 pm	–	0	250	70	–	–
Tirunelveli	3 : 00 pm	03 : 05 pm	100 km	₹80	320	90	100	20
Tuticorin	7 : 00 pm	07 : 10 pm	250 km	₹200	150	70	50	30
Madurai	11 : 45 pm	12 : 05 am	430 km	₹310	100	60	230	50
Tiruchirappalli	3 : 35 am	03 : 40 am	670 km	₹450	120	40	80	30
Arakkonam	6 : 30 am	06 : 35 am	820 km	₹590	80	20	90	10
Renigunta	11 : 00 am	terminates	1140 km	₹740	–	–	–	–

11. What is the speed of the train running between Kanyakumari and Madurai?

1) 40 kmph 2) $60\frac{2}{19}$ kmph

3) $62\frac{11}{21}$ kmph 4) 50 kmph

5) $68\frac{15}{22}$ kmph

12. If there is no any stop between Kanyakumari and Renigunta, then what will be the new speed of the train?

1) $47\frac{5}{7}$ kmph 2) $48\frac{4}{9}$ kmph

3) $49\frac{1}{2}$ kmph 4) $50\frac{3}{7}$ kmph

5) $53\frac{11}{17}$ kmph

13. What is the total income of Railways from this train from Kanyakumari to Madurai? (Given – fare for Child is 40% that for an Adult)

1) ₹163400 2) ₹155980 3) ₹173500
4) ₹184000 5) ₹1925000

14. What is the ratio of adults to children who arrive at Renigunta?

1) 3 : 5 2) 47 : 21 3) 39 : 41
4) 47 : 51 5) 5 : 19

15. A 10-member family, in which there are 4 children, boards the train at Tuticorin and deboards the train at Arakkonam. What is the fare paid by them? (Given that the ratio of fare of Adult to Child is 5 : 2)

1) ₹3034 2) ₹2832 3) ₹2964
4) ₹3544 5) ₹3262

16. Two cards are drawn from a well-shuffled pack of 52 cards. Find the probability that both of them are either red or Kings.

1) $\frac{7}{13}$ 2) $\frac{3}{26}$ 3) $\frac{63}{221}$ 4) $\frac{55}{221}$ 5) $\frac{5}{7}$

17. Two dice are tossed. What is the probability that the sum total is a prime number?

1) $\frac{1}{6}$ 2) $\frac{5}{12}$ 3) $\frac{1}{2}$ 4) $\frac{7}{9}$ 5) $\frac{8}{15}$

Directions (Q. 18-20): Study the information carefully to answer the questions given below:

There are 1200 men on an island. Two-thirds of them are Indians. 10% of them are Americans and the remaining belong to other countries. Forty per cent of the Indians are females and the remaining are males. Two-thirds of the Americans are males and the remaining are females.

18. What is the difference between the number of persons belonging to India and the number of persons belonging to other countries (except America)?

1) 240 2) 560 3) 360 4) 450 5) 520

19. What is the difference between the number of Indian males and the number of American males?

1) 280 2) 180 3) 80 4) 400 5) 480

20. What is the ratio of American females to Indian females?

1) 3 : 4 2) 2 : 5 3) 1 : 5 4) 2 : 7 5) 1 : 8

Answers and explanations

1. 4; Time taken by boat A to travel 200 km = $\frac{200}{18-10}$ = 25 hrs

Time taken by boat B to travel 200 km = $\frac{200}{14-12}$ = 100 hrs

$\therefore$ Reqd difference = (100 – 25) = 75 hours

2. 2; Total distance travelled by Shyam = 1000 km

Distance covered by boat A = $1000 \times \frac{40}{100}$ = 400 km

Time taken by boat A = $\frac{400}{18-10}$ = 50 hours

Time taken by boat B = $\frac{1000 \times \frac{18}{100}}{14-12}$ = 90 hours

Time taken by boat C = $\frac{1000 \times \frac{26}{100}}{10-6}$ = 65 hours

Time taken by boat D = $\frac{1000 \times \frac{16}{100}}{14-10}$ = 40 hours

$\therefore$ Total time taken by Shyam = (50 + 90 + 65 + 40) = 245 hours

3. 1; Speed of boat C after 40% increase in its speed

$= 10 \times \frac{140}{100} = 14$ kmph

Speed of stream after 20% decrease

$= 6 \times \frac{80}{100} = 4.8$ kmph

Now, time taken by boat C = $\frac{200}{14-4.8}$

$= \frac{200}{9.2} = 21\frac{17}{23}$ hours

Time taken by boat previously = $\frac{200}{10-6}$

$= \frac{200}{4} = 50$ hours

$\therefore$ Difference = $(50 - 21\frac{17}{23}) = 28\frac{6}{23}$ hours

4. 2; New speed of boat D = $14 \times \frac{110}{100}$ = 15.4 kmph

Time taken to travel 500 km = $\frac{500}{15.4-10}$

$= 92.54 \approx 92.6$ km

5. 5; Time taken by boat C = $\frac{x \text{ km}}{(10+6)}$

Time taken by boat D = $\frac{x \text{ km}}{(10+14)}$

$\therefore$ Reqd ratio = $\frac{x}{16} : \frac{x}{24} = 3 : 2$

6. 4; Part of building costruction by Rituraj in one day $= \frac{1}{20}$

by Amarkant = $\frac{1}{22}$ and by Prithusen = $\frac{1}{24}$

Work of building construction done in 1 day by all three together = $\left(\frac{1}{20}+\frac{1}{22}+\frac{1}{24}\right) = \frac{181}{1320}$

ie they construct a building in $\frac{1320}{181} = 7\frac{53}{181}$ days

7. 2; The part of work of tower installation done by Vishwamohan in one day

$= \frac{1}{24}$, that by Laliteshwar in one day = $\frac{1}{30}$ and that by Rituraj in one day = $\frac{1}{26}$

The part work of tower installation done by all three together in one day = $\frac{1}{24}+\frac{1}{30}+\frac{1}{26}=\frac{177}{1560}$

$\therefore$ 1 tower installation work is done in $\frac{1560}{177}$ days

$\therefore$ 10 tower installation work is done in $\frac{1560 \times 10}{177}$

= 88.13 days

8. 4; The part of work of bridge construction done by Rituraj, Prithusen and Laliteshwar in 4 days

$= \left(\frac{1}{24}+\frac{1}{30}+\frac{1}{26}\right) \times 4 = \frac{177 \times 4}{1560} = \frac{708}{1560} = \frac{59}{130}$

The part of work of bridge construction done by Rituraj, Prithusen and Amarkant in one day

$= \left(\frac{1}{24}+\frac{1}{30}+\frac{1}{20}\right) = \frac{5+4+6}{120} = \frac{1}{8}$

After 4 days the remaining work

$= 1 - \frac{59}{130} = \frac{130-59}{130} = \frac{71}{130}$

Now, $\frac{71}{130}$ work is done by Rituraj, Prithusen and

Amarkant in $\frac{\left(\frac{71}{130}\right)}{\left(\frac{1}{8}\right)} = \frac{71\times 8}{130} = \frac{568}{130} = 4\frac{24}{65}$ days

9. 4; When Rituraj, Prithusen and Viswamohan work together, the work of building construction done by them $= \left(\frac{1}{20}+\frac{1}{24}+\frac{1}{18}\right) = \frac{53}{360}$ per day

Work of road construction $\left(\frac{1}{18}+\frac{1}{22}+\frac{1}{26}\right) = \frac{359}{2574}$

$\frac{53}{360}$ part of building construction is done in 1 day

∴ 5 building construction work is done in $\left(\frac{360}{53}\times 5 = \right)$ 33.96 days

$\frac{359}{2574}$ part of road construction is done in 1 day.

4 roads are constructed in $\left(\frac{2574}{359}\times 4 = \right)$ 28.67 days

∴ Total time taken = (33.96 + 28.67) = 62.63 days

10. 2; Ratio of work done by Rituraj to that by Amarkant in one day in building construction

or, Rituraj : Amarkant $= \frac{1}{20} : \frac{1}{22} = 11 : 10$

Total wage = 50000

∴ Share of Rituraj $= 5000 \times \frac{11}{21} =$ ₹26190.47

11. 1; Speed of train between Kanyakumari and Madurai

$= \frac{430}{11.45 \text{ pm} - 1.00 \text{ pm}} = \frac{430}{10.45} = \frac{430}{10\frac{3}{4}} = \frac{430\times 4}{43} = 40$ kmph

12. 5; Total time taken by the train to travel from Kanyakumari to Renigunta

= 11 am – 1 pm = 22 hours

Total halt time = 5 + 10 + 20 + 5 + 5 = 45 minutes

If there in no halt then time taken

= 22hr – 45 minutes

= 21 hours 15 minutes

∴ Speed $= \frac{1140 \text{ km}}{21 \text{ hrs } 15 \text{ minutes}} = \frac{1140\times 4}{85}$

$= \frac{1140\times 4}{85} = \frac{912}{17} = 53\frac{11}{17}$ kmph

13. 2; Total income of Railways from the train from Kanyakumari to Madurai = (fare of adult × number of adults) + (fare of child × number of children)

$= (250\times 80) + (70\times 80\times \frac{40}{100}) + \{(250+320-100)(200-80) + (70+90-20)(200-80)\frac{40}{100}\} + \{(250+320-100+150-50)\times(310-200) + (70+90+70-20-30)(310-200\times\frac{40}{100})\}$

$= \{(20000+2240) + (56400+6720) + (62700+7920)\}$

= ₹155980

14. 2; Number of adults arriving at Renigunta = (250 + 320 + 150 + 100 + 120 + 80) – (100 + 50 + 230 + 80 + 90) = 470

Number of children arriving at Renigunta = (70 + 90 + 70 + 60 + 40 + 20) – (20 + 30 + 50 + 30 + 10) = 210

∴ Reqd ratio = 470 : 210 = 47 : 21

15. 3; The fare paid by the family = fare of 6 adults + fare of 4 children $= \{6\times(590-200) + 4(590-200)\times\frac{2}{5}\}$

= ₹2964

16. 4; $n(s) = {}^{52}C_2 = \frac{52\times 51}{2} = 1326$

Let E_1 = event of getting both red cards and E_2 = event of getting both Kings

Then, $E_1 \cap E_2$ = event of getting two Kings of red cards

$n(E_1) = {}^{26}C_2 = \frac{26\times 25}{2} = 325$,

$n(E_2) = \frac{4\times 3}{2\times 1} = 6 \quad n(E_1\cap E_2) = {}^{2}C_2 = 1$

Now, $P(E_1) = \frac{n(E_1)}{n(S)} = \frac{325}{1326}, P(E_2) = \frac{n(E_2)}{n(S)} = \frac{6}{1326}$

$\therefore P(E_1\cap E_2) = \frac{1}{1326}$

$P(\text{Both red or both Kings}) = P(E_1\cup E_2) = P(E_1) + P(E_2) - P(E_1\cap E_2) = \left(\frac{325}{1376} + \frac{6}{1328} - \frac{1}{1326}\right) = \frac{55}{221}$

17. 2; n(S) = 6 × 6 = 36

E = event that the sum is a prime number = {(1, 1) (1, 2), (1, 4), (1, 6), (2, 1), (2, 3), (2, 5), (3, 1), (3, 4), (4, 1), (4, 3), (5, 2), (5, 6), (6, 1), (6, 5)}

$\therefore n(E) = 15, \therefore P(E) = \frac{n(E)}{n(S)} = \frac{15}{36} = \frac{5}{12}$

(18-20):

18. 5; Number of people from other countries = 1200 – (800 + 120) = 280

∴ Difference = 800 – 280 = 520

19. 4; Difference of the number of Indian males and the number of American males = 480 – 80 = 400

20. 5; Ratio of American females to Indian females = 40 : 320 = 1 : 8

Practice Set 33

Directions (Q. 1-5): Study the following graphs carefully and answer the questions given below:

Number of students appeared (in thousand) and the percentage of students qualified in a competitive examination over the years.

Number of students appeared (in thousand)

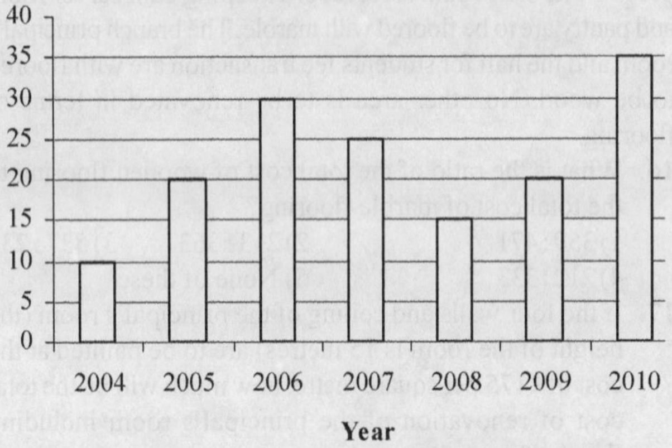

Percentage of students qualified

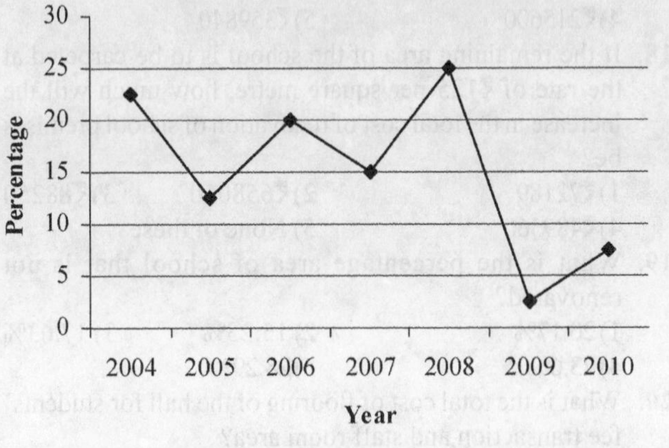

1. What was the ratio of the number of students appeared in 2007 to the number of students qualified in 2006?
   1) 25 : 6 2) 19 : 7 3) 4 : 5
   4) 13 : 5 5) 29 : 12
2. In which of the following years was the number of students qualified the least among the given years?
   1) 2005 2) 2008 3) 2009
   4) 2010 5) 2007
3. What was the percentage drop in the number of students appeared from the year 2007 to 2008?
   1) 40% 2) 54% 3) 60.92%
   4) 71.28% 5) 73.66%
4. How many students qualified in the year 2005?
   1) 2625 2) 2385 3) 2432
   4) 2500 5) None of these
5. The number of students qualified in 2010 was what per cent of the number of students appeared in 2009?
   1) 15.28% 2) 13.13% 3) 21%
   4) 9.25% 5) 23.33%

Directions (Q. 6-10): Study the table carefully to answer the questions given below:

Number of accidents reported in a state in different years

Years	Types of accident			
	Spot death	Handicapped	Major	Minor
2007	86200	43280	28000	26500
2008	72920	18620	20500	22400
2009	60000	24600	18600	23100
2010	54000	29750	24600	20500
2011	62000	32500	30000	21000
2012	68300	35640	25000	18050

6. In which of the following year was the total number of reported accidents the highest?
   1) 2009 2) 2011 3) 2007
   4) 2012 5) 2008
7. What is the approximate percentage reduction in the number of accidents in 2009 from the previous year?
   1) 4% 2) 6% 3) 7%
   4) 8% 5) 12%
8. In how many years, the percentage of spot deaths amongst the total number of accidents in that year was less than 47%?
   1) 3 2) 4 3) 5
   4) 6 5) None of these
9. What is the ratio of the major accidents in the year 2008 to those in the year 2011?
   1) 39 : 48 2) 41 : 60 3) 19 : 33
   4) 53 : 78 5) None of these
10. In which of the following pairs of years is the ratio of the number of handicapped 119 : 130?
    1) 2010 and 2012 2) 2008 and 2009

3) 2009 and 2011 4) 2010 and 2011
5) 2008 and 2012

Directions (Q. 11-15): Study the following pie-chart and answer the following questions.

Percentage distribution of teachers in six different universities

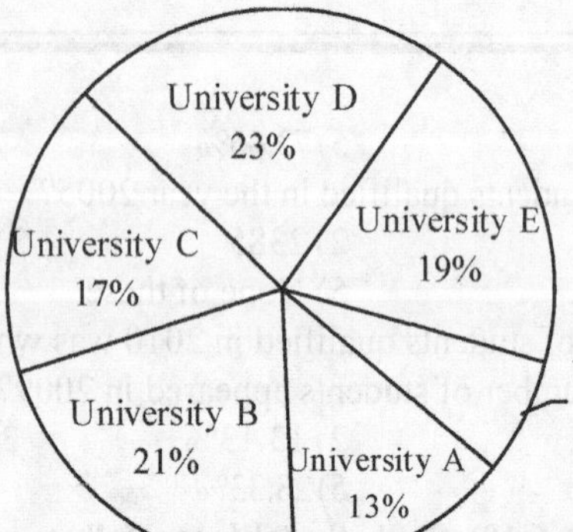

Total number of teachers = 7800

11. If $\frac{1}{38}$ of the number of teachers from University E are professors and the salary of each professor is ₹92000, what will be the total salary of all the professors together from University E?
1) ₹2956400 2) ₹3165900 3) ₹3780600
4) ₹3588000 5) ₹4258900

12. The difference between the total number of teachers in University A, B and C together and University D, E and F together is what per cent of the number of teachers of all universities?
1) 1% 2) 2% 3) 3%
4) 4% 5) 5%

13. What is the average number of teachers in University A, C, D and F together?
1) 1170 2) 1985 3) 1357
4) 2468 5) None of these

14. If 16.66% of the number of teachers in University C are females, what is the number of male teachers in University C? (Approximate)
1) 976 2) 1105 3) 325
4) 723 5) 873

15. The number of teachers in University C is approximately what per cent of the total number of teachers in University A and University E together?
1) 47% 2) 53% 3) 39%
4) 58% 5) None of these

Directions (Q. 16-20): Study the following information carefully and answer the given questions.

The premises of a school are to be renovated. The renovation is in terms of flooring. Certain areas are to be floored either with marble or wood. All rooms/halls and pantry are rectangular. The area to be renovated comprises a hall for students' fee transaction measuring 28m by 32 metres, the branch principal's room measuring 15m by 18m, a pantry measuring 20m × 14 metres, a record keeping cum server room measuring 23m by 17 metres and staff room 33m by 29 metres. The total area of the school is 3500m². The cost of wooden flooring is ₹160 per m² and the cost of marble flooring is ₹180 per m². The staff room area, record keeping cum server room and pantry are to be floored with marble. The branch principal's room and the hall for students fee transaction are with floored to be wood. No other area is to be renovated in terms of flooring.

16. What is the ratio of the total cost of wooden flooring to the total cost of marble flooring?
1) 359 : 471 2) 213 : 363 3) 537 : 239
4) 212 : 333 5) None of these

17. If the four walls and ceiling of the principal's room (the height of the room is 15 metres) are to be painted at the cost of ₹175 per square metre, how much will be the total cost of renovation of the principal's room including flooring?
1) ₹243450 2) ₹263700 3) ₹316590
4) ₹215600 5) ₹359840

18. If the remaining area of the school is to be carpeted at the rate of ₹125 per square metre, how much will the increase in the total cost of renovation of school premises be?
1) ₹72189 2) ₹658050 3) ₹88250
4) ₹489560 5) None of these

19. What is the percentage area of school that is not renovated?
1) 20.17% 2) 15.25% 3) 17.63%
4) 23.6% 5) 28.29%

20. What is the total cost of flooring of the hall for students' fee transaction and staff room area?
1) ₹428969 2) ₹375690 3) ₹528640
4) ₹352086 5) ₹315620

Answers and explanations

1. 1; Number of students appeared in 2007 = 25000
Number of students qualified in 2006

$= 20\% \text{ of } 30000 = \frac{20 \times 30000}{100} = 6000$

Reqd ratio = 25000 : 6000 = 25 : 6

2. 3;

Years	Number of students qualified
2004	22.5% of 10000 = 2250
2005	12.5 of 20000 = 2500
2006	20% of 30000 = 6000
2007	15% of 25000 = 3750
2008	25% of 15000 = 3750
2009	2.5% of 20000 = 500
2010	7.5% of 35000 = 2625

3. 1; Number of students appeared in 2007 = 25000
Number of students appeared in 2008 = 15000

Hence drop percentage $= \frac{25000 - 15000}{25000} \times 100 = 40\%$

4. 4; Number of students qualified in 2005

$= 20000 \times \frac{12.5}{100} = 2500$

5. 2; Number of students qualified in 2010 = 7.5% of 35000 = 2625

Hence, required percentage $= \frac{2625}{20000} \times 100$

$= 13.125\% \approx 13.13\%$

6. 3; Total number of accidents in 2007
= 86200 + 43280 + 28000 + 26500 = 183980
Total number of accidents in 2008 = 72920 + 18620 + 20500 + 22400 = 134440
Total number of accidents in 2009 = 60000 + 24600 + 18600 + 23100 = 126300
Toal number of accidetns in 2010 = 54000 + 29750 + 24600 + 20500 = 128850
Total number of accidents in 2011 = 62000 + 32500 + 30000 + 21000 = 145500
Total number of accidents in 2012 = 68300 + 35640 + 25000 + 18050 = 146990
Clearly, in 2007.

7. 2; Number of accidents in 2008 = 134440
Number of accidents in 2009 = 126300

Reqd % reduction $= \frac{134440 - 126300}{134440} \times 100$

$= 6.054\% \approx 6\%$

8. 2; Percentage of spot deaths in 2007

$= \frac{86200}{183980} \times 100 = 46.85\%$

Percentage of spot deaths in 2008

$= \frac{72920}{134440} \times 100 = 54.23\%$

In 2009 $= \frac{60000}{126300} \times 100 = 47.50\%$

In 2010 $= \frac{54000}{128850} \times 100 = 41.90\%$

In 2011 $= \frac{62000}{145500} \times 100 = 42.61\%$

In 2012 $= \frac{68300}{146990} \times 100 = 46.46\%$

Clearly, no. of years = 4

9. 2; Reqd ratio $= \frac{\text{Number of major accidents in 2008}}{\text{Number of major accidents in 2011}}$

$= \frac{20500}{30000} = \frac{41}{60} = 41 : 60$

10. 4; Ratio of the number of handicapped type of accidents

in 2010 and 2011 $= \frac{29750}{32500} = \frac{119}{130} = 119 : 130$

11. 4; Number of teachers from University E

$= 19\% \text{ of } 7800 = \frac{19 \times 7800}{100} = 1482$

Number of professors from University E

$= \frac{1}{38} \times 1482 = 39$

Total salary of all the professors together from University E = 39 × 92000 = ₹3588000

12. 2; Total number of teachers in University A, B and C

together $= (13 + 21 + 17)\% \text{ of } 7800 = \frac{51 \times 7800}{100} = 3978$

Total number of teachers in University D, E and F

$= (23 + 19 + 7)\% \text{ of } 7800 = \frac{49 \times 7800}{100} = 3822$

Reqd difference = 3978 – 3822 = 156
This number, ie 156, as a percentage of total number

$= \frac{156}{7800} \times 100 = 2\%$

13. 1; Reqd average $= \frac{\text{Total number of teachers in Universities A, C, D and F together}}{4}$

$= \frac{(13 + 17 + 23 + 7)\% \text{ of } 7800}{4} = \frac{4680}{4} = 1170$

14. 2; Number of teachers in University C

$= 17\% \text{ of } 7800 = \frac{17 \times 7800}{100} = 1326$

Number of male teachers in University C

$= (100 - 16.66\%) \text{ of } 1326 = \frac{83.34 \times 1326}{100} \approx 1105$

15. 2;

$$\text{Reqd} = \frac{\text{Number of teachers in University C}}{\text{Number of teachers in University A and E together}}$$

$$= \frac{17\% \text{ of } 7800}{(13+19)\% \text{ of } 7800} \times 100 = \frac{1326}{2496} \times 100 = 53.125\% \approx 53\%$$

16. 4; Area of hall = $28 \times 32\text{m}^2 = 896\text{m}^2$
Area of principal's room = $15 \times 18 = 270\text{m}^2$
Area of pantry = $20 \times 14 = 280\text{m}^2$
Area of record keeping = $23 \times 17 = 391\text{m}^2$
Area of staff room = $33 \times 29 = 957\text{m}^2$
Total flooring area with marble = Staff room + record keeping + Pantry = $957 + 391 + 280 = 1628\text{m}^2$
Cost of flooring = 1628×180 = ₹293040
Total flooring area with wood = Principal's Room + Hall = $270 + 896 = 1166\text{m}^2$
Cost of flooring = 1166×160 = ₹186560
Reqd ratio = 186560 : 293040 = 212 : 333

17. 2; Cost of flooring of principal's room = 270×160 = ₹43200
Cost of painting = $[2(18 \times 15 + 15 \times 15) + 15 \times 18] \times 175$ = ₹220500
Total cost = 43200 + 220500 = ₹263700

18. 3; Total area of school = 3500m^2
Total flooring area = $(1628 + 1166) = 2794\text{m}^2$
Remaining area = $3500 - 2794 = 706\text{m}^2$
Cost of carpeting = 706×125 = ₹88250

19. 1; Area not to be renovated = 706m^2

$$\text{Reqd } \% = \frac{706}{3500} \times 100 = 20.17\%$$

20. 5; Cost of flooring of students' fee transaction hall + staff room = $896 \times 160 + 957 \times 180$ = ₹315620

Practice Set 34

Directions (Q. 1-5): Study the following table carefully and answer the questions give below.

Number of boys of Std XI participating in different games

Game	Class					
	XI A	XI B	XI C	XI D	XI E	Total
Chess	8	8	8	4	4	32
Badminton	8	12	8	12	12	52
Table Tennis	12	16	12	8	12	60
Hockey	8	4	8	4	8	32
Football	8	8	12	12	12	52
Total number of boys	44	48	48	40	48	228

Note:

1. Every student (boy or girl) of each class of Std XI participates in a game.
2. In each class, the number of girls participating in each game is 25% of the number of boys participating in each game.
3. Each student (boy or girl) participates in one and only one game.

1. All the boys of Class XI D passed the annual examination but a few girls failed. If among the boys and girls who passed and entered Class XII D, the ratio of boys to girls is 5 : 1, what would be the number of girls who failed in Class XI D?
1) 8 2) 5 3) 3 4) 2 5) 6

2. Girls playing which of the following games need to be combined to yield a ratio of boys to girls of 4 : 1, if all boys playing Chess and Badminton are combined?
1) Table Tennis and Hockey
2) Hockey and Football
3) Badminton and Table Tennis
4) Chess and Hockey
5) Badminton and Football

3. What should be the total number of students in Std XI if all the boys of Class XI A together with all the girls of Class XI B and XI C were to be equal to 25% of the total number of students?
1) 272 2) 560 3) 656 4) 340 5) 372

4. Boys of which of the following classes should be combined to become four times the number of girls in Class XI B and XI C?
1) XI D and XI E 2) XI A and XI B
3) XI A and XI C 4) XI B and XI E
5) None of these

5. If the boys of Class XI E participating in Chess together with girls of Class XI B and Class XI C participatiing in Table Tennis and Hockey respectively are selected for a course at the college of sports, approximately what per cent of the students of all the sections of class XI will get advantage?
1) 6% 2) 4% 3) 10.51% 4) 13.5% 5) 8%

Directions (Q. 6-10): Study the following table and graph carefully and answer the questions give below.

Income of a company (in ₹ lakh)

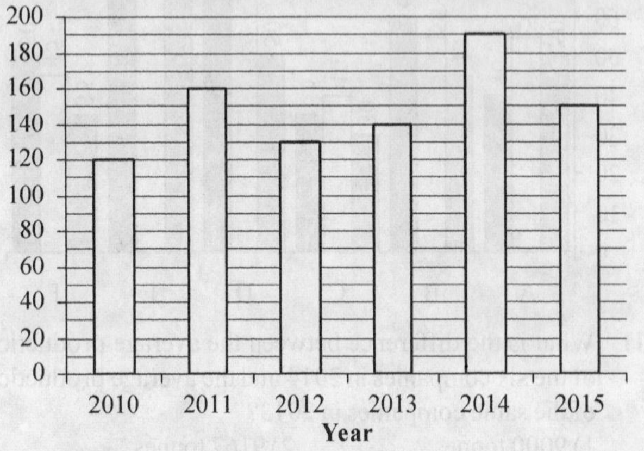

Percentage profit over the years

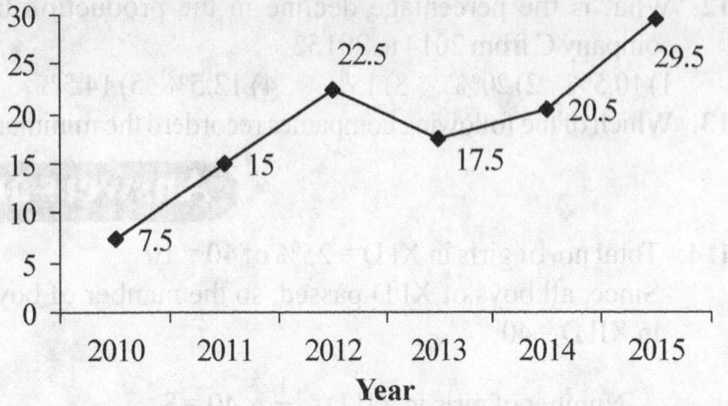

6. In which of the following years was the amount of profit the maximum?
1) 2014 2) 2011 3) 2010 4) 2015 5) None of these

7. Approximately what was the average expenditure for the given years?
1) ₹110 lakh 2) ₹130 lakh 3) ₹120 lakh

4) ₹140 lakh 5) ₹150 lakh

8. In which of the following years was the percentage increase/decrease in percentage profit from the previous year the minimum?
1) 2011 2) 2013 3) 2014 4) 2012 5) None of these

9. Approximately what was the expenditure in 2011?
1) ₹120 lakh 2) ₹160 lakh 3) ₹140 lakh
4) ₹180 lakh 5) ₹135 lakh

10. If the profit percentage in 2014 had been 25, what would have been the expenditure in that year?
1) ₹130 lakh 2) ₹148 lakh 3) ₹120 lakh
4) ₹152 lakh 5) ₹160 lakh

Directions (Q. 11-15): Study the following graph carefully and answer the questions given below.

Production of Aluminium by different companies in three consecutive years (in thousand tonnes)

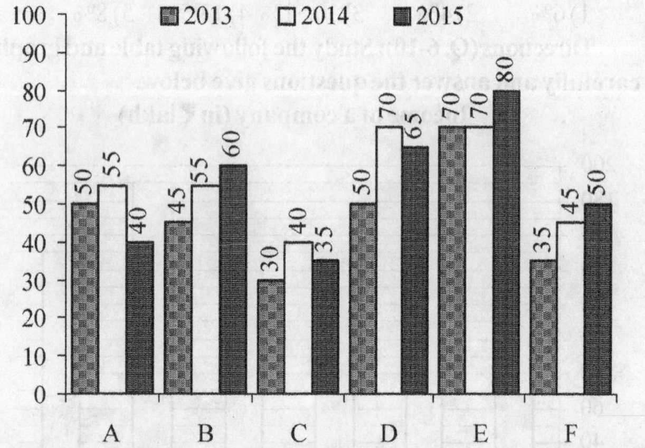

11. What is the difference between the average production of the six companies in 2014 and the average production of the same companies in 2013?
1) 9000 tonnes 2) 9167 tonnes
3) 10002 tonnes 4) 9435 tonnes
5) 9020 tonnes

12. What is the percentage decline in the production by company C from 2014 to 2015?
1) 10.5% 2) 20% 3) 15% 4) 12.5% 5) 14.5%

13. Which of the following companies recorderd the minimum percentage growth from 2013 to 2014?
1) A 2) B 3) C 4) E 5) D

14. The production of company C in 2014 and the production of company F in 2013 together is what per cent of the production of Company B in 2015?
1) 80% 2) 65% 3) 125%
4) $120\frac{1}{2}$% 5) None of these

15. In which of the following pairs of companies is the difference between the average production for the given three years maximum?
1) E and F 2) D and C 3) E and C
4) A and E 5) None of these

Directions (Q. 16-20): The following table gives the population of a locality from 2011 to 2015. Read the table and answer the given questions.

Year	Men	Women	Children	Total	Increase(+) or decrease (–) over preceding year
2011	65104	60387	–	146947	–
2012	70391	62516	–	–	+(11630)
2013	–	63143	20314	152922	–
2014	69395	–	21560	–	(–)5337
2015	71274	65935	23789	160998	–

16. What is the number of children in 2011?
1) 31236 2) 125491 3) 14566 4) 21456 5) 124591

17. The number of children in 2012 is approximately what per cent of the number of children in 2011?
1) 144% 2) 120% 3) 98% 4) 108% 5) 115%

18. The number of women in 2014 is what per cent of the total no. of women of the locality in 2012?
1) 90.58% 2) 94.20% 3) 86.5% 4) 89% 5) 92.60%

19. The increase or decrease in population in 2015 over 2014 is
1) 13413 2) 13413 3) 12493 4) 12493 5) 14103

20. The average number of women in the locality during 2011 to 2015 is
1) 59842 2) 61722 3) 60342 4) 62132 5) 58442

Answers and explanations

1. 4; Total no. of girls in XI D = 25% of 40 = 10
Since, all boys of XI D passed, so the number of boys in XII D = 40

$\therefore$ Number of girls in XII D = $\frac{1}{5} \times 40 = 8$

$\therefore$ Number of girls failed in XI D = 10 – 8 = 2

2. 2; Total no of boys, playing (Chess + Badminton)
= 32 + 52 = 84
(No. of girls playing) (Hockey + Football)
= 84 × 25% = 21

$\therefore$ Ratio = 84 : 21 = 4 : 1
$\therefore$ Required result is Hockey + Football.

3. 1; No. of boys in XI A = 44
No. of girls in XI B = 25% of 48 = 12
No. of girls in XI C = 25% of 48 = 12

$\therefore$ Required result = $\frac{(44+12+12)\times 100}{25} = 272$

4. 4; No. of girls in XI B and XI C = 25% of 48 + 25% of 48
= 12 + 12 = 24
Four times = 24 × 4 = 96

5. 2; No. of boys of XI E participating in Chess = 4
No. of girls of XI B participating in Table Tennis
$= 16 \times 25\% = 4$
No. of girls in XI C participating in Hockey
$= 8 \times 25\% = 2$
$\therefore$ No. of students for sports = 2 + 4 + 4 = 10

$\therefore$ Required % $= \dfrac{10}{\left(228 + \dfrac{25 \times 228}{100}\right)} \times 100 = 3.85\% \approx 4\%$

6. 4; Profit = Income $\left[1 - \dfrac{100}{100 + \%\text{profit}}\right]$

ie The profit was maximum in 2015.

7. 2; Average expenditure

$$= \frac{1}{6}\left[\begin{array}{l} 120 \times \dfrac{100}{107.5} + \dfrac{160 \times 100}{115} + \dfrac{130 \times 100}{122.5} \\ + \dfrac{170 \times 100}{117.5} + \dfrac{190 \times 100}{120} + \dfrac{150 \times 100}{127.5} \end{array}\right] = ₹130 \text{ lakh}$$

8. 1; In 2011 $\rightarrow \dfrac{15 - 7.5}{7.5} \times 100$

= 100% increase

Similarly, In 2012 $\rightarrow \dfrac{22.5 - 15}{15} \times 100$

$= \dfrac{7.5}{15} \times 100 = 50\%$ increase

In 2013 $\rightarrow \dfrac{-22.5 + 17.5}{+22.5} \times 100$

$= \dfrac{-5}{22.5} \times 100 = -\dfrac{50 \times 100}{225} = -\dfrac{50 \times 4}{9}$

$= \dfrac{200}{9} = 22\dfrac{2}{7}\% = 22\dfrac{2}{7}\%$ decrease

In 2014 $\rightarrow \dfrac{20.5 - 17.5}{17.5} \times \dfrac{3}{17.5} \times 100 = 17\dfrac{1}{7}\%$ increase

In 2015 $\rightarrow \dfrac{29.5 - 20.5}{20.5} \times 100 = 43\dfrac{37}{41}\%$ increase

Hence in the year 2011 the percentage increase in percentage profit from the previous year is the maximum.

9. 3; Expenditure in 2011 $= \dfrac{160 \times 100}{115} \approx ₹140$ lakh

10. 4; Expenditure in 2014 $= 190 \times \dfrac{100}{125} = ₹152$ lakh

11. 2; Required difference $= \dfrac{335 - 280}{6} \times 1000$

= 9166.67 tonnes ≈ 9167 tonnes

12. 4; Percentage decline $= \dfrac{40 - 35}{40} \times 100 = 12.5\%$

13. 4; By graph it is clear that E's growth is the minimum.

14. 3; Required % $= \dfrac{40 + 35}{60} \times 100 = 125\%$

15. 3; It is clear that the highest average production is in E and the lowest average production is in C. So the maximum difference would be between E and C.

16. 4; Reqd no. of children = 146947 – (65104 + 60387) = 21456

17. 2; No. of children in 2012 = (146947 + 11630) – (70391 + 62516) = 25670
No. of children in 2011 = 146947 – (65104 + 60387) = 21456

$\therefore$ Reqd % $= \dfrac{25670}{21456} \times 100 = 119.64 \approx 120\%$

18. 1; Women in 2012 = 62516
Women in 2014 = (152922–5337)–(69395+21560) = 56630

$\therefore$ Required percentage $= \dfrac{56630}{62516} \times 100 = 90.58\%$

19. 2; Reqd answer = 160998 – (152922 – 5337) = 13413

20. 2; Reqd no. of women in 2011 = 60387, in 2012 = 62516, similarly, in 2013 = 63143, in 2014 = 56630, in 2015 = 65935

$\therefore$ Average $= \dfrac{60387 + 62516 + 63143 + 56630 + 65935}{5}$

= 61722.2 ≈ 61722

Practice Set 35

Directions (Q. 1-5): Refer to the data given below and answer the questions that follow:

The marks obtained by a student in six subject: Telugu, Hindi, English, Maths, Science and Social Science is 500. He got equal marks in Telugu and Maths, i.e. 89 entire. He got 84 and 85 marks in English and Science respectively. The marks obtained by the student in Social Science is 73.

1. How many marks did the student get in Hindi?
1) 100 2) 90 3) 80 4) 70 5) 75

2. The total marks obtained in Hindi, Maths, English and Social Science is
1) 426 2) 436 3) 346 4) 326 5) 428

3. The sum of the marks obtained in Science and English is equal to the sum of the marks obtained in which of the following subjects?
1) Science and Social Science 2) Telugu and English
3) Maths and Hindi 4) Telugu and Social Science
5) Maths and Social Science

4. What is the average of the marks in Social Science, Maths and English?
1) 80 2) 82 3) 84 4) 85 5) 90

5. If the total marks in all the six subjects is 600, then the overall percentage of marks obtained by the student is
1) $83\frac{1}{3}$% 2) $89\frac{2}{3}$% 3) 85% 4) 79% 5) 80%

Directions (Q. 6-10): Study the following graph carefully and answer the questions given below it.

Target and Actual production of cement (in 1,000 ginny bags) of a factory over a period of six years.

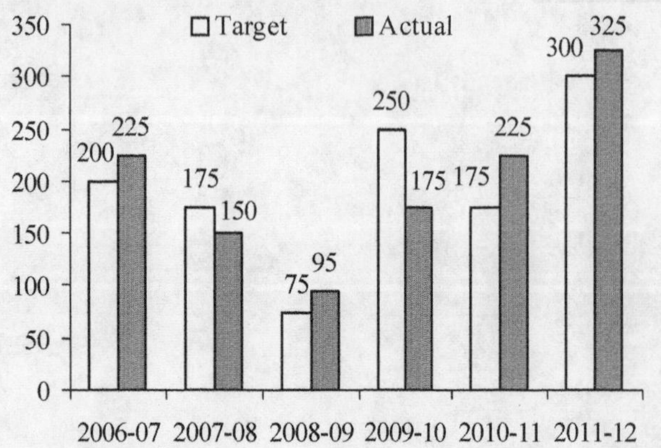

6. If the combined target production in two adjacent years is compared to the combined actual prodcution (over these two years), then in which of the following pairs of years will the sums be equal?
1) 2010-11, 2011-12 2) 2008-09, 2009-10
3) 2006-07, 2007-08 4) 2007-08, 2008-09
5) 2009-10, 2010-11

7. The difference between the target production and the actual production for the year 2009-10 is how much more/less than the total target production for the entire given period? (in '000 ginny boys)
1) 1750 2) 850 3) 1100 4) 800 5) 825

8. In which of the following years was the actual production as percentage of target production the highest?
1) 2010-11 2) 2011-12 3) 2008-09
4) 2006-07 5) 2008-2009

9. The actual production of cement for 2006-07 was how many times the target production for that year?
1) 1.125 2) 0.88 3) 1.088 4) 1.25 5) 0.78

10. What is the ratio of the number of years in which the actual production was above average to that below average?
1) 2 : 1 2) 1 : 2 3) 3 : 2 4) 1 : 1 5) 2 : 3

Directions (Q. 11-15): Study the following graph carefully and answer the questions given below it.

Distribution of candidates enrolled for MBBS (Pie-chart I) and the candidates who successfully completed the course (Pie-chart II) from different institues.

Pie chart-I

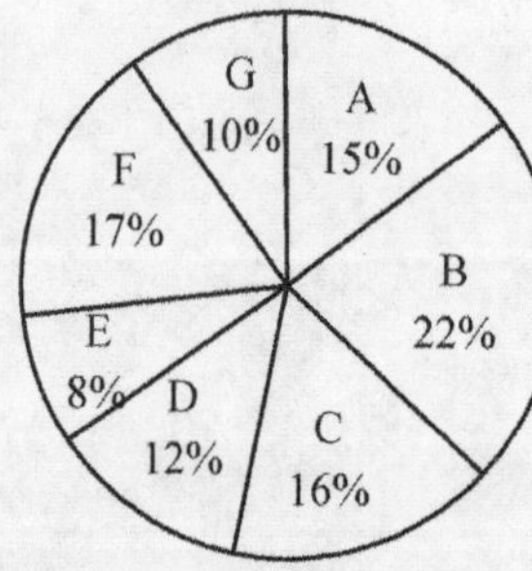

Candidates enrolled = 5000

Pie chart-II

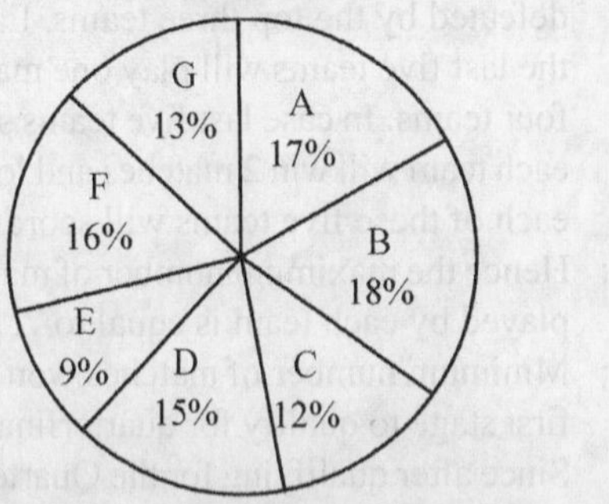

Candidates who have successfully completed the course = 3800

11. Which institute has the highest percentage of successful students as compared to enrolled students?
1) D 2) E 3) A 4) G 5) B

12. What percentage of candidates from Institute D have come out to be successful out of the total candidates enrolled in this institute?
1) 115 2) 95 3) 80 4) 85 5) 105

13. What is the approximate percentage of students successful with respect to those enrolled in institute A?
1) 92 2) 89 3) 86 4) 96 5) 82

14. What is the ratio of candidates successful to those enrolled in institutes B and C together?
1) 5 : 12 2) 5 : 7 3) 12 : 5 4) 3 : 5 5) 7 : 5

15. What is the percentage of students successful from institute E and F together, with respect to the students enrolled in these institues together?
1) 76 2) 105 3) 80 4) 74 5) 108

Directions (Q. 16-21): Read the caselet carefully and answer the questions that follow:

16 teams participated in Eurofootball tournament. These are divided into two groups A and B with each group having 8 teams. At the first stage, each team played against all other teams of its group once and top four teams from each group qualified for the quarterfinals. At the second stage, the team having first rank in group A will play with the team having first rank in group B. Similarly, the team having second rank in group A will play with the team having second rank in group B and so on. After the first stage, every match is a knock-out match (means the team losing any match after the first stage will be out from the tournament.)

In the third stage the winner of the quaterfinals will play the semifinal and in the fourth stage the winner of the semifinal will play the finals. If two or more teams end up with the same score the team with higher number of goals is placed higher in the point table. Two points are given for a win, no point is given for a loss and no match ends in a tie.

16. The minimum number of points scored by a team that qualifies for the quarterfinals can be
1) 4 2) 6 3) 12 4) 10 5) 8

17. The maximum number of matches a team can play that does not qualify for the quarterfinals can be
1) 6 2) 10 3) 8 4) 12 5) Other than the given options

18. What is the minimum number of matches required to be won by a team to qualify for the finals?
1) 6 2) 8 3) 3 4) 2 5) 4

19. What is the total number of matches played before the finals?
1) 48 2) 58 3) 52 4) 62 5) 46

20. What is the total number of points scored by all the teams in the tournament?
1) 130 2) 126 3) 144 4) 138 5) 122

21. What per cent of matches are played by group A team before quarterfinal in comparison to the total number of matches played in the tournament?
1) $42\frac{2}{9}\%$ 2) $44\frac{4}{9}\%$ 3) $53\frac{4}{9}\%$ 4) $54\frac{2}{9}\%$ 5) $38\frac{4}{9}\%$

Answers and explanations

1. 3; Marks in Hindi = 500 – (89 + 89 + 84 + 85 + 73) = 80

2. 4; Hindi + Maths + English + Social Science = 80 + 89 + 84 + 73 = 326

3. 3; Science + English = 85 + 84 = 169
So, Maths + Hindi = 89 + 80 = 169

4. 2; Average marks = $\frac{73+89+84}{3} = 82$

5. 1; Required percentage = $\frac{500}{600} \times 100 = 83\frac{1}{3}\%$

6. 3; Target production = 200 + 175 = 375
Actual production = 225 + 150 = 375

7. 3; In 2009-10 the difference between target production and actual production = 250 – 175 = 75

Total target production in the given period = 200 + 175 + 75 + 250 + 175 + 300 = 1175

∴ Reqd answer = 1175 – 75 = 1100 thousands ginny bags.

8. 1; Reqd percentage in 2006-07 = $\frac{225}{200} \times 100 = 112.5\%$

Similarly, in 2010-11 = $\frac{225}{175} \times 100 = 128.57\%$

In 2011-12 = $\frac{325}{300} \times 100 = 108.33\%$

Hence in 2010-11 the actual production is the highest as compared to the target production.

9. 1; Reqd answer = $\frac{225}{200} = 1.125$

10. 4; Average of actual production

$= \frac{225+150+95+175+225+325}{6} = 199.17$

∴ Actual production is above average in 2006-07, 2010-11 and 2011-12.

∴ above average = 3

And below average = 3

∴ ratio = 3 : 3 = 1 : 1

11. 4; Enrolled candidates in G = $\frac{5000 \times 10}{100} = 500$

Successful candidates from G = $\frac{3800 \times 13}{100}$

∴ Required % = $\frac{494}{500} \times 100 = 98.8\%$

12. 2; Enrolled candidates in D = 5000×12% = 600

Successful candidates = 3800×15% = 570

∴ Required % = $\frac{570}{600} \times 100 = 95\%$

13. 3; Enrolled candidates in institute A

= 5000 × 15% = 750

Successful candidates from institute A

= 3800 × 17% = 646

∴ Reqd % = $\frac{646}{750} \times 100 = 86.16 \approx 86\%$

14. 4; Reqd ratio = $\frac{2 \times (342+228)}{2 \times (550+400)} = \frac{3}{5} = 3:5$

15. 1; Reqd % = $\frac{2 \times (171+304)}{2 \times (200+425)} \times 100 = 76\%$

16. 1; Points scored by a team that qualifies for quarterfinals would be minimum when last five teams of the group score equal points and each of these five teams is defeated by the top three teams. Each team among the last five teams will play one match with the other four teams. In case last five teams score equal points, each team will win 2 matches and lose 2 matches, thus each of these five teams will score 4 points.

17. 2; Hence the maximum number of matches that will be played by each team is equal to 7.

18. 5; Minimum number of matches won by a team in the first stage to qualify for quarterfinals = 2.

Since after qualifying for the Quarterfinals a team has to win quarterfinal and semifinal to qualify for the finals.

∴ Minimum number of matches won by a team to qualify for finals

= 2 + 1 (quarterfinal) + 1 semifinal = 4

19. 4; Number of matches played in each group in the first stage = ${}^8C_2 = 28$

∴ Total number of matches played in the first stage

= 28 × 2 = 56

∴ Number of matches after first stage and before finals = 4 (quarter finals) + 2 (semifinals) = 6

∴ Total number of matches played before finals

= 56 + 6 = 62

20. 2; Total number of matches played in the tournament = 62 (before finals) + 1 final = 63

Since two points are awarded for each win

∴ The number of points scored = 63 × 2 = 126

21. 2; Total number of matches played in Group A before quarterfinals = ${}^8C_2 = 28$

∴ Total number of matches played in the tournament = 28 × 2 + 4 × 2 + 1 = 63

∴ Reqd % = $\frac{28}{63} \times 100 = \frac{400}{9} = 44\frac{4}{9}\%$

Practice Set 36

Directions (Q. 1-5): The table given below shows the proportion of female employees and the proportion of postgraduates. There are 1200 employees in the company, out of which 70% are in the Finance department and the rest are divided equally between the Marketing and the Accounts department.

The proportion of male employees in each department is equal to the postgraduate employees in each department.

Department	Female	Postgraduate
Marketing	0.60	
Finance		0.45
Accounts	0.55	
Total	0.5875	0.4425

1. If in the Marketing department, 25% of the postgraduates are females, then what is the difference between the number of male postgraduates in the Marketing department and that of female employees who are not postgraduates in Marketing department?
   1) 45 2) 36 3) 27 4) 54 5) 26
2. What per cent of employees in the Marketing department are postgraduates?
   1) 32% 2) 58% 3) 40% 4) 55% 5) 66%
3. What is the ratio of the number of postgraduates in the Accounts department to the number of postgraduates in the Marketing department?
   1) 9 : 8 2) 8 : 7 3) 8 : 9
   4) 3 : 2 5) Other than the given options
4. Find the difference between the number of post-graduate employees in the Finance department and the number of female employees in the Accounts department.
   1) 269 2) 279 3) 180 4) 363 5) 178
5. Find is the percentage of female employees in the Finance department.
   1) 45% 2) 55% 3) 45.75% 4) 48% 5) 60%

Directions (Q. 6-10): Study the given graph and answer the following questions:

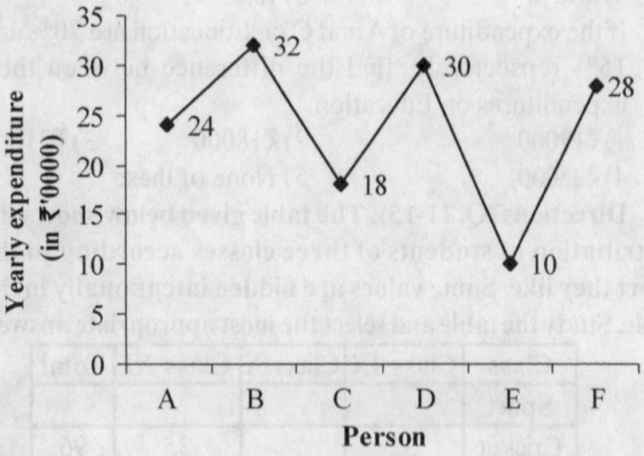

Break-up of expenses of E

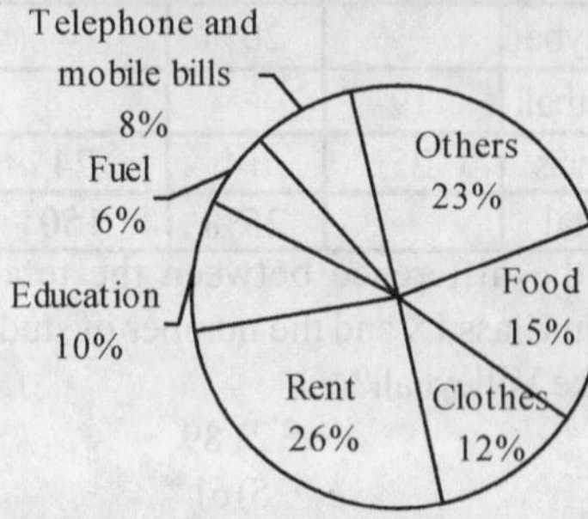

6. If the expenditure of D on Food is 20% more than the average expenditure of all six persons on Food then what is the average yearly expenditure of all six persons on Food?
   1) ₹12500 2) ₹18000 3) ₹14000
   4) ₹15500 5) ₹16500
7. If B spent 10% of his expenditure on Clothes, then by what per cent was the expenditure of D on Clothes more/less than that of B?
   1) 50% more 2) 60% less 3) $62\frac{1}{2}$% more
   4) $62\frac{1}{2}$% less 5) 60% more

8. If the yearly expenses on Food and Fuel for all the six persons are the same, then for how many persons will the expenditure on Fuel be less than 5% of their total yearly expenditure?
1) One 2) Four 3) Three 4) Five 5) Six

9. If the expenditure of D on Others is 10% more than that of E on the same head, then his expenditure on Others is what per cent of his total yearly expenditure?
1) 33% 2) 18% 3) 14.43%
4) 8.43% 5) 10.43%

10. If the expenditure of A and C on Education are 20% and 15% repsectively, find the difference between their expenditures on Education.
1) ₹17000 2) ₹18000 3) ₹21000
4) ₹25000 5) None of these

Directions (Q. 11-15): The table given below shows the distribution of students of three classes according to the sport they like. Some values are hidden intentionally in the table. Study the table and select the most appropriate answer.

Class	Class IX	Class X	Class XI	Total
Sport				
Cricket	32		35	96
Hockey	15%	20	6%	
Volleyball		20%		95
Football	19			
Tennis	25	14	24	63
Total		25%	150	360

11. What is the difference between the total number of students in Class IX and the number of students in Class XI who like Volleyball?
1) 79 2) 89 3) 67
4) 69 5) 61

12. If 18 more students took admission in Class X and all of them like Tennis then what will be the ratio of the number of students of Class X who like Tennis to the number of students of Class IX who like Hockey?
1) 16 : 7 2) 16 : 9 3) 9 : 16
4) 4 : 3 5) 3 : 4

13. The number of students of Class XI who like Football is what per cent of the number of students of Class X who like Volleyball?
1) 72% 2) 172.22% 3) 162.23%
4) 84.22% 5) 152.22%

14. What is the total number of students who like Football and Volleyball together?
1) 144 2) 214 3) 134
4) 124 5) 154

15. What is the difference between the total number of students who like Cricket and the total number of students who like Hockey?
1) 48 2) 46 3) 49
4) 42 5) 44

Directions (Q. 16-18): Given below is the percentage of the number of participants from five different countries who participate in different numbers of seminars.

Country	No. of seminars 1	No. of seminars 2	No. of seminars 3	No. of seminars 4	No. of seminars 5	No. of seminar 6
L	40	15	16	6	–	8
M	–	18	27	–	–	20
N	15	25	20	–	–	–
O	–	–	25	18	10	22
P	15	–	24	–	30	5

Note: Some data are missing in the above table. Find out the missing data and give answer accordingly.

16. The number of participants from country L who participate in more than 2 seminars is what per cent less than the number of participants from country O who participate in at least 3 seminars, if the number of participants who participate in 2 seminars from country L is 48 and the number of participants from country O who participate in 6 seminars is 4 more than the number of participants from country L who participate in 1 seminar?
1) 58 2) 48 3) 68 4) 72 5) 65

17. If the difference between the number of participants from Country P who participate in 3 seminars and the number of participants who participate in 5 seminars is 21, and the total number of participants from Country N is 60% of the total number of participants from Country P, then find the number of participants who participate in at least 4 seminars from Country N.
1) 80 2) 84 3) 74 4) 63 5) 104

18. The total number of participants from Country L who participate in at most 2 seminars is equal to the sum of the number of participants from Country P who participate in 1 seminar and the number of participants from the same country who participate in 6 seminars. Then the total number of particpants from Country L is what per cent of the total number of participants from Country P?
1) $57\frac{1}{7}\%$ 2) $47\frac{1}{7}\%$ 3) $47\frac{4}{7}\%$
4) $36\frac{4}{11}\%$ 5) $54\frac{3}{11}\%$

Directions (Q. 19-23): Study the following pie-charts and table carefully to answer the questions that follow.

The pie-charts show the percentage share of students who passed CBSE X and XII examinations in 2016 from different cities.

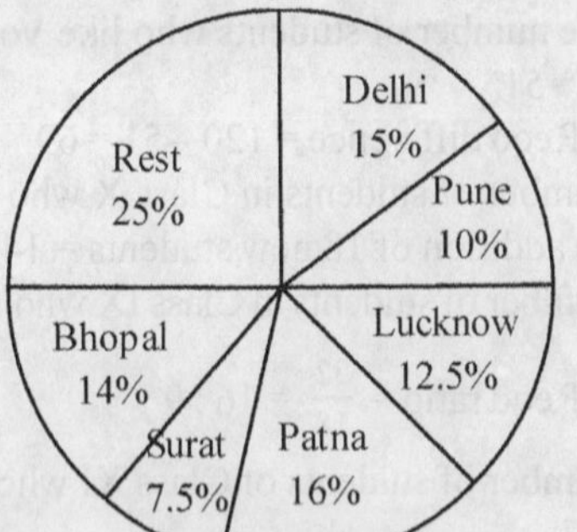

Class X

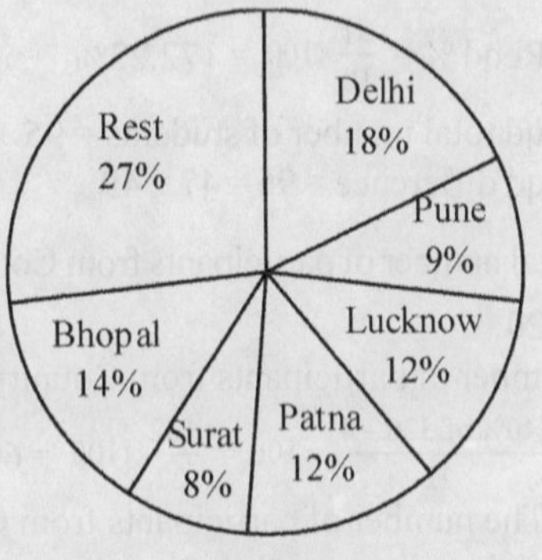

Class XII

The following table shows the ratio of the number of boys to girls passing from different cities.

City ↓	X	XII
	Boys : Girls	Boys : Girls
Delhi	2 : 3	4 : 5
Pune	5 : 3	4 : 7
Lucknow	7 : 5	5 : 7
Patna	9 : 7	7 : 9
Surat	7 : 5	4 : 7
Bhopal	4 : 3	11 : 10
Rest	8 : 7	9 : 7

19. In Class X exam if there are 3000 girls who passed from Surat, then what is the total number of boys who passed from Lucknow in the same exam?

1) 6500 2) 7500 3) 8000 4) 6800 5) 7000

20. If 16200 students passed Class XII exam from Patna, then find the number of girls passing the same exam from Delhi.

1) 12600 2) 12800 3) 11500 4) 13500 5) 16000

21. Which of the following cities shows the maximum percentage of girls in comparison to the total number of students passing Class X exam from the same city?

1) Delhi 2) Rest 3) Patna
4) Pune 5) Lucknow

22. If the difference between the number of boys passing Class XII exam from Bhopal and that from Lucknow is 315, then find the total number of students passing Class XII exam in 2016.

1) 13500 2) 13600 3) 14500 4) 13700 5) 14000

23. In Class X exam if 12000 students passed from Lucknow in 2016 then what is the total number of boys passing from all the cities together?

1) 50820 2) 50280 3) 52080
4) 52800 5) None of these

Answers and explanations

(1-5):

Depart-ment	Total no. of employees	Number of female employees	No. of male employees	Number of post-graduates
Marketing	180	108	72	72
Finance	840	462	378	378
Accounts	180	99	81	81
Total	1200	669	531	531

1. 2; Number of male postgraduates

$= 72 - 108 \times \frac{25}{100} = 72 - 27 = 45$

Number of females who are not postgraduates

$= 108 \times \frac{3}{4} = 81$

∴ Reqd difference = 81 − 45 = 36

2. 3; Reqd % $= \frac{72}{180} \times 100 = 40\%$

3. 1; Reqd ratio $= \frac{81}{72} = 9 : 8$

4. 2; Reqd difference = 378 − 99 = 279

5. 2; Reqd % $= \frac{462}{840} \times 100 = 55\%$

6. 1; Expenditure of E on Food $= \frac{100000 \times 15}{100} = ₹15000$

Average yearly expenditure of all six persons on Food

$= \frac{15000 \times 100}{120} = ₹12500$

7. 4; B's expenditure on Clothes = 10% of 320000 = ₹32000

E's expenditure on Clothes = $\frac{100000 \times 12}{100}$ = ₹12000

$\therefore$ Reqd % = $\frac{32000-12000}{32000} \times 100$

$= \frac{20000 \times 100}{32000} = \frac{2000}{32}\% = 62\frac{1}{2}\%$ less

8. 4; Yearly expenditure on Fuel for all six persons = 6% of 100000 = ₹6000

E's expenditure on Fuel as per cent of his total yearly expenditure = 6%

A's expenditure on Fuel as % of his total yearly expenditure = $\frac{6000}{240000} \times 100 = 2.5\%$

B's expenditure on Fuel as per cent of his total yearly expenditure = $\frac{6000}{320000} \times 100 = 1.875\%$

C's expenditure on Fuel as per cent of his total yearly expenditure = $\frac{6000}{180000} \times 100 = 3.33\%$

D's expenditure on Fuel as per cent of his total yearly expenditure = $\frac{6000}{300000} \times 100 = 2\%$

F's expenditure as fuel as per cent of his total yearly expenditure = $\frac{6000 \times 100}{280000} = 2.14\%$

Hence there are five persons who have less than 5% expenditure on fuel out of their total expenditures.

9. 4; E's expenditure on Others = $\frac{23 \times 100000}{100}$ = ₹23000

D's expenditure on Others = $\frac{23000 \times 110}{100} = 25300$

Thus reqd % = $\frac{25300}{300000} \times 100 = 8.43\%$

10. 3; Reqd difference = $\frac{240000 \times 20}{100} - \frac{180000 \times 15}{100}$

= 48000 – 27000 = ₹21000

(11-15):

Sport	Class IX	Class X	Class XI	Total
Cricket	32	29	35	96
Hockey	15% = 18	20	6% = 9	47
Volleyball	26	18	51	95
Football	19	9	31	59
Tennis	25	14	24	63
Total	120	25% = 90	150	360

The given table can be completed by adding up all the totals and calculating the required percentages. The final complete table is shown above.

11. 4; Total number of students in Class IX = 120

The number of students who like Volleyball in Class XI = 51

$\therefore$ Reqd difference = 120 – 51 = 69

12. 2; Number of students in Class X who like Tennis after the addition of 18 new students = 14 + 18 = 32

Number of students in Class IX who like Hockey = 18

$\therefore$ Reqd ratio = $\frac{32}{18} = 16:9$

13. 3; Number of students of Class XI who like Football = 31

Number of students of Class X who like Volleyball = 18

$\therefore$ Reqd % = $\frac{31}{18} \times 100 = 172.22\%$

14. 5; Reqd total number of students = 95 + 59 = 154

15. 3; Reqd difference = 96 – 47 = 49

16. 3; Total number of participants from Country L = $\frac{48}{15} \times 100$ = 320

Number of participants from Country O

$= \frac{(40\% \text{ of } 320 + 4)}{22} \times 100 = \frac{132}{22} \times 100 = 600$

$\therefore$ The number of participants from Country L who participate in more than 2 seminars

= {100 – (40 + 15)}% of 320

$= \frac{45 \times 320}{100} = \frac{9}{20} \times 320 = 9 \times 16 = 144$

The number of participants from Country O who participated in at least 3 seminars

= 75% of 600 = $\frac{3}{4} \times 600 = 450$

$\therefore$ Reqd % more = $\frac{450-144}{450} \times 100$

$= \frac{306}{450} \times 100 = \frac{306 \times 4}{18} = 68\%$

17. 2; Total number of participants from Country P

$= \frac{21}{(30-24)} \times 100 = \frac{2100}{6} = 350$

$\therefore$ Total number of participants from Country N = 60% of 350 = $\frac{3}{5} \times 350 = 210$

Reqd number of participants who participated in at least 4 seminars = (100 – 60 =) 40% of 210 = 84

18. 4; From the question 55% of L = 20% of P or, $\frac{L}{P} = \frac{20}{55}$

$\Rightarrow$ Reqd % = $\frac{L}{P} \times 100 = \frac{20}{55} \times 100 = 36\frac{4}{11}\%$

19. 5; Reqd number of boys who passed from Lucknow

$= \frac{3000}{5} \times 12 \times \frac{12.5}{7.5} \times \frac{7}{12} = 7000$

20. 4; Reqd number = $\frac{16200}{12} \times 18 \times \frac{5}{9} = 13500$

21. 1; Reqd % for Delhi = $\frac{3}{5} \times 100 = 60\%$ (highest)

Pune = $\frac{3}{8} \times 100 = 37.5\%$

Rest = $\frac{7}{15} \times 100 = 46.7\%$

22. 1; Let the total number of students passing in Class XII exam be x.

Then,

$14\% \text{ of } x \times \frac{11}{21} - 12\% \text{ of } x \times \frac{5}{12} = 315$

or, $\frac{22x}{300} - \frac{5x}{100} = 315$ or, $\frac{22x - 15x}{300} = 315$

$\therefore x = \frac{315}{7} \times 300 = 13500$

23. 3; The number of boys from Lucknow

$= 12000 \times \frac{7}{12} = 7000$

Delhi = $12000 \times \frac{15}{12.5} \times \frac{2}{5} = 5760$

Pune = $12000 \times \frac{10}{12.5} \times \frac{5}{8} = 6000$

Patna = $12000 \times \frac{16}{12.5} \times \frac{9}{16} = 8640$

Surat = $12000 \times \frac{7.5}{12.5} \times \frac{7}{12} = 4200$

Bhopal = $12000 \times \frac{14}{12.5} \times \frac{4}{7} = 7680$

Rest = $12000 \times \frac{25}{12.5} \times \frac{8}{15} = 12800$

Reqd number = 7000 + 5760 + 6000 + 8640 + 4200 + 7680 + 12800 = 52080

Practice Set 37

Directions (Q. 1-5): Study the following information carefully to answer the questions that follow:

In an organisation there are 2800 employees. They work in various departments, viz Logistics, Operations, Marketing, HR, Accounts and IT. 11% of the total employees work in Logistics and 18% of the total employees work in Operations. The number of employees who work in Marketing is 1.5 times of the number of employees who work in Operations, and the number of employees in HR is 1.5 times of the number of employees in Logistics. The ratio of the number of employees in Accounts to that in IT is 3 : 4. The ratio of the male employees in Marketing to the female employees in Marketing is 5 : 4. The number of female employees in IT is equal to 60% of the male employees in Marketing. The number of male employees in HR is 28 more than the number of female employees in IT. The number of male employees in Accounts is 8 more than the number of female employees in HR. The number of female employees in Logistics is half of the number of female employees in Marketing. The number of male employees in Operations is 1.5 times of the number of female employees in Logistics.

1. What is the ratio of number of male employees in Operations and IT together to that of the number of female employees in Marketing and Logistics together?
   1) 57 : 55　2) 53 : 55　3) 57 : 53　4) 55 : 63　5) 63 : 55
2. What is the difference between the total number of employees in HR and Accounts together and that in Logistics and Operations together?
   1) 40　2) 28　3) 20　4) 35　5) 30
3. The number of male employees in Operations is what per cent of the total number of employees in the organisation?
   1) 9%　2) 8%　3) 6%　4) 12%　5) 11%
4. What is the difference between the average number of employees in Logistics and IT together and the average number of employees in Marketing, HR and Accounts together?
   1) 196　2) 142　3) 126　4) 146　5) 186
5. What is difference between the total number of male employees in the organisation and the total number of female employees in the organisation?
   1) 175　2) 150　3) 180　4) 240　5) 140

Direction (Q. 6-10): Study the following pie-chart and graph carefully to answer the questions given below.

Proportion of income of seven companies in a country during the financial year 2016-17

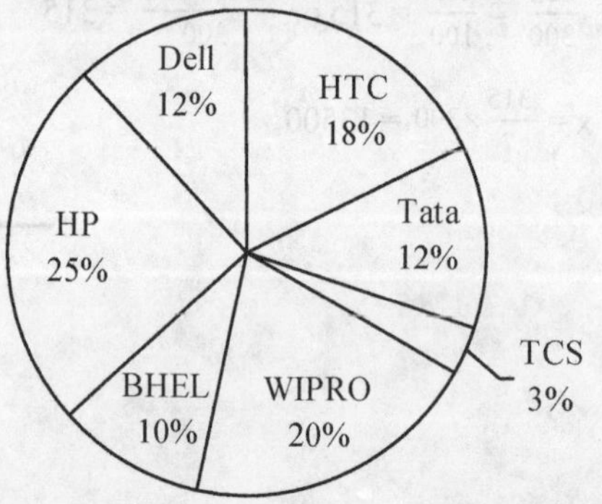

% profit of these companies during the financial year

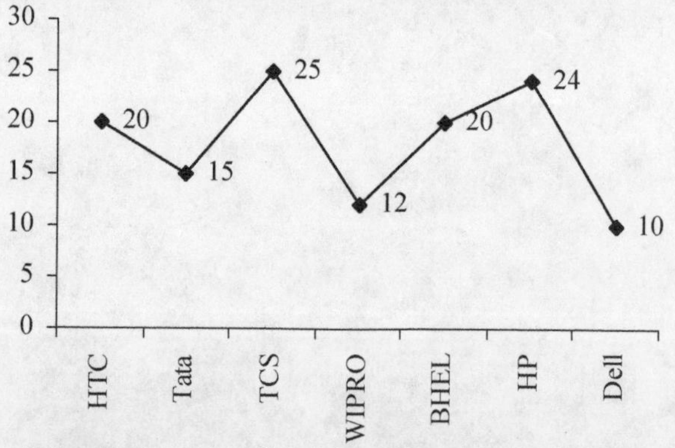

6. What is the ratio of the expenditure of HTC to that of TCS?
   1) 25 : 4　2) 24 : 5　3) 6 : 1　4) Can't be determined　5) None of these
7. If the difference between the income of HTC and BHEL was ₹240 cr, then what was the total expenditure of both the companies together?
   1) ₹740 cr　2) ₹700 cr　3) ₹840 cr　4) Can't be determined　5) None of these
8. Which of the following companies has recorded the maximum profit (in terms of ₹) in the given financial year if the combined income of these companies is ₹3000 cr?
   1) HTC　2) TCS　3) WIPRO　4) BHEL　5) HP
9. If in the financial year 2016-17 the income of WIPRO was

₹535 cr, then what was the approximate expenditure of Tech Mahindra in the same financial year?
1) ₹240 cr 2) ₹250 cr 3) ₹280 cr
4) ₹350 cr 5) ₹275 cr

10. If the expenditure of HP was ₹750 cr then what was the total income of all the given companies together?
1) ₹3680 cr 2) ₹3240 cr 3) ₹3720 cr
4) Can't say 5) None of these

Directions (Q. 11-15): Study the following graph carefully and answer the following questions:

Number (in lakh) of bicycles manufactured and sold by Company X over the years

The pie-chart shows the percentagewise manufacture of bicycles from different plants of Company X in different states in the year 2014

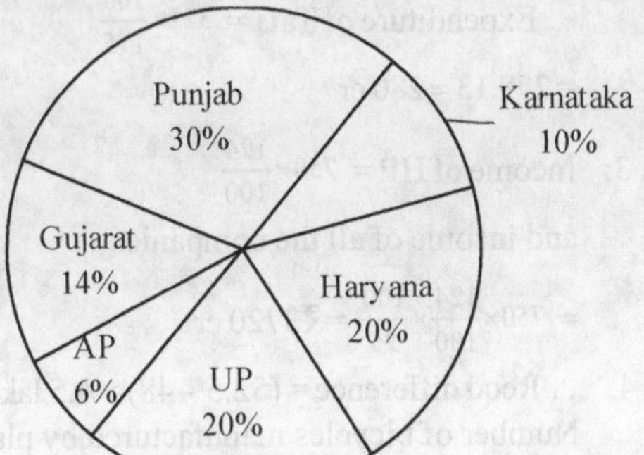

11. The difference between the number of bicycles manufactured by Company X in the year 2016 and that in the year 2015 is what per cent of the number of bicycles manufatured by the plant of Company X in Gujarat in 2014?
1) $65\frac{2}{7}$% 2) $70\frac{4}{7}$% 3) $72\frac{1}{7}$%
4) $71\frac{3}{7}$% 5) $62\frac{3}{7}$%

12. The number of bicycles sold by Company X in the year 2011 is approximately what per cent of the number of bicycles manufactured by plant of Company X Karnataka in that year if the number of bicycles manufactured by the plant of Company X in Karnataka in 2011 is 20% less than the number of bicycles manufactured by plant X in Karnataka in 2014?
1) 681% 2) 667% 3) 656%
4) 671.5% 5) 695%

13. What is the percentage increase in the number of bicycles sold by the Company X in the year 2013 from the previous year?
1) $16\frac{1}{3}$% 2) $42\frac{2}{3}$% 3) $45\frac{2}{3}$%
4) $28\frac{2}{3}$% 5) $33\frac{1}{3}$%

14. What is the ratio of the number of bicycles not sold by the Company X in the year 2014 to that not sold in the year 2012?
1) 3 : 1 2) 5 : 6 3) None of these
4) 1 : 3 5) 6 : 5

15. What is the difference between the average number of bicycles manufactured by the Company X over all the years together and the number of bicycles manufactured by the plant of Company X from state Punjab and Gujarat in 2014?
1) 2655000 2) 2333000 3) 3948000
4) 2481000 5) 2361000

Directions (Q. 16-20): Study the following information carefully and answer the questions given below:

Percentage of employees in various firms of the Tata group of companies and the ratio of males to females.

The total number of employees = 25000

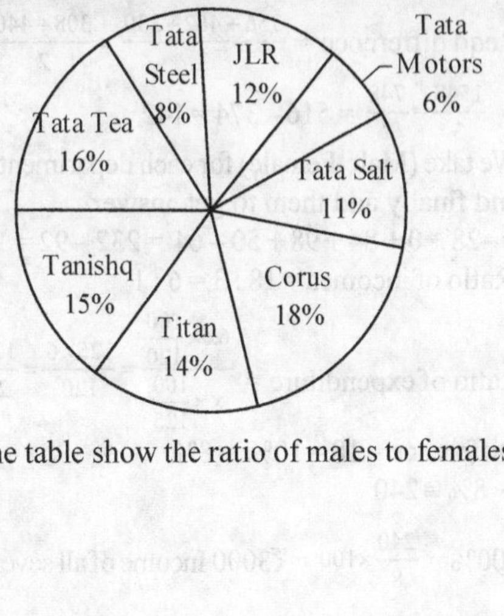

The table show the ratio of males to females.

Firm	Male : Female
JLR	7 : 5
Tata Steel	2 : 3
Tata Tea	5 : 3
Titan	3 : 4
Corus	5 : 4
Tata Salt	6 : 5
Tata Motors	2 : 1
Tanishq	7 : 8

16. What is the ratio of male employees in JLR to those in Tata Motors?
1) 7 : 4   2) 4 : 7   3) 3 : 4
4) 7 : 3   5) None of these

17. What is the difference between the total number of male employees in Titan and that of female employees in Corus?
1) 7500   2) 1500   3) 1000
4) 5000   5) None of these

18. What is the ratio of the total number of males in Tata Tea and Tanishq together to the total number of females in these two firms?
1) 13 : 15   2) 15 : 13   3) 13 : 17
4) 17 : 14   5) None of these

19. How many more/less female employees are there in Tata Tea in comparison to male employees in Tata Motors?
1) 2500   2) 1200   3) 1250
4) 1500   5) None of these

20. The difference between the number of male and female employees in Tata Salt is what per cent of the total number of male employees in Tata Steel?
1) $22\frac{1}{4}\%$ 2) $31\frac{1}{4}\%$ 3) $36\frac{1}{4}\%$
4) $23\frac{2}{4}\%$ 5) None of these

Answers and explanations

(1-5):

Department	Total	Males	Females
Logistics	2800×11/100=308	308–168=140	336×1/2=168
Operations	2800×18/100=504	168×1.5=252	504–252=252
Marketing	504×1.5=756	756×5/9=420	756×4/9=336
HR	308×1.5=462	252+28=280	462–280=182
Accounts	770×3/7=330	182+8=190	330–190=140
IT	770×4/7=440	440–252=188	420×60/100=252

1. 4; Reqd ratio = $\frac{252+188}{336+168}=\frac{440}{504}=55:63$

2. 3; Reqd difference
$=(308+504)-(462+330)=812-792=20$

3. 1; Reqd % = $\frac{252}{2800}\times100=9\%$

4. 2; Reqd difference = $\frac{756+462+330}{3}-\frac{308+440}{2}$
$=\frac{1548}{3}-\frac{748}{2}=516-374=142$

5. 5; We take (Male-Female) for each department separately and finally add them to get answer
$=-28+0+84+98+50-64=232-92=140$

6. 1; Ratio of incomes = 18 : 3 = 6 : 1

Ratio of expenditure = $\frac{6x\times\frac{100}{120}}{x\times\frac{100}{125}}=\frac{125\times6}{120}=\frac{125}{20}=25:4$

7. 2; Difference = 18 – 10% = 8%
$\because$ 8% ≡ 240

$100\%=\frac{240}{8}\times100=$ ₹3000 Income of all seven company

$\therefore$ Expenditure of HTC and BHEL

$=3000\left\{\frac{18}{120}+\frac{10}{120}\right\}=3000\times\frac{28}{120}=25\times28=700$ cr

8. 5; The % of income is maximum of HP
Thus the % profit of HP is also second highest.
Then in term of ₹ the profit is maximum for HP.

9. 3; Income of Tata = $\frac{535}{20}\times12=321$ crore

$\therefore$ Expenditure of Tata = $321\times\frac{100}{115}$

$=279.13\approx280$ cr

10. 3; Income of HP = $750\times\frac{124}{100}$
and income of all the companies
$=750\times\frac{124}{100}\times\frac{100}{25}=$ ₹3720 cr

11. 4; $\therefore$ Reqd difference = (52.5 – 48) = 4.5 lakh
Number of bicycles manufactured by plant of Company X in Gujarat in 2014 = 14% of 45 = 6.3 lakh

$\therefore$ Reqd % = $\frac{4.5}{6.3}\times100=\frac{5}{7}\times100=\frac{500}{7}=71\frac{3}{7}\%$

12. 5; The number of bicycles sold by Company X in 2011 = 25 lakh
The number of bicycles manufactured by plant of Company X in Karnataka in 2011

$=45\times\frac{10}{100}\times\frac{80}{100}=45\times\frac{1}{10}\times\frac{4}{5}=3.61$ lakh

$\therefore$ Reqd % = $\frac{25}{3.6}\times100=\frac{25000}{36}=694.44\approx695\%$

13. 5; No. of bicycles sold in year 2013 = 40
No. of bicycles sold in year 2012 = 30

$\therefore$ Reqd % = $\frac{40-30}{30}\times 100 = \frac{100}{3} = 33\frac{1}{3}\%$

14. 4; No. of bicycles not sold in 2014 = (45 – 42.5) = 2.5
No. of bicycles not sold in 2012 = (37.5 – 30) = 7.5
$\therefore$ Reqd ratio = 2.5 : 7.5 = 1 : 3

15. 5; Reqd average = $\frac{35+37.5+42.5+45+48+52.5}{6} = \frac{260.5}{6}$

= 43.41 lakh

The number of bicycles manufactured by plant of Company X in state Punjab and Gujarat in 2014 = (30 + 14)% of 45

= 44% of 45 = $\frac{45}{100}\times 45 = \frac{44}{20}\times 9$ = 19.8 lakh

$\therefore$ Reqd difference = 43.41 – 19.8 = 23.61 lakh = 2361000

16. 1; Reqd ratio = $\frac{12\times\frac{7}{12}}{6\times\frac{2}{3}} = \frac{7}{4} = 7:4$

17. 4; Reqd difference = $25000\left\{18\%\times\frac{4}{9}-14\%\times\frac{3}{7}\right\}$

= 25000{(8 – 6)%} = 250 × 2 = 5000

18. 4; Total number of males in Tata Tea and Tanishq

$= 25000\times\frac{\left(16\times\frac{5}{8}+15\times\frac{7}{15}\right)}{100} = 250\times 17 = 4250$

Total number of females in Tata Tea and Tanishq

$= 25000\left(16\times\frac{3}{8}+15\times\frac{8}{15}\right) = 250\times 14 = 3500$

$\therefore$ Reqd ratio = 4250 : 3500 = 17 : 14

Method II.
(Neglecting common factors)

Reqd ratio = $\frac{\left(16\times\frac{5}{8}+15\times\frac{7}{15}\right)}{\left(16\times\frac{3}{8}+15\times\frac{8}{15}\right)} = \frac{10+7}{6+8} = 17:14$

19. 5; The no. of female employes in Tata Tea

$= 25000\times\frac{16}{100}\times\frac{3}{8} = 250\times 6 = 1500$

The no. of male employees in Tata Motors

$= 25000\times\frac{6}{100}\times\frac{2}{3} = 250\times 4 = 1000$

$\therefore$ Reqd no. of more employees = 1500 – 1000 = 500

20. 2; The difference between the no. of male and female employees in Tata Salt

$= 25000\times\frac{11}{100}\left(\frac{1}{11}\right) = 250$

$\therefore$ Reqd % = $\frac{250}{8\%\text{ of }25000\times\frac{2}{5}}\times 100$

$= \frac{250}{800}\times 100 = \frac{250}{8} = 31\frac{1}{4}\%$

Practice Set 38

Directions (Q. 1-5): Study the following table carefully and answer the given questions:

Number of students appeared (A) and failed (F) in five departments of university over the years.

Year	Department									
	Medical		Fashion		Commerce		Architect		Biotech	
	A	F	A	F	A	F	A	F	A	F
2010	68	12	67	9	75	11	84	7	78	9
2011	65	19	70	11	63	8	69	5	79	12
2012	75	6	62	13	69	7	70	6	65	17
2013	79	12	76	10	67	13	81	5	74	8
2014	63	10	87	14	82	12	64	16	63	12
2015	72	15	66	4	74	15	70	7	82	4
2016	60	5	60	7	77	5	71	6	75	6

Note: Pass students = Appeared students – Failed students

1. What is the total number of failed students from Commerce for the given years?
   1) 77   2) 83   3) 68   4) 71   5) None of these
2. What is the ratio of the total number of passed students to the total number of failed students for the year 2013?
   1) 139 : 24   2) 329 : 48   3) 90 : 11   4) 325 : 42   5) 377 : 48
3. Which of the following departments has the minimum number of failed students over the years?
   1) Medical   2) Fashion   3) Commerce   4) Architecture   5) Biotech
4. What is the number of passed students for all the departments together in the year 2015?
   1) 319   2) 329   3) 317   4) 314   5) 315
5. What is the overall percentage of passed students with respect to those appeared in Architecture department for all the years together (rounded off to two digits after decimal)?
   1) 87.78   2) 88.24   3) 79.72   4) 86.94   5) 89.78

Directions (Q. 6-9): Study the following table carefully and answer the questions that follow:

Production of Maize (in tonnes) in three different states over the years.

Year → State ↓	2011	2012	2013	2014	2015	2016
Punjab	4.3	4.9	5.6	5.8	6.7	7.4
Haryana	3.1	3.7	4.4	5.1	6.0	6.2
UP	3.9	4.7	5.8	6.6	7.3	8.3

6. What is the approximate percentage increase in the production of Maize in Haryana from 2014 to 2015?
   1) 19   2) 18   3) 15   4) 21   5) 19.25
7. What is the ratio of the total production of Maize in all three states in the year 2014 to that in 2015?
   1) 7 : 9   2) 8 : 7   3) 6 : 7   4) 7 : 8   5) 11 : 12
8. The average production of Maize in UP for all the given years together is what per cent of the average production of Maize in Punjab for all the given years together?
   1) 114.47%   2) 124.47%   3) 94.74%   4) 105.47%   5) None of these
9. What is the difference between the total production of Maize in all three states together in 2016 and that in 2013?
   1) 6.9 tonnes   2) 6 tonnes   3) 6.1 tonnes   4) 6.4 tonnes   5) 5.8 tonnes

Directions (Q. 10-12): The table given below shows the distribution of three classes according to the sports they like and the number of students or percentage of students of that class in a particular sport. Some values are hidden intentionally in the table. Select the most appropriate answer.

Class → Sports ↓	Class VIII	Class X	Class XII	Total
Tennis	45		42	116
Chess	20%	31	18%	
Hockey		20%		98
Cricket			47	
Football	39	15%		82
Badminton	25	24	34	83
Total		140	250	560

10. If 13 more students took admission in Class X and all of them like cricket then what will be the ratio of the number of students of Class X who like Cricket to the number of students of Class XII who like Hockey?
    1) 1 : 3   2) 3 : 1   3) 2 : 3   4) 3 : 2   5) 5 : 3

11. What is the difference between the total number of students who like Chess and the total number of students who like Cricket?
1) 29 2) 27 3) 39
4) 38 5) None of these

12. The total number of students of Clas XII and Class VIII who like Tennis and Football respectively is what per cent more than the total number of students of Class VIII and Class X who like Hockey and Badminton respectively?
1) $118\frac{4}{17}\%$ 2) $128\frac{5}{17}\%$ 3) $108\frac{5}{17}\%$
4) $138\frac{4}{17}\%$ 5) $139\frac{4}{17}\%$

Directions (Q. 13-17): Study the following graph carefully and answer the questions that follow:

The bar-graph shows the number of suitcase models T_1 and T_2 produced by a company in different years.

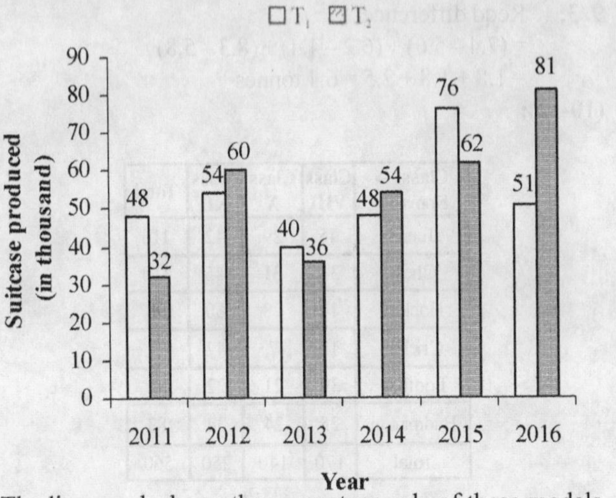

The line-graph shows the percentage sale of these models in different years.

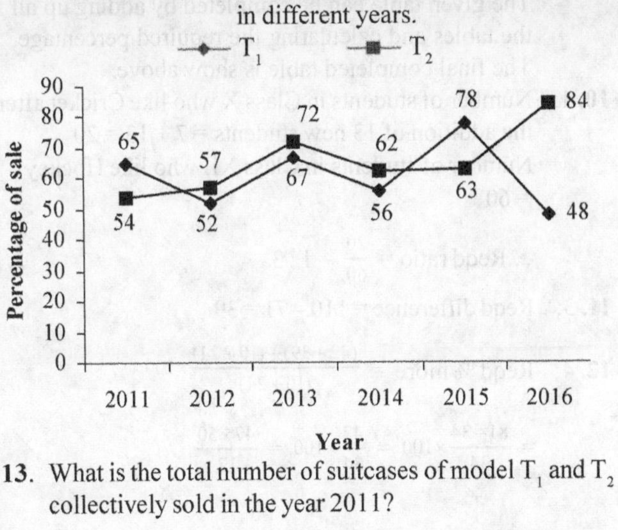

13. What is the total number of suitcases of model T_1 and T_2 collectively sold in the year 2011?
1) 48280 2) 48480 3) 49000
4) 42840 5) None of these

14. What is the ratio of the total number of unsold suitcases of model T_2 in the year 2012 to the total number of suitcases produced of model T_2 in 2013?
1) 43 : 60 2) 42 : 61 3) 41 : 57
4) 41 : 63 5) None of these

15. In which of the following years is the percentage rise/fall in the production of model T_1 the minimum as compared to the previous year?
1) 2016 2) 2011 3) 2012 4) 2015 5) 2013

16. What is the approximate percentage rise in the sale of model T_2 from year 2013 to 2014?
1) 29% 2) 31% 3) 19% 4) 24% 5) 32%

17. What is the total number of suitacases of model T_1 sold over all the six years together?
1) 195240 2) 197340 3) 198020
4) 196720 5) 198280

Directions (Q. 18-21): Refer to the graphs and answer the given questions:

The value of liquor supplied in 5 states in 2014 and the rate of custom duty in each state

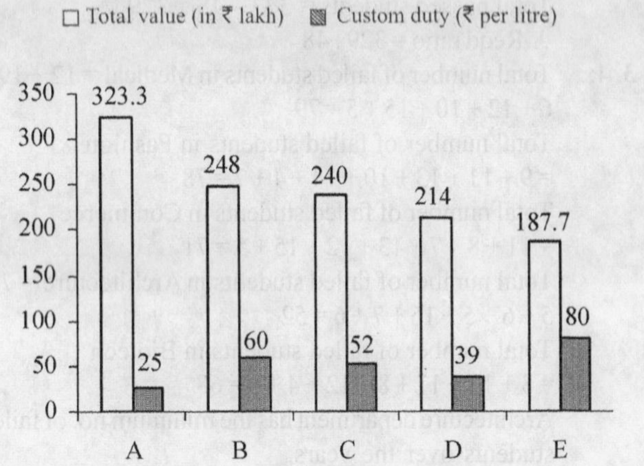

Amount of liquor supplied by Distilleries P, Q, R, S and T in State A (in lakh litres)

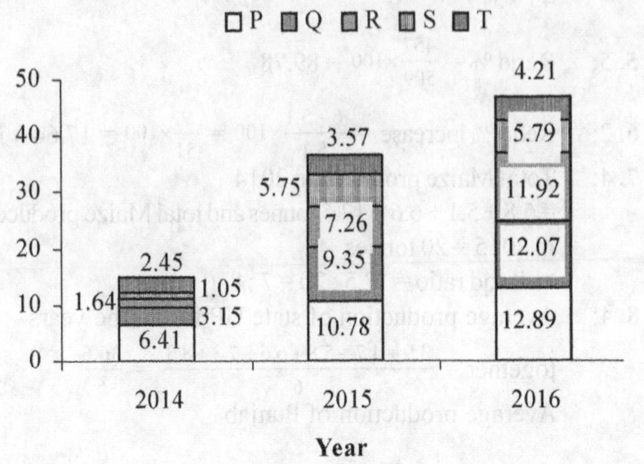

18. The custom duty rate (₹ per litre) of state A and B together is what per cent of the total customs duty rate (₹ per litre) of all the given states?
1) 22.23 2) 20.32 3) 27.30
4) 33.20 5) Can't be determined

19. Which of the five states manufactured liquor of the lowest cost?
1) A 2) E 3) C
4) The state which has the lowest value for (wholesale price – customs duty) per litre
5) Can't be determined

20. If customs duty is levied before the goods leave the factory (on the value of the liquor), then which of the following choices shows the distilleries in ascending order of the customs duties paid by them for the year 2014? (Assume the total liquor in the state A is supplied by only these 5 distilleries.)
1) TSPQR 2) PSTQR 3) SRTQP
4) PQRST 5) Can't be determined

21. If the state A's distillery, with the least average simple annual growth in amount of liquor supplied in the given period, had shown the same rate of growth as the one which grew the fastest, what would that distillery supply have been in 2016 (in lakh litres)?
1) 13 2) 130 3) 141.58
4) 15.35 5) 153.57

Answers and explanations

1. 4; Total number of failed students
$= 11 + 8 + 7 + 13 + 12 + 15 + 5 = 71$

2. 2; Total number of appeared students in the year 2013
$= 79 + 76 + 67 + 81 + 74 = 377$
Total number of failed students in the year 2013
$= 12 + 10 + 13 + 5 + 8 = 48$
Total passed students $= 377 - 48 = 329$
$\therefore$ Reqd ratio $= 329 : 48$

3. 4; Total number of failed students in Medical $= 12 + 19 + 6 + 12 + 10 + 15 + 5 = 79$
Total number of failed students in Fashion
$= 9 + 11 + 13 + 10 + 14 + 4 + 7 = 78$
Total number of failed students in Commerce
$= 11 + 8 + 7 + 13 + 12 + 15 + 5 = 71$
Total number of failed students in Architecture $= 7 + 5 + 6 + 5 + 16 + 7 + 6 = 52$
Total number of failed students in Biotech
$= 3 + 12 + 17 + 8 + 12 + 4 + 6 = 68$
Architecture department has the minimum no. of failed students over the years.

4. 1; Total number of passed students for all the departments together in the year 2015
$= (72 + 66 + 74 + 70 + 82) - (15 + 4 + 15 + 7 + 4) = 364 - 45 = 319$

5. 5; Reqd % $= \frac{457}{509} \times 100 = 89.78$

6. 2; Reqd % increase $= \frac{6 - 5.1}{5.1} \times 100 = \frac{9}{51} \times 100 = 17.64 \approx 18$

7. 4; Total Maize produced in 2014
$= 5.8 + 5.1 + 6.6 = 17.5$ tonnes and total Maize produced in 2015 = 20 tonnes
$\therefore$ Reqd ratio $= 17.5 : 20 = 7 : 8$

8. 4; Average production of state UP for all the years together $= \frac{3.9 + 4.7 + 5.8 + 6.6 + 7.3 + 8.3}{6} = \frac{36.6}{6}$
Average production of Punjab
$= \frac{4.3 + 4.9 + 5.6 + 5.8 + 6.7 + 7.4}{6} = \frac{34.7}{6}$
$\therefore$ Reqd % $= \frac{36.6}{34.7} \times 100 = 105.47\%$

9. 3; Reqd difference
$= (7.4 - 5.6) + (6.2 - 4.4) + (8.3 - 5.8)$
$= 1.8 + 1.8 + 2.5 = 6.1$ tonnes

(10-12):

Class → / Sports ↓	Class VIII	Class X	Class XII	Total
Tennis	45	29	42	116
Chess	34	31	45	110
Hockey	10	28	60	98
Cricket	17	7	47	71
Football	39	21	22	82
Badminton	25	24	34	83
Total	170	140	250	560

The given table can be completed by adding up all the tables and calculating the required percentage. The final completed table is show above.

10. 1; Number of students in Class X who like Cricket after the addition of 13 new students $= 7 + 13 = 20$
Number of students in Class XII who like Hockey $= 60$
$\therefore$ Reqd ratio $= \frac{20}{60} = 1 : 3$

11. 3; Reqd difference $= 110 - 71 = 39$

12. 4; Reqd % more $= \frac{(42 + 39) - (10 + 24)}{(10 + 24)} \times 100$
$= \frac{81 - 34}{34} \times 100 = \frac{47}{34} \times 100 = \frac{47 \times 50}{17}$

$= \frac{2350}{17} = 138\frac{4}{17}\%$

13. 2; Sale $T_1 = 48000 \times 0.65 = 31200$

Sale $T_2 = 32000 \times 0.54 = 17280$

$\therefore$ Total sale $(T_1 + T_2) = 31200 + 17280 = 48480$

14. 1; In 2012, unsold T_2

$= 60000 \times \frac{(100-57)}{100} = 60000 \times \frac{43}{100} = 25800$

In 2013, production of $T_2 = 36000$

$\therefore$ Ratio $= \frac{25800}{36000} = \frac{43}{60} = 43:60$

15. 3; For year 2012 $= \frac{54-48}{48} \times 100 = 12.5\%$ (rise)

$2013 = \frac{54-40}{54} \times 100 = 25.92\%$ (fall)

$2014 = \frac{48-40}{40} \times 100 = 20\%$ (rise)

$2015 = \frac{76-48}{48} \times 100 = 58.33\%$ (rise)

$2016 = \frac{76-51}{76} \times 100 = 32.57\%$ (fall)

16. 1; In 2013, sale of $T_2 = 36000 \times \frac{72}{100} = 25920$

In 2014, sale of $T_2 = 54000 \times \frac{62}{100} = 33480$

$\therefore$ Reqd % rise $= \frac{33480-25920}{25920} \times 100 = 29.16 \approx 29\%$

17. 4; Total T_1 sold $= (48 \times 0.65 + 54 \times 0.52 + 40 \times 0.67 + 48 \times 0.56 + 76 \times 0.78 + 51 \times 0.48) = (31.2 + 28.08 + 26.8 + 26.88 + 59.28 + 24.48) \times 1000 = 196720$

18. 4; Reqd % $= \frac{25+60}{25+60+52+39+80} \times 100$

$= \frac{85}{256} \times 100 = 33.20\%$

19. 5; Here, the total value is given but nothing is mentioned about the amount of liquor manufactured by the states other than state A. So, the answer can't be determined.

20. 3; Since customs duty is collected on the total value of liquor produced by 5 distilleries, this will be in the same order as the order of quantity of the liquor produced by them. Hence the correct order is SRTQP.

21. 4; The simple average annual growth for the 5 distilleries in state A is shown below.

Distilleries	Calculation	Rate
P	(12.89 – 6.41) / (6.41 × 2)	50.54%
Q	(12.07 – 3.15) / (3.15 × 2)	141.58%
R	(11.92 – 1.64) / (1.64 × 2)	313.41%
S	(5.79 – 1.05) / (1.05 × 2)	225.71%
T	(4.21 – 2.45) / (2.45 × 2)	35.91%

Distillery with lowest growth rate is T.

Distillery with highest growth rate is R.

R grew by 313.41% in the 2 years period.

So, the overall supply by T in 2016 would be

$2.45 \times \frac{626.82}{100} = 15.35$ litres

Practice Set 39

Directions (Q. 1-5): Study the following information to answer the questions.

In Reliance Group there are 5200 employees in five different subsidiary companies – Reliance Retail, Reliance Life Services, Reliance Logistic, Reliance Solar and RJIL. Out of the total number of female employees in the organisation, 27% work in Reliance Retail, 22% work in Reliance Logistic, 16% work in Reliance Life Services and the remaining 840 female employees work in Reliance Solar. RJIL has no female employee. Out of the total number of male employees in the group, 14% work in Reliance Retail, 30% work in Reliance Logistic, 25% work in Reliance Life Services, 11% work in the Reliance Solar and the remaining employees work in RJIL.

1. If the no. of male employees in Reliance Life Services increases by 20%, the male employees in Reliance Solar increases by 25%, 60 male employees join RJIL and the numbers of male employees in Reliance Retail and Reliance Logistic remain the same, what is the percentage increase in the number of male employees in the group?
1) 10.12% 2) 7.22% 3) 6.89% 4) 10.42% 5) 9.89%
2. The total number of male employees working in Reliance Logistic and Reliance Life Services together is what per cent of the total number of employees (male and female) working in these two firms?
1) 52.47% 2) 62.8% 3) 68.8% 4) 50.8% 5) 64.6%
3. What is the approximate average number of employees (male and female) who work in RJIL, Reliance Logistic, and Reliance Solar companies together?
1) 1044 2) 1120 3) 1025 4) 986 5) 1004
4. If equal number of female and male employees working in Reliance Life Services leave the job, the ratio of the number of male employees working in Reliance Life Services to the number of females working in the same department reduces to 149 : 70. What is the total number of employees working in Reliance Life Services who left the job?
1) 254 2) 148 3) 52 4) 257 5) 208
5. If 92 male employees of Reliance Retail are transferred to Reliance Solar and 70 female employees of Reliance Solar are transferred to Reliance Retail, then what is the ratio of the number of male employees to the number of female employees in Reliance Solar after the transfer of employees?
1) 40 : 77 2) 4 : 7 3) 6 : 7 4) 41 : 77 5) 52 : 77

Directions (Q. 6-10): Study the following table and answer the questions given below:

Performance of 6 Indian batsmen internationally

Batsman	Total no. of matches played	Average runs scored	Total balls faced	Strike rate
Sachin T	8	–	–	129.6
Saurav G	20	81	–	–
Sunil G	–	76	800	114
Shahid A				72
Sandip P	56	110	2560	–
Sanjay P	–	–	–	66

Note: (A) Strike rate $= \frac{\text{Total runs scored}}{\text{Total balls faced}} \times 100$

(B) Some values are missing. You have to calculate these values as per given data.

6. The ratio of the total number of balls faced by Shahid A to that by Sanjay P is 3 : 4. The total number of runs scored by Sanjay P in the tournament is what per cent more than the total runs scored by Shahid A?
1) $\frac{200}{9}\%$ 2) $\frac{100}{9}\%$ 3) $\frac{250}{9}\%$ 4) $\frac{150}{7}\%$ 5) None of these
7. If the runs scored by Sandip P in the last 3 matches of the tournament are not considered, his average runs scored in the tournament decreases by 9. If the runs scored by Sandip P in the 54th and 55th Match are below 168 but more than 165 (no two scores among these scores are equal), what is the minimum possible runs scored by Sandip P in the 56th Match?
1) 384 2) 160 3) 474 4) 182 5) 464
8. The total number of balls faced by Sachin T is 74 less than the total number of runs scored by him. What is the average runs scored by Sachin T?
1) 40.5 2) 45 3) 38.5 4) 39 5) 44
9. Saurav G faced equal number of balls in the first 10 matches and the last 10 matches. If his strike rate in the first 10 matches and the last 10 matches are 120 and 150 respectively, then what is the total number of balls faced by him?

1) 1150 2) 1050 3) 1250 4) 1200 5) 1025

10. What is the total number of matches played by Sunil G?

1) 13 2) 14 3) 15 4) 9 5) 12

Directions (Q. 11-14): Study the following table and answer the questions that follow:

The number of professionals required by Asia and India for the given years (in lakh)

	2014		2015		2016	
Profession	Asia	India	Asia	India	Asia	India
Doctors	50	4	70	10	80	15
Lawyers	30	0.5	40	2.5	50	5
Engineers	50	4	60	5	75	10
Architects	10	0.5	20	1	25	1.3
Teachers	10	1	10	1.5	20	2
Total	150	10	200	20	250	33.3

11. From 2014 to 2016, which two professions jointly meet more than 60 per cent of the total professionals required by both Asia and India?

1) Doctors and Lawyers 2) Doctors and Engineers
3) Lawyers and Engineers 4) Architects and Teachers
5) None of these

12. Which profession's proportion in the total professionals' demand increases from 2014 to 2015 and decreases from 2015 to 2016 for both Asia and India?

1) Doctors 2) Lawyers 3) Engineers
4) Architects 5) Teachers

13. The proportion of which profession in India decreases continuously from 2014 to 2016?

1) Lawyers 2) Engineers 3) Architetss
4) Teachers 5) None of these

14. The proportion of which profession in comparison to all the professions in Asia remains constant over the period 2014 and 2015 but the proportion in India increases in comparison to the total demand for the same period?

1) Engineers 2) Lawyers 3) Teachers
4) Architects 5) Doctors

Directions (Q. 15-19): Study the following pie-chart and answer the questions that follow:

Distributon of novels (Horror and Romantic) sold by 8 stores in 2016

Total number = 66000

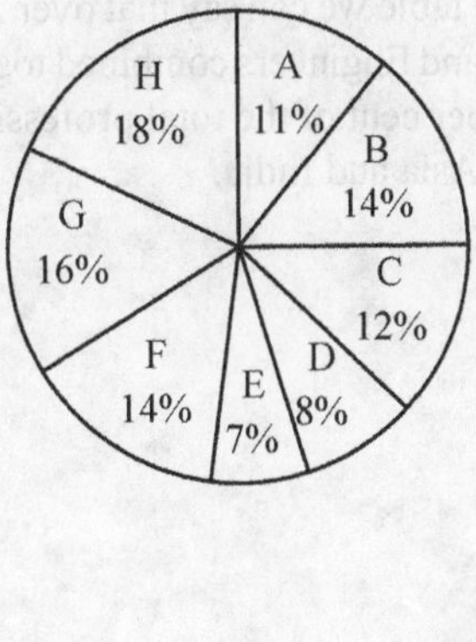

Distribution of Horror novels sold by 8 stores in 2016

Total number = 38000

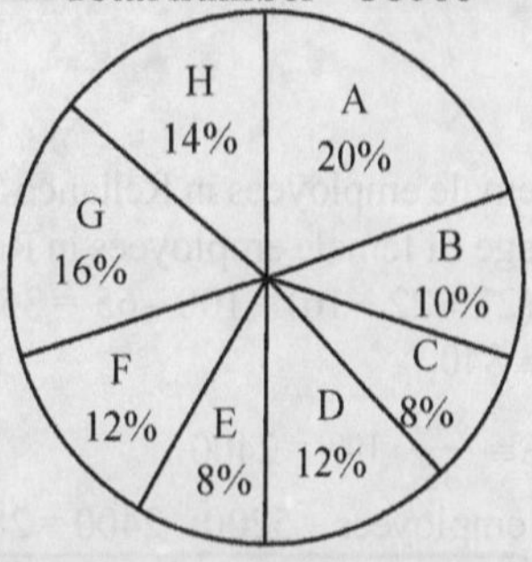

15. Total number of Romantic novels sold by Store C and H together is by what per cent less than the total number of novels (Horror and Romantic) sold by C and D together?

1) $12\frac{2}{3}$ 2) $14\frac{1}{3}$ 3) $13\frac{1}{3}$
4) $18\frac{2}{3}$ 5) None of these

16. The number of novels (Romantic and Horror) sold by Store F is approximately what per cent more/less than the total number of Horror novels sold by store B, C and D together?

1) 14% less 2) 18% more 3) 15% more
4) 19% less 5) None of these

17. What is the difference between the total number of Romantic novels sold by stores B, H and E together and the total number of Horror novels sold by store A, E and D together?

1) 1820 2) 3280 3) 1620 4) 5220 5) 4220

18. If the number of novels sold by store E, G and H increased by 15%, 20% and 35% respectively and so did Horror novels sold by these three stores from 2016 to 2017, what was the total number of Romantic novels sold by these three stores in 2017?

1) 16029 2) 16049 3) 15489
4) 16849 5) None of these

19. What is the central angle corresponding to the number of novels (both Romantic and Horror) sold by store B?

1) 48.4° 2) 56.4° 3) 40° 4) 50.4° 5) 60.4°

Answers and explanations

(1-5):

No. of female employees in Reliance Solar = 840

Percentage of female employees in Reliance Solar $= 100-(27+22+16) = 100-65 = 35\%$

$\therefore 35\% \equiv 840$

$\therefore 100\% \equiv \frac{840}{35} \times 100 = 2400$

$\therefore$ Male employees = 5200 − 2400 = 2800

Company	Male	Female
Reliance Retail	392	648
Reliance Logistic	840	528
Reliance Life Services	700	384
Reliance Solar	308	840
RJIL	560	0
Total	2800	2400

1. 5; Total increase in employees = 20% of 700 + 25% of 308 + 60 = 140 + 77 + 60 = 277

$\therefore$ Reqd % $= \frac{277}{2800} \times 100 = 9.89\%$

2. 2; Total no. of male employees in Reliance Logistic and Reliance Life Services = 840 + 700 = 1540

Total no. of employees in these two companies = 840 + 528 + 700 + 384 = 2452

$\therefore$ Reqd % $= \frac{1540}{2452} \times 100 = 62.8\%$

3. 3; Reqd average $= \frac{560+840+528+308+840}{3} = \frac{3076}{3} \approx 1025$

4. 5; Let the number of male employees who left the job be x

Then, $\frac{700-x}{384-x} = \frac{149}{70}$

or, $70(700-x) = 149(384-x)$

or, $149x - 70x = 149 \times 384 - 700 \times 70$

or, $79x = 57216 - 49000 = 8216$

$\therefore x = \frac{8216}{79} = 104$

$\therefore$ Total number of employees who left the job $= 104 \times 2 = 208$

5. 1; No. of male employees in Reliance Solar after the transfer of 92 males from Reliance Retail = 308 + 92 = 400 and the number of female employees in Reliance Solar = 840 − 70 = 770

$\therefore$ Reqd ratio = 400 : 770 = 40 : 77

6. 1; Total runs scored by Sanjay P $= \frac{66 \times 4x}{100} = \frac{264x}{100}$

Shahid A $= \frac{72 \times 3x}{100} = \frac{216x}{100}$

Reqd % more $= \frac{48x}{100} \times \frac{100}{216x} \times 100$

$= \frac{48}{216} \times 100 = \frac{8 \times 25}{9} = \frac{200}{9}\%$

7. 3; Total runs scored = No. of matches played × Average runs = 56 × 110 = 6160

Total runs scored (excluding last 3 matches) = 53 × 101 (average decreasing by 9) = 5353

Total runs in last 3 matches = 6160 − 5353 = 807

54th and 55th matches are below 168 and more than 165 and no two score among these 3 scores are equal.

So, assume 54th = 166 and 55th = 167

$\therefore$ Run in 56th match = 807 − (166 + 167) = 474

8. 1; Let the total runs scored by Sachin T be x.

Total balls faced by Sachin T = x − 74

$\therefore$ According to the question,

$\frac{x}{x-74} \times 100 = 129.6$

or, $129.6x - 129.6 \times 74 = 100x$

or, $29.6x = 9590.4 \therefore x = 324$

$\therefore$ Average $= \frac{324}{8} = 40.5$

9. 4; Let the total number of balls faced by Saurav G be x.

According to the question,

$\frac{120}{100} \times \frac{x}{2} + \frac{150}{100} \times \frac{x}{2} = 20 \times 81 = 1620$

or, $\frac{6x}{10} + \frac{3x}{4} = 1620$ or, $\frac{54x}{40} = 1620 \therefore x = 1200$

10. 5; Let the total number of matches played by Sunil G be x

Then, $114 = \frac{76 \times x}{800} \times 100$

$\therefore 114 = \frac{38x}{400} \times 100$

or, $38x = 456 \therefore x = \frac{456}{38} = 12 \therefore x = 12$

11. 2; From the table we can say that over 2014 to 2016, Doctors and Engineers combined together meet more than 60 per cent of the total professionals' demand for both Asia and India.

Profession ↓ Total demand →		2014		2015		2016	
		Asia 150	India 10	Asia 200	India 20	Asia 250	India 33
Lawyers	Value	30	0.5	40	2.5	50	5
	Proportion	20%	5%	20%	12.5%	20%	15.01%
Engineers	Value	50	4	60	5	75	10
	Proportion	33.3%	40%	30%	25%	30%	30.3%
Doctors	Value	50	4	70	10	80	15
	Proportion	33.3%	40%	35%	50%	32%	45.4%

12. 1; From the same table we can say that the proportion of Doctors has increased over 2014 to 2015 and decreased over 2015 to 2016 for both Asia and India as compared to the total professionals' demand.

(13-14):

Profession		2014		2015		2016	
Total demand		Asia 150	India 10	Asia 200	India 20	Asia 250	India 33
Lawyers	Value	30	0.5	40	2.5	50	5
	Proportion	20%	5%	20%	12.5%	20%	15.15%
Engineers	Value	50	4	60	5	75	10
	Proportion	33.3%	40%	30%	25%	30%	30.3%
Architects	Value	10	0.5	20	1	25	1.3
	Proportion	6.6%	5%	10%	5%	10%	3.9%
Teachers	Value	10	1	10	1.5	20	2
	Proportion	6.6%	10%	5%	7.5%	8%	6.06%

13. 4; From the above table we can conclude that the demand of Teachers is decreasing over the years in India.

14. 2; Again, from the table we can conclude that the demand for Lawyers remains constant in Asia while it increases in India over the years.

15. 3; Romantic novels sold by Store C and H together = (18 + 12)% of 66000 – (14 + 8)% of 38000 = 30% of 66000 – 22% of 38000 = 19800 – 8360 = 11440

Total number of novels sold by Store C and D together = (12 + 8)% of 66000 = 20% of 66000 = 13200

$\therefore$ Reqd % less = $\frac{13200-11440}{13200}\times 100$

$= \frac{1760}{13200}\times 100 = \frac{440}{33} = \frac{40}{3} = 13\frac{1}{3}\%$ pass

16. 4; Total number of novels sold by store F (Romantic and Horror) together = 14% of 66000 = 14 × 660 = 9240

Total number of Horror novels sold by store B, C and D together = (10 + 8 + 12)% of 38000 = 30% of 38000 = 30 × 380 = 11400

$\therefore$ Reqd % less = $\frac{11400-9240}{11400}\times 100$

$= \frac{2160}{114} = 18.94\% \approx 19\%$ less

17. 3; Number of Romantic novels sold by Store B, H and F together

= (14 + 18 + 7)% of 66000 – (10 + 14 + 8)% of 38000

= 39% of 66000 – 32% of 38000

= 39 × 660 – 32 × 380 = 25740 – 12160 = 13580

Number of Horror novels sold by store A, E and D together = (20 + 8 + 12)% of 38000 = 40% of 38000 = 40 × 380 = 15200

$\therefore$ Reqd difference = 15200 – 13580 = 1620

18. 2; Total number of Romantic novels sold by store E, G and H together

$= \left(\frac{7\times 660\times 115}{100} - \frac{8\times 380\times 115}{100}\right) +$

$\left(\frac{16\times 660\times 120}{100} - \frac{16\times 380\times 120}{100}\right) +$

$\left(\frac{18\times 660\times 135}{100} - \frac{14\times 380\times 135}{100}\right)$

= (5313 – 3496) + (12672 – 7296) + (16038 – 7182)

= 1817 + 5376 + 8856 = 16049

19. 4; Reqd central angle = $\frac{14}{100}\times 360 = 14 \times 3.6 = 50.4°$

Practice Set 40

Directions (Q. 1-5): Study the following graph carefully and answer the given questions.

The bar graph shows the marked price of five different models of car

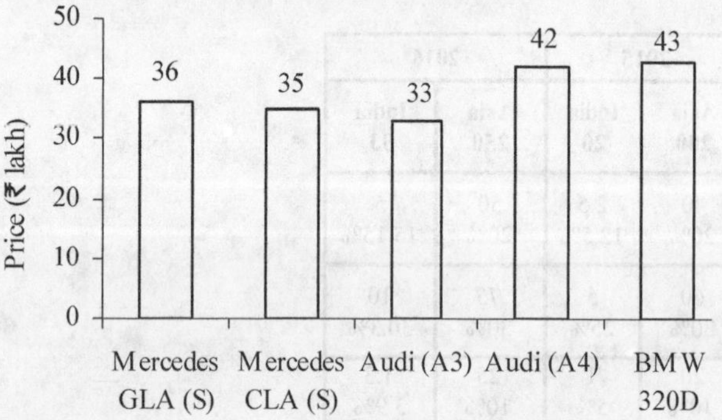

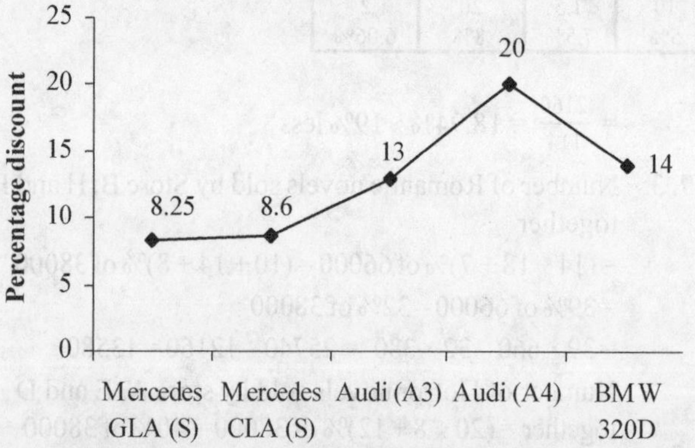

1. A dealer gives an additional discount besides the discount on BMW 320D. After additional discount he sells it for ₹35.131 lakh. Find the percentage of additional discount.
   1) 7.5% 2) 5% 3) 6.25% 4) 6% 5) 7.25%
2. What price should the dealer sell Audi (A4) at so as to make a profit of 25% on his outlay if the dealer makes a profit of 12% after discount at present?
   1) ₹36.5 lakh 2) ₹38.25 lakh 3) ₹36.75 lakh
   4) ₹37.5 lakh 5) ₹42.65 lakh
3. Pawan Singh, a director of a reputed company, purchased two cars – Mercedes GLA(S) and Mercedes CLA(A). If he paid 15% as sales tax on each car, then find the amount paid by him for purchasing both the cars.
   1) ₹6979540 2) ₹6879450 3) ₹6997450
   4) ₹6879650 5) None of these
4. A customer bought Audi (A3). The rate of depreciation is 13% per annum. After one year he sold it at 20% less than the original marked price. Find the difference between the depreciated value and the new selling price of the car.
   1) ₹142230 2) ₹134220 3) ₹153460
   4) ₹143220 5) ₹163420
5. A dealer gets a profit of 25% after allowing discount on Mercedes CLA(S). If he reduced his profit to $12\frac{1}{2}\%$, then find the additional % discount.
   1) 12.5 2) 8 3) 7.5 4) 9 5) 10

Directions (Q. 6-10): Study the following graph carefully to answer the given questions:

The bar-graph shows the number of flats booked in HIG, MIG and LIG categories from different cities in 2016.

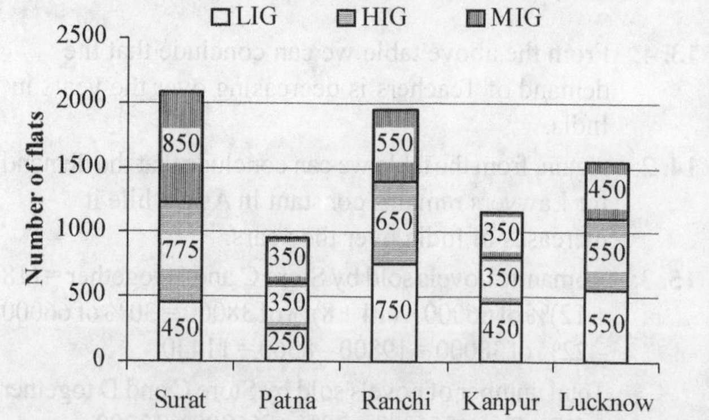

6. The total number of MIG flats booked in Patna, Ranchi and Kanpur is by what per cent less than the total number of LIG flats booked from these three cities together? (Rounded off to the nearest integer)
   1) 10% 2) 7% 3) 14%
   4) 18% 5) None of these
7. Out of the MIG flats booked from Ranchi, 28% were by employees of a financial institution, and out of the remaining flats, those booked by officers from a software company and officers from MHA department of Government of India were in the ratio of 5 : 4. What was the total number of MIG flats booked by officers from MHA department of Government of India?
   1) 172 2) 176 3) 185
   4) 196 5) None of these

8. If for Kanpur the number of LIG flats booked in 2016 was more than that in 2015 by 20%, the number of MIG flats booked in 2016 was less than that in 2015 by 12.5% and the number of HIG flats booked in 2016 was more than that in 2015 by 25%, then what was the total number of flats booked in Kanpur in 2015?
1) 975 2) 1095 3) 1055 4) 1175 5) 1125

9. What is the difference between the total number of MIG flats booked in Surat, Patna, Ranchi and Lucknow together and the total number of HIG flats booked in these four cities together?
1) 148 2) 172 3) 165 4) 125 5) 108

10. What is the ratio of the total number of flats booked in Surat to that in Ranchi?
1) 83 : 78 2) 83 : 73 3) 78 : 89 4) 81 : 73 5) 85 : 71

Directions (Q. 11-15): Study the following pie-charts carefully to answer the questions.

The following pie-charts show the regional distribution of aid from DAC member

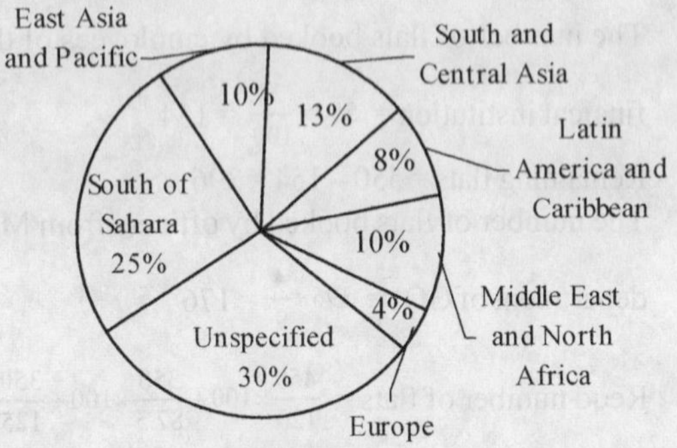

Year 2011

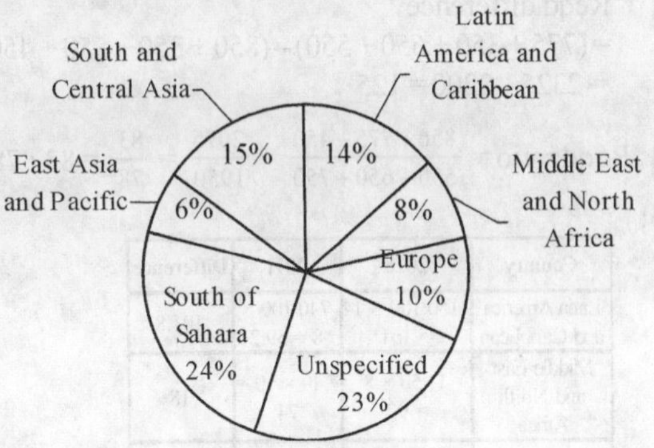

Year 2016

11. If the total aid received by all the countries in 2011 and 2016 was ₹740 billion and ₹1150 billion respectively, then which group of regions show the maximum difference between 2016 and 2011?
1) South and Central Asia 2) Unspecified
3) Europe 4) South of Sahara
5) Latin America and Caribbean

12. The aids received by South and Central Asia in 2011 and by South of Sahara in 2016 are ₹192.4 billion and ₹552 billion respectively. What is the difference between the total aid received by them in 2016 and that in 2011? (in ₹ billion)
1) 780 2) 820 3) 815
4) 860 5) 845

13. If Europe gets ₹74 billion aid in 2011, then the amount of aid received by South and Central Asia and East Asia and Pacific together is how much percentage less than that by South of Sahara and Middle East and North Africa together in the same year?
1) 31.12% 2) 39.82% 3) 24.28%
4) 34.28% 5) 36.78%

14. If the ratio of aids received by Unspecified regions in 2011 to that in 2016 is 22 : 23 and the Unspecified regions get ₹264.5 billion in 2016 then what is the ratio of the aids received by Latin America and Carribbean in 2011 to that in 2016?
1) 1687 : 4025 2) 1683 : 4031 3) 4031 : 1683
4) 4025 : 1686 5) None of these

15. If Middle East and North Africa get ₹148 billion in 2011, then the aids received by Unspecified regions is what per cent more than that received by South of Sahara?
1) 33.33% 2) 23.33% 3) 16.66%
4) 24.68% 5) None of these

Directions (Q. 16-20): Study the following information carefully and answer the questions given below:

There are four banks A, B, C and D. The number of clerical employees in Bank D is 350 more than the number of clerical employees in Bank C and 1350 less than the number of clerical employees in Bank A. The number of clerical employees in Bank B is 14 more than 5.6 times of the number of officers in that bank. The number of clerical employees in Bank C is 38 less than 4.2 times the no. of officers in Bank D. The number of officers in Bank D is 115 more than that of officers in Bank A and 170 less than that of officers in Bank B. The number of officers in Bank A and that in Bank C are 1025 and 1500 respectively.

The number of male clerks in Bank A is 56% of the total number of clerical employees in Bank B. The number of female officers in Bank A is 45% of the total number of officers in Bank D. The number of male clerks in Bank C is 6 times of the number of female officers in Bank A. The number of male clerks in D is double the number of female clerks in C. The number of male clerks in Bank B is 2452 more than the number of male clerks in Bank C. The number of male officers in Bank B is 16% of the total number of clerks of Bank D. The number of female officers in Bank C is 56 less than that of male officers in Bank B. The number of male officers in Bank D is 1.5 times that of female officers in Bank B.

16. What is ratio of the number of female clerks in Bank A and D together to the number of female clerks in Bank B and C together?
1) 2405 : 1674 2) 2054 : 1476 3) 2045 : 1746
4) 2504 : 1467 5) None of these

17. What is the sum of the average number of female officers in Bank B, C and D together and the average number of male clerks in those banks?
1) 4535 2) 4455 3) 4575 4) 4355 5) 4753

18. The number of female officers in Bank A, C and D together is what per cent of the number of male clerks in Bank A and D together?
1) 24.22% 2) 28.72% 3) 32.66%
4) 22.41% 5) 18.27%

19. What is the difference between the number of male clerks in Bank A, B and C together and the number of male officers in all the bank together?
1) 10815 2) 9915 3) 10515 4) 10668 5) 10645

20. In which bank are female clerks the maximum and male officers the minimum respectively?
1) A and B 2) A and C 3) C and B
4) B and D 5) None of these

Answers and explanations

1. 2; After discount the selling price of the car

$= 43\times\left(\frac{100-14}{100}\right) = 43\times\frac{86}{100} = ₹36.98$ lakh

Additional discount $= 3698000 - 3513100 = 184900$

$\therefore$ Additional discount % $= \frac{184900}{3698000}\times100 = 5\%$

2. 4; After discount the selling price of the car $= 42\times\frac{80}{100}$

$= ₹33.60$ lakh

$\therefore$ Selling price of the car to make a 25% profit

$= \frac{33.6}{112}\times125 = ₹37.5$ lakh

3. 5; After discount the selling price of both the cars

$= 36\times\frac{91.75}{100} + 35\times\frac{91.4}{100} = 33.03 + 31.99 = ₹65.02$ lakh

After paying the sales tax, required amount

$= 65.02\times\frac{115}{100} = ₹74.773$ lakh $= ₹7477300$

4. 1; Selling price of the car $= 33\times\frac{87}{100} = ₹28.71$ lakh

Depreciated value after one year

$= 28.71\times\frac{87}{100} = ₹24.9777$ lakh

$\therefore$ Reqd difference $= 33\times\frac{80}{100} - 24.9777$

$= 26.4 - 24.9777 = ₹1.4223$ lakh $= ₹142230$

5. 5; Selling price of the car $= 35\times\frac{91.4}{100} = ₹31.99$ lakh

Selling price of the car after reduced profit

$= \frac{31.99}{125}\times112.5 = ₹28.791$ lakh

Reqd % $= \frac{31.99-28.791}{31.99}\times100 = \frac{3.199}{31.99}\times100 = 10\%$

Quicker Approach:

Here initial % profit = 25%

and reduced % profit = 12.5%

Suppose CP = 100

Then $SP_1 = 125$ & $SP_2 = 112.5$

$\therefore$ Reqd addition % discount

$= \frac{125-112.5}{125}\times100 = \frac{12.5}{125}\times100 = 10\%$

6. 3; Reqd % $= \frac{(250+750+450)-(350+550+350)}{(250+750+450)}\times100$

$= \frac{1450-1250}{1450}\times100 = \frac{200}{1450}\times100 = 13.80 \approx 14\%$

7. 2; The number of flats booked by employees of the finaical institution $= 550\times\frac{28}{100} = 154$

Remaining flats $= 550 - 154 = 396$

The number of flats booked by officers from MHA department of GOI $= 396\times\frac{4}{9} = 176$

8. 3; Reqd number of flats $= \frac{450}{120}\times100 + \frac{350}{87.5}\times100 + \frac{350}{125}\times100$

$= 375 + 400 + 280 = 1055$

9. 4; Reqd difference

$= (775+350+650+550) - (850+350+550+450)$

$= 2325 - 2200 = 125$

10. 1; Reqd ratio $= \frac{856+775+450}{550+650+750} = \frac{2075}{1950} = \frac{83}{78} = 83:78$

11. 5;

Country	2016	2011	Difference
Latin America and Caribbean	1150/100 × 14 = 161	740/100 × 8 = 59.2	101.8
Middle East and North Africa	11.50 × 8 = 92	7.40 × 10 = 74	18
Europe	11.50 × 10 = 115	7.4 × 4 = 29.6	85.4
Unspecified	11.50 × 23 = 264.5	7.40 × 30 = 222	42.5
South of Sahara	11.50 × 24 = 276	7.40 × 25 = 185	91
South and Central Asia	11.50 × 15 = 172.5	7.40 × 13 = 96.2	76.3

Hence the maximum difference is ₹101.8 billion

12. 2; Reqd difference $= \frac{552}{24}\times100 - \frac{192.4}{13}\times100$

$= 2300 - 1480 = ₹820$ billion

13. 4; $\text{Reqd \%} = \frac{(25+10)-(13+10)}{(25+10)} \times 100$

$= \frac{35-23}{35} \times 100 = \frac{12}{35} \times 100 = ₹34.28\%$

14. 1; The aids received by Unspecified region in 2011

$= \frac{264.5}{23} \times 22 = ₹253 \text{ billion}$

$\text{Reqd ratio} = \frac{\frac{253}{30} \times 8}{\frac{264.5}{23} \times 14} = \frac{67.47}{161} = \frac{1687}{4025} = 1687:4025$

15. 5; $\text{Reqd \%} = \frac{30-25}{25} \times 100 = \frac{5}{25} \times 100 = 20\%$

(16-20):

	Clerks			Officers		
	Total	M	F	Total	M	F
A	5100+1350 =6450	7350×56/100 =4116	6450 –4116=2334	1025	1025 –513=512	1140×45/100 =513
B	1310×5.6+14 =7350	3078+2452 =5530	7350–5530 =1820	1140+170 =1310	5100×16/100 =816	494
C	1140×4.2 –38=4750	513×6=3078	4750–3078 =1672	1500	1500 –760=740	816–56=760
D	4750+350 =5100	2×1672=3344	5100–3344 =1756	1025+115 =1140	494×1.5 =741	1140 –741=399

16. 3; $\text{Reqd ratio} = \frac{2334+1756}{1820+1672} = \frac{4090}{3492} = 2045:1746$

17. 1; $\text{Reqd sum} = \frac{494+760+399+5530+3078+3344}{3}$

$= \frac{13605}{3} = 4535$

18. 4; $\text{Reqd \%} = \frac{513+760+399}{4116+3344} \times 100 = \frac{1672}{7460} \times 100 = 22.41\%$

19. 2; $\text{Reqd difference} = (4116+5530+3078) - (512+816+740+741) = 12724 - 2809 = 9915$

20. 5

Practice Set 41

Directions (Q. 1-5): Study the following table to answer the given questions.

The table shows the number of appeared and qualifed candidates (in thousand) in competitive axamination from different states over the years.

States	2012		2013		2014		2015	
	App	Qual	App	Qual	App	Qual	App	Qual
Bihar	88	16	–	14	76	16	95	19
TN	70	17	75	12	69	–	82	15
UP	–	13	78	09	72	12	88	–
Delhi	86	–	84	15	–	8	94	14
Odisha	77	12	68	–	70	12	–	11

1. If the number of appeared students in 2012 and in 2015 from all the states are 407 thousand and 431 thousand respectively, then what is the difference between the number of appeared candidates from UP and that from Odisha in all the given years (in thousand)?
   1) 32 2) 28 3) 47 4) 37 5) 46
2. If in 2013 the number of appeared candidates from Bihar is 9 thousand more than the number of appeared candidates from Odisha in 2012 and the number of qualified candidates in Odisha in 2013 is 125% of qualified candidates from that state in 2012, then the number of qualified candidates in 2013 from all the states is what per cent of that of appeared candidates from all the states in that year?
   1) 7.75% 2) 33.33% 3) 16.63%
   4) 22.22% 5) 9.3%
3. In 2016 the number of appeared candidates from Bihar, TN and Delhi increased by 20%, 15% and 12% from the previous year respectively and the number of appeared candidates from UP and Odisha decreased by 5% and 4% respectively. What is the number of appeared candidates in 2016 from all the given states if the number of appeared candidates from Odisha in 2015 is equal to 12% more than that of appeared candidates from TN in 2013? (in thousand)
   1) 458.76 2) 477.82 3) 476.53
   4) 488.32 5) 473.82
4. If the average number of appeared candidates from UP is 79 thousand and the average number of qualified candidates from that state is equal to that of qualified candidates in 2014, then what is the ratio of the appeared candidates from UP in 2012 to that of qualified candidates in 2015?
   1) 39 : 7 2) 38 : 9 3) 47 : 8 4) 41 : 8 5) 36 : 7
5. If the number of appeared candidates from Bihar in 2013 is 5% less than that of appeared candidates from the previous year and the number of appeared candidates from Delhi in 2014 is 10% more than that of appeared candidates from the previous year then what is the average number of appeared candidates from Bihar and Delhi per year per state?
   1) 80.375 thousand 2) 85.5 thousand
   3) 83.735 thousand 4) 87.75 thousand
   5) None of these

Directions (Q. 6-10): Read the data given in the paragraph carefully and answer the questions:

There are three trains X, Y and Z that travel between different stations. Following is the route that is followed by the three trains and some information regarding the distance between those stations:

Note: All the stations are in a straight line and the distance between any two stations is the same in both the ways.

Train X: A → B → C → D

The distance between station A and C is 115 km and the distance between station B and C can be covered in 1 hour 40 minutes when travelling at speed 42 km/hr.

Train Y: C → P → Q → R

The distance between station C and Q is 75 km. The ratio of the distance between station P and Q to that between station Q and R is 1 : 1 and the distance between station C and P is half of that between station P and Q.

Train Z: Q → D → P → C

The ratio of the distance between station Q and D to the distance between station D and P is 4 : 1.

6. The total distance covered by train X is what per cent more than the total distance covered by train Y?
   1) 12% 2) 15% 3) 25% 4) 20% 5) 35%
7. If the cost of fuel is ₹75 per litre and train X can run 5 km per litre, then what is the total cost of fuel for train X when it runs from station A to station D?
   1) ₹2550
   2) ₹5250
   3) ₹2250
   4) None of the given options
   5) ₹2305

8. What is the ratio of the difference between the total distance covered by train X and Y to the difference between the total distance covered by train Y and Z?
1) 1 : 1 2) 1 : 2 3) 2 : 1 4) 2 : 5 5) 4 : 9

9. If train X goes from station A to station P at the speed of 70 km/hr and from station P to station D at speed 25 km/hr, then what is the total time taken by train X to reach station D from station A?
1) 1.8 hours 2) 2.6 hours 3) 4.8 hours
4) 2.4 hours 5) Cannot be determined

10. The distance between P and Q is what per cent more or less than the distance between P and D?
1) 500% 2) 350% 3) 250%
4) 40% 5) 400%

Directions (Q. 11-13): Study the following information carefully and answer the questions that follow.

A jar P contains 'X' litres milk and jar Q contains 'X – 25' litres water. 'K' litres water is taken from jar Q and mixed with K% milk from jar P to form a mixture A. The remaining quantity of water in jar Q is distributed into two equal parts, one part of which is mixed with 40% remaining milk from jar P to form a mixture B of 64 litres and another part is mixed with the remaining quantity of milk in jar P to form a mixture C. The difference between the quantity of milk in mixture B and that in C is 17 litres.

11. What is the value of 'X'?
1) 125 2) 100 3) 150
4) 75 5) None of the given options

12. If 20% mixture A is replaced by water, then what will be the ratio of the quantity of milk to that of water in the new mixture?
1) 3 : 4 2) 2 : 3 3) 5 : 9 4) 1 : 3 5) 3 : 2

13. If 6 litres of milk and 5 litres of water is added to the mixture B, then **approximately** what per cent milk will be present in new mixture?
1) 49 2) 53 3) 47
4) 62 5) Cannot be determined

Directions (Q. 14-17): Study the following information carefully and answer the questions that follow:

1.8X men can do a work in 5Y days. 1.6X women can do the same work in 3Y days and 2.4X children can do the same work in 5(Y + 1) days. 30 men, 24 women and 48 children can complete the whole work together in $8\frac{4}{7}$ days. When A men and B women work together for 5 days, then the remaining work is completed by 31 children in 36 days. When 5A children work for 4 days, then the remaining work is completed by one woman in 360 days. (X + Y) men and (A + B) women together can do the whole work in D days. When 6 women work for C days, then the remaining work completed by A men in 45 days. **(Note: 4A + C = 16Y)**

14. If BX men and AY women work together for 2 days, then in how much time will the remaining work be completed by C children?
1) 15.5 days 2) 13.5 days 3) 16.5 days
4) 19 days 5) 18.5 days

15. If (3A – 2X) women work for 16 days and the remaining work is completed by 8 men and Z women in $\frac{240}{19}$ days, then in how many days will (Z + 12) women complete the whole work?
1) $11\frac{13}{17}$ days 2) $21\frac{4}{7}$ days 3) $17\frac{1}{7}$ days
4) $19\frac{2}{9}$ days 5) None of the given options

16. If 3XY men, 2AC women and 5B children work together for one day, then approximately what per cent work will be completed?
1) 89.5 2) 95.5 3) 97.5
4) 75 5) Cannot be determined

17. What is the value of (3A – 2XY – BC + 26D)?
1) 56 2) 42 3) 46 4) 61 5) 37

Directions (Q. 18-22): Study the following information carefully and answer the questions that follow.

A shopkeeper purchased five different items and sold them to his customers. The pie-chart given below shows the distribution (in degrees) of purchase price of those five items.

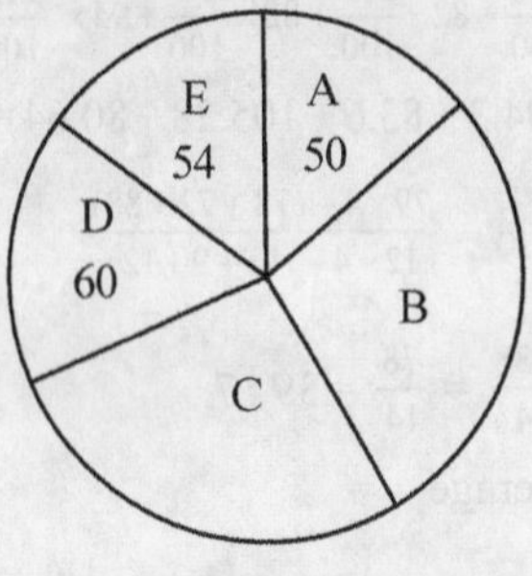

Some other information is also known:

The purchase price of item C is ₹630 more than that of item E and the profit per cent earned when items C and E together are sold at ₹2727 is 21.2% and the purchase price of item B is ___**(P)**___ rupees. The profit per cent earned on item D and E are ___**(Q)**___% and ___**(R)**___% respectively when both the items are sold at ₹1215 each.

18. What is the ratio of the value of Q to that of R?
1) 7 : 9 2) 4 : 5 3) 7 : 10
4) 8 : 11 5) None of the given options

19. Item A is marked 60% above its purchased price and sold at 29.2% profit. Which of the following options correctly shows the two successive discount percentages on that item?
1) 10% and 5% 2) 5% and 15%
3) 10% and 10% 4) 20% and 5%
5) 15% and 15%

20. If items A and F together are sold at 'P' and the profit percent earned on item A and F are 28% and 35% respectively, then at what price is item F purchased?
1) 300 2) 350 3) 600
4) 400 5) 500

21. P is **approximately** how many times the average of Q and R?
1) 35 2) 32 3) 42 4) 30 5) 20

22. What is the value of P – (2Q + 5R)?
1) 1250 2) 810 3) 1200
4) 1180 5) None of the given options

Answers and explanations

1. 4; The number of appeared students from Odisha in 2015
$= 431 - (95 + 82 + 88 + 94) = 431 - 359 = 72$ thousand
The number of appeared students from UP in 2012
$= 407 - (88 + 70 + 86 + 77) = 407 - 321 = 86$
$\therefore$ Reqd difference $= (86 + 78 + 72 + 88) - (77 + 68 + 70 + 72) = 324 - 287 = 37$ thousand

2. 3; The number of appeared aspirants from Bihar in 2013
$= 77 + 9 = 86$ thousand
The number of qualified aspirants from Odisha in 2013
$= 12 \times \frac{125}{100} = 15$ thousand
$\therefore$ Reqd % $= \frac{14 + 12 + 9 + 15 + 15}{86 + 75 + 78 + 84 + 68} \times 100$
$= \frac{65}{391} \times 100 = 16.63\%$

3. 2; The number of appeared aspirants in 2016
$= 95 \times \frac{120}{100} + 82 \times \frac{115}{100} + 88 \times \frac{95}{100} + 94 \times \frac{112}{100} + 75 \times \frac{112}{100} \times \frac{96}{100}$
$= 114 + 94.3 + 83.6 + 105.28 + 80.64 = 477.82$ thousand

4. 1; Reqd ratio $= \frac{79 \times 4 - (78 + 72 + 88)}{12 \times 4 - (13 + 9 + 12)}$
$= \frac{316 - 238}{48 - 34} = \frac{78}{14} = 39 : 7$

5. 5; Reqd average
$= \frac{88 \times \frac{95}{100} + 88 + 76 + 95 + 86 + 84 + 84 \times \frac{110}{100} + 94}{8}$
$= \frac{83.6 + 88 + 76 + 95 + 86 + 84 + 92.4 + 94}{8}$
$= \frac{699}{8} = 87.375$ thousand

(6-10):
Since all stations are in a straight line, after mentioning all the stations in a straight line:
$A \leftrightarrow B \leftrightarrow C \leftrightarrow P \leftrightarrow D \leftrightarrow Q \leftrightarrow R$
Distance between A and C = 115 km
Distance between B and C $= 42\left[1 + \frac{40}{60}\right]$
$= 42 + 28 = 70$ km
Distance between A and B = 115 – 70 = 45 km
Distance between C and Q = 75 km
Let the distance between P and Q and that between Q and R be 'x' each.
Distance between C and P $= \frac{x}{2}$
Now, $x + \frac{x}{2} = 75 \Rightarrow x = 50$
Distance between C and P $= \frac{x}{2} = 25$ km
Distance between P and Q = x = 50 km
Distance between Q and R = x = 50 km
Let the distance between Q and D and that between D and P be 4y and y respectively.
According to the question,
$4y + y = 50 \Rightarrow y = 10$
Distance between Q and D = 4y = 40 km
Distance between D and P = y = 10 km
Distance between P and C = 25 km
Distance between C and D = 25 + 10 = 35 km

45 70 25 10 40 50
$A \leftrightarrow B \leftrightarrow C \leftrightarrow P \leftrightarrow D \leftrightarrow Q \leftrightarrow R$

6. 4; Total distance covered by train X
$= 45 + 70 + 25 + 10 = 150$ km
Total distance covered by train Y
$= 25 + 10 + 40 + 50 = 125$ km
Difference $= 150 - 125 = 25$ km
$\therefore$ Required % $= \frac{25}{125} \times 100 = 20\%$

7. 3; Total distance between station A and D
$= 45 + 70 + 25 + 10 = 150$ km
Total quantity of fuel needed
$= \frac{150}{5} = 30$ litres
$\therefore$ Cost of fuel = 30 × 75 = ₹2250

8. 2; Total distance covered by train X
$= 45 + 70 + 25 + 10 = 150$ km
Total distance covered by train Y
$= 25 + 10 + 40 + 50 = 125$ km
Total distance covered by train Z
$= 40 + 10 + 25 = 75$ km
$\therefore$ Required ratio $= (150 - 125) : (125 - 75)$
$= 25 : 50 = 1 : 2$

9. 4; Distance between station A and P
$= 70 + 25 + 45 = 140$ km

Distance between station P and D = 10 km
Total time taken by train X from station A to D

$= \left(\frac{140}{70}+\frac{10}{25}\right) = 2+0.4 = 2.4$ hours

10. 5; Distance between P and Q = x = 50 km
Distance between P and D = y = 10 km

$\therefore$ Required % $= \frac{50-10}{10}\times 100 = \frac{40}{10}\times 100$

= 400% more

(11-13):

Initial quantity of milk in P = X litres
Initial quantity of water in Q = (X − 25) litres

In mixture A: Quantity of milk = K% of X $= \frac{KX}{100}$

Quantity of water = K

Total quantity $= K+\frac{KX}{100} = \frac{K(X+100)}{100}$

In mixture B:
Quantity of milk = 40% of (100 − K)% of X

$= \frac{0.4\times(100-K)\times X}{100}$

Quantity of water $= \frac{X-25-K}{2}$

Total quantity $= \left[\frac{0.4\times(100-K)\times X}{100}+\frac{X-25-K}{2}\right] = 64$

$\Rightarrow X = \frac{7650+50K}{90-0.4K}$ ...(i)

In mixture C:
Quantity of milk = 60% of (100 − K)% of X

$= \frac{0.6\times(100-K)\times X}{100}$

Quantity of water $= \frac{X-25-K}{2}$

Total quantity $= \frac{0.6\times(100-K)\times X}{100}+\frac{X-25-K}{2}$

Now,

$\frac{0.6\times(100-K)\times X}{100} - \frac{0.4\times(100-K)\times X}{100} = 17$

$\Rightarrow X = \frac{8500}{100-K}$ ...(ii)

Now, from (i) and (ii), we have

$\frac{7650+50K}{90-0.4K} = \frac{8500}{100-K} \Rightarrow K = 15$

Then, $X = \frac{8500}{100-K} = 100$

11. 2; X = 100

12. 2; **In mixture A:**

Quantity of mixture $= \frac{K(100+X)}{100}$

$= 15\left(\frac{100+100}{100}\right) = 30$ litres

Quantity of milk $= \frac{KX}{100} = 15\times\frac{100}{100} = 15$ litres

When 20% of mixture is replaced by water, new quantity of milk = 80% of 15 = 12 litres

New quantity of water $= 15\times\frac{120}{100} = 18$ litres

Then, ratio = 12 : 18 = 2 : 3

13. 2; **In mixture B:**

New quantity of water $= \frac{X-25-K}{2}+5$

$= \frac{100-25-15}{2}+5 = 35$ litres

New quantity of milk

$= \frac{0.4\times(100-K)\times X}{100}+6 = 40$ litres

New quantity of mixture = 35 + 40 = 75 litres

Then, % of milk $= \frac{40}{75}\times 100 = 53\%$ (approx.)

(14-17):

1.8X men can do a work in 5Y days. 1.6X women can do the same work in 3Y days and 2.4X children can do the same work in 5(Y + 1) days. Then,

One day's work of man $= \frac{1}{1.8X\times 5Y} = \frac{1}{9XY}$

One day's work of woman $= \frac{1}{1.6X\times 3Y} = \frac{1}{4.8XY}$

One day's work of child

$= \frac{1}{2.4X\times 5(Y+1)} = \frac{1}{12XY+12X}$

30 men, 24 women and 48 children can complete the whole work in $8\frac{4}{7}$ days. Then,

$\frac{30}{9XY}+\frac{24}{4.8XY}+\frac{48}{12XY+12X} = \frac{7}{60}$

$\Rightarrow XY = \frac{740Y+500}{7Y+7}$ ...(i)

When 6 women work for C days, the remaining work is completed by A men in 45 days. Then,

C days' work done by 6 women $= \frac{6C}{4.8XY} = \frac{5C}{4XY}$

Remaining work $= 1-\frac{5C}{4XY} = \frac{4XY-5C}{4XY}$

Then, $45 = \frac{4XY-5C}{4XY}\times\frac{9XY}{A}$

$\Rightarrow 20A+5C = 4XY$ ...(ii)

Also, we have, 4A + C = 16Y

$\Rightarrow 80Y = 4XY \Rightarrow X = 20$

Now, from (i), we get

$20Y = \frac{740Y+500}{7Y+7} \Rightarrow Y = 5$

Now, one day's work of a man

$= \frac{1}{9XY} = \frac{1}{9\times20\times5} = \frac{1}{900}$

One day's work of a woman $= \frac{1}{4.8XY} = \frac{1}{480}$

One day's work of a child

$= \frac{1}{12XY+12X} = \frac{1}{1440}$

5 days' work done by A men and B women

$= \frac{5A}{900} + \frac{5B}{480} = \frac{A}{180} + \frac{B}{96} = \frac{8A+15B}{1440}$

Remaining work $= 1 - \frac{8A+15B}{1440} = \frac{1440-8A-15B}{1440}$

Then, $\frac{31\times36}{1440} = \frac{1440-8A-15B}{1440}$

$\Rightarrow B = \frac{324-8A}{15}$ ...(iii)

When 5A children work for 4 days, the remaining work is completed by one woman in 360 days.

In 4 days work done by 5A children $= \frac{5A\times4}{1440} = \frac{A}{72}$

Then, remaining work $= 1 - \frac{A}{72} = \frac{72-A}{72}$

And, $360 = \frac{72-A}{72} \times 480$

$\Rightarrow A = 18$

From (ii), we get $20A + 5C = 4XY$

$\Rightarrow 20\times18 + 5C = 4\times20\times5 \Rightarrow C = 8$

From (iii), we get $B = \frac{324-8\times18}{15} \Rightarrow B = 12$

(X + Y) men and (A + B) women together can do the whole work in D days. Then, $\frac{X+Y}{900} + \frac{A+B}{480} = \frac{1}{D}$

$\Rightarrow \frac{25}{900} + \frac{30}{480} = \frac{1}{D} \Rightarrow D = \frac{144}{13}$

14. 3; 2 days' work done by BX men and AY women together

$= 2\times\frac{BX}{900} + 2\times\frac{AY}{480} = \frac{2\times12\times20}{900} + \frac{2\times18\times5}{480} = \frac{109}{120}$

Then, remaining work $= 1 - \frac{109}{120} = \frac{11}{120}$

Now, time taken by C = 8 children to complete the remaining work $= \frac{11}{120} \times \frac{1440}{8} = 16.5$ days.

15. 3; 16 days' work done by (3A – 2X) women

$= \frac{16(3A-2X)}{480} = \frac{7}{15}$

Remaining work $= \frac{8}{15}$

And, one day's work done by 8 men and Z women together $= \frac{8}{900} + \frac{Z}{480} = \frac{64+15Z}{7200}$

Then, $\frac{8}{15} \times \frac{7200}{64+15Z} = \frac{240}{19} \Rightarrow Z = 16$

$\therefore$ Time taken by (Z + 12) women to complete the work $= \frac{1}{\frac{Z+12}{480}} = 17\frac{1}{7}$ days

16. 3; One day's work done by 3XY men, 2AC women and 5B children together

$= \frac{3XY}{900} + \frac{2AC}{480} + \frac{5B}{1440}$

$= \frac{3\times20\times5}{900} + \frac{2\times18\times8}{480} + \frac{5\times12}{1440} = \frac{39}{40}$

$\therefore$ % of work completed $= \frac{39}{40} \times 100 = 97.5\%$

17. 3; Here, X = 20, A = 18, B = 12, C = 8 and $D = \frac{144}{13}$

$\therefore 3A - 2XY - BC + 26D$

$= 3\times18 - 2\times20\times5 - 12\times8 + 26\times\frac{144}{13} = 46$

(18-22): Let the sum of purchase price of all 5 items together = 360x

Let the CP of A, D and E be 50x, 60x and 54x respectively.

CP of C = 54x + 630

CP of B = 360x – 50x – (54x + 630) – 60x – 54x = 142x – 630

SP of C and E together = 121.2% of [(54x + 630) + 54x] = 2727 ⇒ 108x + 630 = 2250 ⇒ x = 15

CP of A = 50x = 750

CP of B = P = (142x – 630) = 1500 ⇒ P = 1500

CP of C = 54x + 630 = 1440

CP of D = 60x = 900

CP of E = 54x = 810

Profit % earned when D is sold at 1215 = Q%

$\Rightarrow Q\% = \frac{1215-900}{900} \times 100 = 35\%$

Profit % earned when E is sold at 1215 = R%

$\Rightarrow R\% = \frac{1215-810}{810} \times 100 = 50\%$

18. 3; Required ratio = 35 : 50 = 7 : 10

19. 2; MP of A $= \frac{160}{100} \times 750 = 1200$

SP of A $= \frac{129.2}{100} \times 750 = 969$

Now, from (2),

SP of item = 95% of 85% of 1200 = 969

Hence, (2) is the correct option.

20. 4; P = 1500 = Total SP of A and F

Let CP of F = F

As per information given,
(128% of 750) + (135% of F) = 1500 ⇒ F = 400

21. 1; Average of Q and R = $\frac{35+50}{2}=\frac{85}{2}$

∴ Required answer

$= \frac{1500}{85} \times 2 = 35.29 \approx 35$ times

22. 4; We have,

$P-(2Q+5R)=1500-[2(35)+5(50)]$
$=1500-[70+250]$
$=1500-320=1180$

Practice Set 42

Directions (Q. 1-5): Following is the information about the time taken to cover 10 km distance by each of the five persons by three modes (running, cycling and swimming). Read the given information carefully and answer the questions that follow.

The sum of the time taken by Vineet to cover 10 km by all three modes (running, cycling and swimming) is 145 minutes. The sum of the time taken by Devender to cover 10 km by all of the three modes is the same as the sum of the times taken by Vineet to cover 10 km by all the three modes. The cycling efficiency of Devender is 50% more than his running efficiency and the running efficiency of Devender is 25% less than his swimming efficiency. The running efficiency of Devender is 25% less than that of Vineet and the swimming efficiency of Vineet is 25% less than that of Devender. The time taken by Sudip to cover 10 km by cycling is 28% less than the time taken by him to cover 10 km by running, and the running efficiency of Sudip is 10% less than his swimming efficiency. The running efficiency of Sudip is 20% more than that of Devender. The sum of time taken by Divika to cover 10 km by all three modes is 8 minutes less than sum of time taken by Sudip to cover 10 km by all three modes. The cycling efficiency of Divika is 25% more than her running efficiency and the ratio of time taken by Divika to cover 10 km by cycling to the time taken by her to cover 10 km by swimming is 6 : 7. The cycling efficiency of Reena is 20% more than her running efficiency and the time taken by Reena to cover 10 km by swimming is 28% more than the time taken by her to cover 10 km by cycling. The cycling efficiency of Reena is 60% more than that of Devender.

1. If Sudip's cycling efficiency is increased by 80%, running efficiency by 100% and swimming efficiency by 62%, then what is the difference between the total time taken by Divika to cover 20 km by all three modes and the total time taken by Sudip to cover 18 km by all three modes?
1) 117 minutes 2) 134 minutes 3) 123 minutes
4) 115 minutes 5) None of the given options

2. The cycling efficiency of Vineet is 25% more than that of A and the swimming efficiency of Reena is 50% more than that of B. The running, cycling and swimming efficiency of A are equal and the running, cycling and swimming efficiency of B are also equal. If on a day A did cycling for 1 hour, running for 30 minutes and swimming for 20 minutes while on same day B did cycling for 60 minutes, running for 36 minutes and swimming for 24 minutes, then what is the total distance travelled by all 3 modes by A and B together?
1) 47 km 2) 37 km 3) 45 km 4) 52 km 5) 56 km

3. If on a day Vineet did cycling for 36 minutes, running for 63 minutes and swimming for 42 minutes and on the same day Devender did cycling for 28 minutes, running for 138 minutes and swimming for 27 minutes, then the total distance covered by Devender is what per cent of the total distance covered by Vineet?
1) 120% 2) 125% 3) 115% 4) 150% 5) 95%

4. What is the ratio of the time taken by Reena in covering 10 km by cycling to the time taken by Devender in covering the same distance by running?
1) None of the given options
2) 5 : 11 3) 4 : 9 4) 9 : 4 5) 5 : 12

5. The time taken by Divika in completing 10 km distance by each of the three modes one after the other is **approximately** what per cent of the time taken by Vineet in completing 10 km distance by each of the three means one after the other?
1) 82 2) 94 3) 85 4) 72 5) 45

Directions (Q. 6-11): Study the following data carefully and answer the questions:

In a cloth shop, there are three sections X, Y and Z with different sizes of jeans - small, medium and large. The total number of small jeans in all the sections together is 90.

In section X, the probability of choosing a small jeans is $\frac{1}{3}$ and that of choosing a medium jeans is $\frac{1}{5}$ while the number of large jeans is 20 more than the number of small jeans.

In section Y, the total number of jeans is 120 and the sum of small and large jeans is 2 times the number of medium jeans. Also, the ratio of probability of choosing small jeans to that of choosing medium jeans is 3 : 4.

In section Z, the total number of jeans is half the total number of jeans in section Y and the probability of choosing large jeans is $\frac{1}{6}$ more than the probability of choosing medium jeans.

6. If 'K' number of small jeans are shifted from section X to section Z and the probability of choosing medium jeans

from section Z decreases by $\frac{1}{12}$ then how many small jeans are shifted from section X to section Z?
1) 20 2) 10 3) 25
4) 30 5) None of the given options

7. One jeans each is selected from section X, Y and Z. Find the probability that all of them are small jeans.
1) $\frac{1}{82}$ 2) $\frac{4}{11}$
3) Cannot be determined
4) $\frac{1}{12}$ 5) $\frac{1}{72}$

8. What is the total number of jeans in all the three sections together?
1) 220 2) 330 3) 243
4) 180 5) 110

9. If a customer takes $\frac{3}{5}$ of the small jeans from section X, all the medium jeans from section Y and $\frac{1}{3}$ of the large jeans from section Z and places them in his shopping basket, what is the probability that when three jeans are chosen from the shopping basket all of them will be small?
1) $\frac{5}{12}$ 2) $\frac{203}{4108}$ 3) $\frac{201}{4108}$
4) $\frac{1}{12}$ 5) None of the given options

10. What is the difference between the number of medium jeans from section X and Y together to the number of large jeans from section Y and Z together?
1) 5 2) 25 3) 15
4) 10 5) 0

11. The average number of medium jeans in all the sections is what per cent of the average number of large jeans in all the sections given?
1) 60 2) 50 3) 75
4) 80 5) 100

Directions (Q. 12-17): Read the following table and bar graph carefully and answer the questions given below:

The table given below shows the amount of work done (in units) per hour by five different persons on Friday. It also shows the ratio of efficiency of doing work of these five persons on Friday to that on Saturday.

Persons	Work done per hour (in units) on Friday	Ratio of efficiency on Friday to that on Saturday
Anushka	2	1 : 3
Ejaz	6	3 : 2
Sumit	4	4 : 9
Pavitra	5	1 : 2
Mukul	3	3 : 1

The bar graph given below shows the time taken by each of the five persons on Sunday to do the work as percentage of time taken by them in doing the same work on Friday.

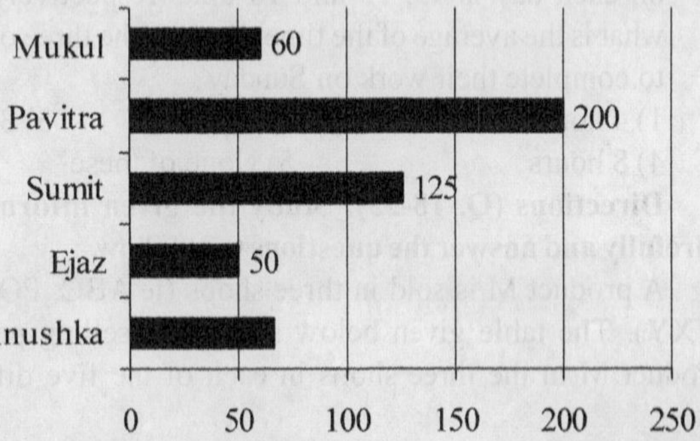

Note: Total work done by each of the five persons individually on each day is the same. For example, if Sumit does N units of work on Friday then he will do N units of work on Saturday and Sunday as well, whereas efficiencies and time taken to complete this work is different as per given conditions.

12. If the amount of work done by five persons is 12 units each individually, then what is the sum of time taken by each of them individually to complete the work on Saturday?
1) 12 hours 42 minutes 2) 20 hours 20 minutes
3) 19 hours 32 minutes 4) 14 hours 12 minutes
5) 22 hours 44 minutes

13. If Anushka took 6 hours to do her work on Friday, then what is the ratio of time taken by her to do her work on Saturday to that on Sunday?
1) 2 : 1 2) 3 : 1 3) 1 : 2
4) 1 : 4 5) Cannot be determined

14. If the total work done by Ejaz is four times the work done by Anushka and the time taken by Ejaz to do his work on Friday is 2 hours more than the time taken by Anushka to do her work on the same day, then what is the sum of time taken by both of them to complete their work on Saturday?
1) 11 hours 2) 14 hours 3) 16 hours
4) 12 hours 5) 17 hours

15. The sum of time taken by Ejaz and Pavitra in completing their work individually is 11 hours. If it is given that total

amount of work done by them is 63 units together (sum of work done by both of them), then what is the ratio of the time taken by Pavitra to that by Ejaz on Sunday to do their work?
1) 3 : 2 2) 1 : 4 3) 3 : 7
4) 3 : 5 5) Cannot be determined

16. If it is given that the time taken by Pavitra to do her work on Saturday is less than the time taken by her to do her work on Friday by 1 hour and 30 minutes, then what is the time taken by her to do her work on Sunday?
1) 2 hours 2) 4 hours 3) 3 hours
4) 8 hours 5) None of the given options

17. If the amount of work done by Mukul, Pavitra and Sumit on each day is 15, 15 and 16 units respectively, then what is the average of the time taken by the three of them to complete their work on Sunday?
1) 4 hours 2) 6 hours 3) 3 hours
4) 8 hours 5) None of these

Directions (Q. 18-23): Study the given information carefully and answer the questions that follow.

A product M is sold in three shops (ie ABC, PQR and WXY). The table given below shows the selling price of product M in the three shops in each of the five different cities.

Cities	ABC	PQR	WXY
Faizabad	3150	3220	2975
Kanpur	2975	2905	3010
Puri	2800	3450	2695
Banaras	3325	2625	2730
Patiala	3150	3115	2800

Note: Marked price of product M is the same in all three stores across all five cities.

18. If the discount offered on product M at ABC in Kanpur is ₹525, then what is average discount offered on product M in WXY in all the cities together?
1) ₹446 2) None of these 3) ₹758
4) ₹568 5) ₹658

19. If the discount on product M at store ABC in Puri is ₹700, then what is the percentage of discount offered on product M in Banaras and Patiala at WXY?
1) 28% 2) 24% 3) 15%
4) 12% 5) 21%

20. If the discount offered on product M at PQR in Patiala is 11%, then what is the ratio of the sum of percentage discounts offered on product M at PQR and WXY in Puri to the sum of percentage discounts offered on product M at ABC and PQR in Banaras?
1) 13 : 12 2) Cannot be determined 3) 14 : 9
4) 10 : 11 5) 11 : 10

21. If the cost price of product M at PQR in Faizabad is 10% less than the cost price of product M at ABC in the same city and the percentage profit on selling the product M at ABC in Faizabad is $16\frac{2}{3}\%$, then what is the percentage profit on product M at PQR in Faizabad?
1) 28.51 2) 34.36 3) 32.51
4) 41.59 5) None of these

22. If the discount offered on product M at ABC in Patiala is in creased by 24% , the discount obtained is ₹204 more than the original discount . What is the marked price of product M?
1) ₹4200 2) ₹3750 3) ₹3500
4) ₹4000 5) Cannot be determined

23. In Banaras, the discount per cent offered on product M at PQR is 25%. If the discount offered on the product M at PQR had been 60% more than the present discount amount, there would have been a profit of 5%. What is the present percentage profit on product M at PQR in Banaras?
1) 33.33% 2) 27.50% 3) 12.25%
4) 37.25% 5) 31.25%

Answers and explanations

(1-5):

Sum of time taken by Devender to cover 10 km by all of the 3 modes = 145 minutes

Suppose Devender took T minutes to complete 10 km by cycling.

Time taken by Devender to cover 10 km by running = 1.5T

Time taken by Devender to cover 10 km by swimming $= 0.75 \times 1.5T = 1.125T$

So, we will have $1.5T + T + 1.125T = 145$

$\Rightarrow T = 40$ minutes

So, time taken by him to do cycling = 40 minutes

Running = 60 minutes

Swimming = 45 minutes

Time taken by Vineet for 10 km running $= 0.75 \times 60 = 45$ minutes

Swimming $= \frac{100}{75} \times 45 = 60$ minutes

Cycling $= 145 - (45 + 60) = 40$ minutes

Time taken by Sudip for 10 km running

$= \frac{100}{120} \times 60 = 50$ minutes

Cycling $= 0.72 \times 50 = 36$ minutes

Swimming $= 0.9 \times 50 = 45$ minutes

Sum of time taken by Divika for 10 km by all 3 modes $= (36 + 50 + 45) - 8 = 123$ minutes

Let time taken by Divika to complete 10 km by cycling and swimming be 6T and 7T respectively.
Time taken by Divika to cover 10 km by running $= 1.25 \times 6T = 7.5T$
Now, $6T + 7.5T + 7T = 123 \Rightarrow T = 6$ minutes
So, time taken by her in 10 km by cycling = 36 minutes
Time taken by her in 10 km by running = 45 minutes
Time taken by her in 10 km by swimming = 42 minutes
Time taken by Reena in 10 km by cycling

$= \frac{100}{160} \times 40 = 25$ minutes

Time taken by Reena in 10 km by running
$= 1.2 \times 25 = 30$ minutes
Time taken by Reena in 10 km by swimming
$= 1.28 \times 25 = 32$ minutes
Tabulising all the information:

Person	Cycling	Running	Swimming
Vineet	40	45	60
Sudip	36	50	45
Devender	40	60	45
Divika	36	45	42
Reena	25	30	32

1. 4; Sudip's cycling efficiency increases by 80%, running efficiency by 100% and swimming efficiency by 62%, Thus, distance covered in 1 minute of cycling

$= 1.8 \times \frac{1}{36} \times 10 = 0.5$ km

Running $= 2 \times \frac{1}{50} \times 10 = 0.4$ km

Swimming $= 1.62 \times \frac{1}{45} \times 10 = 0.36$ km

Total time taken for 18 km by each mode

$= \frac{18}{0.5} + \frac{18}{0.4} + \frac{18}{0.36} = 131$ minutes

Total time taken by Divika to cover 20 km by each mode $= 2 \times (36 + 45 + 42) = 246$ minutes
$\therefore$ Required difference
$= 246 - 131 = 115$ minutes

2. 1; Time taken by A to cover 10 km by cycling $= 1.25 \times 40$ = 50 minutes

In 1 minute he covers $\frac{1}{50} \times 10 = \frac{1}{5}$ km
Time taken by B for 10 km by swimming
$= 1.5 \times 32 = 48$ minutes

In 1 minute, B covers $\frac{1}{48} \times 10 = \frac{5}{24}$ km
Total distance covered by A in 1 hour of cycling, 30 minutes of running and 20 minutes of swimming

$= (60 + 30 + 20) \times \frac{1}{5} = 22$ km

Total distance covered by B in 1 hour of cycling, 36 minutes of running and 24 minutes of swimming

$= (60 + 36 + 24) \times \frac{5}{24} = 25$ km

$\Rightarrow$ Total distance covered $= 22 + 25 = 47$ km

3. 1; Distance covered by Vineet in 1 minute by cycling

$= \frac{1}{40} \times 10 = \frac{1}{4}$

Distance covered by Vineet by cycling in 36 minutes

$= 36 \times \frac{1}{4} = 9$ km

Distance covered by Vineet by running in 63 minutes

$= 63 \times \frac{10}{45} = 14$ km

Distance covered by Vineet by swimming in 42 minutes

$= 42 \times \frac{10}{60} = 7$ km

Total distance covered $= 9 + 14 + 7 = 30$ km
Similarly, distance covered by Devender
$= 7 + 23 + 6 = 36$ km

$\therefore$ Required percentage $= \frac{36}{30} \times 100 = 120\%$

4. 5; Required ratio $= 25 : 60 = 5 : 12$

5. 3; Required percentage $= \frac{36 + 45 + 42}{40 + 45 + 60} \times 100 = \frac{123}{145} \times 100$

$= 84.82\% \approx 85\%$

(6-11):

Section X:
Let number of small jeans = S,
Medium jeans = M and Large jeans = L

$P(S) = \frac{1}{3}, P(M) = \frac{1}{5}$

So, $P(L) = 1 - \frac{1}{3} - \frac{1}{5} = \frac{7}{15}$
Given, $L = 20 + S$
Let total number of jeans = T

Now, $P(S) = \frac{S}{T} = \frac{1}{3}$ and $P(L) = \frac{L}{T} = \frac{7}{15}$

So, $\frac{20 + S}{T} = \frac{7}{15} \Rightarrow \frac{20}{T} + \frac{S}{T} = \frac{7}{15}$

$T = 20 \times \frac{15}{2} = 150$

Thus, $S = 150 \times \frac{1}{3} = 50$

$H = 150 \times \frac{1}{5} = 30$ and $L = \frac{150 \times 7}{15} = 70$

Section Y: T = 120; Given, $2M = S + L$
So, $T = S + M + L = 2M + M = 3M$
$\Rightarrow 120 = 3M \Rightarrow M = 40$

$P(M) = \frac{M}{T} = \frac{M}{3M} = \frac{1}{3}$
Also, $P(S) : P(M) = 3 : 4$

$P(S) = \frac{3}{4} \times \frac{1}{3} = \frac{1}{4}$

Thus, $S = 120 \times \frac{1}{4} = 30$

$\Rightarrow P(L) = 1 - \frac{1}{3} - \frac{1}{4} = \frac{5}{12} \Rightarrow L = 120 \times \frac{5}{12} = 50$

Section Z: Total number of small jeans in section Z $= 90 - 50 - 30 = 10$

Total number of jeans $= \frac{1}{2} \times 120 = 60$

$\Rightarrow P(S) = \frac{10}{60} = \frac{1}{6} \Rightarrow P(L) + P(M) = 1 - \frac{1}{6} = \frac{5}{6}$ ... (i)

Given $P(L) = \frac{1}{6} + P(M)$ ... (ii)

Adding (i) and (ii), $2P(L) = 1 \Rightarrow P(L) = \frac{1}{2} \Rightarrow \frac{L}{60} = \frac{1}{2}$

$\Rightarrow L = 30$

So, $M = 60 - 10 - 30 = 20$

Tabulising all the information:

Section	Small	Medium	Large	Total
X	50	30	70	150
Y	30	40	50	120
Z	10	20	30	60

6. 1; Probability of getting medium jeans in section Z reduces by $\frac{1}{12}$.

So, new $P(M) = \frac{1}{3} - \frac{1}{12} = \frac{1}{4}$

Now, $\frac{20}{60+k} = \frac{1}{4} \Rightarrow 60 + k = 80 \Rightarrow k = 20$

7. 5; Required probability

$= [P(S) \text{ in section X}] \times [P(S) \text{ in section Y}]$

$\times [P(S) \text{ in section Z}] = \frac{1}{3} \times \frac{1}{4} \times \frac{1}{6} = \frac{1}{72}$

8. 2; Total number of jeans $= 150 + 120 + 60 = 330$

9. 2; **In shopping basket:**

Small jeans $= \frac{3}{5} \times 50 = 30$

Medium jeans $= 40$

Large jeans $= \frac{1}{3} \times 30 = 10$

Total $= 30 + 40 + 10 = 80$

$\therefore$ Required probability $= \frac{^{30}C_3}{^{80}C_3} = \frac{203}{4108}$

10. 4; Required difference $= (50 + 30) - (30 + 40)$

$= 80 - 70 = 10$

11. 1; Required percentage

$= \frac{\frac{30+40+20}{3}}{\frac{70+50+30}{3}} \times 100 = \frac{90}{150} \times 100 = 60\%$

12. 3; Time taken by Anushka on Saturday

$= \frac{12}{2 \times 3} = \frac{12}{6} = 2$ hours

Time taken by Ejaz on Saturday

$= \frac{12}{6 \times 2} \times 3 = 3$ hours

Time taken by Sumit on Saturday

$= \frac{12}{9} = 1$ hour 20 minutes

Time taken by Pavitra on Saturday

$= \frac{12}{10} = 1$ hours 12 minutes

Time taken by Mukul on Saturday

$= \frac{12}{1} = 12$ hours

$\therefore$ Reqd sum = 2 + 3 + 1 hour 20 minutes + 1 hour 12 minutes + 12 hours

= 19 hours 32 minutes

13. 3; Time taken by Anushka on Sunday

$= 66\frac{2}{3}\%$ of 6 hours $= 4$ hours

Total work $= 6 \times 2 = 12$ units

Work done by Anushka on Saturday

$= \frac{2}{1} \times 3 = 6$ units/hour

Time taken to do work on Saturday

$= \frac{12}{6} = 2$ hours

$\therefore$ Reqd ratio $= 2 : 4 = 1 : 2$

14. 2; Let total work done by Anushka = W units

Then total work done by Ejaz = 4W units

As per information given, $\frac{4W}{6} - \frac{W}{2} = 2$

$\Rightarrow 4W - 3W = 2 \times 6 = 12 \Rightarrow W = 12$ units

$\Rightarrow 4W = 48$ units

Time taken by Anushka on Saturday

$= \frac{12}{2 \times 3} = 2$ hours

Time taken by Ejaz on Saturday

$= \frac{48}{\frac{6}{3} \times 2} = 12$ hours

$\therefore$ Reqd sum $= 12 + 2 = 14$ hours

15. 1; Let time taken by Ejaz = T hours

Then time taken Pavitra = (11 – T) hours

As per provided information,

$6T + 5(11 - T) = 63 \Rightarrow T = 8$ hours

Time taken by Ejaz on Sunday

$= 8 \times \frac{50}{100} = 4$ hours

Time taken by Pavitra on Sunday

$= (11-8) \times \frac{200}{100} = 6$ hours

$\therefore$ Reqd ratio = 6 : 4 = 3 : 2

16. 5; Let total time taken by Pavitra to do her work on Friday by N hours.

Then, time taken on Saturday = (N – 1.5) hours

Now, $5N = (N-1.5) \times \frac{5}{1} \times 2 \Rightarrow 5N = 10N - 15$

$\Rightarrow N = 3$ hours

Time taken on Sunday = $3 \times \frac{200}{100} = 6$ hours

17. 5; Time taken by Mukul on Friday = $\frac{15}{3} = 5$ hours

Time taken by Mukul on Sunday = $\frac{60}{100} \times 5 = 3$ hours

Time taken by Pavitra on Friday = $\frac{15}{5} = 3$ hours

Time taken by Pavitra on Sunday = $\frac{200}{100} \times 3 = 6$ hours

Time taken by Sumit on Friday = $\frac{16}{4} = 4$ hours

Time taken by Sumit on Sunday = $\frac{125}{100} \times 4 = 5$ hours

$\therefore$ Reqd average = $\frac{3+6+5}{3} = \frac{14}{3}$ hours

18. 5; MP of product M = 2975 + 525 = 3500

Discount offered at WXY in Faizabad

= 3500 – 2975 = 525

Discount offered at WXY in Kanpur

= 3500 – 3010 = 490

Discount offered at WXY in Puri

= 3500 – 2695 = 805

Discount offered at WXY in Banaras

= 3500 – 2730 = 770

Discount offered at WXY in Patiala

= 3500 – 2800 = 700

$\therefore$ Reqd average = $\frac{525+490+805+770+700}{5} = \frac{3290}{5}$

= ₹658

19. 5; MP of product M = 2800 + 700 = ₹3500

Total MP of product M at WXY in Banaras and Patiala

= 3500 + 3500 = 7000

Total SP = 2730 + 2800 = ₹5530

$\therefore$ Required % discount offered

$= \frac{7000-5530}{7000} \times 100 = 21\%$

20. 5; MP of product M = $\frac{3115}{89} \times 100$ = ₹3500

Required % discount offered at PQR (Puri)

$= \frac{3500-3150}{3500} \times 100 = 10\%$

Required% discount offered at WXY (Puri)

$= \frac{3500-2695}{3500} \times 100 = 23\%$

Required % discount offered at ABC (Banaras)

$= \frac{3500-3325}{3500} \times 100 = 5\%$

Required % discount offered at PQR (Banaras)

$= \frac{3500-2625}{3500} \times 100 = 25\%$

$\therefore$ Reqd rate = (10 + 23) : (5 + 25)

= 33 : 30 = 11 : 10

21. 3; Let CP of product M at ABC in Faizabad = 10n

CP of product M at PQR in Faizabad = 9n

SP of product M at ABC

$= 10n + 16\frac{2}{3}\%$ of $10n = 10n + \frac{10n}{6} = \frac{70n}{6} = 3150 \Rightarrow n = 270$

$\Rightarrow$ CP of product M at PQR = 9n = 9 × 270 = 2430

Required % profit = $\frac{3220-2430}{2430} \times 100 = 32.51\%$

22. 4; Let discount offered initially on product M be D.

Now, $\frac{24D}{100} = 204 \Rightarrow D = 850$

MP of product M = 3150 + 850 = ₹4000

23. 5; MP of product M = $\frac{2625}{75} \times 100$ = ₹3500

Discount = 3500 – 2625 = 875

If this discount had been 60% more, ie $875 \times \frac{160}{100} = 1400$,

then SP = 3500 – 1400 = 2100

When there is 5% profit $\Rightarrow$ CP = $2100 \times \frac{100}{105}$ = ₹2000

$\therefore$ % profit = $\frac{2625-2000}{2000} \times 100 = 31.25\%$

Practice Set 43

Directions (Q. 1-6): Seven car manufacturing companies produce a certain number of cars in the first quarter of the year 2019 – January to March. Some of these cars are found to have defects in them.

The Bar graph given below shows the per cent of non-defective cars manufactured by these seven companies out of the total cars manufactured.

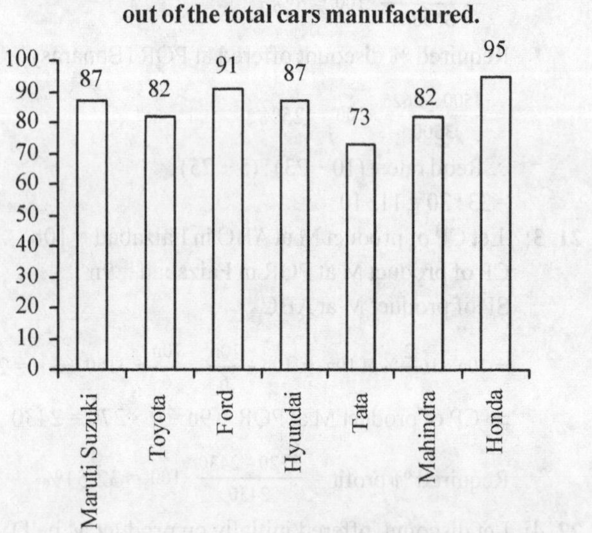

1. If the number of defective cars produced by Toyota in the first quarter of 2019 is 10080 and the number of total cars produced by Mahindra is $14\frac{2}{7}\%$ more than the total number of cars produced by Toyota, then what is the number of non-defective cars produced by Mahindra in the first quarter of 2019?
   1) 52480 2) 64000 3) 11520
   4) 55860 5) 44820
2. The no. of defective cars produced by Toyota is 7020 more than the no. of defective cars produced by Ford and the total no. of cars produced by Honda is 11000 less than the sum of the total no. of cars produced by Toyota and Ford. If it is given that the ratio of the total no. of cars produced by Toyota to that by Hyundai is 2 : 3 and the difference between them is 28000, then what is the number of defective cars produced by Honda?
   1) 9250 2) 1640 3) 4680 4) 3950 5) 1250
3. What is the ratio of the no. of defective cars produced by Maruti Suzuki to that by Honda, if the ratio of non-defective cars produced by them is 87 : 79?
   1) Cannot be determined 2) 247 : 79 3) 231 : 79
   4) 245 : 83 5) 79 : 247
4. If the no. of non-defective cars produced by Hyundai is 61470 more than the no. of defective cars produced by Tata and the ratio of the no. of defective cars produced by Tata to that by Hyundai is 387 : 364, then what is the sum of the total no. of cars produced by Hyundai and Tata?
   1) 113000 2) 105000 3) 91000
   4) 162000 5) 127000
5. It is given that the total no. of non-defective cars produced by Mahindra and Toyota in the first quarter of 2019 is 2460. What could be the maximum number of non-defective cars produced by Toyota in the same time period?
   1) 3000 2) 2289 3) 2419
   4) 2950 5) Cannot be determined
6. If the ratio of the no. of cars produced by Mahindra to that by Ford is 32 : 17 and the difference between the number of non-defective cars produced by Mahindra and that by Ford is 21540, then the no. of defective cars produced by Ford is how much per cent less than the no. of defective cars produced by Mahindra?
   1) 72.80% 2) 73.43% 3) 56.43%
   4) 69.29% 5) 43.73%

Directions (Q. 7-11): Study the following information carefully and answer the questions that follow.

The present age of Hrithik is half of the present age of his father and 5 years ago he was (P) of his father's age. Hrithik will be 28 years after 3 years. Hrithik and his father invested in a business in the ratio of 2 : 3. Hrithik invested some money for 4 months and his father invested for (Q) months. Out of the total profit of ₹2720, profit share of Hrithik's father was ₹160 more than the profit share of Hrithik. Hrithik invested half of the profit he got at simple interest for two years and the other half at compound interest, both at (R)% for the same time period. The difference between the interest obtained in the two investments is ₹14.4. From the amount which Hrithik's father obtained as profit, he started a business of manufacturing toy trains. The labour cost of manufacturing is $\frac{1}{3}$ of the profit and apart from labour cost, there are two other costs, viz raw material and transportation cost, which are in the ratio of 1:1. With that amount he manufactured 20 toy trains. If he wants to earn a profit of 20% on selling all the toy trains that he manufactured then selling price of one toy train is (S). The cost of transportation of four toy trains is (T).

7. What will come in place of P?
1) $\frac{4}{9}$ 2) $\frac{1}{2}$ 3) $\frac{3}{5}$ 4) $\frac{1}{3}$ 5) $\frac{4}{7}$

8. What will come in place of Q?
1) 8 2) 4 3) 3 4) 9 5) 5

9. What will come in the place of R?
1) 10 2) 20 3) 12 4) 15 5) 8

10. What will come in the place of S?
1) ₹72 2) ₹86.4 3) ₹82.6 4) ₹84.6 5) ₹76.2

11. What will come in the place of T?
1) ₹84 2) ₹112 3) ₹480 4) ₹72 5) ₹96

Directions (Q. 12-14): Study the following information carefully and answer the questions given below:

Two persons Raghu and Raman started travelling from point P in their cars separately in the same direction. Raman covers twice the distance covered by Raghu in the same time period. Two hours later, Rishi also starts from point P in his car in the same direction as Raghu and Raman. He overtakes Raman exactly 6 hours and 40 minutes after he overtakes Raghu.

12. If the speed of Raghu's car is 40 kmph, then what is the speed of Rishi's car?
1) 135 kmph 2) 120 kmph 3) 80 kmph
4) 100 kmph 5) Cannot be determined

13. What is the distance covered by Rishi's car till the time it overtakes Raman's car if the speed of Raghu's car is 40 kmph?
1) 400 km 2) 800 km 3) 625 km
4) 900 km 5) Cannot be determined

14. The moment Rishi's car overtakes Raghu's car, Raman increases the speed of his car by 10 kmph. If it is given that the speed of Raghu's car is 40 kmph, then in how much more time will Rishi overtake Raman's car?
1) 8 hours 20 minutes 2) 6 hours 40 minutes
3) None of these 4) 4 hours 30 minutes
5) 5 hours 20 minutes

Directions (Q. 15-19): Study the following information carefully and answer the questions given below:

A 21-member squad is announced from country ABC for the ICC Cricket World Cup tournament. The squad announced consists of 7 batsmen, 5 bowlers, 3 wicket-keepers, 4 batting all-rounders and 2 bowling all-rounders. A team of 11 players needs to be chosen for every match of the tournament. The playing team will include all the five types of players. The minimum and maximum number of different types of players that can be chosen are given as under:

Players	Number of players	
	Minimum	Maximum
Batsman	3	6
Bowlers	2	4
Wicket-keeper	1	1
All-rounder (Batting)	1	2
All-rounder (Bowling)	1	2

15. If the number of batting all-rounders and bowling all-rounders needed to be included in the team are equal and the number of bowlers and batsmen are three and five times respectively of the number of batting all-rounders to be included, then in how many ways can the team be formed?
1) 10050 2) 1250 3) 5040
4) 5850 5) Cannot be determined

16. The number of batsmen to be included in the team is 2 more than the number of bowlers to be included in the team. If it is given that maximum possible number of bowling all-rounders are to be included in the team, then in how many ways can the team be formed?
1) 6300 2) 5250 3) 3012 4) 7200 5) 5040

17. If the number of batsmen to be included in the team is not less than the number of bowlers in the team and the number of bowlers in the team is more than the number of all-rounders (including both bowling and batting all-rounders) in the team, then in how many ways can the team be formed?
1) 4200 2) 5040 3) 8460
4) 9240 5) Cannot be determined

18. What is the difference between the number of ways in which the maximum number of batsmen are included in the team and the number of ways in which the maximum number of bowlers are included in the team?
1) 16820 2) 12600 3) 10980
4) 8830 5) None of these

19. Samrat Kohli and ML Gony are two best batsmen available in the team who hold top two spots in ICC World rankings for batsmen and it is necessary for them to play as it is the Finals of the tournament. Similarly, Jasprit Bumrah is the bowler available in the team who holds top spot in bowlers' ICC World ranking and it is necessary for him to play in the Finals. If it is given that the maximum possible number of all-rounders (both batting and bowling all-rounders) have to play the Finals and the number of batsmen to be played should be more than the number of bowlers to be played in the team, then in how many ways can the team to play the Finals be selected?

1) 3120 2) 720 3) 5040
4) 1080 5) None of these

Directions (Q. 20-22): Study the given information carefully and answer the questions that follow:

A box contains three types of fruits – Apple, Mango and Orange. The average number of these three fruits is 13. The number of mangoes is 3 more than the number of apples in the box. The number of oranges in the box is 7.5 more than the average number of apples and mangoes in the box.

20. If three fruits are drawn at random, what is the probability that all of them are the same fruit?

1) $\frac{795}{9139}$ 2) $\frac{1120}{2389}$ 3) $\frac{1120}{9139}$
4) Cannot be determined 5) None of these

21. If three fruits are drawn at random from the box, then what is the probability that not all of them are of the same colour?

1) $\frac{1120}{9139}$ 2) $\frac{8019}{9139}$ 3) $\frac{1120}{8019}$
4) $\frac{3569}{9139}$ 5) None of these

22. It is given that one more variety of fruits – Chikoo – is added in the box and the number of Chikoos is 1.5 more than the average number of four kinds of fruits in the box. Now, if 5 fruits are drawn at random, 2 of which are oranges, then in how many ways can these five fruits be picked?

1) 1092420 2) 486840 3) 56590
4) 948600 5) 96390

Answers and explanations

1. 1; Number of defective cars produced by Toyota = 10080

Total no. of cars produced by Toyota

$= \frac{10080}{18} \times 100 = 56000$

No. of cars produced by Mahindra = $56000 + 14\frac{2}{7}\%$ of $56000 = 56000 + 56000 \times \frac{1}{7}$

$56000 + 8000 = 64000$

The no. of non-defective cars produced by Mahindra

$= \frac{82}{100} \times 64000 = 52480$

2. 4; $(3-2=)\ 1 \equiv 28000 \therefore 2 \equiv 56000$

Now, total no. of cars produced by Toyota = 56000

The no. of defective cars produced by Toyota

$= 56000 \times \frac{18}{100} = 10080$

The no. of defective cars produced by Ford

$= 10080 - 7020 = 3060$

Total no. of cars produced by Ford

$= \frac{3060}{9} \times 100 = 34000$

Total no. of cars produced by Honda

$= 34000 + 56000 - 11000 = 79000$

Defective cars produced by Honda

$79000 \times \frac{(100-95)}{100} = 79000 \times \frac{5}{100} = 3950$

3. 2; Reqd ratio $= \frac{87}{87} \times 13 : \frac{79}{95} \times 5 = 247 : 79$

4. 5; Let H and T be the total no. of cars produced by Hyundai and Tata respectively.

Now, according to the question,

$$\frac{\frac{13}{100}H}{\frac{27T}{100}} = \frac{364}{387}$$

$$\Rightarrow \frac{13H}{27T} = \frac{364}{387} \Rightarrow \frac{H}{T} = \frac{84}{43}$$

$\Rightarrow H = 84n$ and $T = 43n$; where n is any natural no.

Also, $\frac{87}{100} \times (84n) - \frac{27}{100} \times (43n) = 61470$

$$\Rightarrow \frac{7308n - 1161n}{100} = 61470 \Rightarrow n = 1000$$

$\therefore$ Reqd sum $= 127 \times 1000 = 127000$

5. 3; Let total cars produced by Mahindra and Toyota by M and T respectively.

Non-defective cars produced by them

$= 82M + 82T = 2460 \times 100 \therefore M + T = 3000$

(Total cars produced by them)

Now, for Mahindra the ratio of defective to non-defective cars produced is $18 : 82 = 9 : 41$

Hence, for Toyota to produce the maximum cars Mahindra should produce the least no. of cars. The least no. of cars that Mahindra can produce is $41 + 9 = 50$

In that case, no. of cars produced by Toyota

$= 3000 - 50 = 2950$

Max non-defective cars produced by Toyota

$= \frac{82}{100} \times 2950 = 2419$

6. 2;

	Mahindra		Ford
Production	32	:	17
Defective	32 × 18	:	17 × 9
	64	:	17

$\therefore$ Reqd % $= \frac{64-17}{64} \times 100 = \frac{47}{64} \times 100$

$= 73.4375\% \approx 73.43\%$

Another approach:

According to the question,

$(82\% \text{ of } 32 - 91\% \text{ of } 17) \equiv 21540$

$\Rightarrow (2624 - 1547 =)\ 1077 \equiv 21540 \times 100$

$1 \equiv \frac{21540 \times 100}{1077} = 2000$

$\therefore$ Number of defective cars produced by Mahindra
$= (100 - 82)\%$ of $32 \times 2000 = 18\%$ of $64000 = 11520$

Again, number of defective cars produced by Ford
$= 9\%$ of $17 \times 2000 = 9 \times 340 = 3060$

$\therefore$ Reqd % less $= \frac{11520 - 3060}{11520} \times 100$

$= \frac{8460}{11520} \times 100 = 73.43\%$

7. 1; Present age of Hrithik $= 28 - 3 = 25$ years
His father's present age $= 25 \times 2 = 50$ years
Now, 5 years ago, Hrithik's age
$= 25 - 5 = 20$ years
$\therefore$ His father's age $= 50 - 5 = 45$ years
Now according to question, $20 = P \times 45$

$P = \frac{20}{45} = \frac{4}{9}$

8. 3; Let Hrithik's father get a profit of N. Then, Hrithik's share of profit $=$ ₹$(N - 160)$
Also $N + N - 160 = 2720 \Rightarrow 2N = 2880$
$\therefore N = 1440$
Hrithik's profit $= 1440 - 160 = 1280$

Now, $\frac{2 \times 4}{3 \times Q} = \frac{1280}{1440}$

$\therefore Q = \frac{8 \times 1440}{3 \times 1280} = 3$ months

9. 4; Hrithik's profit $= 1280$

Amount invested in each scheme $= \frac{1280}{2} =$ ₹640

$\therefore$ Difference $= \frac{PR^2}{(100)^2} \Rightarrow 14.4 = \frac{640 \times R^2}{100 \times 100}$

$\therefore R^2 = \frac{14.4 \times 100 \times 100}{640} = 225 \therefore R = 15\%$

10. 2; Profit share of Hrithik's father $=$ ₹1440, which is equal to cost price of 20 toy trains.

So, CP of 1 toy train $= \frac{1440}{20} =$ ₹72

SP of 1 toy train $= 72 \times \frac{120}{100} =$ ₹86.4

11. 5; Cost of transportation for 20 toy trains

$= 1440 \times \frac{2}{3} \times \frac{1}{2} = 480$

Cost of transportation for 4 toy trains

$= \frac{480}{20} \times 4 =$ ₹96

12. 4;

	Raghu		Raman
Ratio of speed	1	:	2
	40	:	80

Now, according to the question,

$\frac{R \times 80}{R - 80} - \frac{2 \times 40}{R - 40} = 6\frac{2}{3} = \frac{20}{3}$

$\Rightarrow \frac{8}{R - 80} - \frac{4}{R - 40} = \frac{1}{3} \Rightarrow \frac{8}{N - 80} - \frac{4}{N - 40} = \frac{1}{3}$

$\Rightarrow 8N - 320 - 4N + 320 = (N - 80)(N - 40)$

$\Rightarrow 12N = N^2 - 120N + 3200$

$\Rightarrow N^2 - 132N + 3200 = 0$

Step I – 100 –32
Step II 100, 32
But $N \neq 32$ [$N > 40$ and > 80, as it overtook both cars].
$\therefore N = 100$ kmph

13. 2; Time taken by Rishi to overtake Raman $= \frac{2 \times 80}{100 - 80}$
$= 8$ hours
$\therefore$ Distance $= 100 \times 8 = 800$ km

14. 3; Time taken by Rishi to overtake Raghu $\frac{80}{100 - 40}$

$= \frac{80}{60} = 1\frac{1}{3}$ hours $= \frac{4}{3}$ hours

$= 1$ hour 20 minutes
Distance between Rishi and Raman

$= 80 \times 2 + 20 \times \frac{4}{3} = 160 + \frac{80}{3}$ km

Relative speed $= 100 - 90 = 10$ kmph

$\therefore$ Reqd time $= \frac{160 + \frac{80}{3}}{10} = \frac{480 + 80}{30} = \frac{560}{30} = \frac{56}{3}$ hours

$= 18$ hours 40 m

15. 3; Let no. of batting all-rounders included in the team be x
No. of bowling all-rounders $= x$
No. of bowlers $= 3x$
No. of batsmen $= 5x$
As per information given,
$x + x + 3x + 5x + 1 = 11 \Rightarrow 10x = 10 \Rightarrow x = 1$
Thus, reqd no. of ways $= {}^2C_1 \times {}^4C_1 \times {}^3C_1 \times {}^5C_3 \times {}^7C_5$
$= 2 \times 4 \times 3 \times 10 \times 21 = 5040$

16. 1; Total no. of players in team should be 11. There must be 2 bowling all-rounders (maximum possible) and 1 wicket-keeper.)
Remaining players $= 11 - 3 = 8$. If we take 3 bowlers, there will be $(3 + 2 =)$ 5 batsmen. Then no place will be left for a batting all-rounder.
So, the bowlers should be in team $= 2$
No. of batsmen $= 2 + 2 = 4$
No. of wicketkeepers $= 1$
No. of batting all rounders $= 2$
No. of bowling all rounders $= 2$
Thus, reqd no. of ways $= {}^5C_2 \times {}^7C_4 \times {}^3C_1 \times {}^4C_2 \times {}^2C_2$
$= 10 \times 35 \times 3 \times 6 \times 1 = 6300$

17. 4; **Possible combinations:**

	No. of batsmen	≥	No. of bowlers	>	All rounders (both)	WK
(i)	4		4		1 + 1	1
(ii)	5		3		1 + 1	1
(iii)	4		4		2 + 1	(ruled out)

Case (iii) is ruled out become no place remain for wicket keeper.

Now,

(i) Bowlers = 3 and Batsmen = 5

$\therefore$ No. of ways = ${}^4C_1 \times {}^2C_1 \times {}^3C_1 \times {}^5C_3 \times {}^7C_5$

$= 4 \times 2 \times 3 \times 10 \times 21 = 5040$

(ii) Bowlers = 4 and Batsmen = 4

No. of ways = ${}^4C_1 \times {}^2C_1 \times {}^3C_1 \times {}^5C_4 \times {}^7C_4$

$= 4 \times 2 \times 3 \times 5 \times 35 = 4200$

$\therefore$ Total no. of ways = 5040 + 4200 = 9240

18. 5; Player distribution when maximum batsmen are playing will be: Batsmen = 6, Bowlers = 2, WK = 1, Allrounder (Batting) = 1

All rounder Bowling = 1

So, no. of ways = ${}^7C_6 \times {}^5C_2 \times {}^3C_1 \times {}^4C_1 \times {}^2C_1$

$= 7 \times 10 \times 3 \times 4 \times 2 = 1680$

Player distribution when maximum bowlers are playing will be: Bowlers = 4, WK = 1

Now, three cases arise:

(1) Batsmen = 4, Batting all rounders = 1, Bowling all-rounders = 1

No. of ways = ${}^5C_1 \times {}^3C_1 \times {}^7C_4 \times {}^4C_1 \times {}^2C_1$

$= 5 \times 3 \times 35 \times 4 \times 2 = 4200$

(2) Batsmen = 3, Batting all rounders = 2

Bowling all rounders = 1

No. of ways = ${}^5C_4 \times {}^3C_1 \times {}^7C_3 \times {}^4C_2 \times {}^2C_1$

$= 5 \times 3 \times 35 \times 6 \times 2 = 6300$

(3) Batsmen = 3, Batting all rounders = 1, Bowling all rounders = 2

No. of ways = ${}^5C_4 \times {}^3C_1 \times {}^7C_3 \times {}^4C_1 \times {}^2C_2$

$= 5 \times 3 \times 35 \times 4 \times 1 = 2100$

So, total no. of ways = 2100 + 6300 + 4200 = 12600

$\therefore$ Reqd difference = 12600 − 1680 = 10920

19. 4; As per information given, players, distribution can be done in the following way:

Batsmen = 4 Batting all-rounders = 2

Bowler = 2 Bowling all-rounders = 2

WK = 1

Hence, no. of ways = ${}^5C_2 \times {}^4C_2 \times {}^3C_1 \times {}^4C_2 \times {}^2C_2$

[As 2 batsmen and 1 bowler are fixed and they must play] = $10 \times 6 \times 3 \times 6 \times 1 = 1080$ ways

(20-22):

Let no. of apples in the box = N

No. of mangoes = N + 3

Also, no. of oranges = $\frac{N + N + 3}{2} + 7.5 = \frac{2N+3}{2} + 7.5$

Sum of these three fruits = 13 × 3 = 39

Now, $N + N + 3 + \frac{2N+3}{2} + 7.5 = 39$

$\Rightarrow \frac{2N + 2N + 6 + 2N + 3 + 15}{2} = 39$

$\Rightarrow 6N + 24 = 78 \Rightarrow 6N = 54 \therefore N = 9$

So, no. of apples = 9

Mangoes = 12 Oranges = 18

20. 3; No. of ways in which all of them are the same fruit

$= {}^9C_3 + {}^{12}C_3 + {}^{18}C_3 = 84 + 220 + 816 = 1120$

Total no. of ways = ${}^{39}C_3 = 9139$

$\therefore$ Probability = $\frac{1120}{9139}$

21. 2; Reqd probability = $1 - \frac{1120}{9139} = \frac{8019}{9139}$

22. 1; Let no. of Chikoos to be added be x.

Then, $\frac{9+12+18+x}{4} = x - 1.5$

$\Rightarrow 39 + x = 4x - 6 \Rightarrow 45 = 3x \Rightarrow x = 15$

Now, reqd no. of ways = ${}^{18}C_2 \times {}^{36}C_3$

$= 153 \times 7140 = 1092420$

Practice Set 44

Directions (Q. 1-5): Study the given information carefully and answer the questions that follow.

The table given below shows total production of bikes by Company ABC from 2013 to 2018.

Years	Total production of bikes
2013	26500
2014	30600
2015	49500
2016	94500
2017	90000
2018	40800

NOTE: Company ABC produces only two types of bikes – Type A and Type B.

The line graph shows percentage production of Type B bikes in excess of Type A bikes during these six years.

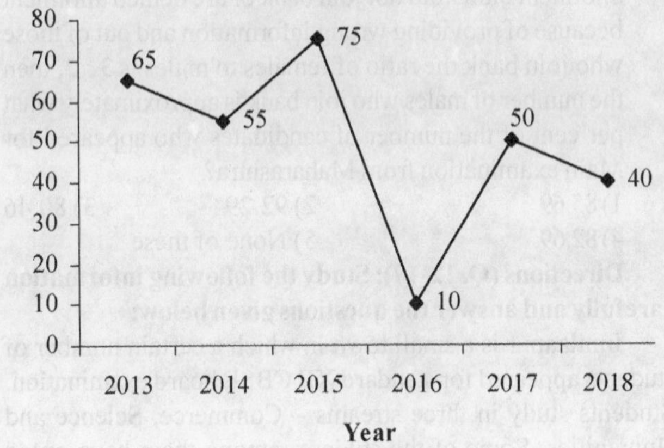

1. The number of Type A bikes produced in the year 2017 is what per cent of the total number of type B bikes produced in 2015 and 2016 together?
   1) 34.33 2) 66.66 3) 55.64
   4) 44.44 5) None of these
2. What is the ratio of the total number of Type A bikes produced in 2017 and 2018 to the number of Type B bikes produced in 2013 and 2016 together?
   1) 53 : 64 2) 66 : 53 3) 52 : 53
   4) 58 : 61 5) None of these
3. If in the year 2019, the total production of company ABC increased by 56% as compared to 2018 and the production of Type B bikes increased by 24% as compared to 2014, then by what per cent was the production of Type A bikes more in 2019 as compared to that of Type B likes in 2018?
   1) 69.44 2) 70.52 3) 54.58
   4) 41.52 5) None of these
4. The average of Type B bikes produced in 2013, 2014, 2016 and 2017 is how much more or less than the average of Type A bikes produced in 2015 and 2018?
   1) 17150 more 2) 16800 less 3) 25900 more
   4) 17150 less 5) None of these
5. In the year 2017, 12% of the total number of Type A bikes produced are found to be defective, which is 886 less than the defective Type B bikes in the same year. What is the total number of non-defective bikes produced by company ABC in the year 2017?
   1) 84074 2) 88794 3) 86528
   4) 80474 5) None of these

Directions (Q. 6-11): Study the following information carefully and answer the questions given below:

An examination for the recruitment of Probationary Officers (PO) in banks is conducted in six states. The examination is conducted in three phases – Preliminary examination, Main examination and Interview. Those candidates who appear for the examination have to clear the Preliminary examination first. Those candidates who clear the Preliminary examination are called for Main examination and those candidates who clear the Main examination are called for Interview. After conducting the Interview, a merit list is prepared in which marks of each candidate in Main examination and Interview are added up to give provisional allotment to candidates as per the vacancies reported by the bank.

The pie-chart given below shows the percentage of students appeared for Preliminary examination from each state out of total number of students appeared.

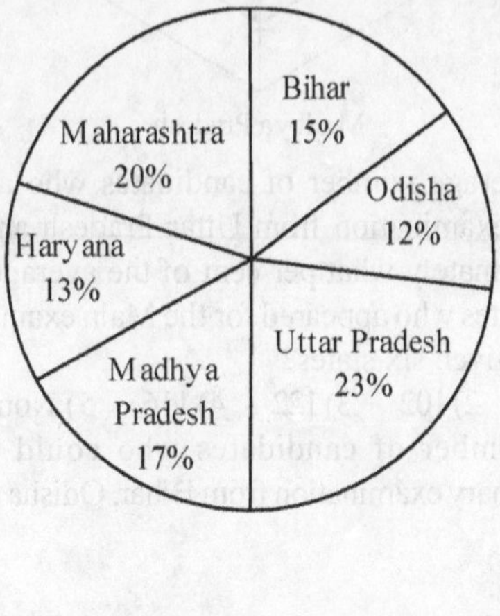

NOTE: The recruitment examination is conducted only in these 6 states across the nation and the total students who appeared for the Preliminary examination in all these states together is 12 lakhs.

The Bar graph given below shows the percentage of candidates who appeared for Mains examination out of the students who appeared for Preliminary examination from each state respectively.

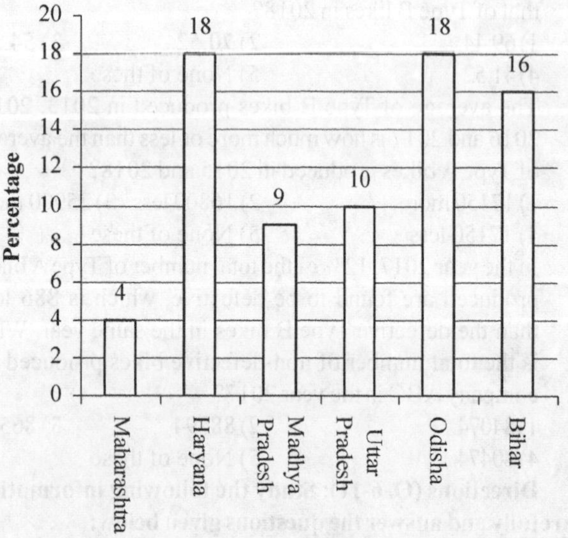

The Radar graph given below shows the percentage of candidates who are called for Interview out of the students who appeared for Main examination from each state respectively.

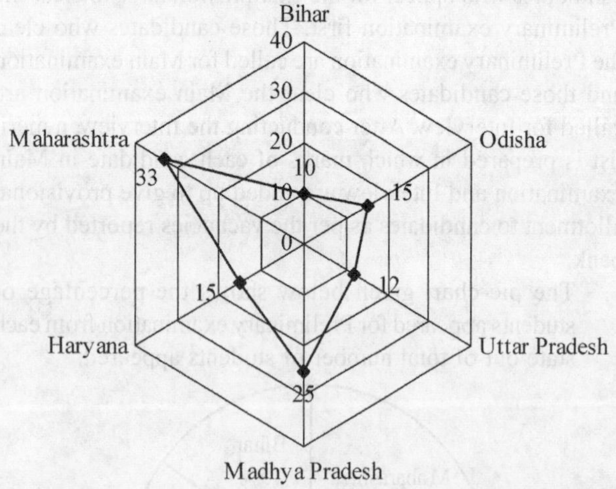

6. The average number of candidates who appeared for Mains examination from Uttar Pradesh and Odisha is approximately what per cent of the average number of candidates who appeared for the Main examination from all the given six states?
   1) 114 2) 102 3) 122 4) 116 5) None of these

7. The number of candidates who could not qualify Preliminary examination from Bihar, Odisha and Haryana is how much more than the number of candidates who could not qualify Main examination from these three states?
   1) 315230 2) 325380 3) 469020 4) 352380 5) 338240

8. If the ratio of candidates who got provisional allotment to the candidates who were called for Interview is 1 : 3 and the ratio of male to female candidates who got provisional allotment is 4 : 3, then the number of candidates who appeared for Main examination from Uttar Pradesh is approximately what times the number of female candidates who got provisional allotment?
   1) 5.5 2) 10.6 3) 9.2 4) 6.4 5) 8.8

9. What is the ratio of the number of candidates who could not qualify Preliminary examination from Maharashtra to the number of candidates who appeared for Main examination from all the six states together?
   1) 1983 : 2019 2) 1150 : 1929 3) 1920 : 1153
   4) None of the given options 5) 1153 : 1920

10. The average number of candidates who did not qualify Preliminary examination is how much more than the average number of candidates who did not qualify Main examination?
    1) 186000 2) 157555 3) 168366
    4) 154344 5) 175555

11. If 10% of the number of candidates who got provisional allotment either did not join bank or are denied allotment because of providing wrong information and out of those who join bank the ratio of females to males is 3 : 2, then the number of males who join bank is approximately what per cent of the number of candidates who appeared for Main examination from Maharashtra?
    1) 85.69 2) 92.29 3) 80.46
    4) 82.69 5) None of these

Directions (Q. 12-17): Study the following information carefully and answer the questions given below:

Jumlaapur is a small town in which a certain number of students appeared for standard XII CBSE board examination. Students study in three streams – Commerce, Science and Humanities. Some of the students among them have opted for two or three streams as well. Each standard XII student has opted for at least one stream.

68% of students study Science stream and students from Humanities only are $\frac{1}{17}$ of the students of Science stream. The number of students from both Humanities and Commerce stream but not from Science stream are 80. Students studying in only Commerce stream are 8 less than 6 times of the number of students studying in only Humanities stream. The number of students studying in only Science stream is 16 more than twice the number of students studying in only Commerce stream.

12. What is the number of students from Science stream but

not only from Science stream?
1) 360 2) 80 3) 160 4) 340 5) 240

13. What is the total number of students studying in standard XII in Jumlaapur?
1) Cannot be determined 2) 1500 3) 180
4) 1800 5) None of these

14. What is the total number of students studying in Commerce stream only?
1) Cannot be determined 2) 160 3) 460
4) 864 5) 424

15. If the number of students in Science and Commerce stream but not in Humanities is 160, then approximately what per cent of the total number of students are there in both Science and Humanities?
1) 21 2) 13 3) 11 4) 15 5) 18

16. The number of students studying in Science or Commerce stream is what per cent of the number of students studying in Science stream only or Commerce stream only?
1) 134.16 2) 136.68 3) 112.24
4) 105.56 5) 145.45

17. It is given that the number of students studying in Science and Commerce but not in Humanities is double the number of students studying in all there streams, which is two-third of the number of students studying in Science and Humanities stream and not in Commerce. Then what will be the ratio of the number of students studying in one stream only to the number of students studying in more than one stream?
1) 34 : 15 2) 34 : 11 3) 33 : 17
4) Cannot be determined 5) 11 : 34

Direction (Q. 18-21): Study the following information carefully and the answer the questions.

A cuboidal box is to be painted at the rate of ₹10 per cm². After painting the box, a certain number of identical cylinders have been kept in the box. The total number of cylinders kept in the box is 24 and after keeping all the cylinders 13440 cm³ of the volume remains vacant in the box. The width of the box is 21 cm and the ratio of its length to height is 3 : 2. An amount of ₹174720 has been incurred for filling the empty space of the cuboidal box with a substance. The perimeter of the floor of the box is 162 cm. The height of each cylinder is equal to the height of the box.

18. What is the cost of painting the surface of the box?
1) ₹55000 2) ₹96000 3) ₹85000
4) ₹9000 5) None of the given options

19. What is the diameter of each cylinder?
1) 5 cm 2) 3.5 cm 3) 12.25 cm
4) 7 cm 5) None of the given options

20. What is the cost per cm³ of the substance used to fill the empty space in the cuboidal box?
1) ₹13 2) ₹12 3) ₹17 4) ₹23 5) ₹19

21. It is mentioned that cylinders are hollow made up of a material of width 0.5 cm and are open from the top. (Assume that the thickness of the material at the bottom of the cylinders is negligible.) If these cylinders are also filled with a substance costing ₹4.9 per litre, then what is the ratio of the cost incurred in the substance used to fill the empty space of the cuboid to the cost incurred in the substance to fill the cylinders?
1) 99 : 130 2) 131 : 85 3) 130 : 99
4) 130 : 97 5) None of the given options

Answers and explanations

(1-5):

Let N = Number of Type A bikes produced by ABC in 2013 $\Rightarrow N + \frac{165N}{100} = 26500 \Rightarrow \frac{265N}{100} = 26500$

$\Rightarrow N = 10000$ and Type B bikes (2013) = 16500

Similary, calculate for every year individually in ratio terms.

Now, In 2014 Type A = $\frac{30600 \times 100}{100 + 155}$

$= 30600 \times \frac{20}{51} = 600 \times 20 = 12000$

Type B = 30600 – 12000 = 18600

In 2015, Type A = $49500 \times \frac{100}{275} = 49500 \times \frac{20}{55} = 18000$

Type B = 49500 – 18000 = 31500

In 2016, Type A = $94500 \times \frac{100}{210} = 94500 \times \frac{10}{21} = 45000$

Type B = 94500 – 45000 = 49500

In 2017, Type A = $90000 \times \frac{100}{250} = 90000 \times \frac{2}{5} = 36000$

Type B = 90000 – 36000 = 54000

In 2018, Type A = $40800 \times \frac{100}{240} = 40800 \times \frac{5}{12} = 17000$

Type B = 40800 – 17000 = 23800

Now, we can draw a table:

Years	Type A	Type B	Total
2013	10000	16500	26500
2014	12000	18600	30600
2015	18000	31500	49500
2016	45000	49500	94500
2017	36000	54000	90000
2018	17000	23800	40800

1. 4; Reqd % = $\frac{36000}{31500 + 49500} \times 100 = \frac{36000}{81000} \times 100 = 44.44\%$

2. 5; Reqd ratio = (36000 + 17000) : (16500 + 49500) = 53000 : 66000 = 53 : 66

3. 2; Total production of ABC in 2019 $= 40800 \times \frac{156}{100} = 63648$

Production of Type B bikes in 2019

$= 18600 \times \frac{124}{100} = 23064$

Type A bikes produced in 2019

$= 63648 - 23064 = 40584$

$\therefore$ Reqd % $= \frac{40584 - 23800}{23800} \times 100 = 70.52\%$

4. 1; Average Type B bikes produced in 2013, 2014, 2016 and 2017 together $= \frac{16500 + 18600 + 49500 + 54000}{4}$

$= \frac{138600}{4} = 34650$

Average Type A bikes produced in 2015 and 2018

$= \frac{18000 + 17000}{2} = \frac{35000}{2} = 17500$

Hence reqd difference $= 34650 - 17500 = 17150$ more

5. 4; Number of defective Type A Bikes in 2017 $= 36000 \times \frac{12}{100}$

$= 4320$

Number of defective Type B bikes in 2017

$= 4320 + 886 = 5206$

$\therefore$ Total non-defective bikes

$= 90000 - (4320 + 5206) = 80474$

(6-11):

In Preliminary examination, candidates who appeared from

Bihar $= \frac{15}{100} \times 1200000 = 180000$

Odisha $= \frac{12}{100} \times 1200000 = 144000$

UP $= \frac{23}{100} \times 1200000 = 276000$

Madhya Pradesh $= \frac{17}{100} \times 1200000 = 204000$

Haryana $= \frac{13}{100} \times 1200000 = 156000$

Maharashtra $= \frac{20}{100} \times 1200000 = 240000$

Candidates who cleared Preliminary examination and appeared for Main examination from Bihar

$= \frac{16}{100} \times 180000 = 28800$

Odisha $= \frac{18}{100} \times 144000 = 25920$

UP $= \frac{10}{100} \times 276000 = 27600$

Madhya Pradesh $= \frac{9}{100} \times 204000 = 18360$

Haryana $= \frac{18}{100} \times 156000 = 28080$

Maharashtra $= \frac{4}{100} \times 240000 = 9600$

Candidates called for Interview from

Bihar $= \frac{10}{100} \times 28800 = 2880$

Odisha $= \frac{15}{100} \times 25920 = 3888$

UP $= \frac{12}{100} \times 27600 = 3312$

Madhya Pradesh $= \frac{25}{100} \times 18360 = 4590$

Haryana $= \frac{15}{100} \times 28080 = 4212$

Maharashtra $= \frac{33}{100} \times 9600 = 3168$

The above calculations can be summarised in a table as:

States	Candidates appeared for Pre exam	Candidates appeared for Main exam	Candidates called for Interview
Bihar	180000	28800	2880
Odisha	144000	25920	3888
UP	276000	27600	3312
Madhya Pradesh	204000	18360	4590
Haryana	156000	28080	4212
Maharashtra	240000	9600	3168

6. 4; Average of candidates appearing for Main examination from Odisha and UP $= \frac{25920 + 27600}{2} = 26760$

Average candidates appearing for Main examination

$= \frac{28800 + 25920 + 27600 + 18360 + 28080 + 9600}{6} = 23060$

$\therefore$ Reqd % $= \frac{26760}{23060} \times 100 \approx 116\%$

7. 2; Number of candidates who could not qualify Preliminary examination from Bihar, Odisha and Haryana

$= (180000 - 28800) + (144000 - 25920) + (156000 - 28080) = 151200 + 118080 + 127920 = 397200$

No. of candidates who could not qualify Main examination from these states $= (28800 - 2880) + (25920 - 3888) + (28080 - 4212) = 71820$

$\therefore$ Reqd difference $= 397200 - 71820 = 325380$

8. 5; No. of candidates who got provisional allotment

$= \frac{2880 + 3888 + 3312 + 4590 + 4212 + 3168}{3} \times 1 = \frac{22050}{3}$

$= 7350$

Female candidates who got provisional allotment

$= \frac{7350}{7} \times 3 = 3150$

Hence required answer $= \frac{27600}{3150} = 8.76 \approx 8.8$ (approx)

9. 3; Reqd ratio $= (240000 - 9600) : (28800 + 25920 + 27600 + 18360 + 28080 + 9600) = 230400 : 138360 = 1920 : 1153$

10. 2; Average candidates who did not qualify Preliminary exam $= \frac{151200 + 118080 + 248400 + 185640 + 127920 + 230400}{6} = 176940$

Average candidates who could not qualify Main examination $= \frac{(28800 + 25920 + 27600 + 18360 + 28080 + 9600) - (2880 + 3888 + 3312 + 4590 + 4212 + 3168)}{6}$

$= \frac{138360 - 22050}{6} = 19385$

Reqd difference $= 176940 - 19385 = 157555$

11. 4; Candidates who join bank

$= \frac{90}{100} \times [2880 + 3888 + 3312 + 4590 + 9212 + 3168]$

$= \frac{90}{100} \times 22050 = 19845$

Male candidates who join bank $= \frac{19845}{5} \times 2 = 7938$

$\therefore$ Reqd % $= \frac{7938}{9600} \times 100 = 82.6875 \approx 82.69\%$

(12-17):

Let total standard 12th students in Jamlaapur be 100x.

Students in Science stream = 68x

Students from Humanities only $= \frac{68x}{17} = 4x$

Students in Commerce only $= 6(4x) - 8 = 24x - 8$

Students in both Humanities & Commerce & not in Science = 80

Students in Science only $= 2(24x - 8) + 16 = 48x$

This can be represented as

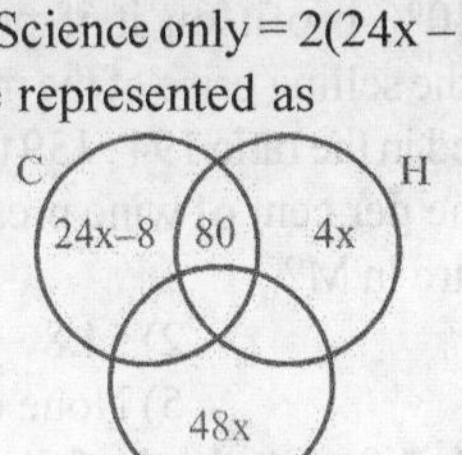

Also, $100x - [(24x - 8) + 4x + 68x] = 80 \Rightarrow x = 18$

So, the above given Venn diagram becomes

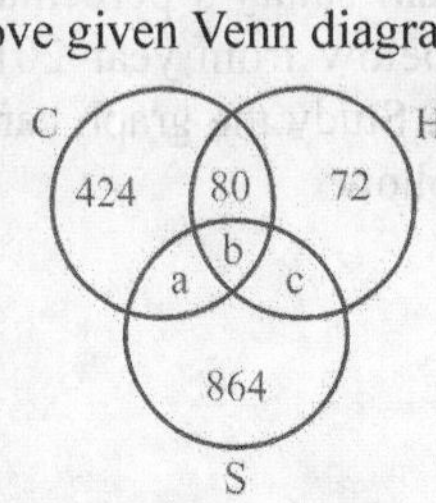

Total students = 100x = 1800

Total students in Science stream $= 68 \times 18 = 1224$

Students in Science stream only $= 48 \times 18 = 864$

12. 1; Total no. of students in Science stream = 1224

Students only in Science stream = 864

$\therefore$ Reqd answer $= 1224 - 864 = 360$

13. 4; Total students = 1800

14. 5; Students in Commerce stream only = 424

15. 3; Referring to the figure, we have a = 160

We know that, $864 + a + b + c = 1224$

$\Rightarrow 864 + 160 + b + c = 1224 \Rightarrow b + c = 200$

$\therefore$ Reqd % $= \frac{200}{1800} \times 100 = \frac{100}{9}\%$ or, $11\frac{1}{9}\% \approx 11\%$

16. 1; No. of students in Science or Commerce stream $= 1800 - 72 = 1728$

Students in Science only or Commerce only $= 424 + 864 = 1288$

$\therefore$ Reqd % $= \frac{1728}{1288} \times 100 = 134.16$

17. 2; It is given that $a = 2b$ and $b = \frac{2}{3}c \Rightarrow c = \frac{3}{2}b$

$a + b + c = 1800 - [424 + 72 + 80 + 864]$

$\Rightarrow 2b + b + \frac{3b}{2} = 360 \Rightarrow b = 80$, $a = 160$ and $c = 120$

Now, required ratio $= (864 + 72 + 424) : (120 + 80 + 80 + 160) = 1360 : 440 = 34 : 11$

(18-21):

Let length of cuboid = 3n and height of cuboid = 2n

Width = 21 cm Then, $2(21 + 3n) = 162$

$\Rightarrow 42 + 6n = 162 \Rightarrow 6n = 120 \Rightarrow n = 20$

So, length = 60 cm Height = 40 cm = Height of cylinder.

18. 5; Area of cuboid $= 2(60 \times 21 + 21 \times 40 + 60 \times 40) = 2(1260 + 840 + 2400) = 2 \times 4500 = 9000\ cm^2$

$\therefore$ Cost of painting $= 10 \times 9000 =$ ₹90000

19. 4; Volume of cuboidal box $(60 \times 40 \times 21)\ cm^3 = 50400\ cm^3$

Volume occupied by cylinders $= (50400 - 13440)\ cm^3$

$= 36960\ cm^3$ Volume of 1 cylinder $= \frac{36960}{24} = 1540\ cm^3$

Let r be the radius of each cylinder.

Then, $1540 = \frac{22}{7} r^2 \times 40$

$\Rightarrow r^2 = \frac{1540 \times 7}{40 \times 22} = 12.25$ $\therefore r = 3.5$ cm $\Rightarrow D = 7$ cm

20. 1; Reqd cost $= \left(\frac{174720}{13340}\right) =$ ₹13

21. 3; Volume of one cylinder $= \frac{22}{7} \times (3.5 - 0.5)^2 \times 40$

$= \left(\frac{22}{7} \times 9 \times 40\right) cm^3$

Volume of all cylinders $= \left(24 \times \frac{22}{7} \times 9 \times 40\right) cm^3$

Cost incurred = ₹$\left(4.9 \times 24 \times \frac{22}{7} \times 9 \times 40\right) =$ ₹133056

$\therefore$ Reqd ratio $= 174720 : 133056 = 130 : 99$

Practice Set 45

Directions (Q. 1-4): Study the given information carefully and answer the given questions:

There are 10 mixtures A, B, C, D, E, F, G, H, I and J of wine and water. The bar graph given below shows the amount of wine in the first five mixtures A, B, C, D and E as a per cent of amount of water in the last five mixtures F, G, H, I and J respectively.

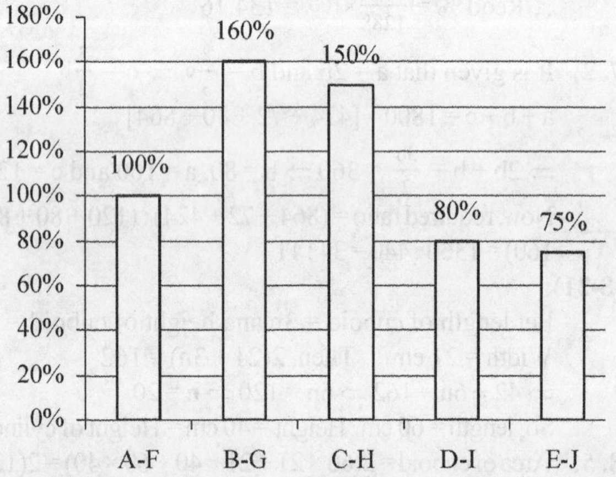

Again, the table given below shows the ratio of the amount of water in the first five mixtures A, B, C, D and E to the amount of wine in the last five mixtures F, G, H, I and J respectively.

Mixture	Ratio
A-F	1 : 1
B-G	4 : 1
C-H	2 : 1
D-I	1 : 3
E-J	7 : 10

1. The quantity of water in mixture H is 25% more than that of wine in the same mixture. Prabhjot, a dealer, mixes 50% of mixture H with $66\frac{2}{3}$ % of mixture C and names it mixture Z. If the cost price of wine is ₹50 per litre and Prabhjot sells mixture Z at ₹35 per litre and still makes a profit of ₹1015, then what is the quantity of wine in mixture C?
   1) 45 litres 2) 48 litres 3) 24 litres
   4) 30 litres 5) None of these
2. The ratio of the total amount of liquid in mixture D to that in mixture I is 4 : 7. Pranav mixes mixture D and mixture I in the ratio 4 : 7 to form a new mixture N. What is the fraction of wine in this new mixture N?
   1) $\frac{7}{11}$ 2) $\frac{239}{308}$ 3) $\frac{323}{539}$
   4) $\frac{4}{7}$ 5) Cannot be determined
3. If the quantity of wine in mixture A is 10 litres less than quantity of wine in Mixture F and the ratio of the total quantity of mixture A to the quantity of water in mixture J is 1 : 1. If the quantity of J is 80 litres more than the quantity of A and the ratio of wine to water in J is 4 : 5, then what is the difference in quantity of wine in A and the quantity of wine in J?
   1) 60 litres 2) 30 litres 3) 80 litres
   4) 45 litres 5) 35 litres
4. If a dealer mixed whole amount of mixture B and G together and sold this mixture at the cost of pure wine, then he would gain 40% profit on it if profit percentage is calculated on the selling price of the mixture. If mixture B and G are mixed in the ratio 194 : 139 to form a mixture M, then what is the per cent of wine present with respect to the total mixture in M?
   1) 45.2 2) 54.8 3) 56.3
   4) 61.3 5) None of these

Directions (Q. 5-9): Study the following information carefully and answer the questions given below:

Rimjhim's annual salary's percentage breakdown of spending is given below from year 2013 to 2018 in the following bar graph. Study the graph carefully and answer the questions that follow.

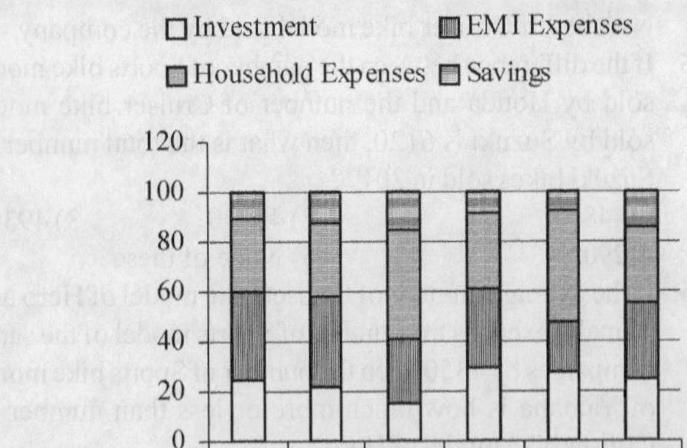

	2013	2014	2015	2016	2017	2018
Savings	10	12	15	9	8	14
Household Expenses	30	30	44	30	44	31
EMI Expenses	35	36	26	31	20	30
Investment	25	22	15	30	28	25

Year

5. If the amount invested in 2014 is $\frac{7}{18}$ of the amount invested in 2016, then what is the approximate difference between the amount spent on EMI and Household expenses in 2014, if it is given that the total income in 2016 is ₹18 lakh?
   1) ₹48000 2) ₹46000 3) ₹42000
   4) ₹57300 5) ₹420000
6. If every year there is an increase of 20% in annual salary as compared to previous year's annual salary, then what is the ratio of the average monthly salary in 2015 to the average monthly expenses on EMI in 2013?
   1) 120 : 89 2) 35 : 144 3) 88 : 23
   4) 144 : 35 5) None of these
7. If the annual EMI expenses in 2014 and annual Household expenses in 2017 are in the ratio 9 : 22, then annual amount invested in 2017 is what per cent more or less than the annual Savings and the annual Household expenses together in 2014?
   1) $33\frac{1}{3}$% 2) $66\frac{2}{3}$% 3) $50\frac{1}{3}$%
   4) $60\frac{2}{3}$% 5) $28\frac{1}{3}$%
8. In 2013, Rimjhim invested in two schemes A and B her entire money to be invested that year. Schemes A and B offer interest rates of 8% and 10% respectively. Scheme A offers compound interest and scheme B offers simple interest. If after 3 years the total interest earned by Rimjhim is ₹42180 then what is the approximate amount invested by her in scheme A if it is given that her savings in 2013 is ₹60000?
   1) ₹65000 2) ₹75000 3) ₹80000
   4) ₹70000 5) ₹60000
9. If the total annual income of Rimjhim in 2016 and 2018 is ₹30 lakhs and the sum of the amount invested in 2016 and 2018 is ₹8,10,000 then what is the ratio of savings of Rimjhim in the year 2018 to that in 2016?
   1) None of the given options
   2) 7 : 3 3) 5 : 3
   4) 9 : 4 5) 3 : 7

Directions (Q. 10–14): Read the following information carefully and answer the questions that follow.

In four different MNC companies – Infosys, TCS, IBM and Wipro – there are only two grades of working employees Grade-B and Grade-C. The ratio of the number of male Grade-B employees in TCS to the number of female Grade-B employees in Wipro is 9 : 10. The number of male Grade-B employees in TCS is $\frac{9}{10}$ times the number of female Grade-C employees in Infosys. The sum of male Grade-B employees and male Grade-C employees in Wipro is 32500, which is in the ratio of 3 : 10. The number of female Grade-B employees in Wipro is equal to the number of female Grade-B employees in IBM.

In Infosys, the total number of employees is 35000 and the total number of Grade-B employees is $\frac{2}{7}$ times of the total number of employees in that company. The number of female Grade-C employees in TCS is half of the number of male Grade-C employees in that company.

The ratio of male to female Grade-B employees in TCS is 9 : 5. The ratio of male Grade-C employees to female Grade-C employees in Infosys is 4 : 1. The total number of male employees in IBM is 40000 and number of male Grade-B employees in IBM is one-fourth of the total number of male employees in that company.

The number of female Grade-B employees in IBM is 50% of the number of female Grade-C employees in the same company. The ratio of the number of male Grade-C employees in TCS to the number of female Grade-C employees in IBM is 7 : 5 and total number of female employees in IBM in grade C is 10000.

The number of female Grade-C employees in Wipro is 50% more than female Grade-B employees in IBM. The number of male Grade-B employees in Infosys is 20% more than the number of female Grade-C employees.

10. The number of male Grade-C employees in TCS and Wipro is what per cent of the number of Grade-C employees in Infosys?
    1) 156% 2) 178% 3) 133%
    4) 150% 5) None of these
11. If it is given that 20% of Grade-B employees in IBM are

below 30 years of age and 45% of Grade-B employees are under 45 years of age, then what is the ratio of IBM Grade-B employees aged 30 to 45 years to the male Grade-C employees in TCS?
1) 56 : 15 2) 29 : 55 3) 15 : 56
4) 13 : 52 5) None of these

12. In TCS, $28\frac{4}{7}$% of male Grade-C employees left the company and joined Wipro and Infosys in the ratio of 15:17 at the same posts. What is the difference between total male Grade-C employees in Infosys and Wipro together and female Grade-B employees in the same companies?
1) 18500 2) 49000 3) 44000
4) 40000 5) 36500

13. The difference between average male Grade-C employees and average female Grade-B employees is
1) 18750 2) 18125 3) 16825 4) 15281 5) 12185

14. Total employees of which of the following companies is greater than the average of total number of employees?
1) TCS, Infosys and Wipro 2) None of the given options
3) Infosys and TCS 4) IBM, TCS and Infosys
5) IBM and Wipro

Directions (Q. 15-18): Study the given information carefully and answer the given questions:

The pie-chart given below shows the per cent of bikes sold out of total bikes sold in the year 2017 by six different bike manufacture companies.

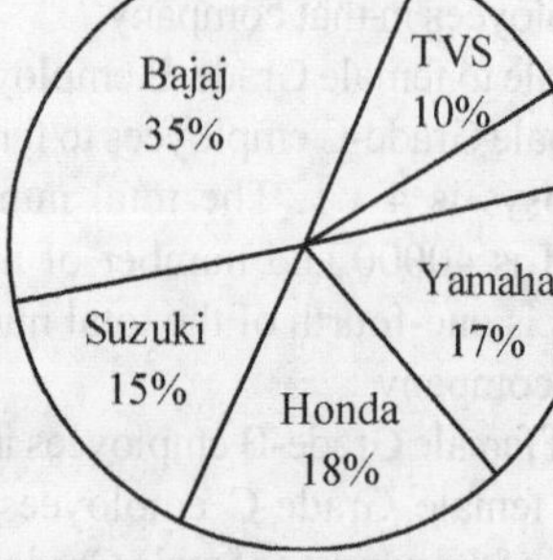

The table given below shows the ratio of Sports bike model to Cruiser bike model sold in the year 2017 by these six companies.

Company	Ratio
Hero	7 : 3
Yamaha	6 : 11
Honda	15 : 14
Suzuki	13 : 12
Bajaj	5 : 2
TVS	16 : 13

NOTE: Total number of bikes sold by a company = Number of Sports bike model sold by the company + Number of Cruiser bike model sold by the company.

15. If the difference between the number of Sports bike model sold by Honda and the number of Cruiser bike model sold by Suzuki is 6120, then what is the total number of Suzuki bikes sold in 2017?
1) 44850 2) 43500 3) 49300
4) 29000 5) None of these

16. If the average number of Cruiser bike model of Hero and Yamaha exceeds the number of Sports model of the same companies by 4350, then the number of Sports bike model of Yamaha is how much more or less than number of Cruiser bike model of Hero?
1) 13050 less 2) 17400 more 3) 2900 less
4) 13050 more 5) Cannot be determined

17. What is the average of all Sports bike models sold in 2017 if it is given that the difference between the number of Sports bike model of Bajaj sold and that of Cruiser bike model of TVS sold is 178500 in the year 2017?
1) 82835 2) 62695 3) 58835
4) 35858 5) None of the above

18. If in the year 2018, sale of all the bike companies increases by 10% as compared to 2017 except for Bajaj and TVS, then find by approximately what per cent the sale of Bajaj and TVS together decreased in 2018 as compared to 2017 if it is given that the total sales of all the bike companies together in 2017 and 2018 remain the same?
1) 15 2) 14 3) 18
4) Cannot be determined 5) 12

Directions (Q. 19-21): Read the following information carefully and answer the questions given below:

Aakash started a journey from Hissar to Delhi by train. The train ran with speed **(A)** kmph for the first hour of the journey. For the journey of next two hours, it increased and decreased its speed by 20% and 25% from the previous hours respectively. It is mentioned that the average speed of the total journey in 3 hours was 62 kmph. Aakash has **(B)** coins in his pocket out of which 4 are ₹1 coins and remaining ₹2 coins. If he takes out two coins randomly from his pocket, then the probability that an amount more than ₹2 is taken out is $\frac{13}{15}$. A salesman entered the train for selling a product. If his product is marked at ₹ **(C)** and he sold it at 60% discount, then Aakash can buy it with all the coins in his pocket.

19. What is the value of A?
1) 60 2) 50 3) 10 4) 120 5) 40

20. What is the ratio of B to A?
1) 1 : 6 2) 2 : 3 3) 6 : 1
4) None of the given options 5) 1 : 4

21. A + B is what per cent of C?
1) 75% 2) 150% 3) 175%
4) 145% 5) 200%

Answers and explanations

1. 1; Let quantity of wine in mixture H = 4x
Then, quantity of water in mixture H = 5x

In mixture C, wine = $\frac{150}{100} \times 5x = 7.5x$

In mixture C, water = $\frac{2}{1} \times 4x = 8x$

In 50% of mixture H,
Wine = 50% of 4x = 2x
Water = 50% of 5x = 2.5x

In $66\frac{2}{3}\%$ of mixture C, wine = $7.5x \times \frac{2}{3} = 5x$

Water = $8x \times \frac{2}{3} = \frac{16}{3}x$

Wine in mixture Z = 2x + 5x = 7x
Now, CP of mixture Z = (2x + 5x)50
= 7x × 50 = 350x

SP of mixture Z = $(2x + 2.5x + 5x + \frac{16}{3}x)35 = \frac{1557.5x}{3}$

Now, according to the question,

$\frac{1557.5x}{3} - 350x = 1015$

$\Rightarrow \frac{1557.5x - 1050x}{3} = 1015 \Rightarrow 507.5x = 1015 \times 3 \Rightarrow x = 6$

∴ Quantity of wine in mixture C = 7.5 × 6 = 45 litres

2. 4; Let quantity of wine in mixture D = 4x
Then quantity of water in mixture I = 5x
Let quantity of water in mixture D = y
Then quantity of wine in mixture I = 3y
As per information,

$\frac{(4x + y)}{(5x + 3y)} = \frac{4}{7}$

$\Rightarrow 28x + 7y = 20x + 12y \Rightarrow 8x = 5y$

$\Rightarrow \frac{x}{y} = \frac{5}{8}$ ... (i)

Part of wine in D = $\frac{4x}{4x + y} = \frac{20}{20 + 8} = \frac{20}{28} = \frac{5}{7}$

Part of wine in I = $\frac{3y}{5x + 3y} = \frac{24}{25 + 24} = \frac{24}{49}$

Now, let the new mixture be N and its part of wine be n.
Then,

$\frac{5}{7}$ $\frac{24}{49}$
n
4 7

Now, $\frac{\frac{5}{7} - n}{n - \frac{24}{49}} = \frac{7}{4} \Rightarrow \frac{\frac{5 - 7n}{7}}{\frac{49n - 24}{49}} = \frac{7}{4} \Rightarrow \frac{35 - 49n}{49n - 24} = \frac{7}{4}$

$\Rightarrow 140 - 196n = 343n - 168 \Rightarrow 308 = 539n$

$\Rightarrow n = \frac{308}{539} = \frac{4}{7}$

3. 5; Quantity of wine in A = x
Quantity of water in F = x
And quantity of wine in F = x + 10
Quantity of water in A = x + 10
Quantity of water in J = x + x + 10 = 2x + 10
Total quantity of J. 2x + 10 + 80 = 2x + 90
∴ Quantity of wine in J = 2x + 90 − (2x + 10) = 80

$\Rightarrow$ Quantity of water in J = $\frac{80}{4} \times 5 = 100 = 2x + 10$

$\Rightarrow x = 45$
∴ Reqd difference = 80 − 45 = 35 litres

4. 3; Let water quantity in G = 5x
Wine quantity in B = 8x
Let wine quantity in G = y
⇒ water quantity in B = 4y
If cost price of pure wine is ₹a per litre
Then, CP of mixture B and G = (8x + y)a
SP of mixture B and G = (13x + 5y)a
Profit = 13ax + 5ay − 8ax − ay = (5x + 4y)a

Now, $\frac{(5x + 4y)a}{(13x + 5y)a} = \frac{40}{100}$

$\Rightarrow \frac{x}{y} = \frac{10}{1}$ ... (i)

Part of wine in B = $\frac{8x}{4y + 8x} = \frac{80}{84} = \frac{20}{21}$

Part of wine in G = $\frac{y}{y + 5x} = \frac{1}{51}$

Let the fraction of milk in mixture M be T.
Then,

$\frac{20}{21}$ $\frac{1}{51}$
T
194 139

$\Rightarrow \frac{\frac{20}{21} - T}{T - \frac{1}{51}} = \frac{139}{194}$

$\frac{(20 - 21T)}{21} \times \frac{51}{(51T - 1)} = \frac{139}{194} \Rightarrow \frac{(20 - 21T)}{7(51T - 1)} = \frac{139}{194}$

$\Rightarrow 340 \times 194 - 357T \times 194 = 357T \times 139 - 7 \times 139$

$\Rightarrow 357T(139+194) = 340 \times 194 + 7 \times 139$

$\Rightarrow \frac{66933}{333 \times 357} = \frac{201}{357} \Rightarrow T = \frac{201}{357}$

$\therefore$ Reqd % $= \frac{201}{357} \times 100 = 56.3\%$

5. 4; Amount invested in 2016 $= \frac{18 \times 30}{100} = 5.4$ lakh

Amount invested in 2014 $= 5.4 \times \frac{7}{18} = 0.3 \times 7 = 2.1$ lakh

$\because 22\% \equiv 2.1$ lakh

$\therefore$ Reqd difference $= (36-30)\% = 6\%$

$\therefore 6\% \equiv \frac{2.1}{22} \times 6 \approx 57300$

$= \frac{12.6}{22}$ lakh $= 0.57272$ lakh ≈ 57300

6. 4; Let annual salary in 2013 be ₹N.

Annual salary in 2014 $= \frac{120 \times N}{100}$

Annual salary in 2015 $= \frac{6N}{5} \times \frac{6}{5} = \frac{36N}{25}$

Average monthly salary in 2015 $= \frac{36N}{25 \times 12} = \frac{3N}{25}$

Average monthly expenditure on EMI in 2013

$= \frac{35}{100} \times \frac{N}{12} = \frac{7N}{240}$

Reqd ratio $= \frac{3N}{25} : \frac{7N}{240} = 144 : 35$

7. 1; Let total annual income in 2014 and 2017 of Rimjhim be ₹M and ₹N respectively.

Then, $\frac{36M}{44N} = \frac{9}{22} \Rightarrow N = 2M$

Annual amount invested in 2017 $= \frac{28}{100} \times N$

$= \frac{28}{100} \times (2M)$

Annual savings & houshold expenses together in 2014

$= \frac{30+12}{100} \times M = \frac{42M}{100}$

$\therefore$ Reqd % $= \dfrac{\frac{28 \times 2M}{100} - \frac{42M}{100}}{\frac{42M}{100}} \times 100$

$= \frac{14M}{42M} \times 100 = \frac{100}{3}\% = 33\frac{1}{3}\%$

Another Method:

EMI_{2014}	HE_{2017}
9x	22x
$\frac{9x}{36} \times (30+12)$	$44\% = 22x$
$= \frac{9x}{36} \times 42 = \frac{21x}{2}$	$\therefore 28\% = \frac{22x}{44} \times 28$
$= 10.5x$	$= 14x$

$\therefore$ Reqd % more $= \frac{14x - 10.5x}{10.5x} \times 100$

$= \frac{3.5x}{10.5x} \times 100 = \frac{100}{3}\% = 33\frac{1}{3}\%$

8. 4; Amount to be invested by Rimjhim in 2013 $= \frac{60000}{10} \times 25$

$=$ ₹15000

Let amount invested by her in scheme A be ₹N. Then, as per information,

$= \left[N\left\{\left(1+\frac{8}{100}\right)^3 - 1\right\}\right] + \frac{(150000-N)10 \times 3}{100} = 42180$

$\Rightarrow N\left[\left(\frac{27}{25}\right)^3 - 1\right] + \frac{450000-3N}{10} = 42180$

$\Rightarrow \frac{4058N}{15625} + \frac{450000-3N}{10} = 42180$

$\Rightarrow 40580N + 7031250000 - 46875N$

$= 156250 \times 42180 = 6590625000$

$\Rightarrow -6295N = -440625000$

$\therefore N = \frac{440625000}{6295} = 69996 \approx 70000$

9. 2; Let the total annual income of Rimjhim in 2016 be L. Then, as per given information,

$\frac{30}{100}L + \frac{25}{100}(3000000 - L) = 810000$

$\Rightarrow \frac{3L}{10} + \frac{3000000 - L}{4} = 810000$

$\Rightarrow 6L + 15000000 - 5L = 16200000$

$\Rightarrow L = 1200000 =$ ₹12 lakhs

$\Rightarrow$ Total income in 2018 = ₹18 lakhs

$\therefore$ Reqd ratio $= \frac{14}{100} \times 18 : \frac{9}{100} \times 12 = 7 : 3$

(10-14):

The information given can be classified in a table as follows:

Company	Grade B		Grade C		Total
	Male	Female	Male	Female	
Infosys	120% of 5000=6000	4000	25000×4/5 =20000	25000×1/5 =5000	35000
TCS	5000×9/10 =4500	4500/5×9 =2500	7/5×10000 =14000	7000	28000
IBM	40000×1/4 =10000	50% of 10000 =5000	30000	10000	55000
Wipro	32500×3/13 =7500	5000	32500×10/13 =25000	150% of 5000 =7500	45000

10. 1; Reqd % $= \frac{14000+25000}{20000+5000}\times100 = \frac{39000}{25000}\times100 = 156\%$

11. 3; In IBM, Grade B employees under 30 years of age

$= \frac{20}{100}\times15000 = 3000$

Remaining employees $= (15000-3000) = 12000$

Grade B employees below 45 years of age

$= \frac{45}{100}\times15000 = 6750$

So, Grade B employees in IBM of the age of 30 to 45 years $= 6750-3000 = 3750$

$\therefore$ Reqd ratio $= 3750 : 14000 = 15 : 56$

12. 4; Male Grade C employees who left TCS

$= 28\frac{4}{7}\%$ of $14000 = \frac{2}{7}\times14000 = 4000$

Employees who joined Wipro $= \frac{4000}{15+17}\times15 = 1875$

Employees who joined Infosys $= \frac{4000}{15+17}\times17 = 2125$

Male Grade C employees in Infosys

$= 2125+20000 = 22125$

Male Grade C employees in Wipro

$= 1875+25000 = 26875$

$\therefore$ Reqd difference $= (22125+26875)-(4000+5000) = 49000-9000 = 40000$

13. 2; Reqd difference

$= \frac{1}{4}\{(20000+14000+30000+25000)-(4000+2500+5000+5000)\} = \frac{1}{4}(72500) = 18125$

14. 5; Average total number of employees in four companies

$= \frac{35000+28000+55000+45000}{4} = \frac{164000}{4} = 40750$

Hence only IBM and Wipro have employees more than this.

15. 2; Let total bikes sold during 2017 by all the companies be N.

Then, Sports bike sold by Honda

$= \frac{18N\times15}{100\times29} = \frac{270N}{2900} = \frac{27N}{290}$

Cruiser bikes sold by Suzuki $= \frac{15N}{100}\times\frac{12}{25}$

$= \frac{180N}{2500} = \frac{9N}{125}$

As per information given,

$\frac{27N}{290} - \frac{9N}{125} = 6120$

$\Rightarrow \frac{675N-522N}{7250} = 6120 \Rightarrow 153N = 6120\times7250$

$\Rightarrow N = \frac{6120\times7250}{153} = 290000$

Total Suzuki bikes sold $= \frac{15}{100}\times290000 = 43500$

16. 4; Let total bikes manufactured of Hero and Yamaha be 5x and 17x respectively.

Then, as per information,

$\frac{\frac{5x}{10}\times3+\frac{17x}{17}\times11}{2} - \frac{\frac{5x}{10}\times7+\frac{17x}{17}\times6}{2} = 4350$

$\Rightarrow \frac{3x}{2}+11x-\frac{7x}{2}-6x = 8700$

or, $5x-2x = 8700$ or, $3x = 8700 \Rightarrow 6x = 17400$

$\Rightarrow x = 2900$

So, Sports bike model of Yamaha $= \frac{17\times2900}{17}\times6 = 17400$

Cruiser bike model of Hero $= \frac{5\times2900}{10}\times3 = 4350$

$\therefore$ Reqd difference $= 17400-4350 = 13050$

17. 1; Let total bikes manufactured in 2017 be T.

Then, Sports bike model of Bajaj $= \frac{35}{100}\times T\times\frac{5}{7} = \frac{T}{4}$

Cruiser bike model of TVS $= \frac{10T}{100}\times\frac{13}{29} = \frac{13T}{290}$

As per information given; $\frac{T}{4}-\frac{13T}{290}=178500$

$\Rightarrow \frac{145T-26T}{580}=178500 \Rightarrow T=870000$

Sports bike model of Hero

$=\frac{5}{100}\times 870000\times\frac{7}{10}=30450$

Similary, that of Yamaha = 52200
Honda = 81000
Suzuki = 67860
Bajaj = 217500
TVS = 48000

$\therefore$ Reqd average

$=\frac{30450+52200+81000+67860+7217500+48000}{6}$

$=\frac{497010}{6}=82835$

18. 5; $\because$ 10% of (5 + 17 + 18 + 15) = x% of (35 + 10)
$\therefore$ 10% of 55 = x% of 45

$\Rightarrow x=\frac{550}{45}=\frac{110}{9}=12.2\approx 12$

(19-21):
Speed of train in 1st hour = A kmph

Speed of train in 2nd hour = $A\times\frac{120}{100}=1.2A$ kmph

Speed of train in 3rd hour = $1.2A\times\frac{75}{100}=0.9A$ kmph

Total distance travelled in 3 hours = 3 × 62 = 186 km
$\Rightarrow A+1.2A+0.9A=186 \Rightarrow 3.1A=186$
$\therefore$ A = 60 kmph

For amount to be more than ₹2 at least one coin must be of ₹2.
Thus, P(no coin is of ₹2) = 1 – P (Amount taken is more than ₹2)

$\Rightarrow \frac{{}^4C_2}{{}^BC_2}=1-\frac{13}{15}=\frac{2}{15} \Rightarrow \frac{4\times 3}{B(B-1)}=\frac{2}{15}$

$\Rightarrow B(B-1)=\frac{4\times 3}{2}\times 15=90=10\times 9 \Rightarrow B=10$

Total coins = 10, ₹1 coins = 4,
₹2 coins = (10 – 4) = 6
Total amount Aakash has with him = (4 × 1) + (6 × 2) = ₹16

As per given information, C = $16\times\frac{100}{40}$ = ₹40

Thus, A = 60
B = 10
C = 40

19. 1; A = 60
20. 1; Reqd ratio = 10 : 60 = 1 : 6
21. 3; Reqd % = $\frac{60+10}{40}\times 100=\frac{70}{40}\times 100=175\%$

Practice Set 46

Directions (Q. 1-5): The given bar graph shows the percentage of questions solved by three students Aarush, Amrish and Aatish out of the total number of questions attempted by them from two books, ie Book-1 and Book-2.

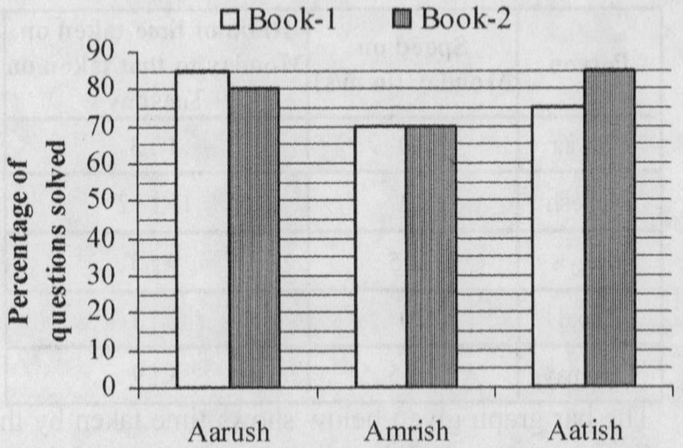

NOTE: The total number of questions attempted from each book need not be the same for each of the students; ie the number of questions attempted from Book-1 by Aarush need not be the same as the number of questions attempted from Book-1 by Amrish or Aatish.

1. If the number of questions solved by Aarush from Book-1 and Aatish from Book-2 is 510, then what could be the maximum number of questions that were not solved by Aarush from Book-1?
   1) 89 2) 87 3) 45
   4) 93 5) Cannot be determined
2. The number of questions solved by Amrish from Book-2 is 175 and the total number of questions attempted from Book-2 by him is 50 less than the number of questions solved by Aatish from Book-1. Find the total number of questions attempted from Book-1 by Aatish.
   1) 300 2) 400 3) 250 4) 325 5) 450
3. The number of questions attempted by Aarush and Aatish each from Book-2 exceeds that from Book-1 by 6.25% and the average number of questions solved by them from Book-2 is 245 more than that the average number of questions solved from Book-1. Find the difference between the number of questions attempted by Aatish from Book-1 and that from Book-2.
   1) Cannot be determined 2) 185 3) 255
   4) 250 5) 200
4. The number of questions solved by Aatish from Book-1 is 75% of the questions solved by him from Book-2. The number of questions solved by Amrish from Book-2 is equal to the sum of the number of questions solved by Aatish from both the books. What will be the ratio of the number of questions attempted by Amrish and Aatish each from Book-2?
   1) 85 : 28 2) 23 : 21 3) 64 : 23
   4) 28 : 85 5) None of these
5. What is the ratio of the number of questions attempted by Aarush, Amrish and Aatish from Book-1, if the numbers of questions solved by them from Book-1 are in the ratio of 5 : 5 : 6?
   1) 1050 : 1275 : 1211 2) 1428 : 1275 : 1050
   3) 1050 : 1275 : 1428 4) Cannot be determined
   5) 1858 : 1275 : 1429

Directions (Q. 6-10): Study the given information given below carefully and answer the following questions:

The bar graph given below shows the time taken by 5 friends Prakash, Deepti, Rajan, Neha and Shikhar in completing an assignment in week-1 (in hours).

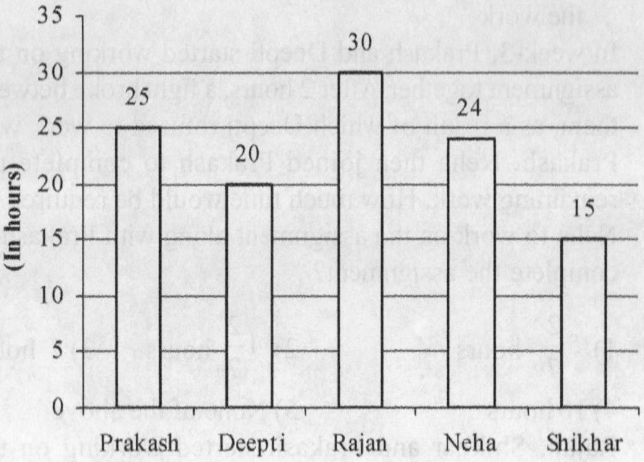

The table given below gives the ratio of time taken by 5 friends – Prakash, Deepti, Rajan, Neha and Shikhar – in completing the same assignment in week-1 to that in week-3.

Persons	Ratio of time taken in week-1 to week 3 in completing assignment
Prakash	5 : 3
Deepti	5 : 2
Rajan	10 : 11
Neha	6 : 5
Shikhar	5 : 9

The line chart shows the percentage of efficiencies of 5 friends, ie Prakash, Deepti, Rajan, Neha and Shikhar, in week-2 with respect to their efficiencies in week-1.

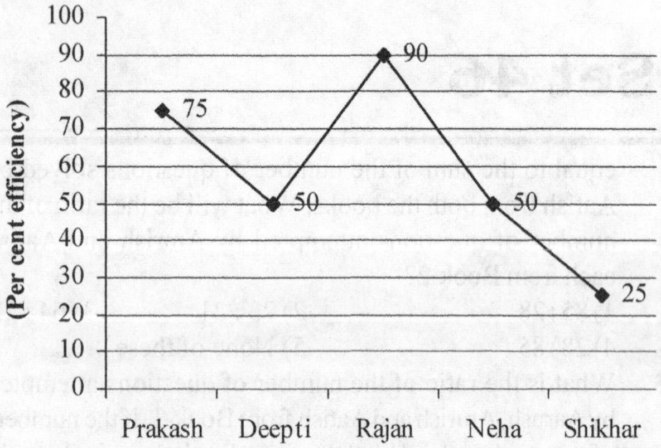

6. Deepti, Neha and Shikhar worked on the assignment in rotation in week-2 such that each one of them works exactly for 1 hour. Who should start working on the assignment first so that $\frac{5}{6}$ of the assignment is completed in the least possible time?
1) Cannot be determined 2) Neha 3) Shikhar
4) Deepti
5) Same time would be taken regardless of who starts the work

7. In week-3, Prakash and Deepti started working on the assignment together. After 2 hours, a fight broke between them, as a result of which Deepti refused to work with Prakash. Neha then joined Prakash to complete the remaining work. How much time would be required by Neha to work on the assignment along with Prakash to complete the assignment?
1) $5\frac{2}{7}$ hours 2) $4\frac{2}{7}$ hours 3) 7 hours
4) 10 hours 5) None of the above

8. Rajan, Shikhar and Prakash started working on the assignment alternately in week-3 such that each one of them works for an hour. If ₹3980 is paid to them for completing of the total assignment, then find the share of Shikhar and Prakash.
1)₹2580 2)₹2680 3)₹2080
4)₹2480 5)₹3080

9. In week-2, Rashika, who is $\frac{1}{3}$ as efficient as Shikhar, worked for 20 hours and left the assignment. The remaining assignment is completed by Deepti and Neha together. Find the time taken (approximately) by them to complete the remaining assignment.
1) 8.2 hours 2) None of these 3) 4.3 hours
4) 6.3 hours 5) 4.6 hours

10. In week-2, all of them started working together. After working for 3 hours, Rajan left. After working for another 2 hours, everyone left except Neha. Find the time taken by Neha to finish the remaining assignment.
1) 21.48 hours 2) 20.88 hours
3) 15.48 hours 4) Cannot be determined
5) 25.58 hours

Directions (Q. 11-14): Read the following table and bar graph carefully and answer the questions given below:

The table given below shows the speed of five different persons on Monday and the ratio of time taken by them on Monday to that on Tuesday.

Person	Speed on Monday (in m/s)	Ratio of time taken on Monday to that taken on Tuesday
Garvita	10	1 : 3
Mahesh	22	11 : 12
Pragya	12.5	9 : 5
Rupal	20	2 : 3
Chinmay	12.5	5 : 9

The bar graph given below shows time taken by these five persons on Wednesday as a per cent of the time taken by them on Monday.

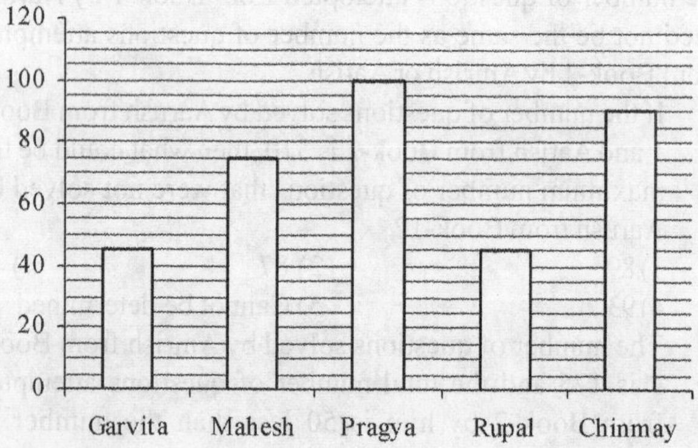

NOTE: Each person travels the same distance on each of the mentioned days, ie Garvita travels the same distance on Monday, Tuesday and Wednesday and so on.

11. Rupal covers a certain distance and goes to her office on Monday and reaches office 20 minutes late. On Wednesday, she reaches her office 25 minutes earlier. What is the distance of her office from her home?
1) 98.18 km 2) 90 km 3) 92.46 km
4) 102.23 km 5) 96.18 km

12. Priyank leaves his house at a certain time to pick up his girlfriend Pihu from her office daily at 6 pm. One day, Pihu left her office at 4 pm and started towards Priyank's home at a speed of 40 km/hr and met Priyank on the way,

who left his home at his usual time. Priyank than picked her up and they reached Priyank's home 40 minutes earlier than their usual time. Then speed of Priyank is (approx) what per cent of the speed of Chinmay on Monday?

1) 423% 2) 450% 3) 564%
4) 444% 5) Cannot be determined

13. Chinmay goes to a certain place on Monday and returns on Wednesday. Find his approximate average speed (in kmph) during the entire journey.

1) 45.58 2) 47.37 3) 54.66
4) 47.20 5) None of these

14. Garvita goes to visit a historical monument on Monday in a certain time and returns on Tuesday in a certain time. Find the distance between her house and the historical monument if it is given that whole journey took her a total of 44 hours.

1) 454 km 2) 264 km b3) 400 km
4) 396 km 5) Cannot be determined

Direction (Q. 15-18): Study the given passage carefully and answer the questions.

Three friends – Kanta, Kamli and Shanta – invested in a business in the ratio of 6 : 7 : 13. At the beginning of the 5th month, Shanta withdrew ₹59 from her investment and Kanta added ₹12 to her investment.

At the beginning of the 7th month, Kamli added to her investment an amount that is ₹28 more than the sum of what Kanta had withdrawn and Shanta had added at the beginning of the 5th month.

At the beginning of the 11th month, Shanta made an addition of double the deduction she made from her investment at the beginning of the 5th month. After 8 more months, Kamli increased her investment by ₹50.

It is given that at the end of 2 years, the ratio of profit shared by Kanta and Shanta is 201 : 434.

15. The profit of Kanta is what per cent of the total profit?

1) None of the given options 2) 22.42%
3) 23.65% 4) 21.71%
5) 28.28%

16. What is the difference between the profit shares of Shanta and Kamli if the total profit is ₹1036.91?

1) ₹160.37 2) ₹102.69 3) ₹112.89
4) ₹174.74 5) None of these

17. By what approximate per cent is the initial investment of Kanta and Shanta more than the initial investment of Kamli?

1) 82.26 2) None of the given options
3) 56.42 4) 156.3
5) 171.42

18. Maggie invested in a scheme which offers 8% per annum simple interest for a period of 2 years and 12% per annum thereafter. What will be the total interest earned by Maggie at the end of 7 years, if it is given that she invested 325% more than the initial investment of Kanta?

1) ₹728.28 2) ₹850.16 3) ₹833.34
4) ₹632.78 5) ₹920.50

Directions (Q. 19-23): Study the following pie-charts to answer the given questions.

The first pie-chart shows the distribution of cost of heavy artilleries production and the second pie-chart shows the distribution of cost of maintaining of heavy artilleries in different countries in 2017.

Total cost of production of heavy artilleries = $1440 billion

Israel 57°
Russia 72°
France 60°
Others 36°
UK 54°
USA 81°

Total cost of maintaining of heavy artilleries = $950 billion

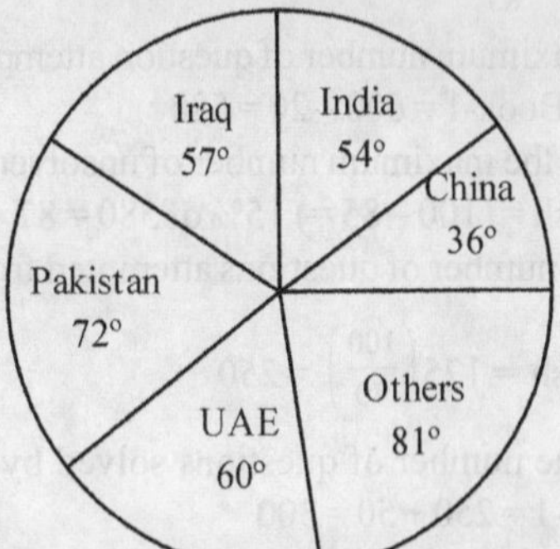

19. Due to pressure from UNO, if USA reduces the production of heavy artilleries by 25%, Russia by 30%, UK by 15% and France by 28%, then what will be the total cost of heavy artilleries production in the given countries?

1) $825 billion 2) $801 billion 3) $845 billion
4) $960 billion 5) $887 billion

20. If the cost of maintaining of heavy artilleries of China is increased by 18% and that of India by 12% in 2018, then how much amount will China have to spend less than India in maintaining of heavy artilleries? (Assume that distribution remains the same as in 2017)

1) $59.8 billion 2) $46.8 billion 3) $47.5 billion
4) $65.5 billion 5) $85.6 billion

21. What the ratio of the difference in the cost of heavy artilleries production of Russia and UK to the difference in the cost of maintaining heavy artilleries of Others and Iraq?

1) 108 : 85 2) 108 : 95 3) 107 : 75

4) 107 : 81 5) None of these

22. The total cost of heavy artilleries production of Russia in 2016 was 14% less than that in 2017. The cost of heavy artilleries production of USA and UK in 2016 were 12% and 15% more than that in 2017 respectively. What is the difference between the cost of heavy artilleries production of Russia and UK together and that of USA in 2016?
1) \$186.8 bn 2) \$175.6 bn 3) \$144.3 bn
4) \$133.2 bn 5) \$139.6 bn

23. If India spent 25% of the cost of the maintaining of heavy artilleries on anti-tank guns, 40% of the remaining on anti-aircraft guns and the remaining on other heavy artilleries, then what is the cost of maintaining of other heavy artilleries by India?
1) \$95.065 billion 2) \$85.625 billion
3) \$64.125 billion 4) \$98 billion
5) \$93.125 billion

Answers and explanations

1. 2; Let the total number of questions attempted from Book-1 by Aarush and from Book-2 by Aatish be p and q respectively.
It is given that 85% of (p + q) = 510 ⇒ p + q = 600
The number of questions solved by Aatish from Book-2 is 85%.
Minimum integral value of 85% = 17
∴ Minimum number of questions solved by Aatish = 17
∴ Minimum number of questions attempted by Aatish

$= 17 \times \frac{100}{85} = 20$

∴ Maximum number of question attempted by Aarush from Book-1 = 600 – 20 = 580
Now, the maximum number of unsolved questions by Aarush = (100 – 85 =) 15% of 580 = 87

2. 2; Total number of questions attempted from Book-2 by

Amrish $= 175\left(\frac{100}{70}\right) = 250$

So, the number of questions solved by Aatish from Book-1 = 250 + 50 = 300
∴ Total number of questions attempted by Aatish

from Book-1 $= \frac{300}{75} \times 100 = 400$

3. 5; Let the total number of questions attempted by Aarush and Aatish from Book-1 be 100P and 100Q respectively.
The questions solved by Aarush and by Aatish from Book-1 will be 85P and 75Q respectively.
Total number of questions attempted by Aarush and Aatish from Book-2 will be 106.25P and 106.25Q respectively.
The number of questions solved by Aarush from

Book-2 $= \frac{80}{100} \times 106.25P = 85P$

The number of questions solved by Aatish from Book-

2 $= \frac{85}{100} \times 106.25Q = 90.3125Q$

As per the given information,

$\frac{85P + 90.3125Q}{2} \quad \frac{85P + 75Q}{2} = 245$

$\Rightarrow \frac{90.3125Q - 75Q}{2} = 245 \Rightarrow 15.3125Q = 490$

$\therefore Q = \frac{490000}{153125} = 32$

∴ Reqd difference = 106.25Q – 100Q
= 6.25Q = 6.25 × 32 = 200

4. 5; Let total no. of questions attempted by Aatish from Book-1 be 100x.
No. of questions solved by him from Book-1 = 75x
∴ No. of questions solved by him

from Book-2 $= \frac{75x}{75} \times 100 = 100x$

As per the given question,
The no. of questions solved by Amrish from Book-2 = 100x + 75x = 175x
The number of questions attempted by Amrish from

Book -2 $= \frac{175x}{70} \times 100$

∴ Reqd ratio $= \frac{175x \times 100}{70} : \frac{100x}{85} \times 100 = 17 : 8$

5. 3; Let the total number of questions solved by Aarush, Amrish and Aatish from Book-1 be 500x, 500x and 600x respectively.

Reqd ratio $= \frac{500x}{85} \times 100 : \frac{500x}{70} \times 100 : \frac{600x}{75} \times 100$

= 1050 : 1275 : 1428

6. 4; Time taken by Depti to complete assignment in week-

$2 = \frac{20}{50} \times 100 = 40$ hours

Time taken by Neha to complete assignment in week-

$2 = \frac{24}{50} \times 100 = 48$ hours

Time taken by Shikhar to complete assignment in week-

$2 = \frac{15}{25} \times 100 = 60$ hours

Let total work done on assignment
= LCM of (40, 48, 60) = 240 units

$\frac{5}{6}$ of assignment = $\frac{5}{6} \times 240$ = 200 units

Now, work done per hour by Shikar = 4 units
Deepti = 6 units
Neha = 5 units
In 3 hours work done by them alternatively = (4 + 6 + 5 =) 15 units
In (3 × 13 =) 39 hours work done = 15 × 13 = 195 units
Remaining units = 200 – 195 = 5
Clearly, in week-2 efficiency of Deepti is the maximum. So, she should start the job so that the job is completed in the least time.

Note: You can solve easily when you analyse bar graph and line graph. We find that from the bar graph and line graph, the efficiency of Deepti is more than the efficiency of Neha and Shikhar.
The most efficient person should start first, then the second most afficient person and the least efficient should come at last.

So, $\frac{5}{6}$ of the assignment is completed in the least time when Deepti starts the work.

7. 1; Time taken by Prakash to complete assignment in week-3 = $\frac{25}{5} \times 3$ = 15 hours

Time taken by Deepti to complete assignment in week-3 = $\frac{20}{5} \times 2$ = 8 hours

Time taken by Neha to complete the assignement in week-3 = $\frac{24}{6} \times 5$ = 20 hours

Suppose total work = 120 units
(LCM of 5, 8, 20)

Work done by Neha per hour = $\frac{120}{20}$ = 6 units

Similarly, work done by Prakash per hour = 8 units
Work done by Deepti per hour = 15 units
Now, work done by Prakash and Deepti in 2 hours = 2(15 + 8) = 46 units
∴ Remaining work = (120 – 46 =) 74 units

∴ Reqd time = $\frac{74}{6+8} = \frac{74}{14} = 5\frac{4}{14}$ hours = $5\frac{2}{7}$ hours

8. 5; Time taken by Shikhar to complete assignment in week-3 = $\frac{15}{5} \times 9$ = 27 hours

Time taken by Rajan to complete assignment in week-3 = $\frac{30}{10} \times 11$ = 33 hours

Time taken by Prakash to complete assignement in week-3 = $\frac{25}{5} \times 3$ = 15 hours

Let total work done on assignement
= LCM of (27, 33 and 15) = 1485 units

Work done by Shikhar per hour = $\frac{1485}{27}$ = 55 units

Work done by Rajan per hour = $\frac{1485}{33}$ = 45 units

Work done by Prakash per hour = $\frac{1485}{15}$ = 99 units

Now, the profit will be distributed according to their efficiency.
So, total efficiency = (55 + 45 + 99) = 199 units/hour
Share of Shikhar and Prakash

= $\frac{55+99}{199} \times 3980$ = `3080

Method II.
Note: The amount should be distributed in ratio

= $\frac{1}{27} : \frac{1}{33} : \frac{1}{15}$ = 33 × 15 : 27 × 15 : 27 × 33
= 11 × 5 : 9 × 5 : 9 × 11 = 55 : 45 : 99
∴ Reqd share of Shikhar and Prakash

= $\frac{55+99}{199} \times 3980$ = `3080

9. 3; Time taken by Shikar to do work in week-3 = $\frac{15}{5} \times 9$ = 27 hours

Time taken by Rashika in week-3 = 27 × 3 = 81 hours

Time taken by Deepti in week-3 = $\frac{20}{5} \times 2$ = 8 hours

Time taken by Neha = $\frac{24}{6} \times 5$ = 20 hours

∴ Let total work to be done on assignment
= 3240 units (LCM of 81, 8 and 20)

∴ Work done by Rashika in 1 hour = $\frac{3240}{81}$ = 40 units

Work done by Deepti per hour = $\frac{3240}{8}$ = 405 units

Work done by Neha per hour = $\frac{3240}{20}$ = 162 units

Work done by Rashika in (1 × 20) hours
= 40 × 20 = 800 units
∴ Remaining work = (3240 – 800) = 2440 units

$\therefore$ Reqd time $= \frac{2440}{405+162} = \frac{2440}{567} = 4.3$ hours

10. 1; In week-2: Time taken by Prakash $= \frac{25}{75}\times 100$

$= \frac{100}{3}$ hours

Time taken by Deepti $= \frac{20}{50}\times 100 = 40$ hours

Time taken by Rajan $= \frac{30}{90}\times 100 = \frac{100}{3}$ hours

Time taken by Neha $= \frac{24}{50}\times 100 = 48$ hours

Time taken by Shikar $= \frac{15}{25}\times 100 = 60$ hours

Let total work done to complete assignment = 2400 units

Work done by Prakash per hour = 72 units

Work done by Deepti per hour = 60 units

Work done by Rajan per hour = 72 units

Work done by Neha per hour = 50 units

Work done by Shikhar per hour = 40 unit

$\therefore$ Work done per hour by all of them

$= 72+60+72+50+40 = 294$ units

Work remaining after Rajan left $= 2400 - 3\times 294 = 1518$ units

For next 2 hours work done per hour

$= 294 - 72 = 222$ units

Work remaining for Neha alone to do

$= 1518 - 2\times 222 = 1074$

$\therefore$ Reqd time $= \frac{1074}{50} = 21.48$ hours

11. 1; Let the distance of her office from her house be D km.

Now, speed of Rupal on Monday = 20m/s

$= 20\times \frac{18}{5} = 72$ kmph

Ratio of time taken by Rupal on Monday to that on Wednesday = 100 : 45

Ratio of Rupal's speeds on that on Monday to Wednesday = 45 : 100

$\therefore$ Speed on Wednesday $= \frac{72}{45}\times 100 = 160$ kmph

It is given that, $\frac{D}{72} - \frac{D}{160} = \left(\frac{20+25}{60}\right) = \frac{45}{60}$

$\Rightarrow \frac{20D - 9D}{1440} = \frac{3}{4} \Rightarrow D = \frac{3}{4}\times\frac{1440}{11} = 98.18$ km.

12. 4;

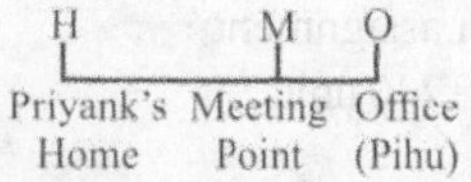

Today, Priyank doesn't need to go from M to O and hence saves 20 minutes each on one way. So he meets Pihu at 5 : 40 pm.

Ratio of time taken by Pihu to that by Priyank in reaching M from O

$= (5:40 - 4:00) : 20 = 100 : 20 = 5 : 1$

Ratio of speed of Pihu to that of Priyank = 1 : 5

Thus, speed of Priyank = 40 × 5 = 200 kmph

Speed of Chinmay on Monday

$= 12.5\times\frac{18}{5} = 45$ kmph

$\therefore$ Reqd % $= \frac{200}{45}\times 100 = 444\frac{4}{9}\% \approx 444\%$

13. 2; Speed of Chinmay on Monday

$= 12.5$ m/s $= 12.5\times\frac{18}{5} = 45$ kmph

Ratio of time taken by Chimmay on Monday to that on Wednesday = 100 : 90 = 10 : 9

Ratio of speeds = 9 : 10

Speed of Chinmay on Wednesday

$= \frac{45}{9}\times 10 = 50$ kmph

$\therefore$ Average speed $= \frac{2\times 50\times 45}{50+45}$

$= \frac{2\times 50\times 45}{50+45} = 47.37$ kmph

14. 4; Let total distance from her house to historical monument be N km.

Speed of Garvita on Monday = 10m/s

$= 10\times\frac{18}{5} = 36$ kmph

Ratio of time taken on Monday to that on Tuesday = 1 : 3

Ratio of speed on Monday to that on Tuesday = 3 : 1

Speed of Garvita on Tuesday $= \frac{36}{3} = 12$ kmph

It is given that; $\frac{N}{36} + \frac{N}{12} = 44$

$\Rightarrow \frac{N+3N}{36} = 44 \Rightarrow N = 396$ km

(15-18):

Let initial investments of Kanta, Kamli & Shanta be 6x, 7x and 13x respectively.

Then,

Kanta	Kamli	Shanta
First 4 months 6x × 4 = 24x **5th to 24th months** (6x + 12)20 = 120x + 240	**First six months** = 7x × 6 = 42x **7th to 18th months** (7x + 59 + 12 + 28)12 = (7x + 99)12 = 84x + 1188 **19th to 24 months** (7x + 99 + 50)6 = (7x + 149)6 = 42x + 894	**First four months** 13x × 4 = 52x **5th to 10th months** (13x – 59)6 = 78x – 354 **11th to 24th months** (13x – 59 + 118)14 = (13x + 59)14 = 182x + 826
Total = 24x + 120x + 240 = 144x + 240	**Total** = 42x + 84x + 1188 + 42x + 894 = 168x + 2082	**Total** = 52x + 78x – 354 + 182x + 826 = 312x + 472

It is given that; $\frac{144x+240}{312x+472}=\frac{201}{434}$

$\Rightarrow 216x = 9288 \Rightarrow x = 43$

Thus, initial investment of Kanta = 6 × 43 = ₹258

Initial investment of Kamli = 7 × 43 = ₹301

Initial investment of Shanta = 13 × 43 = ₹559

And, ratio of profit will be

Kanta		Kamli		Shanta
144(43)+240	:	168(43)+2082	:	312(43)+472
= 6432	:	9306	:	13888
= 3216	:	4653	:	6944

15. 4; Reqd % = $\frac{3216}{3216+4653+6944}\times 100=\frac{3216}{14813}\times 100=21.71\%$

16. 1; Let profits of Kanta, Kamli and Shanta be 3216x, 4653x and 6944x. It is given, that

$3216x + 4653x + 6944x = 1036.91$

$\Rightarrow 14813x = 1036.91 \Rightarrow x = 0.07$

$\therefore$ Reqd difference = $6944x - 4653x = 2291x$

$= 2291 \times 0.07 = 160.37$

17. 5; Reqd % = $\frac{258+559-301}{301}\times 100$

$=\frac{516}{301}\times 100 = 171.42\%$ (approx)

18. 3; Investment of Maggie = $\left(258\times\frac{425}{100}\right)$ = ₹1096.5

Thus, interest earned = $1096.5\left(\frac{8\times 2}{100}+\frac{12\times 5}{100}\right)$

$= 1096.5 \times \frac{76}{100}$ = ₹833.34

19. 2; After reduction the cost of production of USA

$=\frac{1440}{360}\times 81\times\frac{75}{100} = 81 \times 3 = \$243$ bn

Russia = $\frac{1440}{360}\times 72\times\frac{70}{100} = 0.8 \times 36 \times 7 = \$201.6$ bn

UK = $\frac{1440}{360}\times 54\times\frac{85}{100} = 10.8 \times 17 = \$183.6$ bn

France = $\frac{1440}{360}\times 60\times\frac{72}{100} = 24 \times 7.2 = \$172.8$ bn

$\therefore$ Reqd total cost = \$(243 + 201.6 + 183.6 + 172.8) bn

= \$801 bn

20. 3; Cost of maintaining of heavy artilleries by China in

2018 = $\frac{950}{360}\times 36\times\frac{118}{100} = 19 \times 5.9 = \$112.1$ bn

India in 2018 = $\frac{950}{360}\times 54\times\frac{112}{100} = 19 \times 8.4 = \$159.6$ bn

$\therefore$ Reqd amount = 159.6 – 112.1 = \$47.5 bn

21. 2; Reqd ratio = $\frac{\frac{1440}{360}\times(72-54)}{\frac{950}{360}\times(81-57)}=\frac{4\times 18\times 3}{95\times 2}\times 3 = 108:95$

22. 4; Cost of production by

Russia in 2016 = $1440\times\frac{72}{360}\times\frac{86}{100}$

$= 2.88 \times 86 = \$247.68$ bn

USA in 2016 = $1440\times\frac{81}{360}\times\frac{112}{100}$

$= 81 \times 4.48 = \$362.88$ bn

UK in 2016 = $1440\times\frac{54}{360}\times\frac{115}{100}$

$= 54 \times 4.6 = \$248.4$ bn

Reqd difference = (247.68 + 248.4) – 362.88

= 496.08 – 362.88 = \$133.2 bn

23. 3; Cost of maintaining artilleries by India

$=\frac{950}{360}\times 54 = \$142.5$ bn

Amount spent on anti-tank guns

$= 142.5\times\frac{25}{100} = \$35.625$

Amount spent on other heavy artilleries

$=(142.5-35.625)\times\frac{60}{100}=\frac{106.875\times 60}{100} = \$64.125$ bn

Practice Set 47

Directions (Q. 1-5): Study the following information to answer the given questions.

There are five companies J, K, L, M and N in a certain town. The total number of employees in all the companies together is 2400. The strength of company J and company K are 37.5% and 20% of the total number of employees respectively. M and N have equal strength. 40% of employees of company J know only one language Hindi. $\frac{1}{3}$ of the employees of company M know only English. There are 101 more employees in company K who know only Hindi than the number of employees of company M who know only English. 175 employees of company L know Hindi but not English. 128 employees of company M know both the languages. The strength of company L is 42% of the strength of company J. 37.5% of employees of company K know both the languages. The number of employees of company L who know English but not Hindi is 12 more than the number of the same category of employees of company K. 87 employees of company N know only English and 28% employees of company J know both the languages. 142 employees of company N know both the languages.

1. If $\frac{2}{3}$ of the number of employees who know only Hindi are males and $\frac{5}{9}$ of the number of employees who know both the languages are females, then what is the difference between the number of males who know only Hindi and that of females who know both the languages?
   1) 109 2) 179 3) 169 4) 219 5) 209
2. If 25% of the number of employees of company J who know both the languages also know French, then the number of employees of company J who know French is approximately what per cent more/less than the number of employees of company L who know both the languages?
   1) 48% more 2) 36% less 3) 32% more
   4) 60% less 5) 24% more
3. What is the maximum difference between the number of employees who know only Hindi and only English in the same company?
   1) 96 2) 98 3) 121 4) 116 5) 129
4. Find the percentage of the number of employees who know only Hindi in all the companies together.
   1) 38.375% 2) 32.675% 3) 25%
   4) 42.5% 5) None of these
5. In Company J if 37.5% of the number of employees J who know only Hindi are freshers and 20% of the remaining employees who know only Hindi are 5 years experienced, then the number of employees of company J who are five years experienced and who know only Hindi is what per cent of the number of employees of company L who know only Hindi?
   1) 19.38% 2) 29.67% 3) 38.36%
   4) 21.67% 5) 25.71%

Directions (Q. 6-10): Study the following table to answer the following questions.

The table shows the investments of three persons in five different years.

Year	Investment (in ₹)		
	Prakash	Vikash	Yogendra
2012	150000	175000	190000
2013	–	180000	200000
2014	80000	50000	–
2015	–	–	120000
2016	60000	–	–

6. In 2013 Prakash invested 10% more in comparison to his investment of previous year. After 3 months, 4 months and 6 months Prakash, Vikash and Yogendra withdrew $\frac{1}{11}$, $\frac{1}{9}$ and $\frac{1}{10}$ part of their investments respectively. If at the end of 2013 the total profit was ₹24500, then what is the share of Prakash in the profit?
   1) ₹8150 2) ₹7460 3) ₹7210
   4) ₹7380 5) ₹7750
7. In 2014 Prakash and Vikash started a business. After x months Yogendra joined them with ₹70000 and Vikash left x months before the end of the year. If they share the profit in the ratio of 12 : 5 : 7, then what is the value of x?
   1) 3 2) 2 3) 6 4) 4 5) 5
8. Prakash, Vikash and Yogendra started a business. In 2015, Prakash and Vikash invested double the amount of their investments in the previous year. At the end of the year

Prakash received 14% of the profit being a manager, after which the remaining profit is divided in the proportion of the investment by each of them in 2015. Find the share of Vikash when Prakash received ₹19080.

1) ₹2100 2) ₹1900 3) ₹3400 4) ₹8000 5) ₹8600

9. In 2016, Vikash and Yogendra invested 20% and 15% more than Prakash' investment respecively. At the end of 18 months Yogendra withdrew his total amount. After two years a profit of ₹29400 was earned. Find the share of Yogendra in the profit.

1) ₹7460 2) ₹7520 3) ₹7720 4) ₹8340 5) ₹8280

10. The ratio of time for which Prakash, Vikash and Yogendra invested in 2012 is 4 : 6 : 5. In what ratio would their profit be distributed?

1) 19 : 20 : 23 2) 13 : 16 : 17 3) 12 : 21 : 19
4) 14 : 15 : 16 5) 18 : 17 : 15

Directions (Q. 11-15): Study the following graph to answer the given questions.

The bar graph shows the time taken by five different pipes to fill the cistern.

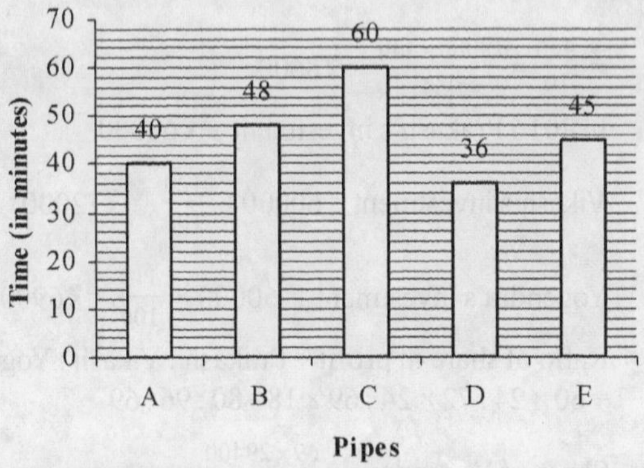

11. Pipe A and B fill the cistern. Another pipe G carries off 19 litres per minute. If the cistern is already full and all three pipes are opened the cistern is emptied in 80 minutes. How many litres of water can the cistern hold?

1) 570 litres 2) 460 litres 3) 525 litres
4) 640 litres 5) 720 litres

12. The cistern is filled by pipes C, D and E. It is emptied by Pipe G in half an hour. The pipes C, D and E are turned on at noon, but the Pipe G is accidentally left open at the same time and not closed for a quarter of an hour. At approximately what time will the cistern be full?

1) 1 : 20 pm 2) 12 : 23 pm 3) 12 : 40 pm
4) 1 : 00 pm 5) 12 : 30 pm

13. Pipe G can empty the full cistern in 30 minutes. If Pipe G is opened 7 minutes after two pipes A and B are opened, then find the time in which the cistern will be full.

1) $58\frac{9}{11}$ minutes 2) $52\frac{1}{11}$ minutes 3) $46\frac{1}{3}$ minutes

4) $61\frac{1}{3}$ minutes 5) $54\frac{1}{3}$ minutes

14. If Pipe C starts working only after Pipe E has been used for filling $\frac{2}{3}$ of the cistern, then the total time taken to fill the cistern is

1) 30 minutes 2) 45 minutes 3) 50 minutes
4) 40 minutes 5) None of these

15. Pipe G is used for emptying the cistern, which lets out water at the rate of 8 litres per minute. If pipes G and B are opened together it would take 24 minutes longer to fill the cistern completely. Find the capacity of the cistern.

1) 1152 litres 2) 1760 litres 3) 1080 litres
4) 1340 litres 5) 1520 litres

Directions (Q. 16-20): Study the following table carefully and answer the questions given below:

Marked price of different items are given on two different days, ie Day 1 and Day 2. There is also a discount % on different items on two different days.

Items	Marked price (in ₹)		Discount %	
	Day 1	Day 2	Day 1	Day 2
A	650	625	18%	16%
B	1150	1175	6%	8%
C	325	450	8%	8%
D	850	925	10%	12%
E	500	625	14%	12%
F	800	750	17%	13%

16. What is the ratio of the cost price (CP) of item D on Day 1 to the cost price (CP) of item E on Day 2, if item D on Day 1 is sold at 50% profit and item E on Day 2 is sold at 12% loss?

1) 20 : 25 2) 25 : 20 3) 102 : 125
4) 21 : 25 5) 25 : 21

17. What is the difference (in ₹) between the total selling price of all the items on Day 1 and the total selling price of all the items on Day 2?

1) 274.50 2) 264.50 3) 284.50 4) 254.50 5) 244.50

18. What is the cost price of item A and item F respectively, if the profits earned on these items are 25% and 16% respectively? (in ₹)

1) 500, 572.5 2) 572.5, 500 3) 420, 562.5
4) 500, 562.5 5) 420, 572.5

19. What is the cost price (in ₹) of item C on Day 2, if it is sold at 8% loss on the cost price?

1) 400 2) 425 3) 450
4) 475 5) Can't be determined

20. What is the total profit earned on items A, C and F on Day 1, if each item was sold at 10% profit? (Calculate the approximate value)

1) ₹158.60 2) ₹138.60 3) ₹150.60
4) ₹136 5) ₹149.60

Answers and explanations

(1-5):

Company	Strength	Only Hindi	Only English	Both
J	2400×37.5/100 = 900	900×40/100 = 360	900 −(360+252) = 288	900×28/100 =252
K	2400×20/100 =480	107+101 =208	480 −(208+180) =92	480×37.5/100 = 180
L	900×42/100 = 378	175	92+12=104	378−(175+104) =99
M	321	321 −(107+128) =86	321/3=107	128
N	321	321 −(142+87) =92	87	142
Total	2400	921	678	801

1. 3; Reqd difference $= 921\times\frac{2}{3} - 801\times\frac{5}{9} = 614-445 = 169$

2. 2; No. of employees who know French

$= 25\%$ of $252 = \frac{1}{4}\times 252 = 63$

Reqd % $= \frac{99-63}{99}\times 100 \approx 36\%$ less

3. 4; Reqd difference $= 208-92 = 116$

4. 1; Reqd % $= \frac{921}{2400}\times 100 = 38.375\%$

5. 5; Reqd % $= \frac{360\times\frac{62.5}{100}\times\frac{20}{100}}{175}\times 100$

$= \frac{45}{175}\times 100 = 25.71\%$

6. 4; Prakash's investment in 2013 $= 150000\times\frac{110}{100} = ₹165000$

Ratio of share in profit

= P : V : Y

$= 165\times 3+165\times 9\times\frac{10}{11} : 180\times 4+180\times 8\times\frac{8}{9}$

$: 200\times 6+200\times 6\times\frac{9}{10}$

$= 495+1350 : 720+1280 : 1200+1080$

$= 1845 : 2000 : 2280 = 369 : 400 : 456$

$\therefore$ Share of Prakash $= \frac{24500}{1225}\times 369 = ₹7380$

7. 4;

Prakash	Vikash	Yogendra
80×12	50(12–x)	70(12–x)
96	60–5x	84–7x

Now, $\frac{(60-5x)+84-7x}{96} = \frac{12}{12}$

$\Rightarrow \frac{144-12x}{96} = 1 \Rightarrow 12x = 144-96 = 48$

$\therefore x = 4$ months

8. 5; Investment of Prakash in 2015

$= 80000\times 2 = ₹160000$

That of Vikash in 2015 $= 50000\times 2 = ₹100000$

Ratio of share in profit

	Prakash	Vikash	Yogendra
=	16	10	12

$= 8 : 5 : 6$

Let the total profit be ₹100

Then, Prakash's share $= 14+(100-14)\times\frac{8}{19}$

$= 14+86\times\frac{8}{19} = 14+\frac{688}{19} = \frac{954}{19}$

Now, $\frac{954}{19} \equiv 19080 \therefore (100-14)\times\frac{5}{19}$

$= \frac{430}{19} \equiv \frac{19080\times 430}{954} = ₹8600$

9. 5; In 2016 Prakash's investment $= ₹60000$

Vikash's investment $= 60000\times\frac{120}{100} = ₹72000$

Yogendra's investment $= 60000\times\frac{115}{100} = ₹69000$

Ratio of share in profit = Prakash : Vikash : Yogendra

$= 60\times 24 : 72\times 24 : 69\times 18 = 80 : 96 : 69$

Share of Yogendra $= \frac{69\times 29400}{80+96+69}$

$= \frac{69\times 29400}{245} = ₹8280$

10. 3;

Prakash : Vikash : Yogendra

Reqd ratio of profit

$15\times 4 : 17.5\times 6 : 19\times 5$

$= 60 : 105 : 95 = 12 : 21 : 19$

11. 1; The part filled in 1 minute by A $= \frac{1}{40}$

The part filled in 1 minute by B $= \frac{1}{48}$

And the part filled by all three pipes in 1 minute $= \frac{1}{80}$

Part emptied in 1 minute by G

$= \frac{1}{40}+\frac{1}{48}-\frac{1}{80} = \frac{6+5-3}{240} = \frac{8}{240} = \frac{1}{30}$

$\because \frac{1}{30}$ part contains 19 litres of water

$\therefore$ 1 part $= 19\times 30 = 570$ litres

12. 2; Let the total time taken be x minutes

Then, $\frac{x}{60}+\frac{x}{36}+\frac{x}{45}-\frac{15}{30}=1$

$\Rightarrow \frac{x}{60}+\frac{x}{36}+\frac{x}{45}=1+\frac{1}{2}=\frac{3}{2}\Rightarrow \frac{9x+15x+12x}{540}=\frac{3}{2}$

$\Rightarrow \frac{36x}{540}=\frac{3}{2} \therefore x=22.5$ minutes

Therefore, the cistern will be full at approximately

$12+22.5\text{min}=12:22.5 \text{ pm} \approx 12:23$ pm

13. 4;

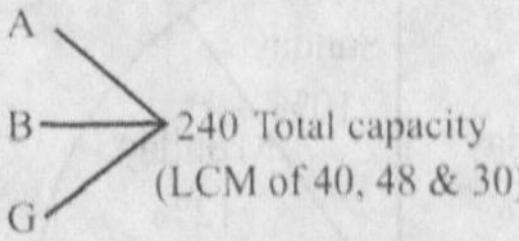

$\Rightarrow$ A fills $\frac{240}{40}=6$ lit/min

B fills $\frac{240}{48}=5$ lit/min

G empties $\frac{240}{30}=8$ lit/min

(A + B) can fill in 7 min = (6 + 5) × 7 = 77 litres

$\therefore$ Remaining part = 240 – 77 = 163 litres

Time taken to fill the remaining part

$=\frac{163}{(6+5-8)}=\frac{163}{3}=54\frac{1}{3}$ minutes

$\therefore$ Total time $=\left(54\frac{1}{3}+7\right)$ min $=61\frac{1}{3}$ min

14. 3; Time taken by E to fill $\frac{2}{3}$ of the cistern

$=\frac{2}{3}\times 45=30$ minutes

Time taken by C to fill $\frac{1}{3}$ of the cistern $=\frac{1}{3}\times 60=20$ minutes

$\therefore$ Reqd total time = 30 + 20 = 50 minutes

15. 1; B fills the cistern in 48 minutes.

Let G empties the cistern in x min.

When both operate, cistern is filled in 48 + 24 = 72 min

$\Rightarrow \frac{1}{48}-\frac{1}{x}=\frac{1}{72} \therefore \frac{1}{x}=\frac{1}{48}-\frac{1}{72}=\frac{3-2}{144}=\frac{1}{144}$

$\Rightarrow$ x = 144 min $\Rightarrow$ Capacity of cistern = 144 × 8 = 1152 litres

(16-20):

Item	Selling Price	
	Day 1 (₹)	Day 2 (₹)
A	650×82/100 =533	625×84/100 =525
B	1150×94/100 =1081	1175×92/100 =1081
C	325×92/100 =299	450×92/100 =414
D	850×90/100 =765	925×88/100 =814
E	500×86/100 =430	625×88/100 =550
F	800×83/100 =664	750×87/100 =652.50
Total	3772	4036.50

16. 3; MP of item D on Day 1 = ₹850

SP of item D on Day 2 = ₹765

SP = CP + P

Now, 150% = 765

$100\%=\frac{765}{150}\times 100=$ ₹510

Similarly, we find

CP of item E on Day 2.

SP of item E on Day 2 = ₹550

It is sold at 12% loss = 100 – 12 = 88%

$\therefore$ CP $=\frac{550}{88}\times 100=$ ₹625

Reqd ratio = 510 : 625 = 102 : 125

Another Method:

Reqd ratio $=\frac{850\times\frac{90}{100}\times\frac{100}{150}}{625\times\frac{88}{100}\times\frac{100}{88}}=\frac{510}{625}=\frac{102}{125}=102:125$

17. 2; From the above table

Total selling price on Day 1 = ₹3772

Total selling price on Day 2 = ₹4036.50

$\therefore$ Reqd difference = 4036.50 – 3772 = ₹264.50

18. 3; CP of item A on Day 2 $=\frac{525}{125}\times 100=$ ₹420

CP of item F on Day 2 $=\frac{652.50}{116}\times 100=$ ₹562.50

19. 3; Item C is sold at 8% loss on CP

So, SP = 100 – 8 = 92

Then, CP $=\frac{414}{92}\times 100=$ ₹450

20. 4; Total SP of item A, C and F on Day 1 = 533 + 299 + 664 = 1496

$\therefore$ Profit on item A, C and F on Day 1

$=1496\times\frac{10}{110}=$ ₹136

Practice Set 48

Directions (Q. 1-5): Study the table carefully and answer the questions that follow. Given data show ratio of illiterate male and female and literate male and female population of six major cities of India and the % of illiterate population.

City	% of illiterate	Illiterate M : F	Literate M : F
Amritsar	52%	7 : 6	3 : 1
Bengaluru	40%	3 : 2	8 : 7
Chandigarh	28%	4 : 3	2 : 1
Delhi	40%	7 : 3	7 : 8
Mumbai	50%	13 : 12	3 : 2
Kolkata	36%	2 : 1	5 : 3

1. The number of illiterate females in Bengaluru is 28760 and that of the literate females in Chandigarh is 48000. By what per cent approximately is the population of Bengaluru less than that of Chandigarh?
1) 10% 2) 12% 3) 14%
4) 18% 5) None of these
2. If the number of illiterate females in Delhi is 38400 then what is the illiterate population in Delhi?
1) 160000 2) 128000 3) 192000 4) 96800 5) 89600
3. If the population of Kolkata is 336000 then find the difference between the number of literate females and illiterate males of Kolkata.
1) 53760 2) 94080 3) 40320
4) No difference 5) Can't be determined
4. If the number of literate female population of Mumbai is 68000, then what is the total male population of Mumbai?
1) 170000 2) 190400 3) 149600 4) 156400 5) 183600
5. If the number of illiterate males in Amritsar is 67200, then find the number of literate females in Amritsar.
1) 86400 2) 57600 3) 28800 4) 14800 5) 7200

Directions (Q. 6-10): Study the data given below and answer the following questions. The pie-charts shows the distance covered by a boat moving upstream and downstream on different days of a week. And the table shows the speed of the stream in kmph on different days of the week.

Total distance covered upstream = 250 km

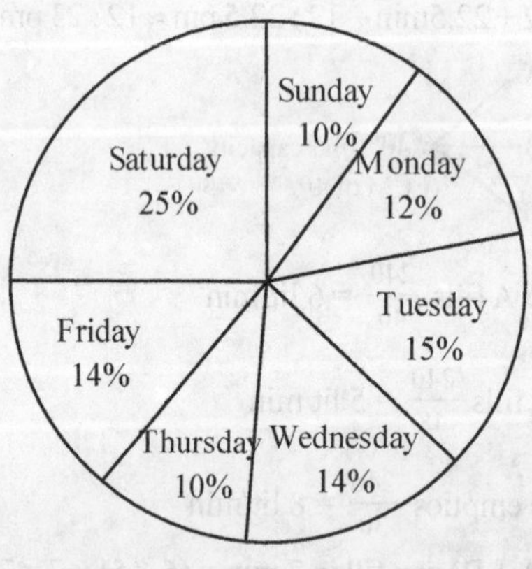

Total distance covered downstream = 150 km

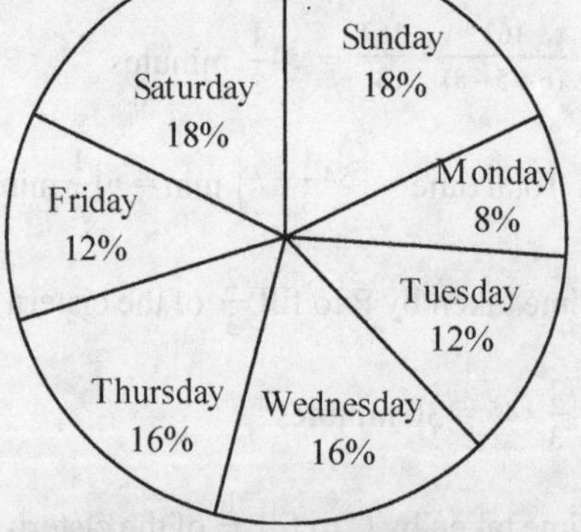

Day	Speed of stream (in kmph)
Monday	–
Tuesday	4
Wednesday	2
Thursday	–
Friday	3
Saturday	1
Sunday	2

6. If the time taken by the boat to travel upstream on Tuesday is $\frac{89}{40}$ hours more than the time taken by it to

travel downstream on the same day then find the speed of the boat in still water on Tuesday.
1) 16 kmph 2) 20 kmph 3) 18 kmph
4) 14 kmph 5) 24 kmph

7. If the time taken by the boat to travel upstream on Friday is 3 hours more than the time taken by it to travel downstream on Wednesday and the speed of the boat in still water on Wednesday is 10 kmph then find the upstream speed of the boat on Friday.
1) 4 kmph 2) 8 kmph 3) 6 kmph
4) 7 kmph 5) 12 kmph

8. The speed of the boat in still water on Monday was 14 kmph and that on Sunday was $28\frac{4}{7}\%$ less than that on Monday. If the time taken by the boat to travel upstream on Monday is $1\frac{2}{3}$ times the time taken to travel downstream on Sunday, then find the time taken by the boat to cover a distance of 32 km upstream when the speed of the stream is the same as that on Monday.
1) 3 hours 2) 4 hours 3) 2 hours
4) 3.5 hours 5) None of these

9. If the time taken by the boat to travel upstream on Saturday is equal to the time taken by it to travel downstream on Wednesday and the speed of the boat in still water on Wednesday is 16 kmph, then find the speed of the boat (in kmph) in still water on Saturday.
1) 47.875 2) 46.875 3) 36.875
4) 24.875 5) None of these

10. Find the ratio of upstream distance covered on Friday, Monday and Tuesday together to the downstream distance covered on Monday and Saturday.
1) 37 : 14 2) 38 : 17 3) 37 : 12 4) 15 : 17 5) 47 : 12

Directions (Q. 11-15): Given below is the information regarding the results of 3 students Tanu, Rishi and Pooja of PO Main examiantion. Read it carefully and answer the following questions.

There are total 4 subjects, ie English, Reasoning, GA and Quant, each carrying different maximum marks. English and GA both carry equal maximum marks, ie 40 marks each. Reasoning carries maximum marks which is 20 more than English. The total of the maximum marks of 4 subjects is 200. Pooja scored 60% marks in English, while Tanu scored 75% in the same subject. Rishi scored only 19 marks in English. Rishi scored 30 marks in Reasoning, which is 60% of the marks scored by Tanu in the same subject. The total of the marks of 3 students in Reasoning is 102. Pooja scored 65% marks in GA, while Rishi scored 40% in the same subject and Tanu scored the highest among the three in GA, which is 28 marks. Tanu scored 24 marks in Quant. The sum of marks of Rishi and Pooja in Quant is 56 while the ratio of the marks in their same subject is 5 : 9.

11. What is the average marks scored by the 3 students in Reasoning?
1) 32 2) 34 3) 36
4) 38 5) None of these

12. Calculate the percentate of marks obtained by Rishi in all the given subjects.
1) 40.5% 2) 32.125% 3) 42.5%
4) 54% 5) 44.5%

13. Find the difference between the total marks scored by all three candidates in English and the total marks scored by all three in GA.
1) 5 2) 6 3) 9 4) 12 5) None of these

14. Marks of Rishi and Pooja together in Reasoning is what per cent more or less than the marks of Tanu and Rishi in GA together?
1) 9.09% 2) 18.18% 3) 11.11%
4) 22.22% 5) None of these

15. If the pass marks in each exam is 40%, then what is the total number of compartments of all three students together? The inability to get pass marks in any subject is categorised as compartment.
1) 0 2) 1 3) 2 4) 3 5) 4

Directions (Q. 16-20): Study the following pie-chart to answer the following questions.

The pie-chart shows the distance travelled by six persons.

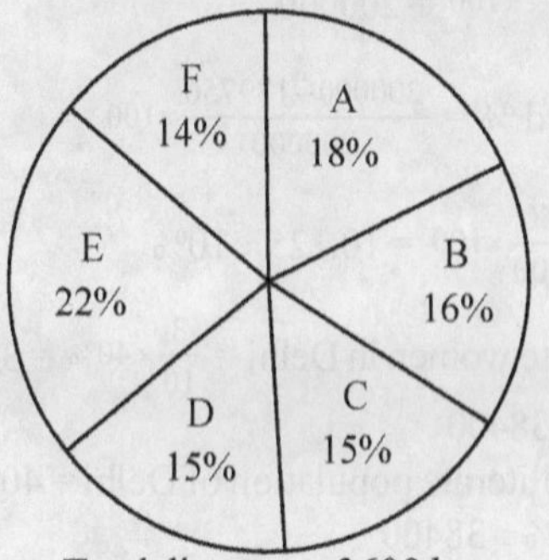

Total distance = 3600 km

16. B travels at the rate of 48 kmph for the first 240 km by bike and then travels by car for the rest of the journey. Howoever, had he travelled 240 km by car and the remaining distance by bike he would have taken half an hour longer to complete the journey. Find the speed of the car.
1) 72 kmph 2) 64 kmph 3) 90 kmph
4) 78 kmph 5) 68 kmph

17. D's speed is 12 kmph less than the speed of C and six-sevenths the speed of F. If F takes 8 hours to cover $\frac{7}{9}$ of his total distance, then what time will be taken by C to complete the whole journey?
1) 12 hours 2) 8 hours 3) 6 hours
4) 10 hours 5) 15 hours

18. E travels 72 km daily. After travelling for 3 days, E doubles his speed. Find the total time taken by him to reach his destination.
1) 14 days 2) 18 days 3) 7 days
4) 16 days 5) 20 days

19. A travels 270 km by air, 288 km by train and the remaining distance by car, taking altogether $6\frac{1}{4}$ hours. The speed of the aircraft is five times that of the train and the speed of the train is 1.2 times that of the car. What is the speed of A in air?
1) 300 kmph 2) 360 kmph 3) 240 kmph
4) 320 kmph 5) 400 kmph

20. C started travelling at the rate of 54 kmph so as to reach just in time. After 2 hours he realised that he had left his purse at the starting point, so he went back and after collecting his purse he began to travel at an increased speed, and reached his destination on time. What was his increased speed?
1) 28 kmph 2) 32 kmph 3) 36 kmph
4) 48 kmph 5) 42 kmph

Answers and explanations

1. 1; Illiterate women in Bengaluru

$= \frac{2}{5} \times 40\%$ of total popⁿ = 28760

So, 16% of total popⁿ = 28760

Total population of Bengaluru $= \frac{28760}{16} \times 100 = 179750$

Literate women in Chandigarh $= \frac{1}{3} \times 72\%$ of total popⁿ

$\therefore$ 24% of total popⁿ = 48000

$\therefore$ Total population of Chandigarh

$= \frac{48000}{24} \times 100 = 200000$

$\therefore$ Reqd % $= \frac{200000 - 179750}{200000} \times 100$

$= \frac{20250}{200000} \times 100 = 10.125 \approx 10\%$

2. 2; Illiterate women in Delhi $= \frac{3}{10} \times 40\% = 38400$

12% = 38400

Total illiterate population of Delhi = 40%

So, 12% ≡ 38400

$\therefore 40\% \equiv \frac{38400}{12} \times 40 = 128000$

3. 4; Total population of Kolkata = 336000

Illiterate population of Kolkata

$= \frac{36}{100} \times 336000 = 120960$

Illitrate males $= \frac{2}{3} \times 120960 = 80640$

Literate population = 336000 − 120960 = 215040

Literate females $= \frac{3}{8} \times 215040 = 80640$

As we can see, there is no difference between the population of illiterate males and literate females.

4. 2; Literate female population of Mumbai

$= 50\% \times \frac{2}{5} = 68000 \therefore 20\% = 68000$

Then male population (literate) = 30% = 102000

Illiterate population = 50% = 102000 + 68000 = 170000

$\therefore$ Male illiterates $= \frac{13}{25} \times 170000 = 88400$

Total males = 88400 + 102000 = 190400

5. 3; Illiterate males in Amritsar $= \frac{7}{13} \times 52 = 28\% = 67200$

Then literate population $= 48\% = \frac{67200}{28} \times 48 = 115200$

$\therefore$ Literate females $= \frac{1}{4} \times 115200 = 28800$

6. 1; Let the speed of the boat in still water be x kmph.

Then, $\frac{15 \times 2.5}{x-4} = \frac{89}{40} + \frac{1.50 \times 12}{x+4} \Rightarrow \frac{37.5}{x-4} - \frac{18}{x+4} = \frac{89}{40}$

If we put x = 16 then the above equation is satisfied.

Hence x = 16 kmph

7. 4; Let the speed of the boat in still water on Friday be x kmph.

Then, $\frac{2.50 \times 14}{x-3} = 3 + \frac{16 \times 1.5}{10+2} \Rightarrow \frac{35}{x-3} = 3 + 2 \Rightarrow x - 3 = 7$

$\therefore$ x = 10 kmph

$\therefore$ Upstream speed = 10 − 3 = 7 kmph

8. 2; Speed of the boat in still water on Monday = 14 kmph

Now, $28\frac{4}{7}\% = \frac{2}{7}$

$\therefore$ Speed of the boat in still water on Sunday

$= 14 - 14 \times \frac{2}{7} = 10$ kmph

Now, $\frac{12 \times 2.5}{14 - x} = \frac{5}{3} \times \frac{18 \times 1.5}{10+2}$

$\Rightarrow \frac{30}{14-x} = \frac{5}{3} \times \frac{27}{12} \Rightarrow \frac{30}{14-x} = \frac{45}{12} \Rightarrow 360 = 45 \times 14 - 45x$

$\Rightarrow 45x = 45 \times 14 - 360 \Rightarrow 45x = 270 \therefore x = 6$ kmph

$\therefore$ Reqd time $= \frac{32}{14-6} = \frac{32}{8} = 4$ hours

9. 1; Let the speed of the boat in still water on Saturday be x kmph.

Then, $\frac{25\times2.5}{x-1} = \frac{16\times1.5}{16+2}$

$\Rightarrow \frac{62.5}{x-1} = \frac{24}{18} \Rightarrow 62.5\times18 = 24x - 24 \Rightarrow 24x = 1125 + 24$

$\therefore x = \frac{1149}{24} = 47.875$

10. 3; Reqd ratio $= \frac{(10+12+15)\% \text{ of } 250}{(8+12)\% \text{ of } 150}$

$= \frac{37\times2.5}{20\times1.5} = \frac{37\times25}{20\times15} = 37:12$

(11-15):

Maximum marks in Engish = 40
and GA = 40, Reasoning = 40 + 20 = 60
∴ In Quant = 200 – (40 + 40 + 60) = 60
Now, we draw the table given below:

	English (40)	Reasoning (60)	GA (40)	Quant (60)
Tanu	30	50	28	24
Rishi	19	30	16	20
Pooja	24	22	26	36
Total	73	102	70	80

11. 2; Reqd average $= \frac{102}{3} = 34$

12. 3; Total marks scored by Rishi
$= 19 + 30 + 16 + 20 = 85$

Reqd % $= \frac{85}{200}\times100 = 42.5\%$

13. 5; Reqd difference = 73 – 70 = 3

14. 2; Marks of Rishi and Pooja in Reasoning

$= \frac{52-44}{44}\times100 = 30 + 22 = 52$

Tanu and Rishi in GA = 28 + 16 = 44

Reqd % $= \frac{52-44}{44}\times100 = \frac{8}{44}\times100 = 18.18\%$

15. 3; Total compartments = 2
Pooja in Reasoning and Rishi in Quants.

16. 2; Total distance covered by B
= 16% of 3600 = 36 × 16 = 576 km
Distance covered by bike = 240 km
Distance covered by car = 576 – 240 = 336 km

Let the speed of the car be x kmph.

Case I. Time taken $= \frac{240}{48} + \frac{336}{x} = \left(5 + \frac{336}{x}\right)$ hours

Case II. Time taken $\frac{240}{x} + \frac{336}{48} = \left(\frac{240}{x} + 7\right)$ hours

According to the question,

$\left(\frac{240}{x} + 7\right) - \left(5 + \frac{336}{x}\right) = \frac{1}{2}$

$\Rightarrow \frac{240}{x} + 7 - 5 - \frac{336}{x} = \frac{1}{2} \Rightarrow -\frac{96}{x} = -\frac{3}{2} \quad \therefore x = 64$ kmph

17. 4; Distance covered by F = 14% of 3600
= 36 × 14 = 504 km

Speed of F $= \frac{504\times\frac{7}{9}}{8} = \frac{392}{8} = 49$ kmph

Speed of D $= 49\times\frac{6}{7} = 42$ kmph

∴ Speed of C = 42 + 12 = 54 kmph
Distance covered by C = 15% of 3600 = 15 × 36

∴ Time taken by C $= \frac{36\times15}{54} = 10$ hours

18. 3; Total distance for E = 22% of 3600
= 36 × 22 = 792 km

Reqd number of days $= \frac{792-(72\times3)}{72\times2} + 3 = \frac{576}{144} + 3$
= 4 + 3 = 7 days

19. 2; Total distance covered by A = 18% of 3600 = 18 × 36
= 648

	Air	Train	Car
Speed	6x	1.2x	x
Distance	270	288	90

Now, $\frac{270}{6x} + \frac{2880}{12x} + \frac{90}{x} = \frac{25}{4} \Rightarrow \frac{540+2880+1080}{12x} = \frac{25}{4}$

$\Rightarrow \frac{4500}{12x} = \frac{25}{4} \quad \therefore x = \frac{4500\times4}{12\times25} = 60$ kmph

∴ Speed of aircraft = 60 × 6 = 360 kmph

20. 3; Total distance covered by C = 15 × 36 = 540 km

Total time $= \frac{540}{54} = 10$ hours

Remaining time = 10 – 2 – 2 = 6 hours

After increase the speed of C $= \frac{540}{6} = 90$ kmph

∴ Increased speed = 90 – 54 = 36 kmph

Practice Set 49

Directions (Q. 1-5): Study the following table carefully to answer the following questions. The table shows various statistics of five different products.

Product	Cost price	MP	Profit/Loss (Percentage)	Profit/Loss (in ₹)	SP
Laptop	₹35000	–	–	–	–
Mobile	–	₹16875	–	1675	–
Tablet	–	₹26250	6.25%	–	₹22312.5
Printer	–	₹22950	–	–	–
Monitor	–	–	–	–	₹16675

1. A shopkeeper marked 30% above the cost price on the Laptop, but he offers 10% discount on the Laptop to all his customers. He offers a further discount of 4% on the reduced price to those customers who pay in cash. What will be the purchase price for a customer who wishes to purchase in cash?
   1) ₹39312 2) ₹36728 3) ₹35273
   4) ₹33918 5) ₹34615
2. If the cost price of a Printer is ₹17,000, then find the % profit of a shopkeeper who offers a discount of 16% on the same article.
   1) 17.6% 2) 13.4% 3) 10% 4) 18.75% 5) 12.8%
3. A shopkeeper sold a Monitor at a discount of 8% on the marked price. He would have earned a profit of 25%, had there been no discount. What was the actual percentage of profit earned?
   1) 10% 2) 12% 3) 15% 4) 8% 5) 20%
4. A shopkeeper marked the price 35% and 25% above the cost price of Mobiles and Tablets respectively. What is the difference between the cost price of a Tablet and the selling price of a Mobile?
   1) ₹6786 2) ₹8338 3) ₹6532
   4) ₹7857 5) ₹6825
5. A shopkeeper sold a Mobile at a discount of 4%. If on this sales tax is 12%, then the find the selling price of a Mobile.
   1) ₹14188 2) ₹16177 3) ₹17716
   4) ₹18144 5) ₹15750

Directions (Q. 6-10): Study the following information to answer the following questions.

Rangoli Paint Company (RPC) is in the business of manufacturing paints. RPC buys Red, Green and Blue paints and produces Yellow, White, Magenta and Cyan. Yellow colour is prepared by mixing Red and Green in the ratio of 2 : 3. White colour is prepared by mixing Red, Green and Blue in the ratio of 2 : 1 : 2. The company prepares Magenta colour by mixing Red and Blue in the ratio of 4 : 1. The cost prices of Red, Green and Blue paints are ₹35, ₹40 and ₹45 per litre respectively.

6. Cyan colur is prepared by mixing Green and Blue colour in the ratio of 3 : 2. Assume that Yellow, Magenta and Cyan each colour is sold for the same price. Which of the three is the most profitable to produce?
   1) Only Yellow colour 2) Only Magenta colour
   3) Only Cyan colour 4) Either Yellow or Cyan
   5) Either Magenta or Cyan
7. The company prepared a packet of Cyan colour of 20 litres of which $\frac{1}{3}$ is Green and the rest is Blue, which is mixed with another 30 litres of Cyan colour, of which $\frac{1}{4}$ is Green and the rest is Blue. What is the ratio of Green to Blue in the final mixture?
   1) 16 : 41 2) 17 : 41 3) 19 : 43
   4) 17 : 43 5) 16 : 43
8. The company prepared a packet of Magenta colour of 30 litres. When from the Magenta colour packet 10 litres is taken out and X litres of Blue colour is poured into the packet the ratio of Red to Blue becomes 2 : 3. How many litres of Blue colour was poured into the packet?
   1) 25 litres 2) 32 litres 3) 20 litres
   4) 22 litres 5) None of these
9. The company prepared a packet of White colour of 40 litres. What price should it sell on the packet at to make a profit of 10%?
   1) ₹1760 2) ₹1440 3) ₹1890
   4) ₹1680 5) ₹1560
10. The company sells 30 litres of Red colour at a profit of 10%, 45 litres of Green colour at a profit of 15% and 50 litres of Blue colour at a profit of 20%. What is the total profit of the company?
    1) ₹900 2) ₹670 3) ₹750
    4) ₹1000 5) ₹825

Directions (Q. 11-12): Read the following information carefully and answer the questions.

Ritu, Shamita and Ragini invested ₹360, ₹640 and ₹280

in a business which gives returns at the end of each year. They further increased their investments at the end of each quarter. They invested additional amount in the ratio of 3 : 4 : 4 at the end of the first quarter and invested further additional amount in the ratio of 2 : 5 : 2 at the end of the second quarter. Again after the end of the third quarter they invested further additional amount in the ratio of 7 : 6 : 7. They invested the whole amount for one year from the time of initial investment.

11. Shamita and Ragini invested a total amount of ₹4200 in the entire year and Shamita and Ritu invested ₹3600 in the entire year. What will be the amount invested by Ritu, Shamita and Ragini at the beginning of the second quarter?
1) ₹4600 2) ₹6480 3) ₹6800
4) ₹7480 5) Cannot be determined

12. Find the profit of Ragini at the end of one year, if Ritu, Shamita and Ragini had invested additional amount at the end of each quarter in the same ratio as they had invested after the end of the second quarter and the initial investment was also in the ratio of 2 : 5 : 2 instead of that mentioned in the given information and the total profit at the end of the year is ₹540.
1) ₹160 2) ₹220 3) ₹120
4) ₹190 5) Cannot be determined

Directions (Q. 13-18): Given below is the table showing investment of five persons in a business, time for which investment is made, share of profit of each person and percentage share of total profit earned.

Some values are missing in the table, you have to calculate these values if necessary to answer the questions.

Persons	Investment (in ₹)	Time (in months)	Share of profit	Percentage share of total profit
Arjun	—	8	—	480/23
Biplab	25000	—	—	—
Chirag	—	—	900	—
Divya	—	8	—	400/23
Elle	35000	—	945	—

13. What is the sum of the total profit of Arjun and Chirag together if the investment of Arjun and Chirag together is 200% of the investment of Biplab and the investment of Arjun is 50% more than the investment of Chirag (Arjun invested for two months less than Chirag)?
1) ₹1200 2) ₹1890 3) ₹1980 4) ₹1840 5) ₹2100

14. What is the profit of all five persons if profit per cent of Elle is 5% more than the profit per cent of Divya?
1) ₹6545 2) ₹3755 3) ₹4575
4) ₹5250 5) ₹5175

15. What is the total investment of Elle and Chirag if Elle invested for four months less than Chirag and the ratio of the time of investment of Chirag to Elle is 5 : 3?
1) ₹55000 2) ₹20000 3) ₹45000
4) ₹64000 5) None of these

16. The profit of Arjun is what per cent of the profit of Chirag if the profit of Chirag is $16\frac{2}{3}\%$ less than the profit of Arjun?
1) 135 2) 120 3) 125
4) 80 5) Cannot be determined

17. For how many months more is investment made by Divya in comparison to Elle if the profit of Divya is equal to the profit of Chirag and the investment of Divya is $71\frac{3}{7}\%$ of the investment of Elle?
1) 3 2) 4 3) 6 4) 2 5) 5

18. What is the percentage share of Biplab out of the total profit earned if it is given that the profit earned by Biplab is 50% more than the profit earned by Chirag, which in turn is $17\frac{9}{23}\%$ of the total profit earned by all the five persons?
1) $\frac{600}{23}$ 2) $\frac{450}{23}$ 3) $\frac{420}{23}$
4) $\frac{400}{23}$ 5) Cannot be determined

Directions (Q. 19-21): Study the given information carefully and answer the questions that follow.

Abhay is thrice as efficient as Bajrangi and therefore he is able to complete an assignment in 80 hours less than Bajrangi. If Abhay and Bajrangi complete $\frac{5}{8}$ of the assignment and then Abhay is replaced by Akhandita, the remaining assignment is completed by Bajrangi and Akhandita in 15 hours. If Abhay and Bajrangi complete $\frac{5}{12}$ of the job and then Bajrangi is replaced by Dhwani, the remaining assignment is completed by Abhay and Dhwani in 10 hours.

19. How long will it take for Abhay, Bajrangi, Akhandita and Dhwani to complete the assignment working together?
1) 18 hours 2) 16 hours 3) 12 hours
4) 9 hours 5) 15 hours

20. The assignment is completed in the following manner: Abhay and Bajrangi work in 1st hour, Bajrangi and Akhandita in 2nd hour, Akhandita and Dhwani in 3rd hour, Dhwani and Abhay in 4th hour and this order gets repeated.
How long will it take for the assignment to be completed in this manner?

1) 30 hours 2) 18 hours 3) 20 hours
4) 24 hours 5) 36 hours

21. How long will it take to complete the assignment if in 1st hour Bajrangi, Akhandita and Dhwani do the assignment and Abhay destroys it; in 2nd hour Abhay, Akhandita and Dhwani do the assignment and Bajrangi destroys it; in 3rd hour Abhay, Bajrangi and Dhwani do the assignment and Akhandita destroys it; and in 4th hour, Abhay, Bajrangi and Akhandita does assignment and Dhwani destroys it and this process keeps on repeating? (It is mentioned that working capacity of a person is equal to the destroying capacity of that person.)
1) 24 hours 2) 36 hours 3) 48 hours
4) 12 hours 5) 30 hours

Answers and explanations

1. 1; Reqd amount = $35000\times\frac{130}{100}\times\frac{90}{100}\times\frac{96}{100}=₹39312$

2. 2; Cost price = ₹17000

Selling price = $22950\times\frac{84}{100}=19278$

$\therefore$ Reqd % profit = $\frac{19278-17000}{17000}\times100$

$=\frac{2278}{17000}\times100=13.4\%$

3. 3; Marked price = $\frac{16675}{92}\times100=₹18125$

$\therefore$ Cost price = $\frac{18125}{125}\times100=\frac{18125}{5}\times4=₹14500$

Selling price = ₹16675

$\therefore$ Actual profit % = $\frac{16675-14500}{14500}\times100$

$=\frac{2175}{14500}\times100=\frac{2175}{145}=15\%$

Quicker Method:

Let CP = 100 $\Rightarrow$ MP = 125

$\Rightarrow$ SP at 8% disc = $125\times\frac{92}{100}=115$

$\Rightarrow$ % profit = $\frac{115-100}{100}=15$

4. 5; Reqd difference = $\frac{26250}{125}\times100-\left(\frac{16875}{135}\times100+1675\right)$

$=21000-(12500+1675)=21000-14175=₹6825$

5. 4; Marked price of Mobile = 16875

Net price of the Mobile = $16875\times\frac{96}{100}=₹16200$

$\therefore$ Selling price of the Mobile = $16200\times\frac{112}{100}=₹18144$

6. 2; Cost price of Cyan colour

$=40\times\frac{3}{5}+45\times\frac{2}{5}=24+18=42$

$\therefore$ Cost price of Yellow colour

$=35\times\frac{2}{5}+40\times\frac{3}{5}=14+24=38$

$\therefore$ Cost price of Magenta colour

$=35\times\frac{4}{5}+45\times\frac{1}{5}=28+9=37$

Therefor cost price is minimum for Magenta colour paint.
Hence Magenta colour is the most profitable to produce.

7. 4; Reqd ratio = $20\times\frac{1}{3}+30\times\frac{1}{4}:20\times\frac{2}{3}+30\times\frac{3}{4}$

$=\frac{20}{3}+\frac{30}{4}:\frac{40}{3}+\frac{90}{4}$

$=\frac{80+90}{12}:\frac{160+270}{12}=\frac{170}{12}:\frac{430}{12}=17:43$

8. 3; Total quantity = 30 litres
Taken out quantity = 10 litres
Remaining quantity = 30 – 10 = 20 litres
$\because$ Magenta colour is prepared by mixing Red and Blue in the ratio 4 : 1.

Quantity of Blue colour in remaining 20 litres = $20\times\frac{1}{5}$
= 4 litres

Now, $\frac{4+x}{20+x}=\frac{3}{5}\Rightarrow20+5x=60+3x\Rightarrow5x-3x=60-20$

$\Rightarrow2x=40\;\therefore\;x=20$ litres

9. 1; Reqd selling price = $40\left(35\times\frac{2}{5}+40\times\frac{1}{5}+45\times\frac{2}{5}\right)\times\frac{110}{100}$

$=\frac{110}{100}\times40(14+8+18)=\frac{110}{100}\times40\times40=₹1760$

10. 5; Total profit

$=30\times35\times\frac{10}{100}+40\times45\times\frac{15}{100}+45\times50\times\frac{20}{100}=105$

$+270+450=₹825$

11. 4; Let the amount invested by Ritu, Shamita and Ragini after the first quarter 3x, 4x and 4x respectively.
After second quarter 2y, 5y and 2y respectively.
After third quarter 7z, 6z and 7z respectively.
Then, amount invested by Shamita and Ragini

$=(640+280)+8x+7y+13z=4200$

$\Rightarrow8x+7y+13z=3280$ ...(i)

And amount invested by Ritu and Shamita

$=(360+640)+7x+7y+13z=3600$

$\Rightarrow7x+7y+13z=2600$ ...(ii)

Solving (i) and (ii), we get x = 680

$\therefore$ required answer = $(3+4+4)x=11x$

$=11\times680=₹7480$

12. 3; At the end of the second quarter. ratio of new investment is 2 : 5 : 2 (given).
According to the information in this question, this is the ratio in which they had invested at the end of each quarter. Now, it is evident that profit shared by Ragini

in the entire year is $\frac{2}{9}$ of the total profit.

$\therefore \frac{2}{9} \times 540 = ₹120$

13. 3;

	Arjun	Chirag	Biplav
Investment →	150% of C	C	25000

Now, according to the question,

$(3C + 2C) = 200\%$ of $25000 = 2 \times 25000 = 50,000$

$\therefore C = 10000$

So, investment of Chirag = 20000

And investment of Arjun = 30000

Ratio of profit of C to A $= 20000 \times 10 : 30000 \times 8$

$= 2 \times 5 : 3 \times 4 = 5 : 6$

$\therefore$ Sum of profit $= \frac{900}{5} \times 11 = ₹1980$

14. 5; Profit % of Elle $= \frac{105}{100} \times \frac{400}{23} = \frac{420}{23}\%$

Now, $\frac{420}{23}\% \equiv 945$

$\Rightarrow 1\% \equiv \left(\frac{945}{420} \times 23\right)$

So, $100\% \equiv \frac{945}{420} \times 23 \times 100 = ₹5175$

15. 1; Let Elle and Chirag invest for 3x and 5x months respectively.

Then, $5x - 3x = 4 \Rightarrow 2x = 4 \Rightarrow x = 2$

Again, $\frac{N \times 10}{35000 \times 6} = \frac{900}{945}$ (where N = amount invested by Chirag) $\Rightarrow N = 20000$

$\therefore$ Reqd answer $= 20000 + 35000 = ₹55000$

16. 2;

Arjun	Chirag
100	$100 - \frac{50}{3} = \frac{250}{3}$

$\therefore$ Reqd % $= \frac{100 \times 3}{250} = 120\%$

17. 4; Investment of Divya

$= 71\frac{3}{7}\%$ of $35000 = \frac{5}{7} \times 35000 = 25000$

Profit of Divya = Profit of Chirag = 900

Then, $\frac{8 \times 25000}{35000 \times t} = \frac{900}{945}$ (where t = time of investment of Elle) $\Rightarrow t = 6$ months

$\therefore$ Reqd answer $= 8 - 6 = 2$ months

18. 1; Profit earned by Biplab $= \frac{3}{2} \times 900 = ₹1350$

Now, $17\frac{9}{23}\% = \frac{4}{23} \; \therefore \; \frac{4}{23} \equiv 900 \; \therefore 1 \equiv \frac{900}{4} \times 23 = 5175$

$\therefore$ Reqd answer $= \frac{1350}{5175} \times 100 = \frac{600}{23}\%$

19. 3; Let Abhay and Bajrangi take n and 3n hours respectively to complete the assignment.

Then as per information given, $3n - n = 80$

$\Rightarrow n = 40$ hours

$\Rightarrow$ Abhay takes 40 hours and Bajrangi takes $(40 \times 3) = 120$ hours to do the assignment alone.

Now, let Akhandita do the work in y hours.

Then, $15\left(\frac{1}{120} + \frac{1}{y}\right) = 1 - \frac{5}{8} \Rightarrow 15\left(\frac{y+120}{120y}\right) = \frac{3}{8}$

$\Rightarrow \frac{y+120}{120y} = \frac{1}{40} \Rightarrow \frac{y+120}{3y} = 1 \therefore y = 60$ hours

Let Dhwani take d hours to complete the assignment alone. Then, $10\left(\frac{1}{40} + \frac{1}{d}\right) = 1 - \frac{5}{12}$

$\Rightarrow d = 30$ hours $\therefore$ One day's work of all of them

$= \frac{1}{40} + \frac{1}{120} + \frac{1}{60} + \frac{1}{30} = \frac{1}{12}$

$\therefore$ Required answer = 12 hours

20. 4; **(Using solution Q. 19):**

Part of assignment done in 1st hour

$= \frac{1}{40} + \frac{1}{120} = \frac{1}{30}$

Part of assignment done in 2nd hour

$= \frac{1}{60} + \frac{1}{120} = \frac{1}{40}$

Part of assignment done in 3rd hour

$= \frac{1}{60} + \frac{1}{30} = \frac{1}{20}$

Part of assignment done in 4th hour

$= \frac{1}{30} + \frac{1}{40} = \frac{7}{120}$

Part of assignment done in 4 hours

$= \frac{1}{30} + \frac{1}{40} + \frac{1}{20} + \frac{7}{120} = \frac{20}{120} = \frac{1}{6}$

Hence, the work will be completed in $(6 \times 4 =)$ 24 hours

21. 1; In 1st hour, part of assignment done

$= \frac{1}{120} + \frac{1}{60} + \frac{1}{30} - \frac{1}{40} = \frac{4}{120} = \frac{1}{30}$

In 2nd hour, part of assignment done

$= \frac{1}{40} - \frac{1}{120} + \frac{1}{60} + \frac{1}{30} = \frac{3-1+2+4}{120} = \frac{8}{120} = \frac{1}{15}$

In 3rd hour, part of assignment done

$= \frac{1}{40} + \frac{1}{120} - \frac{1}{60} + \frac{1}{30} = \frac{3+1-2+4}{120} = \frac{6}{120} = \frac{1}{20}$

In 4th hour, part of assignment done

$= \frac{1}{40} + \frac{1}{120} + \frac{1}{60} - \frac{1}{30} = \frac{3+1+2-4}{120} = \frac{2}{120} = \frac{1}{60}$

So, in 4 hours, part of work done

$= \frac{1}{30} + \frac{1}{15} + \frac{1}{20} + \frac{1}{60} = \frac{2+4+3+1}{60} = \frac{10}{60} = \frac{1}{6}$

$\therefore$ Time taken $= 6 \times 4 = 24$ hours

Practice Set 50

Directions (Q. 1-5): Study the information carefully and answer the given questions:

There are five mixtures of wine and water in five different vessels—P, Q, R, S and T. Given below are two pie charts. Pie chart A shows the percentage distribution of wine in each of the vessels out of the total wine in these five vessels. Pie chart B shows percentage distribution of water in each of the vessels out of the total water in these five vessels.

Pie Chart A

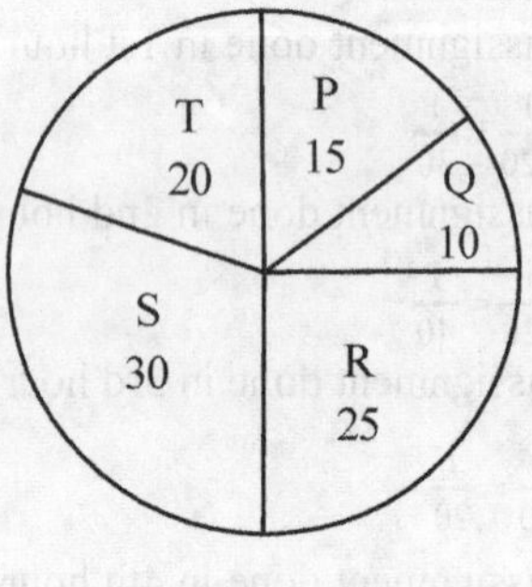

Pie Chart B

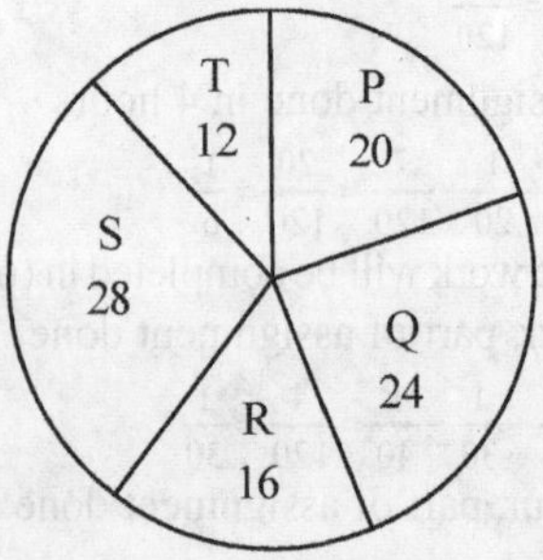

Note: The total amount of water in these five vessels is 2.5 times the amount of wine in these five vessels.

1. The mixtures of vessel P and R are mixed into another vessel W. If 26 litres of mixture from W is taken out and 12 litres of wine is added then the ratio of wine to water becomes 5 : 9. What is the quantity of wine in vessel Q?
   1) 28 litres 2) 7 litres 3) 35 litres
   4) 14 litres 5) 18 litres
2. Rupal pours the mixtures of vessel S and T in another vessel K, which already contains only water which is equal to 75% of water in vessel S. If Rupal professes to sell the whole mixture in vessel S at the cost price and the cost price of the mixture is due to wine only, then find the percentage profit of Rupal in selling the whole mixture of vessel S.
   1) 75 2) 205 3) 305
   4) 145 5) Cannot be determined
3. If the total quantity of wine and water in vessel Q is 98 litres, then the quantity of wine and water in vessel T is how much less than the quantity of water in vessel S?
   1) 98 litres 2) 42 litres 3) 28 litres
   4) Cannot be determined 5) 35 litres
4. Some quantities of mixtures from vessel Q and T are taken out and the ratio of the quantities taken out from vessel Q and T are in the ratio 2 : 3. Then find the ratio of wine to water in the final mixture.
   1) 53 : 93 2) 53 : 125 3) 21 : 75
   4) None of these 5) Can't be determined
5. All the contents of the mixtures from all the vessels except R are poured into a bigger vessel and only 52 litres of mixture from R is poured into the bigger vessel. If the ratio of wine to water in the bigger vessel is 125 : 326, then what is the total quantity of water in all five vessels?
   1) 240 litres 2) 140 litres 3) 350 litres
   4) 420 litres 5) Cannot be determined

Directions (Q. 6-11): Study the information given below carefully and answer the questions that follow.

The pie chart given below shows percentages of bikes sold by six dealers.

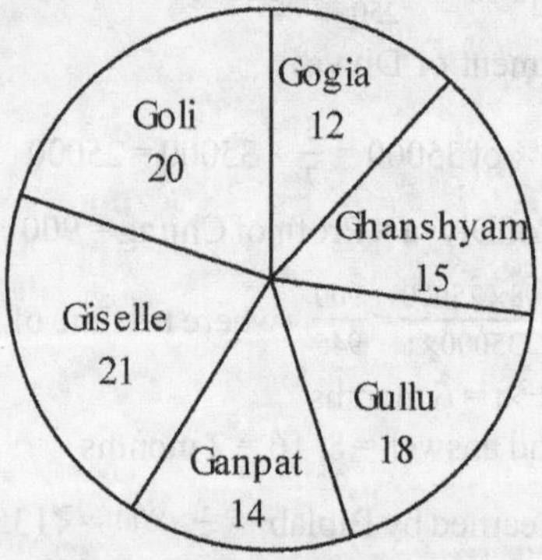

Total bikes sold in 2018 = 15 lakh

Each of these sellers sold three different models of bikes—P, Q and R—in the year 2018. The table given below shows the ratio of the models of bikes sold by each of these sellers.

Persons	Ratio of models P, Q and R sold by the dealers
Gogia	4 : 3 : 2
Ghanshyam	3 : 4 : 3
Gullu	9 : 7 : 9
Ganpat	6 : 4 : 5
Giselle	3 : 2 : 1
Goli	4 : 5 : 3

6. What is the ratio of P and Q model bikes sold by Ghanshaym to model P bikes sold by Giselle and Goli together?
1) 306 : 301 2) 63 : 103 3) 103 : 306
4) 306 : 103 5) None of the given options
7. The average of P model bikes sold by all the six given dealers in 2018 is
1) 97700 2) 96500 3) 84200
4) 102500 5) None of the given options
8. What is the difference between model P and Q bikes sold by Gullu together and model R and P bikes sold by Goli together?
1) 2000 2) 1800 3) 2200
4) 2400 5) 2800
9. Model P and R bikes sold by Gogia is what per cent more or less than the model Q and R bikes sold by Goli?
1) 60 2) 40 3) 20 4) 120 5) 80
10. The ratio of the total model Q bikes sold by all the six dealers to the total model R bikes sold by all six dealers is
1) 2885 : 2011 2) 2558 : 2561 3) 2011 : 2023
4) 2558 : 2011 5) None of these
11. The average model Q bikes sold by all the six dealers together is more than model R bikes sold by how many of the given dealers?
1) Five 2) Four 3) Three
4) None 5) Two

Directions (Q. 12-15): Study the given information carefully and answer the questions that follow.

Kajal's mother gave her some money and asked her to give the money to four beggars. Kajal could only find one beggar and gave him $\frac{1}{4}$ of the money. After a while, Kajal saw another beggar and then she gave $\frac{1}{4}$ of the remaining money to each of the first and second beggar. After some time, Kajal found another beggar and then she gave $\frac{1}{4}$ of the remaining money to each of the three beggars. Finally, Kajal found the fourth beggar and then distributed the remaining amount of money equally among all of them.

12. What is the ratio of amount that the first beggar got to the amount that the fourth beggar got?
1) 64 : 3 2) 71 : 3 3) 9 : 1
4) 81 : 4 5) Cannot be determined
13. If the fourth beggar got a total of ₹48, then how much money did Kajal's mother give her?
1) Cannot be determined 2) ₹3448 3) ₹1728
4) ₹2098 5) ₹2048
14. If the difference between the amount that the second and the third beggar got is ₹72, then what is the total amount that the first beggar got?
1) None of the given options 2) ₹223 3) ₹208
4) ₹213 5) Cannot be determined
15. The amount received by the fourth beggar is what per cent of the amount received by the second beggar?
1) $7\frac{9}{13}$ 2) $8\frac{2}{5}$ 3) $16\frac{2}{3}$
4) $14\frac{2}{7}$ 5) Cannot be determined

Directions (Q. 16-21): Read the following table and bar graph carefully and answer the questions given below:

The table given below shows the amount of work done (in units) per hour by five different persons on Monday. It also shows the ratio of the efficiency of doing work of these five persons on Monday to that on Tuesday.

Persons	Work done per hour (in units) on Monday	Ratio of efficiency on Monday to that on Tuesday
Jhilmil	2	1 : 3
Satwik	6	3 : 2
Rituraj	4	4 : 9
Kishwar	5	1 : 2
Prince	3	3 : 1

The bar graph given below shows the time taken by each of the five persons on Wednesday to do the work as a per cent of time taken by them in doing the same work on Monday.

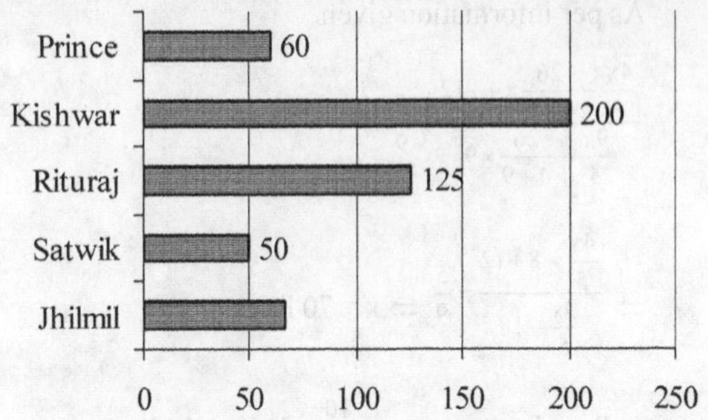

Note: Total work done by each of the five persons individually on each of the three days is the same. For example, if Rituraj does N unit work on Monday then he will do N units of work on Tuesday and on Wednesday as well, whereas, efficiencies and the time taken to complete this work is different as per given conditions.

16. If Jhilmil took 6 hours to do her work on Monday, then what is the ratio of time taken by her to do her work on Tuesday to that on Wednesday?

1) 2 : 1 2) 3 : 1 3) 1 : 2
4) 1 : 4 5) Cannot be determined

17. If it is given that time taken by Kishwar to do her work on Tuesday is less than the time taken by her to do her work on Monday by 1 hour and 30 minutes, then what is the time taken by her to do her work on Wednesday?

1) 6 hours 2) 4 hours 3) 3 hours
4) 8 hours 5) Cannot be determined

18. If the total work done by Satwik is four times the work done by Jhilmil and the time taken by Satwik to do his work on Monday is 2 hours more than the time taken by Jhilmil to do her work on the same day, then what is the sum of the time taken by both of them to complete their work on Tuesday?

1) 11 hours 2) 15 hours 3) 16 hours
4) 12 hours 5) 14 hours

19. If the amount of work done by Prince, Kishwar and Rituraj on each day is 15, 15 and 16 units respectively, then what is the average of the time taken by the three of them to complete their work on Wednesday?

1) 5 hours 2) 6 hours 3) $3\frac{2}{3}$ hours
4) 8 hours 5) $4\frac{2}{3}$ hours

20. If the amount of work done by the five persons is 12 units each individually then approximately what is the sum of time taken by each of them individually to complete the work on Tuesday?

1) 12 hours 42 minutes 2) 19 hours 32 minutes
3) 20 hours 20 minutes 4) 14 hours 12 minutes
5) 22 hours 44 minutes

21. The sum of time taken by Satwik and Kishwar in completing their work individually is 11 hours. If it is given that the total amount of work done by them is 63 units together (sum of work done by both of them), then what is the ratio of time taken by Kishwar to that of time taken by Satwik on Wednesday to do their work?

1) 2 : 3 2) 1 : 4 3) 3 : 2
4) 3 : 5 5) Cannot be determined

Answers and explanations

1. 4; Total amount of water in all the five vessels in 2.5 times that of wine.

Let total wine and water in all five vessels be 2x and 5x respectively. Then,

$$\text{Wine in P and R} = \frac{15+25}{100}\times 2x = \frac{4x}{5}$$

$$\text{Water in P and R} = \frac{20+16}{100}\times 5x = \frac{9x}{5}$$

So, ratio of wine to water in vessel W

$$= \frac{4x}{5} : \frac{9x}{5} = 4:9$$

As per information given,

$$\frac{\frac{4x}{5} - \frac{26}{4+9}\times 4 + 12}{\frac{9x}{5} - \frac{26}{4+9}\times 9} = \frac{5}{9}$$

$$\Rightarrow \frac{\frac{4x}{5} - 8 + 12}{\frac{9x}{5} - 18} = \frac{5}{9} \Rightarrow x = 70 \text{ litres}$$

$$\therefore \text{Required answer} = \frac{10}{100}\times 70\times 2 = 14 \text{ litres}$$

2. 3; Let total wine quantity = 200n litres

And total water quantity = 500n litres

Total wine in vessels S and T

$$= \frac{20+30}{100}\times 200n = 100n$$

Total water in vessels S and T

$$= \frac{28+12}{100}\times 500n = 200n$$

Water present initially in K

$$= \frac{75}{100}\times\frac{28}{100}\times 500n = 105n$$

So, total water in K = 105n + 200n = 305n

∴ Total mixture in vessel K = 305n + 100n = 405n

If CP of 1 litre of wine is ₹1.

Then, CP of mixture in vessel K = 100n

SP = 405n

$$\text{Required \% profit} = \frac{405n - 100n}{100n}\times 100 = \frac{305n}{100n}\times 100$$

$$= 305\%$$

3. 3; Let total quantity of wine and water in all 5 vessels be 2n and 5n respectively. Then,

$$\frac{10}{100}(2n) + \frac{24}{100}(5n) = 98$$

$$\Rightarrow \frac{n}{5} + \frac{6n}{5} = 98 \Rightarrow n = \frac{98\times 5}{7} = 14\times 5 = 70 \text{ litres}$$

Quantity of water in vessel S

$$= \frac{28}{100}\times 5\times 70 = 98 \text{ litres}$$

Quantity of wine and water in vessel T

$= \frac{20}{100}(70\times 2) + \frac{12}{100}(70\times 5) = 28 + 42 = 70$ litres

$\therefore$ Required difference = 98 – 70 = 28 litres

4. 4; Ratio of wine to water in vessel Q

$= \frac{10}{100}x : \frac{24}{100}\times\frac{5}{2}x = \frac{x}{10} : \frac{3x}{5} = 1 : 6$

Ratio of wine to water in vessel T

$= \frac{20}{100}x : \frac{12}{100}\times\frac{5}{2}x = 2 : 3$

By alligation: (Part of water)

$\frac{3}{5}$ $\qquad$ $\frac{1}{7}$

M (reqd ratio)

3 : 2

Now, $\frac{3}{2} = \frac{\frac{6}{7} - M}{M - \frac{3}{5}} \Rightarrow M = \frac{123}{175} = 123 : 175$

Part of wine = 175 – 123 = 52

$\therefore$ Required ratio of wine to water = 52 : 123

5. 3; Let total wine in all five vessels be 200x.

Let total water in all five vessels be 500x.

Then, wine in all vessels except R

$= \frac{75}{100}\times 200x = 150x$

Water in all vessels except R $= \frac{84}{100}\times 500x = 420x$

Ratio of wine to water in vessel R

$= \frac{25}{100}\times 200x : \frac{16}{100}\times 500x = 50x : 80x = 5 : 8$

According to the question,

$\frac{150x + \frac{5}{13}\times 52}{420x + \frac{8}{13}\times 52} = \frac{125}{326} \Rightarrow x = \frac{7}{10}$

Hence, total quantity of water

$= 500x = 500 \times \frac{7}{10} = 350$ litres

(6-11): In 2018,

Bikes sold by Gogia $= \frac{12}{100}\times 1500000 = 180000$

Bikes sold by Ghanshyam $= \frac{15}{100}\times 1500000 = 225000$

Bikes sold by Gullu $= \frac{18}{100}\times 1500000 = 270000$

Bikes sold by Ganpat $= \frac{14}{100}\times 1500000 = 210000$

Bikes sold by Giselle $= \frac{21}{100}\times 1500000 = 315000$

Bikes sold by Goli $= \frac{20}{100}\times 1500000 = 300000$

Bikes of model P sold by Gogia $= \frac{180000}{9}\times 4 = 80000$

Bikes of model Q sold by Gogia $= \frac{180000}{9}\times 3 = 60000$

Bikes of model R sold by Gogia $= \frac{180000}{9}\times 2 = 40000$

Similarly, calculating for all the sellers, we get

Person	P model bikes sold	Q model bikes sold	R model bikes sold
Gogia	80000	60000	40000
Ghanshyam	67500	90000	67500
Gullu	97200	75600	97200
Ganpat	84000	56000	70000
Giselle	157500	105000	52500
Goli	100000	125000	75000

6. 2; Required ratio = (67500 + 90000) : (157500 + 100000)

= 157500 : 257500 = 1575 : 2570 = 63 : 103

7. 1; Required average

$= \frac{80000 + 67500 + 97200 + 84000 + 157500 + 100000}{6} = 97700$

8. 3; Required difference

= (100000 + 75000) – (97200 + 75600)

= 175000 – 172800 = 2200

9. 2; P and R model bikes sold by Gogia

= 80000 + 40000 = 120000

Q and R model bikes sold by Goli

= 125000=75000=200000

Required % $= \frac{200000 - 120000}{200000}\times 100$

$= \frac{80000}{200000}\times 100 = 40\%$

10. 4; Required ratio = (60000 + 90000 + 75600 + 56000 + 105000 + 125000) : (40000 + 67500 + 97200 + 70000 + 52500 + 75000) = 511600 : 402200 = 2558 : 2011

11. 1; Average model Q bikes sold by all dealers

$= \frac{60000 + 90000 + 75600 + 56000 + 105000 + 125000}{6} = 85266\frac{2}{3}$

Hence, this average is more than model R bikes sold by Gogia, Ghanshyam, Ganpat, Giselle and Goli.

12. 2; Total amount that 1st beggar got

$= \frac{N}{4} + \frac{3N}{16} + \frac{3N}{32} + \frac{3N}{128} = \frac{32N + 24N + 12N + 3N}{128} = \frac{71N}{128}$

Thus, required ratio = $\frac{71N}{128} : \frac{3N}{128} = 71 : 3$

13. 5; According to the question, $\frac{3N}{128} = ₹48$

$\Rightarrow N = ₹\left(\frac{48 \times 128}{3}\right) = ₹(16 \times 128) = ₹2048$

14. 4; As per information given,

$\left(\frac{3N}{16} + \frac{3N}{32} + \frac{3N}{128}\right) - \left(\frac{3N}{32} + \frac{3N}{128}\right) = ₹39$

$\Rightarrow \frac{3N}{16} = 72 \Rightarrow N = \frac{72 \times 16}{3} = 24 \times 16 = 384$

Amount that 1st beggar got

$= \frac{N}{4} + \frac{3N}{16} + \frac{3N}{32} + \frac{3N}{128} = \frac{71N}{128} = \frac{71 \times 384}{128} = ₹213$

15. 1; Reqd % $= \frac{\frac{3N}{128}}{\frac{3N}{16} + \frac{3N}{32} + \frac{3N}{128}} \times 100 = \frac{\frac{3N}{128}}{\frac{39N}{128}} \times 100$

$= \frac{1}{13} \times 100 = 7\frac{9}{13}\%$

16. 3; Time taken by Jhilmil to do her work on Wednesday

$= 66\frac{2}{3}\%$ of $6 = \frac{2}{3} \times 6 = 4$ hours

Total work = 6 × 2 = 12 units

Work done per hour by Jhilmil on Tuesday

$= 2\left(\frac{3}{1}\right) = 6$ units

Time taken to do work on Tuesday = $\frac{12}{6} = 2$ hours

∴ required ratio = 2 : 4 = 1 : 2

Note: Efficiency of M to T is given.

So, efficiency = 1 : 3

Time = 3 : 1

So, he takes 6 : 2

Then, 2 hours on Tuesday.

∴ required ratio = 2 : 4 = 1 : 2

17. 1; Let total time taken by Kishwar to do her work on Monday be N hours.

Then, time taken on Tuesday = (N – 1.5) hours

Now, $5 \times N = (N - 1.5) \times \frac{5}{1} \times 2 \Rightarrow 5N = 10N - 15$

$\Rightarrow N = 3$ hours

Time taken on Wednesday $= \frac{3 \times 200}{100} = 6$ hours

Note: Ratio of efficiency of Kishwar M to T is 1 : 2.

Time 2 : 1

∴ Difference (2 – 1 =) 1 ≡ 1.5 hours

Time taken on Monday = 1.5 × 2 = 3 hours.

∴ Time taken on Wednesday

= 200 % of 3 = 6 hours

18. 5; Let total work done by Jhilmil = W units

Then total work done by Satwik = 4W units

As per information,

$\frac{4W}{6} - \frac{W}{2} = 2$

$\Rightarrow 4W - 3W = 2 \times 6 = 12 \Rightarrow W = 12$ units

∴ 4W = 48 units

Time taken by Jhilmil on Tuesday

$= \frac{12}{2 \times 3} = 2$ hours

Time taken by Satwik on Tuesday $= \frac{48}{\frac{6}{3} \times 2} = 12$ hours

∴ Reqd sum = 12 + 2 = 14 hours

19. 5; Time taken by Prince on Monday $= \frac{15}{3} = 5$ hours

Time taken by Prince on Wednesday

$= \frac{60}{100} \times 5 = 3$ hours

Time taken by Kishwar on Monday $= \frac{15}{5} = 3$ hours

Time taken by Kishwar on Wednesday

$= \frac{200}{100} \times 3 = 6$ hours

Time taken by Rituraj on Monday $= \frac{16}{4} = 4$ hours

Time taken by Rituraj on Wednesday

$= \frac{125}{100} \times 4 = 5$ hours

∴ Reqd average $= \frac{3 + 6 + 5}{3} = \frac{14}{3} = 4\frac{2}{3}$ hours

20. 2; Time taken by Jhilmil to do work on Tuesday

$= \frac{12}{2 \times 3} = \frac{12}{6} = 2$ hours

Time taken by Satwik to do work on Tuesday

$= \frac{12 \times 3}{6 \times 2} = 3$ hours

Time taken by Rituraj to do work on Tuesday

$= \frac{12}{9} = 1$ hour 20 minutes

Time taken by Kishwar to do work on Tuesday

$= \frac{12}{10} = 1.2$ hours = 1 hour 12 minutes

Time taken by Prince to do work on Tuesday

$= \frac{12}{1} = 12$ hours

∴ Reqd sum = 2 hrs + 3 hrs + 1 hr 20 min + 1 hr 12 min + 12 hrs = 19 hrs 32 min

21. 3; Let time taken by Satwik = T hours

Then time taken by Kishwar = (11 – T) hours

According to the question,

$6T + 5(11 - T) = 63$

$\Rightarrow 6T + 55 - 5T = 63 \Rightarrow T = 8$ hours

Time taken by Satwik on Wednesday

$= 8 \times \frac{50}{100} = 4$ hours

Time taken by Kishwar on Wednesday

$= (11 - 8) \times \frac{200}{100} = 6$ hours

$\therefore$ Reqd raetio = 6 : 4 = 3 : 2